The Harvard Lectures of Alfred North Whitehead, 1925–1927

The Edinburgh Critical Edition of the Complete Works of Alfred North Whitehead

General Editor: George Lucas, US Naval Academy Emeritus
Executive Editor: Brian G. Henning, Gonzaga University
Assistant Editor: Joseph Petek, Claremont School of Theology

The complete, collected critical edition of the unpublished and published manuscripts of British-American philosopher Alfred North Whitehead

This Critical Edition brings together for the first time, in a series of critically edited volumes, the complete, collected published works and previously unpublished lectures, papers and correspondence of Alfred North Whitehead, one of the 20th century's most original and significant philosophers.

Newly discovered materials, long thought lost or destroyed, including illustrations, equations and chalkboard diagrams, which Whitehead used in classroom settings, have never before been seen by contemporary scholars. A projected six volumes of unpublished material will illuminate many factors influencing the development of Whitehead's initial and later thought, as well as elucidate, in considerably greater detail than ever before, many of the principal concepts later set out in his body of published philosophical reflection.

New critical editions of his famous lecture series at Harvard University, such as *Science and the Modern World*, *Symbolism* and *The Function of Reason*, his world-renowned Gifford lecture series at Edinburgh University in 1928, *Process and Reality*, together with new editions of justifiably famous collections of later essays and public lectures, such as *Adventures of Ideas* and *Modes of Thought*, will round out this ambitious and authoritative Critical Edition.

Editorial Advisory Board
The editorial advisory board is composed of respected Whitehead scholars from the United States, Canada and Europe who will ensure the scholarly integrity and quality of the Critical Edition of Whitehead.

George Allan, Paul Bogaard, Ronny Desmet, Daniel A. Dombrowski, Roland Faber, Nancy Frankenberry, Michael Halewood, Jude Jones, Helmut Maassen, Leemon McHenry and Robert Valenza.

Available

The Harvard Lectures of Alfred North Whitehead, 1924–1925: Philosophical Presuppositions of Science edited by Paul A. Bogaard and Jason Bell

The Harvard Lectures of Alfred North Whitehead, 1925–1927: General Metaphysical Problems of Science edited by Brian G. Henning, Joseph Petek and George Lucas

The Harvard Lectures of Alfred North Whitehead, 1925–1927

General Metaphysical Problems of Science

Edited by Brian G. Henning, Joseph Petek and George Lucas

Edinburgh University Press is one of the leading university presses in the UK. We publish academic books and journals in our selected subject areas across the humanities and social sciences, combining cutting-edge scholarship with high editorial and production values to produce academic works of lasting importance. For more information visit our website: edinburghuniversitypress.com

© editorial matter and organisation, Brian G. Henning, Joseph Petek, George R. Lucas, Jr, 2021, 2026

Edinburgh University Press Ltd
13 Infirmary Street, Edinburgh, EH1 1LT

First published in hardback by Edinburgh University Press 2021

Typeset in Garamond and Cambria
by R. J. Footring Ltd, Derby, and
printed and bound by CPI Group (UK) Ltd, Croydon, CR0 4YY

A CIP record for this book is available from the British Library

ISBN 978 1 4744 1693 1 (hardback)
ISBN 978 1 3995 5232 5 (paperback)
ISBN 978 1 4744 1694 8 (webready PDF)
ISBN 978 1 4744 1695 5 (epub)

The right of Brian G. Henning, Joseph Petek, George R. Lucas, Jr to be identified as the editors of this work has been asserted in accordance with the Copyright, Designs and Patents Act 1988, and the Copyright and Related Rights Regulations 2003 (SI No. 2498).

Contents

General introduction   vii
   George Lucas, *General Editor*
   Brian G. Henning, *Executive Editor*
Editorial principles   xiii
Chronology for Alfred North Whitehead   xvi
Published works of Alfred North Whitehead   xx
Introduction to *The Harvard Lectures of Alfred North Whitehead, 1925–1927*   xxv
   Joseph Petek, *Assistant Editor*
   Brian G. Henning, *Executive Editor*

Philosophy 3b: Philosophy of Science
Radcliffe lectures, fall semester 1925   3
Harvard lectures, fall semester 1925   46
Harvard lectures, spring semester 1926   113
Harvard lectures, fall semester 1926   170
Harvard lectures, spring semester 1927   291

Seminaries and guest lectures for 1926–7
Philosophy 20h: Seminary in Metaphysics, fall semester 1926   341
Philosophy 20i: Seminary in Logic, spring semester 1927   371
Social Ethics 20a: Fundamentals Underlying the Social Sciences, fall semester 1926   391
Philosophy A: History of Philosophy, spring semester 1927   408

Appendix 1. Tables of student notes by date   414
Appendix 2. Samples of original notes   421
Appendix 3. Diary entry of George Conger on Whitehead   435

List of primary sources   438
Bibliography   439
Index   444

General introduction

George Lucas, *General Editor*
Brian G. Henning, *Executive Editor*

Alfred North Whitehead, a British-born philosopher who attained widespread fame in America in the first half of the twentieth century, is perhaps best known among the wider public for his famous saying that the European philosophical tradition 'consists of a series of footnotes to Plato'.[1]

A student of mathematics at Trinity College, Cambridge, in the 1880s, Whitehead was elected a Fellow of the College in 1884, where he mentored the mathematical studies of such notable figures as John Maynard Keynes and Bertrand Russell, and was also inducted as a member of one of the most elite societies in the English-speaking university world at the time, the famed 'Cambridge Apostles'.

In 1910, Whitehead resigned his fellowship at Trinity College and moved to London, where (after a year spent in research and writing) he obtained a lectureship in mathematics at University College London. In 1914, he began lecturing at the newly organised Imperial College of Science and Technology (now Imperial College London) before being elected Dean of the Faculty of Science at the University of London in 1918 and Chairman of its Academic Council in 1920.[2]

While at the University of London, Whitehead successfully lobbied for a new history of science department, helped establish a bachelor of science degree in 1923, and made the school more accessible to less wealthy students. Finally, at the age of 63, Whitehead retired from his position at the University of London and sailed to America to accept a coveted chair at Harvard University, becoming a naturalised citizen and remaining an active and prolific scholar until his death on 30 December 1947 in Cambridge, Massachusetts.

At the beginning of the twentieth century, Whitehead began a collaboration with his student and protégé Lord Bertrand Russell that lasted well over a decade and resulted in the publication (in 1910, 1912 and 1913) of the three-volume *Principia Mathematica*, a monumental study intended to establish the foundations of mathematics in formal logic. Subsequently, in 1922, Whitehead himself concluded two decades of study of the geometry of space-time in *The Principle of Relativity*, a path-breaking work of theoretical cosmology explicitly intended to pose an alternative to Albert Einstein's General Theory. Other

---

1. Alfred North Whitehead, *Process and Reality* (1929) (New York: Free Press, 1979), p. 39.
2. Both University College London and the Imperial College of Science and Technology were member colleges of the University of London.

works spanning Whitehead's academic career in England include *A Treatise on Universal Algebra* (1898), 'On mathematical concepts of the material world' (1906), *An Introduction to Mathematics* (1911), *The Organization of Thought* (1917), *An Enquiry Concerning the Principles of Natural Knowledge* (1919) and a significant work on the philosophy of science, *The Concept of Nature* (1920). These works cemented Whitehead's reputation as one of the leading figures in the early development of analytic philosophy, alongside Russell, G. E. Moore and Ludwig Wittgenstein.

Upon coming to the United States, however, and with inspiration allegedly derived from the uniquely American philosophy of 'experience' (particularly that of William James and John Dewey), Whitehead undertook a series of works on far broader philosophical themes. His later work encompasses the history and philosophy of science, the sociological development of civilisation, the philosophy of history, philosophical reflections on education and, most famously, an ambitious attempt to develop a descriptive metaphysical system commensurate with early twentieth-century relativistic cosmology and quantum mechanics, which scholars now commonly label 'process philosophy'. Works during this American period of his career include *Science and the Modern World* (1925), *Religion in the Making* (1926), *Symbolism* (1927), *The Function of Reason* (1929) and his best-known work, *Process and Reality* (1929), based upon his Gifford lectures at the University of Edinburgh delivered in June 1928. In addition to subsequent books, such as *Adventures of Ideas* (1933) and *Modes of Thought* (1938), Whitehead also published a number of lectures and essays on diverse topics during this period, many of which he later published in collections such as *The Aims of Education* (1929) and *Essays in Science and Philosophy* (1948).

Whitehead's stature as a pivotal figure in American philosophy, his significant contributions to the rise of analytic philosophy, and the recent and worldwide renewal of interest in the constructive contribution of his seminal ideas to a number of important contemporary metaphysical and cosmological problems in philosophy argue for the appropriateness and timeliness of a complete critical edition of his works – an edition intended to rank alongside critical collected editions already produced or in progress on the works of his eminent predecessors and contemporaries, including William James, John Dewey, Josiah Royce, George Santayana and C. S. Peirce, as well as Einstein, Russell and Wittgenstein.

The need for a complete critical edition of the unpublished and published manuscripts of Whitehead is compelling. Beginning around 2010, an enormous body of unpublished material steadily began to come to light, thus helping to dispel the myth that all of the Whiteheadian *Nachlass* had been lost or destroyed.[1] The new discoveries include substantive correspondence with students and leading intellectual and political figures of the period, along

---

1. For more on this see Brian G. Henning, 'Preface: A brief history of the Critical Edition of Whitehead', in Brian G. Henning and Joseph Petek (eds), *Whitehead at Harvard, 1924–1925* (Edinburgh: Edinburgh University Press, 2020), and Brian G. Henning, 'On the recently discovered Whitehead papers', Whitehead Research Project website, 14 January 2019, <http://whiteheadresearch.org/2019/01/14/on-the-recently-discovered-whitehead-papers> (last accessed 17 August 2020).

with copious and detailed lecture notes taken by both students and faculty colleagues attending Whitehead's classes. These lecture notes were recorded by philosophers who became quite accomplished in their own right, and some of whom (such as W. V. O. Quine) are characterised by an eminent historian of philosophy, Professor Jerome B. Schneewind, as numbering among the most significant philosophical figures of the twentieth century.[1]

Despite the fact that much of his work undertaken in America was written comparatively recently (mostly during the early part of the last century), scholars at present do not have a clear sense of what motivated Whitehead or what led to the development of his thought. Part of the reason for this has to do with the fact that his personal correspondence with colleagues – along with the lecture notes of his students which were not either discarded, donated or destroyed following his death – had been scattered in libraries and archives across the United States, Canada and the UK.

The editors and staff of the Whitehead Research Project have invested considerable time and effort locating, collecting and cataloguing a substantial body of these extant unpublished materials (many of which were mistakenly thought to have been lost to scholars forever). The newly discovered materials in particular shed considerable light on the factors influencing the development of Whitehead's later philosophy, and also often elucidate – in considerably greater detail than ever before – many of the principal concepts encompassed within that body of philosophical reflection (e.g. through the apparent use by Whitehead himself of illustrations, equations and blackboard diagrams in classroom settings which have never before been seen by contemporary scholars).

Whitehead's published works, meanwhile, remain in disarray: some are out of print, while others remain in print from multiple sources, replete with inconsistencies and extensive uncorrected typographical and textual errors. Many lack even a cursory index. Apart from a newly reprinted edition of Whitehead and Russell's *Principia Mathematica*, the sole exception was the re-issue (in 1978) of a so-called 'Corrected Edition' of *Process and Reality*. This proved to be a helpful interim work but it did not fully adhere to the rigorous protocols since established for scholarly editions generally.[2] Finally, while multiple copyrights for extant works are claimed by several publishers, in point of fact all of Whitehead's materials (published and unpublished) continue to remain legally in the sole possession of the Whitehead family estate, whose sole executor[3] has granted full permission for the future publication of both unpublished and published works to the Whitehead Research Project.

When finally completed, the *Edinburgh Critical Edition of the Complete Works of Alfred North Whitehead* will encompass the entire collected works of the author, published and unpublished. Furthermore, by organising, archiving,

---

1. J. B. Schneewind, Chair, Department of Philosophy, Johns Hopkins University (letter of reference to the National Endowment for the Humanities, 30 June 2012).
2. See for example Mary-Jo Kline and Susan Holbrook Perdue, *A Guide to Documentary Editing* (3rd edition) (Charlottesville: University of Virginia Press, 2008).
3. George W. Whitehead (a grandson).

digitising, transcribing, editing and indexing all of his writings, the full breadth and significance of Whitehead's diverse work will, perhaps for the first time, come fully into view. Not only will this make available materials that have never been published, but it will also improve the scholarly understanding of previously published items. Perhaps the most useful and exciting aspect of this project to many scholars, however (beyond the publication of newly discovered material), will be the creation of a fully searchable electronic archive of these primary source materials.[1] In these ways, this *Critical Edition* should facilitate and energise the scholarly study of one of the twentieth century's most original and influential intellectual figures.

Outline and methodology of the Harvard lectures

The *Critical Edition* begins with a series of volumes devoted to the considerable body of recently discovered and almost entirely unpublished lecture notes, followed by two volumes of correspondence. Upon completion of the publication of all of the hitherto unpublished materials, the *Critical Edition* will turn, in chronological sequence, to the re-issuing of critically edited volumes of published works, from *Universal Algebra* (1898) through to the later American works, up to the date of Whitehead's death in 1947.

Whitehead mainly taught three courses during his Harvard career: Phil 3b ('Philosophy of Science'),[2] Phil 20h ('Seminary in Metaphysics') and Phil 20i ('Seminary in Logic'). This might imply a tedious and repetitive chronology of the same or similar topics over time, but this is not how Whitehead worked. Unlike the majority of academics – who most often teach a repertoire of courses for students in a major or graduate programme while attempting to reserve their own time for original and publishable scholarly research – Whitehead carried out his original research in the classroom and in public lecture halls, in dialogue with the undergraduate and graduate students in his core classes and seminars, and changed the course content based on the focus of his research at the time.

These changes are reflected to some degree in the shifting sub-titles for his Phil 3/3b, which during his 13-year teaching career at Harvard was variously called 'Philosophical Presuppositions of Science', 'Cosmologies Ancient and Modern' and 'The Function of Reason', among other titles. But in fact, topics changed more frequently than even changes in sub-titles suggest; every year was different. Louise R. Heath, who took Whitehead's Phil 3b two years in a row, wrote at the top of her notes for the second year: 'Theoretically [this was the] same course as 1924, but I credited it because actually it was quite different'.[3]

---

1. Digital scans of many items can be reviewed on site at the Whitehead Research Project (WRP) in Claremont, California. Finding aid information for all items can be obtained by contacting the WRP staff. Visit http://whiteheadresearch.org for more information.
2. A course that Whitehead taught during both semesters, it was later split into two courses: Phil 3b (fall semester) and Phil 3 (spring semester).
3. Louise R. Heath, 'Whitehead, Fall 1925', MS 284, Victor Lowe Papers, Box 2.9, Special Collections, Sheridan Libraries, Johns Hopkins University, <https://catalyst.library.jhu.edu/catalog/bib_556595> (last accessed 17 August 2020).

Whitehead did not tie himself to any particular set of topics from year to year, but simply taught his most current thought on whatever he was working on, often months before similar material would appear in print. Hence, the overriding significance of the materials included in these volumes of lectures is that they provide long-missing insight into the formation and development of Whitehead's thought during this crucial period.

It has long been believed, for example (as the record of his formally published work seems to suggest), that Whitehead first developed a provisional metaphysical synthesis of and foundation for modern science (in his first published American work, *Science and the Modern World*, in 1925) that differed substantively from his 'later' and quite distinct reformulation of these foundations in *Process and Reality*. Volume I of this *Critical Edition* demonstrates that this widespread interpretation is inaccurate, inasmuch as his later mathematical and geometrical foundations (especially Part IV of *Process and Reality*) are presented largely intact in the Emerson Hall lectures of 1924–5, while a more general, historical and publicly accessible account of these (same) foundations is offered in the Radcliffe College lectures (nominally under the same course heading) delivered at the same time (which formed the basis of *Science and the Modern World*). Having found during that first year that the technical account was somewhat daunting for his students – even for Harvard graduate students – Whitehead proceeded to alter the focus of the 'master course' significantly during the next two years, taking a more historical and descriptive approach to the materials presented in class as his thinking about these issues continued to evolve.

The lecture notes over the ensuing two years thus reflect the origins of at least some of the several divisions, or 'Parts', that would come to compose the formal publication of *Process and Reality* in 1929. These lectures themselves lead up to the delivery of the Gifford lectures in Edinburgh toward the end of the academic term in June 1928 (during which Whitehead reported encountering similar difficulties with audience comprehension and developing the proper 'pitch' for his lectures). What these notes together reveal is that the alleged 'transformation' of his thought from an 'early' (1925) to a quite distinctive 'later' version (1929) cannot be sustained on the basis of this new evidence. Instead, what we see is a more subtle 'evolution' of concepts and theoretical foundations, captured in a decided transformation in public dissemination and style. Indeed, the textual evidence suggests that Whitehead encountered a problem similar to that described by Wittgenstein in his own post-*Tractatus* lectures, in which the methodology involves abandoning a straightforward sequential-logical approach for a somewhat less systematic piecemeal criss-cross of the same subject-terrain from alternative perspectives, utilising varying modes of expression in order to gain insight into the complex whole of the subject more adequately.

In Whitehead's case, these lecture notes also demonstrate how he used his teaching and public presentations as the portrait or drawing board upon which to sketch and re-sketch his evolving thought, searching for a proper mode of presentation and delivery that would succeed in capturing the whole of a metaphysical vision that he himself had described to his son, North, in 1924 as 'the right way of looking at things', lacking only the opportunity that his Harvard years finally presented to set it all out systematically. This was not an easy task, of course, nor was it accomplished in a single year, or in a single course. Instead, we witness the true 'compositional history' of Whitehead's thought not in some hypothetical reconstruction, but in his very own words, during his own presentations, as recorded meticulously by his own students, all wrestling together with the problem of a proper reformulation of the metaphysical picture of nature as presented in the varieties of discoveries constituting modern science at the dawn of the twentieth century.

The annual succession of lecture notes in these volumes thus supplies the long-absent background for understanding the development and maturation of Whitehead's thought. For anyone interested in Whitehead, in process philosophy specifically, or in the evolution of early twentieth-century Anglo-American philosophy generally, these notes are a discovery of extraordinary significance.

Editorial principles

Lecture notes taken during Alfred North Whitehead's classes were recorded not only by his students but also by recent graduates and both junior and senior faculty colleagues. Some sets of notes were deposited in various library archives with which their owners were affiliated, while others were privately retained and discovered later by Whitehead's biographer, Victor Lowe, or by members of the Whitehead Research Project.

In editing lecture notes taken during Whitehead's classes, the editors have operated on a policy of minimal interference with the text. Although we are dealing for the most part with notes on Whitehead's lectures taken by others, the text is the closest thing we have to Whitehead's words. This being the case, we correct what is clearly wrong (such as typographical errors and incorrect bibliographic information) but make no attempt to edit the text aggressively.

The following principles, listed alphabetically, have governed the way in which the text has been edited, standardised or silently corrected, across the *Critical Edition*. Elaborations and additions specific to each volume may be made as a matter of editorial discretion.

- *Angle brackets*. Angle brackets (⟨ ⟩) have been used to indicate editorial intervention, since both parentheses and square brackets have been used by the original note-takers.
- *Capitalisation*. Capitalisation has been standardised without record according to the sixteenth edition of the *Chicago Manual of Style*.
- *Contractions/shorthand*.
  - If the shorthand or contraction is unambiguous, it has been silently expanded without record. This includes ditto marks.
  - If a contraction or word(s) seems legible, but its meaning is ambiguous or unclear, a footnote has been added explaining the difficulty.
  - If the editors have a strong guess but cannot be sure about the reading of a word or a portion of a word, then they have placed angle brackets around those markings with a question mark at the end (e.g. ⟨example?⟩); or a footnote has been added.
- *Dashes*. Dashes have all been standardised as en dashes.
- *Deletions*. Legible deletions have been retained and marked with strikethroughs (~~deletion~~). Insignificant accidental deletions have been silently removed without record. Insignificant accidental deletions include misspellings (~~freind~~ friend) and false starts (too~~m~~ much).
- *Diagrams/figures*. Whenever possible, diagrams and figures that would have appeared on the blackboard (and therefore were drawn by

Whitehead) have been faithfully recreated or scanned and inserted in their original location relative to the rest of text.
- *Doodles.* Insignificant doodles have not been reproduced, but footnotes will indicate their existence.
- *Illegible words.* If a single word is completely illegible, the editors have inserted a question mark in angle brackets (⟨?⟩). If more than one word is illegible, the editors have inserted an ellipsis or series of ellipses of the approximate length of the illegible text within angle brackets and a question mark at the end (⟨......?⟩); or a note added.
- *Interlineations.* Authorial interlineations have been placed in their intended locations and marked with carets. Carets pointing upward (∧interlineation∧) indicate that the marked word has been moved to its present location from below, while carets pointing downward (∨interlineation∨) indicate that the marked word has been moved to its present location from above.
- *Italics.* All book titles and foreign words have been italicised. If a book title is underlined or enclosed in quotation marks, this has been silently removed and italics used instead.
- *Line and page breaks.* The finished editorial text will not retain the author's original line or page breaks, in most cases, and will not generally mark where line breaks occur, but for page breaks a record will be inserted between upright bars (|example|).
- *Line spacing.* Unusually large or small amounts of space between lines or paragraphs have not been retained in the finished text, in most cases, and no record has been made of them; but where deemed important to understanding the note-taker's intention some spacing may have been retained or a note added.
- *Marginal text.* Text sometimes appears in odd places on the page (e.g. vertical text, or text that has been circled and placed in the corner of the page or in the margin). Placement of such text is at the editors' discretion, on a case-by-case basis. A footnote has been added explaining the original positioning of any text whose intended location within the larger text is ambiguous (e.g. 'This line originally appeared in the upper-left corner of the page').
- *Markings.* Marginal marks for emphasis, such as vertical lines, braces, arrows, or check marks, have been retained or not at the editors' discretion.
- *Markings not made by original author.* Any markings not made by the original author have been removed without record. These include archival markings, or any markings made by previous transcribers. If ambiguous, a footnote has been added.
- *Misspellings.* Misspellings have been corrected without record.
- *Notes.* The classes of footnotes have been used.
  - *Substantive notes/contextual information.* These types of notes provide further information and context for the reader (e.g. information on a person or book that Whitehead mentions).

- ◦ *Editorial notes/textual difficulties.* These notes explain textual treatment (e.g. difficulties with textual interpretation or describing odd text positioning).
- *Page headers (including dates).* Headers have been standardised to a uniform format.
- *Paragraph indentation.* The indentation for paragraphs has been made uniform. However, for any outline-style notes with a clear hierarchy, the different levels of indentation have been preserved at the editors' discretion.
- *Punctuation.* Punctuation may be changed without record for purposes of clarity. The editors have been very conservative in this practice when the text employs little shorthand. Where extensive shorthand has been used, changes and additions to punctuation are more frequent.
- *Quoted text.* At times when a book or article is being read aloud, these portions of the text have been **bolded** to distinguish them from commentary on the text being read.
- *Separator lines.* Lines or other marks that the author has used to clearly separate one piece of text from another may be retained or silently removed at the editors' discretion.
- *Supply, editorial.* Editors have inserted missing articles, prepositions or pronouns within soft angle brackets (⟨supply⟩).
- *Underlining.* Underlining of book titles has been replaced with italics. All other underlining and double underlining that occurs in the edition has been preserved from the original. The editors have not added underlining.

Chronology for Alfred North Whitehead

1861 15 February. Birth as the last of four children.
1875 September. Whitehead leaves home to attend Sherborne School, a boarding school for boys (through to 23 June 1880).
1877 June. Whitehead's grandfather dies.
1880 October. Whitehead attends Trinity College, Cambridge, as a student (through to October 1884).
1884 17 May. Election to Cambridge Apostles.
1884 9 October. Whitehead elected a Fellow of Trinity College, Cambridge, and begins teaching mathematics there.
1888 First two papers published.
1888 Begins afternoon teaching at Girton College, Cambridge (then a women's college), probably for no pay, until 1913.
1890 16 December. Marriage to Evelyn Wade.
1891 31 December. Birth of T. North Whitehead.
1894 23 February. Birth of Jessie Whitehead.
1895 October. Bertrand Russell elected a Fellow of Trinity College.
1898 March. Whitehead's father dies.
1898 27 November. Birth of Eric Whitehead.
1899 Whitehead moves from Cambridge to Grantchester.
1901 Whitehead is appointed to the Council of Newnham College, Cambridge, although he never taught there.
1901 Bertrand and Alys Russell move in with the Whiteheads and live with them for about a year. Russell and Whitehead begin collaboration on the *Principia*.
1903 13 February. Whitehead is elected a Fellow of the Royal Society.
1907 January. Whitehead's brother-in-law, John Branch (married to his sister Shirley), kills himself. Whitehead visits to help put affairs in order.
1907 April. Whitehead moves back to Cambridge.
1907 May. Whitehead becomes Chairman of the Cambridge branch of the Men's League for Women's Suffrage.
1910 April. Whitehead resigns his Trinity lectureship and soon moves to Chelsea, London. He and his wife also buy a country home in Lockeridge, Wiltshire.
1910 December. First volume of the *Principia* is published.
1911 July. Whitehead is appointed to a teaching position at University College London.
1912 Whitehead is elected President for a year of both the South-Eastern Mathematical Association and the London branch of the Mathematical Association.
1914 10 July. Whitehead is appointed to a professorship at Imperial College London.
1914 15 July. Whitehead resigns from University College London.

Chronology for Alfred North Whitehead

1914 31 July. Gertrude Stein and Alice Toklas stay with the Whiteheads for six weeks.
1914 1 September. Whitehead begins teaching at Imperial College London.
1915 Whitehead joins the Aristotelian Society, in which he is active through to his departure for America in 1924 (serves as President, 1922–3).
1915 Whitehead is elected President of the Mathematical Association, and serves for two years.
1916 11 July. Russell is dismissed from his Trinity lectureship due to his anti-war views.
1917 May. Eric Whitehead is enlisted in the Royal Flying Corps.
1917 The Whiteheads sell their country home in Lockeridge. They buy another in Oxted, Surrey.
1918 13 March. Eric Whitehead is killed in action.
1918 6 May. Russell is imprisoned for his anti-war views until 11 September of the same year.
1918 31 October. Whitehead is elected Dean of the Faculty of Science at the University of London and holds the post for four years.
1919 18 October. Whitehead delivers the first of his Tarner lectures (he gives seven in total, through to 29 November that year).
1920 Whitehead is appointed Chairman of the Academic (Leadership) Council of the Senate of the University of London and holds the post for four years.
1920 July. Whitehead is appointed Chairman of the Delegacy for Goldsmiths' College, London, and holds the post until he leaves for Harvard in 1924.
1920 3 November. T. North Whitehead marries Margaret Schuster.
1921 Eric Alfred North Whitehead is born, T. North's son and Whitehead's grandson.
1922 Whitehead accepts first invitation to cross the Atlantic to America in April for a conference at Bryn Mawr College in honour of mathematics professor Charlotte Angas Scott.
1924 2 February. Whitehead's mother dies.
1924 24 February. Whitehead accepts a five-year appointment at Harvard.
1924 1 April. Whitehead agrees to give the Lowell lectures, responding to the invitation of 18 March.
1924 16 August. Whitehead leaves England for Cambridge, Massachusetts.
1924 27 August. Whitehead arrives in Cambridge.
1924 25 September. Whitehead gives his first lectures at Harvard.
1924 4 October. Whitehead moves into a new flat in Radnor Hall (now part of the Memorial Drive Apartments Historic District), overlooking the Charles River.
1925 2 February. Whitehead delivers the first of his Lowell lectures, which he proceeds to give through to 2 March, every Monday and Thursday at 5 p.m., with the exception of 23 February (these would become *Science and the Modern World*).
1925 5 April. Whitehead delivers a lecture on 'Religion and science' at Phillips Brooks House at Harvard.

1925	14 April. Whitehead gives a lecture on 'Mathematics as an element in the history of thought' to the Mathematical Society at Brown University, Providence, Rhode Island.
1925	29 June. Jessie Whitehead arrives in Cambridge, Massachusetts, and begins working in the Harvard library on 20 July.
1925	30 December. Whitehead attends his first meeting of the American Philosophical Association and gives a paper on the subject of time.
1926	February. Whitehead delivers a second series of Lowell lectures (these would become *Religion in the Making*).
1926	February. The 'Committee of Four' begins meeting (Whitehead, L. J. Henderson, John Livingston Lowes, Charles P. Curtis). Together they choose four to eight PhD students per year for the Society of Fellows for a term of three years each with an option for three more (among these Junior Fellows was Quine, chosen in the first batch).
1926	During Harvard's spring break, Whitehead delivers lectures at McGill University (Montreal, Canada), the University of Michigan and the University of Illinois.
1926	Whitehead delivers lectures at Dartmouth College.
1926	September. Whitehead attends the Sixth International Congress of Philosophy at Harvard, and gives a paper entitled 'Time'.
1927	27 February. Whitehead accepts an invitation to deliver the Gifford lectures for 1928.
1927	April. Whitehead delivers the Barbour-Page lectures at the University of Virginia (these would become *Symbolism: Its Meaning and Effect*).
1928	1 June. Whitehead delivers the first of the Gifford lectures (which he proceeds to give through to 22 June).
1929	March. Whitehead delivers the Vanuxem lectures at Princeton University, New Jersey (these would become *The Function of Reason*).
1929	Whitehead delivers a series of four Mary Flexner Lectures at Bryn Mawr College, which would become chapters in *Adventures of Ideas*.
1930	Whitehead attends the Seventh International Congress of Philosophy in Oxford.
1931	14 February. Whitehead attends a symposium for his seventieth birthday, arranged by James Woods.
1931	Whitehead delivers an address at the Harvard Business School.
1931	February. T. North Whitehead joins a human relations study group at Harvard Business School and moves to Cambridge, Massachusetts.
1931	29 December. Whitehead delivers his presidential address to the eastern division of the American Philosophical Association at New Haven.
1931	Whitehead is elected a Fellow of the British Academy.
1932	March. Whitehead delivers the Davies Lecture in Philosophy at the Institute of Arts and Sciences, Columbia University, which later become a chapter in *Adventures of Ideas*.
1933	October. Whitehead delivers two lectures at the University of Chicago, which subsequently become *Nature and Life*, and, later, two chapters in *Modes of Thought*.

1935 25 October. Whitehead gives a short address to graduate students of the Harvard and Radcliffe Philosophical Departments, which would adapted into the epilogue of Modes of Thought.
1937 7 May. Whitehead delivers his final Harvard lecture.
1937 29 October. Whitehead delivers the first of a series of six inaugural Calkins Lectures at Wellesley College, which later become the first six chapters of *Modes of Thought*.
1941 15 February. Whitehead attends a party for his eightieth birthday, organised by his Harvard colleagues.
1945 1 January. Whitehead is awarded the Order of Merit.
1947 30 December. Whitehead dies from a cerebral haemorrhage.

Published works of Alfred North Whitehead

1886 10 February. 'A celebrity at home. The clerk of the weather'. *Cambridge Review*, vol. 7, pp. 202–3.
1886 12 May. 'Davy Jones'. *Cambridge Review*, vol. 7, pp. 311–12.
1888 6 March. 'A visitation'. *Cambridge Fortnightly*, vol. 1(4), pp. 81–3.
1888 'On the motion of viscous incompressible fluids: a method of approximation'. *Quarterly Journal of Pure and Applied Mathematics*, vol. 23, pp. 78–93.
1888 'Second approximations to viscous fluid motion. A sphere moving steadily in a straight line'. *Quarterly Journal of Pure and Applied Mathematics*, vol. 23, pp. 143–52.
1891 20 February. 'The Fens as seen from skates'. *Cambridge Review*, vol. 12 (attribution to Whitehead not wholly certain).
1896 14 May. 'On ideals: with reference to the controversy concerning the admission of women to degrees in the University'. *Cambridge Review*, vol. 17, pp. 310–11.
1898 10 March. 'The geodesic geometry of surfaces in non-Euclidean space'. *Proceedings of the London Mathematical Society*, vol. 29, pp. 275–324.
1898 *A Treatise on Universal Algebra*. Cambridge University Press Warehouse.
1899 2 February. 'Sets of operations in relation to groups of finite order'. *Proceedings of the Royal Society of London*, vol. 64, pp. 319–20.
1901 April. 'Memoir on the algebra of symbolic logic'. *American Journal of Mathematics*, vol. 23(2), pp. 139–65.
1901 October. 'Memoir on the algebra of symbolic logic, part II'. *American Journal of Mathematics*, vol. 23(4), pp. 297–316.
1902 'On cardinal numbers'. *American Journal of Mathematics*, vol. 24, pp. 367–94.
1903 'The logic of relations, logical substitution groups, and cardinal numbers'. *American Journal of Mathematics*, vol. 25, pp. 157–78.
1903 14 May. 'The University library'. *Cambridge Review*, vol. 24, p. 295.
1904 'Theorems on cardinal numbers'. *American Journal of Mathematics*, vol. 26, pp. 31–2.
1905 'Note'. *Revue de Metaphysique et de Morale*, vol. 13, pp. 916–17.
1906 29 March. 'On mathematical concepts of the material world'. *Philosophical Transactions of the Royal Society of London*, vol. 77(517), pp. 290–1.
1906 Through to 1910. *The Axioms of Projective Geometry*. Cambridge University Press Warehouse.
1906 5 November. 'Liberty and the enfranchisement of women'. Cambridge Women's Suffrage Association, pamphlet.
1907 March. *The Axioms of Descriptive Geometry*. Cambridge University Press Warehouse.
1910 (With Bertrand Russell) 'Non-Euclidean geometry'. *Encyclopedia Britannica* (11th edition), vol. 11, pp. 724–30.

1910 'Axioms of geometry'. *Encyclopedia Britannica* (11th edition), vol. 11, pp. 730–6.
1910 October. 'The philosophy of mathematics'. *Science Progress in the Twentieth Century*, vol. 5, pp. 234–9.
1910 December (with Bertrand Russell) *Principia Mathematica, Volume 1*. Cambridge University Press.
1911 *An Introduction to Mathematics*. Williams and Norgate, Henry Holt.
1912 'The place of mathematics in a liberal education'. *Journal of the Association of Teachers of Mathematics for the Southeastern Part of England*, vol. 1(1).
1912 (With Bertrand Russell) *Principia Mathematica, Volume 2*. Cambridge University Press.
1913 (With Bertrand Russell) *Principia Mathematica, Volume 3*. Cambridge University Press.
1913 'The principles of mathematics in relation to elementary teaching'. *Proceedings of the Fifth International Congress of Mathematicians*, vol. 2, pp. 449–54. Also published in *L'Enseignment Mathematique*.
1913 March. 'Presidential address to the London branch of the Mathematical Association'. *Mathematical Gazette*, vol. 7, pp. 87–94.
1914 'Report of the Council of the Royal Society of London'. *Year-Book of the Royal Society*, pp. 177–87.
1915 'Report of the Council of the Royal Society of London'. *Year-Book of the Royal Society*, pp. 176–85.
1916 January. 'The Aims of education: a plea for reform'. *Mathematical Gazette*, vol. 8, pp. 191–203.
1916 'Space, time, and relativity'. *Proceedings of the Aristotelian Society*, vol. 16, pp. 104–29.
1916 'The organisation of thought'. *Report of the 86th Meeting of the British Association for the Advancement of Science*, pp. 355–65. Also published with slight differences in *Proceedings of the Aristotelian Society*, vol. 17, pp. 58–76.
1916 'La théorie relationniste de l'espace'. *Revue de Métaphysique et de la Morale*, vol. 23, pp. 423–54.
1917 *The Organisation of Thought*. Williams and Norgate, Greenwood Press.
1917 March. 'Technical education and its relation to science and literature'. *Mathematical Gazette*, vol. 9(128), pp. 20–33. Also published in *Technical Journal* vol. 10 (January), pp. 59–74.
1917 (With A. W. Siddons) 'Letter to the Editor'. *Mathematical Gazette*, vol. 9, p. 14.
1918 'Graphical solution for high-angle fire'. *Proceedings of the Royal Society*, Series A 94, pp. 301–7.
1919 'Fundamental principles of education'. *Report of the 87th Meeting of the British Association for the Advancement of Science*, p. 361.
1919 (With Oliver Lodge, J. W. Nicholson, Henry Head, Adrian Stephen and H. Wildon Carr) 'Symposium: time, space and material: are they, and if so in what sense, the ultimate data of science?' *Proceedings of the Aristotelian Society, Supplementary Volumes*, vol. 2, 'Problems of Science and Philosophy', pp. 44–108.

1919 *An Enquiry Concerning the Principles of Natural Knowledge*. Cambridge University Press.
1919 15 November. 'A revolution in science'. *The Nation*, vol. 26, pp. 232–3.
1919 'Address on founder's day [Stanley Technical Trade School, South Norwood, London]'. Coventry and Son.
1920 *The Concept of Nature*. Cambridge University Press.
1920 12 February. 'Einstein's theory: an alternative suggestion'. *Times Educational Supplement*.
1921 'Science in general education'. *Second Congress of the Universities of the Empire*, pp. 31–9.
1921 (With many others) *Report of the Committee Appointed by the Prime Minister to Inquire into the Position of Classics in the Educational System of the United Kingdom*. His Majesty's Stationary Office.
1922 20 February. (With H. W. Carr, T. P. Nunn and Dorothy Wrinch) 'Discussion: the idealistic interpretation of Einstein's theory'. *Proceedings of the Aristotelian Society, New Series*, vol. 22, pp. 123–38.
1922 18 April. 'Some principles of physical science', presentation at Bryn Mawr College conference put in print as a booklet and also published later that year as a chapter in *The Principle of Relativity*.
1922 16 July. 'The philosophical aspects of the principle of relativity'. *Proceedings of the Aristotelian Society New Series*, vol. 22, pp. 215–23.
1922 *The Principle of Relativity, with Applications to Physical Science*. Cambridge University Press.
1922 November. 'The rhythm of education'. *Bulletin of the American Association of University Professors*, vol. 9(7), pp. 17–19.
1922 6 November. 'Uniformity and contingency: the presidential address'. *Proceedings of the Aristotelian Society New Series*, vol. 23, pp. 1–18.
1923 (With H. W. Carr and R. A. Sampson) 'Symposium. The problem of simultaneity: is there a paradox in the principle of relativity in regard to the relation of time measured and time lived?' *Aristotelian Society*, Supplementary 3, 'Relativity, Logic and Mysticism', pp. 15–41.
1923 'The place of classics in education'. *Hibbert Journal*, vol. 21, pp. 248–61.
1923 'The rhythmic claims of freedom and discipline'. *Hibbert Journal*, vol. 21, pp. 657–68.
1923 'The first physical synthesis'. In *Science and Civilization*, pp. 161–78. Oxford University Press.
1923 17 February. 'Letter to the Editor: Reply to review of *The Principle of Relativity*'. *New Statesman*.
1925 August. 'Religion and science'. *Atlantic Monthly*, vol. 136, pp. 200–7.
1925 'The importance of friendly relations between England and the United States'. *Phillips Bulletin*, vol. 19, pp. 15–18.
1925 October. *Science and the Modern World*. Macmillan.
1926 September. *Religion in the Making*. Macmillan and Cambridge University Press.
1926 '*Principia Mathematica*: to the Editor of *Mind*'. *Mind*, vol. 35(137), p. 130.
1926 Autumn. 'The education of an Englishman'. *Atlantic Monthly*, vol. 138, pp. 192–8.

1927 'England and the narrow seas'. *Atlantic Monthly*, vol. 139, pp. 791–8.
1927 'Time'. In *Sixth International Congress of Philosophy*, pp. 59–64. Longmans, Green & Co.
1927 November. *Symbolism: Its Meaning and Effect*. Macmillan.
1928 'Universities and their function'. *Atlantic Monthly*, vol. 141, pp. 638–44.
1929 *Process and Reality*. Macmillan and Cambridge University Press.
1929 *The Aims of Education and Other Essays*. Macmillan, Williams & Norgate.
1929 *The Function of Reason*. Princeton University Press.
1930 January. 'An address delivered at the celebration of the fiftieth anniversary of the founding of Radcliffe College'. *Radcliffe Quarterly*, vol. 14, pp. 1–5.
1930 'Prefatory note'. In Susanne K. Langer, *The Practice of Philosophy*, p. vii. Henry Holt & Co.
1931 'On foresight'. Introduction, in Wallace Brett Donham, *Business Adrift*, pp. xi–xxix. McGraw-Hill.
1931 'Objects and subjects'. *Proceedings and Addresses of the American Philosophical Association*, vol. 5, pp. 130–46.
1932 'Symposium in honor of the seventieth birthday of Alfred North Whitehead', speech included in a booklet of symposium proceedings printed by Harvard University Press (pp. 22–9).
1933 *Adventures of Ideas*. Macmillan and Cambridge University Press.
1933 'The study of the past – its uses and its dangers'. *Harvard Business Review*, vol. 11(4), pp. 436–44.
1934 'Foreword'. In *The Farther Shore: An Anthology of World Opinion on the Immortality of the Soul*. Houghton Mifflin.
1934 *Nature and Life*. University of Chicago Press. (This book, which comprises two essays, was republished in its entirety as Part 3 of *Modes of Thought*, 1938.)
1934 'Philosophy of life'. In Dagobert D. Runes (ed.), *Twentieth Century Philosophy: Living Schools of Thought*, pp. 131–44. Philosophical Library.
1934 'Foreword'. In Willard van Orman Quine, *A System of Logistic*, pp. ix–x. Harvard University Press.
1934 July. 'Indication, classes, numbers, validation'. *Mind*, New Series, vol. 43(171), pp. 281–97.
1934 October. 'Corrigenda. Indication, classes, numbers, validation'. *Mind*, New Series, vol. 43(172), p. 543.
1935 'Minute on the life and services of Professor James Haughton Woods'. *Harvard University Gazette*, vol. 30, pp. 153–5.
1935 'The aim of philosophy'. *Harvard Alumni Bulletin*, vol. 38, pp. 234–5.
1935 'Eulogy of Bernard Bosanquet'. In *Bernard Bosanquet and His Friends: Letters Illustrating the Sources and the Development of His Philosophical Opinions*, p. 316. George Allen & Unwin.
1936 'Memories'. *Atlantic Monthly*, vol. 157, pp. 672–9.
1936 'Harvard: the future'. *Atlantic Monthly*, vol. 159, pp. 260–70.
1937 'Remarks'. *Philosophical Review*, vol. 46, pp. 178–86.
1938 *Modes of Thought*. Macmillan and Cambridge University Press.
1939 'An appeal to sanity'. *Atlantic Monthly*, vol. 163, pp. 309–20.

1939 'John Dewey and his influence'. In Paul Arthur Schilpp (ed.), *The Philosophy of John Dewey*, pp. 477–9. Northwestern University Press.
1940 'Aspects of freedom'. In Ruth Nanda Anshen (ed.), *Freedom: Its Meaning*, pp. 42–67. Harcourt, Brace.
1940 'The issue: freedom'. *Boston Daily Globe*, 24 December.
1941 'Autobiographical notes'. In Paul Arthur Schilpp (ed.), pp. 1–15. *The Philosophy of Alfred North Whitehead*. Northwestern University Press.
1941 'Mathematics and the good'. In Paul Arthur Schilpp (ed.), *The Philosophy of Alfred North Whitehead*, pp. 666–81. Northwestern University Press.
1941 'Immortality'. In Paul Arthur Schilpp (ed.), *The Philosophy of Alfred North Whitehead*, pp. 682–700. Northwestern University Press.
1942 February. 'The problem of reconstruction'. *Atlantic Monthly*, vol. 169, pp. 172–5.
1942 October. 'Statesmanship and specialized learning'. *Proceedings of the American Academy of Arts and Sciences*, vol. 75(1), pp. 1–5.
1945 Preface to 'The organization of a story and a tale', by William Morgan. *Journal of American Folklore*, vol. 58(229), p. 169.
1947 *Essays in Science and Philosophy*. Philosophical Library.

Introduction to *The Harvard Lectures of Alfred North Whitehead, 1925–1927*

Joseph Petek, *Assistant Editor*
Brian G. Henning, *Executive Editor*

This second volume of Whitehead's Harvard lectures was a much more complex and challenging book to edit than the first. The first volume (HL1) covered a single academic year and was drawn from three archival sources, all of which were original, covered the full academic year (or very near to it) and were fairly consistently dated, well organised and easy to follow.

In contrast, the present volume covers two academic years (so far as student notes are available) and draws from the notes of 10 different authors for the Philosophy 3b portions alone, some of which cover a full academic year, and others only about half a semester. For some lectures we have as many as five different student accounts, and for others only one, or none at all.[1] For some of our sources the original handwritten notes have been lost, leaving us with a transcribed version of them. Many of the notes were inconsistently dated, or not dated at all. Some of the undated notes were disorganised; one set of them (Charles Hartshorne's) could hardly have been more out of order if the pages had been thrown up in the air and picked up at random. And in some cases, the structure of the notes was such that it was difficult even to put them in a linear order, with 'blocks' of text spread across the page seemingly at random.

All of these difficulties mean that it is particularly important for readers to understand at the outset some of the steps that we have taken as editors to turn these disparate sets of student notes into a coherent and readable volume. But first, we will start with an account of Whitehead's activities during the period in which the student notes were taken. Following this, we will discuss the most salient editorial decisions made across the whole of the volume, and finally provide a description of the individual sets of notes and the people who recorded them.

---

1. The student notes available collectively relate to just one semester at Radcliffe College but all four semesters at Harvard of Whitehead's Philosophy 3b course (details of the coverage are given on pp. xxxvi–lv, in the section 'The note-takers and their notes'). In addition there are notes for one semester for each of Whitehead's seminary classes, as well as for a lecture Whitehead gave as a guest speaker for Richard Clarke Cabot's Social Ethics 20a seminary and for the four lectures he contributed to Harvard's Philosophy A undergraduate introductory course. Appendix 1 details the notes available and how and where they are used.

Whitehead at Harvard, 1925–7

Whitehead's second and third academic years at Harvard were in some ways a transitional period in which he slowly ceased being the exciting new arrival and instead became a staple of the Harvard University scene. In at least one sense, there is nothing vague about this transition: Harvard's original offer to Whitehead had been for a five-year term. In December 1926, however, Whitehead's appointment was made permanent, with Harvard President Abbott Lawrence Lowell writing to Henry Osborn Taylor that 'everybody appreciates that [Whitehead] has been an enormous benefit to the University, for he has been a great stimulus. We shall certainly want him for more than five years.'[1] Another concrete change that took place during this time had to do with the enrolment in Whitehead's classes. While his lectures typically saw a healthy attendance of 30–40 people, few during the first two years were brave enough to take Whitehead's classes for credit; only about 6–10 Harvard students per term did so. But in the autumn of 1926, that number suddenly jumped to 41, and thereafter stayed in that general range for the remainder of his Harvard career (during his final year, the number was closer to 60).[2]

But perhaps we should back up and start at the beginning, in this case just after Whitehead's first year of lectures at Harvard had concluded in May 1925.

Whitehead's first spring term at Harvard had been an unusually busy and tiring one. Not only did he have his normal teaching load, but he also had to deliver his Lowell lectures – which would become *Science and the Modern World* – on Mondays and Thursdays for a month. He wrote to his son, North, in mid-March that the lectures 'amounted to writing a book in about two months . . . they were a great strain on me; and I am only just feeling sufficient rebound to be able to think of anything else'.[3] In late May, he discussed his feelings about the completion of his first academic year:

> My first session of lectures is now over. It has been rather an effort, and therefore a strain. But I have enjoyed it immensely. I have had the same feeling as you have in examinations – the joy of defeating the examiners. On the whole, I think that I have done it – It might have been done much better, but it was done. My class, which largely consisted of postgraduates who come for their own pleasure, increased in the latter part of the session. So I am in good spirits, though I now know what I ought to have said as distinct from what I did say.[4]

---

1. Letter from A. Lawrence Lowell to Henry Osborn Taylor, 15 October 1926, UAI 5.160, Records of the President of Harvard University, Abbott Lawrence Lowell, Box 238, Folder 576, Harvard University Archives, <https://id.lib.harvard.edu/ead/c/hua03003c11946/catalog>. Websites and URLs cited in the Introduction were all last accessed 18 August 2020.
2. Alfred North Whitehead, 'Student Record Book for Harvard and Radcliffe Classes', HUG 4877.10, Papers of Alfred North Whitehead, 1924–47, Harvard University Archives, <https://id.lib.harvard.edu/ead/c/hua10017c00002/catalog>.
3. Letter from Alfred North Whitehead to T. North Whitehead, 15 March 1925, MS 282, Alfred North Whitehead Collection, Box 2, Folder 19, Special Collections, Sheridan Libraries, Johns Hopkins University, <https://catalyst.library.jhu.edu/catalog/bib_505857>.
4. Letter from Alfred North Whitehead to T. North Whitehead, 31 May 1925, MS 282, Alfred North Whitehead Collection, Box 2, Folder 19, Special Collections, Sheridan Libraries, Johns Hopkins University, <https://catalyst.library.jhu.edu/catalog/bib_505857>.

Whitehead spent the first month of summer turning his Lowell lectures into the manuscript for *Science and the Modern World*. He submitted it to Macmillan for publication on 9 July and urged for a speedy publication.[1] In the meantime, Whitehead's daughter Jessie had emigrated from England in late June.[2] He asked his friend James H. Woods, the Philosophy Department Chair, to recommend her for a position in Harvard's Widener Library; they needed someone who could read Arabic, with which Jessie had some familiarity. She started her new job on 20 July and did well at it; she was promoted in early November.[3] Whitehead seems to have spent the remainder of the summer resting, including spending most of August at Lawrence J. Henderson's cabin in Vermont.

Whitehead made a few changes to his classes for the 1925–6 academic year. He changed the title of his Philosophy 3b lectures from 'Philosophical Presuppositions of Science' to the more straightforward 'Philosophy of Science'. The Harvard and Radcliffe catalogues had slightly different subtitles: 'General metaphysical problems' and 'General metaphysical and logical problems', respectively. His two seminaries[4] remained 'Philosophy 20h: Seminary in Metaphysics' and 'Philosophy 20i: Seminary in Logic', but he inverted their order from the previous year, when he had taught the logic seminary during the first term. In his student record book (a grading notebook), he titled them 'Principia' for the first term and 'Space-Time-Alexander' for the second.[5] As in his first year, he taught his Philosophy 3b on Tuesdays, Thursdays and Saturdays from 9 to 10 a.m. at Radcliffe,[6] and noon to 1 p.m. at Harvard, and his seminaries on Fridays from 7:30 to 9:30 p.m. at his home; the seminaries did not have separate sessions for the Harvard and Radcliffe students, but brought them all together.

Detailed accounts of Whitehead's teaching style have been published elsewhere,[7] but suffice it to say that Philosophy 3b was Whitehead's primary

---

1. Letter from Alfred North Whitehead to Macmillan Company, 9 July 1925, MssCol 1830, Macmillan Company Records, Series 1 (Author Files), Whitehead, Alfred North, <http://archives.nypl.org/mss/1830#c1048570>).
2. For more on Jessie Whitehead, see Brian G. Henning, 'Whitehead's daughter, Jessie', Whitehead Research Project website, 15 January 2020, <http://whiteheadresearch.org/2020/01/15/jessie-marie-whitehead>.
3. Letter from Alfred North Whitehead to T. North Whitehead, 1925, MS 282, Alfred North Whitehead Collection, Box 2, Folder 21, Special Collections, Sheridan Libraries, Johns Hopkins University, <https://catalyst.library.jhu.edu/catalog/bib_505857>.
4. 'Seminary' is an older term for 'seminar'.
5. Whitehead, 'Student Record Book', p. 13, 15.
6. At the time, the repetition of Harvard classes at Radcliffe was strictly optional for each professor, and the increase in pay was not to scale with what they were already making. Whitehead's salary at Harvard was $8,000; he would receive $1,000 for lecturing at Radcliffe. Harvard and Radcliffe classes would not be integrated until 1943, six years after Whitehead's retirement. See Letter from James H. Woods to Whitehead, 18 June 1924, LET1003, Whitehead Research Library, <http://wrl.whiteheadresearch.org/items/show/1438>.
7. See especially Paul Bogaard's Introduction to the first volume of Harvard lectures, and Joseph Petek's Introduction to *Whitehead at Harvard, 1924–1925*: Paul A. Bogaard and Jason Bell (eds), *The Harvard Lectures of Alfred North Whitehead, 1924–1925: Philosophical Presuppositions of Science* (Edinburgh: Edinburgh University Press, 2017) (henceforth referred to as HL1 throughout the present volume); Joseph Petek, 'Introduction: Tales from the Whitehead mines – on Whitehead, his students and the challenges of editing the Critical Edition', in Brian G. Henning and Joseph Petek (eds), *Whitehead at Harvard, 1924–1925* (Edinburgh: Edinburgh University Press, 2020), pp. 1–37.

venue for developing and communicating his own thought. He prepared his lectures in advance, but did not simply read them; he was more extemporaneous than this. He would also get up to draw figures on the blackboard. He did not object to questions, but they were not encouraged (see the section on Lester Snow King, below). As already mentioned, there were typically 40-plus students and faculty in attendance, although many in the first two years were not taking the course for credit. The seminaries, by contrast, were less popular, drawing somewhere in the vicinity of a dozen students for the first few years.[1] They took place at Whitehead's home rather than in a classroom, and were centred as much around discussion of student presentations/papers as they were around Whitehead's teaching. Accounts of the seminaries are scarce in comparison with accounts of the lectures.

For his Philosophy 3b, Whitehead assigned *Science and the Modern World* to his students on the first day of class, despite the fact that it had not yet been published and would not be for another month.[2] Upon submission of the manuscript, he had asked Macmillan for a second set of proofs so that he could keep one set, and he could have had these on hand to teach from if he wished. Aside from his own books, he assigned reading on Aristotle, Descartes, Berkeley and Hume; among contemporary philosophers, he assigned books or articles by John Dewey, Samuel Alexander, Bertrand Russell, Henri Bergson, William James and C. D. Broad.

Broad is perhaps worth discussing a little further. Aside from a brief mention of Broad during Whitehead's 70th birthday celebration that later appeared in print, Whitehead does not discuss him at all in his published writings.[3] But for his classes, Broad served as an important foil, something that no one could have known about prior to the publication of Whitehead's Harvard lectures.[4]

Broad was younger than Whitehead by about a quarter century, and studied at Trinity College, Cambridge, near the end of Whitehead's tenure. He became a Fellow of Trinity in 1911, a year after Whitehead's departure. Broad was an admirer of Whitehead, at least since he reviewed *The Principles of Natural Knowledge* in 1920, but the thing that probably brought Broad to Whitehead's attention was the Tarner lectures at Trinity: Whitehead had delivered the first of these lectures in 1919 (which would become *The Concept of Nature*) and Broad

---

1. Whitehead's first Seminary in Logic in the spring of 1925 was credited by only two students, one of whom was J. Robert Oppenheimer, the father of the atomic bomb. He got a 'B' (Whitehead, 'Student Record Book', p. 5).
2. A letter from Whitehead's publisher informed him that the book was published in the last week of October. Letter from Curtice N. Hitchcock to Alfred North Whitehead, 4 November 1925, MssCol 1830, Macmillan Company Records, Series 1 (Author Files), Whitehead, Alfred North, Archives and Manuscripts, New York Public Library, <http://archives.nypl.org/mss/1830#c1048570>.
3. Speeches at the celebration were recorded and Whitehead's later appeared in Alfred North Whitehead, *The Interpretation of Science: Selected Essays*, ed. A. H. Johnson (Indianapolis: Bobbs-Merrill, 1961), chapter 16.
4. For more on Broad and Whitehead, see Brian G. Henning, 'Whitehead in class: do the Harvard–Radcliffe course notes change how we understand Whitehead's thought?', in Brian G. Henning and Joseph Petek (eds), *Whitehead at Harvard, 1924–1925* (Edinburgh: Edinburgh University Press, 2020), pp. 337–56.

the second set of lectures, in 1923.¹ No doubt Whitehead would have been interested in the work of his successor to the Tarner lectureship.

In Broad, Whitehead would find a philosopher with whom he was in fundamental disagreement on certain key points, but who had the virtue of expressing himself clearly. Broad's *Scientific Thought* and, later, *The Mind and Its Place and Nature* would become standard reading for Whitehead's students during his entire Harvard tenure, chiefly, it seems, as an example of the kind of anti-metaphysical philosophy that he opposed. Whitehead would go so far as to read several pages of Broad's books aloud in class, with interruptions for commentary.² Broad, for his part, never ceased being an admirer of Whitehead's work, though in the obituary he wrote for *Mind* in 1948, he noted that *Process and Reality* was 'one of the most difficult philosophical books that exist', and that 'I cannot pretend to understand much of it, and I cannot help thinking that many of its enthusiastic admirers must simply be counted among those who "wonder with a foolish face of praise"'.³ Whitehead had once famously said that Bertrand Russell considered him muddle-headed, while he thought Bertie was simple-minded;⁴ Broad seems as though he could have taken Russell's place in this comparison.

In the autumn of 1925, Whitehead not only taught his own classes, but also attended at least one regularly. His pocket appointment book for the year lists 'Woods at 3–4' every Monday, Wednesday and Friday.⁵ This was probably Woods's 'Philosophy 12: Early Greek philosophy, with especial reference to Plato'. Woods may have been a greater influence on Whitehead than is generally realised, especially with regard to Plato and Buddhism.⁶ The appointment book also reveals frequent individual meetings with students, faculty meetings on Tuesdays at 4 p.m., and social engagements with people such as Henry Osborn Taylor, William McDougall⁷ and Felix Frankfurter.⁸

During the winter recess after the autumn term, Whitehead attended his first meeting of the American Philosophical Association (APA), and gave a paper on the topic of time on 30 December 1925. This was never published, though he would give another paper at the Sixth International Congress of Philosophy that would be published (see below). It seems probable that much of the content

---

1. Incidentally, the third set of Tarner lectures would be delivered by Bertrand Russell in 1926.
2. See the lecture of 16 October 1926, pp. 189–90.
3. C. D. Broad, 'Alfred North Whitehead (1861–1947)', *Mind*, vol. 57(226) (1948), p. 144.
4. This apparently originated from Whitehead's introduction of Russell for the latter's William James lectures at Harvard in 1940. See George Lucas, '"Muddleheadedness" vs. "simplemindedness" – comparisons of Whitehead and Russell', *Process Studies*, vol. 17(1) (spring 1988), pp. 26–39.
5. Alfred North Whitehead, 'Pocket Engagement Book, 1925–26', MS 282, Alfred North Whitehead Collection, Box 7, Folder 3, Special Collections, Sheridan Libraries, Johns Hopkins University, <https://catalyst.library.jhu.edu/catalog/bib_505857>.
6. Joseph Petek, 'Whitehead and James Haughton Woods', Whitehead Research Project website, 8 October 2018, <http://whiteheadresearch.org/2018/10/08/whitehead-and-james-haughton-woods>.
7. See note 1, p. 70.
8. Felix Frankfurter (1882–1965) held a chair at Harvard Law School and became one of Whitehead's closest friends after his arrival in America. For more on the relationship between Frankfurter and Whitehead, see Joseph Petek, 'Whitehead and Felix Frankfurter', Whitehead Research Project website, 13 November 2019, <http://whiteheadresearch.org/2019/11/13/whitehead-and-felix-frankfurter>.

for Whitehead's APA paper appeared in his Harvard lectures (his lectures of 12 December 1925 and 14 January 1926 suggest themselves here); Whitehead would not only share some of his work in his lectures that would later appear in print, but he would also on occasion 'recycle' recently published work or work recently delivered elsewhere with his classes, often with accompanying commentary on it.

In February 1926, the 'Committee of Four' – consisting of Whitehead, Lawrence J. Henderson, John Livingston Lowes and Charles P. Curtis – began to meet.[1] Their purpose was to choose four to eight 'Junior Fellows' per year for the newly created 'Society of Fellows', based on a system of Prize Fellowships at Trinity College, Cambridge. Each chosen Fellow would devote three years to the research that most interested them, with an option for three more. The first Fellows chosen were W. V. O. Quine, B. F. Skinner, Garrett Birkhoff, John C. Miller, Frederick M. Watkins and E. Bright Wilson, Jr. Though meetings began in 1926, the Society was not officially established until 1933, thanks to a donation from Harvard President Abbott Lawrence Lowell shortly before his resignation in 1932.

The spring semester of 1926 also proved to be something of a repeat for Whitehead in that he gave a second set of Lowell lectures – this time four instead of eight – on religion. He titled them: 'Religion: Its Passing Forms and Eternal Truths'. But in a letter of 10 March to Curtice Hitchcock, Whitehead's editor at Macmillan, he said that he had chosen the title *Religion in the Making* for the new book based on these lectures, as he did not like the original title: 'It is pompous and turgid'.[2]

During Harvard's spring break, Whitehead delivered lectures at McGill University (Montreal, Canada), the University of Michigan and the University of Illinois.[3] Whitehead's appointment book[4] reveals a tightly packed schedule for the trip. He took a night train to Montreal on Saturday, 17 April, after delivering his usual Philosophy 3b lectures that morning. He delivered his lecture in Montreal on 19 April, travelled to Ann Arbor on 20 April, and delivered his lecture at the University of Michigan on 21 April, followed by a day of travel to Urbana, where he delivered a series of lectures at the University of Illinois from 23 to 28 April. He arrived back in Boston shortly after noon on Friday, 30 April, in time to hold his seminary at 7:30 p.m. that night.

After another busy spring term, Whitehead took some time to decompress, staying with Henry Osborn Taylor and Julia Isham Taylor – the people who had provided the money for his salary, unbeknownst to him – in New York for about 10 days in early June, just after his Philosophy 3b students had sat their exams on 3 June. He followed this with a trip to the University of Wisconsin at

---

1. Victor Lowe, *Alfred North Whitehead: The Man and His Work, Volume II: 1910–1947* (Baltimore: Johns Hopkins University Press, 1990), pp. 254–6.
2. Letter from Alfred North Whitehead to Curtice N. Hitchcock, 10 March 1926, MssCol 1830, Macmillan Company Records, Series 1 (Author Files), Whitehead, Alfred North, Archives and Manuscripts, New York Public Library, <http://archives.nypl.org/mss/1830#c1048570>.
3. The content of these lectures is unknown. See Lowe, *Alfred North Whitehead, Vol. II*, pp. 206–7.
4. Whitehead, 'Pocket Engagement Book, 1925–26'.

Madison from 19 to 22 June, and returned to Boston in time for 'degree day' on 24 June.

Religion in the Making was published in late August, in time for the Sixth International Congress of Philosophy at Harvard, which ran from 13 to 17 September, at which Whitehead would present his paper 'Time', likely a refined version of the unpublished paper on time that he had delivered in December 1925. This paper was published in the proceedings of the Congress,[1] and Whitehead would re-present it to his seminary students about two weeks later as a lead-off to the autumn 1926 term, passing out a printed abstract for students to keep.[2]

Whitehead's son, North, and his wife, Margot, would sail to America for a visit during the term, arriving in New York on 11 October. Whitehead's appointment book reveals that North stayed for about a month, and Margot about two months. They emigrated to America permanently in 1931, where North would join the faculty of the Harvard Business School.

As during the previous year, in 1926–7 Whitehead participated in some classes other than his own. One was an appearance in Richard Clarke Cabot's Social Ethics seminary. Whitehead was the guest speaker in this class on 18 October, but probably attended other sessions of it as well. A transcript of the 18 October session has been included in this volume; see the discussion of it below. We also know that he was a frequent visitor to the classes of Étienne Gilson, who was a visiting professor for the autumn term from the University of Paris.[3] In the spring of 1927, Whitehead also delivered four lectures in Harvard's 'Philosophy A', an undergraduate introductory course that was co-taught by various members of the department. We have notes for these lectures, as well; see the discussion of them below.

On 30 November and 2 December, Charles Hartshorne guest lectured in Whitehead's Philosophy 3b; Raphael Demos did the same thing on 14 December. It seems likely that Whitehead was absent on these days, though it also seems possible that he was present and simply wanted to give the two men a venue to express some of their ideas. A few of our student note-takers recorded these lectures, while others specifically omitted them; we have not included these lectures in the volume.

Whitehead discussed C. Lloyd Morgan a great deal at the beginning of the spring 1927 term. Morgan had given the presidential address to the Aristotelian Society on 1 November 1926, with the title 'Objects under reference'.[4] It explicitly discusses and works through ideas from Whitehead's *Science and the*

---

1. Alfred North Whitehead, 'Time', in Edgar Sheffield Brightman (ed.), *Proceedings of the Sixth International Congress of Philosophy* (New York: Longmans, Green and Co., 1927), pp. 59–64.
2. See the seminary of 1 October, pp. 342–7. Whitehead would also teach the content of the same paper to his Philosophy 3b students, but with significant additions and commentary; see the lectures of 4, 7, 9 and 11 December 1926.
3. Joseph Petek, 'Whitehead and Étienne Gilson', Whitehead Research Project website, 10 May 2018, <http://whiteheadresearch.org/2018/05/10/whitehead-and-etienne-gilson>.
4. C. Lloyd Morgan, 'Objects under reference: the presidential address', *Proceedings of the Aristotelian Society*, New Series, vol. 27 (1926–7), pp. 1–20.

Modern World, the preface of which acknowledged indebtedness to Morgan and Samuel Alexander. Whitehead read portions of Morgan's address to his seminary students on 25 February, comparing Morgan's formulation to his own.[1] Whitehead likely did not know at the time that Morgan had since delivered another lecture, entitled 'A concept of the organism, emergent and resultant', on 14 February, less than two weeks before this seminary, in which he had again explicitly discussed *Science and the Modern World*.

Again echoing the previous year, Whitehead spent his April spring break lecturing, this time delivering the Barbour-Page lectures at the University of Virginia, which would become his *Symbolism: Its Meaning and Effect*. Though we have only Paul Weiss's notes for Whitehead's Harvard lecture in early May 1927 and those are rather scant, it appears that Whitehead repeated most or all of this material to his Philosophy 3b students upon his return.

And thus concludes our brief account of Whitehead's activities for his second and third years at Harvard, 1925–7. During the following year (1927–8), he would be much preoccupied with writing his Gifford lectures, and perhaps this is the thing to end on. He had in fact received the invitation to deliver the Gifford lectures at Edinburgh in 1928 on 17 January 1927, just a few days after he had delivered his last lecture of the autumn term, on 15 January. He accepted the invitation on 27 February, and proposed a title for the lectures, 'The concept of organism', in a letter to Norman Kemp Smith dated 6 April 1927.[2] The title would, of course, be changed to *Process and Reality*, and become his most celebrated work.

It is worth noting as a conclusion to this portion of the introduction that in the preface to *Process and Reality*, Whitehead wrote that 'In the expansion of these lectures to the dimensions of the present book, I have been greatly indebted to the critical difficulties suggested by the members of my Harvard classes'.[3] Just as Whitehead found the comments of his students helpful in his own writing, we hope that readers will find their accounts of his lectures illuminating.

Editorial handling of the lectures

Multiple accounts

The first problem we faced in editing this volume was an embarrassment of riches. While the first volume of Harvard lectures included two full duplicate sets of Harvard notes – which were edited in parallel – for the second volume there are sometimes as many as five different accounts for a single lecture.

---

1. See pp. 372–5.
2. Letter from Alfred North Whitehead to Norman Kemp Smith, 6 April 1927, Papers of Professor Norman Kemp Smith, Coll-1038 Gen.1416.5 ff128–129, Special Collections, University of Edinburgh Library, <http://lac-archives-live.is.ed.ac.uk:8081/repositories/2/resources/416>.
3. Alfred North Whitehead, *Process and Reality: An Essay in Cosmology* (New York: Free Press, [1929] 1978), pp. xiv–xv.

Reproducing all five accounts in full in a printed book was never a realistic option, so we were forced to come up with an alternative.

The common-sense solution that we came to fairly quickly was to reproduce in full the best set of notes for a given period. However, we were acutely aware of the ironical sense of the old adage 'A person with one watch knows exactly what time it is, while a person with two watches is never sure'. In short, while there would have been a comforting illusion of certainty in relying upon a single set of notes for Whitehead's lectures, the fact is that these student note-takers not only made errors, but often left out significant portions of what Whitehead was saying. We can hardly blame them for this, since these students were taking notes for an audience of one: themselves. They had no notion that their notes might later be edited and printed for the benefit of future generations, and so they copied down the bits of Whitehead's lectures that they considered to be the most relevant or interesting, while leaving out the rest.

We were thus determined to make use of all the materials at our disposal, using alternative accounts to cross-check and supplement our chosen account through footnotes. The importance of these alternative accounts, and the extent to which they have enriched the volume as a whole, can hardly be overestimated. Through comparison of the different parallel sets of notes, we were able to spot numerous errors and read many otherwise indecipherable words, not to mention to add content that was missing completely in our primary account.

The actual mechanics of the comparison had several stages. First, we compared undated sets of notes with dated ones side by side in order to determine likely lecture break points and dates (this was a complex endeavour in itself – see the next section), then used that data to build a spreadsheet that laid out which note-takers had lecture notes for which dates, and the corresponding page numbers in the original manuscripts where each lecture appeared. After that, we split each set of notes into separate documents by lecture date, which allowed us to quickly reference all different accounts for any given date without needing to track them down in each full original manuscript. When it came time to integrate the various accounts, we picked the most detailed version, and then – theoretically, at least – worked information from the alternative accounts in as footnotes to the base document one at a time. In practice, we usually had all the relevant documents open on screen at the same time – which could be as many as five different transcribed student accounts, plus the original handwritten base account, and possibly a book that Whitehead was reading from or referencing – because if we did locate some element that was important enough to add in as a footnote, it was important to check how many of the other accounts had something similar, and might have expressed it in a more detailed or more elegant way.

It was not always easy to decipher where text from an alternative account should be placed within our chosen primary text, as accounts could vary widely in content and phrasing, with students focusing on different details of Whitehead's lecture and wording. But we were usually able to sufficiently orient ourselves by key words or phrases that were common to all or most accounts of a given lecture. One example of four people catching almost exactly the same phrase is this instance from the lecture delivered on 19 October 1926:

Conger: But process of knowing ought to be something general of which we are only particular modes.

Nelson: The process of knowing has obviously got to be something general of which we are particular modes.

King: The process of knowing is obviously something general of which we are only particular modes.

Jackson: Process of knowing must be general of which you and I are particular molds.

Here Jackson appears to have made an overt error, hearing 'molds' instead of 'modes'; such mis-hearings were not uncommon. But in any case, such key words and phrases acted as signposts for our process of comparison, and generally allowed us to insert additional content as footnotes in the correct place in our chosen primary accounts with a fairly high degree of accuracy.

As a practical matter, we did not usually note where different accounts largely agree with one another, as this would have overburdened the already considerable number of footnotes. However, whenever a set of notes contained material that our primary account did not, or contained significantly different or significantly clearer phrasing, we have included a note at the appropriate place. We only rarely venture an opinion as to which account is more likely to be correct, leaving readers to make their own judgements.

It should be noted that in the midst of the editing process, we enacted one important systemic change. We had originally envisioned choosing a single set of notes for a given time period and sticking to it, which had the benefit of providing a higher degree of stylistic consistency for readers. But in beginning to edit notes for the spring 1926 term, we discovered that Edward Robinson's partial set of notes (covering about half the term) were considerably more complete on average than those of Fritz Roethlisberger, who had covered the whole academic year. We also found that sometimes our chosen note-taker would have an off day, with an alternative account being more thorough and complete for one particular lecture. This was leading to some lectures having more content in the footnotes than the body of the text, since we were filling in a less complete account with footnotes from a more complete one. In the end, we decided to abandon the idea of sticking to a single account for a given period of time, and instead choose our primary account on a lecture-by-lecture basis. Thus, each lecture in this volume has the name of the note-taker just below the date, so that there is never any confusion about whose account forms the primary presentation.

Though this process of cross-comparison of alternative accounts slowed down editing considerably, we believe that the end result provides readers with a text that most nearly approaches Whitehead's complete original words, and which is in some ways even more useful than a full reproduction of every available archival source, since it picks out the most salient differences while eliminating the redundant portions. Nonetheless, it is important to us that the unused alternative accounts, the ones that we have not reproduced here in full, be available to Whitehead scholars who wish to see them. We are thus making all of these available – as far as is possible under copyright restrictions – at the Whitehead Research Project website (whiteheadresearch.org).

For a full listing of all notes available to us in editing this volume broken down by date, see the tables in Appendix 1 (pp. 414–20).

Lecture dates

Correctly dating the notes – particularly those taken during the autumn of 1925 – was a serious problem early on. Our two Harvard accounts for autumn 1925 (Roethlisberger and Hartshorne) did not date consistently, leaving us unsure as to where the lecture breaks were. The only person who did date consistently was Louise Heath, who was a student at Radcliffe rather than Harvard. It seemed dangerous to try to date the Harvard notes by comparison with Heath, since Whitehead lectured at Harvard and Radcliffe separately, even though nominally the same course was delivered at each. Further, we knew from preparing the Harvard lectures for the first volume of the Critical Edition that frequently Whitehead was not lecturing on the same material on the same day at both Harvard and Radcliffe.

However, what we discovered through a close comparison of these different sets of notes is that when Roethlisberger and Hartshorne did provide dates, the content of their notes did largely match the content from the corresponding date in the notes of Heath. This fact led us to decide to try to supply dates for the Harvard notes whenever we could make a credible guess – based partly on Heath's notes from the Radcliffe lectures – despite the inherent danger of misdating material. We came to believe that lecture dates were too important as an organisational apparatus to exclude.

A few things should be made clear here. First, supplied dates are always bracketed to indicate that they are editorial insertions not found in the original document (e.g. '⟨Thursday, 8 October 1925⟩'). Second, comparison with Heath's notes was not the *only* thing we used to date the Harvard notes (indeed, Heath's notes were available only for autumn 1925); we also made use of contextual clues within the Harvard notes themselves. For instance, sometimes a lot of blank space would be left at the bottom of a page, while at other times there was evidently a change of pen or of ink quality, a change in the quality of the handwriting, or a line drawn between one paragraph and the next. None of these things by itself provides surety of a lecture break. But when taken together, in most cases these clues have allowed us to make credible guesses at lecture dates with a reasonable degree of confidence. In most cases we provide a note accompanying date insertions to explain our reasons for thinking that the material was presented on that day. In a few cases we could not confidently estimate the date and have instead provided a heading with a range of likely dates for the material.

Text standardisation

A full list of standardisations can be found in the Editorial principles (pp. xiii–xv), but we want to discuss in more detail a few of the most important standardisations here.

First, shorthand has been expanded silently. This is not a practice that is generally recommended for critical editions; normally, such expansions would be marked in the body of the text, or there would be a back-of-book record of the changes. However, while this practice makes perfect sense for artefacts such as letters, unpublished essays and drafts, it is impractical to the point of impossibility for lecture notes of students, which in some cases employ shorthand for nearly every word. Marking expansions would make the text so cluttered as to be unreadable, while a back-of-book record would be as large as the rest of the volume itself. We thus adopted the practice of silent expansion of shorthand out of necessity. Of course, we could not always be sure of the correct expansion of a word, and in these cases we have placed the word in angle brackets and/or provided a footnote describing the difficulty.

Second, in some sets of notes (particularly George Conger's) it is not easy to discern a linear order. For instance, Conger sometimes wrote his notes in 'blocks' of text on different parts of the page (see the example in the section discussing Conger's notes below, p. xlix). At other times, a note-taker would make a marginal addition for which the correct insertion point was not obvious. In all cases we have done our best to put this ambiguously placed text in a linear order, often aided by comparison with alternative sets of notes that maintain a more linear presentation. Text that was particularly difficult to place has been accompanied by a footnote describing the problem.

Third, in a number of places Whitehead was clearly reading portions of a text aloud to his class (sometimes his own work and sometimes the work of others). We decided that it in these cases it would be useful to distinguish what was being read from Whitehead's comments on those passages. Thus, text being read aloud is rendered in **bold**. As a practical matter, this has been done solely in the notes of Conger, since only his notes caught Whitehead's phrasing in exact enough detail to discern when a text was being quoted verbatim. And while we certainly cannot guarantee that we have caught every place in the lectures where such reading aloud occurs, the portions that we have bolded are ones that we are quite sure about. We sometimes accompany these bolded portions with the original text as a footnote (particularly in places where the student has really butchered a passage), both to give a wholly accurate reading of some key passages, and to provide the reader with a better sense of just how much of Whitehead's lecture the note-taker was catching versus missing, providing a window into the overall fidelity of the student's notes.

The note-takers and their notes

The main course that Whitehead offered at both Harvard and Radcliffe was Philosophy 3b, which could be 'taken as a half-course in either half-year',

Introduction to *The Harvard Lectures of Alfred North Whitehead, 1925–1927*

though in practice many students would take it for the whole year. The bulk of this volume consists of notes from this class. Our source texts for Philosophy 3b are four sets of notes for 1925–6, and six sets of notes for 1926–7. These are discussed below for each academic year, under the names of the note-takers, where some general information is given about the note-takers themselves, together with an overview of the state of their notes and the attendant difficulties, and a description of how they are used within this volume. Similar consideration is then given to Whitehead's seminaries and other lectures for 1926–7 for which notes were available. An example page for each set of notes is presented in Appendix 2. For full citations of all the archival sources that make up the text of this volume, see the Acknowledgements section at the end of this Introduction.

1925–6

Louise Robinson Heath (1899–1988)

We begin with Louise Heath, who is both the only returning note-taker from the first volume of Harvard lectures and the only representative of Whitehead's Radcliffe lectures in either volume. As Paul Bogaard detailed in his Introduction to HL1, she was born in Iowa in 1899, graduated from Newton Public High School in Massachusetts with honours in 1917, and attended Mount Holyoke as a 'Mary Lyon Scholar' (named for Mount Holyoke's founder) in Philosophy and Biblical Literature, earning her AB in 1921. She began her PhD at Radcliffe shortly after, earning her degree in 1927. She then taught for 20 years at Hood College, in Frederick, Maryland, as a professor of philosophy and psychology, and was dean of Keuka College in New York from 1947 until her retirement in 1954. She died in 1988.[1]

In the preface to her one major publication, *The Concept of Time* (1936), Heath wrote: 'It is evident, however, that on this subject my thought has been very much influenced by Professor Whitehead. To him I owe thanks not only for sharing his thoughts on time but also for his time, both in class and in conference.'[2] Thanks to our recent acquisition of Whitehead's 1925–6 appointment book, we know now that she wasn't kidding about spending time in conference with Whitehead. She met with him at least half a dozen times during the spring 1926 term, usually at 10:30 a.m. on Saturdays, between the end of his Radcliffe lecture at 10 a.m. and the beginning of his Harvard lecture, at noon.[3] We also know from a page of Heath's notes[4] that for this year she was attending or considering attending seminaries taught by Whitehead, William Ernest Hocking and Ralph Barton Perry, along with Hocking's lecture course on metaphysics, and C. I. Lewis's course on Kant. Whitehead's grading notebook

---

1. HL1, pp. xxxiv–xxxv.
2. Louise Robinson Heath, *The Concept of Time* (Chicago: University of Chicago Press, 1936), p. vii.
3. Whitehead, 'Pocket Engagement Book, 1925–26'.
4. Page 83 of Heath's notes, which we have omitted from the body of the notes, since it contains nothing other than a course listing.

also confirms[1] that she attended his spring 1926 seminary, titled 'Space-Time-Alexander' in the notebook, receiving an 'A' for the course, though we never found any of her notes for this seminary (nor any others for the seminaries in the academic year 1925–6). She is not listed in Whitehead's notebook as an attendee of Philosophy 3b for autumn 1925, despite the fact that she claims to have 'credited it', but she was the only one of Whitehead's four Radcliffe students in 1924–5 to receive 'straight A's'.[2]

It is rather gratifying for us as editors of this volume (and, indeed, this series of volumes) that at the top of Heath's notes she wrote that this autumn 1925 session of Whitehead's Philosophy 3b was 'Theoretically same course as 1924, but I credited it because actually it was quite different'.[3] This reinforces our argument for the desirability of publishing Whitehead's student notes across all his Harvard years: he was not one to repeat the same material year after year, but instead taught whatever he was thinking about at the moment.

Heath's notes were sent to Victor Lowe and currently reside in the Victor Lowe Papers at Johns Hopkins University. They consist of 88 original, handwritten pages for the autumn 1925 term only, beginning on 1 October 1925 and ending on 7 January 1926. The notes are consistently dated and well organised. The pages are also numbered consistently on both the fronts and backs of the sheets, though this numbering does not seem to be original, and was probably added by Victor Lowe, who had also numbered Heath's notes for 1924–5, complete with notes in pencil to his student assistant, Bruce Epperly. Her attendance prior to the Thanksgiving break was good, though afterwards it became somewhat spottier; in total, she attended 29 of the 41 autumn 1925 lectures. We have omitted a page that appears to have been second-hand notes for a Whitehead seminary, though we cannot be certain; see note 1 on page 8 for a fuller discussion of this.

Heath's notes are of a quality consistent with those from the previous year, and are about as thorough as any of the notes taken by Roethlisberger and Hartshorne. At times her notes are actually considerably clearer than those of her Harvard counterparts,[4] though we cannot be sure if Heath was taking better notes at these places, or whether Whitehead himself was explaining things more clearly.

Since Heath's notes for autumn 1925 represent the only Radcliffe lectures in this volume, we have reproduced them in full. They are thus the only notes published in this volume which might be considered 'repetitious', since Whitehead was nominally teaching the same material to Roethlisberger, Hartshorne, Edward Robinson and the rest of his Harvard students, but they are no less valuable for it. We have provided footnotes for each of the Radcliffe lectures pointing the reader to the page number of the corresponding Harvard

---

1. Whitehead, 'Student Record Book', p. 15.
2. Whitehead, 'Student Record Book', p. 3.
3. See p. 3.
4. Certain sections from the 19 November 1925 and 5 January 1926 lectures are good examples. See note 2, p. 83, and note 3, p. 100.

lecture, and vice versa, but unlike the Harvard notes, for which we have made every effort to provide detailed footnotes on the differences between the various archival sources, we have done little of this for the notes of Heath, seeing as the Radcliffe lectures technically constituted a separate class. We have duplicated some footnotes in the Harvard and Radcliffe lectures in the 1925 fall semester to save the reader needing to flip back and forth between them.

Fritz Jules Roethlisberger (1898–1974)

Fritz Roethlisberger is probably best known as a key social science researcher in the Hawthorne experiments of the 1920s and 1930s under Elton Mayo, which studied ways to improve worker productivity at a Western Electric factory in Cicero, Illinois, just outside Chicago. In 1927, a year after his course with Whitehead, Roethlisberger put his PhD studies in philosophy aside in order to become an instructor of industrial research and Mayo's assistant at the Harvard Business School, and would spend the rest of his career there, eventually becoming the Wallace Brett Donham Professor of Human Relations from 1950 until his death in 1974.[1] He published multiple books on management theory, but the most famous was his 1939 *Management and the Worker*, co-authored with William J. Dickson, which presented the first comprehensive results from the Hawthorne experiments.

Though it would not occur until years after the notes for this volume were taken, Whitehead ended up with an oblique connection to Roethlisberger through his son, T. North, who migrated to America in 1931 to join the faculty of the Harvard Business School. Like Roethlisberger, North would also work on the Hawthorne experiments, and would publish his *The Industrial Worker: A Statistical Study of Human Relations in a Group of Manual Workers* in 1938, a year before Roethlisberger and Dickson published their results. The two men would have known each other well, and though we have no direct evidence of it, it seems somewhat likely that Roethlisberger and Whitehead would have encountered one another at least sporadically in the years following North's arrival.

Roethlisberger is the only one of our three Harvard note-takers for 1925–6 who was taking the class for credit; Hartshorne, who completed his PhD in 1923, was sitting in as Whitehead's assistant and an instructor in the department, while Robinson was auditing. Roethlisberger received an 'A-' for the first half of the course and an 'A' for the second half.[2]

Roethlisberger's notes are held by the Baker Library of the Harvard Business School, and consist of 89 original, handwritten pages covering the entire 1925–6 academic year, beginning on 1 October 1925 and ending on 25 May 1926. The notes were bundled together with Roethlisberger's four essays for the course,

---

1. Jeffrey Mifflin, 'Biographical Note', Fritz J. Roethlisberger Papers, Harvard Business School Archives, Baker Library, Harvard Business School, <https://id.lib.harvard.edu/ead/bak00040/catalog>.
2. Whitehead, 'Student Record Book', p. 16.

totalling 41 pages, which we have not published here.¹ The bundle also included an abstract of Whitehead's paper 'Time'² and a copy of the mid-year exam for 1925–6, which appears at the end of the notes for the autumn 1925 lectures (see page 112). Finally, Roethlisberger's notes contain five pages of material on Whitehead that we cannot identify; it is possible that they are Roethlisberger's own 'review notes', or study material for an exam, or seminary notes. We have omitted these five pages from the volume.

The notes are consistently numbered, probably by Roethlisberger himself (though this numbering contains some errors), with the numbering resetting at the beginning of the spring term and, outside of some confusion surrounding the 16–23 March lectures, they are well organised. They are not, however, consistently dated, particularly during the autumn term. As discussed earlier in this Introduction,³ we have endeavoured to supply dates for Roethlisberger's notes in places where he omitted them, based partly on a comparison with the notes of Heath, Hartshorne and Robinson, and partly on contextual clues within the notes themselves. Though we cannot be sure of all dates, from what we can tell, Roethlisberger's attendance was remarkably consistent; if he missed any sessions at all, they were toward the end of May as the class was wrapping up. But since no one else has any notes for these dates either, we cannot say for sure whether they even took place.

Roethlisberger's notes are reasonably thorough, though not spectacularly so; he generally recorded around 300–600 words per lecture in the autumn term and 200–400 per lecture in the spring term. Where they *are* spectacular is in neatness and organisation. He had by far the neatest handwriting of any of our note-takers, a gorgeous longhand script that at times could almost be mistaken for a printed font. He was also meticulously neat and precise in his habits; lacking lined paper, he drew his own left marginal line on every page with a straight edge for the purpose of creating a place for notes, and similarly often drew horizontal lines when Whitehead moved on to what Roethlisberger considered to be a new topic. We have moved Roethlisberger's marginal notes into the body of the text with a footnote indicating the move, except in cases where Roethlisberger was clearly making his own comment or judgement on the content; these instances have been moved to footnotes.

Roethlisberger was also in the habit of going back through his notes at some point after the class was over and amending them with his own descriptive headings (which were usually in printed rather than cursive handwriting) and other comments. Early on in the editing process, we attempted to indicate to readers which bits of Roethlisberger's notes appeared to have been later additions, but we eventually decided to abandon this practice, for a number of reasons: (1) the additions are by Roethlisberger himself; (2) in many cases it

---

1. Their titles are: 'Problem of Kant', 'The Method of Logical Analysis', 'A Comparison of Bergson and Dr. Whitehead on Time' and 'Approaches to a Philosophy of Nature'.
2. The presence of this abstract in Roethlisberger's notes is a little odd, since Whitehead would not deliver the paper until September 1926, months after this course was over.
3. See 'Lecture dates', p. xxxv.

is unclear what is a later addition and what is merely an interlineation inserted during the lecture, and we do not want to engage in guessing, or the illusion that what we have marked as definitely additions are the *only* additions; and (3) in some cases it is clear that such later amendments are not any kind of guesswork by Roethlisberger, but were made through consultation with either Whitehead or another student, as they contain examples which match up with other student notes and are too specific to be coincidence.[1]

Out of the 78 lectures for 1925–6 for which we have notes, we use Roethlisberger's account as the primary one 57 times. In all but five cases we found Roethlisberger's notes preferable to Hartshorne's, though in some cases it was a close call, and we tended to default to Roethlisberger's account for the sake of consistency. Robinson's notes, when they were available, were more thorough, but since the majority of Robinson's notes were lost (see the section on Robinson below), Roethlisberger's account was usually the best available to us.

Charles Hartshorne (1897–2000)

For Whitehead scholars, Charles Hartshorne needs no introduction. Along with Whitehead himself and, later, John B. Cobb, Jr, Hartshorne is one of the pivotal figures in the development of Whiteheadian 'process philosophy' and 'process theology'.

Born in 1897, the son of Francis Cope Hartshorne and Marguerite Haughton, he attended Haverford College and spent two years as a hospital orderly in the US army before attending Harvard University, where he received his BA, MA and PhD degrees in consecutive years from 1921 to 1923. After spending two years in Europe on a Sheldon Fellowship studying under Husserl and Heidegger (among others), Hartshorne returned to Harvard to teach a course on the 'History of the Theory of Perception', assist Whitehead with his Philosophy 3b course (chiefly by helping him grade papers) and begin editing the Charles Peirce papers with Paul Weiss.[2] Following three years at Harvard, he was a professor at the University of Chicago from 1928 to 1955,[3] where he taught with a number of other professors interested in Whitehead's thought, including Henry Nelson Wieman, Bernard Loomer, Bernard Meland and Daniel Day Williams. Following his departure from Chicago, he taught at Emory University from 1955 to 1962, and at the University of Texas from 1962 until his retirement.[4]

Hartshorne's notes on Whitehead's 1925–6 lectures were by far the most problematic set of notes that we were faced with editing. Hartshorne had rediscovered the notes by chance in 1978 and 'edited' them by typing up otherwise indecipherable portions and attempting to correctly order them chronologically,

---

1. For example, in the lecture on 22 October 1925. See note 5, p. 63.
2. Charles Hartshorne, 'Some causes of my intellectual growth', in Lewis Edwin Hahn (ed.), *The Philosophy of Charles Hartshorne* (La Salle: Open Court, 1991), p. 24.
3. Hartshorne, 'Some causes of my intellectual growth', p. 26.
4. Hartshorne, 'Some causes of my intellectual growth', p. 37.

leaving a total of 75 original handwritten manuscript pages and eight typed pages, which he then sent on to the Center for Process Studies. In 2001, Roland Faber published a full transcription of the notes in the journal *Process Studies*.[1] Then, sometime between the publication of the notes in 2001 and the beginning of Petek's tenure at the Whitehead Research Project in 2013, the original notes were lost.

What we were left with as we began editing was Faber's transcription of the original notes, two photocopies of Hartshorne's notes held in the Hartshorne Archives at Claremont School of Theology (one of which was incomplete) and a third photocopy of the notes given to us by Lewis Ford (who will likewise be well known to many readers as the inaugural editor of *Process Studies*). All versions of the notes had different handwritten annotations; all versions had different handwritten page orders. In beginning to work on the notes, we chose to transcribe Ford's version first, and address the differences between the versions at a later stage in editing.

But the turning point in working on the Hartshorne notes came when we decided that we needed to compare them closely with the notes of Roethlisberger in order to verify the page order. What we discovered, somewhat to our shock, was that none of our archival photocopies was in anything close to the correct order. Hartshorne had neglected to date consistently when he originally recorded his notes, hence making a sure discernment of their correct order impossible; his later guesswork in the 1970s while 'editing' them probably did much more harm than good. In fairness, there was simply no way for either Hartshorne or Faber to know the correct order, as they had no reference point. Only comparison with a second set of notes by another student who had been sitting in on the same lectures could have accomplished a correct ordering, which was happily the situation we found ourselves in with the discovery of Roethlisberger's notes. To give the reader a sense of the extent of the disorder, what we now know to be the first six pages of Hartshorne's notes had been labelled in Ford's version as pages 1, 2, 6, 72, 22 and 19, despite the consequent syntactical and other problems.

With the re-ordering complete, we could finally begin to assess the true value of Hartshorne's account of Whitehead's lectures. As already mentioned, Hartshorne's notes consisted of 75 handwritten pages (photocopy rather than original) and eight typed pages of otherwise indecipherable handwritten pages. Even after comparison with the Roethlisberger notes, one of the pages could not be dated at all, and two more had so little content that we could not be sure of their date. The bulk of the notes range from 13 October 1925 to 16 March 1926, though there are significant gaps in Hartshorne's attendance; he also recorded a single lecture on 4 May, but this constitutes his only notes in the last two months of the course. In total, he seems to have recorded notes for about 37 or 38 lectures (the lack of consistent dating means we cannot be sure), next to the 78 recorded by Roethlisberger, averaging a little over 300 words per

---

1. Roland Faber, 'Charles Hartshorne's handwritten notes on A. N. Whitehead's Harvard lectures 1925–1926', *Process Studies*, vol. 30(2) (2001), pp. 289–373.

lecture. Unlike Roethlisberger and Robinson, Hartshorne did not often record Whitehead's figures. But one virtue of Hartshorne's notes is that he seemed fairly consistent in placing square brackets around his own comments on Whitehead's lectures, which were usually observations about the similarity of some idea of Whitehead's to ideas he had run across in his recent years studying in Germany under Husserl.

When we compared Hartshorne's notes to those of Roethlisberger, in most cases Roethlisberger's notes provided the more detailed account. Out of 78 lectures for 1925–6, we use Hartshorne's account as primary only five times. At times when the two sets of notes seemed about equal in level of detail, we tended to default to the notes of Roethlisberger, partly because lingering problems with the Hartshorne notes made us leery of them, including a few outstanding page order questions, and the fact that some of the handwritten pages were completely illegible in the photocopies, so that we were forced to rely on Hartshorne's typed account, itself somewhat suspect.[1] However, we do make frequent use of Hartshorne's account in footnotes to the notes of Roethlisberger and Robinson.

It may be a little shocking to some Whitehead scholars that we have not made more prominent use of Hartshorne's notes, given who he was and his importance in the history of Whiteheadian process thought generally. But we have discovered in our years of editing such material that a person's level of fame in the process community or the wider philosophical community has absolutely nothing to do with the quality of their personal notes, and have judged them solely on level of detail, fidelity and clarity. In the end, Hartshorne's notes simply were not as good as those of Roethlisberger or Robinson.

Edward Schouten Robinson (1904–68)

Out of all our note-takers, Robinson's story, and the story of his notes specifically, is surely the most tragic. An accident that took place in the late 1960s has had the effect of permanently impoverishing Whitehead scholarship.

Edward S. Robinson was born in 1904 in Vermont. He attended Harvard University, where he earned his AB in 1926, MA in 1928 and PhD in 1932. After stints of teaching at Harvard, Northeastern University, Kenyon College and Oklahoma State, he spent the bulk of his career at the University of Kansas. Arriving in 1946, he became professor of philosophy in 1961 and chaired the philosophy department from 1963 to 1965. His most significant scholarly contribution was a 1962 English translation with John Macquarrie of Heidegger's *Being and Time*.[2]

---

1. Hartshorne does not seem to have made any egregious changes that would significantly alter meaning, but he was also not endeavouring to transcribe the exact wording of his original notes. For example, at one point his original notes had the following: 'Plato and Aristotle over-emphasized the one aspect, the other, the other'. Hartshorne transcribed this as: 'Plato overemphasized the one aspect, Aristotle the other'. But since parts of Hartshorne's original notes are indeed completely illegible now, and not merely difficult to read, we simply cannot always be sure about the accuracy of Hartshorne's typed pages.
2. Richard T. De George, 'Edward Schouten Robinson 1904–1968', *Proceedings and Addresses of the American Philosophical Association*, vol. 41 (1967–8), p. 135.

In 1963, at around the same time that Robinson began chairing the University of Kansas philosophy department, Paul Weiss was encouraging the Yale Philosophy Club to initiate a project of collecting and transcribing Whitehead lecture notes taken by his students, much as the Whitehead Research Project is doing today.[1] Robinson was one of six former Whitehead students to send the Club his notes. They consisted of 410 consecutively numbered pages for 1925–6, and an unspecified additional number of pages for spring 1925.[2]

However, in 1966, after three years working on the project, the Yale Philosophy Club came to the conclusion that it had bitten off more than it could chew. With no money, working on typewriters and employing only the volunteer work of interested students, the Club decided to abandon the project, store the transcriptions they had completed in the Yale library and send the original notes back to their owners.[3] In the case of Robinson, they had transcribed only 79 pages, or less than 20% of what Robinson had sent them for 1925–6 (and nothing at all from the spring of 1925).

Here the tragedy ensued. In 1968, Robinson was killed by a car while crossing the street.[4] He had never married and had no close relatives. In a 2016 email exchange with Robinson's friend and colleague in the University of Kansas philosophy department, Richard De George – who had been with the department since 1959, and would go on to teach there for more than 50 years, until his retirement in 2012 – we learned that Robinson's heir had turned out to be a distant cousin from Switzerland. His effects were disposed of by his lawyer and the cousin; his books were mostly donated to the library at University of Kansas, but the fate of the remainder of Robinson's possessions remains unknown. De George opined that Robinson's notes were most likely destroyed, with his cousin and lawyer not knowing their value. Our efforts to track down the notes came to naught.

At first, we were not overly distraught by the apparent loss of Robinson's account of Whitehead's lectures. The notes of Hartshorne and especially Roethlisberger seemed perfectly adequate. Furthermore, the fact that the few Robinson notes we had were a typescript rather than original, and, in the words of the Yale Philosophy Club, '[had] not [been] proofread against the manuscripts',[5] made us believe that they would not be of much use in our project anyway, except perhaps in verifying or augmenting our other accounts. Then we read them. As it turned out, despite all the problems that came with

---

1. Brian G. Henning, 'Preface: a brief history of the Critical Edition of Whitehead', in Brian G. Henning and Joseph Petek (eds), *Whitehead at Harvard, 1924–1925* (Edinburgh: Edinburgh University Press, 2020), pp. ix–xxi.
2. Graduate Philosophy Club of Yale University, 'Notes from "Lectures of A. N. W. at Harvard" compiled by students, 1926–1937', Philosophy and Social Science Manuscripts Collection, MS 644, Box 10, Folder 98, Manuscripts and Archives, Yale University, <https://archives.yale.edu/repositories/12/archival_objects/1262622>, p. 1.
3. Graduate Philosophy Club of Yale University, 'Notes from "Lectures of A. N. W. at Harvard" compiled by students, 1926–1937', pp. v–vi.
4. Joe D. VanZandt, 'Editor's introduction', *Auslegung*, vol. 1(1) (1973), p. 4.
5. Graduate Philosophy Club of Yale University, 'Notes from "Lectures of A. N. W. at Harvard" compiled by students, 1926–1937', p. v.

Robinson's notes not being the original handwritten version, their content shone through as wholly superior to our other accounts. Not only were they generally more detailed, but they often caught Whitehead's own idiomatic phrasing where the others had failed to do so. Numbers-wise, Robinson's notes typically consisted of 600–800 words per lecture, significantly more than Roethlisberger's 300–500 for this same period. In hindsight, the fact that Robinson's original notes were composed of 410 pages, next to Roethlisberger's 89 and Hartshorne's 75, probably should have been a clue that they were a great deal more detailed (even allowing for the fact that Roethlisberger's handwriting was quite small, and that he fit a great deal of text onto each page).

In total, Robinson's notes as typed by the Yale Philosophy Club total 44 pages, not including a title page. In addition, a copy of the Club's transcription made by Victor Lowe, now held by Johns Hopkins,[1] includes Whitehead's mid-year exam for 1926–7. The inclusion of this exam with Robinson's notes is curious, since it was for the year after Robinson attended the class; quite possibly Lowe got it from somewhere else, and he or an archivist incorrectly bundled it together with Robinson's notes. In any case, we have included the exam at the end of the student notes for the autumn 1926 lectures (see pages 289–90).

As already mentioned, there were problems that came along with the notes being unverified transcriptions of the originals. They had been transcribed by two different people, Fred Oscanyan and James McGilvray, with the former beginning with the notes from the start of the spring 1926 term, on 9 February, and leaving off at the conclusion of the 9 March lecture, while the latter began with the 1 April lecture and continued through to 10 April. The fact that the Yale Philosophy Club had not standardised the transcription methods meant that these two groups of lectures were handled somewhat differently. The main differences are that the earlier group of 12 lectures in February and March did not keep track of Robinson's original pagination, but did contain drawings of the accompanying figures, while the later group of five April lectures did track Robinson's original pagination, but left large blank spaces for drawing in accompanying figures that were never filled in. Both groups of lectures contain numerous blanks in places where the transcribers could not read portions of the text, and both contain numerous corrections and additions – handwritten and typed. Both contain what we know through comparison with the other sets of notes to be numerous typographical and reading errors, though these do not seem to be more numerous than our own typical first drafts of transcriptions. It is also entirely possible that both transcribers were expanding shorthand and 'smoothing out' the language to make the notes more readable, though without the original we cannot be sure of this.

There are several different sets of numbering for the Robinson notes. One is handwritten numbers beginning with the title page; these are the numbers that

---

1. Edward S. Robinson, 'Notes on 3b Philosophy of Science. General Metaphysical Problems', MS 284, Victor Lowe Papers, Box 2.2, Special Collections, Sheridan Libraries, Johns Hopkins University, <https://catalyst.library.jhu.edu/catalog/bib_556595>.

we have adopted as references. Another set of typed numbering begins with the first page of notes, but does not continue through the April lectures. Lastly, as already mentioned, a third set of numbering refers to Robinson's original manuscript pages, and appears in the transcriptions of the April lectures. References to these latter two sets of numbering have been removed.

The state of Robinson's notes required special handling. Specifically, in certain circumstances we broke our self-imposed rule of never including the notes of another student in the body of the text of another – for the most part, we believe that it is not responsible scholarship to intermingle different sources this way. But for Robinson, we did the following. (1) For the second (April) group of Robinson's lectures, we supplied missing figures from Roethlisberger's notes when available; these are always accompanied by footnotes to indicate their source, and we have similarly left notes for blanks in Robinson's notes for which we could not find a corresponding figure in Roethlisberger (and may or may not have constituted a missing figure). (2) In places where the Yale Philosophy Club left blanks to indicate indecipherable words, we have supplied these from other sets of notes where available, though always in brackets and with an accompanying note. (3) Lastly, and again through comparison with the notes of Roethlisberger and Hartshorne, we altered certain text in the Robinson transcriptions that was a product of the limitations of the Yale Philosophy Club's typewriters, such as substituting the Greek letters α, β and γ for the letters a, b and y in places where the other note-takers used these Greek letters. We regard these as necessary steps to make the Robinson notes as intelligible as possible.

Out of the total of 17 lectures recorded by Robinson, we use his account as the primary one 16 times. If the remainder of his notes had survived, we almost assuredly would have used them as our primary account for the majority of Whitehead's 1925–6 lectures. Sadly, this was not to be. Whitehead scholarship is all the poorer for it.

It is perhaps worth noting that Robinson was auditing the class as an undergraduate, while Roethlisberger was taking it for credit as a graduate PhD student, and Hartshorne was attending as Whitehead's assistant, and yet Robinson's notes were the most thorough. This is one example of a case in which greater ability or experience in a field did not lead to better notes. In fact, it may very well have been Robinson's relative lack of experience and familiarity with the material that led to his greater level of detail. While the other two were more apt to summarise and pick and choose what they wrote down, Robinson – presumably with less knowledge of what may or may not have been important in Whitehead's lectures – seemed to have been endeavouring to take down as much of what Whitehead said as possible, and as near to his exact phrasing as possible. We are the beneficiaries of his diligence.

1926–7

Before getting into the separate note-takers for 1926–7, we should point out that Charles Hartshorne delivered two guest lectures in Whitehead's class, on 30 November and 2 December 1926, while Raphael Demos delivered one guest lecture, on 14 December 1926. Some of our note-takers provide accounts of these lectures (King, Jackson and Burch), while others appear to have deliberately excluded them (Conger and Nelson). We have decided not to reproduce these three lectures in this volume, as it is intended to be an account of Whitehead's lectures, and not necessarily the lectures of others that happened to take place in his classroom.

George Perrigo Conger (1884–1960)

The notes of George Conger are without question the most important archival source for this volume. They are considerably more detailed than any of the other notes we have discovered for Whitehead's second and third academic years at Harvard, and compare favourably with the notes of Winthrop Pickard Bell covering Whitehead's first year of lectures.[1]

George Perrigo Conger was born in New York in 1884. He graduated from Cornell University in 1907, then earned a BD from Union Theological Seminary in 1910, and was ordained a Presbyterian minister in 1913. After spending some time as a pastor, he earned his PhD from Columbia in 1922, two years after he had already begun teaching at the University of Minnesota as an assistant professor of philosophy in 1920. He became a full professor of philosophy at Minnesota in 1937, and chaired the department from 1940 until his retirement in 1952, after which he spent a few years teaching at Ohio Wesleyan University. He died in 1960.

For the autumn 1926 term and part of the spring 1927 term, Conger, then 42 years old, was on sabbatical, and decided to spend it at Harvard. While there, he seems to have attended as many of Whitehead's classes as he possibly could. He says in a diary entry – reproduced in Appendix 3 (pp. 435–7) – that he 'fairly haunted [Whitehead] – went to all his lectures, to his seminars, to the famous Sunday evening gatherings at his house, and usually about once a week for a personal conference and tea'. Conger and Whitehead developed a friendship over that year. Whitehead recommended Conger's 1924 *A Course in Philosophy* to his students at the top of his 16 November 1926 lecture,[2] and wrote letters of introduction for Conger to several academics upon his departure in March 1927.[3] Moreover, Conger's 1941 letter of congratulations to Whitehead on his 80th birthday suggests that the two kept in touch, and that Conger and his wife had gone on to meet more of Whitehead's family in London.[4]

Conger's notes consist of more than 300 original, handwritten pages and cover every lecture of Whitehead's 1926–7 Philosophy 3b, from the first lecture on 30 September up until 19 March, soon after which Conger returned to

---

1. See Bogaard's account of Bell in the Introduction to HL1, pp. xxvii–xxxii.
2. See note 2, p. 226.
3. See Conger's diary entry, p. 437.
4. Letter from George P. Conger to Alfred North Whitehead, 17 February 1941, LET1123, Whitehead Research Library, <http://wrl.whiteheadresearch.org/items/show/1433>.

Minnesota. In addition, they cover 10–12 of Whitehead's seminaries during the same period (the exact number is unclear, since some are undated), and one of Whitehead's four lectures for Philosophy A, an introductory survey course taught by different members of the department. He also made a few sparse notes on Whitehead's paper 'Time', but we omitted these from the volume, largely because Whitehead's paper was published in full anyway.

The notes were initially sent to the Yale Philosophy Club in 1963 (three years after his death) by his wife, Agnes. After the Club returned the notes, they were donated to the University of Minnesota Library in the early 1970s. At some point along the way either Agnes, or the Yale Philosophy Club, or an archivist at the University of Minnesota sorted the notes into separate folders by date and class. They made a few errors, largely due to the fact that Conger had neglected to date his notes for the first four Philosophy 3b sessions and first two seminary sessions (thankfully, we were able to date these notes through a comparison with other student accounts). But starting on 9 October, Conger began to date consistently, and from that point on his notes are well organised.[1] Conger also usually numbered his pages, though, unlike other students, his page numbers reset at the beginning of each new lecture. In places where he failed to provide his own numbering, we have inserted our own page numbers for ease of reference.

It would be hard to overstate the level of detail of Conger's notes. The notes of most other students in this volume seldom (or never) exceeded 500–600 words; Conger routinely recorded more than 1,000, at times going as high as 1,500–2,000. They are, in fact, so detailed that we were able to discern numerous places in his notes where material was being read verbatim from a book, with Conger catching nearly the exact phrasing.

That said, Conger's notes were not without their editorial difficulties. For one, he employed more shorthand than most of the other students, some of which proved difficult or impossible to interpret with certainty. When we were uncertain, we either bracketed the expansion with a question mark, or left a note describing the various possible alternatives. Another problem was that at times Conger would write 'blocks' of text in a seemingly random configuration across the page, making it very difficult for us to discern a correct linear order (see Figure 1 for an example). At times a comparison with the notes of other students helped with this problem, but Conger's notes were often so much more detailed than our other accounts that we could not find a parallel in the other notes for the problematic text. At these times we ordered the text as best we could and left a footnote indicating the difficulty. Lastly, on a few occasions Conger would record his notes on the backs of notes for something else. In most cases this was easy to discern, and we excised the unrelated material with a note to the reader indicating that we were doing so. But for the 7 January seminary, it was not clear whether the material on one side of eight different pages was for Whitehead's class or not. We decided against publishing this material; see

---

1. One exception is a few pages of seminary notes that we could not definitively date, though by process of elimination they should fall between 22 October and 17 December 1926. See note 1, p. 358.

Introduction to *The Harvard Lectures of Alfred North Whitehead, 1925–1927*

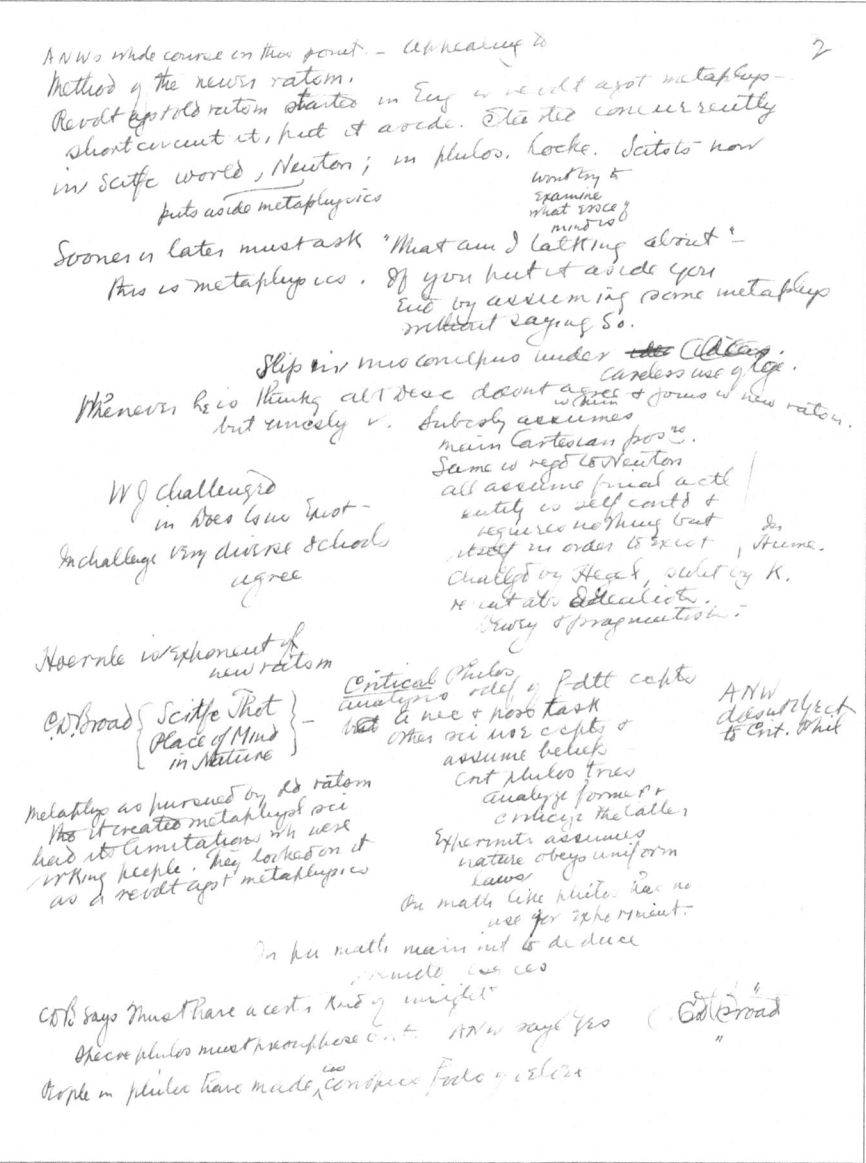

Figure 1. Second page of George Conger's original manuscript for the lecture of 16 October 1926. From George Perrigo Conger autographs and papers, Mss020, Box 4. A transcription of this page appears on pp. 188–90.

note 2 on page 362 for a more detailed account of this issue. A further example of Conger's notes is presented in Appendix 2 (p. 425).

Out of the 47 Philosophy 3b lectures that Conger recorded, we used his notes as our primary account 45 times. The two exceptions, both near the beginning of the term, were lectures for which we found the notes of Everett Nelson slightly preferable. For the seminaries we used Conger's account as the primary in every case, though in most cases his account was the only one. For the one Philosophy A lecture that Conger recorded, we edited the official notebook for the class in preference to Conger's notes, which were used as a supplement.

Everett John Nelson (1900–88)

Everett J. Nelson was born in Washington state in 1900. He received his AB and AM from the University of Washington in 1923 and 1925, and a second AM as well as a PhD from Harvard in 1928 and 1929. Upon graduation from Harvard, he did postdoctoral work in Europe on a Sheldon Fellowship, somewhat echoing the path of Charles Hartshorne. He spent the first half of his career at the University of Washington, where he began as an assistant in philosophy in 1923, and was later promoted to assistant professor, associate professor, full professor and executive officer of the Department of Philosophy. In 1952, he departed the University of Washington and chaired the philosophy department at Ohio State University until his retirement in 1968.[1]

Nelson's notes are for the autumn 1926 term only; he would become a visiting assistant in philosophy at Harvard in 1927. The notes are not original, but rather a typed version sent in 1970 to Victor Lowe, who photocopied them and returned the original to Nelson. They consist of 39 numbered pages, not counting a title page and two back-of-page notes. No dates are provided and few explicit lecture breaks are indicated. We know through comparison with other sets of notes that the dates range from 30 September 1926 to 4 January 1927; Nelson did not miss any of Whitehead's 1926 lectures, but the notes from 4 January are his only material from after Harvard's winter break.

We do not know who typed up the notes, though it seems likely to have been Nelson himself. Because the original notes seem to be lost, we cannot speak to the accuracy of the transcription. Their readability suggests that the transcriber(s) may well have been expanding shorthand and 'smoothing out' the language in the notes, though we can only guess at this.

As for the content, Nelson's notes were fairly thorough, typically falling in the 300–700-word range per lecture. He was the only note-taker for the autumn of 1926 whose account sometimes rivalled Conger's level of detail. Still, out of the 31 lectures he recorded, we use Nelson's account as primary only twice, both for lectures near the beginning of the term – 30 September (the first lecture) and 9 October. For the rest of the term, we use Nelson's notes as an important supplement to Conger's, citing his account frequently in footnotes.

---

1. Virgil Hinshaw, 'Everett John Nelson, 1900–1988', *Proceedings and Addresses of the American Philosophical Association*, vol. 62(3) (January 1989), pp. 561–2.

Paul Weiss (1901–2002)

Paul Weiss has already been mentioned in this Introduction as the man who in 1963 encouraged the Yale Philosophy Club to begin gathering and transcribing student notes from Whitehead's classes – in some ways the precursor to the current Whitehead Research Project – and his name is well known among Whiteheadian process philosophers.

The son of Hungarian and German emigrants, Samuel Weiss and Emma Rothschild, Weiss grew up in New York City, where he earned his BA from City College of New York in 1927. He received his MA and PhD from Harvard in 1928 and 1929, with Whitehead as his adviser. He also worked with Charles Hartshorne on editing the papers of Charles Sanders Peirce. Upon his departure from Harvard in 1931, he began teaching at Bryn Mawr, a premiere women's liberal arts college in Pennsylvania. In 1946, he began teaching at Yale University, during which tenure he founded the scholarly journal *The Review of Metaphysics* in 1947 and the Metaphysical Society of America in 1950. Following Yale, he taught at the Catholic University of America, in Washington, DC, from 1970 until his retirement in 1994. He died in 2002.[1]

The provenance of Weiss's notes is a little unusual. Lewis Ford first photocopied the notes in 1974, then wrote to Weiss in 1978 asking if he could borrow the notebook again to make clearer copies.[2] Weiss responded that he was pledged to give his papers to the Southern Illinois University Library, but that he could possibly donate the notebook outright to the Center for Process Studies.[3] A follow-up letter from Weiss said that he did not remember where he had put it.[4] Fast-forward 35 years, and Ford donated his photocopy of the notes to the Whitehead Research Project in 2013. It is not clear to us if Weiss ever found the original notes again in 1978 or not; what we do know is that we have been unable to find them in the Southern Illinois University Archives or at the Center for Process Studies, so they appear to be lost, leaving us with only Ford's photocopy, which is rather faded and difficult to decipher in places.

Sadly, the quality of the content of Weiss's notes is remarkably poor. Part of this may have to do with a difference in accents between a native New Yorker who had just arrived at Harvard in February 1927 and a recently emigrated Englishman, as Weiss recalled some 53 years later:

> I sat right in the front row and couldn't understand a single word. Years later I spoke to Whitehead and told him this. He laughed and said, 'I couldn't understand a single word you said when you spoke.' Our syllabifications or emphases were so radically distinct that we couldn't understand one another. Later on, of course, when

---

1. Paul Weiss, 'Lost in thought: alone with others', in Lewis Edwin Hahn, *The Philosophy of Paul Weiss* (La Salle: Open Court, 1995), pp. 3–45; and Lewis Edwin Hahn, 'Preface', in *The Philosophy of Paul Weiss* (La Salle: Open Court, 1995), pp. xvii–xix.
2. Letter from Lewis Ford to Paul Weiss, 14 July 1978, LET636, Whitehead Research Library, <http://wrl.whiteheadresearch.org/items/show/1085>.
3. Letter from Paul Weiss to Lewis Ford, 18 July 1978, LET637, Whitehead Research Library, <http://wrl.whiteheadresearch.org/items/show/1086>.
4. Letter from Paul Weiss to Lewis Ford, 7 August 1978, LET639, Whitehead Research Library, <http://wrl.whiteheadresearch.org/items/show/1088>.

I understood just how he was speaking, I found him remarkably lucid and his expressions very clear and could understand every single word.[1]

Whatever the reasons, Weiss's notes for Whitehead's Philosophy 3b in spring 1927 are quite brief, consisting of just 14 handwritten pages for the entirety of the term. Only once did he write more than a single page of notes for a session (for 1 March 1927). He seldom recorded more than 150 words for a lecture, and at times wrote only a sentence or two. There is also evidence of much confusion on Weiss's part, culminating in a list of 19 mathematical expressions on the fifth page of his notes which he numbered from 1.0 to 1.18, but which we know from other sets of notes were never meant to go together; rather, they were given by Whitehead across three different class sessions to discuss very different things. Meanwhile, Weiss did not record any of the context according to which these expressions might make some sense. His notes also include a fair amount of illegible text in the margins.

Despite the fundamental inadequacy of Weiss's notes, in many cases they were the only account we had of Whitehead's spring 1927 lectures. Conger had departed for Minnesota after Whitehead's 19 March lecture, and the notes of Nelson, Gardner Jackson and George Burch had ended even earlier. Lester King did not regularly attend Whitehead's class (or at least did not regularly take notes) after 10 March, and we have notes from him for only three lectures following Conger's departure. In short, aside from these three lectures recorded by King, Weiss was our only option after 19 March, and so we use his account as primary for 13 lectures only because we had no other choice. Frankly, if the rest of the notes in this volume were of a similar quality to these notes of Weiss, then the volume itself would not have been worth publishing, but we present them here in the interest of giving as complete an account of Whitehead's lectures for 1925–6 and 1926–7 as we possibly can.

Entirely different from Weiss's notes for Philosophy 3b are four pages of typed notes for the 4 March Seminary in Logic that appear in the photocopy to have been pasted into his pre-numbered notebook. It seems likely that these were not his notes at all, but taken from another student. For more on this, see the section on 'Seminary in Metaphysics/Seminary in Logic' below, p. lvii.

Lester Snow King (1908–2002)

Lester S. King graduated from Harvard College at the young age of 19 and went on to do graduate work in philosophy, but ultimately changed his focus and earned his MD from Harvard Medical School in 1932. After completing his residency at the Rockefeller Institute for Medical Research in New York City in 1939, he joined the army and worked as a pathologist at William Beaumont

---

1. Paul Weiss, 'Recollections of Alfred North Whitehead', *Process Studies*, vol. 10(1–2) (1980), p. 44. Despite Weiss's confusion, he did quite well in the class grades-wise, one of only two students to receive an 'A+' for both his first and second report (Whitehead, 'Student Record Book', p. 25). The other was Felix Cohen, the son of Morris Cohen, whom Weiss had studied under at City College of New York, and with whose work Whitehead himself was familiar (see note 5, pp. 193–4).

General Hospital in El Paso, Texas; he moved to Chicago and joined the staff of the University of Illinois Medical School upon the war's conclusion. He became a senior editor of the *Journal of the American Medical Association* in 1963, and remained with the journal until his retirement in 1991.[1] He also gave lectures at the University of Chicago on the history of medical science beginning in the late 1960s.[2] He died in 2002.

About a third of Whitehead's 40-odd students for 1926–7 were undergraduates, and King was one of them, less than 20 years old. He discussed his experience of Whitehead's class in a 1978 letter to Lewis Ford:

> [Whitehead] was up from time to time with a cherubic smile, as if to ask whether everything was clear (which it wasn't); and if anyone asked a question (which he did not object to but, as I remember, did not encourage) he would get enveloped in a cloud of explanation. . . . I remember having cram sessions with [classmate Philip Stanley] before exams, trying to decipher just what Whitehead might have meant. I believe I got an A in the course,[3] but I certainly had only the most confused notions of what Whitehead was trying to say. I learned some of the vocabulary, to be sure, and was able to transpose some of his terms into more familiar notions. I remember discussing the relations of Whitehead's concepts to those of Plato, but all was quite vague. How much intelligible material my notes contain I do not know, for I have not gone over them since I graduated.[4]

King's notes, held in the Harvard University Archives, consist of 81 original, handwritten pages beginning on 30 September 1926 and ending on 12 April 1927. Most of his notes are for the autumn term, where they cover all but five lectures. He has notes for only 10 lectures from the spring term: for the first seven, from 24 February through to 10 March, and three somewhat later, from 29 March, 7 April and 12 April. Despite the doubts King voiced to Ford in his 1978 letter, his notes are no less intelligible than anyone else's, and typically consist of around 200–500 words per lecture.

Though King's notes seem reasonably competent, particularly during the first term, they were never as detailed as Conger's, and so are rarely used as primary. In fact, we print King's account only of the last three lectures he attended in full, when his notes were our only alternative to the notes of Weiss. Still, King's notes provide an important supplement to Conger's account, and we cite him with some frequency in footnotes.

---

1. Rudolph Bush, 'Lester King, 94', *Chicago Tribune*, 10 October 2002, <https://www.chicagotribune.com/news/ct-xpm-2002-10-10-0210100161-story.html>.
2. 'Bibliographical Avocation: The Lester King Collection', University of Chicago Library, <https://www.lib.uchicago.edu/collex/exhibits/bibliographical-avocation-lester-king-collection>.
3. King did in fact receive an 'A' for the autumn 1926 semester, though the only grade Whitehead lists for him during the spring 1927 term is for a report, a 'B'. Whitehead, 'Student Record Book', pp. 21, 25.
4. Letter from Lester S. King to Lewis S. Ford, 3 May 1978, LET322, Whitehead Research Library, <http://wrl.whiteheadresearch.org/items/show/565>.

liii

Gardner Jackson (1896–1965)

Born in 1896 in Colorado, the son of wealthy railroad magnate William Sharpless Jackson, Gardner Jackson was a journalist, government official and political activist. He attended Amherst College from 1914 to 1917, then fought in the First World War, and attended Columbia University upon his discharge from the army. After brief stints at an investment firm and as a reporter at the *Denver Times*, he was an editorial writer and reporter at the *Boston Globe* from 1920 to 1926. From 1927 to 1930, he was a publicist and strategy adviser to the Sacco-Vanzetti Defense Committee.[1] From 1931 to 1933, he was a Washington, DC, correspondent for several Canadian newspapers, and in 1933 was named Assistant Consumers' Counsel in the Agricultural Adjustment Administration (AAA) under President Franklin Roosevelt. After being fired from the AAA over disagreements concerning milk marketing policy and the treatment of sharecroppers in the cotton states, he spent several years in the private sector as a researcher and lobbyist, before again serving in the Roosevelt administration as specialist assistant to Under-Secretary of Agriculture Paul Appleby from 1941 to 1942. He would later take on such varied jobs as attending the United Nations Food and Agriculture Organization meeting in Copenhagen in 1946, serving as special assistant to Welch Grape Juice Company President J. M. Kaplan from 1948 to 1949, and working for the American Federation of Labor and Congress of Industrial Organizations (AFL-CIO). He died in 1965.[2]

In the autumn of 1926, Jackson was still working as a reporter for the *Boston Globe*, but started attending some Harvard classes as a 30-year-old 'special student'.[3] His notes, which reside at the FDR Presidential Library, consist of 82 original, handwritten pages, not counting a title page. They are both unnumbered and undated, but we know through comparison with other notes that they span Whitehead's lectures from 30 September to 7 December 1926, with one absence, on 20 November. He was a little less thorough than most of the other note-takers in this volume, typically recording about 200–400 words per lecture.

Jackson's notes are one of two accounts of Whitehead's Philosophy 3b for 1925–7 that we never use as the primary source. This is largely because Conger has notes for all the same lectures that Jackson recorded, and they are wholly

---

1. Nicola Sacco and Bartolomeo Vanzetti were accused of murdering a guard in a 1920 robbery. They were found guilty of first-degree murder and sentenced to death in a 1921 trial that was widely perceived as influenced by anti-Italian and anti-immigrant bias. They were executed in 1927 after many appeals and public protests. Other Defense Committee members included Felix Frankfurter and Bertrand Russell. Whitehead discussed the case in a letter to his son, North, opining that 'there seems very little doubt but that they were entirely innocent', citing Frankfurter's famous examination of the case in *The Atlantic*. Letter from Alfred North Whitehead to T. North Whitehead, 25 March 1927, MS 282, Alfred North Whitehead Collection, Box 2, Folder 21, Special Collections, Sheridan Libraries, Johns Hopkins University, <https://catalyst.library.jhu.edu/catalog/bib_505857>.
2. 'Collection Historical Note', Gardner Jackson Papers, 1912–1965, Franklin D. Roosevelt Presidential Library, <http://www.fdrlibrary.marist.edu/archives/collections/franklin/index.php?p=collections/findingaid&id=461>.
3. This was his official designation in Whitehead's notebook. He received a grade of 'B' for his work in the class (Whitehead, 'Student Record Book', p. 21).

superior. We do occasionally cite material from Jackson's notes, but significantly less often than we cite from the notes of Nelson and King.

George Bosworth Burch (1902–73)

George Bosworth Burch was born in Connecticut in 1902. He earned all his degrees from Harvard: his AB in 1923, his AM in 1927 and his PhD in 1939. Following a year as an assistant in the Philosophy Department at Harvard, he was Professor of Philosophy and Psychology at the College of Idaho from 1942 to 1946. In 1946, he became the Fletcher Professor of Philosophy at Tufts University, Massachusetts, and taught there until his retirement in 1967. He died in 1973.[1]

Burch's notes, which reside in the Harvard University Archives, are a mixed bag. They are not the original handwritten notes, but rather a typed version that have been labelled 'permanent notes'. The Whitehead portions consist of 14 pages, oddly organised. The last three pages are labelled as being from 26 February and 1 March 1927, but there is no indication of a break between. Meanwhile, the first 11 pages are not dated at all, and have some headings which turn out on closer inspection to be misleading. For instance, the first two pages are titled 'Lectures by Professor Whitehead – Introduction', which one would think was Whitehead's first lecture of the term, but in fact these first two pages contain material from three lectures: the first, third and fourth of the term. Without other notes to compare them to, one would never know that Burch had summarised the content from three non-consecutive lectures together. All in all, Burch has notes from 17 different Whitehead lectures between 30 September 1926 and 1 March 1927, most of them for the autumn term, and he usually did not record more than about 150 words per lecture.[2]

Bundled together with Burch's Whitehead notes are notes for the guest lectures in Whitehead's class delivered by Charles Hartshorne and Raphael Demos, the two assistants, along with notes on a lecture or lectures by William Ernest Hocking *about* Whitehead, probably from his 'Philosophy 9: Metaphysics'. Somewhat inexplicably, these notes for the lectures by Hartshorne, Demos and Hocking are more detailed than the notes on those delivered by Whitehead himself.

As with the notes of Gardner Jackson, we never use Burch's notes as our primary account. They are simply too brief to be of much use. We do cite Burch's notes occasionally in the volume, but these instances are quite rare. Note that they were previously published in *Process Studies*.[3]

---

1. Juliana Kuipers, 'Biographical note', George Bosworth Burch personal archive, 1919–1943. HUC 8919.300.10, Harvard University Archives, <https://id.lib.harvard.edu/ead/hua03013/catalog>.
2. The exception is for the 1 March 1927 lecture, at around 500 words, where Burch's notes are uncharacteristically detailed.
3. George B. Burch and Dwight C. Stewart (ed.), 'Whitehead's Harvard lectures 1926–27', *Process Studies*, vol. 4(3) (1974), pp. 199–206.

Whitehead's seminaries and guest lectures for 1926–7

Philosophy 3b was not the only class nor the only lectures that Whitehead gave at Harvard from 1925 to 1927. He also held a seminary every Friday, either 'Philosophy 20h: Metaphysics' or 'Philosophy 20i: Logic', depending on the term. In addition, in the autumn of 1926 he was a guest in Richard Clarke Cabot's seminary on the fundamentals of social ethics, and in the spring of 1927 he delivered four lectures in 'Philosophy A', an introductory history of philosophy survey course for undergraduates.

Seminary in Metaphysics/Seminary in Logic

Notes from Whitehead's Friday seminary courses have been harder to come by than notes for his Philosophy 3b lecture course. This is probably due primarily to the format of the seminaries themselves: they were discussion-based, with a focus on student presentations, and took place in Whitehead's home – typically around the dining room table. Understandably, and probably appropriately, this kind of environment seems to have made students less inclined to take detailed notes. Between this and the smaller number of students enrolled in the seminaries – around a dozen seems to have been typical for this period, next to the 40-plus for the Harvard Philosophy 3b lectures – we simply have not been able to find many students from Whitehead's seminaries who both took notes and kept them.

That said, we were lucky enough to discover the notes of a few seminary students for 1926–7 (though none for the previous year). Here again Conger is our most important source. He attended and took notes for Whitehead's first three seminaries, on 1, 8 and 15 October, and also the last six seminaries before his departure back to Minnesota – 7 and 14 January, 25 February, and 4, 11 and 18 March. There is a large and continuous gap in the middle of these two groups of notes – nine seminaries that took place between 22 October and 17 December – and we have inserted a few undated pages of Conger's seminary notes into this gap, since by process of elimination they must fall somewhere into that date range.[1] It is not clear if Conger simply did not attend most of these nine seminaries, or if they were mostly composed of student presentations, and hence Conger did not bother to take notes, or did not bother to keep them.

Conger's seminary notes had the same editorial difficulties as his Philosophy 3b notes (see above), plus some other problems besides. The most important difficulty is that, since Conger's notes are for a discussion-based class, we cannot always be sure when it is Whitehead talking and not someone else. Readers should keep this problem at the forefront of their minds when reading or quoting the seminary notes. There are times when we can be fairly certain that Whitehead is speaking – such as the first seminary, on 1 October, in which Whitehead is re-presenting the 'Time' paper that he had delivered at the Sixth International Congress of Philosophy some weeks earlier – and other times when Conger has

---

1. See note 1, p. 358.

made some effort to distinguish between speakers, such as the final seminary that he attended (18 March). But most of the time we simply cannot be sure.

One other oddity to Conger's seminary notes is that, unlike the portrait orientation of the pages for his notes for Philosophy 3b, the pages are given a landscape orientation with three distinct columns, often with one page proceeding from left to right and the next page from right to left, seemingly based on whether he was writing on the front or back of a sheet. Usually he numbered these columns so that the order was clear, but not always. Whenever we are uncertain of a page order or column order, we have left a footnote describing the difficulty.

We also have notes for the first two seminaries of autumn 1926 from Sinclair Kerby-Miller,[1] an assistant in the department. Their chief virtue in the context of this volume is that they allow us to date Conger's notes on these occasions. We refer to Kerby-Miller's notes occasionally in Conger's notes for these seminaries.

Lastly, we have a few lines from Weiss for 11 March, and, more importantly, four typed pages of notes for 4 March. The nature and source of these typed notes is not entirely clear. The typed sheets appear to have been pasted into Weiss's pre-numbered notebook. In a letter to Weiss, Ford described them as 'some sort of class hand out',[2] but given the presence in those typed pages of a few question marks in parentheses that pretty clearly indicate confusion, this seems unlikely. If it was a handout, there would be no confusion. Given the brevity of the rest of Weiss's notes, it also seems unlikely that Weiss himself recorded them. The most likely scenario seems to be that Weiss got the notes from another student and pasted them into his notebook after the fact, but we cannot be sure of this. Regardless of their origin, these typed notes match Conger's account fairly closely, and were used to fill in the spotty numbering in Conger's account, along with some other additions.[3]

Social Ethics seminary

The notes from Whitehead's guest appearance in Richard Clarke Cabot's Social Ethics seminary on 18 October 1926 are a little unusual, but in a good way: not only are they perhaps the only thing we have from Whitehead that is exclusively an extended discussion of his view of ethics, but, unlike the other notes in this volume, these notes appear to be almost an exact transcript of what Whitehead actually said. To explain how this came to be, a little bit of background on Cabot, the Department of Social Ethics and the class Cabot was presiding over are in order.

---

1. Kerby-Miller will be an important figure in the third volume of Harvard lectures, so we will leave a biographical introduction of him for that volume.
2. Letter from Lewis Ford to Paul Weiss, 14 July 1978.
3. Ford would eventually collate the notes of both Conger and Weiss for this session and publish them as an appendix to his 1984 *Emergence*. See Lewis Ford, *The Emergence of Whitehead's Metaphysics, 1925–1929* (Albany: State University of New York Press, 1984), pp. 317–22.

Cabot was born in 1868 in Massachusetts. He received a BA in classics and philosophy from Harvard College in 1889 and his MD from Harvard Medical School in 1892. Following his graduation, he began working in the outpatient department of Massachusetts General Hospital, and in 1905 established the first hospital social service department in the United States.[1] The hospital refused to support the new department, leading to Cabot (a millionaire) himself paying the salaries of all its employees for 12 years.[2] In the meantime, Cabot began teaching at Harvard in 1902, first in philosophy and then in clinical medicine (the latter he taught at Harvard for 30 years), and later took up the chair in social ethics in 1919.

A department of social ethics was a new idea at the time, straddling a line somewhere between philosophy, economics and 'Christian morals'. Harvard's department had been officially established in 1905 and housed on the second floor of the newly constructed Emerson Hall. The department's existence was almost exclusively due to the gifts of Alfred T. White, who gave $150,000 for its establishment and who would later almost double that amount to support its running. Its first chair was White's long-time friend Francis Greenwood Peabody, whose classes in the early 1880s 'anticipated by many years the earliest teaching of social work in [the United States]', to quote Cabot.[3]

And so we come to Cabot's seminary itself. The full course name as it appeared on Cabot's syllabus was 'Social Ethics 20a: Fundamentals Underlying the Social Sciences'.[4] His stated objective was to 'work out cooperatively the fundamentals of the social sciences'.[5] By 'cooperatively', he meant with other departments in the university. Here Cabot is worth quoting at length, in a statement with which Whitehead was undoubtedly in full agreement:

> My aspiration is to knock down some of the interdepartmental lines of Harvard or to weaken at any rate the defences and dykes that keep departments apart. I feel strongly that one of our greatest evils here is the lack of any synthesis. Each department teaches the best it knows, but with no considerable awareness of what the others are doing. I cannot help thinking, when I visited some of the courses last spring, how good it would be for other departments to be hearing that teaching.[6]

The general format was for Cabot to invite members from across Harvard's various university departments to give their own views as to what constituted the social sciences. The speaker would give a presentation, which would ideally include answers to six specific questions that Cabot posed in the syllabus,[7]

---

1. Mike Cadogan and Andrew Robbins, 'Richard Clarke Cabot', <https://litfl.com/richard-clarke-cabot>.
2. Sarah Gehlert, 'The conceptual underpinnings of social work in health care', in Sarah Gehlert and Teri A. Browne (eds), *Handbook of Health Social Work* (New York: Wiley, 2006), p. 11.
3. Richard Clarke Cabot, 'A. T. White and the Department of Social Ethics', *Harvard Alumni Bulletin*, vol. 23(30) (5 May 1921), p. 700.
4. Richard Clarke Cabot, 'The fundamentals of social science, 1926–1927', Papers of Richard Clarke Cabot, HUG 4255, Box 90, Harvard University Archives, <https://id.lib.harvard.edu/ead/c/hua02998c00424/catalog>, Syllabus, p. 1.
5. Cabot, 'The fundamentals of social science', First meeting, p. 1.
6. Cabot, 'The fundamentals of social science', First meeting, p. 2.
7. See note 1, p. 402.

followed by questions from the audience. Meanwhile, the students, again to use Cabot's words, were 'the small end' of the course, which seems to have been his polite way of saying that he was more concerned with getting the various faculty departments to learn from each other than he was with teaching students per se, at least for this course.

This helps to explain the situation we find ourselves in with the notes of Whitehead's guest appearance in the class. Cabot believed that the discussions between the various 'Great Men' of the Harvard faculty in this class were going to be very important, and so he wanted to keep an accurate record of what was said. Being independently wealthy,[1] it appears that he hired a professional stenographer to keep that record (it seems very unlikely that the university itself would have paid for such a thing). Given the voluminousness and apparent word-perfect accuracy of these notes, this is the only explanation that makes sense. One oddity that helps substantiate this theory is that the stenographer made a few errors suggesting a lack of philosophical training, such as typing 'entological' when Whitehead clearly would have said 'ontological'; a Harvard student taking a class in Emerson Hall probably would not have made errors of this kind.

There are actually three distinct sets of notes for this session of Cabot's seminary, which appear in the Cabot papers at the Harvard University Archives. One is the aforementioned typed record of the discussion, which is 23 pages long, consecutively numbered, and weighing in at a hefty 8,700 words. This is the account we are presenting in full. There are also six pages of Cabot's own handwritten notes of Whitehead's lecture; these notes stop once Whitehead's presentation ends and the questions begin, presumably because Cabot had begun to facilitate the discussion and so could no longer focus on taking his own notes. Very occasionally we were able to use Cabot's notes to make corrections to the stenographer's account. Lastly, there are three pages which Cabot has labelled 'obiter dicta, after seminary', which appear to be Cabot's own thinking-through of Whitehead's presentation for his own stated purpose of synthesising a new theory of the fundamentals of social ethics. Cabot's 'obiter dicta' are not included in this volume.

It is interesting to note that Cabot was a close family friend of William Ernest Hocking, whose notes are included in the first volume of Harvard lectures. Later, money from the Hocking and Cabot estates was given to a

---

1. Whitehead actually discussed Cabot's wealth and his attitude toward it in a letter to his son, North: '[Agnes Hocking] told Richard Cabot – an overconscientious New Englander who has an important engagement for every half-hour of the day – to call for Mummy at 3:15 and take her to a school entertainment about a mile off. Accordingly Cabot turned up . . . that Mrs Hocking should have thought it possible to tell an immensely busy man of some importance to fetch Mummy in his car, and that he should of course have complied at great inconvenience, is just like them. Of course no one, not a millionaire, keeps a chauffeur. Cabot is a millionaire, via his wife, but is much too conscientious to spend money in that way. The idea of New Englanders flaunting wealth is quite wrong. They are much more likely to be living on half their incomes, and either investing the rest or giving it away – about equal chances which.' Letter from Alfred North Whitehead to T. North Whitehead, 21 December 1924, MS 282, Alfred North Whitehead Collection, Box 2, Folder 17, Special Collections, Sheridan Libraries, Johns Hopkins University, <https://catalyst.library.jhu.edu/catalog/bib_505857>.

permanent trust – the Hocking-Cabot Fund for Systematic Philosophy – which was for years overseen by Hocking's son, Richard Hocking. The Hocking-Cabot Fund helped to support the first two editorial conferences of the Critical Edition of Whitehead.[1]

Philosophy A

'Philosophy A: History of Philosophy' was a general introductory course in philosophy intended for undergraduates. In March 1927 Whitehead lectured for four sessions of Philosophy A. Two years earlier (during Whitehead's first year) it had been two separate courses: 'Philosophy A: History of Ancient Philosophy' and 'Philosophy B: History of Modern Philosophy', with the two taking place in consecutive terms. Starting in 1925–6, the distinction between ancient and modern philosophy was kept for the two terms, but the classes themselves were combined into one year-long introduction. For 1926–7 the primary instructors listed in the course catalogue were Ralph Barton Perry and Winthrop Pickard Bell,[2] but the reality was that the course was co-taught by various members of the department according to their areas of specialisation. Whitehead's four lectures for Philosophy A were during the second term (the 'modern' half), on Monday and Wednesday for two weeks running. We know that the class also met on Fridays, so it is not entirely clear why there are no Friday lectures, but it seems possible that Fridays were discussion sessions, for which the instructor of the moment need not have been present. According to the course schedule, Whitehead should have been lecturing on Descartes and Spinoza; in actual fact, he did not discuss Spinoza at all, and focused mostly on Newton.

We have two sources for Whitehead's Philosophy A lectures. The first, which we used as the primary account in all cases, was the 'official notebook' for the course, which resides in the papers of Winthrop Pickard Bell at Mount Allison University in Canada. This notebook was maintained by various Harvard assistants as necessary, so we cannot be sure who actually took the Whitehead notes. Some possibilities include Kerby-Miller, Bell and Robert L. M. Underhill, all of whom are listed on the course schedule. In fact, the notes may be by all three men; the handwriting clearly changes from one week to the next, and from the third lecture to the fourth. Except for the changes in authorship, these notes were fairly straightforward to edit and devoid of many oddities, aside from an irregularity in the page numbering at the beginning: the notebook features large, pre-printed page numbers and the first page of Whitehead notes is on page 87, while the second is on page 94; there is a note on both these pages referring to one another (e.g. 'continued on p. 94'). Following this oddity, the pages are numbered consecutively.

Our second source is once again the notes of George Conger, but uncharacteristically for Conger, he attended only one of Whitehead's Philosophy A

---

1. For more on this, see Henning, 'Preface: a brief history of the Critical Edition of Whitehead'.
2. Bell took notes for Whitehead's first year of lectures, and his notes make up the bulk of the first volume of Harvard lectures. He would continue to teach at Harvard until his resignation in 1927.

lectures: the third one, on 14 March. As with other such alternative accounts, we used Conger's notes to augment the primary account.

Acknowledgements

We would like to thank Roland Faber for giving the Critical Edition of Whitehead a home at the Whitehead Research Project, and Claremont School of Theology for their support of both the Center for Process Studies and the Whitehead Research Project.

Editorial staff for the Whitehead Research Project have been paid for by many generous donors. We offer special thanks to Nancy K. Frankenberry and especially Frederick and Nancy Marcus. Without their support, this volume would not have been possible. We owe them a debt of gratitude that can never be repaid.

We relied on a number of people for support during the editing of this volume. Paul Bogaard gave us invaluable practical advice as we were first finding our editorial feet; we are the beneficiaries of his experience editing the first volume of Whitehead's Harvard lectures. Robert Valenza, Gary Herstein and Ronny Desmet made great efforts to help us verify, understand and correct the mathematical and logical portions of the text that we were ill-equipped to handle; they caught numerous errors that we might otherwise have overlooked. John Becker and Tyler Huson, former editorial assistants for the Whitehead Research Project, helped to do the initial transcription of the notes for this volume back in 2014 and 2015. Lastly, current editorial assistant Jenna Petsche helped with the preparation of the figures.

The following is a list of the archival sources that make up the text of this volume. All are used with the permission of their respective archives.

- Bell, Winthrop P., 'Philosophy A 1926–7 Official Note-book', Winthrop Bell Fonds, Series L, 6501-11-2, No. 3.8, Mount Allison University Archives.
- Burch, George B., 'Philosophy 3b. Philosophy of Science. General Metaphysical Problems', Permanent notes of George Bosworth Burch, Volume 15, George Bosworth Burch personal archive, 1919–1943, HUC 8919.300.10, Box 5, Unit 1, Harvard University Archives, <https://id.lib.harvard.edu/ead/c/hua03013c00016/catalog>.
- Cabot, Richard Clarke, 'The Fundamentals of Social Science, 1926–1927', Papers of Richard Clarke Cabot, HUG 4255, Box 90, Harvard University Archives, <https://id.lib.harvard.edu/ead/c/hua02998c00424/catalog>.
- Conger, George P., 'Notes on Whitehead's class lectures at Harvard University, 1926–1927', George Perrigo Conger autographs and papers, Mss020, Box 4, University of Minnesota Library, <https://archives.lib.umn.edu/repositories/16/archival_objects/81029>.
- Hartshorne, Charles, 'Whitehead Lecture Notes: Hartshorne's Notes on Whitehead's Lectures', STU112, Whitehead Research Library, <http://wrl.whiteheadresearch.org/items/show/1228>.

- Heath, Louise R., 'Whitehead, Fall 1925', MS 284, Victor Lowe Papers, Box 2.9, Special Collections, Sheridan Libraries, Johns Hopkins University, <https://catalyst.library.jhu.edu/catalog/bib_556595>.
- Jackson, Gardner, 'Philosophy 3b: Philosophy of Science', Gardner Jackson Papers, 1912–1965, Series 6: Bibliographical Materials, Box 96, Notebooks (3): History, Philosophy, etc., Franklin D. Roosevelt Presidential Library, US National Archives <http://www.fdrlibrary.marist.edu/archives/collections/franklin/index.php?p=collections/findingaid&id=461>.
- Kerby-Miller, Sinclair, 'Whitehead Lecture Notes: A. N. Whitehead Seminaries', STU116, Whitehead Research Library, <https://catalyst.library.jhu.edu/catalog/bib_556595>.
- King, Lester S., Student Papers, 1923–1928, HUC 8923.45, Box 2, Folder Philosophy 3B: Notes – 1926–1927, Harvard University Archives, <http://id.lib.harvard.edu/alma/990100059270203941/catalog>.
- Nelson, Everett J., 'Philosophy of Science: Lectures by A. N. Whitehead', MS 284, Victor Lowe Papers, Box 2.9, Special Collections, Sheridan Libraries, Johns Hopkins University, <https://catalyst.library.jhu.edu/catalog/bib_505857>.
- Robinson, Edward S., 'Spring 1926: 3b. Philosophy of science. General metaphysical problems', in Graduate Philosophy Club of Yale University, 'Notes from the Lectures of Alfred North Whitehead at Harvard University, 1926–1937', Philosophy and Social Science Manuscripts Collection, MS 644, Box 10, Folder 98, Manuscripts and Archives, Yale University, <https://archives.yale.edu/repositories/12/archival_objects/1262622>, pp. 1–45.
- Roethlisberger, Fritz J., 'Philosophy of Science (Whitehead, A.N.)'. Fritz J. Roethlisberger papers, Arch GA 76, Carton 9, Folder 14, Baker Library Special Collections, Harvard Business School, <https://id.lib.harvard.edu/ead/c/bak00040c00396/catalog>.
- Weiss, Paul, 'Whitehead Lecture Notes: Whitehead on Metaphysics', STU063, Whitehead Research Library, <http://wrl.whiteheadresearch.org/items/show/590>.
- Weiss, Paul, 'Whitehead Lecture Notes: Seminary in Logic 20', STU064, Whitehead Research Library, <http://wrl.whiteheadresearch.org/items/show/591>.

Philosophy 3b: Philosophy of Science

Radcliffe lectures, fall semester 1925

Thursday, 1 October 1925
Heath's notes[1]

|1| ~~Sam~~ Theoretically same course as 1924, but I credited it because actually it was quite ∧different∧.[2]
Reading
Whitehead: *Concept of Nature*
Whitehead: *Science and the Modern World*[3]
Whitehead: *Principles of Natural Knowledge*
Whitehead: *Principle of Relativity*
C. D. Broad: *Scientific Thought*[4] ✓[5]
S. Alexander: *Space, Time and Deity*[6]
B. Russell: *Knowledge of External World* ✓
B. Russell: *Analysis of Mind*[7]

---

1. The corresponding Harvard lecture can be found on p. 46. All the Radcliffe lecture notes presented here are those taken by Louise Heath. Refer to Appendix 1 for a full list of fall semester 1925 Radcliffe lectures by date and their corresponding Harvard lectures, and see also the Introduction for a detailed discussion of each note-taker and their notes.
   The pages of Heath's notes are numbered consecutively. We suspect this numbering was done by Victor Lowe rather than Heath herself, as was the case for her 1924–5 notes, which were published in HL1.
2. This is a meaningful note by Heath, in that it confirms that Whitehead did not simply repeat the same course each semester. Though there is of course some overlap, as subsequent volumes of the Critical Edition will reveal, Whitehead was working out in class with his students the ideas that would be presented to philosophers and later published.
3. Though Whitehead put this book on the reading list for the course, it had not yet been published, and would not be until late October. Whitehead had sent the completed manuscript to Macmillan in July (Whitehead, Letter to Macmillan Company, 9 July 1925). A letter from his contact at Macmillan, Curtice Hitchcock, informed him that the book had been published in the last week of October (Hitchcock, Letter to Alfred North Whitehead, 4 November 1925).
4. Broad, *Scientific Thought*, available at <https://archive.org/details/in.ernet.dli.2015.6694> (all URLs and websites cited in the footnotes throughout the transcriptions were last accessed 18 August 2020). Charlie Dunbar Broad (1887–1971), usually cited as C. D. Broad, was an English philosopher. Like Whitehead, he was a member of the Aristotelian Society, serving as its President from 1927 to 1928. Broad's philosophy served as important foil for Whitehead as he developed his course. See the discussion of Broad in the Introduction (pp. xxviii–xxix), and in Henning, 'Whitehead in class', pp. 343–5.
5. We do not know why Broad's *Scientific Thought* and Russell's *Our Knowledge of the External World as a Field for Scientific Method in Philosophy* have tick marks next to them, but corresponding marks also appear in Roethlisberger's notes (p. 46). Note also that Roethlisberger has an entry for John Dewey that is not present here.
6. Alexander, *Space, Time, and Deity*, available at <https://archive.org/details/spacetimedeitygi01alexuoft>. This book is based on his Gifford lectures, delivered in Glasgow, 1916–18. Samuel Alexander (1859–1938) was a British philosopher important to Whitehead's thought. Like Whitehead, he was a member of the Aristotelian Society. In the preface to *Science and the Modern World*, Whitehead writes: 'There has been no occasion in the text to make detailed reference to Lloyd Morgan's *Emergent Evolution* or to Alexander's *Space, Time and Deity*. It will be obvious to the readers that I have found them very suggestive. I am especially indebted to Alexander's great work.' Whitehead, *Science and the Modern World*, p. xi.
7. Russell, *Our Knowledge of the External World as a Field for Scientific Method in Philosophy*, available at <https://archive.org/details/ourknowledgeofex00inruss>; and Russell, *The Analysis of Mind*, available at

3

Ross: *Aristotle*[1]
Descartes: *Meditations*, Vespecially VI.V Translated by Haldane and Ross.
Descartes: *Principia*[2]
Berkeley: <u>Alciphron</u>
Berkeley: *Inquiry*[3]
Hume: *Treatise*
Hume: <u>Enquiry</u>[4]
Bergson: *Creative Evolution*[5]
William James: *Radical Empiricism*, especially "Does Consciousness Exist?"[6]
|3|[7]
Philosophy of Science

Is not a general description of conclusions of science, but it is taking the ~~usual~~ problems of philosophy which develop when dwell upon the concepts used in science.

As space and time ⟨etc?⟩.

As justification of induction.

Must first understand the scientific state of mind. Must get at this historically. Appeared in Europe in 16th century, and fully active in 17th century. Sporadic occurrences before. – of great genius – examples: Aristotle, Archimedes.

Scientific state of mind.

1. Natural interest in certain irreducible and stubborn facts.

<https://archive.org/details/analysisofmind032971mbp>. Bertrand Russell (1872–1970) was a student of and later collaborator with Whitehead.

1. Ross, *Aristotle*, available at <https://archive.org/details/in.ernet.dli.2015.536932>. William David Ross (1877–1971), usually cited as W. D. Ross, was a Scottish philosopher known for his work in ethics and his critical translations of many of Aristotle's works. Like Whitehead, he was a member of the Aristotelian Society, serving as its President from 1939 to 1940.
2. Both the *Meditations* and *Principia* (*Principles of Philosophy*) were included in the same volume of philosophical works translated by Haldane and Ross: Descartes, *The Philosophical Works, Vol. I*, available at <https://archive.org/details/philosophicalwor01desc>.
3. Berkeley, *Alciphron, or the Minute Philosopher*, available at <https://archive.org/details/alciphron00berk>; Berkeley, *Siris: A Chain of Philosophical Reflexions and Inquiries Concerning the Virtues of Tarwater, And divers other Subjects connected together and arising one from another*, available at <https://archive.org/details/sirischainofphil00berk>. Roethlisberger's notes also list Berkeley, *Three Dialogues Between Hylas and Philonous*, available at <https://archive.org/details/threedialoguesbe00berkrich> (p. 47).
4. Hume, *An Enquiry Concerning the Human Understanding*, available at <https://archive.org/details/humeenquiry00humerich>; Hume, *A Treatise of Human Nature*, available at <https://archive.org/details/treatiseofhumann00hume_0>. Roethlisberger's notes do not list the *Treatise* (p. 47).
5. Bergson, *Creative Evolution*, available at <https://archive.org/details/creativeevolutio00berguoft>. Henri Bergson (1859–1941) was a French philosopher and writer. In the preface to his Gifford lectures, Whitehead acknowledges that he is 'greatly indebted to Bergson, William James, and John Dewey', but that one of his 'preoccupations has been to rescue their type of thought from the charge of anti-intellectualism, which rightly or wrongly has been associated with it'. Whitehead, *Process and Reality*, p. xii.
6. William James (1842–1910), American philosopher and psychologist. In his *Science and the Modern World*, Whitehead describes James as 'that adorable genius' (p. 3). See James, *Essays in Radical Empiricism*, available at <https://archive.org/details/essaysinradicale00jameuoft>. The cited essay was originally published in the *Journal of Philosophy, Psychology, and Scientific Methods* in 1904; see James, 'Does consciousness exist?', available at <https://archive.org/details/jstor-2011942>. Roethlisberger's notes specify only 'Does Consciousness Exist?' and do not mention the book *Radical Empiricism*.
7. Page |2| is the blank back page of |1|.

2. Also having an equal interest in the general theory.

Scientific state of mind is not the inevitable product of civilization – witness India and ⟨China?⟩ etc.

Steps in its development in Europe:
Greek drama
Roman Law (Stoics)
Church
Roman Empire[1]
Revival of Aristotle Logic (⟨Precision?⟩) and Scholasticism (theology Medieval belief of nature of God.)
⟨?⟩ Limit is <u>Personalism</u>

|4| and Greek Rationalism and therefore every detail could be rationalized. [English Empiricism amounted to a complete refutation of this belief in rational details: but the belief was so well founded that even a contrary philosophy did not disturb it.][2]

Whitehead – Science has always had an anti-rationalistic basis and founded itself on a simple faith.

This is why Hume's distinction of rationalism disturbed the ~~sci~~ clergy but not the scientists.

⟨Saturday, 3 October 1925⟩

Heath's notes[3]

Characteristics of Period of Rise of Scientific ∧Mind.∧
1. The Historical Revolt (cf. Bacon).
Aristotle's followers insisted on the importance of the "final cause." [Relation of final and efficient causes (or of philosophy of value and philosophy of nature) is a key problem of philosophy.]
Bacon abandoned looking for final cause in nature in form of the efficient cause.
  a. Appears in recourse to historical method.
  b. Appeal to experiment.
  c. Appeal against intelligibility.
    (Final cause endeavors to see thing as having a reason).
    Suspend reasoning and have a look at what happens.
|5|[4] It is an emphasis on the limitations of abstract reasoning. <u>Science has anti-rationalistic bias</u>. This isn't a novel point of view – it's exactly

---

1. Heath has a brace to the right of 'Church' and 'Roman Empire' with the words 'great organizations' next to it. She also has the words 'Discovery of mathematics' in the left margin; it is not clear whether this is meant to be associated with 'Roman Empire' or 'Revival of Aristotelian Logic'.
2. Closing bracket supplied.
3. The corresponding Harvard lecture can be found on p. 48.
4. Note that, as Heath transitions from one page of her notes to the next, the hierarchy of indentation becomes somewhat ambiguous.

what the people of the time said. cf. Father Paul ⟨blank⟩. History of Council of Trent.¹

With observation of particular instances you raise problem of how can get beyond the particular fact. i.e., <u>Problem</u> of Induction. Took up Mill. Does not attack this <u>root</u> of problem. "Law of Uniformity of Nature."

This was a difficulty that Hume had already plainly stated.

Tuesday, 6 October 1925

Heath's notes[2]

Thought is always abstract and "you are fronting experience with a certain bundle of ideas." Any bundle of ideas leaves out something, for can never exhaust the particular ∨concrete individual∨ by universal ideas. If you have a good bundle it will internally be coherent and it will express facts of experience which are important to you, but it will leave out some. If you have good bundle and neglect <u>all</u> <u>other</u> <u>factors</u> you have <u>two</u> disturbances,

1. Separate factors as Materialism vs. Theory of values.
2. Arbitrary starting point. Why?

|6| So ⟨they're?⟩ from a larger group embracing both groups of concepts.

Hume – Kant broadened the question from problematical inductive laws, but to find that inherent in ∨the∨ away we front experience is our unquestioned assumption of universal ideas as applying to every possible experience. Is the universality merely the universality of the principle of analysis? "*Dictum de omne et nullo*".[3] Cf. New book chapter = "Abstraction".[4] Kant said, are there other universal necessary truths which can't be brought under principle of analysis, i.e. are synthetic?

Whitehead urges a different answer than Kant, i.e. that every particular occasion of cognizance discloses as essential in its own being that there was a beyondness other than itself. ~~Immediate occasion is exhibited as a ψ~~.

Aristotle – Every immediate occasion is ~~of~~ union of being and not-being in process. What Aristotle and Hegel called not-being, Whitehead calls beyondness.

Kant's solution accepts Hume's point of view of <u>atomic</u> nature of the immediately given [cf. also Descartes, Berkeley, etc., and wrong side of Aristotle, i.e. his logic was good |7| methodology but ruined metaphysics.] But, says Kant, to be aware of the world means to have reference to beyondness, therefore it is not in <u>given</u> element of ~~per~~ experience, but universality comes in the process of

---

1. Pope Paul III convened the Council of Trent (1545–63), so it seems likely that this is the Paul to whom Whitehead was referring.
2. The corresponding Harvard lecture can be found on p. 50.
3. 'The maxim of all and none'. This is a principle of Aristotle which states that whatever can be said of an entire class can be applied to any member within that class.
4. This certainly refers to Whitehead's *Science and the Modern World*; its 10th chapter is titled 'Abstraction'. The book had not actually been published yet. See lecture of 1 October, note 3, p. 3.

perceiving. ~~therefore~~ i.e. given is chaotic and articulation of it arises in process of knowing. What process adds is relational concepts – having no content in themselves. ⟨?⟩ i.e. world we know is phenomenal.

Kant contrasts knowledge by sense perception and ⟨our?⟩ <u>practical</u> knowledge of <u>values</u> which come in in process of ⟨fronting?⟩ world. These concepts ∨(God, Freedom and Immortality)∨[1] you have concepts which you know qualify the noumena, but that's all you know of it.

Whitehead – does not see that Kant has got rid of Hume's difficulty. If you took line that the totality of the given is before us and is then organized you're all right, but insofar as you admit any isolation of the given into groups of given and the different occasion, Whitehead does not see that you've related the given at all. Sees how he's related within one specious present but not the ~~gr~~ different presents. <u>Yesterday</u> I could say <u>it</u> would issue into something or other; <u>today</u> I say <u>it</u> has issued from a something or other. |8| How do I identify yesterday's something or other, from today, or vice versa.

i.e. If you admit the isolation of given occasion, Kant does nothing to relate them.

That is "getable over" by the statement that the totality is in the organizing unity *in toto*.

Kant is always assuming that the given occasion ~~as extrinsic~~ is limited.

Thursday, 8 October 1925

Heath's notes

"It is our business to seek simplicity and distrust it" – Whitehead.[2]
[? Apollonius "Conic Sections" look up.][3]
Critique of Kant and his followers is not that they don't get around the difficulties, but they've heaped up a mountain of distinctions at end which have some bearing but are still superficial, i.e. are making evanescent characters support the whole thing.

An example of this obvious but superficial classification is Aristotle's distinction of <u>natural</u> and <u>violent</u> motions, and on this physics was built for generations, but still no clear cut ~~classificati~~ precision was possible.

---

1. Parentheses supplied.
2. This quote comes from Whitehead's 1920 book *The Concept of Nature*, p. 163. The corresponding Harvard lecture can be found on p. 51. It is possible that some of the following notes are actually for a different day. See note 1, p. 8.
3. This likely refers to Thomas Little Heath, *Apollonius of Perga: Treatise on Conic Sections*, available at <https://archive.org/details/treatiseonconics00apolrich>. Whitehead would have known Heath as a fellow graduate of Trinity College (Heath was awarded an ScD in 1896, 12 years after Whitehead had graduated and been elected a Fellow in 1884), and made several references to Heath's translations of Euclid in his 1924–5 lectures: HL1, pp. 222, 482, 502. See also the 13 February 1926 lecture, note 5, page 118.

|11|[1] Norman Kemp Smith on Kant, page 27.[2] vSummarizing Kant's thought.v "The two inseparable criteria of the *a priori* are necessity and universality. That neither can be imparted to a proposition by experience was Kant's confirmed and unquestioned belief. He inherited this view both from Leibniz and from Hume." This Whitehead denies.

Whitehead says if you admit that neither can be imparted to a proposition by experience you must

   a. (Rationalists) state that reason antecedent to experience has in it a discernment of conditions that must be satisfied by any experience.
   b. (Consistent empiricist) that we find ourselves believing this proposition without a ghost of a reason.
   c. (Critical (of Kant)) which looks on world we know via our apprehensions through sense as the product of our function of knowing, and therefore having in itself such factors as are introduced in function of knowing and that therefore given and "what is not" in knowing are disconnected.

Whitehead says – if you are going to have any theory ⟨positing?⟩ the universal, the immediate occasion must somehow include in itself occasions beyond itself.

In the first place therefore your universality |12| and necessity are not *a priori* statements with regard to vany occasionv ⟨t⟩hat you can see, but are statements with regard to what this occasion is, i.e. with regard to that community of occasions which are implicated in unity of immediate occasion. i.e. must have whole world implicated in immediate actual occasions, which are internal, and thus you have real world within ~~this~~ vwhichv this occasion is implicated.

All generality is compiled within the particularity of this real world. Cannot convince himself that any general laws extend beyond the bounds of the particular world given by the particular occasion and that all knowledge is

---

1. We have omitted what Victor Lowe labelled as page |9|, as it appears to have been incorrectly inserted at this point in Heath's notes. Heath wrote at the top of the page in question: 'Whitehead Oct ⑫ 11 . . . Ask him date' (Heath 8). In fact there would have been no Whitehead class on either 11 or 12 October; his seminary met on Friday 9 October and he gave a lecture on the next day, being a Saturday. But Heath writes at the top of her notes for the lecture on 13 October that 'Saturday omitted . . . Lecture omitted in which received general situation in philosophy with which philosophy of science begins' (Heath 11). That she knew the missed lecture was on a Saturday does not fit with her date confusion on this page. The content also does not match Roethlisberger's notes, even allowing for possible differences between the Harvard and Radcliffe sessions. We believe it more likely that the page of notes marked as page 9 were from Whitehead's 9 October seminary and were likely copied from another student, leading to Heath's date confusion; she may not have known on what day of the week the seminary met. Page |10| is the blank back page of |9|.
2. Smith, *A Commentary to Kant's 'Critique of Pure Reason'*, available at <https://archive.org/details/commentarytokant00smituoft>. Smith's *Commentary* is an important work of Kant scholarship and is keyed to the pagination of the 1787 second edition of Kant's *Critique*. The material following the citation makes clear that Whitehead is in fact referring to page 27 of the commentary proper, rather than to page 27 of the introduction (i.e. p. xxvii). Both Roethlisberger's and Heath's notes are close enough to the Smith text that we can assume that Whitehead read the following portion aloud: 'The two inseparable criteria of the *a priori* are necessity and universality. That neither can be imparted to a proposition by experience was Kant's confirmed and unquestioned belief. He inherited this view from both Leibniz and from Hume.'

grounded in the evidence in the particular occasion.

[⟨..........?⟩ an <u>organic</u> <u>empiricism</u>.]¹

⟨?⟩ all, P

A coming together of everything in sphere of discernment (actuality) or thought (possibility), if it is to fill in universality of your thought, if you are to run a theory of organic empiricism.

|13| Application of Kant on time.

Time is a form of intuition, i.e. is supplied in our function of knowing. Because the process is supplied by the knowing you must not talk of the process of knowing, but of the knowing of process, and then you're left with nothing to connect one function of knowing with any other.

What can we say of the entities which come together (component) and v①v how is the concretion to be described, in analysis v②v how to be described as a unit emergent entity other than analysing it as many,² and what is then in the concretion qua real or actual which is additional to the concretion qua possibility in the character of the components (old problem of one and many.) Thus what we want is actual universe as concretion of actual events, in ⟨turn?⟩ concretion of actual events composed, organized or synthesized into definite concretion.³

In next lecture – on Descartes – different point of view. <u>Substances</u> vas concretev which last through many occasions.

Tuesday, 13 October 1925

Heath's notes⁴

Lecture omitted in which received general situation in philosophy with which philosophy of science begins.

Summary:– you can take your stand on

|14|

    1. vPlurality ofv the <u>individual substances</u>. (vGhost ofv Aristotelians)

    2. or <u>Physical</u> occasion. (Heraclitus)⁵

        Associated with a certain scepticism. But here stands Whitehead and hopes to show that is <u>only</u> <u>view</u> which can rescue a thoroughgoing empiricism from scepticism.

    Call our general view <u>organic empiricism</u>.

    3. or ~~Points~~ <u>Functioning</u> as basis – i.e. have a <u>concretion</u> of functioning vorganismv. (Leibniz monad)

---

1. This is Whitehead's first known use of this phrase to refer to his own work. It does not subsequently appear in his published work. He uses the same phrase in the corresponding lecture in Emerson Hall (p. 52).
2. This second point has a brace to the right with the word 'important' next to it.
3. Heath marks this paragraph with a vertical line in the left margin.
4. The corresponding Harvard lecture can be found on p. 55. It appears that Heath missed the class on 10 October, as she wrote at the top of this lecture: 'Saturday omitted'.
5. Heath marked the next three paragraphs with vertical lines in the left margin.

That view as in Leibniz was associated with <u>substantial view</u> for each monad <u>induced</u> through many occasions. Whitehead will associate idea of ultimate <u>organism</u> with the <u>physical occasion</u>.

Scepticism of Heraclitus ~~because~~ \result of considering/ physical occasions as <u>flash in the pan</u> and ~~is~~ gone – but actually each occasion ⟨contains?⟩ <u>under limitations</u> all physical occasions.

Applies not only to justification of induction, but also to explanation of status of laws of thought – pure mathematics, – i.e. every universal judgment.

Abstraction is justified by fact that there are characters which enter into every occasion but may be considered apart from any actual occasion.[1]

You can discern that some are so related that they cannot be jointly completely effective in same actual occasion.

|15| Plato misled philosophy. As he was stuck with beauty and value of contemplation of geometric truth, ~~That led him with what~~ how geometric truth could be discerned as ⟨for?⟩[2] <u>all</u> occasions. i.e. rose above the flux. This led him to weave philosophy around conception of world of <u>Ideas</u> abstracted from world of flux, ~~which~~ \thus/ preserved beauty of absolute attainment. Plato's false step – was ~~not~~ \in saying/ mathematics as abstracted from real world but ~~mathematics as~~ \while really it should be mathematics as/ discernment of mathematical truths as <u>in</u> reality and as an absolute ~~fact~~ condition to which reality is conforming – that it is the absolute as in reality and not absolute as abstracted from reality that has value.

The transformation of Heraclitus comes in seeing the community (a whole) in each particular instance. You cannot get beyond what you discern in particular occasion, but <u>what</u> you discern is a long study.

Leibniz – or Husserl's – discussion of all other <u>possible</u> worlds is an appeal to complete ignorance, because all one has to appeal to is the <u>actual</u>.[3]

But appeal to the alternative within the general conditions is source of art, ethics, ⟨?⟩ etc., but it is an appeal within conditions laid down by the actual. [Cf. <u>Logos</u> of Philo[4] or also Greek philosophy.]

|16| At beginning of modern science Descartes starts from substantial point of view, i.e. a plurality of independent non-mental substances, i.e. bits of matter, which "enjoy" occasions, and in defining these occasions <u>time</u> and <u>space</u> enter into your explanation. Therefore physical science is ultimately based in 17th century is discussion of locomotion of bits of matter in space, during time. Extreme form of idea of <u>simple</u> <u>location</u>.

Order of nature – a harmony between succession of occasions necessitates bringing in completion of relationship between bits of matter, which account for the succession of occasions. i.e. <u>forces</u> in bits of matter. In these forces there is an exclusive appeal to the efficient cause. Simple mechanistic theory.

---

1. Heath marked this paragraph with a vertical line in the left margin.
2. The abbreviation here is 'fr', which could reasonably be expanded as either 'for' or 'from'. This is a problem throughout her notes. When possible, the editors have used context to decide which word to use.
3. Heath wrote 'pure phenomenology' in the left margin next to this paragraph.
4. Philo of Alexandria (20 BCE – 40 CE), also called Judaeus Philo. For a discussion of the doctrine of Logos in Philo's writings, see Hillar, 'Philo of Alexandria'.

How much by ~~this~~ our immediate experience is swept aside as irrelevant by mechanism! i.e. Purpose ⟨etc?⟩. This sweeping aside was an enormous success.

⟨?⟩ yes earlier discussed only <u>final</u> ends. A success for the ends.

Then we come to modern insistence on function (James). This requires extension in <u>time</u> as well as in <u>space</u>, i.e. is not morphology. Therefore must take a certain duration as |17| a whole. i.e. cannot understand the beginning without reference to end, and ~~All~~ all other parts, i.e. is a <u>whole</u>.

Medieval said cannot understand beginning without end.

17th century said cannot understand end without beginning.

Modern says both. i.e. need a fusion of efficient and final cause.

Thursday, 15 October 1925

Heath's notes[1]

<u>Common World</u>.

The standard here also must be the individual occasion and the unity as community of occasions strung together as life of an <u>enduring</u> entity is to be explained on same principle as the total community of the actual world.

Organism and functions are persistent concepts in present science.

Time involves depth or extension.

Extension means divisibility.

But quā <u>real</u> it is one atomic entity.

Therefore when you divide a duration, you mean that quā real the antecedent can only be apprehended by ~~referef~~ reference to the ~~antecedent~~ consequent and vice versa. Therefore in concept of the one real entity you must include the motion of efficient and final cause as in essence of entity itself. You thus get a separation ~~of~~ between the idea of the extensive continuum (four-dimensional) |18| and what we may term the act of realization.

We have the divisibility of what is realized.

In four-dimensional continuum there is a difference between temporality and spatiality. Point is how ~~acts of realization~~ time gets discriminated from space. Temporal series form the impression of the acts of realization.

Mustn't look on realization as another extensive becomingness; it is sheer ~~sh~~ succession of acts which is an impression on that which qua possibility is extensive and as realized is actual extensiveness of past up to present. Total ~~what~~ VthatV is realized is continuous.

In science are two opposite points of view
  1. Idea of continuity is
  2. Idea of atomicity
Cf. Bergson on indivisibility of duration.[2]

---

1. The corresponding Harvard lecture can be found on p. 57.
2. Bergson is well known for his view of the indivisibility of duration (*la durée*) and Bergson's *Creative Evolution* was on the course reading list. Given the context of Kant here, Whitehead may also have had

Even Descartes distinguishes two aspects of time – as measurable and as not measurable.¹

Plato – cf. how <u>time</u> came to be.

|19| Look up if you find this double aspect of time in English Empiricists; or Kant, this is because he had Newton by heart. – talks of prediction of extensive quantity – which is putting in philosophical terms the central doctrine of Newton's fluxions. i.e. in extensive quantity is ⟨counting?⟩ first chapter of differential calculus. But do find the ghost of it in Kant in looking on time and space as <u>forms</u> of intuition as impress on matter or chaotic given. Whitehead thinks given is not chaotic but realization is an impress on given not quā ~~chat~~ chaotic, but as that which is eternally related in every ⟨?⟩ of possibility.

Same ghost appears: Hume when he talks of an impression. i.e. ᵥ1.ᵥ presupposes a mind as given with an extensive temporal ⟨continuum?⟩ ⟨and?⟩ impression (atomic) on the mind.

Again we come round to problem of community.

Whole conception of value and determination of our conations justified themselves as that in us which is for the attainment of value. One of great merits of Kant that he emphasized the idea of <u>value</u> ⟨and?⟩ <u>action</u>, and here finds most fundamental unity.

Saturday, 17 October 1925

Heath's notes²

|20| Turning back on approach via epistemology. Recourse to describe <u>how</u> <u>knowledge</u> is <u>possible</u>. Have to use certain categories. i.e. it must be how knowledge is <u>possible</u> in terms of elements of this situation.

Kant begins by talking about space and time as <u>forms</u> of intuition – They come into his philosophy absolutely uncriticized – ought to first discuss spatiality and temporality. So we are abstracting from the knowing of it and discussing simply the thing known. – if our discussion of thing known makes it impossible to get knowing into known, my metaphysics is obviously incomplete.

Test of metaphysics is coherence and adequacy, and under adequacy, epistemology comes in.

Start ~~well~~ ᵥwithᵥ ? What is immediately known. Whitehead says the <u>universe</u>, a complete all-embracing community, as from the limited stand-point here, now. Which is imposing a limitation on a plurality <u>beyond</u>, and which yet includes that unity, here <u>now</u> in itself. Obviously this is another rendering of Descartes' ~~Cog~~ *cogito ergo sum*. Descartes slipped in the enduring mind surveying a multiplicity of its own occasions.

---

in mind Bergson, *Time and Free Will*, available at <https://archive.org/details/in.ernet.dli.2015.189070>, which was first published in English translation in 1913, and is seen as a critique of Kant.

1. Heath wrote 'look up' in the left margin next to this sentence.
2. The corresponding Harvard lecture can be found on p. 58.

|21|
1. The self as experient ~~is (?)~~ is described by Whitehead as <u>this</u> immediate self here <u>now</u> – i.e. the immediate occasion <u>here, now</u>. And all we know of what we mean by being <u>real</u> – actual must be described in terms of this immediate occasional self. This immediate self is essentially a "prehension." The first character of the prehension is that it proclaims itself <u>as one among others</u>. i.e. as being an entity within a <u>beyondness</u>. i.e. this <u>here now</u> experience is essentially a reference to <u>there, then</u>. There is therefore essentially a duplicity in the experient occasion – <u>it</u> as a <u>unit</u> <u>entity</u> and yet as <u>one</u> <u>among</u> other <u>entities</u>. i.e. Before beginning to talk of space and time we must get at these general and essential characteristics.

2. This synthesis of a common world which is this experient occasion proclaims itself as a synthesis not of a multiplicity of entities *simpliciter*, but a synthesis of the whole under limitation. Yet held apart by that which imposes on them an aspect.

This immediate occasion is VtheV <u>only</u> standard of actual reality.

True way to describe entity is as something for itself – a union of efficient and final cause. Final cause is described in abstraction as value.

Tuesday, 20 October 1925

Heath's notes

|23|[1] Immediate problem presented by cognition. One vs. Many. And this multiplicity is of several types.
  a. Colors, sounds, etc.
  b. Persons, chairs, etc.
  c. Occasions or events.

Yet they are in a <u>community</u>. i.e. a certain <u>one</u>ness, yet not same oneness as that of a sound.

This community is ⟨common?⟩ of things real – something has been achieved, is-for-itself. Where among these types of multiplicity are we to find the most complete exemplification of that which is for itself real?

Aristotelian tradition looks on the enduring entity, the germ, the living thing as the final concrete thing. Put over into modern philosophy by Descartes – many bodies and many minds, each in a sense real things. Cartesian philosophy and all its derivatives has led to inextricable difficulties.

Therefore take another track. Ultimate concrete entity bearing most completely the total community is the "immediate occasion," i.e. that which is happening, i.e. that which has been achieved as real or actual. Then a fact stares you in face which does not on Cartesian philosophy – from[2] this "subjectivism" has |24| already gathered up occasions into a community, i.e. Whitehead looks

---
1. Page |22| is the blank back page of |21|. The corresponding Harvard lecture can be found on p. 60.
2. We have removed an opening bracket that appears here before 'from' because it seems to have been crossed out, but it is impossible to be sure. There is no closing bracket.

on it as our inadequate statement of total community. "Subjectivism" is used in broad sense of any philosophy which makes reality at root the "subject for occasion" (is not necessity mentalism). ~~This f~~

When start with immediate occasion you see at once – that there is

1. No actual world apart from vmultiplicity ofv actual occasions.
2. No occasion without the community.

Whitehead feels that ought to go straight from physical occasions to community and <u>enduring entity</u> to be explained in terms of these two concepts. So put aside <u>enduring entity</u> for the present.

Last time was talking about "beyondness", "isolation", "concreteness", etc. in discussing what was first category we must introduce ~~I~~ in talking of "immediate physical occasion" or "the event." That means that in searching for a category in which to describe immediate occasion, you have to describe it in terms of the community. But you can't talk of this community except in terms of multiplicity of physical occasions. Therefore cannot describe immediate physical occasion except in terms of multiplicity of other physical occasions. But each physical occasion has its own character or |25| essence. Other physical occasions are for <u>It</u> something that is peculiar to <u>It</u> alone. That peculiarity, spatiality which attaches to other occasion as in the synthesis of the occasion which is It, is "mode of entry" or the "aspect" or "perspective" or "limitation under which the entry of the other occasion is conditioned as it is synthesized in <u>It</u>." Then another way – Descartes glimpsed it when he made the distinction between

Objective	Formaliter
as "an object before mind." [Whitehead is talking of object in <u>occasion</u>, not before mind, calls it 'modal limitation'].[1]	That which is under its own form, for itself.

Point is the reality – the being something – in case of physical event depends essentially upon its imposition of limitation. i.e. extending what it otherwise might be – i.e. excluding other occasions *simplicter* and only including them under strict limitations. Here, Whitehead is only insisting on multiplicity side, i.e. that individual event is something in itself, but because in being itself ⟨is?⟩ in synthesis of other things and enters into synthesis of other things ("events are members one of another")[2] each |26| event is limitation of other things – an abstraction on what other things might be otherwise, and this is just because it is limited. An essential part of his metaphysics – cannot describe what an event is in itself without reference to it as extrusion of the whole realm of ideality. Here he diverges from Plato – i.e. cannot tear apart the realm of Ideas from each particular event, nor vice versa.

Each event can only be described as what it is among what it might be as well as what it is among community of all other things that are.

Each event is something made actual, actuality of event-in-itself. In description ~~of~~ that actuality is to be looked on as an end in itself. What you've

---

1. Closing bracket supplied.
2. Opening quotation mark supplied.

not brought in as main category can never be brought in now, except as under that main category.

[Aristotle's categories are able, but we've lived 2,000 years. Two fatal things: 1. To neglect past. 2. To be slave to it.]

The event is one achievement viewing it under guise of isolation and separation, is the attainment of a certain definite pattern of value, shaped, ~~informed~~ informed of value, and that particular form is analysed by the how – i.e. by analysis of the particular modal limitations which are impressed on totality as synthesized.

|27| And therefore Whitehead holds that the limitation of things is primary characteristic of achieved value. Achievement of a particular value arises by extrusion of neutralizing elements. It is a keeping at bay the other elements because apart from this you have nonentity. Therefore in ultimate analysis of how of event we shall find the concept of incompatibility. i.e. if it is this, it can't be that.

As far as an event is for itself, it is emerging value. vConcept ofV value at once brings in a gradation [embodied as intensive quantity]. So an event as for itself may be a more or less vivid entity. Individuality viewed as separable – has gradations. (own note – cf. Bosanquet on examples of individuality).[1] Those gradations depend on completeness of the extrusion. In analysing the event quā achievement of value by extrusion, ~~and in calling all~~ Whitehead must illustrate it by these fields in human experience where we are ~~of~~ dwelling on concept of value – i.e. Art is essentially succession, i.e. arranging the environment so that as synthesized in yourself there is a ready extrusion.

Thursday, 22 October 1925

Heath's notes[2]

|28| An aspect of antagonism between art and ethics.

Aesthetic considerations are more fundamental than those of ethics in their philosophical implications. Because art has to do with immediate value as an end in itself, i.e. as isolatable unity (the superject from the immediate prehension), but ethics has to do with the comparison of occasions, whereby the status of occasions {?} vamongV realized values may or may not lead to endurance. i.e. (ethics) is concerned with survival power and progress. Art, with immediate value of achievement for its own sake. Thus ethics presupposes art,

---

1. Bernard Bosanquet (1848–1923), British idealist philosopher and political theorist. Though Heath notes that this is her own aside, Whitehead was familiar with Bosanquet's work and mentioned him several times during his first year of lecturing at Harvard and Radcliffe. Whitehead later contributed the following to a 1935 book celebrating his work and life: 'Bosanquet's death is a great loss – a big man gone. Of recent years I have been more and more appreciating his size. Also his broad outlook and his single-minded devotion to truth have made him an inspiring figure. He is one of the outstanding men who have collectively made the epoch of thought of the last forty years. I am sure that some of the main principles for which he contended will be found embodied in the slow philosophic reconstruction of the future' (Muirhead, *Bernard Bosanquet and His Friends*, p. 316).
2. The corresponding Harvard lecture can be found on p. 62.

and art requires an ethics derivative from itself. Thus ethics should not be made fundamental in metaphysics.

Art is selection, and thus exclusion – the conscious arrangement of the environment so that some immediate occasions may have the utmost vividness of grade in realization. Every work of art depends on the ~~significance~~ VseparationV ⟨of?⟩ its positive content from irrelevant affairs. Chinese art as an extreme example. But also true of Italian Renaissance – Vitality of a work of art depends on rigid selection.

Art's motive power is envisagement of some definite value – but achievement of art is to secure that limitation |29| which realizes that value [in being given there is extension and vice versa]. Example – Architecture which wins at voluminousness does not leave building ~~app~~ open to unbounded sky – the inner surface of dome delimits and makes evident the soaring volume it contains, balancing itself above the lower volumes.

Further – ~~valu~~ effect of volume due to proportion rather than volume size. The larger volumes defining themselves by reference to smaller, and final reference is your body.

The endurance of insistent individuality of great work of art [Question of survival must be considered later as whole]. The work of art has achieved an enduring independence of being, realizing itself as outcome of limiting occasions and impressing itself on its environment. This atomic individuality achieved by structural limitation and enduring among the passage of things – the recapture of enduring ground of all reality. Thus although only one substance, there is an emergence of that substance in every realized value.

The actual occasion thus includes formal cause and final cause and endurance.

|30| The intense value of this capture of the eternal by some passing occasion, is illustrated by poetry of survival of past. Keats – Last stage of "Eve of St. Agnes."[1]

The ⟨?⟩ past is on its great side the relevant past.

The eternal is ~~th~~ always relevant, but in its actuality it has limited relevance. This particular occasion is falling by shadow of truth on that which otherwise would escape actuality due to its generality. i.e. There is community of many occasions, but apart from ~~man~~ particular occasions there is nothing.

This passing from particular to eternal is theme of religious art. Gothic architecture in authentic French form, is best example of finite pointing to infinite.

---

1. The last stanza of Keats's poem reads:
    'And they are gone: ay, ages long ago
    These lovers fled away into the storm.
    That night the Baron dreamt of many a woe,
    And all his warrior-guests, with shade and form
    Of witch, and demon, and large coffin-worm,
    Were long be-nightmar'd. Angela the old
    Died palsy-twitch'd, with meagre face deform;
    The Beadsman, after thousand aves told,
    For aye unsought for slept among his ashes cold.'

But there is a nature a more direct embodiment of the infinity beyond the finite – wide-open prairie – of ⟨?⟩ desolate marsh – mid-ocean – Even here it's not sheer unboundedness, but the limited in direct contrast with the unlimited. Increased effect of vastness due to VaV single object as a ⟨?⟩, or by the association with detailed events in far past.

Saturday, 24 October 1925

Heath's notes[1]

|31| Difference between the experient occasions and imaginal occasions.
Experient occasion – are ends in themselves as fact.
Imaginal occasion – derivative for experient occasions and are still emergence of value, but quā occasion of knowledge. The knowing expresses a definite relationship to an experient occasion, and that one is value quā <u>fact</u>, and other is value quā <u>knowing</u>.

The most concrete is joint, i.e. experient and imaginal. Cannot describe imaginal until have described experient. [Nor can you describe the experient <u>fully</u> until you have describe the imaginal.]. Each is a synthesis – There a component in experient occasion will be imaginal occasions quā experient.

Experient occasion (several lectures).
1. Described as far as possible without reference to its imaginal occasion. Each experient in being itself is its own end, i.e. as considered with respect to its own intrinsic reality and can be described as individual value. A synthesis.
  a. What is synthesized and what is kept out.

|32| Our occasions are not synthesized *simpliciter* because then every occasion would be like every other. Therefore it is synthesis under an aspect, i.e. something and something. Now how are we going to describe the <u>modes</u>?

Among things synthesized are
1. Other occasions.
2. Something else ⓧ. Therefore need some classification of entities (excluding sheer knowledge) which we find in an experient occasion. Here must have recourse to our immediate experience. There is a flux – each occasion as it passes is gone forever. Therefore each occasion is just what it is. But there is no interest in applying concept of identity to an entity; but when we compare different occasions, you at once see that the whole fact that they are describable depends on this concept of identity – i.e. that there is something in <u>one</u> which is identical with ⟨?⟩ what is in another. This use of concept of identity is |33| fruitful, and the foundation of all knowledge.

There are two main divisions of entities to which we apply "identity" in different ⟨senses?⟩.

<u>More</u> <u>complex</u> = The identity of <u>endurance</u>. i.e. of concrete objects as tables. "perceptual objects."

---

1. The corresponding Harvard lecture can be found on p. 64.

Less complex = identity of <u>disposition</u> of colors etc. – patterns – geometrical shape. Artist or mathematician. Endurance has nothing to do with this.

<u>Eternal</u> <u>objects</u> (universals but doesn't use term because of its difficulty with "fallacy of misplaced concreteness" cannot divest an "eternal object" from ⟨its⟩ relations, while universals are completely abstract.)

But the point is that you get the absolute identity of this object – an extreme <u>logical</u> <u>realism</u>. If you run this view of occasions as concrete, Whitehead thinks you are bound to be a logical realist. (cf. William James.) i.e. it's not sufficient to say "similarity," for this involves possibility of "identity." Though components in occasion are what they are in some independence of the occasion.

|34| Therefore the green has a certain indeterminateness with respect to the occasion. The specific type of its ∧(⟨green's⟩)∧ ingression into this occasion is indeterminate in essence of green. But in essence of each particular occasion, there is a definite determination as to the ingression of <u>green</u>. i.e. ~~the~~ "∨each∨ occasion is a particular solution of the indetermination of eternal object."[1] That is why the eternal objects in abstraction from actual world are world of possibility – Very meaning of "possibility" is that in talking of things as in themselves you find indetermination. Whereas actuality is definite solution of indeterminations in actual occasions. cf. Art lecture – on <u>exclusion</u>.[2]

Tuesday, 27 October 1925

Heath's notes[3]

|35|

<u>Possibility</u> and <u>Contingency</u>

Metaphysical situation discloses a <u>self-creative</u> <u>activity</u> embodying itself in a plurality, forming <u>one</u> community. Each unity of community is the ~~t~~ embodiment of self-creative activity in some particular limitation. In embodying itself in each unity, it in some sense determines the community and requires community. Unity ~~needs~~ cannot be divorced from community and community cannot be divorced from unity.

[Spinoza – too little emphasis on activity of substance. Correct in thinking that activity has a certain content which we can determine as its attributes].[4] First determination of attributes is that of individuality under limitation, as required for creation. (synthesis) and as the realm of 'eternal objects', the given subject matter always for creation. In respect to this total multiplicity of eternal objects – call it <u>realm</u> (not chaotic). can't be turn into detached bits – there is always the creative synthesis – the achieving of mutual relevance. – quā real they are not relevant – need the creative impress for this. Therefore cannot describe the actual as torn apart from the totality of possibility. [a sad error in

---

1. Opening quotation mark supplied.
2. This is likely referring to the previous lecture, 22 October.
3. The corresponding Harvard lecture can be found on p. 67.
4. Closing bracket supplied.

traditional metaphysics – |36| which comes from Descartes' dualism of mind [~~an~~ and matter.]. Cannot take actual as merely actual, but in respect to totality of what it might have been. The untrue propositions about it are part of it. Formula of ~~the~~ ∨realism∨ is just as stunted as pure subjective idealism. "As soon as realist becomes indignant (or has approval) he is an idealist."

Every occasion exhibits itself as analysable into the realization or making actual (eliciting of value [later]) of relationships between eternal objects, which might have been otherwise, but are these relationships between these objects. When we say these relations might have been actual, we do not say this with regard to its reference to previous determinations, but ∨of∨ the concept of any event of community apart from a specially designed status ~~of~~ ∨in∨ community.

In some sense the realization has ⟨to?⟩ achieve in respect especially to certain relationships in preference to other relationships. An occasion of realization is a mode of dealing with whole of relationships in realm of eternal objects; keeping some back and eliciting value from others.

|37| ~~Alternat~~

Each occasion defines the general character of community of occasions by defining

① What any occasion in community <u>must be</u>.
② What any occasion in community <u>may be</u>.
③ What other particular occasions, each with a determinate status related to itself, <u>must be</u> in addition to limitation of ① imposed ~~by~~ ∧on∧ possibilities ~~by~~ ∨of∨ ② in virtue of this definite status.

Platonic myth

α determines what each occasion ∨①∨ <u>must</u> be, ∧②∧ <u>may</u> be {?} ∨③∨ β has perfectly definite status relationship to α, and vice versa.

③ is usually muddled in metaphysics and smuggled in under space and time. These are really just a particular way of representing that definite status. Q complete knowledge of <u>α</u>, by reason of definite status of α relationship to β – discloses the conditions ③ must fulfill.

④ Part of general conditions that any pair of occasions have a definite specific relative status.

Again, there are ① impartial conditions for all occasions ② impartial possibilities for all occasions ③ partial (opposite of impartial) conditions – namely additional specific conditions imposed on ③ by virtue of its relation to α.

|38| These "partial" conditions can be equally well expressed as restriction for β of impartial possibilities ② in virtue of its relation to α.

Point of this theory – no other occasion can have same status relatively to <u>α</u> that β has – i.e. never can get away from "principle of individuality or ɫ uniqueness of relative status". Underlies whole theory of <u>time</u> and <u>space</u>. Put in another way:

Each occasion α determines a general scheme of relations throughout the community and in this scheme there is one and only one niche for each occasion.

⟨Again?⟩ β – from point of view of knowVingV α, you can tell that there is a β occupying that niche, ~~but is~~ i.e. is known by relationship, not by adjective.

[cf. illustration of Gothic architecture.[1] Outside building not known by adjective, but indicated by inside building in spatio-temporal relationships.]

Those who deny any <u>contingency</u>, must hold that the 'partial' conditions provided by antecedent occasions completely determine an occasion β. Those who maintain <u>contingency</u> must |39| hold that the complete character of β cannot be determined from an empirical knowledge of complete character of all antecedent events. – They must hold that it is not necessary that any characteristic of β is explicable by reference to conditions from β which are inherent in character of antecedent occasions V$α_1$ $α_2$ $α_{3v}$. On the other hand – a knowledge of antecedents occasions will determine that β must exhibit some definite characteristics, perhaps of general character capable of alternative VspecificV determinations.

Another question. When we consider the subsequent occasion. – Then also have VeachV a definite status relative to β, and $γ_1$ $γ_2$ etc. requires that β should have possessed certain characteristics. ~~But~~ Thus we must hold that knowledge of $γ_1$ $γ_2$, and $α_1$ $α_2$ will ⟨determine?⟩ β.

But if we hold <u>no</u> contingency, we must hold that complete knowledge of any α will reveal determinations of any β.

But if there be contingency, it is not true. Contemporary occasions $β_1$ $β_2$ $β_3$. These impose no 'partial' conditions whatsoever on β. ⟨?⟩ i.e. are completely independent as far as 'partial' conditions – i.e. "doctrine of mutual independence of VmutuallyV contemporary occasions." [They share in |40|[2] VsameV general scheme of relatedness.]

Doctrine can be expressed thus –

Occasions mutually contemporary, experience in respect to own[3] relations, the purpose of past occasions, together with our free spontaneity. Thus free spontaneity though individually effective, does not transcend among its contemporaries. Also present occasions experience in respect to their future occasions, their own purposes, as conditioned by own past[4] and own experiences of own mutual relations, ~~but not~~ as enriched by own free spontaneity. [Contemporary events experience mutual relationships but don't condition them.] I see a yellow pencil there, but I don't condition it.]

More ⟨care?⟩ –

Present occasions with respect to ⟨sum?⟩ mutual relationships experience purpose of past occasions as enriched by own free spontaneity [individually,

---

1. See 22 October lecture, p. 16.
2. We have deleted a duplicate 'in'.
3. Heath's handwriting makes it impossible to definitively distinguish an 'our' from an 'own', of which there are quite a number of instances in the next few paragraphs. However, Roethlisberger's and Hartshorne's notes from the corresponding Harvard lecture (p. 68) support the notion that most or all of them are 'own'.
4. What is likely the word 'past' is partially occluded by a later hole punch.

not mutually effective] and also as conditioned by our purpose respecting future occasions. i.e. What you experience in present is conditioned by purpose for future so far as not already conditioned by own past and are issue of own free spontaneity.

① Free spontaneity as to mutual relationship of present occasions and
② free spontaneity as to purposes for future occasions, condition each other.

Thursday, 29 October 1925
Heath's notes[1]

|41|
Relations
   1. Eternal relationships *inter se* of eternal objects. No real togetherness of eternal objects, therefore isolation of individual essences, and a formal generality of relationship. Realization is an achievement of a real togetherness – outcome of value of relevance. (Internal because stands in nature of each object that it has these relationships.)[2]
   2. Relationships of eternal objects to actual ∧occasions∧. "Ingression" (External to eternal objects and internal to occasion.)
   3. Relationships of occasions. *inter se*. "Aspects" "perspectives"[3] – conditions – determinations – relative status – causation. (External. But some of relations of contemporary ~~events~~ ∨occasions∨ are external to one and internal to other.)

Each experient occasion as embodiment of creative activity which has in mind total community of actual world. How far is creative emergence of any particular event already determined? Whitehead holds to element of contingency because
   1. Total community of actual occasions is contingent to total possibility. Any judgment of <u>value</u> of world implies a possible alternative.
   2. Each unity prehends in itself the total community. i.e. it is total community under its own limitations and therefore in itself shares in every character of community. And therefore embodies also the contingency.
   3. Direct experience of spontaneous choice under conditions limiting freedom.
   4. Complete arbitrariness of doctrine of determinism. (for any empirical and pluralistic metaphysics. Not arbitrary for monism.)
   |42| New point. Imaginal occasions. i.e. of knowing.
   Each experient occasion gives rise to its corresponding imaginal occasion. i.e. the occasion of knowing the experiences. [Final concrete entity = ultimate occasion – here cannot avoid some dualism. i.e. is di-polar and two poles are

---

1. The corresponding Harvard lecture can be found on p. 68.
2. Parentheses supplied. The parenthetical comments appear in the left margin, as do those in the next two items.
3. Ending quotation mark supplied.

experient occasion and imaginal occasion].[1] An occasion of knowing that experient occasion and thus knowing of an aspect of total community but what is known is experient occasion. In some sense to be identified with immediate occasion of bodily life. Experient occasion is datum in complete independence of its ~~experient~~ ∨imaginal∨ occasion (as they are contemporary).[2] On other hand imaginal occasion – its field ∨⟨?⟩∨[3] of knowledge is <u>purely</u> and only experient occasion.

Occasion of knowing presupposes cognition, but occasion of knowing is determined by cognition, which is presupposed.

Inadequacy, fitfulness – ⟨error?⟩ of knowledge cannot be derived from cognition, but ⟨...?⟩ ⟨and?⟩ fact that occasion of knowing has elements in it, limited, derived from other occasions. Imaginal occasion, like experient occasion, is emergence of ⟨superjicient?⟩[4] value – i.e. knowledge value. Grades of ⟨?⟩ realization of value and therefore you have a large gradation of type of ultimate occasion.

    1. Empty occasion.[5]
        Both experient and imaginal are of ∧negligible vividness∧
    2. Material occasion.
        Experient occasions ⟨are?⟩ with ⟨enduring?⟩ inheritance.
        Imaginal ⟨are?⟩ ⟨?⟩ of
    3. Biological.
        ⟨Experient?⟩ ⟨occasion?⟩ with and ⟨?⟩ are fitful.
    4. Rational.
        Experient ⟨are?⟩ with ⟨enduring?⟩ ⟨inheritance?⟩.
        Imaginal with ⟨enduring?⟩ ⟨inheritance?⟩.
    5. Spiritual.
        Experient without ⟨enduring?⟩ inheritance.
        Imaginal with ⟨enduring?⟩ inheritance.

Saturday, 31 October 1925

Heath's notes[6]

|43| Whitehead is identifying the distinctions in respect to <u>time</u> (before, after – simultaneity) with the mutual causal relations between ultimate occasions; i.e. different types of mutual determinations which are in fact different types of temporal relations. If ~~y~~ we do that first thing is idea of

---

1. Closing bracket supplied.
2. Closing parenthesis supplied.
3. This interlineation appears above 'field' with a bracket encompassing both on the right, suggesting it is supposed to be a synonym or at least an equivalent word.
4. The handwriting here is difficult to decipher, but 'superjicient' does seem likely. It is plausibly a variant of 'superject'. If correct, this would be the first known use of the term.
5. From this point, to the end of the lecture, the writing is very cramped so as to fit into the bottom of the page, making it challenging to decipher with any confidence.
6. The corresponding Harvard lecture can be found on p. 70.

contemporaneous occasions. These have to distinguish between (2 or 3) meanings which are habitually muddled.

vContemporaneous are thoseV[1] 1. Occasions which realize themselves in relative ~~interpr~~ independence. Insofar as there is any spontaneity in occasion, the contemporaneous are completely independent, though bound together by definite ~~relat~~ status. What they are for each other does not depend on what they are for themselves. Whereas of non-contemporaneous occasion, what they are for each other flows from what they are for themselves. Are there as datum for us, but not as a determination. Issue from a common past. cf. Physics, psychology, etc.

[Self – Time relations ~~are~~ vgiveV more fundamental unity and closer organization than do space relations. Is this basis for distinguishing time from space with Space-Time].

vPresent event in sense of presented.v 2. Are displayed in us, not *simpliciter*, but under mode of being loci of eternal objects, which are really |44| relationships of presentation between them and us. This is one way in which relational essence of eternal objects is relevant to explanation of what an occasion is in itself (sense-perception). Proper and orthodox to object to this and say now you are talking of private psychological field and that is different from physical event in physical space. Reply. If you hold to that distinction you never can get physical and private space together. You've got to hold as we all do that what you perceive is red brick building over there, i.e. What <u>that over there</u> is for <u>me here</u>. Sense data are relational in sense that they impose mode as to how present occasions are synthesized in this occasion.

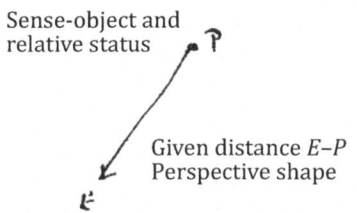

Sense-object and relative status

Given distance E–P
Perspective shape

System of internal relations. E in its essence includes the modifications of relationship to P. Internal on E's end, but it's (almost) external at P's end from its very trivial relation to essence of P. But issue from <u>common</u> past, but does not preclude some ∧spontaneity.∧

(Pathology of perception is not nearly enough considered.)

Two points:

1. What P is in itself is irrelevant to E except so far as vmutualityV relative status, and 2. to that extent, present events are also <u>contemporaneous</u> events. But that does not tell you that contemporaneous events are present events. |45| Objects to modern (relativity) way of putting it, i.e. that sweep away simultaneous events – because immediate datum relative to which whole map of events is made out in space and time, is made via what is immediately before you and therefore that is fundamental, i.e. we fit things into various schemes of presented events. vIn RelativityV You first rule out everything you know as irrelevant and then you have nothing on which to found your measurements.

Whitehead says what you know are coincidences in present occasion and then you somewhat conjecturally fit together present occasions.

---

[1]. We have deleted a redundant 'which' from the interlineation.

Measurements ultimately relate to aspects of presented occasions.

Root of objection to prevalent belief is that doesn't believe in curvature of space – fundamental fact that we have to deal with is succession of immediate "presents." i.e. the ~~kn~~ what man is doing in London now is quite intelligible as distinct from what I now <u>learn</u> by letter ~~of~~ concerning him. Vs. Einstein Whitehead says that measurements of presented are in terms of presented space, i.e. in terms of a uniform scheme and as presented is only externally related to observer.

i.e. P is external relation – E is internal – and therefore |46| general scheme is only discovered by analysing E and not P and while Einstein ⟨?⟩ would analyse E and P. This argument only holds if take "presented" as fundamental.

Tuesday, 3 November 1925

Heath's notes[1]

|47| Distinguished contemporary (independent occasions) and present occasions. (Contemporary – related by presentational ∧relation∧).

Sense data – talked of under guise of high abstraction. i.e. Green is really a presentational relation of another occasion to ⟨me?⟩. It is an external relation, so far as presented occasion is concerned, and internal so far as ego relation is concerned. Externality is demonstrated by physical means of varying presented occasion. The presented occasion is presented via its relative status, which is internal to it – but the greenness is <u>external</u>.

Question arises – Are contemporary events all presented? No, according to modern science occasions which are there as present are not selected via what they are in themselves, and therefore general presentation is systematic and independent of their intrinsic characters.

Contrary to Einstein – holds that there is immediate three-dimensional continuum presented which is selected ∨systematically∨ on basis of relative status.

Einstein – it is warped by the intrinsic essence of occasion.

Question as to whether X is or is not non-contemporaneous, as E is made up of relative status and essence of E as modified by what X is in itself. i.e. Non-contemporaneous |48| might well depend on character of X, but presentation ought not to. i.e. All present – events – are contemporaneous – but not all contemporaneous are present.

In handling of this problem, you get ∨modern∨ physical theory of relativ⟨ity⟩.[2]

Einstein pushes aside presented occasions as irrelevant. Whitehead says must be relevant, for all measurement depends on the presented.

Experient occasion is in complete independence of its imaginal occasion – therefore imaginal occasion is variant type of being "now."

---

1. The corresponding Harvard lecture can be found on p. 71.
2. Heath wrote 'relative', but it seems that 'relativity' was intended.

~~Non-contem~~

Idea of endurance. Simplest way of expressing endurance is continuity of structural repetition, ᵛself-inherited.ᵛ Have a succession of instants, each ᵛa synthesisᵛ capable of analysis ~~of~~ as a structure.

① A structure – an eternal object as exemplified. Repetition – get same eternal object as exemplified throughout the series.

② ᵛRelativeᵛ continuity of the occasion. Has regard to a special property of relative status, i.e. spatio-temporal.

③ A ~~mu~~ successive inheritance. Structure of antecedent occasions should be a determining element in ~~pre~~ following. Not real <u>repetition</u> but "because of antecedents."

This is termed "an enduring object." This is a |49| complex idea – derived from idea of eternal object. Which has to ~~due~~ ᵛdoᵛ with an "historical route" and effective self-inheritance.

Quite essential that relative status be dominant fact in mode of realization.

1. Part and whole relative status of two occasions.
2. Continuity in historical route (time and space), which promotes effective inheritance.
3. Externality of environment.[1]
4. Experient to corresponding imaginal occasion.

When you are dealing with grades of reality, that basis for intensive quantity. That is outcome of being an occasion in route of endurance – structure gives a depth of value when it embodies the inherited memories of the past. ~~Then~~ Under that circumstance each occasion has a vividness of reality. Comes from embodying a past which reinforces the lines of present.

This is first suggestion as to variation of importance of events in community. Grades –[2]

1. –[3] (halfway between Sun and Sirius)
2. material
3. living
4. ~~mental~~ mental
5. spiritual (divorced from ~~mater~~ historical route).

Dipolar imaginal occasion
experient occasion

Imaginal occasions are relative to experient, "but owing to independence of experient of imaginal occasion they may be looked on as mutually "now".

|50| It looks as though we ought to say that imaginal occasions were caused by experient occasion, but denies this. Imaginal occasion is both analysis and synthesis of experient occasions. Experient occasion is a datum for imaginal occasion in additi~~onal~~ to eternal objects being datum.

~~Not a A~~ Experient occasion is not a <u>cause</u> but a datum of imaginal occasion.

---

1. A brace appears in the left margin next to the first three items with the words 'present occasions'.
2. Numbers have been added to this list, both for the sake of clarity and to match the list at the end of this lecture.
3. That is, empty space.

The cause is inheriting from past.
Five possibilities of
1. Void occasion – Experient occasion and imaginal occasion may be devoid of endurance
Not absolute ∧gap.∧[1]
2. Material occasion – Experient occasions have endurance.
Imaginal occasions have negligible (endurance).
3. ~~Living~~ Biological – Experient occasions have ∨impartial∨ endurance
Imaginal occasions have smaller range of endurance.
4. ~~Mental~~ Rational – Experient occasions have ∨impartial∨ endurance.
Imaginal occasions have impartial endurance.[2]
5. Spiritual – Experient occasions have lost endurance.
Imaginal occasions have endurance.

Thursday, 5 November 1925

Heath's notes[3]

|51|
Paper, December 4
1. Extensiveness and relations of space.
2. Process.
3. Types of relation between occasions ∨characterized by∨ ~~(?)~~ time.
4. Time as separated from idea of extensiveness. I.e. time as <u>epochal</u>, as mere succession of epochs.
⟨5.⟩ <u>Descartes</u> on time.
Distinguishes between time as measurable and time as mere becomingness. "Principles of Philosophy."[4]
⟨6.⟩ <u>Hume</u>
Contiguity.

___

Lecture.
Distinction between
1. Relationships of status – i.e. spatio-temporal from point of view of extensiveness or perspective.

___

1. These three words appear between item 1 and item 2 near the right margin. Whether the phrase properly belongs between the two, or is associated with one or the other, is ambiguous.
2. There is some ambiguity here. This entire line is actually just a series of ditto marks, which indicate repetition of the line above. But clearly Heath did not intend to have a second line discussing experient occasions. We have thus interpreted these marks as a repetition of the line above aside from the first word. Alternatively, it is possible that Heath meant to copy the line about imaginal occasions from item 3.
3. The corresponding Harvard lecture can be found on p. 72.
4. Whitehead had assigned the Haldane and Ross translation of *The Philosophical Works of Descartes*, of which *Principles of Philosophy* was a part. He may well be referring to Principle LVII specifically. See Descartes, *The Philosophical Works, Vol. I*, p. 242, available at <https://archive.org/details/philosophicalwor01desc>.

2. Presentational relationships.
   Matter of relation is what one terms an <u>eternal</u>-object.
   Entities related in this way are (in narrow sense) <u>now</u> to each other. The originality of occasion E is largely concerned with presentational relationships.
   ⟨3⟩.[1] Inspectional relationships, {from point of view of E} to another occasion X, is how, what X is in itself, modifies what E is in itself. [As soon as say word <u>how</u> you have presupposed limitation. I.e. nonsense to think of X and E |52| as simpliciter together. I.e. in asking How?, are also asking How not?][2]

~~Re~~
e.g. Presentational relations of X as modifying E, not simpliciter, but under a perspective, as in past (memory).

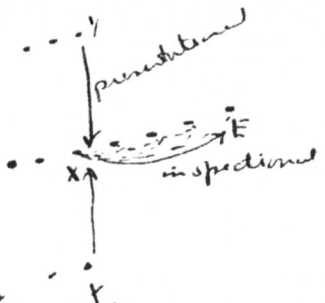

Whole make up of X is in E, and therefore E is what it is partly because of X.

Never get jump from X to E unless also a systematic transition all way along.

But there is <u>also</u> a <u>direct</u> relationship from X to E, although this is trivial in its vividness.

Course of evolution in time is course of evolution in depth of importance, of various ways, although others have lost importance.

Mechanism of an enduring entity is twofold.

1.[3] Via an historical route – get contiguity – a route of successive inheritance of peculiar vividness.

When you have endurance of structure, ~~you~~ a part of fact makes endurance possible is way in which the causal influence of environment is dealt with – taking along with peculiar vividness all relationships of each instant. Structure, preserved |53| intact as result of process of synthesis and causal experience of each instant which is transmitted; the type of causal experience and type of modification has ⟨to?⟩ be such that main structure S_1 is reproduced in successive instants S_2, S_3, etc.

Have endurance in various grades.

T, u, u' are grades of minor endurance all in major endurance vS_1v.

In order to get an important enduring object it has to be such that minor modifications of structure promote reproduction of S_1.

---

1. Heath wrote '4' here, but '3' seems clearly intended. Coincidentally, there is also some number confusion in the corresponding Harvard lecture (p. 73), because Whitehead apparently said that there were two types of relationships, then corrected himself and said that there were three.
2. Closing bracket supplied.
3. Heath does not have a subsequent '2'.

Emphasis on differences or ~~identity~~ vendurancev depends on importance of factor which endures as identical.

Peculiar congruity of each occasion with total past of route that constitutes an important enduring object.

Suppose another occasion $\underline{P}$. Relationship of P with E is no different in principle with relationship of E with its past.

Inspectional relationships with P in past are unsystematic and trivial – lack of reinforcement.

|54| ~~Wh~~ Organisms survive when inspectional relationships are correlated with presentational relations. Though there is sudden jump from one relation to other.

Saturday, 7 November 1925

Heath's notes[1]

|55| The perceptual object.
Difficult problem – stated by Descartes.
See Meditation II. (Haldane and Ross, ⟨Volume⟩ I, 154–155).[2]

              "The wax"

Extension	Thought
(matter)	(mind)
Qualities which cause	vSecondaryv qualities are cogitations in mind

Locke – (meanwhile Newton had made mass a fundamental property of matter).

Matter –	Mind –
Mass was added as primary quality to extension.	Secondary qualities

Earlier vthan Descartesv – Galileo vfirst in modern set tov quite clearly say that unless there be noses, eyes, mouths, there would be no smells, sights, tastes.

Quite open to attack of scepticism.

This <u>inspection</u> of mind is arbitrary while what is clear is apprehension of qualities – Why not make this inspection just another *cogitationes*?

<u>Hume</u> – spatial relationships are relationships between way in which qualities exhibit themselves.

---

1. The corresponding Harvard lecture can be found on p. 74.
   This lecture bears little resemblance to its Harvard counterpart, particularly its second half. In it, Whitehead mentions a half-dozen names that do not show up in Roethlisberger's or Hartshorne's notes anywhere in any lecture: Christian Wolff, Lord Kelvin, Thomas Young, Augustin-Jean Fresnel, John Henry Poynting and Clerk Maxwell (though Maxwell's name shows up once in the notes of Robinson for 13 February, p. 118). The near absence of Maxwell in the Harvard notes for this year is particularly surprising, given that Whitehead wrote his Trinity fellowship dissertation on Maxwell's *A Treatise on Electricity and Magnetism* (1873), and makes somewhat frequent mention of him in his first of year of lectures. See HL1.
2. Descartes, *The Philosophical Works, Vol. I*, available at <https://archive.org/details/philosophicalwor01desc>.

Kant – Leibnizian tradition through Wolff.[1] Idea of ∨enduring∨ monad, ultimately real, as center of organization.

How chaotic sense data is organized in monad.

Whitehead cannot see how Kant's phenomenal world is a common world. Ought to be able to fuse the two Critiques.

|56| In modern science idea of <u>mass</u> ∨(quantitative permanence)∨[2] reigned until recently. Has given way now to <u>energy</u> [another quantitative permanence, in origin it <u>energy</u> was derivative from <u>mass</u>. ∨I.e.∨ Matter with its extension and mass.]. Then two types of <u>energy</u> – <u>kinetic</u> ∨($\frac{1}{2}mv^2$)∨[3] – The obvious type – presuppose mass and its velocity (relations[4] in space and time.) Then potential energy [∨1.∨ May say it's a concealed form of kinetic energy. (Lord Kelvin's vortex ∧rings∧)][5]

[∨2.∨ Another way to look on matter as having not only mass and motion, but property of conveying strain and stress, and behind everything the <u>ether</u> having certain laws of stress – mass ⟨when?⟩ in motion. (Clerk Maxwell ∨(earlier than Kelvin)∨[6] – Strain and stress in ether according to law} and ordinary matter was peculiar knot of strains and stresses. Predominant 1870 – {Began with production of wave theory of light by Young ∧(England)∧ and ⟨Fresnel⟩ ∧(France)∧)).[7]

[<u>Elucidation</u> a great test of scientific theory. This accounts for success of Maxwell's complicated theory and failure of Kelvin's beautifully simple theory].

Another question as to whether in changes of a thing you could trace the streaming of energy from one point to another.

|57| Suppose you look on energy as one thing (slipped into science). Poynting[8] of Birmingham, England showed the laws according to which (electro-magnetic equations) energy streams. Derivative from ether, so looked on like a wave-form passing through ether.

Now idea arises. Ind Can't? <u>energy</u> ⟨be⟩ the fundamental type and ether with mass a derivative, and <u>mass</u> ⟨be⟩ what registers how knol knots of energy hang together?

Now it has been proved that mass is another name for concentration of energy. In modern physics identify mass and energy, and energy is fundamental idea.

Now idea of extended substance is a little fading. Further another type of permanence – the electrical ∨(Charges)∨ and magnetic forces –. Now it has

---

1. Christian Wolff (1679–1754), German philosopher.
2. Parentheses supplied.
3. Parentheses supplied.
4. The abbreviation here is 'rel.', which could be expanded in several different ways, such as 'relation', 'relative', etc.
5. A vortex ring is a vortex in a fluid or gas that forms a closed loop.
6. Parentheses supplied.
7. Thomas Young (1773–1829) and Augustin-Jean Fresnel (1788–1827). Parentheses supplied. Heath has a question mark in place of Fresnel's name. It is not clear whether Heath simply did not catch it or Whitehead had forgotten Fresnel's name but remembered that he was French.
8. John Henry Poynting (1852–1914), English physicist. Poynting was the discoverer of the 'Poynting vector', which shows the flow of energy in a field. This is one of Whitehead's 'root metaphors', as it shows direction and change in something thought to be static and uniform.

been found that molecule of matter can be looked on as simply charges of electricity; also that magnetic effects produced by currents. Gives another point of view, that is it's natural to ~~try~~ look on electricity as outcome of certain organization of energy.

Note that science has varied enormously in conceptions of what it's talking about.

Thursday, 12 November 1925

Heath's notes

|59|[1] Contrast of morphological and functional view of world.

Pre-Socratics – two were intermixed. which makes it more valuable, though difficult to follow, since we commonly distinguish the two. I.e. more valuable – as less abstract. Less valuable, as not recognizing distinctions.

Zeno – comes down on fundamental gap in morphological point of view. Reincarnated in Hume. I.e. if fundamental fact in <u>conformation</u> at an instant – then there is nothing to connect instant number one with instant number two.

[Last lecture (missed) considered morphological –]

Functional point of view. Is essentially that required by biology and psychology. I.e. that the time depth is essential ~~to~~ ∨in∨ the ultimate actual entity. Furthermore that the ultimate entity is not to be described as a shape, but as an achievement, an activity.

∨Any∨ time depth is always divisible ⟨?⟩. ∨But∨ the parts are what they are because of their relation to the whole – how they modify what the whole is. While the whole is what it |60| is because of the way the parts enter in to it. ~~as~~ Therefore the functional relationship is one of parts achieving the whole, and the whole being an achievement resulting from an activity.

What do we mean by being <u>actual</u>?

1. For example Descartes – "*Cogito ergo sum*" calls for an analysis of <u>knowing</u>. Our experience of knowing is a <u>knowing</u> <u>cognita</u> and then the <u>cognita</u> is the immediate fact.

Knowing ⟨vs.⟩ knowing *cognita* ∧(*cognitum*)∧.[2]

While Descartes analyses knowing into ego-knowing.

But the immediate act is "knowing <u>*cognita*</u>" ∨(*cognitum*)∨,[3] i.e. presents a unity of multiplicity. While what Descartes speaks of is Knowing | Knowing *cognita* ∨(*cognitum*)∨.[4]

2. Take Berkeley's formula – "*Esse est percipi*"

[He again seems to be true, just as Descartes was.]

Unless <u>percipiens</u> is very highest brand |61| of actuality, this formula cannot hold. Here again we have a secondary formula. Whitehead has been asserting

---

1. Page |58| is the blank back page of |57|. It appears that Heath missed the 10 November lecture. The corresponding Harvard lecture can be found on p. 77.
2. Parentheses supplied.
3. Parentheses supplied.
4. Parentheses supplied.

all along that everything entered in to everything else, which equals *"esse est percipi."* But the first metaphysical formula this requires is *"esse est percipere"* [This was true of Berkeley – note his reduction of nature to ideas in the mind of God – i.e. God as *percipiens* was ultimate reality – as also our minds.].

Whitehead writes *cognitum/cognita*[1] as given.

Cognitum ∧as unit∧ = *percipiens*.

I.e. ultimate fact is an activity bringing the *cognita* into the unity of one actual entity. It is the whole spread (thought, feeling, sight, etc.) brought into the unity of this immediate actual fact which is ego (∨*percipiens*∨)[2] now.

As entity it is <u>getting</u> things together. Viewed as product it is <u>one</u> for its own sake.[3]

Not two things but the act of synthesis <u>is</u> the achievement. An abstraction if these are separated.

Note in all theories of perception the knowing of this activity has been muddled with the activity. As a matter |62| of fact, that is where Kant comes in. Says what world is to be discovered by analysis of this immediate synthesis and whatever is required by this is what is inherent in actual world. I.e. what is required for act of knowledge is therefore creative of world (therefore knowing it creates it).

But if with Whitehead you divorce knowing and *cognitum* – the *cognitum* being the primary fact, and not act of knowing.

Muddling up ∨act∨ of knowing and perception, gives us that awkward divorce of mind and matter as in either Descartes' dualism or Kant's phenomenalism. (This fitful knowing of a more permanent reality)

Percipiens = taking account of.

{?}

Agrees with Descartes – Sun ∨<u>itself</u>∨ is in {?} ∨eye∨ objective {?}, while in heavens *formaliter*.[4] [Quite different from his representative theory of knowledge]

I.e. the immediate *percipiens* viewed as unity, is constituted by entities ∨(*cognita*)∨[5] in the field and via how they enter constitute unity which is the field.

Synthesis of many constituted into <u>one</u> via limitations of mode. Through these limitations |63| the individuality of the one is achieved. Further that synthesis also has peculiarity of constituting the achieved <u>one</u>, as <u>one</u> in the community of the many.

Namely it is ~~how~~ the actual world – the unity is not an external unity above the *cognita*, but <u>one</u> among the *congita*. Descartes' phraseology. Synthesis

---

1. Slash added; the two terms appear one above the other with braces on either side.
2. Parentheses supplied. The word '*percipiens*' appears below 'immediate' and above 'ego'. Where it should be inserted is unclear.
3. Heath marks this sentence with a brace in the left margin.
4. Heath wrote 'Cf. book' in the left margin here, presumably referring once again to the Haldane and Ross translation of Descartes. See Descartes, *The Philosophical Works, Vol. I*, available at <https://archive.org/details/philosophicalwor01desc>.
5. Parentheses supplied.

into one of the *cognita objectivè*, thereby constituting the one as one in the community of the *cogniter formaliter*.

ᵛThere is anᵛ inspection of *cognita* as in and for themselves (inherent in how they are in the elements which constitute the synthesis).

Tuesday, 17 November 1925

Heath's notes

|65|[1] ("Time?") as form of becoming"
                                    Demos.[2]

The Future

If you take line of traditional empiricism, then any connection is entirely arbitrary. You can neither know the details of the future nor that there will be any future. Question – How do we know that there is a future (or that there <u>was</u> a past)?

(1) In given present we find established a scheme of relatedness which discloses as other *relata* a total community of occasions, ᵛbutᵛ <u>not</u> except as *relata* in that universal scheme. And not as <u>made</u> by the cognition (Kant), but we've discerned it – <u>it is there</u>. To be related to this occasion is ᵛ(1)ᵛ to be related via spatio-temporal scheme, and (2) the immediate occasion discloses this complete scheme of relatedness, i.e. the real world has a meaning as referring to the complete scheme of relatedness.

[This is why objects to saying that space-time has purely contingent qualities – unless there is something general in way of relatedness there can |66| be no general knowledge at all – when look from this <u>general</u> relatedness, the spatio-temporal relatedness and logical relations seem to stand out. This difficulty is one of these difficulties which always arise if one emphasizes either "inspectional" (Plato) or "presentational" (Aristotle) point of view to exclusion of the other.]

(2) Every unit occasion is a unit in the community, which is oneness or "togetherness" of the units. It looks as though there was no difference between unit and community, but there is a fundamental difference, namely – the actual unit is finished – the community is never actual and finished – it is union of being and not-being (Aristotle). It always is <u>beyond</u> the actual – in the possible – but it is not merely a reference to possibility *simpliciter* in abstract, but to that realm as limited by <u>how</u> the community is actual. The systematic coherence of future with past – always presupposed by empiricists and never faced by them.
|67|

(3) How details of future are foreshadowed in present?

~~Final datum is~~

---

1. Page |64| is the blank back page of |63|. Heath appears to have missed the 14 November lecture. The corresponding Harvard lecture can be found on p. 80.
2. Raphael Demos was Whitehead's first teaching assistant. His name appears in the upper-left corner of the page just next to the short quotation. It is unclear if Demos said just this one thing, or gave the entire lecture, as he did a year later, on 14 December 1926.

The basis of all our naive behavior (as making plans) is final datum.

We always know with respect to the ∨a∨ normality, but there may be abnormalities. Yet the normality turns up in science as inertia, that will go on by its own momenta unless. There ∨it∨ is always a reference to the patent fact of endurance – i.e. that which in favorable environment is reproducing itself. – The environment shows a systematic type combined with individual variations, which happen to be irrelevant for inheritance of S along its path.

Then the irrelevant variations may or may not have certain degree of relevance – i.e. may determine ⟨result?⟩ (⟨until?⟩ it curves) without {?} preventing the endurance of S.

Note first law of motion as exemplification of this.

The inertia of existence is better expressed as Self-repetition or will to be itself, which is calculable and basis of probability. {?}

(Observation of an apparently isolated system} is not ⟨disturbed?⟩ by systematic character of |68| rest of universe (requires something definitely active). Unless have systematic whole and ∨general character of∨ self-{?} repetition you can have no knowledge.)[1]

Thursday, 19 November 1925

Heath's notes[2]

|69|
The Future

Immense difficulty – the future is not actual, and therefore is nothing. On other hand when we are talking of future we are talking of something that is definite. If only the present is definite then we're talking of only of present – but obviously we're not talking only of present when we are talking of the future.

Nor is future merely an abstract idea. (*Arabian Nights*.)[3] Any set of abstractions leaves something out and futurity is one of things not accounted for in abstraction.

Immortality of the Past. – Past is not done with.

What concepts do apply to a Future Occasion?

1.[4] A future occasion ∨(*f*)∨ modifies essence of (*a*) ∨(past occasion)∨, and therefore is a relation (internal) to *a*, and therefore (Descartes) it is existing in *a objectivé*. (*a*) could not be what it is apart from its relationships to (*f*). or. The transcendence from (*a*) to (*f*) is a necessary requirement of actuality of

---

1. Closing parenthesis supplied.
2. The corresponding Harvard lecture can be found on p. 82.
3. A collection of Middle Eastern folk tales with a frame story in which the ruler, Shahryār, is told a series of tales by his wife, Scheherazade, that end each night with a cliffhanger designed to so engross Shahryār that he postpones her execution until the following night so that he can hear the rest of the story.
4. There is no '2'.

(*a*). Thus (*f*) is vav determinate entity in respect to its relationship to (*a*), but it is not an actual entity. |70| The relationships of (*f*) to other ~~entit~~ occasions between (*a*) and (*f*) are not yet actualized. So relationships of (*f*) to its antecedents are in process of becoming, as antecedents become. But (*f*) is <u>not itself</u> <u>actual</u> and yet it is <u>determinate</u> in respect of its status. It cannot be actual until all antecedent occasions have been actualized. The substantial creativity which issues in ~~reality~~ v(*f*)v is in process of being formed in actual world – i.e. what is actual and past is the formation of the creative activity which is the future.

[Here come to limitations of concepts we've been using – i.e. analysis of occasion into "substantial activity" and "achievement" or "value." Obviously this is a metaphor of <u>human</u> activity, where <u>maker</u> and <u>made</u> are separate. <u>In reality the achievement is fact of</u> ~~of~~ <u>the achieving</u>. (We're ~~almost~~ in <u>danger</u> of <u>static</u> view.) But there must be a "prime mover" as limiting the statement that character of achieving is its achievements. There are always antecedents – i.e. eternal objects and prime determination of limitation.]¹

|71|

A is individual embodiment of creative activity – but of <u>whole</u> of creative activity, and in this whole there is the <u>transition</u> <u>to</u> *F*, and this vcharacter ofv transition to *F* is embodied in every actual individualization. It is because what is actual is not something beyond the activity, but the activity procuring its own character. [Future is however contingent within a determined character. This contingency assures creativity or process, and determined character assures there being something definite. This is also an underlying determination in ⟨?⟩ which has determined this course of events (as 4 rather than 15 dimensional world). There can be no achievement without limitation. Has laid on achievement not only a character which must be obeyed, but an <u>ideal</u> with respect to which there is an immediate freedom of choice. I.e. creation is in reference to an ideal and in obedience to a character.

Saturday, 21 November 1925

Heath's notes

|73|²
Time.
  Last lecture – Summary – Creativity cannot be separated from creature. Concrete fact is creativity entering into creature, and creature thereby <u>informs</u> the creativity. Thus in creation there is an otherness of creativity.
  Distinction of creator (unitary) and creativity. [But how can this be always passing beyond itself if one runs an ~~ep~~ epochal view of time?]³

---

1. Closing bracket supplied.
2. Page |72| is the blank back page of |71|. The corresponding Harvard lecture can be found on p. 84.
3. Closing parenthesis changed to bracket for consistency.

Future is in itself a definite creature, due to immortality of past, but it's not fully determined.

Present – What is that which achieves actualization in present? Runs epochal theory. Must not consider what happens as gradual coming into being.

Kant – *Critique of Pure Reason* on Extensive Quantity – "Representation of whole is rendered possible by representation of its parts and therefore necessarily preceded by."[1] Whitehead denies the conclusion.

Vicious Regress.[2]

Zeno's Difficulty

1. *A* cannot ⟨come?⟩ into being before its antecedent ∧parts etc.∧

2. No number of points can be made up of points.

|74| Peculiarity of time is that it is an epoch – a who (?) hold. of whole a whole from point of view of actualized occasion.

Holds epochal view on these grounds.

1. Zeno difficulty. Whitehead – Zeno is not really a quantitative difficulty, but that there is no end to start from, i.e. a qualitative difficulty. Asking what end of infinite series which has no end. I.e. Continuity (which has no difficulties in idea) is inconsistent with becomingness.[3]

(2 and 3 come back to Zeno.)[4]

2. If hold that point is mere relationship.

Creature requires a time depth. Creature and creativity cannot be separated. The idea of something which is sectional is nonsense because there's no creature ahead divorced from creativity. I.e. Creativity does not create creature by successive design but is creation of its whole creature. I.e. No creature from creativity.

I.e. Must say there are definite occasions which become. (only alternative is Kantian position).

3. Deals with science – Balance of ⟨?⟩ which ⟨?⟩[5] pure continuity or pure ∧atomicity∧.

---

1. The quotation here comes from the second part of Friedrich Max Müeller's 1881 translation of Kant's *Critique of Pure Reason*, p. 143: 'I call an extensive quantity that in which the representation of the whole is rendered possible by the representation of its parts, and therefore necessarily preceded by it'. Kant, *Critique of Pure Reason*, available at <https://archive.org/details/immanuelkantscr07kantgoog>. Interestingly, Heath wrote in the left margin 'See book p. 147', rather than 'p. 143'. It possible that Whitehead simply got the page number wrong, but it seems more likely that he quoted from page 143 while pointing students to a more detailed discussion of intensive and extensive quantity starting on page 147 in a section entitled 'Anticipations of Perception'. Roethlisberger, by contrast, wrote the reference as '177–8', which seems clearly to be wrong (see p. 84).
2. The placement of 'Vicious Regress' makes it unclear whether it refers to the paragraph above or below (although it seems to apply to both).
3. A marginal note to the left of this paragraph reads: 'Ask Whitehead what is relation of this epochal view and specious present'.
4. Written in the left margin. Parentheses supplied.
5. Cf. Roethlisberger: '3. From consideration of science. Founded on both continuity and atomicity. Science needs both. Cannot exclude one or another. Each has a status.'

Tuesday, 24 November, 1925
Heath's notes[1]

|75|
Time.

Epochal theory – time looked on as relation among things actual exhibited itself as a relationship between things actual in past, actual in present and about to be actual in future. Immediate actuality is epochal, but.

World as actualized is continuous: Draw distinction between <u>time</u> as immediate activity of actualization and time as an extensive element in continuum of relatedness – of things actual.

Time as measurable vs. Time as one duration – haunts all philosophy.

But it always appears paradoxical.

Descartes – shows how ideas ∨of epochal time∨ are in ordinary thought.

Current view: graduality of becomingness vs. Whitehead's view: epochal becoming ∧(*naturans*)∧ of graduality ∧(*naturata*)∧.[2]

Basis of current view ∨①∨ arises from idea of enduring substances. Substance is an <u>actual entity</u> – or ~~it~~ ∨substance∨ is the entity which is actuality. ② To be actual is to endure through time, and this is inherent in the substance (as Descartes – ⟨extension is?⟩ inherent in corporeal substance.) ~~3.~~ Plurality of substances. |76| ③ ∨(relationship between substance)∨[3] Thus an occasion at an instant is correlation of one instant in one substance with an instance in other substance. On this theory the common instant of time is implicitly derivative from substantial instants. Thus there is really an epochal view of time here only inadequately defined – i.e. in dealing with a substance you are really considering a portion of its life history.

I.e. if to exist is to endure, then to abstract from endurance is to abstract from existence.

Problem of becomingness is really obscured by this common view of plurality of ∨enduring∨ substances.

An evil of substantial point of view is that it gives no <u>natural</u> epoch with which to overcome the Zeno difficulty. How does arrow in its quiver get from one moment to another?[4]

Whitehead – gives complete functioning (science = vibration) and it is the totality of that function which is unit of something actual.

Descartes Prin. Sec. 55 ~~etc.~~ 57; 62 etc. "Duration is only distinct from substance by thought."[5]

---

1. The corresponding Harvard lecture can be found on p. 85.
2. Parentheses supplied for these two interlineations.
3. Parentheses supplied.
4. This sentence is written in a smaller size in the margin.
5. This is an exact quote from Principle 62, 'On the distinction created by thought': 'For example, because there is no substance which does not cease to exist when it ceases to endure, duration is only distinct from substance by thought; and all the modes of thinking which we consider as though they existed in the objects, differ only in thought both from the objects of which they are the thought and from each

|77| Thus given the individual substances there are given endurances, vaguely defined – condition between points in endurances constitutes ⟨common?⟩ occasion.

As in that there is not gradual becomingness of actuality – assumed in epochal character of a life history which is ~~an actual~~ v becomeingv graduality not an ~~act~~ gradual becomingness.

As soon as get hold of epochal view it supports the ~~idea~~ theory starting from physical occasions, which require idea of a function which in order to be itself requires a definite period.

Saturday, 28 November 1925

Heath's notes

|79|[1] The <u>Organic</u> View of Affairs (epochal view of time) has become relevant in modern science.

17th century and common sense –

1. vDescartes Extended.v <u>Matter</u> v(i.e. Substance. – desk etc.)²v – enduring – enjoying certain properties which may change, but how much without ceasing to be itself. Accidents or essential attributes (a bit of a muddle).

2. <u>Mass</u> – (Galileo and Newton) = <u>Quantity</u> of Matter ∧(Pythagorean)∧ with idea of <u>simple</u> <u>location</u>.

3. But everything perceivable is not the <u>mass</u>, but <u>functioning</u> of the mass.

4. Then <u>interconnection</u> <u>of</u> <u>behavior</u> which must be expressed.

5. Behavior is always expressed either (a) changes of relative configuration (spatio-temporal) vregulatedv or (b) in the sense of processing interconnection of things in some mysterious way, i.e. <u>regulative</u>.

Field of force.

Two ways of measuring forces

   1. In terms of effects

   2. In terms of origin

Mass x acceleration² = Force.

effects = origin

As soon as you think of process there is *natura naturata* = *natura naturans*.

|80| Ways of expressing force

1. $\dfrac{mm}{d^2}$

2. Shock (billiard ball)

3. Tension Strain and stress (stretched string)

Action and Reaction are equal and opposite. (Newton)

---

other in a common object'. Descartes, *The Philosophical Works, Vol. I*, p. 245, available at <https://archive.org/details/philosophicalwor01desc>.

1. Page |78| is the blank back page of |77|. Thursday, 26 November was Thanksgiving holiday, so there are no notes. The corresponding Harvard lecture for 28 November can be found on p. 86.
2. Parentheses supplied.

Falling body[1]

$$M \times b = v \frac{ME}{a^2}$$
E = earth's mass
v = constant a = Earth's radius

$b = v \dfrac{E}{a^2}$ i.e. acceleration is equal in all ˅falling˅ bodies.

Perplexity

Concerning treating earth as <u>one</u> bit of matter. Took Newton fifteen years to find that can treat force of sphere as from center.

No <u>natural</u> particular if think of matter as just extended just as no natural epochs in the differentiated duration.

⟨Thus?⟩ conceptions of forces at a point.

1. Action at a distance (A mysterious influence behind the veil).[2]

2. Idea of checking momentum producing ⟨the?⟩ force and rate of change of momentum being the force, i.e. attempt to reduce all forces to changes in momentum. ⟨?⟩ ch (Vortex ⟨theories?⟩).

3. Stress and strain of elastic string. A stationary ether slightly displaced in strains and then produces stresses.

Epochal difficulty turns up here. I.e. since there are no natural units, [⟨illegible⟩] infinite regress.

|81| A further difficulty over question of strain, for any configuration of matter is as good as any other. I.e. is only ⟨covered?⟩ way of dealing with forces between bits of matter and therefore epochal difficulty turns up.

All attempts to explain matter as differentiations within a continuous ether has to deal with that difficulty. Further have to deal with arbitrary statement of field of force accompanying simply located masses.[3]

Saturday, 5 December 1925

Heath's notes

|85|[4] To say that anything is divisible is to say that it is divisible.
Here is an objection to saying that a personality is divisible.
Quite obvious that world has the aspect of extensiveness. Descartes' fault was "Fallacy of Misplaced Concreteness."

---

1. Whitehead is not using the standard notation. Had he done so, this would lead to:
    Newton's law of gravity: $F = G \frac{mM}{r^2}$ with G the gravitational constant, m a first mass, M a second one, and r the distance between the two masses (notice that this would be better than $\frac{mm}{d^2}$).
    Newton's second law of dynamics is $F = ma$, with m the mass and a the acceleration.
    Combining the two leads to $ma = G\frac{mM}{r^2}$ and hence $a = G\frac{M}{r^2}$.
    By taking M = the earth's mass, E, and r = the earth's radius, a, and by writing a as b, and G as v, we get Whitehead's expression $b = v\frac{E}{a^2}$.
2. Closing parenthesis supplied.
3. The page labelled |83| is a list of courses that Heath was either taking or considering taking. It seems to have been incorrectly inserted at this point of her notes, possibly by Lowe, who likely organised and numbered them. See the Introduction p. xxxvii for more on this.
4. Page |84| is the blank back page of |83|. We do not have notes from Heath for the lectures on 1 December and 3 December. The corresponding Harvard lecture can be found on p. 89.

Gradual Introduction to Science of <u>Atomic</u> View

a. Inertial point of view succeeded by view of <u>energy</u> (still extended) as fundamental. A muddled idea of <u>energy</u> as fundamental and <u>electron</u> or <u>proton</u> as fundamental.

b. Atomic theory first acquired significance from modern science with John Dalton (1824).[1]

Explained laws of chemical combination by atoms. I.e. essentials – in dealing with matter there are actual units that one must take as wholes.[2]

Criticism – essence of matter is divisibility, what is half ⟨an⟩ atom? I.e. then two ideas don't go together. I.e. if matter is essentially atomic, ⟨then⟩ half ⟨an⟩ atom is not matter.

Other natural units appear.
  Living body.
  Especially when having intellect.

<u>Cell</u> theory in biology introduced at about same time as atomic theory.

|86| (Must describe <u>unit</u> in terms which are other than itself.)

Now instead of atom being *x* it is now looked on as complex structure made up of charges of electricity, in constant activity. Modern idea of atoms is that they are in state of passing from one activity to another. Best conception of a lump of granite is group of excited people talking to each other. – The <u>functioning</u> seems to be of the essence of matter. Goes very well with idea of aggregate of energy. (Later).

When ask what is an electron? Answer usual – It is charge of electricity. To say ⟨it is⟩ is taking ~~only~~ old extended idea, i.e. still have put material behind the functioning. I.e. <u>charges</u> of electricity preserve the Dalton atomic theory in atomic electron and protons.

As like charges repel – nothing ⟨is?⟩ in extended view can explain why every electron (and every proton) isn't blown to pieces. Therefore idea of electricity spread out and every ⟨proton?⟩ having properties of an electron won't work.

|87| There's another point of view that proton is an aggregate of energy.

Individual behaviors of atoms is known only through its emission of light (or energy).

Tuesday, 8 December 1925

Heath's notes[3]

~~The activity in producing the action is~~

Natura naturans and *natura naturata* are separable in abstract, but not in concrete.

---

1. John Dalton (1766–1844) was an English chemist, physicist and meteorologist, best known for introducing atomic theory into chemistry. The significance of the 1824 date is unclear.
2. Heath marks this sentence with a pair of vertical lines in the left margin.
3. The corresponding Harvard lecture can be found on p. 91.

Chemical atom is made of functioning. <u>Subjects</u> of functioning have been driven back to two types of primates, i.e.

+e   -e
proton   and   electron.
mass = M mass = m
radius = b radius = a

All electrons seem to have same mass. = quantity of energy.

$M = \lambda \frac{e^2}{b}$ $m = \lambda \frac{e^2}{a}$ $\frac{1}{\lambda}$ = square of a velocity

                                   = $M \cdot c^2$

$M = 1700m$ M = a number
$A = 1700b$ c = velocity of light

I.e. a thing is massive in proportion as it is concentrated.

Mass measures concentration of energy in a sense; at least it measures concentration of something. One can't definitely say it's <u>energy</u>, for according to Clerk Maxwell the energy is all over the place, but in fixed geometrical relation. [Analogy for cork in infinite ocean where mass is ½MV v(V = volume)v in water and is looked on as distributed through whole ocean].

|88| Now we have connected electric view (⟨?⟩ Cartesian with energetic view. (more fundamental according to ∧Whitehead∧)).[1]

Although the fact that can't divide one of atomic primates is argument for considering electric view as more fundamental. Whereas can divide energy apparently. But when consider carefully – the energy also puts up an atomic structure (Quantum Theory Vetc.V).

Distribution of energy in electron

F (electric force) = $\frac{1}{8\pi} F^2$ × volume

Can take with F or volume as small as you like, i.e. apparently a <u>continuous</u> affair.

But when deal with atom get energy as atomic. But even energy is not completely atomic. It's the <u>action</u> which is completely atomic.

Thursday, 10 December 1925

Heath's notes[2]

|89| Ultimate physical entity:–

Whitehead – When analyse the structure the data are not natural. Data of physical science are abstracts simply considered in respect to change in spatio-temporal.

---

1. Closing parenthesis supplied.
2. The corresponding Harvard lecture can be found on p. 92.

Concrete entity is *Esse est percipi et percipere* \percipientes\.[1]

Take only half of Berkeley's meaning of *percipi*. I.e. "To take account of."

Einstein – Electron simply marks a peculiarity of geometry. Geometrical are not uniform.

In one sense a going back to Descartes' "Matter is extension". Plato would be delighted.

    Four ideal numbers – Four dimensions.

    Mathematics – really all {?} mathematics.

Quantum of energy turns up.

Whitehead – near to Irving Langmuir.[2]

|90| Thinks below picture is better than solar system for relation of electron and proton.

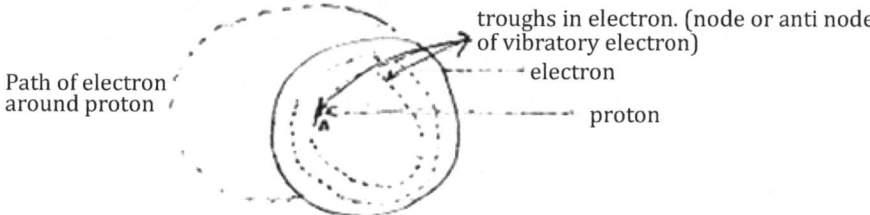

Path of electron around proton

troughs in electron. (node or anti node of vibratory electron)
electron
proton

[See Langmuir on compartment.[3]]

Electron is attached to proton at trough *A*. When energy is given off or absorbed, it slips to another trough (this is a <u>reason</u> for <u>Quantum</u> character).[4]

$q = \dfrac{h}{T}$ ∴ $qT = h$ T = time

                           q = energy

Little *h* is most mysterious constant.

Little *h* is energy through a time.

Little *h* is unit of action.

i.e. Action= energy through a ⟨*T*?⟩.

This is consonant with Whitehead's epochal idea. A definite creative act is looked on as handing over to physics the ultimate unit, i.e. little <u>h</u>. This has a <u>time</u> <u>depth</u>, *T*. I.e. it isn't ⟨in?⟩ <u>at a time</u> but <u>through a time</u>. The smaller the time, the greater the energy.

---

1. This seems likely to be a mishearing of Berkeley's famous phrase 'esse est percipi, aut percipere' (to be is to be perceived, or to perceive).
2. Irving Langmuir was an American chemist and physicist (1881–1957) who won the Nobel Prize in Chemistry in 1932. Whitehead is likely thinking of his famous 1919 article 'The arrangement of electrons in atoms and molecules'.
3. This is likely referring to experiments on oils (in what are now called Langmuir films) reported by Langmuir in 1917, for which he won the Nobel Prize. See Langmuir, 'The constitution and fundamental properties of solids and liquids').
4. Parentheses supplied. The parenthetical material appears in the right margin.

⟨Tuesday, 15 December 1925⟩

Heath's notes[1]

|91|
Knowledge
   Prominent Question in modern philosophy emerges because of collapse of Cartesian philosophy. But Whitehead says answer must be formed in terms of what we know and therefore
   1. Give account of categories that apply to *cogito*.
   2. See if critical discussion of know⟨ing?⟩[2] applies within a special field as science or ethics.
   ⟨?⟩
   3. System must be internally consistent and provide niche for knowing.
   Easy to see causes of Descartes' error, i.e. <u>Duality</u> of <u>substance</u>. But also accords with common-sense, especially through his <u>unity</u> of plan.
   Kantian reformation makes world emerge from knowing of it.
   Whitehead is opposite, i.e. knowing emerges from world.
   ⟨One?⟩ ⟨is?⟩ question how kn⟨owledge?⟩ is possible. Must be through showing what |92| knowledge is.
   Kant started with kn⟨owing?⟩ and then described the possible world. Whitehead does not recognize Kant's world.
   ⟨One?⟩ to answer is that cannot separate active and passive factors.
   Can know no machinery behind the ⟨veil?⟩.
   <u>Synthetic</u> activity is true of <u>creatures</u>.
   Envisagement = creativity as conditioned by
   1. Eternal objects
   2. Immortality of fact vis general
   3. Particular environment
   4. By substance of contiguity from historical route
   5. General influence of future
   ~~what~~
   Knowledge is actual ⟨as?⟩ a ⟨creature?⟩.
   Knowledge is emergence of envisagement into ∧creative∧ actual world.

---

1. Interestingly, the handwriting for the two pages of this lecture is uncharacteristically messy and bears little resemblance to Heath's hand; it is unclear if Heath was injured, writing on an uneven surface, had someone else take notes for her, or something else. Accurately dating this lecture is also difficult. First, it is clear that Heath's notes for 10 December match up with Roethlisberger's notes at his p. 40, which, like most of Roethlisberger's fall semester notes, is undated. It then appears that Roethlisberger's p. 41 (in his notes for the fall semester) must be for the lecture following, which would have been on 12 December. *Then*, his content for pp. 49–50 seems to match Heath's content here, and the lecture following lecture, 12 December, would have been on 15 December. Therefore, it would be reasonable to infer that Heath missed the 12 December lecture and that the date for these oddly written notes is for the lecture on 15 December 1925. This is only an educated guess; it is possible that at times we are misreading when exactly lectures begin and end in Roethlisberger.
   The corresponding Harvard lecture can be found on p. 94.
2. Heath has the ambiguous abbreviation 'know' here, which could mean 'knowledge', 'knowing' or 'knower'.

Saturday, 19 December 1925

Heath's notes[1]

|93|
Knowledge

When you analyze a creature the elements are not creative, nor actual – except so far as other actual things may enter into a single actual thing. Elements are however ideas.

In abstraction do not get a class of unrelatedness (e.g. Plato's world of ideas) because the relational character is of the very essence of eternal objects. Presupposed in Plato and Aristotle but ⟨invoked?⟩ in Middle Ages through influence of Aristotelian logic.[2] This relational side of universals was entirely lost in Cartesian reformation, thus the relational side comes in as "mysterious".

<u>Description of Thought</u>

Knowledge is confrontation of what is for synthesis, vorv fr⟨om?⟩[3] the creature, with the creature. I.e. Confrontation of abstract with the concrete and is the value which arises from that confrontation being actual.

[Togetherness – Red spot alters whole picture. How then is formal logic possible?][4]

Whole realm of eternal objects is only separable in idea from the concrete occasion.

[Is this realism?]

Every ⟨?⟩ concrete occasion is how the whole realm of eternal objects is dealt with in respect to ~~relat~~ togetherness.

[Look up Kant on Intensive Quantity.][5]

In the occasion of knowledge you can confront the abstract situation with the experient occasion as not realizing it. Fact that there are finite truths must ultimately be based on fact that realm of eternal |94| objects is analyzable ⟨?⟩ into a multiplicity of complex situations which can be conceived in isolation.

---

1. Heath appears to have missed the lecture on 17 December. The corresponding Harvard lecture can be found on p. 97. According to Whitehead's appointment book, this was the second-to-last lecture before the Christmas break, which he has marked as 'Recess' on every day starting Wednesday, 23 December through to Saturday, 2 January. His appointment book lists the times of the class for Tuesday, 22 December, but we do not have notes from this date from any of our three note-takers. It is possible that the lecture was cancelled, but we have no documentary evidence to confirm this.
2. This whole sentence seems to be an interlineation or later addition.
3. The abbreviation here appears to be 'fr', which could be expanded as 'from' or 'for'.
4. The bracketed portions in this lecture and the next all appear to be Heath's own thoughts. She is not entirely consistent about using brackets in this way.
5. See the 21 November lecture, note 1, p. 35.

Tuesday, 5 January 1926

Heath's notes[1]

|95| "Art as Exclusion"

Ultimately metaphysics is a descriptive science – i.e. must describe what you find, and as far as one accepts this one is calling oneself an empiricist.

Four general principles which rather require each other.
1. Principle of Otherness
2. Immortality (in a sense Sameness)[2]
    [Whitehead says Sheldon[3] had dropped Principle of Immortality. It seems to me he had dropped Principle of Otherness].
3. Activity (otherness)
4. Eternal Objects (immortality)[4]

1 and 2 apply to Actual Objects.
3 and 4 abstraction from actuality, i.e. an analysis into factors which are not actual.
Two opposed tendencies –
Conformation.
Passage into Otherness.
A diversity of mode of information but an identity of total potentiality of forms. Any actual occasion is a retention.

Picture of Time

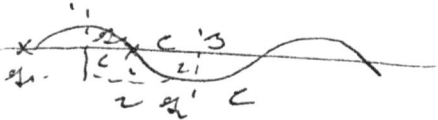

I.e. physical inheritance is |96| really that new epoch has to be conformed to old epoch by actually retaining its last half.

If you look on it as really separate you are taken only every other epoch.
Life of Erasmus – Preserved Smith.[5]
Experient occasion is the becoming of a unit. Ground and consequent is in each epoch.

Hegelian principle of contradictories is exhibited in each duration.

---

1. The corresponding Harvard lecture can be found on p. 99.
2. Heath indicates with a brace and a marginal note that items 1 and 2 are '*natura naturata*'. She also writes 'Contrasting in actual world'.
3. This seems likely to be a reference to Wilmon Henry Sheldon (1875–1980), who was educated at Harvard and taught at Dartmouth and Yale. He wrote a book published in 1918 in which he attempted 'to maintain the integrity of a given thing, person, principle, institution, in the modifications which the environment imposes upon it. In the dialect of technical philosophy this is called the problem of harmonizing the principle of external relations with that of internal relations'. Sheldon, *Strife of Systems and Productive Duality*, p. iii, available at <https://archive.org/details/strifeofsystemsp00shel>.
4. Heath indicates with a brace and a marginal note that items 3 and 4 are '*natura naturans*'.
5. Smith, *Erasmus*, available at <https://archive.org/details/erasmusastudyofh013578mbp>.

Saturday, 9 January 1926

Heath's notes[1]

|97| Epochal unit of actual occasion is essentially a fusion of <u>yes</u> and <u>no</u>, i.e. Hegelian. Intrinsic reality of actual occasion is to ~~p~~ be conceived as a blind perceptiveness. A fusion of contrast within a higher identity. This is very character of Space-Time. There is an identity (⟨homotropic?⟩) of principle but also a difference. In any actual occasion the <u>yes</u> is the ground.

Imaginal occasion is E_1 ⟨expce?⟩

Whereas experience is synthesis, knowledge is abstraction.

I.e. In experient ⟨occasion?⟩ the eternal objects express themselves in <u>event</u>, while in imaginal occasion the eternal objects are ⟨selected?⟩ analysed out of event. Also in ⟨................?⟩.

Think of thought as another dimension. ~~Equally~~ On same principles.

The principle of reversion.

I.e. a Five dimensional world, of which four are measurably structured, but thought dimension is not measurable.[2]

---

1. Heath missed the lecture on 7 January. The corresponding Harvard lecture for this 9 January one can be found on p. 102.
2. These are the last of Heath's notes. Both Roethlisberger and Hartshorne have notes for four more lectures before the end of the spring 1926 term: 12, 14, 16 and 19 January.

Harvard lectures, fall semester 1925

Thursday, 1 October 1925
Roethlisberger's notes[1]

Philosophy of Science
Professor Whitehead

Bibliography[2]

Whitehead: *The Concept of Nature*
Whitehead: *Science and Modern World*[3]
Whitehead: *Principles of Natural Knowledge*
Whitehead: *Principle of Relativity*
*[4]C. D. Broad: *Scientific Thought*[5]
Dewey: Philosophy and Science[6]
Alexander: *Space, Time and Deity*[7]
*Russell: *Knowledge of External World*

---

1. The corresponding Radcliffe lecture can be found on p. 3. There are two sets of notes available for this term: Roethlisberger's notes are used as the primary account for 36 lectures, and Hartshorne's notes for the remaining 5. Refer to the table on p. 415 for a full list of fall semester 1925 Harvard lectures by note-taker and date and their corresponding Radcliffe lectures, and see also the Introduction for a detailed discussion of each note-taker and their notes.
2. There are tick marks next to the titles of some book titles, the meaning of which is not apparent. They have been omitted.
3. Though Whitehead put this book on the reading list for the course, it had not yet been published, and would not be until late October. Whitehead had sent the completed manuscript to Macmillan in July (Whitehead, Letter to Macmillan Company, 9 July 1925). A letter from his contact at Macmillan, Curtice Hitchcock, informed him that the book had been published in the last week of October (Hitchcock, Letter to Alfred North Whitehead, 4 November 1925).
4. Roethlisberger places stars next to both C. D. Broad's *Scientific Thought* and Bertrand Russell's *Our Knowledge of the External World*. These correspond to the tick marks next to these same titles in Louise Heath's notes (p. 3). The exact meaning is not clear, but it is likely that Whitehead called special attention to these two texts. In contrast, the underlines of 'Whitehead' and 'Hume' find no corresponding marks in Heath, and do not seem to have any special significance.
5. Broad, *Scientific Thought*, available at <https://archive.org/details/in.ernet.dli.2015.6694>. Charlie Dunbar Broad (1887–1971), usually cited as C. D. Broad, was an English philosopher. Like Whitehead, he was a member of the Aristotelian Society, serving as its President from 1927 to 1928. Broad's philosophy served as important foil for Whitehead as he developed his course. See the discussion of Broad in the Introduction (pp. xxviii–xxix), and in Henning, 'Whitehead in class', pp. 343–5.
6. This entry does not appear in Heath's reading list (Heath 1), and does not appear to be a specific book. William T. Myers, in email correspondence, suggests that it could refer to Dewey's *Reconstruction in Philosophy*, which came out in 1920 and contains a chapter on the role of science in the reconstruction of philosophy. But this is speculative. See Dewey, *Reconstruction in Philosophy*, pp. 53–76, available at <https://archive.org/details/reconstructionin00deweuoft>.
7. Alexander, *Space, Time, and Deity*, available at <https://archive.org/details/spacetimedeitygi01alexuoft>. This was based on his Gifford lectures, delivered in Glasgow 1916–18. Samuel Alexander (1859–1938) was a British philosopher important to Whitehead's thought. Like Whitehead, he was a member of the Aristotelian Society. In the preface to *Science and the Modern World*, Whitehead writes: 'There has been no occasion in the text to make detailed reference to Lloyd Morgan's *Emergent Evolution* or to Alexander's

Harvard lectures, fall semester 1925

Russell: *Analysis of Mind*[1]
Ross: *Aristotle*[2]
Descartes: *Meditations*[3] – (Six)[4]
Berkeley: *Alciphron, Dialogues* and *Enquiry*[5]
Hume: *Enquiry*[6]
Bergson: *Creative Evolution*[7]
William James: Does Consciousness Exist?[8]

———————————————————————————————————— [9]

———

Space, Time and Deity. It will be obvious to the readers that I have found them very suggestive. I am especially indebted to Alexander's great work.' Whitehead, *Science and the Modern World*, p. xi.

1. Russell, *Our Knowledge of the External World as a Field for Scientific Method in Philosophy*, available at <https://archive.org/details/ourknowledgeofex00inruss>; and Russell, *The Analysis of Mind*, available at <https://archive.org/details/analysisofmind032971mbp>. Bertrand Russell (1872–1970) was a student of and later collaborator with Whitehead.
2. Ross, *Aristotle*, available at <https://archive.org/details/in.ernet.dli.2015.536932>. William David Ross (1877–1971), usually cited as W. D. Ross, was a Scottish philosopher known for his work in ethics and his critical translations of many of Aristotle's works. Like Whitehead, he was a member of the Aristotelian Society, serving as its President from 1939 to 1940.
3. The Heath notes (Heath 1) further specify the Haldane and Ross English translation (1911), and also lists Descartes's *Principia* (*Principles of Philosophy*) on the reading list, which was included in the same volume of philosophical works. See Descartes, *Philosophical Works, Vol. I*, available at <https://archive.org/details/philosophicalwor01desc>.
4. While Roethlisberger has this ambiguous '(Six)', Heath's notes say '*especially* six' (p. 4).
5. Berkeley, *Alciphron, or the Minute Philosopher*, available at <https://archive.org/details/alciphron00berk>; Berkeley, *Three Dialogues Between Hylas and Philonous*, available at <https://archive.org/details/threedialoguesbe00berkrich>; and Berkeley, *Siris: A Chain of Philosophical Reflexions and Inquiries Concerning the Virtues of Tarwater, And divers other Subjects connected together and arising one from another*, available at <https://archive.org/details/sirischainofphil00berk>. Heath's notes do not list the *Dialogues* (Heath 1).
6. Hume, *An Enquiry Concerning the Human Understanding*, available at <https://archive.org/details/humeenquiry00humerich>. Heath's notes also list Hume, *A Treatise of Human Nature*, available at <https://archive.org/details/treatiseofhumann00hume_0>.
7. Bergson, *Creative Evolution*, available at <https://archive.org/details/creativeevolutio00berguoft>. Henri Bergson (1859–1941) was a French philosopher and writer. In the preface to his Gifford lectures, Whitehead acknowledges that he is 'greatly indebted to Bergson, William James, and John Dewey', but that one of his 'preoccupations has been to rescue their type of thought from the charge of anti-intellectualism, which rightly or wrongly has been associated with it' (Whitehead, *Process and Reality*, p. xii).
8. William James (1842–1910), American philosopher and psychologist. In his *Science and the Modern World*, Whitehead describes James as 'that adorable genius' (p. 3).
   Heath's notes specify the book *Essays in Radical Empiricism*, published after James's death in 1910, and then say '*especially* "Does Consciousness Exist?"' (emphasis added). See James, *Essays in Radical Empiricism*, available at <https://archive.org/details/essaysinradicale00jameuoft>. This essay was originally published in the *Journal of Philosophy, Psychology, and Scientific Methods* in 1904; see James, 'Does consciousness exist?', available at <https://archive.org/details/jstor-2011942>.
9. Roethlisberger frequently drew long dividing lines that spanned the page horizontally. These are not always lecture breaks; sometimes they merely indicate what Roethlisberger considered to be a change in topic.

I. Scientific Thought[1]

Philosophy of Science apt to degenerate by taking definite concepts of science and talking generally. [To examine categories of thought employed by science and test their validity ∨and application∨.[2] Time, space, substance, quality, continuity, function. What do they mean?][3]

Scientific thought – how did it arise? Scientific mentality starts about 1500 and large quantities ⟨in⟩ seventeenth century. (1) Interest in irreducible and stubborn facts. (2) general principles. –

The combination of these two interests makes "scientific mentality."

1. Instilled faith in order in details –[4]
2. Interest in ∨non-∨exceptional details
3. Scientific imagination – important – Greek
4. Conception of "law" – Roman

|2|[5]

5. Precise and accurate stating of ideas
6. Instinct belief in that details can be unraveled

Note. – When one asks a scientist "what is his philosophy," nine out of ten will answer Hume. Curiously, however, Hume's philosophy gives no more grounds for a belief in an "order" of in the universe than it gives grounds for belief in God. This belief on the part of scientists is seien instinctive. He firmly believes that the details can be unraveled.

Saturday, 3 October 1925

Roethlisberger's notes[6]

Mediaeval Mind: ∨⟨?⟩∨ To understand nature is through conception of "end."
Historical revolt: Observing particular facts and connecting ∨immediate∨

---

1. Roethlisberger liked to impose order on his notes and, in addition to his dividing lines, he often labelled sections with what seem to be his own invented headings. In some cases such headings appear to be later additions, presumably as he read his notes over after a lecture and was attempting to make sense of them. Frequently such headings are printed (as this one is) rather than written in a cursive script (as are the rest of his notes). The roman numeral here appears to have no special significance; succeeding sections are numbered consecutively, but at one point he starts over again at 'I', then abandons the practice altogether towards the end of the first semester.
2. In some cases Roethlisberger amended his notes, sometimes filling in a blank he left for himself when he knew he had missed something, and in other cases making a correction, addition or editorial comment. In this case, the words 'and application' appear in pencil rather than pen, and are clearly a later addition. However, from this point forward we will typically not take any special pains to distinguish these additions from the rest of the text. See the section on Roethlisberger's notes in the Introduction for further discussion of this (pp. xl–xli).
3. The word 'justification!' was added later in pencil after this sentence.
4. This dash was added later in pencil; it is probable that Roethlisberger thought to add a note similar to those for '3' and '4' below, but then decided against it.
5. Numbers between these short vertical lines indicate Roethlisberger's own pagination, which he wrote in the upper-right corner of each page, probably after each lecture was over, as it was done in pencil while most of the notes are written in ink. The numbering resets for the second semester. Occasionally there are irregularities or errors in this numbering, which we note as they occur.
6. The corresponding Radcliffe lecture can be found on p. 5.

antecedents to consequences. [Appeal to efficient cause and not final cause.] Leads to a certain anti-rationalistic bias. Unwillingness to analyze the irreducible and stubborn fact, and obtaining the "why." This is not a movement as a protest ~~against~~ Von behalf of reasonV. Rather partly anti-rationalistic.[1]

Scientific attitude of last 300 years leads to philosophical difficulties.
(1) Divorcing realm of values from realm of nature
(2) Theory of nature concerned with antecedent and consequent
(3) Two distinct philosophies and jumping (unwarranted) between them

---

II. How does scientific method work?

Bacon:– Method of science is inductive logic – Generalization of particular incident and deriving a general rule "general law" applies to particular incidents not observed. – formula applies to other incidents not observed. Question is crux of any rational explanation. How do you get beyond the particular ~~incidences~~ V⟨instance⟩V?[2]

Induction always depends on a number of ~~incidents~~ VinstancesV. Mill's logic admirable but out of fashion.[3] Whitehead here agrees with <u>Hume</u>. If each instance[4] tells you nothing about the future, how can 100 instances tell you any more? It is not true that science requires a number of instances. (Hume explains but it does not justify its rightness! Russell agrees with Hume in the appeal to practice).[5] Einstein predicted a shift in spectral lines from his formula. It is the single good observation and not multiplicity of instances which counts. VOne then trusts general law.V Formula applies to more than the immediate observation. Problem of "beyondness" of immediate instance [Science as description is inadequate as it is does not explain predictive function].

|3| About Spencer[6] – "knew more about the unknowable than it was decent to know."

Science is a purged appeal to common sense. – Whitehead

<u>Unless you are to chuck rationalistic universe, philosophy must ask whether particular instance involves something beyond itself. Memory is in same boat as induction.</u> If memory is immediate impressions now, how can it tell us anything about the <u>past</u>. Something which lies beyond itself – immediate experience.

Mill:– an antecedent induction has already taken place establishing uniformity of nature on a low probability. Then dragging in all "laws" you obtain high probability of reign of laws. But he appeals only to number (which Hume rejected) in order to get "beyond."[7]

---

1. The words 'interesting observation' appear here with a brace, apparently referring to the text starting with 'Appeal . . .' up to this point.
2. Roethlisberger actually wrote 'instant' here, but as he corrected several occurrences of 'instants' to 'instance' below, we can surmise that 'instance' was his intention.
3. There are lines here that initially look like hyphens (i.e. 'out-of-fashion'), but are probably lines indicating words Roethlisberger had missed and filled in later.
4. Here and two other times below, Roethlisberger has written 'instance' or 'instances' over 'instants'.
5. The text in parentheses appears in the left margin. Parentheses supplied.
6. 'About Spencer' appears in the left margin, apparently referring to this quote.
7. This final paragraph on Mill appears along the left margin of the page.

Harvard lectures, fall semester 1925

Tuesday, 6 October 1925

Roethlisberger's notes[1]

III. Arise of Philosophy from inadequacy of scientific systems.
   Association theory of Hume reducible to principle ∨no connection between occasions apart from knowing process,∨[2] a function of knowing. Function of philosophy: abstract nature of thought.
   Science is a classification ∨or system∨ of concepts (universals) by which we confront[3] reality (contra pragmatism). Concrete individual ∨and experient occasion[4]∨ cannot be exhausted by universals. Any system of universals always omits. The omission varies in importance (practical). Material system omits all value concepts. Number of systems with which to face reality. You get a multiplicity of systems. Each system should be (1) logically coherent (2) actually interpret immediate occasions to which we apply them {Correspondence theory of truth}. (1) is easy, but (2) brings in fallacy of misplaced concreteness.[5] Error is "misplaced concreteness," misapplication of things and relations. Philosophy comes in when you are dissatisfied. (a) Arbitrary postulates at the base of each system. (b) Isolation of systems unsatisfactory. (c) Contradiction of systems[6] – (you inevitably find a common ground among systems.) (d) Omission from all systems – you do not exhaust the concrete individual – Literature and history gives discernment about reality not expressed in any system. Not concerned with abstract selection but concrete experience. Great literature expresses something which is permanent in R. Cannot deny permanent. Better to admit contradictions than deny plain facts. Facts overlap, bound to be contradictions. Hold contradictions provisionally – Efficient causes of science |4| and final causes. Admit both. To be brought together.
   Hume's solution only expressible in terms of knowing-process. Empiricism must find in occasions something that is not an occasion.[7] Kant broadens Hume. Just as difficulty to find something universal in one occasion. Kant assumes a multiplicity of occasions to which universal must apply. Can we reduce all judgements to the principle of analysis? ∨If more general∨ concepts ∨are true,∨ ⟨they⟩ are analyzable into subordinate concepts ∨which are true.∨ Assert detail simplicita. Kant, Descartes, Hume do not convey information about other occasions.[8] There are synthetic judgements not to be obtained by analysis. Whitehead: All universal knowledge arises from analysis, but deny the

---

1. The corresponding Radcliffe lecture can be found on p. 6.
2. Roethlisberger actually put a series of dashes in the space below this interlineation, presumably because he missed what was said and wanted to fill it in later.
3. It is not clear why Roethlisberger struck out 'con'.
4. Roethlisberger actually has 'O$_E$' here. Through an examination of the rest of his notes, we have concluded that it is his abbreviation for 'experient occasion'. The abbreviation does not appear frequently, but has been silently expanded in each instance.
5. This sentence appears in the left margin.
6. The following appears in the left margin: 'Better to entertain contradictions than deny fact'. A slightly rephrased version of this sentiment appears a few lines later.
7. The word 'Induction' appears in the left margin here.
8. The text 'Hume – experient occasion conveys nothing about other occasions' appears in the left margin.

isolation of occasions – You must have a principle of multiplicity – find in this occasion all other occasions. Aristotle analyzed occasion into "union of being and not-being." – "Not being" is Whitehead's "beyondness." Logic use occasion as substantive and predicates.

IV. Kant's Answer to Problem

Kant asks – "how are universal synthetic propositions possible?" To analyze immediate occasion there is "the given" on one side and function of knowing on other. Given elements are chaotic. Order is introduced in the "function of knowing." Chaotic elements expressed as sense-data. Unity of knowing – "F of knowing" introduces the "relations" and you obtain the organized occasion. Relational elements are universals. Perceptual object arises from organizing faculty of knowing. For if organizing process only introduces universals, multiplicity of occasions vanishes into phenomenal. E.g., your function of knowing Vrelating given as a process and not a multiplicityV only introduces relational elements, because but organization only introduces relations suitable to ⟨blank⟩.[1] (Only one occasion of knowing introducing universals among data, and as no new data are introduced, perceptual object issues from and into something or other, but not data.)[2] "Something or other" cannot be identified with yesterday or tomorrow. Theory makes world a function of mind. Kant left with Hume in sheer solipsism.

Kants is in same predicament as Hume. Bradley's (objective idealist)[3] point of view – monistic – a system of appearance into a phenomenal world. Does not explain the multiplicity of reals and multiplicity of occasions –[4]

⟨Thursday, 8 October 1925⟩

Roethlisberger's notes[5]

|5|

V. Disagreement with Kant

As philosophy is developed, difficulty always comes up. – ① Full of subtle distinctions and elaborate distinctions Vclassifications V. Does Kantianism

---

1. The Heath notes suggest that the missing word may be 'isolation'. See p. 7.
2. Parentheses added. The parenthetical text appears in the left margin.
3. This parenthetical appears after the last sentence of the lecture, with an arrow pointing up toward 'Bradley', or possibly to the space before 'Does not explain . . .'.
4. It appears that this is probably the end of the 6 October lecture, since Roethlisberger clearly switches pens on the next page. Following this, Roethlisberger does not provide another date until 24 November. Hence, the only way to date the lectures in between is to match content with notes from Hartshorne or Heath. Heath, one must remember, was taking the class at Radcliffe rather than Harvard, so there is danger that content may sometimes match up even though it was delivered at different times in the two institutions. However, through the use of all the clues at our disposal, including changes in the quality of the ink or handwriting, we can make inferences about dates with a fairly high degree of certainty.
5. This appears to be a new lecture, since Roethlisberger clearly switches pens from the previous page. The material he has here matches up with elements that Heath has for the two following Radcliffe lectures (pp. 7–9), but there is some uncharacteristic date confusion in the Heath notes around this time. See the final note of this lecture, as well as note 1, p. 8, for the 8 October Radcliffe lecture.

depend on (1) classifications which are vague – "fallacy of misplaced concreteness" – and (2) somewhat trivial?[1] A classification which impeded physics is Aristotle's division of "motion" into natural motion and violent motion. – Danger of ~~following~~ Aristotelean classifications.

② Example of over elaboration.
$$\left\{ \begin{array}{l} \text{time} = f(\text{knowing}) \\ \text{a knowing-of-process and not a process of knowing.} \end{array} \right\}$$
③ Norman Kemp Smith's Commentary, page 27.[2]

Two inseparable criteria of *a priori* are necessity and universality – Kant's firm belief. Inherited from Leibniz and Hume. [Neither universality or necessity can be imparted to a proposition by experience] (Whitehead denies against Descartes, Leibniz, Hume, and Kant.)[3] Idea of "simple location." You can get a bit of experience and ask what is "cognita", you do not have to lug in diverse experience. If you want simple location, three alternatives.

(1) rationalism – an *a priori* discernment by reason in virtue of which we obtain universal conditions for any actual world.

(2) skeptical empiricism – we find ourselves believing and making universal judgements. We have an explanation, but this explanation ∨by association∨ does not justify the belief. Depends on assumption. Hume appeals to practice something beyond own principles.

(3) critical phil – here the data to which the idea of simple location is applied becomes one factor in the cogito. ∨Data arranged by function of cognition.∨ You assume whole problem. – One group of data organized in one f (knowing). Plurality is not in the data but in the unity of your function of knowing. (There is one group of data in one function of knowing. Substitutes something beyond experience. Leads into (1) solipsism or (2) Bradley's absolute.)[4]

VI. What is our job? (Organic empiricism)[5]
  1. Plurality of actual occasions where actual occasion is most ultimate concrete entity
  2. Cognizance is cognition of one actual occasion.

---

1. The '(1)' and '(2)' here were originally circled numerals, but have been altered so as not to compete with the numbered list which contains them.
2. Smith, *A Commentary to Kant's 'Critique of Pure Reason'*, available at <https://archive.org/details/commentarytokant00smituoft>. Smith's *Commentary* is an important work of Kant scholarship and is keyed to the pagination of the 1787 second edition of Kant's *Critique*. The material following the citation makes clear that Whitehead is in fact referring to page 27 of the commentary proper, rather than to page 27 of the Introduction (i.e., xxvii). The notes in both Roethlisberger and Heath are close enough to the Smith text that we can assume that Whitehead read the following portion aloud: 'The two inseparable criteria of the *a priori* are necessity and universality. That neither can be imparted to a proposition by experience was Kant's confirmed and unquestioned belief. He inherited this view from both Leibniz and from Hume.'
3. Parentheses added. This text appears in the right margin.
4. Parentheses added. This text appears in the left margin.
5. This is Whitehead's first known use of this phrase to refer to his own work. It does not subsequently appear in his published work.

3. Cognizance is one kind of occasion.
   ① experiential occasion¹
   ② imaginal occasion

|6|

3. Each actual occasion is a concretion of occasions other than itself. The most fundamental thing is "growing together".

4. Concretion is a plurality of things growing together. The components of concretion: wherever you get universality, it is to be discerned in the experienced occasion – the "all" of universal judgement is limited by components of experienced occasion. The components will be of 2 types: (1) other actual occasions (2) eternal objects.

5. Actual universe is universe of components in my immediate experienced occasion. Its evidence is immediate evidence.

6. No knowledge of any actual universe except as a content? Object of reason is to say something extreme. We only discern law of identity in immediate occasion.² Philosophy is the wonder of the obvious.

7. The concretion of the concrete is not a Cartesian substance.³

⟨Saturday, 10 October 1925⟩

Roethlisberger's notes⁴

Different Approaches to a philosophy of nature.
VII. Descartes
   To obtain precise concepts and explain universe ultimately in those concepts. Modern philosophy based on subjectivism, ancient philosophy based on objectivism. What is problem of subjectivism and objectivism? Descartes starts with himself as a cogitating being. Is that which is within your cogitation objective? He assumes you ~~get to~~ \have\ a plurality of cogitating subjects. Easy ⟨runs?⟩ to solipsism. Speaks from point of view of individual substances (1) cogitating substance (2) corporeal substance. But how are you to get to know the corporeal substance [Meditation VI]?⁵

---

1. 'Experiential' is clearly written in the text, but it seems likely that 'experient' may have been intended. See the 24 October lecture, note 1, p. 65, for a similar confusion.
2. The words 'Eternal objects only valuable to Oi' appear in the left margin here. We are confident that 'Oi' means either 'immediate occasion' or 'imaginal occasion', but unclear which. Subsequent unclear instances will also be brought to the reader's attention with a footnote.
3. This appears to be the end of the 8 October lecture, both because the quality of the ink and handwriting is different, and because it matches up with Heath's notes for 8 October (pp. 7–9).
4. There is no corresponding Heath material for this lecture. But at the top of her notes for the following lecture (13 October), Heath wrote: 'Lecture omitted in which received general situation in philosophy with which philosophy of science begins' (p. 9). The Roethlisberger notes which follow match Heath's description of the 'omitted' lecture, and are sandwiched between the 8 and 13 October lectures, which correspond fairly closely in the Harvard and Radcliffe accounts, so we are confident that this content is indeed for 10 October.
5. Whitehead had pointed to the importance of Descartes's sixth meditation from his *Meditations* on the first day of class.

53

James: In his essay "Does Consciousness Exist", he denies what Descartes assumes. Cartesian subjectivism[1] ⟨is⟩ outcome of broader subjectivism – (Aristotle's subject-predicate)

Heraclitus: ~~For D~~ It is something which is flowing is the most ultimate. For Descartes, flowing is an accident of the thing. Due to the flowing the things gets occasional attributes – relations. But what is the occasion? Individual substances are ultimate reals |7| subjected to occasional experiences of attributes and relations. Occasions are derivative from substance. Whereas for Heraclitus, the occasions form in themselves a factor of flowing. Beings in the process for concretion. The particular concretion is an essence. For Descartes, occasion is accidental and eternal to substance.

VIII. Summary

1. Occasion represents[2]

2. (Cartesian difficulty)[3] On Cartesian point of view, corporeal bodies are subjects, but not cogitative. How can he get away from single cogitating subject?

3. (Fundamental problem becomes)[4] Finding ultimate reality in individual substances subject to occasions. How can you get the object out of cogitations?

4. What is real? The ultimate enduring things to which certain things happen or ~~physical things~~ process. (Enduring substance vs. flux (physical entity) are two points of view)[5] Aristotle plays with both points of view. Both still in mediaeval ages. In 16th century back turned on Aristotle. You never quite turn your back on past. Always something which you retain and don't question. They took Aristotelean logic. With it went substance and attributes, from which you are led to subjective predicament.

5. The subjective point of view is congenial to "simple location" idea. If occasion is to be explained in terms of substance. Each occasion is just itself Vwith no referenceV. [How you are going to get substance out of immediate occasion – a plurality of occasions].

6. Spinoza starts with substance. Only one – starts with plurality – inadequate, so he went to one. – Modes of Spinoza similar to flowing of Heraclitus.

7. Individual entities are not in the enduring things, but in the physical entities, such as McTaggart's "sneeze".[6]

---

1. The letters 'subj' have here been expanded as 'subjectivism' due to context. This is a relatively common abbreviation for Roethlisberger and has usually been silently expanded to 'subject', unless otherwise indicated.
2. It seems likely that Roethlisberger missed most of this first item and intended to fill it in later, but never did.
3. Parentheses added. The text appears in the left margin with an arrow pointing to the number 2.
4. Parentheses added. The text appears in the left margin with an arrow pointing to the number 3.
5. Outer parentheses added. The text appears in the left margin.
6. John McTaggart Ellis McTaggart (1866–1925), usually cited as J. M. E. McTaggart, was an important idealist metaphysician at Trinity College, Cambridge. He had a teaching fellowship at Trinity at the same time as Whitehead, and he was C. D. Broad's adviser. Whitehead's reference here is to section 72 of McTaggart, *The Nature of Existence*, available at <https://archive.org/details/cu31924007699600>. 'The conception of substance will be of cardinal importance throughout the rest of our enquiries, and it will be essential to keep closely in view the definition which we have adopted. . . . The name of substance is

Harvard lectures, fall semester 1925

⟨Tuesday, 13 October 1925⟩

Roethlisberger's notes[1]

|8|

IX. <u>Points of departure</u> (continued)

History of philosophy is the laboratory of philosophy. Criticism of general concepts which are used in periods of history. In criticizing forms of beliefs there are three provincialities (1) time (2) space (3) nature or type of concepts which is selected. <u>Provinciality of youth and provinciality of age</u> [Predicaments].

(1) Aristotle: plurality of substances with occasions. Passes into modern thought via Descartes.

(2) Heraclitus used to be associated with a certain amount of scepticism. His view properly reconstructed is only view that can save a thorough empiricism from scepticism.[2]

(3) ∨Reality as function∨ Performance of function – (Leibniz was a coalescence of (3) and (1)) plurality of individual substances. (Whitehead is a coalescence of 2 and 3)

(4) Physical occasion plus idea of function is Whitehead's position. Each occasion is a con⟨cretion⟩.[3]

X. <u>Whitehead's View</u>

1. Consider each occasion as a <u>concretion</u> or totality of every possible entity you can think about. Grades of efficiency. Definite status of each occasion in each entity defines its efficiency. Justifies induction and universal judgement.[4]

2. <u>Apply principle in explaining not only induction but all universal judgements</u>.

3. Every universal judgement is found in actual occasion?[5]

---

often confined to that which, among other characteristics, is either timeless or persistent through time, or is more fundamentally one than many, or is held to be a unity of special importance. A sneeze would not usually be called a substance, nor would a party at whist, nor all red-haired archdeacons, be considered as a single substance. But each of the three complies with our definition, since each of them has qualities and is related, without being a quality or a relation; and each of them would therefore be called a single substance, although each of the two latter are obviously also an aggregate of several substances, and, as we shall see later, the first (and indeed every other substance) is also such an aggregate.'

1. Here we get more assurance as to the likely lecture date. Besides another seeming change in ink quality, Hartshorne's notes dated 13 October (actually, Hartshorne has 13 *September*, but October is clearly what he intended) also uses the phrase 'laboratory of philosophy' at the start of the lecture. The corresponding Radcliffe lecture can be found on p. 9.
2. Hartshorne has here 'Organic Empiricism – Heraclitus' (Hartshorne, p. 1). Heath's notes are more thorough and nuanced, and seem to identify 'Organic Empiricism' as Whitehead's name for his *own* view, while also identifying it as Heraclitian.
3. This expansion of 'con' is confirmed by Health (p. 9).
4. Roethlisberger added a question mark in pencil to the right here, presumably to indicate his confusion about this point.
5. Since 'found in actual occasion?' is written in pencil, and hence is probably a later addition, the question mark here may indicate Roethlisberger's uncertainty over whether he had captured/remembered this point correctly, rather than simple confusion about the concept. Hartshorne has 'Some entities necessarily in every occasion. ⟨This?⟩ = source of pure math' (Hartshorne, p. 1). Heath has an important

4. "Necessarily" means you discern in immediate occasion that qualification, namely "each occasion has relationship to every other occasion."

---

5. Plato misled philosophy – "harmony" is emotional word. – beauty. Thought is in actual world. Transferred beauty from this world to ideas.¹ Universal truths transcend flux for Plato. For us the truth is in the harmony of flux. – [You cannot get beyond what is discernible in an immediate occasion.]. There is no antecedent reason to the particular world. All we can appeal is to ∨the∨ actual. But we can appeal to alternatives which can fall in the general conditions. Community of actual occasions realizes partly a universal harmony. Appeal to reason in things and not beyond them. |9| This appeal to "alternatives" is basis for ethics and religion.

6. Idea of sheer contingency – My immediate experience, besides showing "universals" or "harmony", it shows something of contingency.

Modern philosophy starts with plurality of bits of mind and matter which are subjected to occasions. Defined occasions and modes in ~~ideas~~ ∨terms∨ of time and space. Notions of 17th century is "bits of matter in space and time" – Extreme "simple location" – "any piece of matter ⟨blank⟩² Conception of order of nature in succession of occasions. In the antecedent you can observe or discern subsequent occasions. Arise of idea of "force." "Appeal to efficient cause." – Simple mechanistic theory.

(1) How much of immediate experience is swept away? (by dismissal of final cause)³ your ends or my ends are merely "barren virgins". – Why has this astounding abstraction been so successful? only as you keep within a certain sphere of interest – Final causes had been extremely successful in explain things for the 12th and 13th century – If you say mediaeval philosophy is wrong, you have to say something of modern science. Modern science asserts functions – psychologist and biologist use function – but function is becoming keyword for physical science. Whether really we cannot get some way of defining function without having recourse to ~~efficien~~ mechanism, which ~~only~~ employs only efficient causes.

Beginning only understand in terms of ends and ends in terms of beginnings [Concept of function demands a fusion of efficient and final causes.]. Function requires a depth of time.⁴

---

qualification (underline in original): 'each occasion ⟨contains?⟩ under limitations all physical occasions' (p. 10).
1. The words 'Emergence of ideas in actual world' appear to the left here. Hartshorne's notes seem to capture Whitehead's point more clearly: 'Plato felt beauty of mathematical ideas, and of world as embodying these. This beauty transferred illegitimately to general ideas apart from world. Beauty attaches to abstract only as harmony of the concrete' (Hartshorne, p. 1).
2. There is no closing quotation mark; Roethlisberger presumably missed the end of this item.
3. This text is in the right margin. Parentheses added.
4. Through comparison with the Heath and Hartshorne notes, this appears to be the end of the 13 October lecture. The 15 October lecture follows.

⟨Thursday, 15 October 1925⟩

Roethlisberger's notes[1]

|10|
7. Plurality of elements in a common world:
 (1) (Cartesian view)[2] <u>Individual enduring substance</u>. Community of occasions form the life history of the substance. Plurality of occasions are inherent in one substance. Occasions are derivative. Cogitating subject of Descartes and non-cogitating subjects. No principle for a community of subjects. Hume shows cogitation inherent in each occasion. Subjective method obtains subordinate community of occasions – Then needs a new principle to obtain whole world. Swept away original problem.

---

 (2) (Functional view)[3] Science now concentrating on functions. Immediate occasion is <u>an</u> <u>epoch</u>. Structure of happening – Epoch occasion is one. That epoch, that function becomes real – <u>One</u> occasion; yet divisible with regard to its status in realized community. What is realized as one is yet divisible and continuous in totality of occasions {achieved totality}. Demands a fusion of efficient and final causes. {<u>Antecedent</u> R whole.} {Subsequent R antecedent}. Time becomes double notion.

---

8. Realization
 Arrive at notion of four dimensional continuum and realization. <u>Notion of realization is pure succession</u>, but what precedes is VimpressiveV actuality on entities in scheme of continuum. Scheme = given for realization. If you consider pure extensiveness, you cannot distinguish time and space. But when you consider epochal community, you consider in ⟨blank⟩.[4] What is this impress of actuality?
 Two aspects of <u>time</u>: ⟨(1)⟩ time as <u>sheer sequence</u> and (2) <u>what is realized</u> in respect to ~~four dimensional continuum~~[5] time depth.
 (1) time as epochal – indivisible
 (2) time as divisible
 <u>Bergson</u> – indivisible is flow but allows measurable time.
 <u>Descartes</u> gives both.
 <u>Plato</u> uses both – divisible time from sun and moon (2) time as indivisible in origin beyond nature.

---

1. The corresponding Radcliffe lecture can be found on p. 11.
2. Text appears in the left margin. Parentheses added.
3. Text appears in the left margin. Parentheses added.
4. It is not clear what Roethlisberger might have missed here, but, around the same place, Hartshorne has 'Time as such in <u>how</u> of realization, not in extensiveness or continuum' (Hartshorne, p. 2).
5. It is possible that 'four dimensional continuum' is sloppily underlined rather than struck out, but the latter appears more likely.

(Our awareness of time is as measurable in nature as succession of our awareness)[1]

Seeking of time as measurable in nature and the process of awareness of time.[2] English empiricists are superficial in account of time.

Impressions in Hume are very much like <u>epochs</u>. – atomic overemphasized. Hume loses the community.

For Kant, time is a <u>form of intuition</u>. Unity of apperception is form of unity which gives life history of the individual. Exhibits phenomenal as divisible actuality.

What is left out of science? – Value! Physical science is an "abstraction."

Community is necessary to justify induction and universal truth.[3]

⟨Saturday, 17 October 1925⟩

Roethlisberger's notes[4]

|11|

9. Philosophy of nature deals only with "<u>what is perceived</u>" and not the "<u>perceiver</u>". Description of immediate occasion in widest categories.[5]

   1. Physical occasion is ultimate entity from which we can derive others.

   2. Occasion is a "concretion" or "prehension" – that which is cognized – postponing the problem of knowledge – against modern tradition, Descartes, Locke, Kant. Act of knowing can only be translated by terms supplied by <u>cognitor</u>. Time and space a form of intuition <u>vs</u>. what we mean by time and space. What in *cognita* is there for use?

Universals limit your analysis – wider universal to include what has been omitted. What is the widest universal? Rob the concrete of what you can by universal. Criticism of abstraction. Description of particular in terms of general.[6]

   1. How is description of immediate *cognitum* possible?[7] What are the widest form of categories? What does the *cognitum* present for

---

1. From 'Bergson' up to this point is all an addition in the left margin. We have placed the text here based on comparison with the Heath notes (p. 11).
2. Hartshorne has here 'Never an instant before you, but a process, specious present ($1/10$ of second perhaps). Might be a whole era (Royce) 1000 yrs. to see joke?' (Hartshorne, p. 2).
3. Through comparison with the Hartshorne notes, this is likely the end of the 15 October lecture.
4. The corresponding Radcliffe lecture can be found on p. 12.
5. From '9. Philosophy' up to this point appears in the left margin.
6. Hartshorne mentions Husserl here by name (and again a little further down): '<u>Describe before theorizing</u> [Husserl]. <u>Mankind hamstrung by abstractions. Universals hinder analysis</u>. First task of philosophy: criticism of universals. [Husserl begins so, but criticism too naive and hasty, does (not) apply it to universals <u>he is using</u> enough]' (Hartshorne, 3). Since Roethlisberger does not mention Husserl at all, it seems likely that Hartshorne's brackets indicate that the comparison with Husserl was Hartshorne's own thought, and not Whitehead's. Hartshorne had just spent two years abroad (1923–5) on a Sheldon Fellowship after earning his PhD, including time in Freiburg, where he 'saw and heard [Husserl] many times, [and] read several of his early books, especially *Ideen*' (Hartshorne, 'Some causes of my intellectual growth', p. 22).
7. In Hartshorne's notes this is the 'first problem of metaphysics' (Hartshorne, p. 3).

immediate thought? *Cognitum* include terms or categories in which ⟨blank⟩
2. Coherence and adequacy of description –
3. Immediate act of cognition is not a component of its own ∨immediate∨ cognition.
4. We describe a physical occasion an experienced occasion leaving out what is not in that occasion, i.e. cognition of it.

---

10. <u>Immediate Occasion, Other Occasions and Modes of Limitation</u>[1]
    1. First thing is *cogitatum* ∨(unity of immediate occasion)∨ and not *cogito ergo sum* ∨(I knowing)∨.[2]
    2. A unity which is imposed on a multiplicity – <u>not one, but a concretion</u> of many. <u>The one which emerges is a synthesis of many components</u>.
    3. A denial of Kant's chaotic data. The many and the one are disclosed as involving (here and now) ∧for the one∧ and (there and then) ∧for the many∧.[3] One is disclosed synthesizing "those" which are beyond itself. In synthesis is a category of "beyondness."
    4. "Here and now" are in same community and on same level as "there and then." Refer to a partial community.[4] The entity which is "there and then" is presented as actual. Impartiality of relationship by its very form admits of particularity of standpoint, here and now as distinct from there and then. Particulars synthesized under category of there and then. ("There and then" enters "here and now" as a how of limitation).[5] Correlation of occasions occur in synthesis, not *simpliciter*, but limited. Each occasion from its own standpoint is limited by its own forms. <u>Its</u> own forms is synthesis [⟨?⟩ –[6]
    5. Immediate occasion is synthesis of other occasions[7]
|12|
    6. There is a community of the many in a common mutual beyondness, and that is synthesized in the mode characterized by the <u>beyondness</u>.
    7. These are the most general categories – A coming-together and a synthesis refers to that which apart from synthesis would be an isolation. Concept of "isolation" is to be discovered in "this occasion" as a component. In synthesis there is again the "cause itself". Here is the aboriginal germ of "value".[8] [Immediate occasion is fusion of efficient and final causes]. (Efficient

---

1. From '10' up to this point appears in the left margin.
2. Parentheses added around the last two interlineations in order to preserve meaning.
3. 'Problem of one and many' appears in the left margin here.
4. Hartshorne's notes refer to an '*im*partial community' (Hartshorne, p. 3, emphasis added).
5. Text appears in the left margin. Parentheses added.
6. Hartshorne's formulation here seems a bit cleaner and clearer: 'Correlation of occasions means that the components of occasions enter not *simpliciter*, but as limited by their common relations to this particular experienced occasion' (Hartshorne, p. 3).
7. Roethlisberger seems to have missed the second half of this thought, which Hartshorne caught: 'Immediate occasion is the synthesis of other occasions prescribed by definite order of other occasions as from the standpoint of this occasion' (Hartshorne, p. 4).
8. Hartshorne goes on: 'This is the aboriginal germ of value, value as in form, because it has abolished, isolated, and synthesized into something worthwhile' (Hartshorne, p. 4).

cause is a synthesis, final cause is a value.)[1] Occasions are not only separated in space and time, but together in space and time. Synthesis and isolation are unescapable.[2]
  1. Immediate Occasion
  2. Other Occasions
  3. Modes of limitation[3]

⟨Tuesday, 20 October 1925⟩

Hartshorne's notes[4]

|5| Form of intuition itself indivisible. Given chaotic – this wrong. Given its inherent relations quā merely given, = relation of possibility. Formation not all in impress, but ~~in given~~ preformed in given.
Cognitum
Always a multiplicity of cognita
a) Colors, sounds, shapes – ⟨eternal⟩[5] objects.
b) Persons, chairs – subjects.[6]
c) Occasions, events.
Community of things real, achieved, are for themselves = real world.
What type of unity in multiplicity is most complete exemplification of being-for-self?
Ethics (Socrates) has ruined metaphysics. As man of science feels so. Pre-Socratics getting along – then Socrates spoiled things.
Art vs. ethics. Art for the immediate good. Ethics looks beyond given. Solution in concept of God.
Art prior to ethics in width of its categories.
Aristotelian tradition says – look beyond immediate to enduring entity. System in logic and ethics spoiled his metaphysics. <u>Descartes</u>' many bodies and minds carries this on. God comes in in unfortunate manner – to rise superior to metaphysical difficulties in which we have involved ourselves [= definition of *deus ex machina*].
Subject has subsumed occasions in itself. Unity in subject. But ~~⟨?⟩~~ many subjects and their community.

---

1. Text appears in the left margin. Parentheses added.
2. Hartshorne writes: 'Each entity poses itself as entity which in being itself is to that extent separated from others, and yet in being itself includes the unity of the others' (Hartshorne, p. 4).
3. Through comparison with the Heath and Hartshorne notes, this appears to be the end of the 17 October lecture.
4. Although we will most often use Roethlisberger's notes as the primary source for 1925–6, we will occasionally use an alternative set of notes if it is more thorough for a particular lecture. Here we are using Hartshorne as the primary text for the first time. The corresponding Radcliffe lecture can be found on p. 13.
5. Hartshorne clearly wrote 'internal objects' here, but Whitehead just as clearly intended 'eternal objects', as is confirmed by Roethlisberger (fall semester p. 13).
6. Instead of just 'subjects', Roethlisberger's notes have here: 'enduring subjects and objects' (Roethlisberger, fall semester p. 13).

|6| "Here and now", occasion fully individual. But Aristotle obscures this: that no actual world apart from multiplicity of occasions, and no occasions apart from community of occasions. Isolated occasion meaningless.[1]

Enduring objects, and ethics secondary.

World = *primär*[2] community of occasions.

To describe occasion, must introduce actual world – a concretion of diverse occasions.

Upper and lower community – lower = organism, concretion of all others. Upper = actual world, impartial community of total multiplicity.

Organic empiricism [(*Gestalttheorie*)][3]

Matter = an aggregate of organisms. Statistical survey of their actions, (?) occasions.

Each occasion its own individual essence, and every other as synthesized in it "It" has this [?].[4]

Something in it is for It alone.

Descartes: "in the mind" and "in the sky" (sun) (inconsistent with his philosophy?). In the occasion vs. to be for itself (*formaliter*).[5] This = distinction of image and real.

Imposition of limitation ⟨is⟩ the means of making this distinction. Modal limitation (whole of metaphysics).[6] Total environment.

Impartial synthesis of multiplicity of occasions.

"Members one of another".[7]

1. Modal limitation of being just that alone.
2. Entering into all events.

1. Might be otherwise but isn't. But if were otherwise, others would be otherwise. Hold |7| up obvious by scruff of its neck.

To say what event is = extrude alternatives. Concretion or synthesis, and extrusion (modal).

---

1. In Roethlisberger's notes, the reference is to Descartes rather than Aristotle: 'Now if you have many individual subjects, you cannot show relation to community. – Descartes' difficulty' (Roethlisberger, fall semester p. 13).
2. 'primary'. Hartshorne occasionally slips into German in his notes for no apparent reason other than he had just spent a few years studying abroad in Germany. See note 6, p. 58.
3. Hartshorne consistently uses square brackets to indicate insertions of his own thoughts or references. Here again he notes what he sees as a similarity between Whitehead's thought and theories he encountered in Germany.
4. Cf. Roethlisberger: 'Idea of Organism is not dependent on idea of matter. Get rid of concept of matter and describe in terms of organism. Each occasion (IT) – ∧has its own essence, and every other occasion is synthesized in it∧' (Roethlisberger, fall semester p. 13).
5. Roethlisberger puts this in the form of a helpful chart:

	Objective	Subjective (*Formaliter*)
Descartes	in mind	in sky
Whitehead	in occasion	for itself

6. Cf. Roethlisberger: 'Object in the occasion instead of object in mind: Actual occasion depends on ⟨im⟩position of limitation, excluding other occasions *simpliciter* – admitting them in modal limitation. It is this limitation which preserves multiplicity. The occasion is an organism' (Roethlisberger, fall semester p. 13).
7. Roethlisberger's notes identify this phrase as an example of 'religious language' (Roethlisberger, fall semester p. 13).

Plato? vW.v believes Plato errs here – whole ideal world inseparable from occasions.

Describe event = describe it vasv exclusion of what it does exclude.

Say what it is or what it is not – both equally good, sometimes one better, sometimes another. "Being blown up" = to be told what one is not.

Essential to actual = confrontation with ideal, and to ideal its confrontation with actual.

"Multiplicity" means there are entities which can be conceived in some sense apart. Must start with a one, being finite minds. Descartes starts with Ego. Something for itself, an achievement in itself. An occasion is <u>an end in itself</u> = a value. No such thing as undifferentiated value. Individuality, for-itself-ness, means value is always definite pattern-value. Value-in-itself. ~~def~~ Achievement of value involves exclusion of neutralising elements, keeping them at bay.

Incompatibility: if event is this, it can't be that. Laws of thought.

Emerging definite value = event. But this denies isolation – for value supposes gradation in value. How much value? Brings us back to community of value. Intensive quantity = value in science. Events as comparable, more or less vivid entities. Gradations of <u>importance</u>, of achievement – depends on completeness of extrusion. Art = arrangement of environment of an occasion so that modal synthesis, |8| which is that occasion, vis achievedv with a completeness of extrusion, thus giving correlative definiteness of inclusion. Leaving out condition of what it is.[1]

⟨Thursday, 22 October 1925⟩

Roethlisberger's notes[2]

|14|[3]

Art as exemplified in limitation

Primary position is a community of many entities, i.e. occasions. Occasion is to be analyzed into (1) sub. activity and (2) super.[4] value.

Antagonism between art and ethics. Ethics is of less importance than art. Art has to do with the immediate value, an end in-itself. More immediate connection with immediate occasion. Prehension ≠ Synthesis (inadequate) ∧(as it is as much exclusion as intrusion)∧. Apprehension = cognition (why not use it?).[5]

---

1. Through comparison with the Roethlisberger and Heath notes, this appears to be the end of the 20 October lecture (that almost the entire bottom half of Roethlisberger's page here is blank is especially telling; Roethlisberger often preferred to start a new day of notes on a separate page).
2. The corresponding Radcliffe lecture can be found on p. 15.
3. The previous page has also been numbered '14'. Roethlisberger apparently realised his mistake later and added a subscript '1' to the previous page's number.
4. Since the intended expansion of 'sub.' and 'super.' is not entirely clear, they have been left unchanged. 'Subjective' and 'superjective' or something like them are reasonable inferences.
5. Hartshorne has here: 'Prehension vs. apprehension. Latter brings in (?) cognition, another story' (Hartshorne, p. 8).

Art brings you to fundamental metaphysical situation: "<u>a multiplicity in a community</u>" – each occasion prehends in itself the whole community. A metaphysics:– If Generality based on immediate occasion, then it must <u>include</u> community of occasion; otherwise no escape from Hume's conclusions.[1]

Ethics has to do with comparison of occasions + <u>idea of endurance</u>. <u>Concerned with survival value and progress</u>. Ethics presupposes art. Art requires ethics derived from itself. Socrates' emphasis on ethics was a wrong turn and precursor of Descartes. Aristotle – substance and attribute. Medieval ages occupied with logic.[2] Descartes turns back, retaining (1) Christianity and (2) logic. Arises mind, body. –[3]

Individual occasion has some <u>good</u> for itself. Grades of <u>value</u>, <u>grades</u> of individuality.[4] Ethically evil is always by comparison with something else. (1. lack of survival power 2. diminish another('s) survival power 3. hindering progress 4. ~~some in~~)[5] <u>Immediate value is a product of exclusion</u>. Attainment of art is selection – disengaged from irrelevance. If you put in more, you get less value. Chinese literature suppresses everything irrelevant to <u>rhythm</u> and <u>adjustment</u>. Vitality of art depends on rigid selection. <u>No irresponsibility in art</u>. Motive in art. Procedure of art is to attain value. Volume in architecture only valuable by its selection.[6]

Endurance of great work of art depends on the way it impresses itself. Enduring independence of being – "<u>Individuality enduring among things that pass</u>." "Identity of form through diversity of occasions" – an end in itself. Permanent impress on all times – <u>Superstition of ancestors</u> is better than triviality of one who can only appreciate that it <u>happened yesterday</u>. Eternal has relevance to each passing occasion – relating what will be to what has been.[7] Limitation in art makes vividness of value –[8]

---

1. Hartshorne has here: 'Either Hume or an *a priori* rationalism, which knows of itself conditions of all existence' (Hartshorne, p. 8).
2. Hartshorne has a little more on Aristotle here: 'Socrates precursor of Descartes as enemy of true metaphysics. Greater influence is Aristotle – <u>enduring</u> entities stressed. But these derivative. Aristotle inverts logic, which hardens idea of subject' (Hartshorne, p. 8).
3. Hartshorne adds: 'Occasions derivative (for Descartes). <u>Descartes</u>' clarity, brevity, straightforward exposition good method' (Hartshorne, p. 9).
4. Hartshorne follows this with an underlined phrase in quotes, which seems likely to be an exact Whitehead quote: '"<u>So far as it is something, so far a success</u>"' (Hartshorne, p. 9).
5. This text appears in the left margin. Parentheses added. The text seems to be a later addition (he actually began writing the examples immediately following the preceding sentence, then seems to have realised that there was no space, and wrote them in the margin instead). Hartshorne has a fourth example that Roethlisberger does not have: 'it might have (freely) made itself better' (Hartshorne, p. 9).
    This marginal addition is particularly noteworthy because it appears to demonstrate that Roethlisberger consulted either Whitehead or other students for material he missed; there does not seem to be any other way that he could get the exact same three examples that Hartshorne had. This is part of the reason why we have not generally taken special pains to point out what seem to be later additions in Roethlisberger's notes. (See Introduction, pp. xl–xli.)
6. This illustration is more detailed and clear in Hartshorne: 'Whole based on relevance to human body (in architecture). Limit as dome emphasizes <u>volume</u> by its balance with other volumes of building' (Hartshorne, p. 9).
7. Hartshorne has a particularly nice turn of phrase here: 'Relevance of past in its enrichment of substance as ground of eternal present' (Hartshorne, p. 10).
8. Hartshorne additionally has here: 'Always <u>definite</u> value. No indefinite general value. Always particular. Particular in a community of particulars – can't get away from this.'

|15|
Summary
There is always something to be excluded in synthesis. Why call immediate occasion "prehension"? (1) divest of notion of cognition (2) more neutral regarding positive and negative side.

The whole of religious art consists in making what is definite and limited point beyond itself.[1] Achieved only <u>by</u> <u>limitation</u>. Not achieved by "anything, anyhow." – instead by restriction, by keeping out, by <u>exclusion</u>.

Nature
In nature we have more embodiment of beyondness. Nature using same means for direct conveyance of value. What is given is limited – It is "<u>something</u>" there and not "<u>nothing</u>" which gives us this sense of <u>unboundedness</u>. Uniformity – a type of limitation.[2]

[Philosophy has for its workshop <u>the immediate concrete experience</u> –]*[3]

Memories of the past which limit the present give it that haunting beyondness. Without limitation, we have <u>mere indefiniteness</u>.[4]

Saturday, 24 October 1925

Roethlisberger's notes[5]

I. <u>Dualism – Ultimate entity is bi-polar.</u>
Two different types of occasions (1) experient occasions (2) imaginal occasions. Discard notion of <u>permanent knowing self</u>.[6] Imaginal occasion is important <u>in theory of knowledge</u>. Experient occasion is a value for its own sake. Cognition is VfromV without. – Does not include its own cognition. <u>Imaginal occasion is also actual entity in actual world, but derivative from</u>

---

1. Hartshorne's notes use Gothic architecture as a somewhat extended specific example: 'Religious art – transition from particular entity to eternal which comprehends it. Gothic architecture – purest example of finite referring to infinite. Upward lift as VitsV organic function – ["infinity above me"] everything strains upwards. Horizontal flow also – richness here, in decorated capitals. Strength flows upward, richness horizontally to center of religious rites. Slightest impurity means sinking in value in Gothic' (Hartshorne, p. 10).
2. Hartshorne additionally has here: 'Detailed foreground emphasizing monotony of expanse beyond. |11| One type of limitation throws light on another. [Ratzel's rhythms, in part]' (Hartshorne, pp. 10–11). The bracketed reference to Friedrich Ratzel (1844–1904) is very likely Hartshorne's own, rather than Whitehead's.
3. The significance of the asterisk here is not clear. In Hartshorne's notes this phrase is followed by: 'Pragmatists have done a service here. Metaphysics (is) a learned science, concepts handed down growing more and more abstract [Heidegger]' (Hartshorne, p. 11). Again, the bracketed reference to Heidegger is almost certainly Hartshorne's own thought rather than Whitehead's.
4. Through comparison with the Heath and Hartshorne notes, this is likely the end of the 22 October lecture. However, this is a more difficult determination to make than usual. There is no discernible break in the Hartshorne notes at all. Roethlisberger's notes have a horizontal line spanning the page, and begin with a heading that is numbered with a roman numeral 'I', both of which seem to suggest a lecture break, though the quality of the ink and handwriting is not noticeably different. Our best clue is that Heath, who is the only one consistently dating at this point, begins the next lecture with the difference between experient and imaginal occasions, which matches up with the following text in Roethlisberger.
5. The corresponding Radcliffe lecture can be found on p. 17.
6. Hartshorne follows this comment with 'like James' (Hartshorne, p. 11).

experient occasion. Also an individual value, but <u>presupposes</u> a community of all occasions. Imaginal occasion is synthesis of all occasions via its fundamental exp.Verient∨ occasion and obtains type of value because of exp.Verient∨ occasion.

This is in contrast with Kant, for whom the Given apart from knowing is chaotic. For Whitehead, the Given apart from knowing is real and <u>not chaotic</u>.

How is knowledge possible? Two questions

(1) How is ⟨experient⟩[1] occasion ∨in itself (universal)[2]∨ possible?

(2) How is knowledge of experient occasion possible?[3]

Description of <u>imaginal occasion</u> comes after ⟨<u>experient</u>⟩ <u>occasion</u>. Here is divorce. (Value in experient occasion rather than in imaginal occasion).[4] <u>Gradations of value</u>. How extraordinarily different in values are imaginal occasions – variable {example: thinking, sleep}.

Whereas in world in general – imaginal occasions may be variable and negligible. There is always the couple {<u>imaginal and experient</u>} but you cannot describe im∨aginal∨ before experient.

|16| Experient occasion synthesis ∨with∨ its imaginal occasions in sense of "taking account of" – Imaginal occasion is an abstraction from experient occasion.[5] What is synthesized and what is excluded? Leads to a classification of entities. Among included are <u>other occasions and other entities</u>. One occasion does not <u>synthesize</u> *simplicita*. <u>Modal</u> synthesis arises from interplay of occasions and other entities – (also not *simplicita*).

II. <u>Two fundamental types of entities</u> –

(1) <u>Other occasions</u> (2) <u>eternal objects</u> – something like universals – each unity of occasions is a mode of imposing actuality on whole of occasions and eternal objects.

Description of immediate experience

1. Flux of occasions: each as it <u>passes is gone forever</u>.
2. When we compare different occasions, it depends: describability) on concept of identity – (components in one occasion are identical with components of other occasion.
3. <u>Components</u> is one occasion identical with <u>components</u> of another.
4. Idea of "enduring identity" – permanent objects, table, chairs, etc. <u>extended objects</u> i.e. conceptual object. When we apply it to sense data – reiteration of pattern thru <u>continuity</u> of occasions. What is identical is <u>eternal</u> and independent of any spatial or temporal

---

1. Here and two lines down Roethlisberger inexplicably has 'experienced', but it seems clear from context that he should have 'experient'.
2. Closing parenthesis supplied.
3. Cf. Hartshorne: 'False idea that to describe anything = describe knowing of it' (Hartshorne, p. 11).
4. This text appears in the left margin. Parentheses added. Where the text is best inserted is difficult to determine.
5. Hartshorne also has: 'Emotion arises from synthesis of imaginal occasion into experiential occasion' (Hartshorne, p. 12).

continuity (Sense data – chaotic, no relational tinge, hence use eternal objects). Misplaced concreteness.[1]
5. Practical man interested in <u>enduring objects</u>.
6. Artist and philosopher? interested in <u>eternal objects</u>.[2]
7. Green has a relational aspect; relational entity; greenness is green minus the relational aspect.
8. <u>Lowest eternal objects are relational</u> (Extreme logical realism).[3]
9. Every one occasion has to do with an <u>eternal object</u> – Question is how?[4]
10. Notion of relation.
   (1) eternal relationship, timeless – R⟨elationship of⟩ eternal objects ⟨to one another⟩.[5]
   (2) eternal object R⟨elationship to⟩[6] <u>occasion</u> (prehension into definite) – <u>ingression</u>. An eternal object has an element of indetermination. But at the particular occasion, the mode is decided.
11. Each particular occasion is ᵛsolution ofᵛ the indeterminateness of each eternal object.

|17|
III. Necessity, Possibility, Contingency and Actuality[7]
   Possibility ᵛ<u>means</u>ᵛ depends on ingression of eternal objects in occasion, <u>the eternal objects form a realm of possibility</u> – can be thought as independent. What is possible includes the <u>realm</u> of actuality. It is inherent in what the universe is is that it might be.[8] <u>You cannot divorce actual from possible</u>.[9]

---

1. Cf. Hartshorne: 'Sense data often taken atomistically, no relational tinge (Fallacy of misplaced concreteness – really abstract)' (Hartshorne, p. 13).
2. Roethlisberger has a brace connecting items 5 and 6. Hartshorne's notes have the word 'mathematicians' in place of 'Artist and philosopher' (Hartshorne, p. 13).
3. Hartshorne is more thorough here: 'Fundamental Principle here – one of extreme logical realism. If reject "stuff," must be a logical realist. e.g. William James proclaimed himself a logical realist. Lowest form of abstraction, <u>individual</u> occasion <u>neglected</u>' (Hartshorne, p. 13).
4. Hartshorne follows this with 'But eternal object can be considered, leaving manner of ingretion (?) indefinite (wholly?)' (Hartshorne, p. 13). 'ingretion' is, of course, a misspelling of Whitehead's invented term 'ingression'. Hartshorne's question mark may indicate that this is the first time he heard the term.
5. These two insertions are supplied from Hartshorne's notes (Hartshorne, p. 13). The editors have at times used Hartshorne's notes to supply words missed by Roethlisberger. These instances will be marked by ⟨brackets⟩ according to the edition's editorial conventions and called out with a corresponding footnote.
6. Insertion supplied from page 13 of Hartshorne's notes.
7. This heading is in the left margin with a brace encompassing the entire manuscript page.
8. Hartshorne additionally has here: 'Realism in art – without at romance, cannot see real as it is. Bertrand Russell, "Freeman's worship." Bertrand Russell Indignant at universe. Universe inherently refers to what it might be' (Hartshorne, p. 13). The intended reference is surely to Russell, 'The free man's worship'.
9. Through comparison with the Heath and Hartshorne notes, this is likely the end of the 24 October lecture. However, this determination is less than certain than most. Heath's notes at Radcliffe (pp. 18–21) do not appear to be quite synchronised with those at Harvard (that, or Heath's notes are simply much more voluminous for this lecture, as she has about two handwritten pages of material before it all neatly matches up with the Harvard material again). There also seem to be multiple viable lecture break points in both Roethlisberger and Hartshorne. The lecture break point we have chosen here marks a page break in Hartshorne, a mention of 'art' in Hartshorne at the very end (as there is in Heath, p. 18) and perhaps a *very* slight change in ink quality for Roethlisberger. But, as far as lecture break points matter, the reader should be aware that the editorially inserted lecture break point here is less certain than most.

⟨Tuesday, 27 October 1925⟩

Hartshorne's notes[1]

|14| What might have been otherwise. Each definite occasion has determinate status with respect to previous. But merely as "an occasion," might have been otherwise.

Any definite occasion defines <u>general</u> character of community of occasions determines:

(1) What <u>any</u> occasion <u>must</u> be.

(2) What <u>any</u> occasion <u>may</u> be. (for any occasion contains <u>all</u> eternal objects, all possibilities)

(3) What each ⟨other⟩ definite particular occasion with a determinate status to given occasion must be. ⟨This⟩ Limitation ⟨is⟩ additional to ⟨any limitations⟩[2] (1) imposed on general possibilities of (2). Causation and final causes here.

Most general idea underlying space and time.

Part of (1) that any two occasions must have definite specific relative status.

α β
● ● No other dot can have same relation to α as β. Relation which comes from joint particularity of two entities. Relative status. Absolute status of α can only be described in terms of its relative status to all other entities.

~~Shape~~

Internal relations affirmed.

(1) Impartial conditions ~~of α~~ from standpoint of α.

(2) Impartial possibilities.

(3) Partial (opposite to <u>impartial</u>) conditions of β by virtue of status relative to α. An exclusion of impartial possibilities.

|15| Principle of uniqueness of relative status underlies time and space. Each occasion determines a scheme having one and only one niche for every other occasion. In knowledge of one occasion may know about some other occasion simply by some general relationship, not by adjective. When we point, e.g. The "that" without adjective.

Denial of contingency means partial conditions provided by antecedent occasions completely determine occasion. But: antecedent occasions are those which provide conditions (past <u>defined</u> – to an extent – by causality – this later).

Knowledge of antecedent occasions will determine <u>some</u> characters of occasion – otherwise no induction. And knowledge of consequent occasions would provide premiss for knowledge of <u>some</u> characters:

---

1. The corresponding Radcliffe lecture can be found on p. 18, though the Harvard and Radcliffe lectures do not seem to line up particularly well here. See previous note. Heath seems considerably more thorough here than either of her Harvard counterparts.
2. Insertions supplied through comparison with the Roethlisberger notes (Roethlisberger, fall semester p. 17).

Nothing in β for itself alone.

Contemporary events – must be independent as such. One not cause of another. Only connected through antecedents.

Holds for contingency – otherwise perhaps no past-present-future.

Has purpose of past occasions together with its free responsibility – their own purpose conditioned by purposes of previous occasions and by their own experience of displayed relations, enriched by spontaneity. But two outbursts of spontaneity: (1) own immediate display, (2) in relation to future.[1]

Contemporary occasion in relation to future merely experiences[2] purpose of past occasion.[3]

⟨Thursday, 29 October 1925⟩

Hartshorne's notes[4]

|16|

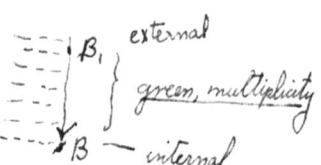

Mutual relations of contemporary events is for β_1 as displayed – eternal objects give content. Mode in which β_1 is in β ~~is~~ involves intervention of eternal objects.

Internal and external. Internal to β_1, external to β. Apprehension external to object. Analysis of β_1 gives no idea of this relation. Yet this analysis would give knowledge of existence of a β [via causes?]

Displayed = what is present – private psychological field. Yet "privacy"!? Must get public world into private field.

Field of display.

Present events are contemporary, but vice-versa? Relativity – ⟨band?⟩[5] of events neither past (cause) nor future (effect) is it all present psychologically.

<u>Grounds for belief</u> in contingency. (ought to be but one, ought to be obvious)

1. Total community of actual occasions is contingent with respect to total realm of possibility. Datum for action = total realm of possibility. In discerning

---

1. Cf. Roethlisberger: 'A pair of mutually related events have in them the purpose of the past with an element of contingency for itself. So they to their future subsequents. Making the immediate occasion what it is in the present and with respect to its purpose for the future' (Roethlisberger, fall semester p. 17).
2. Hartshorne clear has 'exper.' for 'experiences' here, but Roethlisberger instead has 'expresses' (Roethlisberger, fall semester p. 17).
3. Cf. Roethlisberger: 'Present occasions with respect to their contemporary ~~occasions~~ Vmutual relationsV merely express the purpose of past occasions as enriched by its own VfreeV spontaneity and conditioned with respect to their own purposes for the future' (Roethlisberger, fall semester p. 17).
  This appears to be the end of the 27 October lecture.
4. The corresponding Radcliffe lecture can be found on p. 21.
  The figure below has been supplied from the Roethlisberger notes; Hartshorne's notes clearly refer to this same figure, but do not reproduce it.
5. It is unclear whether this word is 'band' or 'bond'.

this datum, we discern total actual as contingency. Approval or disapproval (judgements?).[1]

Why must there have been a world |17| in which Charles I had his head cut off?[2]

2. Each unity prehends total community, and thereby exhibits characters of total community – under limitations. Hence shares in spontaneous contingency of community.

Unit contingent because whole is.

Whole is contingent because unity is.

3. Direct experience of spontaneous choice. Unity given as choosing – under limitation. If no experience of freedom, none of limits (Mongoose).[3]

4. ~~Determination~~ Determinism gratuitous for pluralists and empiricists – who hold that individual occasions must be consulted in knowledge. Comfortable, tight feeling of d monism, plus pleasure of empiricism. Can't have both – Wonderfully baseless doctrine.

Whitehead[4] Sheltered himself behind William James.

Imaginal Occasions, occasions of knowing.

Each experient (occasion) has its correlate imaginal occasion = <u>occasion of knowing that experient occasion</u>. Ultimate concrete = unity of both – that whole = <u>ultimate occasion</u>.[5]

Imaginal occasion = knowing whole community via its experient occasion.

Shy of ego. Descartes. Not *grund wesens*.[6]

Imaginal occasion contemporary with experient occasion because |18| of causal independence (in measure).

Experient occasion as datum is in complete independence of ᵥitsᵥ imaginal occasion. And imaginal occasion has experient occasion <u>qua</u> datum, but datum not cause of knowing. Experient bears to imaginal occasion <u>similar</u> relation as eternal objects to experient occasion, i.e., eternal objects not cause of real world.

Yet theory of causation required in respect to imaginal occasion. Otherwise imaginal occasion gave complete knowledge, or else intrinsically unknowable entities (= "nonsense").

Knowledge erratic because imaginal occasion conditioned by non-contemporary ultimate occasion. Warped from outside.[7]

---

1. What appears to be written is 'jm'ts', which we have expanded to 'judgements', but the handwriting is difficult to decipher. Cf. Roethlisberger: 'we have notions of approval and disapproval which have no meaning without reference to what might have been' (Roethlisberger, fall semester p. 18).
2. This likely refers to the execution of Charles I in 1649 and the subsequent abolition of the monarchy in the United Kingdom.
3. The mongoose reference seems likely to be to a fable originating in India: see <https://en.wikipedia.org/wiki/The_Brahmin_and_the_Mongoose>.
4. The 'Whitehead' here is a later pen addition, but it is not clear if Whitehead was indeed saying that it was he who was appealing to the authority of William James, or if this sentence refers to the people whom Whitehead was criticising.
5. Hartshorne apparently missed a notable Whitehead term here: '"<u>Dipolar</u>" is final concrete ultimate entity' (Roethlisberger, fall semester p. 18).
6. Again, this is Hartshorne switching to German, not Whitehead. See note 6, p. 58.
7. Through comparison with the Roethlisberger and Heath notes, this appears to be the end of the 29 October lecture.

Harvard lectures, fall semester 1925

⟨Saturday, 31 October 1925⟩
Roethlisberger's notes[1]

|19|
VI. Present Occasions and Contemporary Occasions[2]
Distinction "before, now, and after". Take occasion *E* and occasion *N*.[3] Different types of mutual relations between *E* and *N*. Two distinct meanings of "now" which are relevant according to Whitehead. ① If *N* and *E* are now, they are <u>contemporary occasions</u> ②, realized in mutual \physical\ independence. What *N* is \in itself\ does not modify *E*. \But both modified by past and future events is directly determined. *P* is datum for *E*, but not modified for *E*\. In order to explain any connection between *N* and *E*, it has to be done derivatively[4]

Although *N* is in a sense a datum of *E*, it is not a <u>modification</u>. [In physics, all physical influence requires time].

---

② <u>Present occasions</u> – mutually present because one occasion is present with another. *P*'s displayed for *E* not *simpliciter*, but ~~as lo~~ under a mode as a locus of certain <u>eternal objects</u>. Sense prehension is a datum in private psychological field, but is a fact in external world. Mode is a fusion of the relative aspect of the presentation with ⟨blank⟩

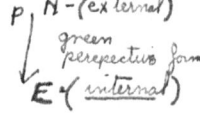

P is present for *E*.
Duration is aggregate of all <u>present occasions</u>.

~~Externality~~   Whitehead's sense data includes relation.
~~S/t presents~~   Present = aggregate of all presentational occasions.
<u>All present occasions are contemporary occasions, but not all contemporary are present occasions</u>. Succession of present events for enduring entity is given scheme where ⟨?⟩ are ordered by perception. Measurements of science are all relative to this scheme. (All measurement is derivative from presentational occasion)[5] {What you perceive is sun 8 minutes ago – no, you see spot over there}. All scientific knowledge is relative to the <u>presented</u>

---

1. The corresponding Radcliffe lecture can be found on p. 22. Whitehead's appointment book indicates that he ended this lecture 15 minutes early. For the previous class session, on 29 October, he wrote: 'Warn about Saturday lecture'. For 31 October, he wrote: 'McDougall – Copley Plaza, Foreign Policy Association, End Lecture at 12:45 – 3:30' (Whitehead, 'Pocket Engagement Book, 1925–26'). William McDougall was a colleague and friend of Whitehead in the Psychology Department (see note 2 for the 17 December lecture, p. 97). According to the Association's 'brief history of the FPA' web page <https://www.fpa.org/about/>: 'The Foreign Policy Association was founded in 1918 as the League of Free Nations Association. It was formed by 141 distinguished Americans to support President Woodrow Wilson's efforts to achieve a just peace. The Association was reconstituted in 1923 as the Foreign Policy Association with a commitment to the careful study of all sides of international questions affecting the U.S. John Foster Dulles and Eleanor Roosevelt were among the incorporators.'
2. This heading appears in the left margin. There is also an illegible false start just below it.
3. The capital 'N's in this paragraph are all written over another letter that is now indecipherable.
4. The word 'What' appears to the right of the following diagram. Its significance or meaning is unclear.
5. This text appears in the left margin. Parentheses added.

scheme. ~~This presented s~~ Contemporaneous occasions is internal on both sides. Contemporaneous may exhibit distortion due.

Distortion = f^1 (presented structural scheme). Contemporaneous occasions[2]

⟨Tuesday, 3 November 1925⟩

Roethlisberger's notes[3]

|20|
VII. Inspectional and Presentational Relationships[4]
   1. Relations between non-contemporary occasions ᵛareᵛ internal. We get from present some information about the future and some about the past. ᵛInᵛ a relationship of presentation which two non-contemporaneous occasions may have to one another. {p is in e by presentational character ᵛrelationᵛ of greenness}. All measurements are made via presentational relationships. Presentational relationships are definite and sharp.
   2. Ultimate occasion is dipolar – ⟨experient⟩[5] and imaginal. Both have a type of independence. The imaginal is the actuality of exemplification ᵛbetween eternal objects and experient occasionᵛ. Actualizes the realm of eternal objects. Relation of exemplification actualizes E with eternal objects.[6] Reason why knowledge is inadequate, limited and erroneous.

When we look on non-contemporary occasions, we find grades of effectiveness among relations. Effectiveness varies. Consider the conditions for effectiveness. We find two dominating conditions.
A. ① Spatial and temporal aspects – why all scientific laws reduce themselves to spatial and temporal. Expressed by occasions form(ing) a historical route.[7] Two conditions (1) time lapse (2) continuity, spatial and temporal. ②[8] Also must be <u>systematic relationship</u> which <u>characterizes</u> the intrinsic relations along the route. Various kinds of systematic relationships. Another way in which group may be effected.[9]
B. <u>Relation of whole and part</u>[10] have a peculiar effectiveness in modifying occasion as a whole. Made more difficult than it is.

---

1. At times Roethlisberger writes the letter 'f' in a different script, which we have interpreted as intending the 'function' symbol and have silently rendered it as such here and subsequently.
2. This is likely the end of the 31 October lecture.
3. The corresponding Radcliffe lecture can be found on p. 24.
4. This underlined heading appears in the left margin.
5. Again Roethlisberger had 'experienced' here when Whitehead must have said 'experient'.
6. The exact significance of the diagram to the right here is not entirely clear. The E here refers to the drawing, but it seems likely it is also referring to an experient occasion. Hartshorne's and Heath's notes seem to suggest that X is 'other occasions' (see Hartshorne, p. 19, and the 5 November Radcliffe lecture, p. 27).
7. See the figure on the right.
8. This character looks very much like a '3', but Roethlisberger seems to have written something over it; that there is no other circled '2' suggests that he meant to change it to '2'.
9. Roethlisberger clearly has 'effected' here, but it is possible Whitehead said 'affected'.
10. See the figure on the right.

Endurance.[1]
> (1) historical route of occasions.
> (2) repetition of structure.
> (3) effective inheritance – because of the modification made by antecedents.

Enduring object is very complex – structure is expressed <u>in terms</u> of eternal objects. It gets its individuality via its historical route: <u>Continuity</u> is very important in notion of enduring object. Verification of individual is gotten from historical route.

Relation between non-continuous occasions is <u>internal</u> to both. ●↔● In order to be internal you need time lapse, structure, etc. Enduring object is the most complete example of ⟨blank⟩

Relationships which are not <u>presentational</u> are <u>inspectional</u>
$A● ↔ ●E$ Inspectional – insistent but <u>vague</u>
$P● → ●E$ Presentational – <u>sharpness</u> of definition –
All modes of expressing inspectional <u>via</u> presentational relation[2]

⟨Thursday, 5 November 1925⟩

Roethlisberger's notes[3]

|21|

VIII. <u>Perceptual Object</u>[4]

Doctrine of substance or subject fails to explain perceptual object. ⟨This is⟩ why Whitehead starts with "occasions". How one occasion synthesizes with another? – relationship between occasions. – how other occasions modify the essence of E. ① What is fundamental are the <u>other occasions</u> – relationship between X and E ⟨is⟩ internal to E.[5] ② Analyze essence of E from standpoint of realm of <u>eternal objects</u>. Two relationships are

$X =$ per object
↓
E

---

1. The phrase 'character of endurance' with a bracket encompassing the numbered list below appears in the left margin.
2. There are date difficulties here again. Some of the content on this page definitely matches with what Heath has for 3 November, but it seems Harvard and Radcliffe were getting somewhat out of synchronisation again. It is not clear when the transition to 5 November happens; it is most likely either here at the end of the page, or at the line Roethlisberger drew four lines up.
3. The corresponding Radcliffe lecture can be found on p. 26.
4. Interestingly, this phrase also appears at the top of Heath's notes for the following session, 7 November, although the content here seems to match much more neatly overall with Heath's notes for 5 November. It is safe to say that at this point the Harvard and Radcliffe lectures are not neatly synchronised.
    At the beginning of this lecture, Heath lists what appear to be six possible paper topics for a paper due on 4 December (p. 26). Hartshorne's notes list only two of these possible topics (presumably the two that caught his interest), but does not identify them as paper topics or reference a date (Hartshorne, p. 19). Roethlisberger has none of this. Hartshorne also references Descartes's second meditation as the lecture begins (Hartshorne, p. 19).
5. For the figure on the right, note that Roethlisberger has written what may be 'per object' for 'perceptual object', but the handwriting is not clear. Both the Hartshorne and Heath notes define 'X' as simply 'other occasions/another occasion' (p. 27; Hartshorne, p. 19).

presentational and inspectional (*Inspectio* from Descartes).¹ ⟨There is⟩ also ⟨the⟩ relationship of "relative status" (perspective and extensive).² A presentational relationship "green" (X is "green" for E).³ Universal rejected because aspect omitted in ordinary treatment. Also E = experient occasion.⁴ E is what it is in itself because of "green". Presentational rel∨ation∨ ~~although it~~ designates :X: via relative status – nothing else, hence relationship is internal to E and external to X.⁵ Inspectional relationships are relationships which only hold when there is a time lapse in the occasions. When you have a relationship internal at both ends (E and Y mutually internal),⁶ what Y is in itself is what does enter into E. ∨How∨ what Y is in itself [in addition to the mere relative status] enters into the essence of E. – Not a mere putting together – but under a mode of limitation. If there was a mere synthesis *simpliciter* of Y and E, there would be no "how". Essentially refers to "how not" (Luther: "When I pray, I curse").⁷ If what Y is in itself enters into essence of E, then E can only be that self which is synthesizing Y. Presentation relationships of Y ∨to Z_1 and Z_2∨ enter into what E is. A peculiarly intimate relationship with occasions of past life. Memory comes in as inspectional relationship.⁸ Occasions contemporary to E are devoid of inspectional relationship. Relationship between past and future not same as presentational ⟨blank⟩⁹

Grades of vividness in what your occasions. What is graded? ∨Birth of intensive quantity∨. It is the grades in vividness of values as things in itself. What are conditions for relation between Y and E should promote a depth of actuality in E. (Perceptual object is a historical route)¹⁰ Historical route gives depth to E. Many historical routes which lead up to E. [The importance of E depends on fact that E issues from its past]. Historical route is a route of contiguous occasions. Each occasion represents

---

1. Hartshorne's notes also reference Descartes's 'lump of wax': 'Descartes' *inspectio* and lump of wax, mere data don't give us identity of wax in two states, but we know it by a certain *inspectio*' (Hartshorne, p. 19).
2. Hartshorne also originally wrote that there were '*two* main types of internal relations', but then crossed out 'two' and wrote 'three' when Whitehead mentioned 'relative status' (Hartshorne, p. 19).
3. See the figure on the right.
4. Hartshorne's notes add that 'E is here experiential occasion, *cognition aside*' (Hartshorne, p. 19).
5. Hartshorne's notes add here: '"Bifurcation of nature" leads to sceptical ruin (merit of Hume). Above relationship is a public fact, apart from private cognition' (Hartshorne, p. 20).
6. Parentheses added.
7. It is unclear whether this reference to Luther was made by Whitehead or Roethlisberger, as neither Hartshorne nor Heath makes any mention of it. The line originally comes from Luther's 1531 treatise *Against the [Character] Assassin at Dresden*, and reads as follows: 'For I cannot pray without thereby having to curse. If I say: "Holy be Thy name," I must in addition say: "Cursed, damned, and disgraced must be the papists' name and all who slander Thy name".' Edwards, *Luther's Last Battles*, p. 51. As applied to Whitehead's point, it illustrates the need for exclusion/limitation within a synthesis (the 'how' and 'how not') in order to achieve value and vividness.
8. Hartshorne's notes add that 'Causality ⟨is⟩ an inspectional relationship' (Hartshorne, p. 20).
9. It is not clear if Roethlisberger omitted text here or merely forgot a full stop.
10. This text appears in the left margin. Parentheses added.

some structure. Some generic type of structure which they exemplify. Endurance is in type of structure which is inherited from antecedent.[1]

⟨Saturday, 7 November, 1925⟩

Hartshorne's notes[2]

We have lost our own merits through Germans without gaining the German merits. No longer write as in 18th century or 17th century – neither in England nor in France.

Galileo – colors, etc. "in sensitive <u>body</u>." This less bifurcation than Descartes' "merely *in cogito*."[3]

<u>Shape and motion only</u>[4] in ~~body ex~~ external cause of sensation.

|22| Descartes: "perceptible under these forms." "A certain extended thing" ⟨alone/above?⟩ <u>there</u>. ~~In Extension~~ Flexibility not mere product of imagination, extension also. For flexibility = an <u>infinity</u> of possible changes. Imagination insufficient to infinity. Sheer presentation of datum does not give wax,[5] but "inspection of mind."

Broad vs. Russell's <u>class</u> theory of ~~su~~ thing.[6] Descartes rejects this, for class = an infinity of forms, not perceived as such at all. ~~Class~~ Unity of class, <u>intension of class</u> given by notion of entity according to Descartes. This notion got by inspection (very "hot," says Whitehead). Russell *müsste* ~~sg~~ *sagen*[7] <u>how</u> data are classified much more definitely than he does.[8]

---

1. Hartshorne's notes contain important additions here: 'If successive states form a unity, [express same theme] – melody! – "S endures" = mere identity. "Important" when endurance depends on S and not primarily on external environment. Then structure really inherited from previous S, not merely reproduced by milieu. Historical group with enduring structure = is an "<u>important</u>" entity' (Hartshorne, p. 21).
   This appears to be the end of the 5 November lecture.
2. The corresponding Radcliffe lecture can be found on p. 28. Note that the Radcliffe lecture bears little resemblance to its Harvard counterpart, particularly its second half. In it, Whitehead mentions a half-dozen names that do not appear in Roethlisberger's or Hartshorne's notes anywhere in any lecture: Christian Wolff, Lord Kelvin, Thomas Young, Augustin-Jean Fresnel, John Henry Poynting and James Clerk Maxwell (though Maxwell's name shows up once in the notes of Robinson, for 13 February, p. 118). See also the Radcliffe lecture for 7 November, note 1, p. 28.
3. Roethlisberger's notes preface this line with 'Galileo – separation into primary and secondary qualities' (Roethlisberger, fall semester p. 22).
4. Roethlisberger records that 'shape, *quantity* and motion remain' (Roethlisberger, fall semester p. 22, emphasis added).
5. Descartes famously discusses a piece of wax in Meditation 2, part 2.
6. Roethlisberger's notes say that for Russell, 'substance = Class of sense-data, but classified with association with a certain entity, but if the entity is not, the class is undetermined' (Roethlisberger, fall semester p. 22). On the first day of class, Whitehead had assigned Broad's *Scientific Thought* and Russell's *Our Knowledge of the External World* (pp. 202–7) and *The Analysis of Mind* (pp. 194–7). The relevant sections of Russell have been indicated, but an examination of Broad's *Scientific Thought* does not reveal any discussion of class theory.
7. This translates as 'would have to say'. Again, these transitions into German are almost certainly not things that Whitehead said.
8. Roethlisberger has this same table, but with a few differences. He has the word 'Result' in the last line of the first column, an arrow pointing from 'Existence' to 'endurance', an arrow pointing from 'secondary qualities' to 'unknown qualities', and identifies 'Matter' with science and 'Minds' with philosophy (Roethlisberger, fall semester p. 22).

Substance	Bits of Matter		Minds
Attribute	extension		cogitation
Existence	endurance		endurance
	unknown qualities causing:		secondary qualities (*cogitata*)
	matter *formaliter*	*inspectio* →	matter <u>objective</u>

But: substance-quality? Cogitation, endurance, secondary qualities, all <u>qualities</u> of mind?? How then is <u>world known</u> if world is non-mental?

However: as map of scientific work for two or three centuries, couldn't have been better. Science took care of left hand part, philosophy of right hand part. Science meant physics (biology less than 100 years old).

|23| Balance has ~~put~~ ∨been∨[1] upset from side of science by rise of physiology and psychology. Come back to Galileo's sensitive body (= experient occasion)

Whitehead drops substance, and gets sensitive occasion as ultimate entity.

Locke and Newton in London together. Locke full of Newtonian ideas. Newton saw extension was insufficient. We ~~en~~ need <u>mass</u>, which = <u>quantity of matter</u> (with {?} extension, two measurable attributes). Mass = inertia, external to ∨its∨ motion. Matter occupies space (Descartes: space = matter)[2]

(Mass as pushiness of things, not separable from their sight, etc.)

Hume: spatial relations merely manner of display of secondary qualities.

Hume: "a few superficial qualities of objects" only shown us by nature, who keeps her secrets well hidden from us. "Influences and powers" unknown. Why bread nourishes, e.g.

"Wonderful power" = satiric of Newton [?].

Cause = essence of substance for Hume in comparison to Descartes.[3]

Sensible qualities in unknown relation to secret causes.

Hume presumes we know past experience. But memory on his scheme = merely present experience. Future no more a puzzle than past.

Like sensible qualities always with like secret powers.

|24| Hume jumps question of what "<u>object</u>" is, here. "No immediate intercourse (Descartes' *inspectio*) between mind and object" (Hume says).

"Energy of mind itself." "Cause unknown to us." Mind experiences no connection of mind with objects, and therefore cannot reason to justify such connection.[4]

---

1. The word 'been' was added in pen over white-out, one of the edits made when these notes were rediscovered in the 1970s. For a discussion of these changes, see the Introduction, pp. xli–xlii.
2. Roethlisberger adds: 'Descartes' *inspectio* and Locke's primary qualities open to sceptical criticism' (Roethlisberger, fall semester p. 22).
3. Roethlisberger writes: 'Hume relates problem of induction to the problem of the object' (Roethlisberger, fall semester p. 22).
4. Through comparison with the Roethlisberger and Heath notes, this appears to be the end of the 7 November lecture.

⟨Tuesday, 10 November, 1925⟩
Roethlisberger's notes[1]

|23|
IX. Morphological vs. Functional
   There are two competing concepts: (1) morphological (2) functional.
   (1) ⟨is⟩ succession of structural forms (2) looks on such description as high abstraction. Morphological view inherent in Descartes and Hume. – main characteristic of Bergson and James of getting away from morphological. Recast your ideas. Science and philosophy interpreted by the morphological point of view which you are trying to get away from. (To explain the more fundamental by less fundamental.) Morphological
   Matter is morphological, energy is functional. Biological functions not capable of being expressed in morphology. Substance comes in morphological view in order to have something to tie together successive instants. What holds successive instants? Same substance. How do these difficulties especially come up in perception? What is it you perceive? Under morphological point of view, your mind is enjoying sense data. Connection between patch of color and "table" is indirect. "Table" does not depend on "sense data", and "sense data" does not seem to depend on "table". A disconnection – Trying to explain in two substance terms of Descartes, you have great difficulty. Not only disconnection, but also a dislocation in time. Look at sun. Sense data indicating object over there. Yet perceiving sense data of eight minutes ago? You can trace a transmission. When you get to brain, it doesn't perceive, it only waggles. Complete gap! You start in with "mind". But you never explain external world. – you reduce it to a world on same level as ourselves – purely conceptual. But our body is part of the external world – "real body in a real world or a conceptual body in a conceptual world, but not a real body in a conceptual world." [Story of mongoose].[2] Gap between function of knowing and ⟨blank⟩.[3]
   Why is it actual perceptions fail to acquaint you with actual world? Difficulty of Hume – do not allow him to slip in "memory". There is the medium which relates occasions separated by time. (Hume denies medium for "future")[4] If you stick to morphological point of view, human scepticism is inevitable. By taking

---

1. There is no corresponding Radcliffe lecture for 10 November; Heath seems to have missed the class (see her note on p. 30).
2. Whitehead made the same mongoose reference on 29 October. See note 3, p. 69.
3. Hartshorne has here: 'Knowledge is functional, known world on same level as Knowing only if morphological view is rejected. World is functional as knowledge is. The body cannot prevent us from knowing an other than ourselves, for in knowing it, the body, we know such an other' (Hartshorne, p. 75). Note, however, that most of Hartshorne's handwritten notes for this session are now so faded as to be completely illegible. Hartshorne himself endeavoured to transcribe the illegible pages when he rediscovered his notes in the 1970s, and it is from this typescript that we derive the quoted passage (and likewise with the other Hartshorne references in this lecture). The reader should also be aware that we know through comparisons with his handwritten notes (where we can read them) that Hartshorne's typescript is not always a word-perfect transcription of the original; he tended to smooth out awkward phrasing and change punctuation.
4. This text appears in the left margin. Parentheses added.

perception at any instant. Whitehead. Cartesian of matter and simple location |24| and mind and simple location. <u>What</u> we ⟨are⟩ living in is the present as issuing from the ~~present~~ ⱽpastⱽ, and is in present as determining the future, and is the present as a functioning partly in its own sake.[1] The very texture of your perceptions is on the same level as yourself. Morphological point of view leaves out what is essential in your immediate experience.[2] Cartesian point of view is too high abstraction – you leave something out – <u>enduring substance</u> and <u>simple location</u> are extremely abstract – allow science to explain certain things very simply with great logical simplicity. Very useful. Modern science wants to express biological facts, something which has time-depth. Difficult to express in terms of strict Newtonian physics (expressing functions in morphological terms).

Science also started with "mass" at an instant, gradually introduced "energy" – mass = name for quantity of <u>energy</u>. Activity needs time-depth. "Atoms" are at an instant. <u>You cannot express a world whose most concrete aspect is function in terms of morphology.</u>

<u>Green is relational</u> – Relating my experient occasion with other occasions. Think of relationship "greenness" as abstracted from its function of relating.

1. External world as <u>atoms</u> is conceptual <u>in morphological terms</u>. Conceptual world is an abstraction from real world. – Reality is only more fundamentally expressed by <u>functional terms</u>.[3]

⟨Thursday, 12 November 1925⟩

Roethlisberger's notes[4]

1. <u>Morphological point of view</u> renders difficult explanation of <u>causality</u>, <u>induction</u>, <u>memory</u>, etc. Zeno is <u>reincarnated in Hume</u> – pointing out difficulties of morphological view – Difficulties of idea of simple location – nothing to relate isolated occasions at an instant. This matter in this conformation now was that matter in that conformation then.

2. <u>Functional point of view</u> – <u>inadequate</u> language, <u>inadequate</u> mental habits. "You don't know how bad opinion I have of myself and how little I ~~know~~ ⱽdeserveⱽ it."[5] Rises out of <u>science</u>, <u>modern biology</u>, <u>modern physics</u>

---

1. These preceding three to four sentences in Roethlisberger are a bit choppy and confusing, and seem clearer in Hartshorne's notes: 'Hume doesn't say an impression is at an instant, but means it. Immediate rendering of experience shows present and functional past and future. |76| Life a doing, not a being at successive instances. Looks back and forwards. Both past and future in present for their own sakes; note symmetry" (Hartshorne, pp. 75–6).
2. Hartshorne's notes add to this the wry remark that 'No wonder if couldn't give a metaphysics' (Hartshorne, p. 76).
3. This appears to be the end of the 10 November lecture. For Roethlisberger there is a change in ink quality, while Hartshorne draws a double line. Moreover, there is an especially clean match for all three note-takers in the content following, with all of them having the phrase 'Zeno is reincarnated in Hume' near the beginning.
4. The corresponding Radcliffe lecture can be found on p. 30.
5. This quote comes from *Ruddigore; or, The Witch's Curse*, an 1887 opera by Gilbert and Sullivan. Text of this passage available online at <https://www.gsarchive.net/ruddigore/web_opera/rudd06d.html>.

and psychology. Time-depth enters into actual entity. Ultimate entity cannot be described |25| by shape. It has to be something which embraces all time in some sense. You have to have an activity, an achieving, ① Synthesis, prehension ∧② product. – Abstraction from a whole.∧ Activity produces something – pattern view. The whole function is one fact – These parts are what they are in relation to whole, and whole is what it is in relation to its parts.[1]

A. Descartes' formula:– "*Cogito ergo sum*"

    Aboriginal   Knowing → *Cognitum*① – what is known
    Descartes   Knowing → {knowing → *cognitum*} – highly complex situation
                              ↓ (*Cognitum*)②
                           Occasion of knowing (ego)

*Cognitum*① is fundamental thing to start with and not Descartes' *Cognitum*②. The given is immediate matter of fact and you reflect on it later on. When you cross Harvard Square you do not regard yourself as "knowing-subject". What is description of immediate fact to start philosophy with – "Many entities synthesized into one occasion" – The immediate unity of that one occasion is the one experiencing. It is the many becoming one or the many being one. – Analysis of *Cognitum*①

B. Berkeley's formula. – "*Esse est percipi*."

The ~~many~~ nature of the many ∨derive (?)∨ is the "one." All the meaning of the many is to be perceived ~~which~~ as one. Existence of what is perceived cannot be more ultimate than that of the percipient "*Esse est percipere*." Experient occasion is primary – all the rest is talk about it.[2]

How does the many enter one? – "The sun itself objectively" – unless you put this in, you cannot get out of private world.[3] It enters under some limitation (how it enters). The unity of experient occasion is constituted by how the ⟨*perceptum*⟩[4] enters into the percipient field. The ⟨perceptum⟩ is the other actual entities perceived. Percipient field qua unity is set among the ⟨percepta⟩ as in communion with them: Unity is a synthesis of many, and yet one among the many entities. – One in a common world. Percipient unity completes conceived unity. Not only enter objectively, but as they are for themselves. Presentation side and inspectional side.[5]

---

1. Hartshorne's notes add here: '17th century great because it oversimplifies and rather superficially eliminates difficulties and complexities' (Hartshorne, p. 28).
2. Cf. Hartshorne for this paragraph: 'You are that experiencing fact. Opposite to Descartes. Many are in the one, in the unity and through it. Perception, not knowledge, as in Descartes. Berkeley better here. No real reciprocity between knower and known, but between perception and perceived there is such. *Esse est percipere*, *Esse est percipi* (reciprocity). Together = experience' (Hartshorne, p. 29). Note that here again Hartshorne's handwritten notes are rather faded, and we are relying partly upon his own transcription to help decipher particularly faded words (see Hartshorne, p. 78).
3. Hartshorne's notes importantly point out that this is Descartes's theory being discussed: 'Descartes: "The sun itself objectively" is in my mind. Yet in general, his theory seems a representative one. Everything hangs on the "itself"; also must be some qualification. Otherwise only one experient occasion of sun possible' (Hartshorne, p. 30).
4. Roethlisberger clearly wrote 'perceptor' here and two more times below, but, through comparison with the Hartshorne notes, it is very likely that Whitehead intended '*perceptum*' or '*percepta*' (see Hartshorne, p. 30).
5. This appears to be the end of the 12 November lecture.

⟨Saturday, 14 November 1925⟩

Roethlisberger's notes[1]

|26| Almost any idea has relevance. Some ideas have a more fundamental ⟨relevance⟩.[2] Perceptiveness – distinguished from consciousness.[3] Divest consciousness from a great amount which has been irrelevantly put into it – experient occasion is one thing; imaginal occasion another.[4] Perceptiveness is "taking account of" – is the datum of consciousness; Every actual <u>thing</u> is a process.[5] ~~You can find~~ Modern physics talks in terms of perception. All you know about two charges of electrons is mutual perceptiveness. Mutual taking account of. Metaphysical idea, first substantial stuff – then focus on it. Science, on the other hand, takes inverted point of view in that $S = f^6$ (forces) = a certain character. Extraordinarily misleading – if you talk of <u>stuff</u>.[7]

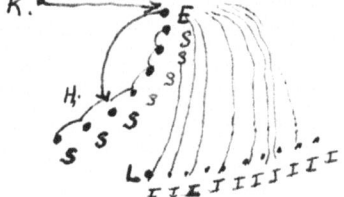

<u>Problem of perceptual object</u> – Consciousness of an actual occasion is the knowledge of a definite <u>experient occasion</u>. Mutual determination of ultimate entities which are the experient occasions.[8] <u>Datum is realm of eternal objects</u>. Ingression of these ⟨eternal⟩[9] object has a relational character – relating occasions to each other. Mode of relationship constitutes "<u>stuffing</u>" of actual occasions. <u>Perceptiveness</u> is expressing the internal relationship between occasions – it allows itself to be distinguished ① "presentational" ② inspectional type.

One occasion as ⟨blank⟩ in the life history of an enduring structure. What K^{10} is in itself is its remoteness as a factor of E.[11] What E is in itself comes as an inspectional – has little individuality outside of its consonance with H.

The world is full of exceptional circumstances. Peculiarity of S is that

---

1. There is no corresponding Radcliffe lecture for 10 November; Heath seems to have missed the class.
2. Cf. Hartshorne: 'No ~~idea~~ VwordV simply wrong or simply right' (Hartshorne, p. 30).
3. Cf. Hartshorne: '"Perceptiveness" good but dangerous' (Hartshorne, p. 30).
4. Cf. Hartshorne: 'Consciousness = Imaginal occasion. Perception = Experient occasion' (Hartshorne, p. 31).
5. Cf. Hartshorne: 'Consciousness = sort of analysis of perception. <u>Every actual thing = process of taking account of everything else</u>. (Bacon)' (Hartshorne, p. 31).
6. Contextually, an uppercase F for force would be expected here, but Roethlisberger clearly has lowercase.
7. Cf. Hartshorne: 'Stuff explained through forces, i.e. perceptive relations. Electron = identity of structure in a series of occasions' (Hartshorne, p. 31).
8. Hartshorne's notes add to this: 'Vs. Kant. Not via consciousness, but via perceptiveness of experient occasion = way to *perceptum*' (Hartshorne, p. 31).
9. Roethlisberger recorded 'internal' here, but this is almost certainly an error. This interpretation is supported by Hartshorne's notes (Hartshorne, p. 31).
10. See the figure on the right. Hartshorne identifies K as 'any other antecedent occasion' (Hartshorne, p. 32).
11. Cf. Hartshorne: 'In principle, what K is in itself is in E, under mode of remoteness, just as truly as S is in E. Contribution may be very small' (Hartshorne, p. 32).

inspectional relationship along historical route is that character of E will be dominated by the S-ness of the route. The whole inspection of the route. How does this arise in definite knowledge? Primary knowledge is that of your antecedent life.[1]

Direct action in principle because of systematic transmission. Peculiar important relation of contiguity. ~~Direct~~ Inspection of internal character is vague and fuses Presentational and Inspectional relationships

"We perceive individual beings but the true object of perception is the universal man."[2]

(1) we perceive single occasions
(2) we perceive historical route of I⟨ndividual⟩[3]
(3) true object of perception is common "I⟨ndividual⟩"[4]

⟨Tuesday, 17 November 1925⟩

Roethlisberger's notes[5]

|27|

X. <u>Future</u> (copied from PS's notes).[6]

Broad and others say it is nothing at all. But it fills all our thoughts – doctrine of final causes. Yet in some senses the future isn't! A crucial point of traditional empiricism. <u>Hume: the relation of experient occasion to the other occasion is entirely arbitrary. Not to be discerned in either occasion.</u> W:– Doubtless the future <u>is</u> uncertain, but so is the past, and the past is something. So the concept of the future arises from something – if only the verb "will be". "Will be and was" are relations – but of what, and vhowv do we know them?

Is now, will be and was express a definite relation to an immediate occasion. <u>So there must be</u> a relata. <u>Immediate occasion is relation to what?</u> The question

---

1. Hartshorne has a particularly nice turn of phrase here: 'In Knowledge, inspectional relationships are primarily of ourselves to our own antecedent occasions as given in memory' (Hartshorne, p. 32).
2. Cf. Hartshorne: 'Aristotle. Perceive individual beings, but true object of perception = universals' (Hartshorne, p. 32).
3. The bare 'I' seems to refer back to the above figure. Cf. Hartshorne: 'But we <u>also</u> perceive (2) historical route of occasion. (= Aristotle's individual)' (Hartshorne, p. 33).
4. Cf. Hartshorne: 'Whitehead. True object of perception is indeed eternal objects, common enduring structure' (Hartshorne, p. 33).
   This appears to be the end of the 14 November lecture. It is the end of the page for Roethlisberger, and there is a particularly pronounced change in ink quality for Hartshorne.
5. The corresponding Radcliffe lecture can be found on p. 32. Though Roethlisberger provides no date here, he has written '<u>8th week</u>' at the top, which would seem to indicate that this is indeed the beginning of a lecture.
6. There is one student in Whitehead's grading notebook with these initials: Philip Edwin Stanley (1901–63), whose 1928 dissertation was titled 'Hume's doctrine of necessary connection' (see <http://id.lib.harvard.edu/alma/990039714310203941/catalog>). Stanley was hired as a professor of philosophy at Union College in 1927 on the strong recommendation of William Ernest Hocking, where he proved to be a very popular teacher for almost 30 years. He temporarily left Union College in 1943 to serve in as a volunteer during the Second World War (as he was too old to be drafted), achieving the rank of lieutenant-commander upon his discharge in 1945. Stanley then continued to teach at Union College, with an emphasis on Hume and Plato, until he was disabled by a series of strokes in 1957 (Somers, *Encyclopedia of Union College History*, pp. 669–71).

is answered in the present occasion – it points beyond itself. The generality in all occasions is their inclusion in relations – The relative status. Kant up to here, but no further. Kant: general scheme inherent in act of cognition. W:– it is inherent in the experient occasion of which there is cognition. To be related to this occasion is: (1) to be related in this spatio-temporal scheme (2) The immediate occasion via this general scheme determines close community of interrelated occasions.[1] Space-time is not purely contingent to a subjective mind. General knowledge is only in general relatedness.

The general scheme must not be taken too rigidly. Cognition is fitful and inadequate. We discern the immediate occasion as related via general scheme, but other faintly important relations must not be barred out because we can't see them. These other relationship may ⟨evolve⟩[2] into importance to our actual world. The spatio-temporal relations may conceivably have been/∨will be∨[3] of very faint depth and importance and ~~others~~ thus irrelevant. The imaginal occasions are something of this sort. – The indistinct vision of a greater sweep of actuality of which this is but a moment.[4] But we are immediately concerned with an actual world. Generality is dangerous if overemphasized (Plato emphasized mathematics above experiment). Aristotle emphasized the detailed facts in the specificity, which leads to the classificatory logic and hence to mathematics. Plato's mathematics was concerned only with numerical relationships devoid of specific characteristics. Aristotle got rid of mathematics in its theoretical function [Only Plato and Aristotle together give modern science].[5] Aristotle's good sense via geocentric earth – put science back 2000 years.[6] Neither was wholly right or wrong.

Generality tells us of every unit occasion (here, now) and it is a unit in a general community – |28| the togetherness of all disclosed occasions. But the community is not a unity like the actual occasion. The actual occasion is irrevocably finished, but the community is never disclosed as actual and finished. The static philosophy, finished and definite, with the unfinished part merely illusion, seems fake to Whitehead. (Aristotle's being and not being seem right here). The future is only to be expressed as indicating future occasion and is not yet actual, but an entity with a relation to a possibility, and limited in its entry to actuality by a how or limitation. Future occasions have not achieved a definiteness. The future → present → past → by change of its relationship to the eternal objects (What difference if Napoleon had won Waterloo). The

---

1. Hartshorne's notes add to this: '"Our real world" as <u>analyzed</u> (not made) by our knowing, refers to this community or scheme as so determined' (Hartshorne, p. 34).
2. Roethlisberger actually wrote 'evolute' here, but it seems very likely that he meant 'evolve', and Hartshorne's notes confirm it (Hartshorne, p. 34).
3. Slash added. Roethlisberger wrote 'will be' above 'has been', but did not cross out the latter, instead drawing a brace encompassing both verbs, indicating that both apply.
4. Cf. Hartshorne: 'Imaginal occasions (which bring in knowledge) may have a mutual relevance, and to them relation to experient occasion or spatial relations may cease to dominate them. Our Cosmology founded on Space Time actual community does not exclude a deeper cosmos' (Hartshorne, p. 34).
5. Cf. Hartshorne: 'Modern science synthesized both. Neo-Platonists farthest from science' (Hartshorne, p. 35).
6. Cf. Hartshorne: '~~Aristotle~~ Plato saw earth not as Center of universe. An ideal center, mathematically conceived. Aristotle <u>common sense</u> man, put back science 2000 years!' (Hartshorne, p. 35).

actual occasion included the incomplete occasions of the future, which may change, and is sometimes completed by its definite limitation by the eternal objects. Actual occasion includes both being and not being in its process, via the community. Each actual occasion includes the creative determination of the future.

The systematic coherence of future and past has always been presumed by empiricists, but never faced by them.

The details of the future are known in the present on the presumption of specific normality – called in science – "inertia" – endurance in a favorable environment – a community of circumstances which favor each other – presupposing a systematic type of inheritance – Also – the irrelevance of differences in endurance.[1]

⟨Thursday, 19 November 1925⟩

Roethlisberger's notes[2]

|29|

Future – continued

Secluding from philosophy things which are interesting – Not, how is knowledge possible vs. what is it we do know. (2.)[3] What you mean by perceptual object? Perplexity not adequately discussed. "What do we mean by future occasion?" It has something definite about it! Must account for such a simple fact as Coop diary.[4] A metaphysical theory must make sense of future. A future ≠ actual occasion. By future we mean something definite, beyond, not adequately described by present occasion. In any finite scheme, something left ⟨out⟩.[5] Actual analyzed into

1. substantive activity.
2. eternal object.
3. individual achievement.

Yet omitted something in three abstractions. Something can be added to make intelligible. Past is gone as well as future. Past more stuffing than future. Whitehead:–

1. immortality of past
2. definiteness of future

---

1. Hartshorne's notes add: 'But environment is in flux – therefore its variations must be irrelevant to the endurance. Degrees of irrelevance. Here science comes in. Roots of endurance = "world-lines" for science' (Hartshorne, p. 36). We referred to Hartshorne's typed transcription of this material for illegible portions of his handwritten notes (Hartshorne, p. 80) (see Introduction).
   This appears to be the end of the 17 November lecture. Roethlisberger leaves half a page blank, and there is a very noticeable change in ink quality for Hartshorne.
2. The corresponding Radcliffe lecture can be found on p. 33. There do not appear to be any Hartshorne notes for this lecture.
3. Roethlisberger seems to have later added '(2.)'. Its meaning is unclear.
4. Referring to the Harvard Coop Diary (self-described as 'a handy bound pocket calendar' provided to students and faculty at Harvard).
5. Supplied from the Heath notes (p. 33).

(2) is so by reason of (1), and past is immortal because it survives in future. Past occasions are VnotV (1) additions to realm of eternal objects,[1] not (2) immediately actual. <u>Present is immediately actual, past immortally actual, and future definitely actual</u>. Past is not merely qualified by <u>present</u> – Whitehead – escapes reference to present. Past and Future not anchored to present occasion. [<u>Present occasion is, however, qualified by past and future occasions.</u>] – by something which has actuality beyond itself. Because of this qualification, it is a process.

A's essence is modified by f, ⟨blank⟩[2]

Objects for A are synthesized in A so that it could not be what it is if ⟨blank⟩[3]

From A to F is a <u>necessary requirement</u> to immediate actuality of A, i.e. a process. Relationship to other occasions <u>subsequent</u> to A and <u>antecedent</u> to A are not determined until actualized. F, though definite, has not yet received <u>adequate</u> determination, for to be immediately actual requires to be in a definite realized relationship to all antecedent entities. Immediately actuality of F requires immortal actuality of antecedent occasions.

Immortal act of past. Creative activity from its achievement. The metaphor of the watchmaker and watch is wrong ("<u>The true ship is the ship builder</u>" – Emerson).[4] Language unfitted to express what I want. Achievement is character of achieving, and achieving has transformed itself as antecedent of its achievement. |30| No finished <u>creation</u>. If creative activity passes into creature, it passes beyond itself. Creatured creation ⟨blank⟩

Immortality of past is definite character impressed upon it by creative activity, and it is this creative activity which gives it its definiteness.

Static error = error finished creation.

[<u>Something you deplore and something you don't know anything about.</u> – Bradley's absolute]. What primarily evolves is <u>creative activity</u>. This general achieving is the community as one – character evolved in its achievements – activity in evolution. <u>Future is a fact in creativeness</u>.

A is individual embodiment of whole creative activity – and in embodiment is a definite transition to F. What is actual by being A <u>does not pass</u>.[5]

---

1. Comma supplied. There is a space here that suggests punctuation; also, it seems probable that Roethlisberger added *both* instances of 'not' in this sentence, even though it is visually only the first one that is obviously a later insertion.
2. In Heath's notes, 'a' is a past occasion and 'f' is a future occasion modifying it. Heath's notes add to this statement that 'therefore ⟨this⟩ is a relation (internal) to $\underline{a}$' (p. 33). Readers are advised to refer to Heath's notes for this section, which are more complete on this point. Note that Roethlisberger shifts from the lowercase 'f' to an uppercase 'F' in the subsequent paragraph. It is not clear whether the shift is significant or intentional.
3. Cf. Heath: '($\underline{A}$) could not be what it is apart from its relationships to ($\underline{f}$)' (p. 33).
4. Emerson, 'History', p. 15, available at <https://archive.org/details/essays20emergoog>.
5. This appears to be the end of the 19 November lecture. The determination had to be made through comparison with the Heath notes only, since Hartshorne missed this lecture. However, the content for both matches up fairly neatly, and Roethlisberger leaves more than half a page blank, which strongly suggests a lecture break here.

Harvard lectures, fall semester 1925

⟨Saturday, 21 November 1925⟩
Roethlisberger's notes[1]

|31|
XI. Epochal Theory of Time

Creativity and creature cannot be separated. Spinoza {*Natura naturans* v(atomicity)v and *natura naturata* v(continuity)v[2]}. Watchmaker simile false because he may sell the watch. Creature remains in the creativity. What essentially becomes other is creativity. Creature passes over to another. Always another creativity, hence creature. Process. Time becomes an illusion if you fail to consider both together. When you take creativity alone, you get the creator a finished product. Start with absolute and you end with a determined world. Whitehead does not use creator as it refers to a definite determined entity. Creativity is creativity in an occasion. Individual embodiment. Creativity for this occasion. Thereby modifies itself. If time is not ⟨i⟩llusion,[3] you need nature as created, vand whichv is never complete and always other than itself. In this Whitehead finds immortality of past. This definite character of creativity attained by the past is the definiteness of future. Future not actually determined for immediate actuality, only for definite actuality.

Present – What achieves actuality in present. Epochal theory of time. Not a graduality of becoming – (Kant's *Critique* p. 177–8. "Extensive quantity and intensive quantity")[4]

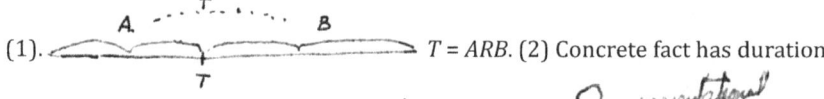

(1). $T = ARB$. (2) Concrete fact has duration

Hence concrete occasion has a time depth, gradual but not a gradual becoming, and becomingness is epochal.

What becomes is. Time is becomingness.

Three reasons for this view.

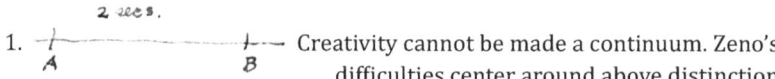

1. Creativity cannot be made a continuum. Zeno's difficulties center around above distinction.

---

1. The corresponding Radcliffe lecture can be found on p. 34. There do not appear to be any Hartshorne notes for this lecture.
2. Parentheses added for 'atomicity' and 'continuity'.
3. Roethlisberger has 'allusion' here, but it seems clear that he means 'illusion'.
4. Referring to Kant's *Critique of Pure Reason*. While Roethlisberger has the reference as pp. 177–8, Heath has it as p. 147. It is possible that they are referring to different editions, but we think it more likely that Roethlisberger simply copied down the reference incorrectly, as we cannot find a pre-1924 edition for which this page reference would make sense. Heath's reference is to the second part of Friedrich Max Müeller's 1881 translation of the *Critique*, specifically to the section on 'Anticipations of Perception'. See Kant, *Critique of Pure Reason*, available at <https://archive.org/details/immanuelkantscr07kantgoog>.

Infinite number of steps from *A.B.* 1 + ½ + ¼ + ⅛ + ...
No Achilles at an instant.¹ Before *A* can reach
C, ½ has to be realized, etc. Zeno's difficulties not
a mathematical one. Main one is "something has to become real". An occasion
has to have a time depth. Arrow at an instant. Not can't get out of place,
but can't get out of <u>time</u>. <u>To make becomingness gradual involves a vicious regression</u>. Difficulty not quantitative, but qualitative.

Time viewed as expressing an abstraction of *natura naturans* as <u>epochal</u> and *natura naturata* (as continuous?)

2. Creature requires a time-depth. Creativity and creature cannot be divorced. Creativity is pure act. If creature wants time-depth, then becomingness must have time depth and time is epochal.

3. From consideration of science. Founded on both continuity and atomicity. Science needs both. Cannot exclude one or another. Each has a status.

Tuesday, 24 November 1925
Roethlisberger's notes²

|32| General question: what categories characterize in general things known? If epochal theory is true, how vhasv it becomes obscured. ① Time is a relation among actual things. [<u>Immediate becoming is epochal, and</u> ② <u>as extensive element among things actual is continuous</u>].³ Distinction between these two views of time. Double aspect of time haunts philosophers.⁴ "<u>For the well-educated man, life presents no problems</u>".

(1) Basis of Descartes' view arises from notion of enduring substances (1) to be actual is to be individual substance? When you ask this, you mean what primary substance are you talking about. Actual occasion is actual by having something to do with actual substances.⁵

(2) To be actual is to endure through time, and this is inherent of any actual substance. Each substance given with its endurance. Actual individual substance is substance as in an epoch of its life history. Epoch belongs to substance and constitutes actuality.

(3) Each substance is primarily given with its endurance.

(4) Implicit⁶ (common epoch is correlation of individual epochs) Is a concern of actual entities for each other. (*ad aliquid*) – to something else. Actual substance as given is an element in *natura naturata* – substance is not a

---

1. This refers to Zeno's paradox of Achilles and the tortoise.
2. For the first time since 6 October, Roethlisberger has provided a date. This was the last lecture prior to Thanksgiving, on 26 November. The corresponding Radcliffe lecture can be found on p. 36.
3. Cf. Hartshorne: 'Immediate actuality is epochal, but world as actualized is continuous. Time as immediate becoming, and time as VanV extensionality of things which have become' (Hartshorne, p. 36).
4. Cf. Hartshorne: 'Time as measurable and as *durée* haunts all philosophy. Descartes slips this in unconsciously. He holds becomingness is gradual, but this implies an epochal becomingness' (Hartshorne, p. 36).
5. Cf. Hartshorne: 'Actual occasion = a system of substances' (Hartshorne, p. 36).
6. Instead of 'implicit', Hartshorne has: '(Here slipped in naively)' (Hartshorne, p. 37).

85

becoming, but what has already become. There is α as instants as R. of epochs and ⟨blank⟩[1]

Problem of time becomes correlation of substance $\underline{A}$ to time t_A, and substance B to time t_B - Correlation in abstract of an instant t. According to this view, there is epochal view of time inadequately defined. In dealing with S. You are considering a portion of life history. If to exist is to endure.

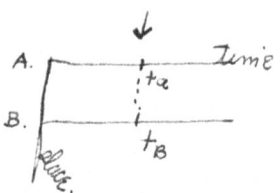

Problem of becomingness or process is obscured by doctrine of multiplicity of enduring substance as ultimate entities. In taking S as ultimate; you have jumped problem of continual becomingness – an inc gives us no natural epoch. Whitehead holds Zeno did not do himself justice?[2]

|33| Zeno obscured problem by formulation. How is process possible if production is gradual and if that which is produced is actual? is Zeno's big question.

Aristotle has process, scholastics emphasize substance over process although retaining the same, finally Descartes and followers drop process and take over substance. Whitehead starts with process, the physical occasion. Aristotle tried to reconcile both – process and substance. Broad and Russell revive Cartesian substance in sensa[3] and this "being = being actual" supercedes process. For W – the sensa (eternal objects) are only factors in actuality of functioning-through-time.[4]

Saturday, 28 November 1925

Roethlisberger's notes[5]

|34|

XII. Scientific Theories (starting 17th century)

Correlating epochal theory of time with science. Scientific Theories commencing with 17th century. Descartes a good representative of his age,

---

1. It appears that Roethlisberger missed some material. Hartshorne has here: 'α) Definition of instants. (Kant: a limit) β) correlation of instants. Each substance its own instant. t = correlation of instants (private to each substance)' (Hartshorne, p. 37).
2. Cf. Hartshorne: 'Really an epoch-view here, only lack of natural epochs provides no ground for refuting Zeno. Zeno should not have asked how arrow gets from one position to another, but how does arrow in its quiver get from one occasion to another' (Hartshorne, p. 37).
3. The entire second half of Broad's *Scientific Thought* is devoted to a discussion of sensa, i.e. 'Part II: The Sensational and Perceptual Basis of Our Scientific Concepts'. See Broad, *Scientific Thought*, available at <https://archive.org/details/in.ernet.dli.2015.6694>.
4. The words 'Important in showing Whitehead's approach' appear in the left margin here with a brace referring to this final paragraph. Cf. Hartshorne for this last sentence: 'Functional point of view provides for natural epochs. Functioning through time = the thing itself. Completion of function is required for entity which is actual. Physical existence = essentially vibratory (to speak in terms of . . .' (Hartshorne, p. 37). Hartshorne presumably completed his incomplete parenthetical comment on the following page, but that page is missing.
5. The corresponding Radcliffe lecture can be found on p. 37. There are no Hartshorne notes for this lecture (in fact, there are no more Hartshorne notes until 10 December).

hence invaluable. Idea of matter as constituting external world. Changing qualities of table and essential attribute as extension. Next step by Galileo and Newton. Addition of "mass" – new quantitative aspect following Pythagorean tradition. Mass is something you can measure. "Mass is quantity of matter" – Newton. Study of spatio-temporal behavior of matter. This point of view makes it difficult to explain transmission theories. – Newtons corpuscles and other. Leads to bifurcation between behavior of matter and knowing mind. Then comes Newton's laws of motion. Mass × acceleration = Force. Force is another aspect of behavior √of matter√ for Newton – matter as regulating behavior. Both sides of dynamical equation correspond to Spinoza's *natura naturata* and *natura naturans*[1] – How does force spring from matter? Nature as behaving vs nature as regulating behavior. Matter enters both in the creating and the creature.

How is there a force between two bits of matter (1) ⟨F?⟩ is rate of <u>transfer of momentum</u> (*mv*) This is billiard ball theory (2) <u>stress and strain idea</u>: Arises from stretching of piece of elastic (3) <u>Action at a distance</u>. Science has always revolted against this idea. One piece of chalk cannot affect another without something in between to transmit the force.

$G = \lambda \frac{Mm}{d^2}$. In case of apple and earth, what is *d*?

Tuesday, 1 December 1925 ⟨and Thursday, 3 December 1925⟩
Roethlisberger's notes[2]

<u>Descartes</u> – matter
<u>Galileo</u> – mass, matter as measurable
<u>Newton</u> – laws of motion
A. Importance of Cartesian view in development of science[3]

Enormous merit of this way of thought is "<u>departmental clearness</u>". All properties of matter explained in terms of mass, force, etc. Corresponding defect is that synthesis of compartments is impossible. "<u>Synoptic arbitrariness</u>". "<u>Anti-rationalistic bias</u>" – to obtain a general view of world is foolish. Authority of mediaeval age was the authority of a <u>harmonious whole</u>, a successful harmony – successful fusion of Aristotelean doctrines with Christian religion. Harmony did not meet the fact. Revolt against harmony. Let us view the facts. But says Whitehead, facts are not <u>departmental</u>. All your departments in some relation.

---

1. There are a pair of lines connecting these two underlined terms and the 'Mass × acceleration = Force' equation above. Specifically, there is a line connecting '*natura nauturata*' with 'acceleration', and '*natura naturans*' with 'Force'.
2. This 1 December date is the last that we get from Roethlisberger for a while (until 17 December), and both Hartshorne and Heath seem to have missed the lectures on 1 and 3 December, leaving us with a dearth of clues for discerning where the 1 December lecture ends and the 3 December lecture begins. Based on the amount of material present in relation to Roethlisberger's other notes taken around this time, we do believe that the following material probably constitutes two lectures rather than one.
3. This heading appears in the left margin with a brace referring to the entire paragraph following.

|35|

B. Arbitrariness in Cartesian system
- (1) Arbitrariness of relation between matter and mind.
- (2) Matter with mass and then relation between bits of matter, where do forces come from?[1]
- (3) Matter as extension (divisible). Capable of subdivisions. Concrete fact shows atomism + extension.
- (4) Difference <u>between</u> organism and matter or function ~~of~~ VandV matter. Inadequate to explain life.

What is <u>force</u>?[2] Entirely arbitrary. Human difficulty. Newton – force = relation between two bits of matter. Three ways of considering stress: (1) action at a distance (2) interchange of momentum (3) introducing ether as a medium. Some entity related to some definite entity when there is a stress; otherwise force means <u>nothing</u>. [Time is becoming, something becoming, if what becomes is continuous, earlier part comes before later. – but "nothing" definitely becomes] Same with force.

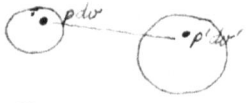

(1) No scientist for last 50 years believes in action at a distance.[3]

(2) But what is "push" acting on?[4] Whitehead does not question "push" but adequacy of concept "<u>force</u>". You never can find "the" bit of matter force is acting <u>on</u>. A relation must have <u>relata</u>. What is it? "<u>There ain't any</u>".

(3) Rise of differential calculus[5] ≈ rise of physics. Newton gives a hazy statement where clear statement is <u>needed</u>. Leibniz wasn't hazy, but <u>wrong</u>. – You do have infinitesimal entities – Leibniz way ahead of the <u>analysis</u> of principles. – 17th century – Theory of infinitesimals blown to pieces by <u>Weierstrass</u>.[6] Makes Newton clear at <u>hazy</u> point. You only deal with finite entities, something which is true about each one of these <u>entities</u>.

We come to an atomic theory of matter[7] – ⟨Dalton⟩.[8] This, however, did not cause a revolt of Newtonian mechanics.

---

1. '1. Extended matter' and '2. Mass' appear in pencil in the left margin next to (1) and (2) here, which are almost certainly additional headings that Roethlisberger added some time after the lecture was over. We have relegated these two added headings and the four others following to footnotes, as they are not only superfluous, but also compete with the original hierarchy of headings in a confusing way.
2. '3. Force' appears in the left margin here.
3. See the figure on the left.
4. See the second figure on the left.
5. '4. Differential Calculus' appears in the left margin here.
6. The German mathematician Karl Theodor Wilhelm Weierstrass (1815–97) was a major contributor to modern analysis during the 19th century, concerned (among other issues) with the soundness of calculus.
7. '5. Atomic Theory of matter' appears in the left margin here.
8. Roethlisberger wrote 'Galton', but Whitehead is almost certainly referring to the English chemist John Dalton (1766–1844).

|37|[1] But here we have another example of <u>arbitrariness</u>. You cannot mention, with ⟨decency?⟩,[2] a part of an atom.

According to Newtonian and Cartesian point of view, with extensiveness and theory of space starts with notion that the part explains the <u>whole</u>. Leads to the Zeno difficulty. No natural whole is provided by VaV concept. "<u>Science is getting to natural wholes</u>"

(2) Theory starts with (1) extended mass as passive subject of external activity. It functions because it is made to function from without –

(2) activity – fact of functioning arises from external relations. Relation of force to matter has certain arbitrariness. <u>Conclusion</u>. Activity lies in the <u>motion</u> – This leads to collision theory.

C. Concept of Energy.[3]

Another definite physical quantity, apparently indestructible. You get idea of energy of position (Potential Energy). What is potential energy? Two particles tied to the end of an elastic. Energy arises from stretching of elastic. General idea from compression, extension and torsion arises from distortion of some medium (strain). <u>Potential Energy</u> – you need a vehicle for your potential energy – strain energy of some intervening medium –

Joule's experiment in 1850.[4]

Energy has been a quantitative property, but it is not <u>individual</u>. Individualization of energy creeps into science.

Scientist (1) makes definite what is vaguely familiar (2) elucidatory power.

Whole upshot leads to: Have we correct relationship between matter and energy? Isn't latter more fundamental? Mass becomes another name for quantity of <u>energy</u>. Measured in other units. Where mass starts from <u>inertia</u>; energy starts from <u>activity</u>. Here is entire <u>inversion</u>.

⟨Saturday, 5 December 1925⟩
Roethlisberger's notes[5]

|38|

<u>Summary</u>:

Descartes "<u>extended material</u>," some sense to be made of it. Newton said it had "<u>mass</u>". You have no natural unit: Leads to Zeno difficulties. Essence of

---

1. Note that page 36 is skipped. It appears that this was a numbering error on Roethlisberger's part, rather than a missing page.
2. What Roethlisberger actually has here is 'deceny'; 'decency' is the most likely correction, with Whitehead perhaps making a wry joke similar to his frequent reference to half a sheep being mutton (see next lecture, p. 90).
3. '6. Energy' appears in the left margin here.
4. The referenced experiment by James Prescott Joule (1818–89) attempted to measure the mechanical equivalent of heat. Joule, 'On the mechanical equivalent of heat', available at <https://archive.org/stream/philtrans00608634/00608634>.
5. The corresponding Radcliffe lecture can be found on p. 38. We believe this to be the beginning of the 5 December lecture due to similarities with Heath's notes (e.g., their discussion of divisibility, Dalton and granite) and to a certain amount of blank space being left at the bottom of the previous page.

Newton's idea of mass is expressed by "inertia". What looks as inertia is derivative from a more fundamental concentration of "energy". Concept has shifted to activity. Half way on to a concept of "function". Still energy is distributed through volume. Yet here arise mathematical difficulties. You cannot add the energy of two electrons. But simplicity of extended material and simple location knocked to pieces. Your energy is distributed throughout space. Energy-concept blurs sharpness of location.

Electro-magnetic theory of matter — ext⟨ended⟩ matter is regarded as electrical.

C. Rise of atomic theory.

(1) Chemistry[1]

Start with John ⟨Dalton⟩.[2] Democritus clears away rubbish — "hard-headed" — otherwise not very clear, workable stating of atomic theory. ⟨Dalton⟩. Matter is essentially atomic — spatially extended. Half an atom is still extended and of same genus as of an atom (whole). (Half a sheep is mutton — idea of atomic theory) analysis of atom into something of a different genus. [Descartes — analysis gives same genus — Whitehead — objection]. If you divide into two, you have to explain how two parts hold together. Quantity of each material turn up as multiple of definite units. Leads to 90 elements.

---

(2) Physics[3]

Electro-magnetic theory of matter gives atoms of electricity — proton and electron. On such a theory you build up an atom by solar systems. You bind positive atoms by negative atoms, thus obtaining a nucleus.

What is size of atom?

Radius of orbit? (10^{-8}) Energy of electron = $\dfrac{ke^2}{a}$,

Mass $\dfrac{ke^2}{a}$, $\dfrac{ke^2}{b}$

$\dfrac{ke^2}{a} = m \quad \dfrac{a}{b} = 1700$
$\dfrac{ke^2}{b} = 1700 \quad a = 1700b$

Huge bloated electron is "b" and (little mass) with wee wee "a" (with enormous mass).

Atom has turned into an organism. Reduced species from 90 to 2. Function of electric atom makes material atom. New difficulties, law of attraction between bits of matter. Out of electron and how parts do not explode becomes a mystery — Analysis of electric atom into parts, you ought to find something else.

---

3. Biology[4]

Ultimate unity of ⱽorganicⱽ matter is cell. Life is functioning of the cell. Atomism rises in science from all sides in 19th century.

---

1. This heading appears in the left margin.
2. See note 8, p. 88.
3. This heading appears in the left margin.
4. This heading appears in the left margin.

History of a particle of granite. Not always the same. Respectable travel, then a flash of energy, then a relapse into passiveness. Where does energy come from? ① Intrinsic energy of a and b (mass energy) ② kinetic energy of a ③ kinetic energy of molecule as a whole. Disturbance of orbit a into another orbit, allowing flash of energy $E_1 - E_2$. But you can only obtain an atomic amount of energy released. Why? Only can obtain integral multiples of a constant amount.[1]

⟨Tuesday, 8 December 1925⟩
Roethlisberger's notes[2]

|39|
D. <u>Atomic Theory and Quantum Theory.</u>
  (1) Chemical atoms (92) species
  (2) Atomic primates – 2 species, protons and electrons ⊕ ⊖
  (3) Atoms of action – 1 species, quantum of action – "h"
What do we mean by an "atom" and what relation ~~by~~ ∨between∨ species? – Two observations lead to two diametrically opposed laws, conceptions.

Atomic primate is a nucleus of protons bound together by electrons. – Physicists are in favor of "solar system"; chemists are doubtful. Picture of chemist is an odd way of tending toward the truth. Merit of solar-system point of view is that fundamental element is not <u>static</u>. "a definite structure of happenings". Aggregation of periodic happenings. Series of periods.

Primates regarded as a concentration of energy. Energy can only be explained in terms of activity. Energetic view illustrates metaphysical principle that *natura naturans* and *natura naturata* are <u>inseparable</u>. Story about "<u>take that silly smile off your face</u>".

	Proton	Electron
Charge	+e	–e
Radius	b	a
Mass	M	m

c = velocity of light *in vacuo*.
Principle of simplicity – take the simplest ideas that work.

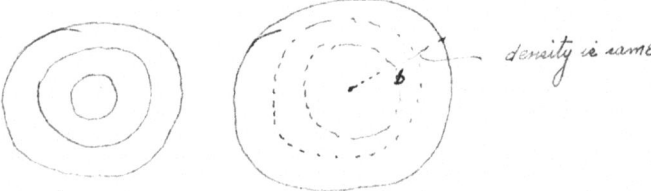
density is same.

---
1. This appears to be the end of the 5 December lecture.
2. The corresponding Radcliffe lecture can be found on p. 39. Note that while there is matching content between the two lectures, parts of them do not align particularly well. For example, Heath's notes have '*natura naturans* and *natura naturata*' right at the beginning, while Roethlisberger has this same phrase nearer the middle of the lecture. It seems that once again the Harvard and Radcliffe lectures may have been getting a little out of synchronisation.

N is ~~found~~ ∨some∨ one number

$M = M = N \dfrac{e^2}{c^2 b}$

$m = 1 \quad N \dfrac{e^2}{c^2 a}$

$M = 1700\, m$

$a = 1700\, b$

Why is proton spherical? Allows you to illustrate doctrine of similarity. Allows you to make math computations – most neutral form – so simple that it is easily calculable.[1]

⟨Thursday, 10 December 1925⟩

Roethlisberger's notes[2]

|40| Where is the energy located? <u>Everywhere</u>. Distribution of energy all over space. Energy structure which theoretically extends throughout space, although for practical purposes it is surrounding electron $e \propto \dfrac{1}{r^4}$.

Vortex theory fails.[3] (1) it does not work in detail[4] (2) You have to give matter many odd properties (3) it doesn't give you hint of relativity or quantum theory (Piece of cork in middle of ocean illustrates ∨focal∨ structure extending throughout water).

Reverse:– space being qualified by charge in field. Modern physicist:– spatial and temporal properties as an abstraction of the concrete charge. – (Whitehead).[5]

③ Third atomic genus – quantum of action.[6]

periodicity' $T_1, T_2, T_3, T_4 \cdots T_n'$ $\quad T_1', T_2', T_3', T_4' \cdots T_n'$ $\qquad$ Period $= \dfrac{1}{\text{frequency}}$
$\qquad\quad e_{1}, e_{2}, e_{3}, e_{4}$ $\quad M$-atom $\qquad N$-atom

You study atom by studying light it emits ~~or light it absorbs~~. Amount of energy which you can obtain will always be an integral number of eq_1 or eq_2.[7]

---

1. This appears to be the end of the 8 December lecture.
2. The corresponding Radcliffe lecture can be found on p. 40. For this date we have corresponding Hartshorne notes, the first since 24 November. Though Hartshorne's notes here are quite sparse, they are dated 10 December, and hence allow us to date Roethlisberger's notes definitively.
3. This is likely referring to the late 19th-century theory popular with British physicists that an atom was a vortex in ether.
4. Hartshorne also has the numbers (1), (2), and (3), but there is no text following the two latter numbers. For (1), he has: 'In detail becomes so arbitrarily complicated. Ether becomes <u>so</u> complex' (Hartshorne, p. 38).
5. Note that in the Radcliffe lecture, around this point Whitehead discusses Irving Langmuir (1881–1957), saying that he is 'near to Irving Langmuir' (p. 41). Whitehead may well have been referring to Langmuir's famous article 'The arrangement of electrons in atoms and molecules'.
6. Hartshorne's notes add to this: 'Only <u>one species</u>' (Hartshorne, p. 38).
7. Cf. Hartshorne: 'One finds that in emitting energy (e.g., light), can only get energy-changes as multiples of a given amount' (Hartshorne, p. 38).

Is there any relation between <u>period and quantity of energy</u> $e_q = \frac{h}{T}$, $e_q \times T = \underline{h}$. h is the same for every kind of molecule. There is not a different h for *Na*, *H*, etc. h is the <u>quantum of action</u>.[1] Physicist's nightmare is "little h"!. "Little h" insists on having a time-depth. It's an activity through a time – not at an instant. Action seems to have an atomicity. As you concentrate in time, you gain in energy. Concentration of time increases energy. Quantitative aspects of nature arise out of concentration or limitation of the impress. Spatial and temporal aspect of VisV quantification is an aspect of creative impress. Cq = intensive side T = extensive side. h = essentially one (atomic). eqT = essentially <u>continuous</u>. h is analyzed into components of structure. eqT more abstract than concrete physical entity "h".

Community is not more abstract than the entities, and the entities are not more abstract than the community.

⟨Saturday, 12 December 1925⟩
Roethlisberger's notes[2]

|41|
E. <u>Relation of "little h" to Whitehead's metaphysics</u>
   You cannot sunder the individual from the community.
   You cannot sunder the objective from the subjective.
   You cannot sunder the creature from the creativity.
   Each individual is an element in a community and the community involves in itself a principle of unit[3] multiplicities. To be perceived is to be an element in community for the other. It is perceiving the community. Space and time exhibit ⟨the⟩ individual in itself. There is a pattern which has relationships to different parts of space and time. Space and space-time is being described from ⟨a⟩ too-limited point of view.
   Each individual actual occasion is immortal; creature qualifies creativity. Immortality and causation are same thing. Each individual is subject to the immortality of other beings – Everything enters into everything else. Persistent difficulty: You cannot have finite truths apparently. You can say something (Whitehead). <u>You cannot say something about individual without saying something about community. How things are apart and brought together under limitation. See *Science and Modern World*, p. 66.</u>[4]

---

1. Hartshorne's notes add that this quantum of action is '(Planck's quantum)' (Hartshorne, p. 38).
2. There are no Heath or Hartshorne notes for this lecture. However, we can guess that these notes are from Whitehead's 12 December lecture with a relatively high degree of certainty, because we have Heath notes for the *following* class session, and these match up with Roethlisberger's next few pages.
3. The word 'unit' is very clear in Roethlisberger's notes. It is difficult to discern whether it is meant as an abbreviation for 'unity' or some other variation.
4. This reference is to the middle of Chapter 3 of *Science and the Modern World*, 'The century of genius'. The first line at the top reads 'the concept of an ideally isolated system', which Whitehead acknowledges is necessary for science and knowledge, but that is 'not a solipsist system, apart from which there would be nonentity'. *Science and the Modern World* was hot off the presses, having been published and printed in late October. Curtice Hitchcock, Whitehead's contact at his publisher, Macmillan, sent him a letter in

Space = *R* (Creatures)
Time = *R* (Creativities)
Time has two meanings: ① ordering of creative acts vatomicv, and each creative act is conditioned by immortality of actual community ② ordering of creatures as a development from creative acts. In this second way time is divisible and continuous. Epochs in continuum refer to creative acts (time as becoming is epochal; time as having become is continuous).

Space and time express how exclusion is possible, how isolation of eternal objects may be maintained (the world of possibility = world of eternal objects). Isolation does not effect togetherness nor togetherness, isolation.

⟨Tuesday, 15 December 1925⟩

Roethlisberger's notes[1]

|42|
I. Theory of Knowledge
From experient to imaginal occasion. Philosophy of last 130 years. "How is knowledge possible" is the fundamental approach to metaphysics. Not way Plato and Aristotle approached. Origin vof problemv starts with breakdown of Cartesian system. Prime assumption:– drop process and assume that world was an aggregate of individual substances with attributes. Relational side of world minimized. Endurance an attribute of individual substance. Public and private time? How about common space? Cogitations are attributes of mental substances. But what about cogitations about other substances? Answer to all these questions and how is knowledge possible? To answer in terms of Cartesian – all publicity fails to be explained. You say cogitations refer to other substances. But what is relation?

How is publicity possible? – Descartes' question.

Answer:– What knowledge is – a description in terms of your metaphysics. You have weighted your criticism unless you criticize the terms in which you begin. First give a description of the first things known. Tests:– ① Refer your test to various specialized fields of thought. ② By their coherence with each other ③ By their adequacy – do they include everything we know about? Should be a possible description of knowledge in terms of those primary categories.

How are we going to describe *k* in terms of the categories we have been thinking by? Principle: You cannot hold apart nature as self-created from nature as a creature. Creativity is pure act. Whatever you assign to creativity is to be found in a creature. Knowledge as a creature is real and actual. Actualization of answer: How the creature is created? You're asking something

---
the first week of November that *Science and the Modern World* 'was duly published last week'. Hitchcock, 'Letter to Alfred North Whitehead', 4 November 1925.
1. The corresponding Radcliffe lecture can be found on p. 42. There do not appear to be any Hartshorne notes for this lecture.

Harvard lectures, fall semester 1925

about creativity: $\xrightarrow{\text{creativity}}$ E. How E? But the "how" is behind the veil. E is the superject. The "how" is another occasion. Knowledge is attainment of value by fusing experient occasion with elements that have gone before me. It is exemplification as an actual value.

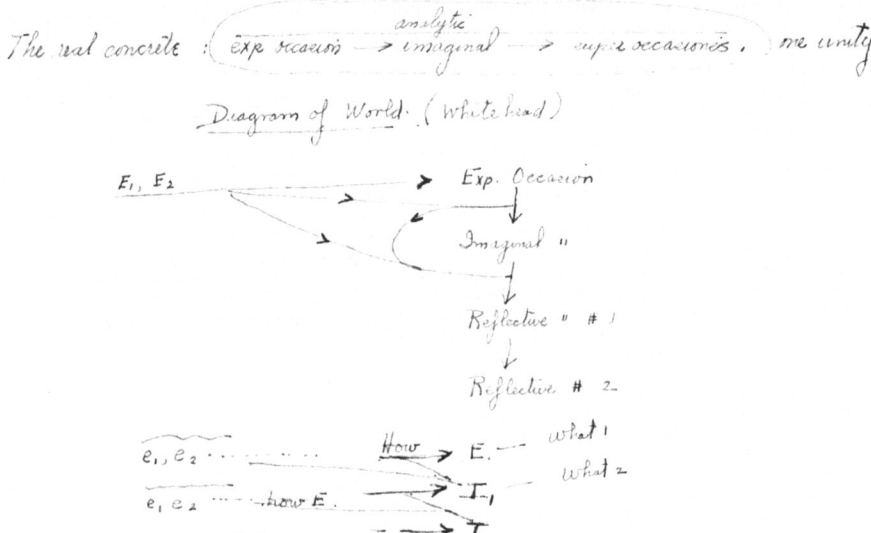

The imaginal occasion is one; duality is ⟨?⟩[1] there is perceptive ego with multiplicity of details.[2] You can get higher types of knowing occasion.
|43|

Envisagement is an attribute of creativity. Envisagement is conditioning creativity by (1) realm of eternal objects (2) immortality of past (when Whitehead talks of past as conditioning creativity, he regards as immortal) (3) by particular environment in question (4) by inheritance to contiguity via historical route (5) ...?..[3] by references to Future and Present. Envisagement two-fold (1) of eternal objects (2) of actual world. Experient occasion is creature conditioned by elements envisaged with such freedom as you ascribe to you⟨r⟩ creative activity. Experient occasion is analyzed (1) envisaged

---

1. There is an indecipherable character here. It appears that Roethlisberger lost the thread of the sentence.
2. Due to textual ambiguity, we have inserted the above figure along with one line of accompanying text. Note that we have repeated one line of this text to clarify where the image leaves off and our transcription begins.
3. Heath has the same list of five items (albeit with some differences). Her item 5, which Roethlisberger apparently felt he did not completely catch, is 'General influence of future' (p. 42).

elements (2) free ∨selective∨ determination. Reflexive synthesis of occasion with analytic elements: that synthesis = knowledge = imaginal occasion. Not a perfect synthesis – room for error and ignorance.

Thursday, 17 December 1925
Roethlisberger's notes[1]

|44| Knowledge is an epiphenomenon. Philosophy is a pretentious attempt. Comes from the fact that ultimate obviousness must be pretentious. Absence of convenient phraseology (habitual). Technical language has danger as "explanatory phrase." Retention of obvious facts in right relations to one another. Paradox in history of culture.

Attempt to give in <u>general terms the obvious facts of knowledge</u>. (1) dependence on bodily senses (2) knowledge ∨arises∨ is going on within body – psychology is not of great importance to metaphysics (3) knowledge is in some way distinct from what is going on within body – (fact and knowledge of fact are distinct).

General principle: <u>Knowledge is actual occasion arising from given (datum) occasion</u>. Datum is function of body. Knowledge is comparison of datum with realm of abstractions. The comparison enters as a natural fact. It makes exemplification real. It makes realization that fact is so (experient occasion being so-and-so) is realized – into a value. – James: there is no <u>stuff</u> which is thinking-perceiving subject but body is accompanied by a function of knowing. [One of first to twist around.][2]

Whitehead: in physics, <u>stuff</u> also goes. – occasion of consciousness is to be treated in same way as physical occasion – Experient occasion is first being in physics. Imaginal occasion is first brick in theory of knowledge. Not to be explained in terms of a stuff. [Every new idea goes through two stages].

Epiphenomenon derivative from function of matter, but distinct from it – Tyndall's answer.[3] to consciousness. You should observe your philosophical facts – not mere counters without observation.

---

1. There do not appear to be any Heath or Hartshorne notes for this lecture. Roethlisberger provides a date for this lecture, the first time he has done so since 1 December.
2. Opening bracket supplied.
3. Whitehead is likely referring to John Tyndall's 1868 address to the Mathematical and Physical Section of the British Association at Norwich, entitled 'Scientific materialism', reprinted in *Fragments of Science*, a collection of Tyndall's essays that proved to be very popular; by 1879 it was in its sixth edition. A relevant excerpt is the following: 'The passage from the physics of the brain to the corresponding facts of consciousness is inconceivable as a result of mechanics. Granted that a definite thought, and a definite molecular action in the brain, occur simultaneously; we do not possess the intellectual organ, nor apparently any rudiment of the organ, which would enable us to pass, by a process of reasoning, from the one to the other. They appear together, but we do not know why. Were our minds and senses so expanded, strengthened, and illuminated, as to enable us to see and feel the very molecules of the brain . . . and were we intimately acquainted with the corresponding states of thought and feeling, we should still be as far as ever from the solution of the problem, "How are these physical processes connected with the facts of consciousness?"' (Tyndall, 'Scientific materialism', pp. 86–7, available at <https://archive.org/details/fragmentsofscien02tyndrich>).

An assumption in epiphenomenon, you call it an ideal real which can be dismissed as not important. Denies assumption of interconnection of things – a scientific principle. Only relations important are relations[1] among bits of matter. Why? You can express facts of nature without any reference to mentality – This is what Whitehead means by mind is closed to nature. There are finite truths which can be expressed without reference to mind [McDougall on Mental Evolution].[2]

Higher is always to be explained in terms of lower? Why – arbitrary postulate.

Saturday, 19 December 1925

Roethlisberger's notes[3]

|45|

1. Whitehead agrees with James in that there is no conscious or cogitating-stuff.[4] Prior to any metaphysical discussion "Nature is a ⟨rum'un⟩." – Dickens.[5] Erroneousness of knowledge has to be explained.

Imaginal occasion is different from experient occasion – is distinguishable – fundamental entity dipolar: experient occasion ↔ imaginal occasion. Analysis of experient occasion is not into other actual entities, but in the data for its

---

1. Roethlisberger has written 'R' here, which we have expanded as 'relations'. It is of course possible that 'relationships' or some other variant was intended.
2. Whitehead is likely referring to McDougall, *Body and Mind*, available at <https://archive.org/details/bodymindhistorya01mcdo>. William McDougall occupied the William James chair of psychology at Harvard from 1920 to 1927. Since philosophy and psychology were grouped into the same department in the 1920s, Whitehead would have had at least a casual acquaintance with McDougall. (In fact, it was McDougall's empty apartment in Radnor Hall which provided the Whiteheads with temporary accommodation upon their arrival in Cambridge on 28 August 1924, and they liked it so well that they ended up renting an apartment in the same building. See Lowe, *Alfred North Whitehead, Vol. II*, p. 138. McDougall is mentioned a few times in Whitehead's appointment book earlier in the term; once for 24 October (he wrote simply 'McDougalls', for what seems likely to be a social engagement), and again for 31 October, for what seems to have been a meeting of the Foreign Policy Association (Whitehead, 'Pocket Engagement Book, 1925–26'). There is a reference to Whitehead and McDougall together at a 1926 dinner meeting to discuss the establishment of the Harvard Psychological Clinic, to be headed by Morton Prince. See Robinson, *Love's Story Told*, pp. 141–2. Their mutual influence is a largely unexplored topic, but McDougall's later thought was at least partially influenced by Whitehead; see especially McDougall, *Modern Materialism*, pp. 72–3, available at <https://archive.org/details/b29815861>; and Desmet, 'The Gestalt Whitehead'.
3. The corresponding Radcliffe lecture can be found on p. 43. According to Whitehead's appointment book, this was the second-to-last lecture before the Christmas break, which break he has marked as 'Recess' on every day starting Wednesday, 23 December through Saturday, 2 January. His appointment book lists the times of the class for Tuesday, 22 December, but we do not have notes from this date from any of our three note-takers. It is possible that the lecture was cancelled, but we have no documentary evidence to confirm this. See Whitehead, 'Pocket Engagement Book, 1925–26'.
4. Hartshorne's notes cite James, 'Does consciousness exist?' Cf. Hartshorne on this point: 'James' "(Does) Consciousness exist?" only open to question insofar as he treats physical things as having stuff, while consciousness only has or is a function' (Hartshorne, p. 39).
5. This is a quote of the character Mr Squeers from Chapter 45 of Dickens's novel *Nicholas Nickleby*. The exact quote is 'She's rum 'un, is Natur', meaning that nature is odd or mysterious. Dickens, *The Life and Adventures of Nicholas Nickleby*, p. 444.

creation.¹ Data is not actual in sense of experient occasion. There is not a realm of possibility out of which actual is selected.² "Intensive quantity" is what you mean by actuality.³ The data for experient occasion are not a scrap heap of unrelated universals.⁴ Relationship of data lying in general possibility. Expressed by relational character of all abstraction.⁵ Russell treats sense-data as non-relational. Obsessed with Cartesian metaphysics.⁶ Weakness lies in making sense-data do the work of the body. "Green" cannot be divorced from relational aspect. It is relating ego (experient occasion) to other experient occasion.⁷ [For Plato, world of ideas is world of relations. Why, pleased! Aristotle's logic distracted from this notion that every idea is relational].⁸ (Analysis of experient occasion into (1) eternal objects).⁹ Relationship in ideal world is the possibility of measure in real world – Relationship with isolation – there is something in actuality which is not in ideal world. Relationship in ideal world. There is an essential seclusion. In actuality it has same relations as in ideal world, but also to enter the functioning of experient creature, as one, of an actual unity has been achieved. (Color red is relevant to sound of trumpet). Synthesis – one, although analyzable – a definite pattern of value. In ideal world there are additional facts; in actual world there are not – Plato found value in ideal world, Whitehead in actual world. – Creature is whole creativity under limitation.¹⁰

---

1. Cf. Hartshorne: 'Imaginal occasion analyses experient occasion into data for its creation, not into actual parts or part-creatures of it as a creature' (Hartshorne, p. 39).
2. Hartshorne's notes here contain a reference to Whitehead's 1922 book *The Principle of Relativity*. The reference is not specific; it says only '(beginning)' (Hartshorne, p. 39). But we can safely assume that Whitehead is referring to the discussion of 'fact' and 'limitation' that takes place at the beginning of Chapter 2, 'The relatedness of nature'. See Whitehead, *The Principle of Relativity*, available at <https://archive.org/details/theprincipleofre00whituoft>.
3. Hartshorne adds: '"Intensive quantity" as in Kant' (Hartshorne, p. 39).
4. Cf. Hartshorne: 'Data for creation – extreme realism in mediaeval sense. Yet – data not unrelated, not a scrap-heap of unrelated universals. This (is) real stumbling block in realism to nominalist' (Hartshorne, p. 39).
5. Cf. Hartshorne: 'Relationship of data as in general possibility of creativity. Creativity has a character. As abstracted from ~~any~~ VallV particular occasions, and also in relation to any particular occasion. All relations are predicational, and all predicates relational' (Hartshorne, p. 39).
6. Hartshorne's notes cite both Russell and G. E. Moore: 'G.E. Moore and Russell obsessed by ghost of Cartesian substantialism' (Hartshorne, p. 39).
7. Roethlisberger missed Whitehead's invented term 'ingression' here, which Hartshorne caught: 'Ingression. This word aims at relational character of universals. Eternal object is how other experient occasions enter into experient occasion which is ego' (Hartshorne, p. 39).
8. Hartshorne's notes add that this was a problem 'chiefly in later Aristotelians' (Hartshorne, p. 39).
9. Cf. Hartshorne: 'Eternal object not idea or thought, extreme realism here. (Lewis?)' (Hartshorne, p. 39). Presumably the reference is to Whitehead's colleague in the Harvard Philosophy Department, C. I. Lewis.
10. Hartshorne's notes reference Aristotle's 'unmusical man' here: 'Creature = whole under limitation – all of possibility is in it in its allotted measure. Aristotle's "unmusical man"' (Hartshorne, p. 40). This is discussed by Ross in his 1923 *Aristotle* (assigned reading for the class), p. 65. The example was originally given by Aristotle in his *Physics*, chapter 7. From Ross: 'We speak of two different sorts of thing as coming to be; we say "the man becomes musical" and we say "the unmusical becomes musical." In the former case that which becomes persists, in the latter it passes away. But whether we say "a becomes b" or "not-b becomes b," what always happens is that a-not-b becomes ab. The product *contains* two elements (a substratum and a form), but a third element is *presupposed* by the change (the privation of the form). The substratum, before the change, was numerically one, but included two distinguishable elements – that which was to persist through the change and that which was to be replaced by its

Experient occasion and imaginal occasion are not quite matter and mind. Conception of world as <u>creativity</u> as issuing into its <u>creatures</u>. The confrontation of creativity with what and how leads to a new creature (imaginal occasion). Conceive as a perpetual creation. How of creation $\xrightarrow{\text{leads to}}$ what of creators $\xrightarrow{\text{produces}}$ how of creativity.

Possibility of finite truth in realm of eternal objects. Relational character of eternal objects is reducible to a multiplicity of finite relations and makes measure of actual world possible.[1] Actual world is patience of ideal world for actuality. Depth of actuality needs an exclusion.

Thought deals with world of possibilities and actual creatures. The how of the selection of possibility which is to be projected on actual fact is where effective contingency begins.[2]

Tuesday, 5 January 1926
Hartshorne's notes[3]

|41|
<u>Knowledge</u>.
  What is the duality we want to avoid?
  Must not construct world from abstractions. Metaphysics describes, rather than constructs.[4]

  <u>Detached facts not ultimate</u> – they exhibit <u>patience</u> for rest of the universe.
  Descartes' bodies and minds, neither completes the other. Each perfectly happy without the other, or rather happier!
  Nature at an instant[5] – the same lack of patience – mere accident, that other instants are brought in?
  Metaphysics concerns internal relations. Otherwise no generalization beyond the datum. <u>If no internal relations</u>, <u>no metaphysics</u>. Thus Hume and Russell.
  And if no metaphysics, then no knowledge beyond immediacy! Hume and Kant's appeal to practice = to ~~an~~ unanalyzed ~~relations~~ internal relations.

---

opposite. Thus we get three presuppositions of change – matter, form, privation.' Ross, *Aristotle*, p. 65, available at <https://archive.org/details/in.ernet.dli.2015.536932>.
1. Cf. Hartshorne: 'Relational character of eternal objects can be analyzed into multiplicity of <u>finite</u> relations. Objective Idealists, Bradley and Bosanquet, who deny finite truths, see things as in the actual world only, ignore possibility' (Hartshorne, p. 40). F. H. Bradley and Bernard Bosanquet were both giants in British idealist philosophy who had just recently passed away, Bosanquet in February 1923, Bradley in September 1924.
2. Cf. Hartshorne: 'Thought is in imaginal occasion = projection of finite relations as in possibilities upon actual fact with its variety of measure of realization of those possible finite relations. Freedom lies in gap between general possibility and particular actual occasion. Thought has one side of absolute generality. Here freedom becomes really effective' (Hartshorne, p. 40).
3. The corresponding Radcliffe lecture can be found on p. 44.
4. Roethlisberger's notes add here: 'Actual fact receives completion from other elements' (Roethlisberger, fall semester p. 46).
5. Roethlisberger's notes label this the 'morphological view' (Roethlisberger, fall semester p. 46).

Why fact is dipolar – knowing and experient. Each must render other intelligible.

Sameness and diversity – [two threads running inseparably through everything].

1) *Natura naturata*.[1] Actual entities and their otherness. Subj – Obj: only a special case of polarity or otherness. Immortality. ~~Ed~~ Each occasion is immortal in each other. "Otherness" involves presence of the other. Is a contrast effect.[2]

2) *Natura naturans*. Data of activity = eternal objects. Sameness of eternal objects vs. diversity of creations.[3]

Aristotle seems to have muddled up notion with time as creative.[4]

|42| Can always explain simple by complex and complex by simple. Neither method sole one. E.g., man by jelly-fish, and jelly-fish by man. No revelation to effect that only first way is valid (as 19th Century thought).[5]

Experient occasions

Whitehead has been starting with the simple here, and so muddled things up.

Degrees of actuality. Without bodies and minds, mere empty space – which seems trivial.[6]

~~I~~ Each microcosm viewed as ⟨?⟩[7]

Individual identity comes via historical route. New epoch there must conform to old ~~route~~ VepochV, because there is creative identity, but must differ from old epoch because there is creative diversity.[8] Any entity is always passing on, yet by continuity with route remains one. Not mere otherness in some

---

1. Roethlisberger's notes have here: 'world as a creature, multiplicity of actual entities' (Roethlisberger, fall semester p. 46).
2. Cf. Roethlisberger: 'Otherness ⊃ multiplicity ⊃ diversity. Identity is made fundamental as ⟨blank⟩' (Roethlisberger, fall semester p. 46).
3. Cf. Roethlisberger: 'World as creativity, activity, passage into novelty. Eternal objects are abiding entities which are the data for action' (Roethlisberger, fall semester p. 46). Readers are advised that the preceding discussion on *natura naturata* and *natura naturans* is much cleaner and clearer in Heath (p. 44).
4. There is a large paragraph here in Roethlisberger's notes that Hartshorne seems to have missed completely: 'Activity and creature are one thing. We have to speak of nature as an entity. Creativity for creature passes into creativity with creature. Time as mere creativity is more fundamental than measured time of nature. Not to be muddled up with motion or measured time. Fundamental fact. Passing into otherness. Immortality exhibits itself in mutual form of things. ⟨(1)⟩ Conformation (2) passage into diversity. Either of these alone leads to difficulties. Whitehead suggests a proper reconciliation as a view of world' (Roethlisberger, fall semester p. 46).
5. Cf. Roethlisberger: '① Historical method, not adequate but very effective method, no claim to be called sole method ② start with self. [Science appears as a direct revelation]' (Roethlisberger, fall semester p. 46).
6. Cf. Roethlisberger: 'Whitehead starting with simple (experient occasion) and building up more complex. There is other way. To take most developed (enduring bodies and minds). Enduring entities (1) as in any epochal occasion, (2) historical route of such occasions which form the life history of enduring entity' (Roethlisberger, fall semester p. 46).
7. Roethlisberger has here: 'Each occasion is a microcosm, containing all principles discerned. Each route is also a microcosm' (Roethlisberger, fall semester p. 46).
8. Cf. Roethlisberger: 'Each occasion is exhibition in extension of passage into otherness and a sameness V(preservation of type),V thereby revealing same principles of total world. Historical route simulates the ⟨?⟩ creative identity in historical route, but also a diversity' (Roethlisberger, fall semester p. 46).

part – but through and through different, yet through and through retains the old. Hence time not a line of successive epochs. This would leave out retention.¹

2nd event thus includes 1st and 3rd in part.

Thursday, 7 January 1926

Roethlisberger's notes²

|47| Considering enduring organism, only entities worthwhile talking about. Principles of Whitehead should apply to a world of these enduring organisms. Life history of organism is a succession of epochal occasions. Each occasion is a creative achievement, ⟨blank⟩.³

Each occasion is a microcosm (a little world). Each microcosm has ᵛsameᵛ principles (with limitations) of macrocosm. Microscopic and macroscopic equations in physics.⁴ Epochal occasion is definite creature. Historical route has preserved the epocha protean creativity. Each epochal occasion preserves in it the principles of ⟨blank⟩ and passage of nature. Creativity always other than itself. Each subordinate epoch filled through and through with otherness. Each occasion subject to limitation is (1) essential change to otherness (2) retention of definite ᵛtypeᵛ⁵ (3) obtains most definite type of achievement that it is capable. New epoch has to conform to other due ⟨to⟩ creative identity, also has to differ due to creative diversity. Essential diversity amid a unity of type.⁶ Hegel's pun of negative. Every occasion has to exhibit a contrariety in its own type.⁷ Actuality is synthesis of a contrast into a unity. Identity reinforces epoch. In every doing there is the undoing. Space-Time

---

1. Roethlisberger's notes add: 'Idea of undifferentiated actuality is impossible' (Roethlisberger, fall semester p. 46).
2. There are no Heath notes for the corresponding Radcliffe lecture at 9:00 a.m., though Whitehead's appointment book indicates that he was set to meet with Heath individually at 11:15 a.m., just prior to his Harvard lecture at noon.
3. Cf. Hartshorne: 'Not a graduality of becoming – but of achievement. of Becoming of graduality, not graduality of becoming' (Hartshorne, p. 43).
4. Hartshorne's notes mention a 'Lorenz' here, which is probably a reference to Dutch physicist Hendrik Antoon Lorentz (1853–1928). Hartshorne's notes follow this with: 'Presupposed unchanging relations to rest of world (isolated systems)' (Hartshorne, p. 43).
5. Cf. Hartshorne: '2) Historical ⟨route⟩ simulates whole community more than a given epoch does' (Hartshorne, p. 43); 'root' has been corrected to 'route'.
6. Cf. Hartshorne: '3) Creative identity – conformation of event to preceding, though always creative, through and through diversity. Molecule in granite, the same since millions of years' (Hartshorne, p. 43).
7. Hartshorne captures a fair bit of additional material here: 'Hegel always exalting power of negative. Every creature must embody its own negative. Essential extensiveness of creature in time solves how creature is both itself and not itself. For, (union of being and not-being – Aristotle) every occasion has to exhibit contrariety (principle of reversion), has to exhibit its own type the other way on' (Hartshorne, p. 43).

continuum is the abstract general statement of how things are in one another.¹ Every part of creativity plays a double role. – ground and consequent, consequent a
reversion of ground.² [Whitehead: In physics vibration, periodicity and quanta essential]. Physics the exemplification of principles which have been in philosophy since Aristotle. Creative achievement is fusion of the actual with its reversion.³ Cannot consider organism alone but (1) coordination of organisms an adaptation of sub organism to super organism.⁴

Saturday, 9 January 1926

Roethlisberger's notes⁵

|48| Status of the ⟨imaginal⟩⁶ occasion. (Philosophy as striving after a genial or cultivated scepticism). Striving so to describe actual entities of world explained by same principles as mental world. Otherwise no general metaphysics.

① Every epochal occasion v⟨ultimate creature⟩v is a synthesis in a sense of opposites, yes and no, doing and undoing.⁷ This principle is essential in everything that is actual. ② Every epochal occasion also illustrates principle of identity – same actors amid differences. ③ Every epochal occasion illustrates protean character of its creativity. Creativity in being itself passes into otherness. You obtain extensive character⁸ – How avoid formal logical contradictions.⁹ You have a diversity by a synthesis of differences – a difference in an identity of ~~occasion~~ type. Not an abstract identity.¹⁰

---

1. Hartshorne's notes add here: 'overlapping of things = 1st character of extension' (Hartshorne, p. 43).
2. See the figure on the right. Hartshorne's notes identify the 'g's as 'ground', and 'c's as 'consequent', while noting that the diagram is 'absurdly oversimplified'. Hartshorne's notes also add here: 'Fusion of already actual ground with hitherto unactualised consequent. This shows more general principle that what is actual in the past is with the creature in the present' (Hartshorne, p. 44).
3. Cf. Hartshorne: 'Epoch gives the minimum reversion. Fusion of already actual with its reversion = epoch. Doing and undoing' (Hartshorne, p. 44).
4. Cf. Hartshorne: 'Human body as example. Cells = organisms. Molecules = organisms. ~~Ulti~~ Whether infinite regress or not, we don't know. Our long past. Coördination of organisms. Parts and whole mutually adaptive' (Hartshorne, p. 44).
5. Roethlisberger misdated this lecture as 8 January. The corresponding Radcliffe lecture can be found on p. 45. This is Heath's final day of notes for the fall semester, though lectures continued through to 19 January. Heath did not continue the course in spring 1926, though she did take the full course the previous academic year.
6. Roethlisberger clearly wrote 'imaginative' here, but Whitehead almost surely said 'imaginal'.
7. Hartshorne's notes add to this: 'grow with consequent. (= reversion)' (Hartshorne, p. 45).
8. Cf. Hartshorne: 'From this extensive character, a ~~re~~ potential simplicity of subordinate occasions' (Hartshorne, p. 45).
9. Cf. Hartshorne: 'Formal logical contradiction not meant by union of opposites' (Hartshorne, p. 45).
10. Cf. Hartshorne: 'Negative is not abstract – concrete opposition' (Hartshorne, p. 45).

(1) various types of identity preserved and types of reversion exhibited. Identity of type is not one thing, but capable of many exemplifications. An essential going into otherness, and yet a preservation of some entity. Producing of contrast does not mean (necessarily) the weakening of identity. May strengthen it. Characteristic mythical diagram to illustrate vmaterialv existence.¹ Any characteristic in space-time not to be treated as trivial. For Whitehead these exhibit fundamental relations vin actual worldv. Duplicity in material existence.

Past occasion is immortal in the present via its aspect.² Environment provides a uniformity of environmental grounds. Modal limitation is in the occasion. ① Analysis of occasion ($g_1 c_1, g_2$) into its <u>relationships</u>. ② Another analysis of occasion, analyzable into entities not actual, but which are present due to synthesis. [Realm of eternal objects and creative synthesis which is the achievement by limitation. Represents a certain selectiveness for a <u>definite achievement</u>. Always a definite achievement. More definite ⊃ more exclusive. This is one way of analyzing epochal occasion]. Holding principle. Whatever is ever to be stated of creature is to be stated of creativity. Synthesis gives opening for analysis. (1) One world line of experient entities → (2)

Thought is out of time.³ Measurability is not built out of creative successiveness. Creative successiveness does not mean measurability. Has character which procures measurability. Whenever experience is directed on one dimension, {?} measurability vanishes.⁴

---

1. Hartshorne has a broadly similar diagram, but it is much simpler, containing only the line, the curve, and the letters *A* and *B* above the first top portion of curve (on either side of the dividing line), just above where Roethlisberger has g_1 and c_1. Hartshorne then writes: '*A* and *B* each the reverse of the other. Below the line gives an opposite to above the line. Often a deeper contrast gives a more definite law or ~~unity~~ identity. Above = characteristic picture of a world-line of a particle' (Hartshorne, p. 45).
2. Cf. Hartshorne: 'Creative synthesis involves creative analysis. Not one serial line of time. This idea has gone to pieces in physics. Past isn't just dropped to non-entity – philosophy has always suspected this. Confused their insight to mean time is an illusion. Two kinds of confusion: knowing ⟨blank⟩' (Hartshorne, p. 45).
3. Cf. Hartshorne: '<u>Thought = another dimension of being</u>. Thought out of time, yet embodies time of exper(ienced) world' (Hartshorne, p. 46). It is not entirely clear how 'exper' should be expanded in this context.
4. Cf. Hartshorne: 'Creative successiveness not in itself measurable as to time. <u>A dimension of being by itself gives no measurability</u>. (Haldane gently slammed) In a "brown study", time seems suspended because other dimensions are almost suppressed. Mystics' (Hartshorne, p. 46). The reference to 'Haldane' here is likely to Lord Richard Burdon Haldane (1856–1928), a British politician and philosopher who was a family friend and correspondent of Whitehead. As noted in HL1 (p. 185, n. 1), it was at Lord Haldane's home in 1921 that Whitehead met Einstein. In his 1924–5 lectures Whitehead also references 'Jack Haldane' – John Burdon Sanderson Haldane (1892–1964) – a physiologist and evolutionary biologist, and the son of a physiologist, John Scott Haldane (1860–1936), Lord Richard Haldane's brother. See HL1, p. 49, n. 1.

World is known to us under a variety of dimensions (5).¹ From variety of dimensions, measurability of experience arises.²

The imaginal occasion is eternal object in thought confronting emergence of ~~the~~ a creature via selection.– knowledge of exemplification or non-exemplification, knowledge of knowledge and so on. Measurable time is correlation of imaginal occasion with actual occasion – although imaginal occasion is out of time, it is grounded in it.³

⟨Tuesday, 12 January 1926⟩

Roethlisberger's notes

|49| How mentality comes into ⟨scheme⟩.⁴ First compare abstraction and concretion. One is reverse of other. Concretion is growing together. Abstraction = drawing away something from else.

Primary datum for coming together in actual world = eternal objects, possible world.

Secondary datum is realm of determination of actual occasions. Actual occasion is concrete, the act of togetherness in world of eternal objects. Community of experient occasions is exemplification of eternal objects into realization.

Depths of actuality. Intensiveness determines gradations of actuality. Diversity and sameness are necessary for effective definiteness.⁵ Definiteness of type and diversity: Always a ground and consequent.⁶ A ground is a datum already actual. The consequent is a novelty now actual by synthesis with ground. [Note distinction between synthesis and concretion – synthesis, regard to result, emphasis on creature rather than creativity – concretion regards creature identical with creativity.]⁷ A dimension⁸ is a route of derivation of

---

1. Heath's notes explain this odd reference to five dimensions: 'Five dimensional world, of which four are measurably structured, but thought dimension is not measurable' (p. 45).
2. Cf. Hartshorne: 'Dimensionality comes from variety of types of creative derivativeness ∨(ground and consequent)∨ – yet how explain three dimensions of space? A dimension need not be measurable' (Hartshorne, p. 46).
3. This final paragraph is odd. Nothing like it appears in Hartshorne's or Heath's notes. There is an arrow pointing from this paragraph to the paragraph that begins 'Thought is out of time', or perhaps to the diagram in the same area which appears to have been crossed out; it is not possible to know which. It is possible that this paragraph is the result of Roethlisberger seeking clarification of an earlier point either from Whitehead or another student, or that he simply wrote his own clarification later on when reviewing his notes.
    Roethlisberger neglects to date the following lecture, but through comparison with the Hartshorne notes, it is likely that this is the end of the 9 January lecture.
4. What Roethlisberger actually has here is 'stream', but Hartshorne has 'scheme of things', which seems altogether more likely (Hartshorne, p. 47).
5. Cf. Hartshorne: 'Endurance of self-identical entity important if diversity is marked' (Hartshorne, p. 47).
6. Cf. Hartshorne: 'Definiteness of type, and of contrast within type (reversion). Enshrines ground and consequent' (Hartshorne, p. 47).
7. Cf. Hartshorne: 'creature as one with its creativity' (Hartshorne, p. 47).
8. Hartshorne adds here in parentheses: '(Montague's generalized sense)' (Hartshorne, p. 47). This is probably a reference to William P. Montague (1873–1953), who taught at Columbia University from 1903 to 1947. Montague had just published the book *The Ways of Knowing or the Methods of Philosophy*

actual occasions in which each actual occasion furnish⟨es⟩ dominant ground for successor. $A \to B$. Ground for B is in some sense an element from A. But A as providing ground is patient of certain type of analysis. Undoing of A provides ground for doing B. Concretion i.e. B involves abstraction from A.[1] In ⟨historical route⟩[2] in experient world, the ground is potentially <u>epochal occasion that is part</u> of A (half, part).[3] <u>Consequent is potentially epochal</u> occasion which is novel part of B. These two occasions are synthesized as B. Consequent is reversion of ground.[4] Yet same type. Marked type and opposition. Definiteness demands exclusion.

When you come to imaginal occasion you have different treatment of A. The ground is A in its character as a concretion of eternal object. Consequen⟨t⟩[5] is complex of eternal objects, i.e. a complex eternal object. Consequent in a way is actual[6] – Consequent ⟨is⟩ synthesized with ground. Concrete occasion which emerges is cognizant perception of A as exemplifying or not exemplifying elements of complex.[7] [Ineffectiveness of bad art is suggestive of definiteness, but does not achieve it].

Dimension of mentality is thoroughgoing reversion. Going into actuality not in same sense as the ground. First imaginal occasion = per⟨ceived⟩ occasion[8] Second imaginal occasion = knowledge of knowledge. Dimension of mentality does not require any other principle than dimension of ⟨historical route⟩. Each mental occasion in so far as it takes rise from experient occasion has a time dimension. Time route. Occasions in mental world rapidly dimension.[9]

(1925). The following two passages from this book sum up Montague's generalised sense of 'dimensions': 'The only limit to the process of successively higher generalizations in any direction is the simplicity or unanalysableness of the essences to which we attend. Mere "being" or "thinghood" is perhaps the simplest, as it is certainly the broadest, of our concepts. But besides this *summum genus* there are universals that are, as it were, off on the side, in a dimension of their own. Examples of such universals are "temporality," "spaciality," and "consciousness." We call them *sui generis*, because of the difficulty of analysing them into further significant genera' (p. 73); 'Sense-data are "in" their universals or qualitative dimensions as much as they are "in" their spatio-temporal dimensions. And universals are in particulars not as apples are in boxes or small spaces in large spaces, but as all time is in each spatial point or all space in each temporal instant' (p. 88). See Montague, *Ways of Knowing or the Methods of Philosophy*, available at <https://archive.org/details/in.ernet.dli.2015.69104>.

1. Cf. Hartshorne: 'B involves A as providing such and such ground of contrast' (Hartshorne, p. 47).
2. Here, and again several paragraphs later, Roethlisberger uses the shorthand 'h.r.'. It is difficult to be sure of the intended expansion, but, given context, 'historical route' is the most likely.
3. Hartshorne's notes have 'last half' (Hartshorne, p. 47).
4. Cf. Hartshorne: '<u>If B is to have depth of actuality, consequent must be reversion of ground</u>' (Hartshorne, p. 47).
5. Roethlisberger has 'Consequence' here, but context and Hartshorne's notes tell us it should be 'Consequent'.
6. Cf. Hartshorne: 'Consequent is actual, but not in way of experient occasion, but as thought, as image' (Hartshorne, p. 47).
7. Hartshorne's notes add here: 'Is this perception? "I am not Vwell∨ read in perception." But A seen as excluding something as well as including something. If we could only perceive positive exemplification, no negative perceptions' (Hartshorne, p. 48).
8. Roethlisberger has here the abbreviation 'per. Occ.'. The intended expansion is not entirely certain, but 'perceived occasion' seems likely.
9. Cf. Hartshorne: 'Dimension of mentality – idea of idea of etc. This not a time-succession. Each mental occasion has a time aspect inside it, but from point of view of exper⟨ienced⟩ world, simultaneous. Both in and out of time. In this dimension, importance rapidly decreases (idea, idea of idea ----)' (Hartshorne, p. 48).

What is negligible is not therefore non-existent. Scale of intensity makes negligible.[1] The most complete fact is an epochal occasion (exp⟨erience⟩[2]) in an important experient occasion with whole route of mental occasions.[3] Relation between experient occasions include finite truths that ⟨to a large extent⟩[4] can be expressed without reference to imaginal occasions. You cannot explain exp⟨erienced⟩ world alone. Not only experient occasions ⟨inherit ⟨of?⟩⟩. Imaginal occasions must inherit from other imaginal occasions and experient occasions.[5] You cannot get on without them, though vague. [Historical route of important mental route]

Principle of General Inheritance ① Whatever "is" is thereby attribute of creativity.[6] ② Whatever is creature is thereby attribute of creat⟨ivity⟩. ② Whatever is creativity emerges into creature. Whatever is determina⟨te⟩[7] creature emerges into new creature[8] – ③ Hence experient occasions ⟨inherit⟩[9] from mentality of antecedent occasions. But mentality of antecedent occasions is undoing of experient occasion.[10] When experient occasions inherit ⟨mental occasion⟩[11] they inherit evaluation and active purpose of creativity. This inheritance is metaphysical basis of feeling, emotion, and blind conation.[12]

|50| Whatever we mean by freedom is predominant⟨ly⟩ the attribute in mental sphere. You have in mental sphere actuality is less bound. Our experience of freedom is via mentality. Consequen⟨ts⟩[13] in route of mentality ⟨are⟩ derivative from non-actual. When you have merely creativity and

---

1. Cf. Hartshorne: 'As one goes toward plants, then atoms, mentality seems to fade away. But this does not mean it ceases altogether. Always a completion of creativity, but not always intensive importance' (Hartshorne, p. 48).
2. It is not entirely clear whether to expand 'exp' as 'experient', 'experience' or some other variant. The same problem recurs two sentences later with 'exp world alone.'
3. Cf. Hartshorne: 'Most complete fact, then, route of experient occasions plus route of mental occasions' (Hartshorne, p. 48).
4. This important qualification is supplied from Hartshorne's notes (Hartshorne, p. 48).
5. Cf. Hartshorne: 'Nature closed to mind. Experient occasions exhibit finite truths which to a very large extent can be expressed without reference to our mentality. Only to a very large extent:– inheritance not merely of experient occasions from experient occasions, but also experient occasions from imaginal and vice-versa' (Hartshorne, p. 48).
6. Hartshorne's notes record the same sentence here with the addition of '(Spinoza)' at the end of the sentence (Hartshorne, p. 48).
7. Roethlisberger has 'determinant' here; we have changed this to 'determinate' based on Hartshorne's notes (Hartshorne, p. 49).
8. Cf. Hartshorne: 'Whatever is attribute of creativity, emerges into creature (only so is it knowable). Therefore, whatever is already determinate creature emerges into new creative' (Hartshorne, p. 49).
9. The original notes had 'inherent', which we have corrected to 'inherit'.
10. Hartshorne's notes add: 'E.g., disentangling of what went to making of experient occasion' (Hartshorne, p. 49).
11. What Roethlisberger actually has here is 'O_m'. He had been using 'O_i' and 'O_e' to denote 'imaginal occasion' and 'experient occasion' respectively, but the meaning of this shorthand is not entirely clear. Comparing this passage and the one below to the Hartshorne notes also makes 'mentality' a plausible expansion, specifically the mentality of an antecedent occasion (Hartshorne, p. 49).
12. Hartshorne's notes add: 'Dog is jealous, but doesn't know this' (Hartshorne, p. 49).
13. Roethlisberger has 'Consequence' here, which we have changed through comparison with the Hartshorne notes (Hartshorne, p. 49).

eternal objects you have no binding or coming together. Need an actual world.¹ Experient occasions with strong inheritance of ⟨mentality⟩ gives you cognizance of feelings – inheritance of experient occasions.

Thursday, 14 January 1926
Roethlisberger's notes

Restatements
   Type of inheritance of enduring object exemplification along historical route. Past is an element in present and determining it. We discern immediate occasion as becoming of itself. Analysis into creativity and creature which cannot be disjoined – two aspects of one fact. Creativity for creature becomes creativity with creature. Deduce time, causation; enduring object. Causation suggests Hume. Where do I find past in experience as determining present? Find none. Causal relation is moonshine. Whitehead's answer. In what Hume assumes point he cannot find. Influence of Past on present is bound up in notion of time. Analyze what we mean by time, we find that past in some sense here now and present is in some sense with past. "Time is a certain ordering of events" – Time as a relationship between events leads to assumption that all our thinking about time follows from it. Mere idea of time as relational does not preclude that time may relate an occasion to itself.² You canVnotV draw denial of reflexiveness of time from idea of time as relational. Can there be a second occurrence of same occasion? Can signing of Declaration of Independence have a double date? To say that time is relational does not make asking of this question impossible. What is most favorable case? Actual world is a repetition of cycles – occurrence (same) in all details. Can the it submit to same concepts? No, the later occasion repeats the earlier³ and earlier does not repeat later. A fundamental fact of experience – anticipation and repetition are contrary relationships. What is ground for <u>irrevocableness of past</u>? What is in actual occasion of repetition. When you repeat, the earlier example is with you – non-entity is non-repeatable. Repetition You repeat immortal past.⁴ Irrevocable because immortal and immortal because irrevocable. We can't help being a person with a past. Each immediate occasion carries in itself its own future. Because we do not know what will happen does not mean we have no knowledge of future. Time as "dead history". Time as "living history" – a novelty. Time looked on as "mere creature". How Time Creature exhibits patience for creation. But in fact you cannot separate creature and creativity. Creature remains |51| with creativity, although watchmaker may sell the watch.

---
1. Cf. Hartshorne: 'Mere creativity plus eternal objects gives complete liberty. Only actual world binds' (Hartshorne, p. 49).
2. Cf. Hartshorne: 'A relation: may be reflexive, self-relating, either contingently or necessarily' (Hartshorne, p. 50).
3. Cf. Hartshorne: 'Eternal recurrence. Later occasion repeats the earlier, that fact alone makes it different' (Hartshorne, p. 50).
4. Cf. Hartshorne: 'Only an immortal past can be repeated' (Hartshorne, p. 50).

Harvard lectures, fall semester 1925

Apart from principle that past abides in present and ~~future~~ determines future, there can be no distinction between past and future. How can past differ from future? By immediate in which........... (blank). Otherwise where is distinction? Agrees with Hume in a way. Hume obsessed with Cartesian metaphysics. His position past is in some sense with future – association of ideas. My previous perceptivity is in some sense with me – So far so good. <u>But</u> your cognizance of perceptivity is knowledge. Occasion of perception is fundamental occasion in physical world. That is what scientist wants. Perceptivity is taking account of relations.[1] Knowledge is not the <u>perception</u>. Whitehead uses Hume in order to show how Descartes' ~~goes w~~ assumptions are wrong.

Mental occasions inherit from antecedent occasions. What relationship among mental occasions?[2]

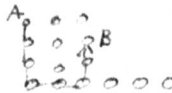

Relation of A to B.
Explain through experient occasions.

⟨Saturday, 16 January 1926⟩

Roethlisberger's notes

Both Hume and Kant placed ultimate fact in an occasion of perceptivity. When Hume dealt with causality, he had in back of head "Cartesian metaphysics". To ~~⟨?⟩~~ explain the "how of immediate occasion of perceptivity" by association. You should not interpret Hume as brain storing up perceptions. Kant points out that "*Anschauung*"[3] was blind, treated as one occasion. Common sense: To preserve a world as a datum of knowledge.

Blind apprehension (prehension) – synthesis vis ultimate factv. Nature of perceptivity is knowledge of ultimate fact which is synthesis of data. Kant leaves us with one <u>occasion</u>, but why call it mental? This is Cartesian emphasis. Thus experient occasion is the creature arising from <u>definite opportunity</u> from creative nature of world. World ⟨divided?⟩.

(1) <u>creativity</u> (passage)	(2) <u>eternal data for creativity</u> (Those things which don't show par relation to vanyv particular occasion "redness")	(3) created data (what is passed that is relevant to present)

Why definite opportunity? Thoroughgoing evolutionary philosophy. Evolution suggests purpose, orderliness. Progress of evolution provides definiteness of opportunity. How does it disclose itself? Systematic scheme of relatedness in created data, a thoroughgoing scheme of <u>internal relations</u>. Causal nature of specific data. Both as systematic and causal opportunity. Nature of world as it is for that |52| opportunity enters into that creature. Every occasion embodies a definite ground – i.e. total opportunity. Opportunity

---

1. Cf. Hartshorne: 'An electron for scientist = merely a bundle of its relations to other electrons. A taking account of, a blind perceptivity' (Hartshorne, p. 51).
2. Through comparison with the Hartshorne notes, this appears to be the end of the 14 January lecture. There is also a distinct change in the quality of Roethlisberger's ink for the text following.
3. That is, 'intuition'.

Harvard lectures, fall semester 1925

analyzed in data, not a scrap heap. How any data enters into particular occasion is by entrance of eternal data with <u>systematic</u> datum ∧(temporal spatial data)∧[1] and causal data. Neither of these data is disconnected. Concrete relationships. How any one datum enters into one occasion is not *simpliciter* but in a mode, a limitation by which it is fused with other datum. Presentation relation relates occasions which are present to us. *P* enters *A* by presentational relation. First regard pure time-space aspect of *P*. But this is a high abstraction. Nothing as such in the concrete. To get to concrete you have to fuse that with some eternal data (red). It is presentation of red under aspect of remoteness in *P*. Or you may say presentation of *P* under mode of it(s) aspect of redness from *A*. Both *P* and red enter *A* under a mode. When you view time and space side (systematic), the *R* is eternal[2] to *A* and *P*. But if you view as red *R*.,[3] it is internal to *A*, but external to *P*. You cannot cast systematic apprehension as external to *P*. – otherwise you lose kindred world. Thus *P* is apprehend by *A* by systematic status in community, and by a mode from eternal data.[4]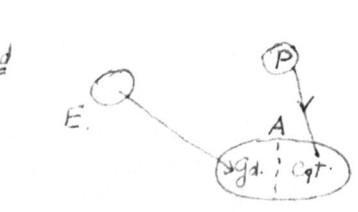

Because consequent has to grow out of ground. The red spatio-temporal relation is the consequent of the ground – (time-spatio) – Consequent is a reversion of ground. Presentational and inspectional relationships – In *R*, it is not only systematic relation, but what it is in itself (causal) enters into ground ∨(Nature of *E* in *A*)∨[5] under a limitation. Consequent is the novelty. In consequent, *A* synthesis *P* in itself. *A* providing eternal objects. Just *A* arises from *E*'s nature, but then you have *P* arising from *A*'s nature. In ground *E* provides <u>causal mode</u>. In consequent *A* provides <u>causal mode</u>.[6]

---

1. This interlineation appears below the underlined word 'systematic' and is connected to it by a line. Parentheses have been supplied to retain the likely intended meaning.
2. That Roethlisberger has written the word 'eternal' is not in doubt. However, there is some question as to whether this is the word Whitehead said. The correct interpretation is difficult to discern and hinges on what the abbreviation 'R' is meant to stand for, context provided by sentence structure, and past habits of abbreviation. It seems most likely that 'R' stands for 'red'. One might think 'R' could be 'relationship', but Roethlisberger consistently abbreviates 'relationship' as 'rel.', including in this lecture. It is more likely that Whitehead did not say 'eternal' here but perhaps 'external', which requires only one letter change, or 'internal' which phonetically sounds most like 'eternal'.
3. The meaning of 'R' here is again uncertain. The most plausible interpretation is still that 'R' stands for 'red' as in 'if you view (it) as red, i.e. *R*, it is internal to *A*, but external to *P*.'
4. On the line below, Roethlisberger wrote 'FIG II'. Presumably he was signalling that the paragraph below is a discussion of the figure above.
5. Parentheses supplied. See the figure above.
6. That there is so much space at the bottom of the page and a change in the quality of the ink and handwriting suggest the end of the 16 January lecture.

109

Harvard lectures, fall semester 1925

⟨Tuesday, 19 January 1926⟩
Roethlisberger's notes

|53| Causality has ground in presentation. Creativity is what it is because of actuality. Inspectional relationship whereby past is in some aspect of limitation concerning immediate occasion. M is in A not *simplicita*, but in a mode. Two higher abstractions: (1) space-time character of M from A + ⟨(2)⟩ character (m). A issues from past in determinate way. What A is in itself is a reversion, the novelty, what A is in itself. Analysis of A reveals ground and consequent (novelty). Considering a detail of ground and detail of consequent. Ground:– space-time aspect + m, Consequent (space-time aspect + a). A = fusion. a = sense data, eternal object. Analogy of presentational relation to cognizant occasion. Confrontation of [A] with concepts or [A] as exemplifying[1] i. Knowledge of what A is or isn't.

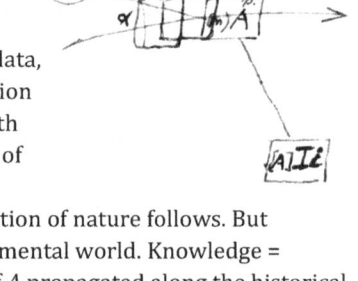

If you put perceptivity in mentality, bifurcation of nature follows. But Whitehead: A = <u>fundamental physical fact</u>. I = mental world. Knowledge = knowledge of A. The fundamental character of A propagated along the historical route. Muddle between blind perceptivity and cognitional perceptiv⟨ity⟩. I takes in character of A as exemplifying (a) or not. Cognizance different from blind perceptivity. Cognizance is analysis of A – in mental world.[2] Presentational relations is what Hume was looking for – Presentation → Action. Force is a presentational relationship. Presentational relationships are those in A which determine tropisms of α.

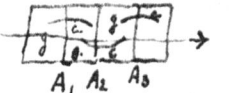

What is historical route of A to be.[3] (Study of tropisms)[4] It is determined by presentational relationships. Immediate facts which determine. What are physical laws? How[5] ultimate entities, presentational relationships – (tropisms of) can be expressed in space-time terms.[6]

---

1. The interlineation 'non or' and a ditto mark appear directly below the word 'exemplifying'. The intended meaning is unclear.
2. Cf. Hartshorne for this paragraph: 'Bifurcation. Redness a fact in nature. Galileo showed what we see has its seat in our own body, grows there as it were. But – mustn't put the perceptivity into the cognition. For A as experient occasion <u>is</u> the physical world and not the mental world' (Hartshorne, p. 51).
3. Roethlisberger clearly writes 'be', but it seems likely that Whitehead said and intended 'B'.
4. Cf. Hartshorne: 'Presentational relationships = those that determine tropism. Mechanics = science of tropisms.' (Hartshorne, p. 51). There is also a single sentence from Hartshorne marked as 19 January which is written on a separate page that is otherwise blank. Given that Hartshorne's notes are notoriously out of order and misnumbered (see Introduction, pp. xli–xlii), it is not clear if this lone sentence belongs at the beginning or end of the 19 January lecture, or even somewhere in the middle. In comparing his notes with those of Roethlisberger, it seems likely that it fits here. It reads: 'The negligible mentality of the lowest organisms, their simple tropisms, gives laws of mechanics' (Hartshorne, p. 52).
5. Roethlisberger has 'How are . . .' here. We have deleted the 'are' after examining context and comparing with Hartshorne, since this does not seem to be an interrogative.
6. Cf. Hartshorne: 'How molecules' presentational relationships to each other determine their spatiotemporal relationships' (Hartshorne, p. 51).

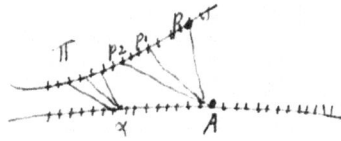
A would not survive unless *P* correlated to environment.[1] *A* is correlated to <u>ground</u> which is enduring object in historical route that leads up to *P*. Historical route is always the route of self-preservation as determined by presentational <u>relationships</u>. The job of evolution is to get enduring entities going.[2]

---

1. Hartshorne's notes make clear that *A* is a molecule, while *P* is a presentational relationship of molecule *A*.
2. This marks the end of the 19 January lecture, the final lecture of the fall semester. According to Whitehead's appointment book, 21–30 January was reserved for examinations, with the exam for Philosophy 3b taking place on Saturday, 23 January (Whitehead, 'Pocket Engagement Book, 1925–26').

Philosophy 3b Mid-Year Exam 1925–6

Harvard University

Philosophy 3b

At least four of these questions are to be answered.

1. 'Science is not explanatory; it is solely concerned with descriptive formulae.'
   Examine this statement and consider whether this characterization of the scope of science evades the difficulties of Induction and Causality.
2. 'If – with Kant as supplementing Hume – the function of knowing introduces the relational elements, any one such act constitutes its corresponding temporal world, and a multiplicity of acts of knowledge would tend to a multiplicity of unrelated temporal worlds.'
   Comment on this statement, and discuss with reference to Hume or absolute idealism.
3. Science in the modern period has employed Descartes' doctrine of individual substances. Give a short account of this doctrine, with some estimate of its influence and value in the development of science.
4. 'Abstraction is justified by the fact that there are characters – i.e. components – which enter into various occasions but may be considered apart from any actual occasion.'
   Discuss the metaphysical doctrine of the experienced world as an activity achieving the reversion of this abstractive process.
5. In the analysis of time as the becoming of novelty, a 'Zeno difficulty' arises. Explain this difficulty and also the lecturer's solution of it by means of an epochal theory of time. Comment.
6. Explain the 'morphological' and 'functional' theories of actual occasions, and compare their respective difficulties and advantages.
7. "Everything actual obtains its individuality by reason of its limitations." Explain this doctrine and illustrate by reference to esthetic experience.
8. Discuss the development of atomic conceptions in physical science. Are such conceptions inconsistent with the retention of any concept of continuity?

Mid-Year. 1926.

Harvard lectures, spring semester 1926

⟨Tuesday, 9 February 1926⟩
Robinson's notes[1]

|2|[2] How is accuracy possible?[3]
This is it.[4]

The idea of scientific and accurate determination of the synthesis – and. This leads you to the one and the many.

The question of comparison – matching – classification. So we get back to the <u>and</u> again.[5]

Measure – definite determination in respect to how much: number and quantity – which refers to number, but all the same is beyond it.[6]

Gradation – inte⟨nsiv⟩eness.[7] Order. Then you have to have some concreteness.[8] <u>What do you mean by the actual world? I run the Platonic point of view, for I am a mathematician.</u>

Confusion and harmony: things that extrude each other – contrariness, and things which supplement and intensify each other in a way. Order and God as a principle of order. The idea of progress – of an end.

Of course I am entirely incapable of carrying out this programme. Accuracy – the idea⟨l⟩s[9] which we import into nature and practically find there.[10]

---

1. There are three sets of notes available for this semester: Robinson's notes are used as the primary account for 17 lectures, and Roethlisberger's for the remaining 21 lectures, while Hartshorne's notes are never used as the primary account. Refer to the table on p. 416 for a full list of spring semester 1926 Harvard lectures by note-taker and date, and see also the Introduction for a detailed discussion of each note-taker and their notes. Readers are especially encouraged to read the Introduction's discussion of the unusual state of Robinson's notes.
    Note that Whitehead was at this time (February 1926) delivering his second set of Lowell lectures, which were subsequently published as *Religion in the Making*.
2. See the Introduction (pp. xlv–xlvi) on the different sets of numbering in Robinson's notes.
3. Comparison with Roethlisberger's notes suggests that Robinson has missed some important context here. Cf. Roethlisberger: 'How is interaction in common world possible? VOld question.V How is accuracy possible? New question. Arouses ideas' (Roethlisberger, spring semester p. 1). Note that Roethlisberger has restarted his numbering for the new semester. Both Roethlisberger and Hartshorne also indicate that 'accuracy' here refers to 'measurement' (Hartshorne, p. 53).
4. Robinson's notes do not really convey the point here. Cf. Roethlisberger: '<u>Most general idea is absolute determinism – "this, it"</u>' (Roethlisberger, spring semester p. 1).
5. Cf. Roethlisberger: '<u>Idea of classification</u>, which brings back to question of extension' (Roethlisberger, spring semester p. 1).
6. Robinson seems to be missing an item here. Roethlisberger has: '<u>Idea of extensiveness</u>. How do you get your <u>exact</u> and <u>precise</u> notions: Why one instrument more precise? Definite ideas of point and instant' (Roethlisberger, spring semester p. 1). Meanwhile, instead of 'extensiveness', Hartshorne has 'Space-time units' here (Hartshorne, p. 53).
7. The Yale transcription has a blank space here. The missing letters have been supplied from Roethlisberger (spring semester p. 1).
8. Cf. Hartshorne: 'Order of concreteness and abstractness' (Hartshorne, p. 53).
9. The Robinson transcription has 'ideas' here, but both the Roethlisberger and the Hartshorne notes have 'ideals'.
10. Hartshorne adds: 'without this ideal, nothing is determinately anything' (Hartshorne, p. 53).

How can you be not precise unless there is a precision which there might be? If there is a meaning, it is that it might be precise but always.[1] God is an ideal which we can't think of nature without importing into nature. We can't talk of nature – there's no such thing as nature. Unless it has this in it. I usually diverge from Kant; but here I am waving friendly signals to him.[2]

IT. Obviously an it is an abstraction. You don't see a bare it; you see a watch. There is not a watch and then specific determinations – you can't separate the what of the watch from the watch.

It is obvious that philosophy started from language and a rather naive trust in grammar. It was a great calamity that Aristotle didn't know Chinese. I have no doubt that it is an equal calamity in China that the Chinese don't |2| know Greek. I don't know that this trust in grammar led Aristotle astray. The beauty of Aristotle is that he was brought up by Plato. He trickled down in his followers until you got something beautifully simple in Descartes. Now I think that the form of the sentence – which really doesn't dominate Aristotle completely – still gives you the it as the subject of predicates – and so gave Aristotle the idea of the absolute subject, with the accompanying relations, predicates, etc., etc.[3] Now I don't believe in this absolute distinction, and I hope I am supported by Chinese grammar. I think you can ask of any entity what and how. This equally refers to the eternal objects and to the events.[4]

If John loves Thomas – John and love and Thomas are as a matter of fact ingredients in a synthesis which is one. All that a sentence can do is to put words in a temporal synthesis. If you abstract from the idea of a temporal sequence you get an even more abstract entity. The it and the and. The S⟨ubject?⟩ which comes after love is the warning that when you have abstracted, that is not what you want to convey;[5] what you want to convey is another synthesis – that enumerative synthesis which has two elements in it – the temporal order – that is to refer to a unity in which those three enter as ingredients. That is the ground – the one of the relation. But Thomas, viewed as an ingredient has its relation of love and John – love has its relational side relating John and Thomas; John his, as relating love and Thomas. When you have an it you always are referring to a specific determination in a community: it may even be an ideal community. The it is an abstraction from that determinat⟨eness⟩[6] – from the specific ground of ⟨determinateness⟩ – a thisness

---

1. Cf. Roethlisberger: 'Sense experience not precise. But if it has any meaning it means that it might have been VgreaterV, but it wasn't' (Roethlisberger, spring semester p. 1).
2. Both Roethlisberger and Hartshorne go into more detail here. Cf. Roethlisberger: 'In ⟨Kant's⟩ first book – discussion of *Anschauung* from *Begriffung* too short. More investigation of *Anschauung* might lead to platonic realism' (Roethlisberger, spring semester p. 1). Cf. Hartshorne: 'Kant – ought to have come to Platonic realism, if he had thought "blind intention" out' (Hartshorne, p. 53).
3. Cf. Roethlisberger: 'Form of the sentence becoming more dominant gives you "it" as subject of predicate → absolute subject → definite specific relationship S⟨ubject⟩-P⟨redicate⟩ → idea of definite relations' (Roethlisberger, spring semester p. 1).
4. Instead of 'events', Roethlisberger has 'epochal occasions' here (Roethlisberger, spring semester p. 1).
5. Cf. Roethlisberger: 'Symbolism is a temporal synthesis of sound or spatial synthesis of marks' (Roethlisberger, spring semester p. 1).
6. Robinson has 'determinatives' here, but through comparison with Roethlisberger and Hartshorne, it seems clear that 'determinateness' is what is meant (Roethlisberger, spring semester p. 1; Hartshorne, p. 54).

divested of its <u>what</u> in itself, and its <u>how</u> among others. But the thing is a what and how. There's nothing apart from a definite answer to these questions. Every entity has an individual and relational essence – it has a patience for all its relationships in itself. So what I object to is the idea of the it as an entity supporting qualities. It is not a fundamental idea, though of course it has derivative importance. The entity is |3| the synthesis of the how and what – they refer to the synthesis and are required by it – they have no meaning apart from it. Every entity refers beyond itself, there is no escape from the synthesis of many into one, and analysis of <u>one</u> as essentially referent to ⟨many⟩.¹ So a relation is nothing else than a definite entity construed in respect to its reference to many things, that is how love is a relation. A subject is a definite entity construed in respect to the many things that are referent to it. Both have an ultimate character as one. [The universe is horribly complicated. I am very sorry, but it is].² A one has more than one side – its what for other things – its what as an ingredient, and its what for itself – at least there may be its what for itself. The eternal objects, however, have no what for themselves. For a what for itself is a matter of experience (⟨experience⟩³ quâ graded – that is value) – In dealing with the actual world there is a concretion of many into a what for itself. I don't think the colour red is a what for itself. But it is contributing to the value – to the finite element which is a unit experience – a what in itself.⁴

⟨Thursday, 11 February 1926⟩

Robinson's notes

Accuracy – a battle ground. If you over-individualize the universe you never can get it together again. You will never be able to get it together again as an afterthought. But if you insist that the totality or community is essential to conceiving of an entity, then you can't have any definite finite statement. When I got to accuracy, I admitted that every individual is essentially referent to the total community which leaves nothing out whatsoever; but that every individual has its what it is as thus related, and <u>how</u> it is related. You can't speak of the how without referring to that what, and vice-versa. Every specific what is always a what in the universe. It refers to every other fact in the universe, but in some systematic way – the general concepts <u>all</u> or any – under which it is cloaked. The most general way is the sheer relationship of diversity. The <u>it</u> is thereby referring to all the rest of the universe as diverse. [That is the

---

1. The original transcription has 'one as essentially referent to one'. But it seems clear that the last word should be 'many'. Cf. Hartshorne: 'One and many each referent to one another' (Hartshorne, p. 54).
2. This certainly reads like a Whitehead aside, but it is unclear if the brackets are Robinson's own, or employed by the Yale Philosophy Club to denote an interlineation, or something else.
3. Supplied from Hartshorne's notes (p. 54).
4. Cf. Hartshorne: 'What for itself = what quâ experience = a value = experience quâ graded. Eternal objects are contributors to value of unit experience of an epochal occasion' (Hartshorne, p. 54).

general waste basket.] That it [bare individuality]¹ is not the substratum but the outcome of the complex ⟨of entities⟩² which is the unity. In dealing with an entity, there is a definite what implying a how. |4| And the it from which you abstract the what and how is not what underlies. Every entity emerges from its relationships and qualities, and cannot underlie them. If anything, it overlies! There are other general reference to the rest of the world which have various leanings on the various sorts of entities. There's a general uniformity of scheme – somewhere else, and some other time. You have gone beyond the bare waste-paper basket of sheer diversity, and considered things in the actual world under a general scheme of thought. Then when you are dealing with coloured things, the ultimate concrete fact – definite specific colours. Then you go to a higher abstraction of color as such, from color to the higher abstraction of sense-datum. Determinables and determinates. By the fact of their being higher and higher abstractions, they are modes by which you refer to other things. I think what I am saying refers to non-actual as well as actual things. There are definite concepts which in their reference to any definite entity, refer to the whole universe in definite layers of generality. The spectacle case as it referring to all the rest of the universe as other; the case as there now referring to everything else as somewhere else in space and time; a definite shape among shaped things; definite color among other things, etc., etc. Layers of generality. You can get a perfectly accurate concept. But that statement in its reference to the rest of the universe does not deal with every other item of the universe one by one, but under the various layers of general reference. The point I run is that it's this perfectly definite accuracy which enables actual things to be actual. They are actual just as much because of what they are not as of what they are. All the logical contraries are simply ways-of – what they mean is that in a sense some event is nebulous because it is not extruding things. Limitation is not an imperfection, but the attainment of actuality. The art of life is accuracy – not to be without detriment of definitions. You must have sharp edges which are not neutralised. Language is so crude that when you come to philosophy, if you really trust to it, you get a much too limited view of the world – whether actual or ideal.

|5| Accuracy therefore is the ⟨exemplification⟩³ of an entity of a definite determinate concept which refers to the remainder of things in respect to these general relationships to the entity, and not under the specific individual relationships of each individual entity to the one in question. And accuracy in particular depends upon also getting hold of the background as well as the entity – it is an apprehension of the class relations of the rest of the universe to the entity in respect to the way that entity expresses that concept.

---

1. These two bracketed portions read like interlineations, suggesting that brackets may have been an apparatus of the Yale Philosophy Club to indicate such.
2. Supplied from Roethlisberger (spring semester p. 2).
3. The original transcription has 'amplifications', but Roethlisberger and Hartshorne have 'exemplification' (Roethlisberger, spring semester p. 2; Hartshorne, p. 56).

The Greeks and accuracy.[1] Euclid and the problem of equality. The axioms. He doesn't define equality. He just states axioms about it. He has assumed that the idea of equality is quite plain and simple. In the first place, there is the idea of a general relationship. Congruence muddled with the idea of a general relationship – a determinable (isoid) and determinate relationship – a characteristic which relations may or may not have.

An isoid relation must have three characteristic activities: 1. It must be transitive. If A is brother to B and B to C, I think A is brother to C – a transitive relationship:[2]

$a \to b$
$\quad b \to c$
$a \to c$

On the other hand, you have a great many relationships which are not transitive. If A is father to B and B to C, A is not to C. 2. It must be symmetrical. If $A \xrightarrow{r} B$, then if it is symmetrical, $B \xrightarrow{r} A$. Brother is symmetrical relationship. But if A is the husband to B, B is not the husband of C. 3. Reflexiveness.

⟨Saturday, 13 February 1926⟩

Robinson's notes

Accuracy – systematic reference to the rest of the universe as a background. Determinable – a genus of predicates. Determinate – a particular predicate.

Euclid's "common notions" or axioms.

Equality. All that Euclid did was to define isoid relations. ⟨blank⟩ as a method of procedure, when you want to analyse a man's thought, what you've got to do is to write down all his accurate statements and then see what ideas are involved.

1. "Things that are <u>equal</u> to the same thing are <u>equal</u> to one another."
|7|
2. "If equals be <u>added</u> to equals, the <u>wholes</u> are equal."
3. "If equals be <u>taken from</u> equals, the <u>remainders</u> are equal."
4. "Things <u>fitting on</u> to each other are ⟨e⟩qual to each other (congruent)."
5. "The <u>whole</u> is greater than its <u>part</u>."

You have to get the most general ideas, and then you must get the most happy particular instance.[3]

---

1. Both Roethlisberger and Hartshorne have additional material on the Greeks here: 'Who started idea of accuracy (complete). Greeks were <u>first</u> to run it vividly. This is their greatest individual contribution of Greeks to civilization' (Roethlisberger, spring semester p. 2); '<u>Who started</u> idea of accuracy? Greeks not first poets, or metaphysicians, artists, etc., but <u>first accurate people</u>. This overlooked in 19th century' (Hartshorne, p. 56).
2. The Yale Philosophy Club typed these arrows as a series of hyphens with a diamond shape at the end, e.g.: ----------◊. But through comparison with the Hartshorne and Roethlisberger notes, it is clear that an arrow is what was intended, and so we have subsequently converted all such marks to arrows.
3. Cf. Hartshorne: 'There are more general ideas at work here. A specific spatial relation of congruence muddled up with a more general ideal (determined in Johnson's language). General idea of isos ⟨(ἴσος)⟩, or equality' (Hartshorne, p. 56). The reference is likely to William Ernest Johnson (1858–1931), who

If aRb, under what circumstances will we call R an isoid relationship? It must be symmetrical, transitive, and refle⟨x⟩ive.[1]
1. Symmetrical : If aRb, then bRa.
2. Transitive: If aRb, and bRc, then aRc.
3. Refle⟨x⟩ive: If a is a relation for R, then aRa.

Then the logician turns up and wants to get a deductive system, bringing things known to the finest statements possible. For psychology is an aesthetic sense. Science has been chiefly deduced not for utility but for aesthetic pleasure.[2] Menaechmus (?)[3] – the pupil of Plato – the first man to investigate conic section [He became the teacher of Alexander the Great, ⟨in⟩cidentally].[4] Apollonius and Pappus (ca. 220 A.D.) – in all this 600 years[5] there wasn't a ghost of an application. Then Kepler[6] discovered that the planets move in conic sections. Cf. also the doctrine of probability and Maxwell's application of it to the ⟨ki⟩netic theory of gases.[7] The logician – (1) aesthetic enjoyment (2) the importance of deductive systems. The principle of ⟨blank⟩ of ultimate premises.

---

had recently finished publishing his three-volume *Logic* in 1924. See Johnson, *Logic*, available at <https://archive.org/details/logicpart01johnuoft> (Part 1), <https://archive.org/details/logicpartiidemon00john> (Part 2), and <https://archive.org/details/logicpart03sparuoft> (Part 3).

1. Through comparison with the Roethlisberger and Hartshorne notes, and with the preceding lecture in these notes, 'reflective' is clearly supposed to be 'reflexive', and likewise in point 3, below (Roethlisberger, spring semester p. 3; Hartshorne, p. 56).
2. Cf. Roethlisberger: '(Reduction to fewest statements possible = to get things beautiful – aesthetic impulse)' (Roethlisberger, spring semester p. 3).
3. Such parenthetical question marks likely indicate confusion or uncertainty on Robinson's part rather than on the part of the Yale Philosophy Club transcribers, since the latter typically just left a blank space in place of indecipherable words.
4. What Robinson actually has here is 'accidentally', but this seems very likely to have been a mishearing of 'incidentally'. Also, the idea that Menaechmus tutored Alexander is not a historical certainty; the theory derives from an anecdote found in the writings of Strobaeus in the fifth century.
5. This 600 years refers roughly to the range of time between Menaechmus (c. 380–320 BCE) and Pappus (c. 290–350 CE). The 220 date seems likely to be an error by someone – whether it was Whitehead misspeaking, or Robinson miswriting, or the Yale Philosophy Club mistyping – as the intended reference is probably to 320 CE, the year of a solar eclipse mentioned by Pappus in his commentary on the *Almagest* of Claudius Ptolemy. Whitehead's brief discussion of these three Greek mathematicians was very likely based on his reading of Heath, *Apollonius of Perga*, available at <https://archive.org/details/treatiseonconics00apolrich>, the first chapter of which is devoted to Menaechmus's discovery of conic sections. Whitehead would have known Heath as a fellow graduate of Trinity College (Heath was awarded an ScD in 1896, 12 years after Whitehead had graduated and been elected a Fellow in 1884), and made several references to Heath's translations of Euclid in his 1924–5 lectures (HL1, pp. 222, 482, 502).
6. Johannes Kepler (1571–1630) was an assistant to astronomer Tycho Brahe (1546–1601) at the end of the latter's life, and later built on Tycho's work to develop his three laws of planetary motion, the first two of which he published in 1609.
7. The notes actually refer to a '*genetic* theory of gases', but this is surely a mishearing on Robinson's part ('kinetic' is also confirmed by Roethlisberger, p. 3). James Clerk Maxwell (1831–79) was a mathematical physicist; Whitehead wrote his Trinity fellowship dissertation on Maxwell's two-volume *A Treatise on Electricity and Magnetism*. Whitehead's dissertation is now lost; Maxwell's *Treatise* is available at <https://archive.org/details/atreatiseonelec03maxwgoog> (Vol. I) and <https://archive.org/details/atreatiseonelec00maxwgoog> (Vol. II). Maxwell first discussed his kinetic theory of gases in a pair of 1860 articles that appeared in *Philosophical Magazine*: 'Illustrations of the dynamical theory of gases. Part I. On the motions and collisions of perfectly elastic spheres' and 'Illustrations of the dynamical theory of gases. Part II. On the process of diffusion of two or more kinds of moving particles among one another'. But Whitehead may well have had a later discussion of this theory in mind.

Now the reflexive aspect of isoid relations is clearly deducible from the symmetrical and transitive aspects.

The next thing you do is to spot instances of isoid relations, which is a matter of direct intuition into things. But this is not always so easy to do, the fewer premises you have to verify, the better. Generalization. Reasoning is over no special instance.[1]

You don't observe a simple thing, but a complex thing. If you never find your |8| propositions contradicted, and find many instances of verification, you have very much extended your inductive power, than if you had merely stuck to direct verification. Now the ancients seemed to believe that the premises existed heaven-borne (?) which isn't true. As a matter of fact there are the simplest premises, but if you take a group of propositions and get the premises from these, you could get premises for the whole system. The premises are not unique. That is essential for the theory of deduction.

The next point is the sort of ⟨blank⟩ which an isoid relation might offer to us.[2] The idea of matching this comes in very much when we think of colors, for instance. I.E. in respect to being colored, two things are instances of the same color. So you get a determinable Y,[3] with specific determinate $c_1\ c_2\ c_3 \ldots$.[4] When we say that $p = q$ with respect to Y [$p = q \rightarrow Y$] that means they both are instances of the same color c. There you have a sort of double use of instances.

$p = q$ in respect to being instances of the same c where c is an instance of Y.

You can generalize that still more:

$p = q$ in respect to being exemplified in the same instance c where c is an instance of Y.

The question as to which is more abstract or concrete doesn't come in this matter of matching.

But if your relation is isoid, then its determinates are contrary to each other. P can't be an instance of two c's. That is with respect to colors. A thing is either red or blue. You get some quite important determinable ⟨blank⟩ where all colored things are very much alike, and yet because one color has a great deal of another in it, still they are contraries – well-marked peculiarities in a well-marked c ⟨blank⟩. Reversion: it is in the nature of reality that there should be a well-marked adherence to type and yet a reversion to a contrary.

---

1. Cf. Roethlisberger for the preceding few paragraphs: 'Logician's questions:– (1) aesthetic interest (2) deductive systems – find consequence just for love of reason. (3) question of direct introspection – finding or spotting this relationship. (4) But you only observe sample (5) Obtain the whole scheme of propositions which can be deduced – all of them are hypotheses' (Roethlisberger, spring semester p. 3).
2. Roethlisberger has here: 'Analysis into relations and relata a trifle artificial' (Roethlisberger, spring semester p. 3).
3. Where Robinson and Roethlisberger have 'Y' or 'y', Hartshorne has a lowercase gamma, 'γ' (Roethlisberger, spring semester p. 3; Hartshorne, p. 57). Of course it is possible that Robinson's original notes used 'γ', and that the Yale Philosophy Club simply had little choice but to type it as 'Y' on their typewriters. We have left these 'Y's in Robinson's notes as they are.
4. Hartshorne again references Johnson here, the only one of the three note-takers to do so: '"Matching". In respect to being colored, two things are instances of same color. (A determinable – "color" – Johnson's term)' (Hartshorne, p. 57).

Suppose $P = Q \rightarrow y \, (c_1)$
And $\quad Q = R \rightarrow y \, (c_2)$
|9| then c_2 has to be c_1 after all, and you have the transitive relationship.[1]

⟨Tuesday, 16 February 1926⟩
Robinson's notes

Every entity is social. You cannot find – either in the realms of abstraction or of fact – any entity which satisfies Descartes' definition of substance, in the sense of something on its own. If there is anything on its own, we can't know anything about it. But our world is presented to us on account of its radically social nature. My theory of systematic reference.[2] It doesn't do to hook up quantity with measure too much. You can't define quantity as that which is measured. Of course it is measurable.[3] ⟨Isoid relation⟩[4] Class Y with attributes c_1, c_2, etc., etc. No entity can have two attributes of the class $P = Q \rightarrow Y$ – two entities matching with respect to that class ⟨blank⟩ relation.

The idea of addition – to get the idea of quantity you must have some sense of parts and wholes.[5]

$K \rightarrow (P, Q, R \ldots)$ another class of the instances of the determinate entities (?) of the class Y. You have a complicated set of instances.

The $Y \rightarrow (c_1, c_2$ etc.) is the class of magnitudes, and the $K \rightarrow (P, Q, R)$ the class of quantities. That is – the magnitude is the length of measurement – a foot, e.g. It corresponds to the quantity.

The relation whereby P and Q can definitely determine another entity of the same class:[6]

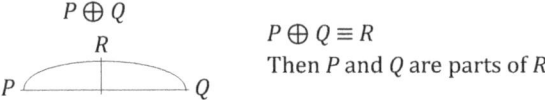

$P \oplus Q \equiv R$
Then P and Q are parts of R

But Euclid's axioms are simply statements of the importance of diversity within a common determinable.

---

1. Through comparison with the Roethlisberger notes, it is likely that this is the end of the 13 February lecture.
2. Roethlisberger has three numbered points at the top of the lecture, the first discussing the radically social character of the universe, the third discussing quantity and measurement. Between these, the second point is: 'Thread of lectures for second term. Idea of accuracy. ⊢: sharp definite truths. This idea does not hitch up so well with (1)' (Roethlisberger, spring semester p. 4).
3. Cf. Roethlisberger: '<u>Quantity is measurable but not that which is measured necessarily.</u> The character which allows measurement is social' (Roethlisberger, spring semester p. 4).
4. The Robinson typescript has a blank here; 'isoid relation' has been supplied from the Roethlisberger notes. Also, Roethlisberger has 'class *of colors*' here, and Hartshorne writes 'e.g. color or magnitude'. Lastly, note that where Robinson and Roethlisberger have Y or y, Hartshorne has γ. (Roethlisberger, spring semester p. 4; Hartshorne, p. 58.)
5. Cf. Roethlisberger: 'Addition – Quantity – ① Class of attributes $y \rightarrow (c_1 c_2 c_3 $ - - - - - -) <u>determinable</u> = Y' (Roethlisberger, spring semester p. 4).
6. In the below diagram recreated by the Yale students, the three variables are in lowercase. However, given context, it is likely that Whitehead wrote or intended for the lowercase letters *p, q* and *r* in the diagram to be uppercase, as reflected in the rest of the lecture.

$P \oplus Q \equiv R$ gives you some other instance of the class R. There is a certain sense in which things are the same; but there is also diversity. A general sameness and a contrast in the instances and some sort of a synthesis – this is the ⟨key⟩[1] of the universe.[2]

$\left. \begin{array}{l} \text{If } A = B \rightarrow Y \\ \text{and } P = Q \rightarrow Y \end{array} \right\}$ Provided they are so related

|10|

$\left. \begin{array}{l} \text{that } A \oplus P \\ \phantom{\text{that }} B \oplus Q \end{array} \right\}$ then $A \oplus P = B \oplus Q \rightarrow Y$

If equals be added to equals the wholes are equal.[3]

II. $\left. \begin{array}{l} A = B \rightarrow Y \\ A \oplus P = B \oplus Q \rightarrow Y \end{array} \right\}$ then $P = Q \rightarrow Y$

Of course P and Q don't have to fit together.[4]

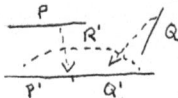

That is a much more abstract idea.

Then Euclid says that the whole is greater than the part. He has the idea of sum nicely enough, but he doesn't get the idea of numerical measurement.

If $P \oplus Q \equiv R$, or rather than

$P \neq P \oplus R \rightarrow Y$ (the whole is not equal to the part). That would be subsumed in a more general postulate. You cannot have

$A = K \rightarrow Y$

$H = B \rightarrow Y$ when you have

You can have one, but not both.

But even here you've not got all you want. Axioms of divisibility. The notion of sequence.

⟨$A_1 \oplus A_2 \oplus A_3 \oplus A_4 \cdots \oplus A_n$⟩[5]

So you can extend your notion of a part.

Suppose a sequence of equal entities.

$A_1 = A_2 = A_3 \cdots = A_n \rightarrow Y$

---

1. Supplied from both Roethlisberger (spring semester p. 4) and Hartshorne (p. 58).
2. Immediately before the equations below, Roethlisberger has 'Postulate set: conditions which you believe satisfy an important idea in the universe. Euclid gave some:–' (Roethlisberger, spring semester p. 4).
3. The Robinson transcription created by the Yale students has the following for the preceding equation 'A O $P = B + Q \rightarrow Y$', with the + written in by hand. Unable easily to insert the '$\oplus$' symbol on a typewriter, the Yale Philosophy Club often used a capital 'O' and then wrote by hand a plus sign inside it. Given context, it is clear that Whitehead intended the exclusive or symbol '$\oplus$' in both cases, which is how it has been rendered here. This interpretation is confirmed by the Roethlisberger notes (spring semester p. 4).
4. Similarly to above, the bottom equation actually reads 'A O $P = B \oplus Q \rightarrow Y$'. The 'O' has been corrected to '$\oplus$'. This change is confirmed by Roethlisberger's notes (spring semester p. 4).
5. The bracketed text has been inserted from Roethlisberger's notes to fill in a blank space in the Yale transcription (Roethlisberger, spring semester p. 4). What Hartshorne has here is much the same, but is accompanied by a horizontal line with vertical lines to separate each letter in the sequence (Hartshorne, p. 59).

Notice in the matter of sketches, I haven't given a suggestion of what difference there is between one sketch and another, tacitly assuming that there is some determinate test of equality as is this notion of sequence of equal lengths; there is a course A itself – the sum of the lot. Suppose C is the predicate of A, and C' of A_1, A_2, etc. etc. Then I can get a convenient |11| system of names. $C = n[C]$ or, I may say, $C' = \frac{1}{n}[C]$. That is ⟨blank⟩ a way of indicating one predicate in terms of another.[1] It simply is a system of family names and Christian names or $\frac{1}{n}$ is then the Christian names.[2]

⟨(1)⟩[3] The axiom of divisibility. If you ⟨have⟩[4] any stretch A, and if N is any number you like, then you can always exhaust A by making it into N equal parts. Also, ⟨(2)⟩ if B be any stretch and C be any magnitude, then you can commence from one end of B and form a sequence of pieces each equal to C, and by ⟨m⟩aking[5] N big enough, can make the sequence lie outside the other end of B, so that B becomes a part of it. This is the axiom of Archimedes.[6] Otherwise you might start on a journey the end of which could not be reached.

⟨Thursday, 18 February 1926⟩

Robinson's notes

The discovery of applied mathematics. Measurement.
Y – class of magnitude
K – corresponding quantities
$P \quad Q$
$P = Q \to Y$[7]
$P \oplus Q \equiv R$ – whole and part.

They there are the various conditions that allow you to use a number as a proper name.

$\frac{m}{n}[C]$ – method of giving a proper name. You can get any ⟨blank⟩ magnitude into this form. So the idea of number comes in as determining the relations between these.[8]

---

1. Roethlisberger's notes add here: 'This does not bring in idea of quantity' (Roethlisberger, spring semester p. 4).
2. The original typescript has an underline under 'or', when it should be the line of the adjacent fraction.
3. Both Roethlisberger and Hartshorne have here 'two axioms necessary/needed' (Roethlisberger, spring semester p. 4; Hartshorne, p. 59). The '(1)' and '(2)' have been supplied for clarity.
4. The original inexplicably has 'love' here. This seems likely to be some kind of Freudian slip.
5. The original has 'taking'.
6. Archimedes' axiom states: 'Given two magnitudes having a ratio, one can find a multiple of either which will exceed the other. This principle was the basis for the method of exhaustion, which Archimedes invented to solve problems of area and volume' (Weisstein, 'Archimedes' axiom'). Roethlisberger (spring semester p. 4) has a figure here which does not appear in the other note sets:
   Cf. Hartshorne: '(e.g. however far away a star is, light from it will reach us – e.g. n times any magnitude is greater V than V any other magnitude) Called Archimedes' Principle' (Hartshorne, p. 59).
7. The Roethlisberger notes identify this as 'Idea of equality' (Roethlisberger, spring semester p. 5).
8. Cf. Roethlisberger: 'Conditions for distribution of magnitudes among quantities. $\frac{m}{n}[C]$ Idea of number as determining relations among quantities' (Roethlisberger, spring semester p. 5).

Harvard lectures, spring semester 1926

Cardinal integral number – the definite multiplicity of a group of things.¹ The discovery that seven fish and seven days had something in common was a tremendous step in abstraction. The essence of definite multiplicity – this comes from the definite fact of a relation – one fish corresponds to one day, etc. The Aristotelian hard and fast classification which led to muddle in philosophy.² [The wedding of thought and practice together is the essence of civilization]. The Egyptians and math.³ The Greeks. The Pythagoreans [who got hold of the |12| idea of the point].⁴

⟨General theory of measurement

Relation of A to B. - $\frac{m}{n}$ ⟩⁵

Some of the most important difficulties were not asked for a thousand years after the Pythagoreans, some not until my lifetime.⁶ The proportion in number which you find in musical sound. The clear recurrence of beat in Greek poetry – scale and slope. The absoluteness of scale in art. But ⟨blank⟩ I imagine that the Greeks quite realised that this absoluteness is with reference to the proportion of the human body. Indeed, what is a proper model? The beginning of the complexity of the idea. The Greeks saw too that if you reduce the side of a triangle, the area is not reduced in the same proportion. Then they discovered that this beautiful idea didn't fit. For the diagonal of the square is not commensurable with its side. Then, of course, they tried to hush it up – as is so typical of humanity.

"We must face the difficulties fairly and squarely and pass on."– ⟨lecturer on theology⟩.⁷ I was brought up in the last stages of passing on. ⟨Passing on by calling it⟩⁸ √2. But just calling it root two doesn't solve the difficulty. If you are ⟨blank⟩. Of course you can easily get around by just describing this as the ratio of side to diagonal – but that is not interpretation in terms of number. [for number is the idea of correlation.] Then philosophers set in and invented the idea of the creative power of the mind. √2 considered as a definite instance of

---

1. Hartshorne's notes add here: 'Human mind doesn't know at first how abstract such ideas are. They are discovered because important. Taking abstractions up by the scruff of the neck & looking at them, = greatness of Greeks. Didn't like vagueness' (Hartshorne, p. 61).
2. Cf. Roethlisberger: 'The Aristotelian categories which separate so hard and fast, qualities, relations and substance have been a great source of error in philosophy' (Roethlisberger, spring semester p. 5).
3. Cf. Hartshorne: 'Math originates with practical man, in Egypt' (Hartshorne, p. 61). Cf. Roethlisberger: 'Land surveying by measurement. Introduced by practical man who used them' (Roethlisberger, spring semester p. 5).
4. Hartshorne's notes add: 'couldn't quite define, appealed to intuition of accurate geometrical boundaries. Got excited over question of √mutual√ commensurability of things' (Hartshorne, p. 61).
5. The Yale students attempted to recreate the board diagrams but, due to the limitations of the typewriter, they misrepresented Whitehead's meaning. As a result, we have used Roethlisberger's recording of the board diagrams as well as the sentence before and after them (spring semester p. 5). For reference, the following is what appeared in Robinson's notes: '_____ $n[c]$ – the length of this. Commensurableness. A may be longer than B – this relation is expressed if you even √can√ find a unit which will fit both. $\frac{B}{n[c]}$ $\frac{A}{n[c]}$'
6. Cf. Hartshorne: 'Some of difficulties in these problems only solved today, after [23] centuries. Americans in a hurry' (Hartshorne, p. 61).
7. Supplied from the Hartshorne notes (p. 62). It is unclear who this might be.
8. Supplied from the Roethlisberger notes (spring semester p. 5).

this.¹ But interpretation of √2 in purely mathematical terms didn't come until my lifetime. Bertrand Russell.² But as a matter of fact mankind worked on with a sort of clumsy compromise that 1, 2, 3 were some sort of abstract entity, and likewise √2. |13| The next step was the Cartesian geometry – another Pythagorean triumph.

1. The idea that all relationships can be named by relationships of number.
2. The more Platonic theory that all relationships <u>are</u> the relationships of numbers.

The logical (relational) side and the individual side. There is no such thing as a simple individual. When you get to the relational aspect, you get the number-side of things. Mathematical beauty. The harmony is a mathematical harmony. The planets in ⟨blank⟩. As a matter of fact, the common idea that mere⟨ly⟩ following the facts leads you to the law is all wrong. The scientist really sees a pretty key to the universe, and fits it in to the facts.³ How Aristotle watched the facts and lost the Platonic neatness. Of course you have to classify. But you must weave measurement and classification together.⁴

Einstein doesn't upset things – he just gives a subtler view of the world. Ignorance and ⟨trenchant⟩⁵; the ignorant man is the member really does the harm. But the ⟨trenchant⟩ man also does harm.⁶ The real moral of the history of <u>culture</u> is infinite patience.

Saturday, 20 February 1926

Roethlisberger's notes⁷

|6| Read Alexander's *Space, Time, and Deity*.⁸ Comparison with Spinoza in order to understand Alexander, giving a different twist to Spinoza, emphasizing a spatio-temporal activity with emerging of spatio-temporal modes. Is a converted absolute idealist.

---

1. Cf. Hartshorne: 'Then phil. stepped in and said "mind creates such entities". Then what has my √2 to do with yours?' (Hartshorne, p. 62).
2. Cf. Roethlisberger: '<u>Dedekind, Cantor</u> supplied proper mathematical interpretation.' (Roethlisberger, spring semester p. 5). Cf. Hartshorne: '<u>What is a number? Frege</u> (and Bertrand Russell rediscovers him) <u>first to answer with full clearness</u>.' (Hartshorne, p. 62).
3. Cf. Hartshorne: '<u>Method of science</u>. "Just observe facts" – they converge to a law of themselves. <u>On contrary, man says, what is most beautiful law that might apply here</u>. Simplicity is key to universe, but not so easy a matter as Greeks thought' (Hartshorne, p. 62).
4. Cf. Hartshorne: '<u>Can't measure until you have classified</u>. For only measurements of things of same class are illuminating. Middle Ages dropped measurement and stuck to classification' (Hartshorne, p. 65).
5. Supplied from Hartshorne (p. 65).
6. Cf. Hartshorne: 'Trenchant man makes one view which has its place, drops out of sight' (Hartshorne, p. 65).
7. Roethlisberger mistakenly dates this lecture 20 February 1925, rather than 1926. There are no Robinson or Hartshorne notes for this class.
8. Samuel Alexander's treatise on metaphysics was based on his 1916–18 Gifford lectures, which were published in two volumes in 1920. We know from Victor Lowe that Whitehead owned a copy of the book and wrote marginal notes in it. Whitehead also told Lowe in August 1942 that Alexander was 'the philosopher of his time from whom he got the most'. See Lowe, *Alfred North Whitehead, Vol. II*, p. 173. For a further discussion of Whitehead and Alexander, see also pp. 173–6.

Addition[1]

Problem of equality and addition. In order to get extensive quantity, your elements must be in a structure. Structure must have an aspect of repetition. Something repeats itself – a structure in spatio-temporal, identity of function in the structure. But what is actual?

Essential incompleteness of the world (actual) and therefore three types of mind/vbeing actualv[2] (1) start with actual final, all-embracing complete world. Problem.

(2) start with idea of incompletion – literary type – "Psalms" – passing of things, "what shadows we are, what shadows we pursue"[3] – If you have idea of structure v(a)v you can hitch it up with a complete structure or (b) a process which is exemplifying of a structural – {Process = structure + passing}.

(3) hard-headed type – struck with paving stones – individual bits of things are real. Here am "I" real. Aristotle was 2 and 3. – idea of ultimate reality to be found in individual substance. If you are a grammarian, this view is strengthened. Difficulties with this view, although should be incorporated among "*Weltanschauungs*".[4]

If you start with substance, it is difficult to give a coherent account of a structured universe. Substance = real; adventures = semi-realities. If you start with individual entity, you can never get your metaphysics real. Aristotle's classification of substance tends to weaken the idea of structure. Moral: Start with abstraction of universe which seems to be perfectly general of the structure of universe. – This is the spatio-temporal character. Universe must have also votherv equally formative elements; Here is where Whitehead disagrees from Alexander.[5]

Part and Whole[6]

What is most general character of spatio-temporal process? Idea of parts. There is a multiplicity of entities, each of which exhibits a part of the universe. "What is going in this room contrasts itself with what is going on outside by a 'beyond'". We can remember yesterday and anticipate Washington's birthday.[7] A part of this process refers to the process as a whole. ② You can divide this room into parts. The first element of structure is idea of extension. Any part you take is vin a wayv within itself and in a way less than itself.

Idea of "whole and part" muddled up with "all and some". Most general = diversity (logical extension). Mind jumps to idea of accuracy – The entity "it"

---

1. This heading appears in the left margin.
2. This interlineation appears above 'mind' with a brace encompassing both terms. It has been rendered with a slash.
3. This quote comes from Edmund Burke's speech at Bristol in 1780 discussing the death of Richard Coombe.
4. German for 'worldviews'. It is unusual for Whitehead to use German philosophical terms.
5. The words 'Digression' and 'See page 7' appear in the left margin with a brace encompassing the text starting with 'Essential incompleteness' and ending here. It seems likely that the page reference is to Roethlisberger's subsequent page of notes.
6. This heading appears in the left margin.
7. George Washington's birthday is 22 February, that is, two days after this lecture.

without parts – final and complete entity – concrete finished definite fact. Time has been regarded as composed of moments without duration (parts). Idea of "point at an instant". Looking for general character of the process, you find an ultimate entity which is without structure or process. Hence you run away from your problem. These finished entities are not what you want. To regard space-time as made up of point-events is such a running away from problem.

⟨Tuesday, 23 February 1926⟩

Robinson's notes

Read Bertrand Russell's *Introduction to Mathematical ⟨Philosophy⟩*.[1] I've now got to a rather fiddling stage. Abstractions. Thought is an analogue of the concrete in terms of the universal. I am coming on extraordinary subtlety which even the unintelligent tram car man has no difficulty about. As soon as there is a certain amount of interest, there is an extraordinary love of abstraction. What is more, language seems to get more abstract as it goes on – English is more abstract than Latin. [⟨Max Müller's⟩ theory of "dialectic ⟨r⟩egeneration" – which is really the progress of abstraction.][2] But when one gets to things in which interest is dead, he is stone blind to abstraction. Language. A curious subtlety and a curious lapse into stone blindness.

|14| Unless philosophy is fattened out by such abstractions of ordinary life, (?) it is lopsided. But if you run to ⟨special⟩[3] sciences, you leave out a lot which is unsystematized.[4]

Two types of philosophic method: the literary tradition and the scientific tradition. Since the 17th century, we have had two classes – those who know a great deal of philosophy, and those who know a great deal of science.[5] The literary philosophy is apt to find contradictions and say that they are engrained in our thought – the idea of infinity for instance.[6]

---

1. Whitehead gets the title wrong here, misidentifying it as *Introduction to Mathematical Logic*. See Russell, *Introduction to Mathematical Philosophy*, available at <https://archive.org/details/introductiontoma00russuoft>.
2. What the typescript actually has here is 'Mac Miller's theory of "dialectical degeneration"', but more likely it is a reference to Max Müller's theory of dialectic regeneration. Müller discusses this theory in Müller, *Lectures on the Science of Language*, pp. 51–62, available at <https://archive.org/details/lecturesonscien07mlgoog>.
3. Supplied from Roethlisberger (spring semester p. 7).
4. Cf. Hartshorne: 'To build philosophy out of results of science = to neglect data not yet systematized by science (No God – like intellects, "every man as stupid as anything somewhere"). But to neglect science = to not get beyond ordinary language' (Hartshorne, p. 63). The parenthetical portion appears likely to be Hartshorne's own thought, rather than Whitehead's. Cf. Roethlisberger: 'Other abstractions are put into special science through special direction of interest. Still, if you use these as a basis for your philosophical system, you commit the sin of omission. You gain, but only by <u>ignoring</u>. ③ If you go to literary expression and abstract your ideas from that, you do not get further than ordinary speech' (Roethlisberger, spring semester p. 7).
5. Hartshorne's notes add here: 'Even Berkeley more all-round than most philosophers today' (Hartshorne, p. 63).
6. Hartshorne is much more thorough here: 'Impatience of people of literary training with contradictions, not seeing that a more subtle analysis than ordinary language removes the contradiction. In mathematics

Space and time and accuracy. They are the great vehicles of accurate knowledge. They are obviously abstractions from the concrete world, expressing certain systematic relations between the parts of the world. The idea of uniformity of systematic relationship comes in here. It is this fact of the general way in which the ⟨rest?⟩[1] of the universe can be finitely expressed which makes finite truth possible. The relation of diversity and the space time idea. What are the accurate statements to be made about space and time? The Greek insistence on clarity. The Greeks brought in the idea of points and of relations between points. Now Euclid defines a point as that which has no parts ("no magnitude" was added afterward, but Euclid knew more than that and didn't put it in). It has position only. A point $\underline{a}$ refers to points – it is negative, but it has positive position. But that means only to be a relation in regard to the space ordering relation. Thus the simplicity of a point means that a point in itself is incapable of analysis into parts which are again relations of this relationship. There is no doubt as to the importance and relevance |15| of this abstract conception of space to the universe. All our ideas of accuracy depend on it. You can't say that our senses are inaccurate unless you have an ideal accuracy. The idea of the point and the idea of complete accuracy. The fallacy of misplaced concreteness.[2] When you talk about space you have ⟨already?⟩[3] made an abstraction about the relation. You've got rid of the concrete universe altogether. Abstract relationships between abstract relation. Our language has presupposed the language of geometry. We look on the space as already there, and the real concrete fact coming in and occupying this abstraction! We think of the table as in a space, not of the space as in the table.[4] Then of course you combine that with the idea of the substantial entity.[5] ⟨Newton⟩ undoubtedly ⟨looked⟩ ⟨upon⟩ space and time as the going concern.[6] The receptacle – and put matter into it.[7] Of course this was very valuable for the rise of science.

The easiest way to take this is to consider two points related to each other by a line between them. •—• Then what is the line? The line is a collection of points. But it is not a mere logical heap of points, but an ordered collection of points – the points as ordered. But to say that the points are ordered, means

---

even we become more and more subtle: e.g. infinity and continuity. If you'll only take the trouble, thing can be unraveled. E.g. Time and space, nothing to be done here without careful consideration of all the distinctions. Royal Society of Edinburgh. Robertson Smith. c. 1860. on Hegel on Differential Calculus' (Hartshorne, p. 63). For the last part, Roethlisberger has: 'Math like cricket. "Hegel understanding dx/dy in ½ hour"' (Roethlisberger, spring semester p. 7). See Smith, 'Hegel and the metaphysics of the fluxional calculus'.

1. The bracketed text has been inserted from Roethlisberger's notes to fill in a blank space in the Yale transcription (Roethlisberger, spring semester p. 7).
2. Cf. Roethlisberger: 'Fallacy of misplaced concreteness to regard points ⟨as⟩ less abstract than ⟨they⟩ actually are' (Roethlisberger, spring semester p. 7).
3. Supplied from the Hartshorne notes (p. 64).
4. Cf. Hartshorne: 'Thus table said to occupy space as already there, concrete occupying an abstract' (Hartshorne, p. 64).
5. Cf. Roethlisberger: 'Combine that with substantial entity – something on its own going on in space and in time' (Roethlisberger, spring semester p. 7).
6. The bracketed text has been inserted from Roethlisberger's notes to fill in blank spaces in the Yale transcription (Roethlisberger, spring semester p. 7).
7. Hartshorne's notes add here: 'Descartes however made spatiality the substance' (Hartshorne, p. 64).

that there is a relation between two individual points, and you are really back where you started. You find that you really have to cut out the intermediate points and content yourself with a mere relation between the two original points. ⟨With this conception⟩[1] you get embroiled in very unob⟨v⟩ious ideas indeed.[2] There is a logical simplicity in the relationship but not in the relationship of the relata.[3]

Thursday, 25 February 1926
Roethlisberger's notes

Idea of Concreteness[4]

Definite accurate truths is pursuit of simplicity. In so far as universe is not simple, it beats us. The addition of simple ideas through generations leads to astounding complications.[5] In the sense it is true in a very abstract character (leaving out a great deal).

Three kinds of simplicity:– ① psychological[6] ② actual. – The most concrete actual fact in universe. ③ logical – a system of entities with relations in which interrelations may be expressed in simple propositions. Things which are logically simple are very complex. Exact statements are logically simple. Relevance to the world is another question – bothersome![7] What is an electron? Relation to this before us. Electron $R_{b.b.c.}$ – Here is a bother. Point R actual world. Unless you have relation of these abstract entities to actual world, you are led to contradictions. Because contradiction is due to muddle of lecturer. ⊃ contradiction in universe. Universe is through and through rational. Enormous difficulties. But be brave and patient. The first 2,000 years are the hardest. Once solved, difficulty becomes obvious. Method of running things up to a contradiction and then saying it lies in things is poor appeal. History of accurate thought is illustrated with respect to mathematics as in no other field.

---

1. The bracketed text has been inserted from Roethlisberger's notes to fill in a blank space in the Yale transcription (Roethlisberger, spring semester p. 7).
2. Cf. Roethlisberger: 'Space as points with ordering relations – conception leads to very unobvious ideas' (Roethlisberger, spring semester p. 7). Cf. Hartshorne: 'Try to view things on obvious lines and you get into trouble, try to be consistent and you reach very unobvious ideas' (Hartshorne, p. 64).
3. Cf. Roethlisberger: '[Logical simplicity in relations among relata, but not in relata]. Only simplicity with regard to one mode of handling' (Roethlisberger, spring semester p. 7).
4. This heading appears in the left margin.
5. There is no punctuation after the word 'complications', though a question mark does appear above and to the right of it. Since it seems likely that the question mark refers to Roethlisberger's confusion, not that Whitehead was formulating a question, and since the next word, 'In', is capitalised, we have supplied a period.
6. Robinson's notes describe psychological simplicity in this way: 'things that strike an individual as simple – my boy thinks me as simple' (Robinson, p. 15).
7. Cf. Robinson: 'All our exact statements are logically simple. But to define their relation to the actual world is ⟨a⟩ deuce of a bother – the fallacy of misplaced concreteness' (Robinson, p. 16). Hartshorne has the exact same phrase: 'a deuce of a bother' (Hartshorne, p. 65).

No philosophy which emerges from (1) <u>science</u> (2) <u>math</u> (3) <u>literature</u> (4) <u>religion</u> but immediate concrete experience. Theoretically possible,[1] but practically mind has insufficient analytic power to discern primary relationships in experience. So you go to 1–4 for suggestion. Analysis of important physical ideas are difficult. History of philosophy becomes important. But to go only to science and history of philosophy, you leave out something. Appeal to concrete experience, life, great literature, etc. No philosophy via any one route. A new idea when introduced, overemphasized. Good as a method. But immensely exaggerated. Periods of recurring sanity. Combination of open + closed minds. Search for accuracy necessitates leaving out many things.[2]

|9|
Idea of Order[3]

Idea of points in serial order. Order made up in way by rest of line. Two orders of telegraph posts (1) <u>the</u> order for motorist (2) <u>the</u> age order. No <u>the</u> order. Increase in the order of cardinal numbers. But what of order, maybe silly but then what is silliness. In either case we have a perfectly definite order. – Brings up types of order. In order 1, 3, 5, 7 … 2, 4, 6, the number 2 is a limit in this type of order. A topic of <u>types</u> of <u>order</u> as semi-math. What is most general ~~relationship~~ ∨definition∨ of ~~rela order~~ a serial relationship representing order. What is theory of types of order? Different order types appeared and things became enmeshed in atmosphere of mystery, of contradiction, difficulties, etc.[4] Philosophy → lie in the nature of things, hence it has to allow for contradiction. "√2 is a creation of the mind". Whitehead against this? Postulated an entity. Will it come when you call for it?[5] <u>Criteria</u>: You have to be able to describe or point to what that entity is. Theory of order types was not conceived until about 1870 – Georg Cantor.[6] Definite rule of correlation between order types. (1) infinite

1, 2, 3, 4, 5, 6 …
2, 1, 4, 3, 6, 5 …

---

1. Hartshorne has here: '(cf. Husserl)' (Hartshorne, p. 66). However, this seems very likely to be Hartshorne's own thought.
2. A bracket referring to this paragraph is marked '<u>Digression</u>'. Cf. Hartshorne: 'No one route (no one man, either) to philosophy. Must try each topic of interest in relation to every other. In so far as you are merely accurate you leave out some major things, in so far as you are not, likewise. Wisdom needed here' (Hartshorne, p. 66).
3. This heading appears in the left margin.
4. Cf. Robinson: 'Types of order. When you think of a limit, you are thinking of a very definite type of order. The most general definition of order. This is the first thing the Pythagoreans should have asked themselves – and ⟨blank⟩ as to the type of order. They didn't ask themselves this, and so they got messed up in different sorts of order' (Robinson, p. 16).
5. Cf. Hartshorne: '√2 a real entity according to Whitehead, doesn't need human mind. Strict *habeas corpus* act of rationalism. No one can invent anything' (Hartshorne, p. 66). Cf. Robinson: '⟨(Whitehead) considers the idea √2 is a product of the human mind is nonsense.⟩ You should never let a philosopher say he has created an entity or postulated one. You should ask him like Hotspur if it will come when he calls it!' (Robinson, p. 17). The Hotspur reference is to Shakespeare's *Henry IV, Part 1*, Act 3, Scene 1. Upon Glendower claiming that he can call spirits from the ocean, Hotspur responds: 'Why, so can I, or so can any man, but will they come when you do call for them?'
6. Cantor's 1883 book *Grundlagen einer allgemeinen Mannigfaltigkeitslehre* (*Foundations of a General Theory of Manifolds*) discusses ordinal numbers as order types of well ordered sets.

class can be correlated with part of itself (2) not necessary that two infinite classes may be correlated.¹

⟨Saturday, 27 February 1926⟩
Robinson's notes

Order types. We wanted to find how measurement is possible. We came to the conclusion that measurement depends on it being applied to data in respect to which we have a particular system ⟨of⟩ relationship(s)² which we can say is isoid – that we have a particular set of entities such that the addition of these makes a thing of the same type and that the property of the isoid relation is such that there can be a certain correlation to numbers. We dealt with elements in structural relationship, and found that in spatio temporal relationships – which are the foundations of extensive quantity and measurements. How then can these exact ideas of measurement be applied? We asked how it was there could be such exact knowledge of space, and found that the idea of space comes from the idea of points with relationships. But I was skeptical of this. Still, unless you have |18| given measuring to points and to the order between points – unless this room is in some sense to be considered a locus of points in order – the whole mathematical theory and the matter of accuracy, being based on this, must be crashed to the ground.... Linea⟨r⟩³ relationship. Serial relationship. Then, having noticed the general character we saw different species within it – order types. The Pythagoreans – the discovery that the order type of points in space could be correlated with that of the fractions. This was the heart of the early Pythagorean theory – although it was busied⁴ in all sorts of irrelevancies. This depends on the correlation of two sets of entities in the <u>same</u> order type. You can't effect this, however, until you have some system of measurement. The Pythagoreans found to their horror that they were too simple minded.

1 2 3 4 5 6

Order type of six entities in order.

Then I may have the letters in the alphabetical order:

a b c d e f

---

1. Robinson has a far more thorough account of the end of the lecture (note that the line between '5' and '4' in the diagram seems to be an error, whether the error is Robinson's or that of the Yale graduate students is unclear): 'There is a definite one to one correspondence between two order types.

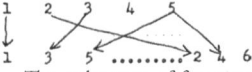

The order type of ~~functions~~ vfractionsv which has no beginning or end – between any two are an infinite number of others. You can correlate all these ~~functions~~ vfractionsv with the integer order type: in such one to one correlation. But you can deal with order types which cannot so be correlated. Infinities. You can have two infinite multiplicities which can not be so correlated. On the other hand you can correlate an infinity with a part of itself. Such investigation as this is exceedingly modern' (Robinson, p. 17).
2. Supplied from Roethlisberger (spring semester p. 9).
3. The original manuscript has 'lineal'. Roethlisberger confirms 'linear' (spring semester p. 9).
4. It seems more likely that Whitehead said 'buried' rather than 'busied'.

It is difficult to get these two types together, so we symbolize them. So:
1→2→3→4→5→6
a→b→c→d→e→f

That's symbolism. The symbols have the same order type, only they're different things. Are not identical with 1 and 2 and a and b, etc. The beauty of this is that we can empirically produce something which brings a relationship between:
a→b→c→d→e→f
↓ ↓ ↓ ↓ ↓ ↓
1→2→3→4→5→6

|19| Now in describing this order type, we don't care about any of these <u>particular</u> arrow relations or for the particular 1 2 3 or $a\ b\ c$ etc. Realize how profoundly we are indifferent to the particular relata and particular relationships when we are discussing order types. The point is this: if any particular set of entities form the relata interconnected by some definite relation <u>R</u>, and if the relationships of these entities as thus connected satisfy <u>such</u> <u>and</u> <u>such</u> general conditions (i.e. which can be stated in abstraction from the particulars) then these relationships satisfy <u>this</u> <u>other</u> condition. This is the blank form in which every mathematical proposition should be put down. (Of course practically mathematics is always taught by reference to a <u>particular</u> set of relations and relata). The standard exemplification of practically any question connected with order which cannot be exemplified by some sufficiently subtle elaboration which starts with the whole numbers – in that way you can get this standard relation for order types. That was the great Pythagorean discovery. The <u>such</u> <u>and</u> <u>such</u> general conditions ⟨blank⟩ which you call the postulates or axioms. All deductive reasoning is always done by an appeal to perfectly general conditions which transcend the particular exemplifications. That is obvious, but it has an enormous philosophical bearing. Your deductive reasoning has its force and validity because of its appeal to the fact that <u>any</u> entities ⟨blank⟩ that as long as the entities or relationships entify[1] these general conditions, then "this other" general condition will also hold.

Any set of entities will do, provided that this hypothesis is exemplified. <u>Seven</u> deadly sins and <u>seven</u> cardinal virtues. You might find that the relation ⟨blank⟩ entities ⟨blank⟩ that ⟨blank⟩ entities put up a definite relation that fits the general conditions. The point is, that |20| you have definitely left the particulars behind. That was a point which the Greeks didn't get.

When instead of saying "any set of ⟨blank⟩" you say "the points of space", and instead of R, "the spatial relations", you ⟨blank⟩ out the two if's, put <u>do</u> before <u>satisfy</u>. Substitute <u>therefore</u> for then – and add "⟨blank⟩ as the particular spatial relations between points."[2] Then the question turns up: how do you know that they do satisfy the conditions? So the absolute certainty of geometry

---

1. It is plausible that Whitehead said some word other than 'entify' here, but without access to Robinson's original handwritten notes there is insufficient documentary evidence to be sure. There are no notes for this lecture from Hartshorne, and Roethlisberger does not clarify the matter.
2. Cf. Roethlisberger: ' <u>If</u> "the points of space" form the relata interconnected by the space ordering relationships and <u>if</u> these relationships of these entities <u>do</u> satisfy - - - - - - - - - - , therefore these

vanishes. A new problem of generality turns up: Can you know everything about the actual world at all? ⟨blank⟩ sense apprehensions <u>now</u>. If I've found a set of points in the room satisfying a set of conditions – how do I know that they apply anywhere else – or in the past? For do I know anything except what is present for me now? (The actual world is always spacey.) The thoroughgoing empiricist says that all you know is what is before you now. I agree. But if you are going to interpret that as it is meant, you fall into difficulty. If you know nothing about the center of the earth, why suppose there is any? If you shut the drawer in which your shirts are, how do you know whether there are any there? At least, how do you know there is space there? You obviously do know this. What is beyond must in some sense or other be what is here, or you wouldn't know anything about it. Time is a worse bother still. How do you know there was a past? Reflection is a <u>present</u> fact, and you can't get away from that. The <u>dream</u> of <u>a</u> half second ago versus the <u>knowledge</u> of <u>the</u> half second ago. There is a problem of generality which is not solved by this generality. Of the reasoning process or intuitions, there are two distinct problems here; and these have been muddled up.[1]

⟨Tuesday, 2 March 1926⟩

Robinson's notes

|21| The application of mathematical ideas to the universe. The difficulty of getting particular facts which fit the abstract conditions.[2] Induction.[3] Equations – statements about the properties of numbers – of groups of whole numbers, ultimately. But how do these relationships between numbers tell you anything about the universe? Measurement involves an appeal to structure – equality – analogy in the functions of <u>this</u> and <u>that</u> in the structure of the universe. Then there is where two things combine together to make a third ~~of~~ VatV the same time.[4] Addition.[5] The types of order which are exhibited by numbers correspond to types of order in the structure of the universe. So you don't have to worry about the universe itself, but can investigate the analogous type of order of numbers. But if it's not the type of order you care about, but something else, then mathematical physics doesn't do you any good. The family with

---

    R <u>do</u> satisfy Vthis other conditionV (<u>exemplified in particular spatial relationships between points</u>)' (Roethlisberger, spring semester p. 10).
1. Cf. Roethlisberger: '<u>Two problems of generality that have gotten muddled up</u>. Hume ran a <u>consistent</u> theory of extreme empiricism' (Roethlisberger, spring semester p. 10).
2. Cf. Roethlisberger: 'Here is a gap. Are there are any entities in physics which satisfy these conditions? Most obvious test of fraud is to see things as they should {Illustration of Dr. Cook}' (Roethlisberger, spring semester p. 11). Our attempts to discover the identity of the referenced 'Dr. Cook' were unsuccessful.
3. Cf. Roethlisberger: 'From this piece of gold → similar things having similar properties – Induction' (Roethlisberger, spring semester p. 11).
4. Cf. Hartshorne: 'Also where two things (e.g. length) combined to make a third thing of same type, i.e., quantity, = an appeal to structure' (Hartshorne, p. 67).
5. Cf. Roethlisberger: 'What sense in idea of addition?' (Roethlisberger, spring semester p. 11).

children named Primus, Secundus … Quintus, Sextus … ⟨blank⟩. This tells you a surprising amount about the family, but leaves out a lot more.¹

Pythagoras – Euclid – Descartes – Einstein.

How is there ⟨?⟩ a structure in the universe ~~in~~ which puts up types of order to be correlated with types of order in number relationship? Measurement.

unit length

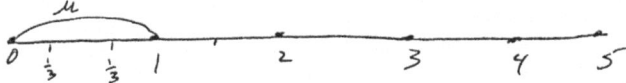

1, 2, 3, 4, are sheer names for these points. But they are so chosen that when you know your unit, they convey information about the measurement – e.g. 3 – 2 = 1, 4 – 2 = 2. etc. Fractions – $\frac{8}{5} - \frac{2}{3} = \frac{14}{15}$ etc. 0 … $\frac{1}{3}$ … $\frac{2}{3}$ … $\frac{1}{1}$ … $\frac{8}{5}$ … $\frac{2}{1}$ … $\frac{z}{1}$ etc. etc.

|22| When you have ⟨once?⟩² made this correlation, anything that simply depends on the order type of this structure, can be got from these numbers. … But these fractions are much too simple. The irrational numbers.³ Now that is further than Euclid got. I have been slipping in some VofV Descartes' ideas.⁴ Euclid thought simply of the relationship of stretches – units to each other. I have gone further, using the relationship of stretches ⟨to?⟩⁵ name the terminal points. Where you use numbers to name the points, you call them coordinates. Then Descartes said, when you are dealing with a plane, you adopt both Christian name and proper name – abscissa and ordinate. The principle is the same.

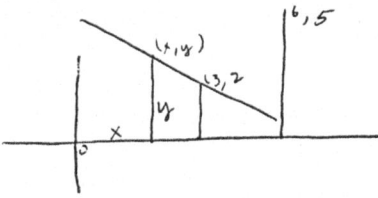

Furthermore, you have qualitative relationships. Straightness, circularity, the great test was whether – suppose any point soever is on a definite straight line and that the straight line is through a certain point (e.g. (3,2)), is there any way of expressing this?

The formula $\frac{x}{3} - \frac{y}{2} = 2$ loci – Any points whose coordinates have that relationship lie on that straight line. But some people have a much clearer feeling for space as such – pure geometry devoid of numbers. The point is not the numbers, but the <u>type of order</u>. But you don't think in terms of simple

---

1. Hartshorne's notes add here: 'Nice or nasty children?' (Hartshorne, p. 67).
2. The bracketed text has been inserted from Hartshorne's notes to fill in a blank space in the Yale transcription (Hartshorne, p. 67).
3. Cf. Roethlisberger: 'Taken whole set of fractions which can be correlated to the points on a line, then anything else which flows or depends on this order can be found by discussing order type of fractions' (Roethlisberger, spring semester p. 11). Cf. Hartshorne: 'When measurements once made, and arithmetical names applied, then interrelations deducible from latter. Fractions, imaginary numbers, etc. merely VveryV complicated ways of stating relations between whole numbers' (Hartshorne, p. 67).
4. Cf. Hartshorne: 'Descartes invented some of this (in bed)' (Hartshorne, p. 67).
5. Cf. Roethlisberger: 'Here we have also <u>named the points</u>' (Roethlisberger, spring semester p. 11).

Harvard lectures, spring semester 1926

abstractions, but you ⟨think⟩[1] with regard to particular examples of numbers or spades according VasV to which you have the finer intuitional sense. Now we have about finished with Descartes. Arbitrary change of area. Area⟨s⟩, of course, do not have to be at right angles, save as they are ⟨blank⟩.

|23|

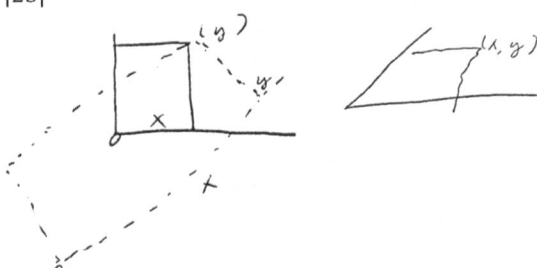

Then somebody else says you can do it this way:

Then somebody claims that there are all sorts of ways of measurement. But notice that you have to have some <u>given</u> element of the structure to which the rest is relative. Any given qualitative part is expressed by formulae. But it isn't the formulae that you're interested in, but the definite <u>line</u> that you are so expressing.[2] Can you elaborate a mathematical method such that you can find a common condition which all formulae must satisfy.[3] Einstein said that there are obviously billions of methods of systematic measurement and that is a detail of physical law, and you ought to be able to express the essence of this physical law in terms of what is common to all formulae. Einstein found that already worked out, and so was able to spring his theory of relativity, which is just as much a theory of absolute, as Bertrand Russell pointed out. Noted the extraordinary abstraction of all this.

⟨Thursday, 4 March 1926⟩

Robinson's notes

|24| The application of number to elucidate the relationships of the physical-actual-world. When you trace it down, it comes to the ⟨blank⟩ importance of order types. The particular entities that you're interested in in the physical

---

1. The bracketed text has been inserted from Roethlisberger's notes to fill in a blank space in the Yale transcription (Roethlisberger, spring semester p. 11).
2. Cf. Roethlisberger: 'Every measurement VrelativeV to some base. Any given qualitative fact is represented by a certain formula: $\frac{1}{3}x + \frac{1}{2}y = z$, $Ax + By = C$. Formula appear alike. Whole group of formulae which express the same qualitative fact, namely a <u>straight line</u>' (Roethlisberger, spring semester p. 11).
3. Roethlisberger's notes add here: 'This worked at by Riemann with <u>dramatic</u> application' (Roethlisberger, spring semester p. 11). Georg Friedrich Bernhard Riemann (1826–66) was a German mathematician, best known for his formulation of the Riemann integral.

world exhibit certain types of order – abstractions from the particular relationships of the particular entities. If you want to find out the implications of a thing, instead of arguing with respect to the actual physical occasions, you can ⟨argue⟩[1] about the special case of numbers. Now in doing that you have abstracted all questions of value. But you get rather near to value. For instance, the colors in the spectrum show order – emotional and aesthetic value can be correlated with the order types. But all the same, you leave out value itself, for all you are talking about is order types.[2] The party of Tertius and Quartus and Quintus – there is here a real value of age limit, if not of dispositions.[3] Remember the <u>naming</u> of points is always relative. The universe discloses itself as having a certain aspect from a standpoint. The universe as an abstraction of a set of points with names. From the point of view of an inch as a measure.... Relative knowledge – the formula. Now you can deduce knowledge which is not relative to the standpoint of the two axes.[4] But the next point is ((that the unit inch is ⟨blank⟩ from its axis)) that you can also have knowledge which is not relative to the unit inch.[5] You can have the ⟨ratio⟩[6] of one length to another – regardless of standpoint or unit. Euclid and proportion.[7] The relativity of ⟨ratio⟩ gives you knowledge which is not without relativity, but gives you ⟨blank⟩ less relativity than you started with.

|25| In dealing with the ⟨blank⟩ of this Pythagorean concept, we have left over some very important things. The order relations between points. ⟨blank⟩ room with a lot of very nice young men in it and chairs and tables, but where are the points? What is ⟨blank⟩ complex relationship between numbers which has the same order type as the complex relation between points? Points on a line – simple serial order with a unit distance between

$0 \quad \frac{2}{5} \quad \frac{1}{3} \quad \frac{1}{2} \quad \frac{1}{1} \quad \frac{3}{2} \quad$ etc.[8]

---

1. The bracketed text has been inserted from Roethlisberger's notes to fill in a blank space in the Yale transcription (Roethlisberger, spring semester p. 12).
2. Roethlisberger's notes add here: 'Values both slip away and "slip in" when dealing with numbers' (Roethlisberger, spring semester p. 12).
3. Roethlisberger's notes add here: 'Cartesian rendering of Pythagorean idea. <u>Giving a point a name</u> Advantage is in numerical formulae involving only numbers expressing geometrical relations – quantitative (distance) and qualitative (straight line)' (Roethlisberger, spring semester p. 12).
4. Cf. Roethlisberger: 'From relative knowledge you can deduce knowledge that is not relative to (some?) <u>standpoint</u>. Importance to theory of knowledge' (Roethlisberger, spring semester p. 12).
5. Cf. Roethlisberger: 'distance not relative to axes x – y but relative to "inch"' (Roethlisberger, spring semester p. 12).
6. The bracketed text has been inserted from Roethlisberger's notes to fill in blank spaces in the Yale transcription (Roethlisberger, spring semester p. 12).
7. Both Roethlisberger (spring semester p. 12) and Hartshorne (p. 69) reference Euclid's 'Sixth Book', almost certainly referring the sixth book of *Euclid's Elements*. See Heath, *The Thirteen Books of Euclid's Elements*, available at <https://archive.org/details/thirteenbookseu03heibgoog>.
8. Here and below, the order of fractions appears to be incorrect, given that 2/5 is larger than 1/3 and should appear to its right, not its left.

Harvard lectures, spring semester 1926

(1) 0, 1, 2, 3, 4, ...
(2) 0, $\frac{1}{4}$, $\frac{2}{5}$, $\frac{1}{3}$, $\frac{1}{2}$ ... $\frac{1}{1}$ ... $\frac{3}{2}$

Now this has the merit that it is everywhere dense. ⟨blank⟩ Pythagoreans thought this order type of fractions would do the trick.

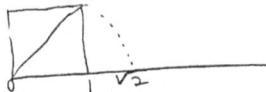

Now this apparently was the negation of the whole Pythagorean system.[1] What struck them was that numbers really could bring you up against values. Music. The idea broke down in just about one generation. As soon as a great idea breaks down, one denies vehemently that this isn't true, next that it is shocking.[2] The problem wasn't finally explained until 1860, when it was found that Euclid had practically hit on the same idea, but just missed it – because of the horrible arithmetical notation of the time ... "Real numbers" or "segmental numbers" (Dedekind).[3] What Dedekind said was this: you can always divide up ⟨blank⟩ let's think of √2. Dedekind noticed you have two classes of segments of fractions:[4]

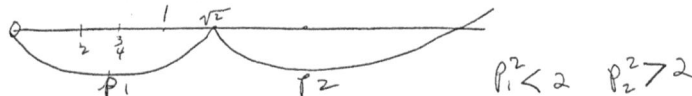

|26| In that way you've defined your contrasted pair of segments. I can always take an $p_1 + p_2$ so near such that

$p_2 - p_1$ is always less than any fraction you care to mention.

~~p2 - p1 is always less than any fraction~~

$p_2 - p_1$ i < $\frac{1}{10^n}$. There is a quasi gap but no finite gap.

$p_1^2 < \frac{4}{25}$

$p_2^2 > \frac{4}{25}$

---

1. Cf. Hartshorne: 'Shows that series of all fractions, though dense, doesn't hit all points on a line. Pythagoreans hit on this difficulty (400–500 B.C.)' (Hartshorne, p. 69).
2. Cf. Roethlisberger: 'When something like this happens two reactions (1) pretty idea but it won't work. (2) not true (3) shocking. (4) crude, more refinement and "analysis" (Whitehead): This took 2000 years' (Roethlisberger, spring semester p. 12).
3. German mathematician Richard Dedekind (1831–1916) found a method of constructing real numbers from rational numbers (in other words, segmental numbers from fractions). Each real number is constructed as a Dedekind cut, that is, as a partition of the set of rational numbers into two non-empty sets A and B, such that all elements of A are less than all elements of B, and A does not contain a greatest element. Whitehead gives the example of √2, which is constructed as the partition of the set of rational numbers into the set of elements whose square is less than 2 and the set of elements whose square is greater than 2.
4. The Yale transcription here is a bit muddled with respect to the variable 'p', which sometimes is alternatively given in uppercase. Given the general context, lowercase seems most appropriate for all instances of the variable, and so we have rendered 'p' as lowercase throughout. This determination is made all the more confusing by the fact that both Hartshorne's and Roethlisberger's notes use the variable 'f' rather than 'p'.

Harvard lectures, spring semester 1926

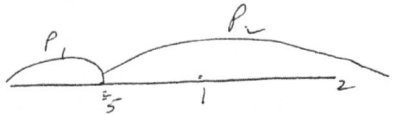

The only difference is that in all cases you exhaust all the fractions in the other. You leave a fraction between.[1]

⟨Saturday, 6 March 1926⟩

Robinson's notes

Any some none diversity etc.[2]

Divine entities such that:; any entities such that:; some entities such that:; etc. Your pure mathematical theorem has always got rid of particulars. The investigations of systematic methods of referring to the total universe – that's mathematics.[3]

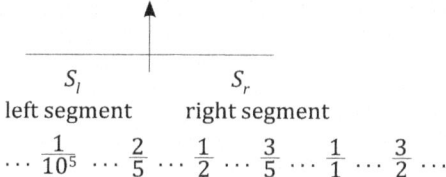

You can divide this into a left segment and a right segment also, at any of these places, also at $\sqrt{2}$.[4]

Now if you divide at $\frac{2}{5}$, you have $\frac{2}{5}$ between the left segment and the |27| right segment. But if you divide at $\sqrt{2}$, you have nothing lying between. This series of fractions is in linear order and everywhere dense. The series of points is also in linear order and everywhere dense. But the order types are different. ⟨blank⟩ always have a point of intersection. But you don't get this in the fraction series. Two order types are mixed up in the idea of density. The gap is the usual

---

1. Roethlisberger's notes add here: 'Same puzzle about differential calculus. Newton and Leibniz both not clear. Dedekind's idea of "cuts" gives complete solution to Pythagorean problem. Identify all order-types in physical world in VwithV order types among sets of cardinal numbers' (Roethlisberger, spring semester p. 13). It is possible that this material belongs at the start of the following lecture, but more likely that it belongs at the end of this one.
2. Cf. Roethlisberger: 'Elaboration of clear ideas (a triumph of) in pure mathematics – notions of "diversity", any, some, or none and their equivalents' (Roethlisberger, spring semester p. 13).
3. Cf. Roethlisberger: 'When you deal with any entity you refer to rest of universe not via particularity but via general systematic relationships such as some, none, any, etc.' (Roethlisberger, spring semester p. 13).
4. Roethlisberger's drawing (spring semester p. 13) is more thorough:

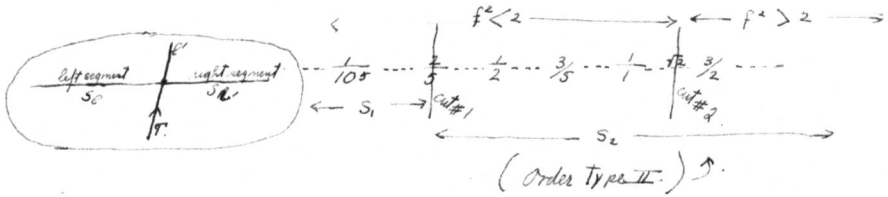

137

state of thing and having a fraction in between is infinitely rare in comparison. The straight line is the densest type – we call it the order type of Dedekind continuity.[1] The fraction series is everywhere dense, but not continuous.

The next step is this: can we define a set of entities in terms of the entities – fractions – which have an order among them and are everywhere dense – by mere reference to cardinal numbers. Take the set of lower segments:

$S_0 \ldots S_{10^5} \ldots S_{\sqrt{2}} \ldots$ etc.

and you will find that they have exactly the order type that you want. There are entities to define (?) entirely by cardinal numbers. Here we have classes – each segment is simply a class or a set – set of fractions less than $\frac{1}{10^5}$, set whose square is less than 2 etc, etc. Dedekind said that this would give you an order type which is exactly that of a straight line.

π and e

The first thing we've got to do is to give a perfectly general definition of what we mean by a lower segment without referring to some particular lower segment?[2]

|28| A lower segment has to have four characteristics:

$S_1 =$ is a lower segment if:

(i) it is a set or class of fractions.

(ii) it does not include all fractions.

(iii) if it be any number of S_1, then any fraction f' such that $f' < f$ also belongs to S_1 (or is a number of S_1).

(iv) if f be any number of S_1, then there is one fraction f' such that f' is a member of S_1 and $f' > f$.

You can also define an upper segment:

(i) and (ii) will both hold for it.

You must change < to > in (iii) and > to < in (iv).

You have to prove that for every lowers segment there is a corresponding upper segment, such that there is either a fraction or nonfraction between them. The next thing you've got to do is to show what you would mean by one segment being greater than another. The one which includes the other is the greater. . . . The arithmetical addition of two segments: but remember that one includes the other. It's not the mere aggregate that you want. If you have two classes – one of all the people in this room, and the other of Mrs. ⟨blank⟩ and myself, if you add us, all you can do is name the larger class.

|29| $S_1 \oplus S'_1$ is the set of fractions found by adding all pairs of fractions of each pair found by taking a number from[3] S_1 and another from S'_1. Until now your labor has increased as soon as you try to be accurate: you've got to prove that you have a real lower segment – and that if there are two fractions standing

---

1. The number line where every real number is defined as a Dedekind cut is a complete continuum without gaps.
2. This sentence is duplicated at the top of the following page, no doubt an error on the part of the Yale Philosophy Club.
3. The following line of text is repeated here (probably the accidental transcription of the same line twice) and has been deleted: 'each pair found by taking a number from'.

between them [e.g. $(S_{\frac{2}{5}}, S_{\frac{2}{5}}) \to \frac{1}{5}$]¹ This is simple enough, but it's got to be done. But this ⟨blank⟩ on the head a great philosophical notion: "the creative power of the human mind which produces entities like √2". Now the basis for that idea of the abstract creative power was that you wanted √2 and didn't have the face to say that you saw it. But I think that is all a bit of sheer romanticism. You may find support for this creative business somewhere else, but you won't find it in mathematics.

⟨Tuesday, 9 March 1926⟩
Robinson's notes

Measurement. Segmental numbers.
The order type of these segmental numbers.² Greater than. Less than. Addition. Notice that in this you've got rather far away from 1, 2, 3,--. The importance of this as knocking away all mathematical basis for so called "creative" power of the mind.³

|30| Then you can find what you mean by addition or subtraction.
$S_2 - S_1$ = that segment (if any) – call it S_3 such that⁴ $S_1 \oplus S_3 = S_2'$
$S_2' - S_1' \ldots S_3' \ldots S_1' \oplus S_3' = S_2'$
Unless S_2 stands over S_1, there won't be any such segment. You've got to prove that you're talking about a lower segment, and that there is one and only one lower segment that will do the trick. You've got to prove that we have a measurable set of things.
Consider the stretches $S_1 \leftrightarrow S_2$ and $S_1' \leftrightarrow S_2'$ etc.⁵
$S_1 \leftrightarrow S_2 {>\atop <} S_1' \leftrightarrow S_2'$
according if $S_3 {>\atop <} S_3'$
$S_1 \leftrightarrow S_2 = S_1' \leftrightarrow S_2'$
if $S_3 \equiv S_3'$

---

1. The Yale transcription originally has here: '$(S_{\frac{1}{5}}, S_{\frac{1}{5}}) \to \frac{1}{5}$'. We have changed the expression based on Roethlisberger's notes (spring semester p. 13).
2. Cf. Roethlisberger: '0 … 1/10, … 1/3, … S_1 — S_2 … S_1' — S_2' Definition of <u>segmental order</u>. Described in terms of classes and numbers.' (Roethlisberger, spring semester p. 14).
3. Cf. Hartshorne: 'Creative power of mind consists in <u>pointing out</u> relations among things, not in <u>putting</u> them there' (Hartshorne, p. 71).
4. The Robinson transcription has 'to' instead of '=' as in 'S_3 to S_2'. Given the context and by comparison with Roethlisberger, who has '=' in place of 'to', it has been corrected (and likewise in the line below). Further, Robinson's notes have S_2', whereas Roethlisberger just has S_2.
5. In the expressions below, some marks which could be interpreted as double diacritic primes have been removed in favour of single marks, as the second marks are faded and likely were intended to be erased. We have also added the diacritic prime to the second S_3 at the bottom, as this is clearly what was intended, and is confirmed by Roethlisberger (spring semester p. 14).

So you have here a measurable segment which satisfies all the measurable segments V⟨?⟩V. There is always the segmental number that corresponds to the stretch.

For the point of view of lower segments there is no measuring to equality unless it is identity. But when we get to the stretches $S_1 \leftrightarrow S_2$ and $S_1' \leftrightarrow S_2'$ we do not have this identity, but have to correlate them with S_3.[1]

I am trying to show that quantity is a complex thing. It is not a mere category as Aristotle thought it was. (Segmental numbers are normally called "real" numbers.) There is a certain formal similarity ~~that~~ VbutV they are really quite different notions.

|31| Notice I am still on ⟨one⟩[2] side of the Pythagorean problem – the correlation of relations between numbers and of those between points. I have just considered the relations between numbers.

There is another point that we have left over – e,g. What is a cardinal number? It obviously has a certain quality of a class.

When you argue about the <u>yellowness</u> of two pieces of chalk, you don't bring it into the argument – you merely talk of the <u>that</u> in which <u>this</u> and <u>that</u> are identical. The beauty of multiplicity is that we can define the matching in terms of mathematical notions.

How am I going to correlate one group of four with another? I can do it by one to one correlations. If you get such one to one correspondence, you⟨r⟩ classes have its same multiplicity. But this is really in terms of the mathematical notions, <u>same, any, such as</u>. Then there is that abstract property of having the same multiplicity. Again, any entity which has a definite correspondence to a particular multiplicity will do as the entity matching that multiplicity. Take the class of all the classes correlated to it – and that will be your cardinal number. The cardinal number two is all the couples in the universe. The advantage of that is that you have defined it. |32| This definition of cardinal number is not necessary for pragmatic purposes, but it is definite and so satisfactory. Number as depending on counting. Now counting depends on order. Now when you are dealing with numbers you doubtless can put them in order. . . . But my definition of multiplicity is independent of order. Though as a matter of fact you may use a serial relation as a method of producing a definite correlation which does the trick; so I quite agree that if you are asked whether there are ten seats in a row, the best thing is to count them. But that is only a practical method of finding the correlation. But the ⟨blank⟩ of the definite multiplicity of a class has nothing to do with order. The fact that there are 120 million people in this country hasn't anything to do with putting them in order one by one.

---

1. We have inserted the two-sided arrows here; there are blanks in the Yale transcription, but the likely intention was to draw in arrows later.
2. The bracketed text has been inserted from Roethlisberger's notes to fill in a blank space in the Yale transcription (Roethlisberger, spring semester p. 14).

Bringing in the idea of counting is a muddle. It's the correlating that's important. That idea of the ⟨blank⟩ multiplicity depends on correlation – I haven't said we were dealing with finite classes at all.

Let us take the cardinal numbers

1 2 3 4 5 6 7 8 . . . .

There's an infinite class. Now you can correlate the numbers of ⟨even integers⟩[1] with each other, viewing them as two classes, ⟨&⟩ but I can't correlate it with part of itself – I can't correlate four with three, for instance. Put in the class 1 2 3 4 5 . . . I can correlate 2 4 5 6 8 10. . . .[2]

[middle of p. 277][3]

Thursday, 11 March 1926

Roethlisberger's notes

|15| In infinite class the whole can be correlated ⌵one-to-one⌵ with any proper part: Is there any difference in the multiplicity of infinite numbers? Can prove there are. Segmental or real number cannot be correlated with the cardinal numbers.

In order to prove that they cannot be done requires more than "I failed to do it". To show that if ⌵assume⌵ there is any such correlation, you run down to a contradiction (*reductio ad absurdum*). Analysis necessary "what? you/we/I? mean".[4]

(a) Can correlate numbers from $0 \to \alpha$ with $1 - \alpha$.
    (1) Can correlate any $x \to x - 1$ As y varies from 0 to ∞
                                $1 - \infty$. $0 \to \infty$ The $y + 1$ varies from 1 to ∞.
    (2) Can correlate $0 < x < 1 - 1 < y < \infty$ $x = 1/y$
           Numbers from 1 to ∞ with numbers from 0 to ∞

---

1. The bracketed text has been supplied from Roethlisberger's notes to fill in an ellipsis in the Yale transcription (Roethlisberger, spring semester p. 14).
2. It would seem that the '5' is out of place in this series. As Roethlisberger notes: 'Finite class can be correlated with itself. But cannot do that with infinite number. Can correlate however with <u>even</u> integers. Infinite class has same multiplicity of a part of itself' (Roethlisberger, spring semester p. 14).
   In addition, Roethlisberger has the following: 'The order type of cardinal numbers, fractions. You can correlate them. Class of fractions $\frac{m}{n}$. Sort out ⌵into⌵ classes $m + n = p$.'

[handwritten diagram showing: $m+n = 1$, $\frac{0}{1}$; $m+n = 2$, $\frac{0}{2}, \frac{1}{1}$; $m+n = 3$, $\frac{0}{3}, \frac{1}{2}, \frac{2}{1}$; $m+n = 4$, $\frac{0}{4}, \frac{1}{3}, \frac{2}{2}, \frac{3}{1}$; with sequence $1, 2, 3, 4, 5, 6, 7, 8, 9$]

(Roethlisberger, spring semester p. 14).
3. This bracketed note is referring to Robinson's original handwritten pages. Whoever was transcribing this portion of the notes stopped here and never picked it up again. There are no notes available for Robinson until those of 1 April. Refer to the Introduction (pp. xliv–xlvi) for further discussion of the state of Robinson's notes.
4. 'we', 'you' and 'I' appear one on top of the other, which we have rendered here with slashes.

Harvard lectures, spring semester 1926

(3) map

$$x = \frac{1}{y+1} \begin{bmatrix} 0 < y < \infty \\ 1 < x < \infty \end{bmatrix}$$

country

Any stretch of segmental numbers can be correlated with the whole set of segmental numbers. No need ⟨to⟩ only think of the segmental numbers between 0 and 1.

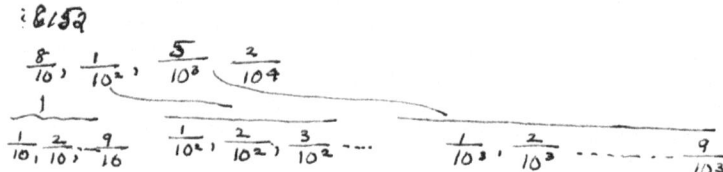

Why nine choices? Because ~~nine figures~~ ten figures are taken as a basis. Arbitrary.

111 on base of 2.
$1 \times 2^2 + 1 \times 2 + 1 =$
$4 + 2 + 1 = 7$.

11 — $1 \times 2 + 1 = 3$
10       $1 \times 2 + 0$ 2
110 — $1 \times 2^2 + 1 \times 2 + 0 = 6$

You can correlate segmental numbers between 0–1 with classes of cardinal numbers. Cardinal numbers and set of classes of cardinal numbers. Can you correlate? Can you <u>correlate</u> the members of a class with the set of ᵛits ᵛ classes? Class named α and sets of α's included from nul class to α. You cannot make this correlation! How can prove this?

⟨Saturday, 13 March 1926⟩

Roethlisberger's notes[1]

|16|
Proof

You cannot correlate a set of entities with the classes you can form out of them.

Notion = $\alpha \to x_1, x_2 \ldots \ldots$ i.e. the citizens

Constituencies ≡ Class $\alpha \to$ any set of citizens you can form.

$i'x_1, i'x_2 \text{-----} ix_p, i'x_q \text{-------}$
$i(x_1 x_2)_1 \text{-----} i(x_p, x_q).$
$i(x_1 x_2 x_3) \text{----} i(x_p, x_q, x_w).$

Every citizen is to appear in house of representatives and to only represent one constituency. To prove by showing it reduces to an absurdity.

---

1. It is possible that this is a continuation of the 11 March notes from the previous page; it is also possible that they are for 13 March. Since neither Hartshorne nor Robinson has any notes for either 11 or 13 March, it is hard to know. Based purely on the fact that Roethlisberger had mostly been taking a single page of notes for each day, this page would seem to be more likely from 13 March. Thankfully, this is the last undated Roethlisberger page. Note that 13 March 1926 is the date given on Whitehead's brief preface to *Religion in the Making*.

American	English
Every ~~voter is a repr~~ ∨representative is∨ a voter in the constituency he represents. Consider the one voter constituency. The one voter must be the representative. This won't work unless for Robinson Crusoe.	There are some representatives not voters in the constituency they represent. Consider those representative who are not voters in the constituency they represent. By hypothesis there are such members. These representatives constitute a class of citizens, i.e., a constituency – call it w. Take any citizen ∨to say that∨ x inhabits w i.e., ∨is equivalent∨. x does not reside in the constituency he represents. Difficulty over constituency w. To say that the representative of w inhabits w is equivalent to saying ∨representative of w∨ does not inhabit w.

Segmental numbers can ∨not∨ be correlated with <u>fractions</u>: Fractions are infinite class which can be correlated with cardinal numbers.

Distinctions among infinities not dependent on order types.

1, 2, 3, 4, 5, 6 → [Infinite] Progression.

All types of orders can be defined in terms of cardinal numbers.

Dedekind continuity. – Has property of being measurable. $2_m > 3_n > s_p > s_q > s_r$

Segmental number s measures the stretch $s_m \to s_n$

$$s_m + s = s_n$$

$s' > s$ $\quad s_p \to s_q > s_m \to s_n$
$s' = s$ $\quad s_p \to s_q = s_m \to s_n$
$s' < s$ $\quad s_p \to s_q < s_m \to s_n$

Segmental numbers play part of quantity. The stretches are the magnitudes.

Tuesday, 16 March 1926

Roethlisberger's notes

|17|

1. $K \stackrel{ab}{=}$ extending over events.

$xK \stackrel{ab}{=} x$ extends over y – Primary relationship – x as a part of y is an element in the constitution of y. Part whole relationship is internal. Irreversible.

$A(x) \stackrel{ab}{=} x$ is determinately actual.

To define overlapping in logic + extension.

2. $xK_0 y \stackrel{reads}{=} x$ overlaps $y \stackrel{dt = means}{=}$ there exists one event z such that $xKz . yKz$

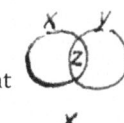

3. A dissection of x is a set of events α such that:– Dissection $(K)x$

(1) every member of α is a part of x.

(2) any part of x must <u>overlap</u> at least one member of α.

(3) no two members of α <u>overlap</u> each other.

Idea of two events which together form one.

4. Relation of adjunction:– When two events which do not overlap together form a dissection of one event.

5. Idea of boundary – y injoined to x
   (1) y is a part of x.
   (2) There exists a z adjoined both to y and to x.

Idea of Point Contact – difficult to define.

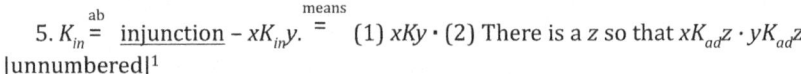

4. K_{ad}^{ab} = adjunction

5. K_{in}^{ab} = injunction – $xK_{in}y$. $\overset{means}{=}$ (1) xKy · (2) There is a z so that $xK_{ad}z \cdot yK_{ad}z$ |unnumbered|[1]

Types of philosopher: (1) hard headed, paving stones, substantial plurality → difficulty with community. Space = extension of substances. Even by filling up space, he did not explain spatial relationship between things. The Cartesian way also found in Aristotle, mediaeval thought, etc., partly Plato.[2]

(2) Start from a common world in the process of creation. Natural point of view. – Poetic view, includes relation in totality of the real. Denial: no actual entity in complete disconnection with everything else. Means a thoroughgoing system of internal relations. Avoid using nomenclature of other point of view. A thing cannot be divorced from its status in the universe. Bradley starts with negating that

3. Where do you find the plurality of entities? In the happening. What is real happens. Avoid morphological point of view. – (At an instant – Actual fact = spread at an instant.)[3] Back to the relation between instants. You cannot leave out process.

Extension in time as well as space. Most concrete and fundamental relation between things that happen. vRelation has to do 2 things.v (1) constitute each thing in itself (2) constituting the community of entities. Consider relation of extension – most general abstraction. Whitehead's difficulty is to account for "paving stone".

---

1. Roethlisberger's notes for 16, 18, 20 and 23 March are, with one exception, dated clearly, but they are not numbered correctly. There are several unnumbered pages inserted in this span. The content following appears on one of these unnumbered page inserts. It is not clear which part of the text is supposed to come first – Roethlisberger's spring semester p. 17 or the insert – because both are labelled 16 March.
2. In the left margin is a note that reads 'See Digression page 6', which may be referring to the whole page or just this paragraph.
3. Closing parenthesis supplied.

Harvard lectures, spring semester 1926

Thursday, 18 March 1926

Roethlisberger's notes

Assumption (1) every event has parts.
kKy etc.   imply that K only gives you one event.[1]

xKy	xK_Oy	$xK_{ad}y$	$xK_{in}y$
x only event	⟨x⟩ only one event but may be different	⟨x⟩ only event	

Route of approximation may be reached by a nest of spheres as well as nest of cubes. We want to say they approximate to ~~same~~ a common point.

If α and β are two classes ~~events~~, A is said to cover B.

$AK_cB \stackrel{means}{=}$ if x be an α then there is an event y such that y is a B & αKy.

Two classes are K-equal when each ~~equals~~ covers the other.

$\alpha AK_{eq}B \stackrel{means}{=} xK_c\beta \cdot BK_c\alpha$

This analysis may be carried on *ad infinitum*. To discern those which are important is the essential thing.

|18|[2]

Whitehead's Communistic Point of View

The most concrete actual fact is social. Radical pluralism leads to fundamental difficulties. Denies there is anything which can exist in itself. In mentioning anything you refer to rest of universe. Extensiveness of events is partial relationship between events.

How is finite truth possible under this view? "There are 14 men in this room"[3] is absolutely true. – only requires a systematic reference to rest of universe. Extension and derivative ideas is the great systematic reference. When you want to get idea of totality, the reference is diversity.

Method of approach by analysis of ideas. What can you say of one relation alone.

---

1. The original chart below has lines pointing from the text to the corresponding 'x'. We have instead inserted 'x's in the text to clarify the meaning. Also, in the expression 'xK_Oy', it is unclear whether the third character should be a zero or the letter O.
2. The following text to the end of this lecture is sandwiched between the above text for 18 March (bottom of Roethlisberger's spring semester p. 17) and the text for 23 March (bottom half of Roethlisberger's spring semester p. 18). As such, the notes are most likely for the lecture on either 18 March or 20 March. In the absence of contrary indications, we are inserting it here as text for 18 March, assuming that it continues the notes from the previous page. But the order of Roethlisberger's notes for 16–23 March is undeniably confused (see note 1, p. 144), so the reader should take the placement of this text with a grain of salt.
3. Whitehead's grading notebook indicates that there were in fact eight men (and four women at Radcliffe) taking the course for credit (Whitehead, 'Student Record Book', p. 16). The other six men at this session would have been auditors/guests. Roethlisberger was the only one of our three note-takers for spring 1926 who was taking the course for credit; Robinson is listed as auditing (p. 9), whereas Hartshorne, a lecturer in the department, was attending the course as a guest, and does not appear in Whitehead's notebook at all.

145

Harvard lectures, spring semester 1926

Saturday, 20 March 1926

Roethlisberger's notes

|unnumbered|[1]
Cartesian Point of View vs. Process.[2]

Most prominent part of the world is process and not tables, chairs. "You cannot stop this infernal rushing of events". Relationships between individual substances are somehow less than real fact. Community has a lower form of reality – "togetherness of two substances". The relationship has to be referred to God. – preestablished harmony.

Aristotle – substance is that to which you attach predicates. A primary subject VsubstanceV can never be a predicate. Tinged with logic. Primary substance is incapable of further analysis. Relation – category does not fit into subject-attribute distinction.

Descartes – primary substance only requires itself. Exaggeration of only one side of Aristotle. Mediaeval – Aristotle + Christianity → Plato.

Something becomes real in process is itself a bit of process, retaining the character of process. Otherwise you get into former difficulty. Take the event as real. What is VatV basis of "process idea" and community?

Are there some fundamental relationships of events which show them to 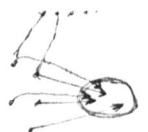 be in a community? Process = activity, Actual entity which becomes what it is because of its activity. Unity of self = multiplicity of relations. Events are social, a process in community You conceive it as the many relations which are for it. Creative synthesis whereby opportunity is one. Relations united in one entity. Status analyzed into many but the – for itself is one. Not an aggregate.

2. Relation to other set of entities – all possible universals.

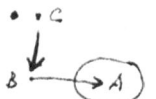
A modified by B under universal C
Something can be said truly of C – B – A
(1) patch of color at that distance – perspective. A definite perspective in relation to a definite yellowness.

Most fundamental relationship is a community of extension. – Also most general. Because of this general scheme of relationships - - -

---

1. As discussed in notes for the previous two lectures, the order of Roethlisberger's notes for 16–23 March is rather muddled. This page is an unnumbered insert that is marked as 'March 20, 1926 (extra)'. We do not know what the 'extra' means. It may indicate that Roethlisberger took other notes for 20 March, such as the section on 'Whitehead's Communistic Point of View' in the previous lecture. It may also simply be an indication that the page was being inserted into the rest of his notes at a later date.
2. In the left margin is a note that reads 'See Morphological vs Functional'.

Tuesday, 23 March 1926
Roethlisberger's notes

Beliefs – "What we mean".
1. K is insymetrical. xKy excludes yKx – (irreversible)
2. If x and y are events then ∴ at least one event z such that $zKx \cdot zKy$
$(x,y) (\exists z) : zKx \cdot zKy$ –
(Unboundedness). There is something beyond.

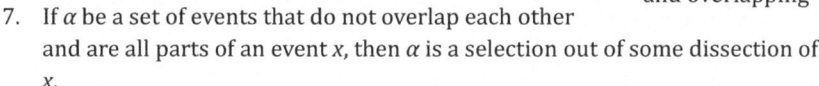
Irreversible side
Boundedness
Transitivity
Being actual
whole actual ⊃ parts actual

3. Any event has parts. – Idea of indivisibility – reverse of #2. continuity idea.
4. If xKy and yKz then xKz – Transitive · $xKy \cdot yKz \supset xKz$.
5. If xKz, then there exists a "y" such that xKy and yKz. – continuity.
6. If there is a class of events α which is a dissection of x and y, then x and y are the same event –

idea of dissection and overlapping

7. If α be a set of events that do not overlap each other and are all parts of an event x, then α is a selection out of some dissection of x.
8. If α is a dissection of x, then (some α's are enjoined to x).
If α is a dissection of x, then every event adjoined to x is adjoined to at least one α.
9.[1] If α is a dissection of x, then every α is adjoined to at least one other α.
$\alpha \, \varepsilon \, \text{diss}(K)'x \, . \supset . \, \overrightarrow{Kad} \, 'x \subset Kad'' \alpha.$ _
Run up against idea of atomicity and idea of continuity. Idea of extension has primarily acquired notion of continuity.
10. If $A(x) \cdot xKy$ then $A(y)$. (whole actual ⊋ parts are actual –) Always an element of uncertainty of an important truth. Psychology of martyrdom.
11. If α be a dissection of x and ~~eve~~ if y be any member of α, then $\underline{A(y)}$, then $\underline{A(x)}$.
|19|[2]

Idea of accuracy.
Instead of talking about room, take a smaller chunk. – Take a part of whole, etc etc. until you obtain simplicity – e.g. density at a point – a certain ideal limit. It has certain advantages, but leaves out things you cannot recover, namely certain simplicity can only be obtained by dealing with whole. If you know everything about each molecule of my body, the group put together would never be a "man". Electron. A period of time smaller than sound. You lose something and gain something. What accuracy can you get by going to an ideal limit? How can you make a route of approximation? Can route of approximation be defined purely in terms of extension?

---

1. This '9' is written over an erased '10'. There is also a '9' in the line above which Roethlisberger apparently attempted to erase, though it remains clear. We have removed it to reflect Roethlisberger's intended numbering.
2. Two unnumbered pages of notes are inserted between these two halves of the 23 March lecture. See notes on Roethlisberger's page order in the notes for the previous three lectures.

Harvard lectures, spring semester 1926

Thursday, 25 March 1926

Roethlisberger's notes

Idea of Extensive Abstraction
   Descartes: extension as a predicate. Whitehead: extension as a relation. Both take extension as fundamental idea. Exact geometrical entities, points, lines, surfaces, instances. Essence of these notions are all elements which have lost some dimension. If the concrete fact is full dimensional entity: ① Point is without parts ∧(predicate view)∧[1] ② utmost simplicity of position ∧(referring to community)∧ ③ utmost simplicity of physical specification. Cannot be defined purely in terms of extension. ① is a procedure of approximation, a limit of a point of approximation, a limiting notion. What do you mean by limit in this connection?
   ---------- ⅔ a limit of class of fractions in order of magnitude
   (1) ⅔ has its position in ordering relation
   (2) any fraction < ⅔ you can find a fraction lying between
   (3) any fraction < ⅔ is in class considered
   It doesn't tell you that you have ⅔. That there is a limit, e.g. $b^2 < 2$. Some stretches have limits, others not. You say that point is a limiting conception. If you start with events, how can you get to points? (physical) Point is a sort of a postulate. These spheres converge to nothing [Whitehead: *An Introduction to Mathematics*] Take the whole class as the $\sqrt{2}$ or point
   A route of approximation – abstractive class.
   α is an abstractive class means:
   (1) every member of α is an event.
   (2) if x and y be any 2 distinct members of α, then either xKy or yKx
   (3) There is a no event such as z with the property that it is contained in every member of α.
   Use and importance. You obtain more simplicity by devolution of extent. Physical simplicities obtained $\alpha = e_1, e_2, e_3, \ldots \ldots e_n$ $\xrightarrow{\text{converges to nothing}}$

|20|
   density = $\frac{m}{V} \searrow_0^0$ → limit[2]
$q(e)$ Class of physical measurements associated with e.
   $q(e_1), q(e_2)\, q(e_3)\, \text{\textendash\textendash\textendash\textendash\textendash\textendash\textendash\textendash} q(e_n) \xrightarrow[\text{a class of definite}]{\text{converges to nothing}} q(l_\alpha)$
   As one goes to nothing, the other becomes more accurate. The convergence of physical measurements goes to a definite limit. Hence all that is important in physics is the abstractive class.
   When α and β are abstract classes
   1. If x be an α, there is a y (belonging to β) such xKy.
   2. If y̶ VxV be any β, there is a y belonging to α such that xKy.
   A geometrical element such as y is a set of abstractive classes such that α is a π means. There is one definite abstractive class β with property that α is K-equal to β.

---

1. Parentheses supplied here and for the following interlineation.
2. This formula appears in the upper-right corner of the page, somewhat apart from the other text.

Saturday, 27 March 1926

Roethlisberger's notes

What did Aristotle discover when he discovered logic? The irrelevance of the particular entity in the cogency of deductive reasoning. The importance of the form. Cogency of reasoning attaches to the form and not the particular entities. In math you also get rid of the particular content. But this leads to "dogmatic" rationalism when you believe you have *a priori* knowledge which tells you something about the world. Knowledge from experience → no points, etc. Arrive at such entities by process of abstraction. What connection between Whitehead's route of approximation has to do with Euclid's points. Same formal relationship. Particular entities do not count. Geometry apart from physical relationships. All pure mathematics starts with an "if". The entities in mathematics may be simple, abstract, etc. – importance lies in same formal relationships.

Concrete fact has four dimensions. Losing of one dimension.

$$\alpha \equiv e_1, e_2 \text{------} e_n \to 0$$

Measurements $q(e_1), q(e_2), \text{-----} q(e_n) \to q(l_\alpha)$ converge to a set of limits. Getting rid of the fallacy of the average illustrated by average density of room. Brings up the atomic features and continuous features of the universe.

Convergence of α conceals different types of convergence. – (1) to a point, surface, etc. two[1] abstract sets equivalent with regard to their convergence.

The point does not depend on <u>squares</u> and spheres. Wish a <u>neutral entity</u> that is equally characteristic of α and β. Nothing defines the point better than the class. The point defined by α $(\omega\alpha)$[2] is a set of abstractive classes such that β with the property $\alpha Keq\beta$. $\bar{\omega}\alpha = \bar{\omega}\beta$

|21| Never get any useful physical information by postulating "point". To produce an entity which corresponds to a point ⟨blank⟩

The convergence of a class to a point is the sharpest type of convergence possible. Whatever VitV covers ~~one~~ covers ~~the other~~ VitV. An abstractive class α is punctually if whenever $\alpha K_c\beta$ and β is an abstractive class then $\beta K_c\alpha$. But now are ⟨there⟩[3] any classes with this characteristic? You have such classes in extension as one of your beliefs. In order to introduce geometry in this world, you need more than <u>extension</u>.

Tuesday, 30 March 1926

Roethlisberger's notes

In order to pass from extension to geometry requires more than idea of extension. Other ideas which need to be weaved. Sets of conditions expressed

---

1. Roethlisberger records 'two' here, but the context suggests that a series may have been intended, so that it should have been '(2)'.
2. Parentheses supplied. The '$\omega\alpha$' originally appears in the left margin with an arrow pointing to the phrase 'The point defined by α'.
3. Roethlisberger clearly has the word 'they', but context would suggest Whitehead likely said 'there'.

in terms of important ideas = σ   α, β, γ, δ --------- Some will satisfy conditions, others not (*Concept of Nature*).[1] Two abstractive classes σ – Prime, σ – Antiprime.

α is a σ – prime means
  (1) α is an abstractive class.
  (2) α satisfies the σ-conditions.
  (3) when β is another abstractive class also satisfying σ, VandV when $αK_cβ$, then $βK_cα$.[2]

⟨This is⟩ the sharpest convergence you can get subject to the conditions σ. ⟨Below is⟩ the least convergence you can get subject to the conditions σ.[3]

α is a σ – antiprime means
  (1) α is an abstractive class.
  (2) α satisfies the σ-conditions.
  (3) when β is another abstractive class also satisfying σ, and when $βK_cα$, then $αK_cβ$.[4]

The ideas left out so far are space and time. Aboriginal idea is shear extensiveness. Extension is ultimate relationship by which things are in a common physical universe. – Similar to Descartes – different "meaning" – For Whitehead there is a distinction between space and time in respect to the physical world. But there is an underlying fact of space and time, i.e. a community of extensiveness. They are correlative. One cannot be talked about without other.

How does space arise? Bergson annoyed over space. Kant and Bergson both think that space imposes a certain form. Kant – pleased. Bergson – unpleased. For Bergson, it holds up the inherent process.[5] The universe as real at an instant. Has it any sense? Three dimensions left. A misinterpretation of ultimate concrete fact. A fact is that which requires nothing but itself to exist. (Descartes)[6]

In dealing with time, it is notion of duration (not instant) which you fall back on. Physical occasion is Vunity arising from ownV internal ~~unity~~ relations to other things.

---

1. Whitehead, *The Concept of Nature*, available online at <https://archive.org/details/cu31924012068593>. See Chapter 4 'The method of extensive abstraction', particularly pp. 87–8, which mirrors this discussion.
2. Line breaks have been added for these three points so that they match the mirrored statements below.
3. There are arrows pointing from these two lines to the descriptions for prime (above) and antiprime (below). Though they have not been recreated, the intention has been retained through the insertion of '⟨This is⟩' and '⟨Below is⟩'.
4. A note in the left margin reads 'See page 23'. This note likely refers to Roethlisberger's own page 23 and is referencing the beginning of this lecture up to this point.
5. Bergson's 1907 *Creative Evolution* – first translated into English in 1911 – appeared on the class reading list, and contains extensive discussion of space. See Bergson, *Creative Evolution*, available at <https://archive.org/details/creativeevolutio00berguoft>.
6. See Descartes, *Philosophical Work*, Vol. I, p. 239, available at <https://archive.org/details/philosophicalwor01desc>.

M = "physical me"

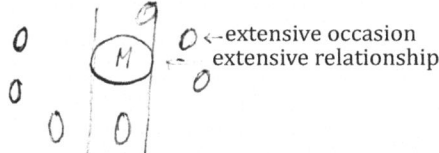

⟨Thursday, 1 April 1926⟩

Robinson's notes

|33| of instantaneous grasping.[1]
How then is the presentation correlated to its past etc.?[2]

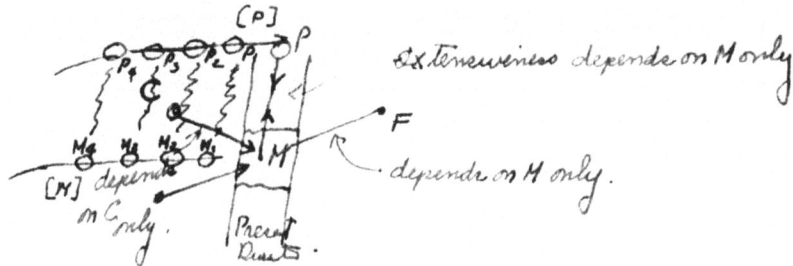

This is the dominant heredity. There has been a continual adjustment of M through millions of antecedent occurrences. This world line is adjusted to that world line.[3] It is entered in the ⟨constitution?⟩[4] of M that it's got to live in the neighborhood of P and vice-versa. You never get anything <u>important</u> of the effect of one thing on another unless you have <u>endurance</u>.

But why should there be an important presentational relationship? It is the outcome of an evolution whereby M takes a character which has survival value.[5] You might have a collision of world lines – when one excludes the other. But

---

1. The transcription of Robinson's notes picks up here, mid-lecture and mid-sentence, after a break from the notes of 9 March 1926. The April Robinson lectures were transcribed by a different Yale graduate student from the one who did the February and March Robinson lectures, with some key differences. See the Introduction (p. xlv) for a discussion of these differences. Cf. Roethlisberger for the beginning of this lecture: 'Something can be said of truth about a single entity – Fallacy which has pervaded all fields of thought. Abstractions as factors in something more concrete. Spatiality and temporality as abstractions from extensiveness. Three types of relationships: (1) presentational for M. (2) conditioning for M. (3) conditioned by M' (Roethlisberger, spring semester p. 22).
2. The figure and accompanying text below come from Roethlisberger's notes (spring semester p. 22). The Yale student who transcribed the April Robinson lectures did not draw in any figures, but instead left spaces to do so at a later time. As a result, we insert Roethlisberger's figures when available. See the Introduction (p. xlvi) for a discussion of this issue.
3. Cf. Roethlisberger, who has something very different here: '(1) What you are for me is not what you are in yourself. Isolation in the present. Philosophy of perception has been muddled by point of view of transmission theory' (Roethlisberger, spring semester p. 22).
4. What the transcription has here is 'institutions (?)'. Given the context, 'constitution' seems far more likely.
5. There is a space left in the middle of this paragraph for a figure that is not present in Roethlisberger's notes.

all that's very vague and may be ~~wrong~~ all wrong. It's obvious I have given no metaphysical reason why the presentational relationship -------[1] what this has to do with P etc. etc. . . . . – this of course is where error turns up. So I insist on the extensional perspective – mirrors, alcohol – this is given you; only the π is apt to be rather large. The conditioning of *M* gives you the presentational relationship; there may be conditioning relationships which do not issue in that.

Let us then consider the causes of error.

1. Abnormality in *M*.
2. Abnormality in ⟨?⟩ *P*. [*P* can go on quite nicely, and suddenly explode – like its stars (?)]
3. Abnormality in the environment – possibly a looking glass.

|34|

4. It is not really *P* that you're thinking of. You're really thinking of the future. You don't say, "Mind that ⟨blank⟩ <u>now</u>", but in the future. . . . So there can be abnormality in the future – error in induction.[2]

I will call the locus of events with a presentational relationship the present endurance.[3]

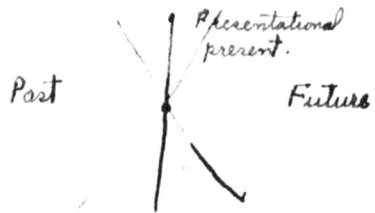

In the idea of the present (for *M*), there are these distinct ideas muddled up.

1. The presentational locus.
2. The idea of events neither conditioning *M* nor conditioned by *M*.
3. Events with the same status of immediacy – namely when *M* for itself is just the last thing – just on the edge of the future.– the last word – a certain community is subject to that.[4]

   This is an instantaneous ~~spa~~ 2 dimensional space – the world as presented instantaneously. _____

---

1. It is likely that the series of dashes and dots here and below refer to a missing figure (see immediately preceding note) and may be illustrating atomicity versus continuity.
2. Cf. Roethlisberger: '(4) abnormality in the future (inductive error). A practical reason for correlation between *M* and *P*, but no metaphysical reason' (Roethlisberger, spring semester p. 22). There is a somewhat faded '8' in the left margin next to the line below. We believe this to be an erased reference to Robinson's original page number 329, and that the transcriber intended to erase the '8' since it was incorrect. We have therefore removed the 8, along with other references to Robinson's original pagination. See the Introduction (pp. xlv–xlvi) for a discussion of this issue.
3. In Roethlisberger, it is 'present duration' instead of 'present endurance' (Roethlisberger, spring semester p. 22).

   The figure below is from Roethlisberger (spring semester p. 22). The following text accompanies it: 'Presentational locus – important. All vivid apprehension of extensional relationship is within. All measurement via presentational locus'.
4. Roethlisberger's notes add here: 'In any discussion ⟨these⟩ three ideas are present. (Good literature languages happy ambiguity)' (Roethlisberger, spring semester p. 22).

But the locus of events which are neither conditioned nor conditioning is wider than that. ---------- and . . .

If you are talking of math-physics the presentational locus is apparently of no interest; but it has two important qualities: 2. all your mind's apprehension of definite extensional relationships is bound up in it. [1. emotionality] The result is that all the measurements of physical science are made by reference to that extensional locus.

⟨Saturday, 3 April 1926⟩
Robinson's notes

The internal relationships of an actual entity to the other entities of a community. I came to the conclusion that geometry requires more than a mere ⟨?⟩ extensive community.

Organism and function seems more fundamental for an entity than mere process.

|35| An organism receives its reality concurrently. ⟨blank⟩ Differentiation in the community appears at once in its past, ⟨present?⟩ duration, and the future.

The differentiations in relation to one entity or epochal occasion:[1] Modern physics of course assumes world line of occasions.

There is an event which qua totality is realized, not as having the gradualness (?) of its extensiveness. ⟨blank⟩ The organism has its full depth. ⟨blank⟩ The individual cannot be extracted from its community; but there is a real pluralism. ⟨blank⟩ Zeno, the notion of becoming – if you take the idea that you want the whole event –[2] ⟨blank⟩ involves a vicious regress. That is what haunted Zeno. Relative motion is an absolutely real fact. But if you have the idea of an instant, there is no time dimension in which to move. So we must have this time depth; if you say this, you get the infinite regress . . . So I have an epochal theory of becoming: the present is an epoch: but in the past what becomes, has extensive continuity; but receiving it as an immediate present there is the atomic becoming. That balance between atomism and continuity haunts all scientific thought. I am not saying that the duration is an indivisible whole; it is distinctly complex. ⟨blank⟩[3] But I do hold that the fact of being real thereby gives you a duration as displayed by that organism.

We have now to ask, what about these durations? Here there is a tendency to go into extreme subjectivism. I hold that the duration is a physical fact of great importance. All our direct apprehensions are apprehensions of presentational relationships. Insofar as everything is related to everything else, these durational relationships mark very important facts with general community.

---

1. The Yale transcription has several blank lines here, likely indicating a missing board drawing or equation.
2. There is a caret within parentheses above this dash that points to the word 'notion'. The meaning intended is unclear.
3. The Yale transcription has several blank lines here that may indicate a missing equation.

Harvard lectures, spring semester 1926

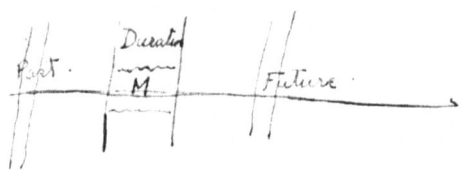

In the first place we have certain beliefs about durations. The community is differentiated throughout thusly.[1] ... I look on the class of durations as a given type of fact which stands before us. There is a <u>now</u> of the world which corresponds to <u>my</u> specious present.[2] I am not, however, |36| saying that my now is identical with yours. (In the modern theory of relativity you assume this difference.) Now what are my beliefs about these durations?

Here, I think, Einstein and his followers have got into confusion in saying ⟨?⟩ that there is meaning in accelerations. I believe with Newton that there is rest. (Rest and uniform motion of a world line is the same.) So there is the uniform state, and the accelerative state. Some world lines are uniform, and some are accelerative. When your world line is uniform, then all the durations connected with that world line have some likeness [?].[3] In such cases you can say, I never moved. But when your world line is relative, you can consider yourself as having moved last Tuesday relatively to yourself now. There is a real question as to whether the various states of the organism give you a motion relative to themselves or not. If they do, there is acceleration.

Two entities can however be at rest from their own respective points of view, but be moving with respect to each other as standpoints.

If we adapt this idea that there are standard systems, we shall get a complete explanation of why there are geometrical elements, and what are the difficulties of modern ~~science~~ physical science.

Consider a system of parallel durations.

A pair of durations in respect to their intersections have 3 alternatives before them:[4]

A. They may not intersect at all.
B. They may have a complete intersection which is a 3rd duration.
C. They may intersect in a complex of events which are not exhaustive of any one duration.

(I look on a duration as one event, for ~~si~~ I think it is a certain systematic whole.)

---

1. Cf. Roethlisberger: 'Beliefs about durations (1) simultaneity (2) time (general ideas about)' (Roethlisberger, spring semester p. 23).
2. Diagram supplied from Roethlisberger (spring semester p. 23).
3. Cf. Roethlisberger: 'Some world lines are uniform and some ~~discriminable~~ accelerated – discriminable. Motion and rest are indiscriminable' (Roethlisberger, spring semester p. 23).
4. Diagrams supplied from Roethlisberger (spring semester p. 23). The perpendicular durations diagram has text accompanying which reads 'Is this an event?'

|37| In case *A* or case *B*, I call the durations parallel. There you have the consistency [?] on which rest and motion take place.[1] (It may be that the only systematic thing which takes place is the dimensional (?) community. But I do also believe in geometry, etc. It seems necessary if we are to have measurement.)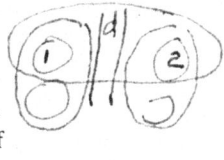

I assume that every duration has parts which are also durations – i.e., it is potentially divisible into other durations. Then, too, I assume that durations which are parallel to the same duration are parallel to each other.

(The rhetorician tries to make the odd things look plausible, while the logician tries to make the plausible look odd.)

From the point of view of modern relativity which assumes alternative time systems

This may be the duration ⟨blank⟩ past and future that the event *E* chose; but it might have chosen one of these:[2]

There are two distinct divisions, one of which has reference to the past and the other to the future.

If If two events belong to the same class, there is an infinite number (at least one) of events which include ⟨?⟩ them both and does not intersect the duration. Any event which contains both the past and future, it has got to include the duration. The duration might be Wednesday between Tuesday and Thursday, for instance.[3]

⟨Tuesday, 6 April 1926⟩

Robinson's notes

Durations. ⟨blank⟩ I was very confused last time. I should have stated it negatively and not positively.

The point is, that I've been dealing with 2 types of relationships of events to each other – physical causality – and how one epochal occasion enters into the existence of a later one. Presentational relationships give you a duration.

|38| The duration is the locus of events which have this presentational relationship.[4]

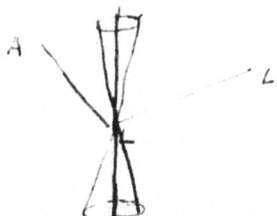
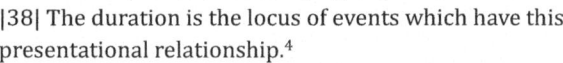

The relation of being presentational means that your set of events is causally independent of *L* and vice-versa . . . that is, *D*, is not *x* or *y*. Of course the

---

1. Cf. Roethlisberger: '(1) (2) durations are parallel – belong to same time system' (Roethlisberger, spring semester p. 23). Robinson's 'A' and 'B' seem to correspond to the '1' and '2' in Roethlisberger's diagrams.
2. This sentence is surrounded by a blank line above, below and to the left, indicating content of some kind left out that the Yale Philosophy Club intended to hand-write, probably diagrams or equations.
3. There are four lines of blank space to the left here, indicating a missing diagram or equations.
4. The Yale transcription has several blank lines here that might indicate missing content, or simply a page break in the original. The figures for this lecture are from Roethlisberger's notes (spring semester p. 24).

physicist is purely interested in the relations Aa and LL, not in D. Still he has to consider these presentationally.[1]

A duration is to be looked on as dividing the whole locus of the physical community into two parts other than itself – the antecedent and the sequent parts. We can define these by reference to extension alone.[2]

Extension is the fundamental community idea. But of course that point of view doesn't give you any functional difference between antecedent and sequent. If you are to have this you must refer to the notion of process.

No event in the sequent set ⟨is⟩[3] physically caus(a)l for any event in D, nor any event in D for any event in the antecedent set. Thus we come up to this idea of parallel durations – you can have parallel durations in the same time system.[4]

But these can also be durations like this:[5]

I will call a complete system of parallel events a time system.

The extensive relationships of durations in one time system satisfy all the axioms I laid down for events in general.

1. xKy and yKx are incompatible.

2. if x, y, are any two durations, z exists in the same s, which contains them both.

|39|

3. Any s of durations includes other relations.

4. If xKy and yKz, then xKz.

5. If xKy, then xKz and zKy.

6. The dissection can only ⟨be⟩[6] the dissection of one duration, etc., etc. But added to all these, there is this:

> If 2 durations overlap, there is one complete duration which contains every event which lies in both.[7]

The antiprime – the least sharp type of convergence (as opposed to the prime – the sharpest).

This involves the assumption that all these durations are in the same time-systems. But you can approximate on the other side too to the same moment.[8]

---

1. Cf. Roethlisberger: 'A is the relatively past for L and L' is relatively future. Relationship of being contemporaneous with L = not causal. Causal independent of L. Present duration = all contemporary events. Physicist interested in A-L-L' relationship. (Physical) But measurements made in terms of contemporary relationships' (Roethlisberger, spring semester p. 24).
2. The Yale transcription has several blank lines here that might indicate missing content.
3. The Yale transcription has 'if', but 'is' is confirmed by Roethlisberger (spring semester p. 24).
4. The Yale transcription has several blank lines here that might indicate missing content.
5. The Yale transcription has several blank lines here that might indicate missing content. Cf. Roethlisberger here: 'To be physically causal = to be relatively future. Belief – you're referring beyond extension. <u>Parallel Events</u>. Durations of this sort has been generally the only ones assumed. But Whitehead sees no reason for X' (Roethlisberger, spring semester p. 24).
6. The notes have a double 'the' here.
7. The Yale transcription has several blank lines here that might indicate missing content.
8. Cf. Roethlisberger: 'If the only way the intellect can do is to start with a moment or instant, β. is correct. But a moment for science is merely a route of approximation. Such a set of durations approaching a

Let us define a σ antiprime:[1] If S is some particular time system (i.e., all the particular parallel durations of that sort), then that satisfies σ, means that is a set S durations: then is an antiprime when

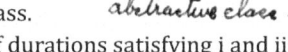

i. It satisfies σ.
ii. It is an abstractive class.
iii. If β be another set of durations satisfying i and ii, then if $βK_c α$, then $αK_c β$.

i.e., cannot cover a σ of that sort without being covered by itself. The beauty of this is that it converges on both sides.

I will call such an antiprime an S-momental abstractive class. The set of such classes is simply what you are talking about when you talk of M. When you talk of M', you talk of a community of durations ⱽeventsⱽ that submit themselves to that type of approximation.

When you speak of a moment, you practically speak of a duration so small that it |40| doesn't bother you.[2] . . . There is an ideal limit in all the physical properties.

An abstractive class which is covered by an S momental abstractive class, may be said to lie in that moment.[3]

An abstractive class which lies in one instantaneous moment, I will call a geometrical abstractive class.

How then, will we get geometry?[4] Euclid: points, straight lines, and planes. Euclid says a plane lies evenly between its end points, and a plane is flat!

Here is a moment of a time system S.

What if there is another time system S'?

This intersection is obviously the assemblage of all the geometrical things that lie in both moments M_s and $M_{s'}$ – the locus of all abstractive classes so covered. The place in such an instantaneous space, is something which could be in another system of time. ⟨blank⟩ The intersection of two planes is a straight line, or they are parallel; if you have a third plane ? ? ? Then there is another point to notice: you might bring in a fourth one

The common intersection of these planes is a point instant.[5]

---

convergence are in one time system. S = particular time system = all parallel durations. α satisfies σ means α is a set of S-duration' (Roethlisberger, spring semester p. 24).
1. Diagram supplied from Roethlisberger (spring semester p. 24). There are a lot of missing Greek letters in the following Yale student transcription of Robinson's notes, perhaps due to the limitations of a typewriter. The Greek letters here have been supplied based on comparison with the Roethlisberger notes.
2. Cf. Roethlisberger: 'You mean a duration so small so that divisibility does not enter into thinking' (Roethlisberger, spring semester p. 24).
3. Cf. Roethlisberger: 'Moment = three-dimensional space' (Roethlisberger, spring semester p. 25).
4. Cf. Roethlisberger: 'How do ideas with definite structure enter into nature?' (Roethlisberger, spring semester p. 25).
5. The Yale transcription has several blank lines here that might indicate missing content.

⟨Thursday, 8 April 1926⟩
Robinson's notes

We are now explaining how there is geometry. This entirely depends on the idea of a definite structural relationship between moments, and the being of alternative systems. That is the whole basis of the measurable structure of things.

Moments: a moment is really a ⟨route⟩[1] of approximation, but as an entity it stands in our mind for
   1. that ⟨?⟩ set of physical statements which is the limit of the ⟨route⟩ of approximation.
   2. a certain psychological grasp of what you mean by an instant.

So you have a physical fact and in trying to make it conceptually definite, you come to the idea of a ⟨route⟩ of approximation. As a concept it represents an idealization |41| which goes beyond what you have actually observed. ⟨Routes⟩ covering each other. ... The moment ... The geometrical elements which lie in moments, i.e., are covered by moments ... alternative time systems.

I want to get the idea of a <u>timeless</u> space – ⟨such⟩[2] as science presupposes to some extent.

Now of course, I have been defining an instantaneous and not a timeless space. ... Now there is a certain absoluteness of space, but it is of a very abstract nature. I come down on the thoroughly Newtonian idea that a uniform velocity is a fact in nature, and is not to be distinguished from rest.[3]

If some actual entity is such that it is the conceptual limit of your presentational [?] field, and you get parallel moments, then you are at rest in that time system.

Two entities are relatively at rest if their presentational moments are so consistent with each other. I assume that the identity of a presentational moment gives you rest.[4]

Suppose you have another entity in another time system S'. (-----------) I come down on uniformity as being a perceptual fact. Now this entity A has its successive actual occasions; but if it's at rest (according to the language of timeless space), it is always at the same point – but the point is the track of occasions ⟨?⟩ T_S. So the point is a pure time dimension. Notice that

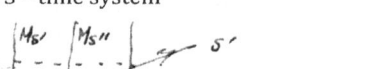

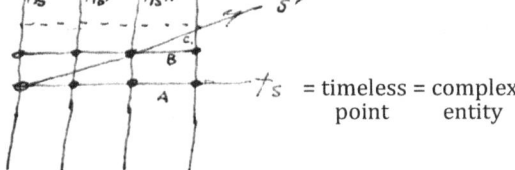

---

1. Here and below the word 'root' has been changed to 'route'.
2. The Yale transcription has 'cuah' here. From context, we have interpreted this as a singularly mangled mistyping of 'such'.
3. The Yale transcription has several blank lines here that might indicate missing content, or simply a page break in the original.
4. The figures for this lecture are from Roethlisberger (spring semester p. 25).

Harvard lectures, spring semester 1926

Alexander says "space is <u>full</u> of time" and "time is full of space". That's where my niggling method strikes me as better.

Enduring objects. ⟨blank⟩ The idea of an instantaneous space squeezes the time ⟨out⟩[1] of space and is a very elaborate logical problem.

Then you take <u>these</u> extraneous ideas of spatio-temporal uniformity as the fundamental fact.

A point is the historical route of an entity relatively at rest. It has S-time, and no S-space.

|42| Both $T_{S^A} T_{S^B}$ are highly complex entities.

Notice that the entity in the S' system is occupying various points at an instant in the S system. I do these intersections of routes which are the final observations that you make.

Let us take up the question of ⟨?⟩ two time systems, S and ~~S⟩~~ S'. If you have two different moments, these intersect. You can take this intersection as one instantaneous plane in either instantaneous space – the locus of all the ⟨routes⟩ of approximation which are covered by both moments. . . . Then we have a more general conception of any number of time systems, $S_1, S_2, \ldots S_n$, with the particular set of moments ⟨?⟩ $M_{S_1}, M_{S_2}, \ldots M_{S_n}$, and ask about the intersection of these moments. I conceive the whole of geometry coming in via the differences of time systems – motion and rest as fundamental facts.

The first idea to have is between a general set $M_{S_1} \ldots M_{S_n}$ and a special set of moments $M_{S_1} \ldots M_{S_n} \ldots$ I will call the set special when the same locus of intersection can be defined by a selection among the moments.

$M_{S_1}, M_{S_2}, \ldots M_{S_g}$ – so that I have a redundant number and the extra numbers of the set don't limit the intersection in any way. When, if you omit any one moment, you get a wider intersection, I call it general. The first stage to get down to three dimensions is this: that all sets of more than four moments are special sets, if they have any common intersections. That really lands you in your four dimensions. Now I don't believe that when you run into a fact like four dimensions, that there is any general metaphysical reason for it. It's part of the nature of the universe to present you with blank facts: particularity is an ultimate irrationality in the universe: and I look on the four dimensions as another ⟨?⟩ one of these curious facts. So when S_1, S_2, S_3, S_4, are different time systems,

|43|
    1. We can have M_{S_1}, M_{S_2} intersecting
    2. We can have $M_{S_1}, M_{S_2}, M_{S_3}$ intersecting
    3. We can have $M_{S_1}, M_{S_2}, M_{S_3}, M_{S_4}$ intersecting

I assume you can always get #2, and #1 – that they always exist, and that #3 may exist.

    #1 is always a general set
    #2 is possibly general and possibly special
    #3 is also possibly general and possibly special

---

1. The Yale transcription has 'our'.

Whenever you have a special case, you can get it back to the case before.

Let us consider only the general intersections: then $M_{S_1} \cdot M_{S_2}$ is a plane in M_{S_1} & M_{S_2}; $M_{S_1} \cdot M_{S_2} \cdot M_{S_3}$ is a straight line; $M_{S_1} \cdot M_{S_2} \cdot M_{S_3} \cdot M_{S_4}$ is a point. (i.e., instantaneous point, plane, or line.) A point is such that each moment either contains it all or doesn't contain it all; it can't be divided up; it is incapable of analysis in that way; it is simple. Then the particular moments it happens to lie in give you its position – its geometrical relations to other points.

The geometry of the timeless space is derivative from the geometry of the instantaneous space.

⟨Saturday, 10 April 1926⟩
Robinson's notes

Descartes said the physical world was made up of extended bodies with endurance. So far he was o.k. . . . Extension, (Process), space, time. I.e. You have (community and process), and then (extension, space time).[1] There is no such thing as an abstract idea all by itself: the number three takes you back to number two. You couldn't have three as the only abstract fact. . . . There's nothing in isolation. The community is many things in community.[2] . . . Then there is that funny idea that metaphysics would be so easy if there weren't any future. But there is a real difference between the future and the past; for the future isn't actual.[3] . . . The community of immediacy. Now Descartes got the wrong idea of extension. . . . The fundamental community idea comes in from the idea of extension. It is the specializing of the identity-diversity relation into the special form which it takes as the most general fact of the physical world. I look on it as a relationship – the extensive relation. It looks on the ultimate physical entities as related by whole and part or overlapping. Why |44| the physical world stands before us as a community is that it is a community of things related by this extensive relation. The molecule becomes a subordinate organism. But that presupposes this general idea of whole and part . . . {?} The next step is the continuity idea. The world is both continuous and atomic. The extensive relation is what gives you the continuity. So you get the transmission idea of connection in continuity – continuous connectedness. When Descartes comes down on the extended body, I agree with him about the extension, but not about the body. It is really an event which you've got to think of. It is, I think, the first instance of general knowledge. A primary general knowledge is that any entity describes itself in . . . . If you take your extension in substances, as Descartes did, you can't get from one substance to another. But if you take your

---

1. Cf. Roethlisberger: 'Primarily concerned with physical world. Three ideas in terms of which all other physical terms are to be defined. (1) extension, space, time, (2) Community and process' (Roethlisberger, spring semester p. 26).
2. Cf. Roethlisberger: 'Community: many in common. – most general reference via "otherness", diversity' (Roethlisberger, spring semester p. 26).
3. Cf. Roethlisberger: 'Big difference between past and future. Past is definite. Scepticism of past different from scepticism about future' (Roethlisberger, spring semester p. 26).

Harvard lectures, spring semester 1926

extension in relationships, you fare better. ⟨blank⟩ Both past and future enter into the immediacy of the event A.[1] Then there are things in the immediacy of A which are neither past nor future, which have a certain independence of A – they are its immediate real world.[2]

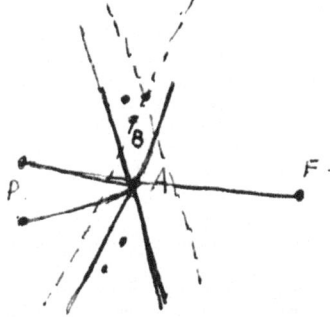

If you are going to deal from the point of view of the immediately real, you would arrange your diagram like this ⟨blank⟩ the immediately real ~~first, present, future~~ past, present, future for our simple-minded parents. ⟨blank⟩ Now do A and B have a common past?[3] They would according to the old common sense view; but not now. But we look at them like this: Of course the parts set off by ⟨?⟩ curved lines are common to both, but their pasts and futures are not

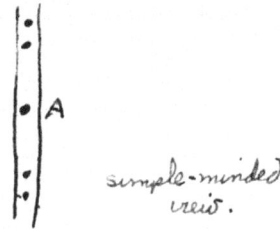

perfectly common. x is contemporary for B but not for A. x is conditioning for A, but not for B, (i.e., A is determinate from the point of view of x). If Caesar hadn't crossed the Rubicon everything else would be different. But still we don't consider that what we are doing now doesn't make any difference whether he crossed the Rubicon. x is settled for A, and A is partially |45| settled by x. There is nothing the case to exclude the case that x and B should be independent in the settlement.

Now there is a prevalent tendency in modern physics to say that that's all there is to it. You are always told that the methods of measurement have no relevance – that your method ~~of measure~~ must always be irrelevant in something that lies below them. But I don't see how you can get any statements about physics if there is no real relevance in your measurement. You can't have any relevance to the fact unless you have something which touches the fact.

Via space and time measurement comes in. Measured time is of course not the same as the mere extension; Descartes saw that. Creative advance from a common whole ⟨blank⟩. In what sense do you have your world spatialized? Obviously as articulate in sense-perception. Redness is not in the president's house, but in the presentational relationship of the house to us. It's not B as settled fact entering into A, but as a certain member of the <u>extensive</u> community in a certain relationship to A, which is determined mainly by A's past and indirectly by B's past – i.e. by the effect of B's past on A's past. Then how A emerges from its past, determines the presentational relationship between A and B. What B in itself is doesn't enter, except insofar as it has its

---

1. The interlineation, '(..............)', appears below 'event A' and above the word 'future' in the following sentence. Its intended placement and meaning are unclear.
2. The figures for this lecture are from Roethlisberger (spring semester p. 26).
3. There do not appear to be any notes from Roethlisberger that correlate to anything in the remainder of Robinson's notes for this lecture, although the latter appear to be still for 10 April.

161

Tuesday, 13 April 1926

Roethlisberger's notes

|27| Moment M_s divides time system S_1 into a system of parallel planes. ($M_s \cdot S_1$) Idea of order comes in space through parallel planes. Order comes in through analysis of "creative ~~analysis~~ advance". Given S_1, there is a definite system of parallel planes $M_s S_1$. A thing at rest in S_1 appears from S to be in uniform motion.

All geometry derived from analysis of creative advance of time systems. Physical world is impartial

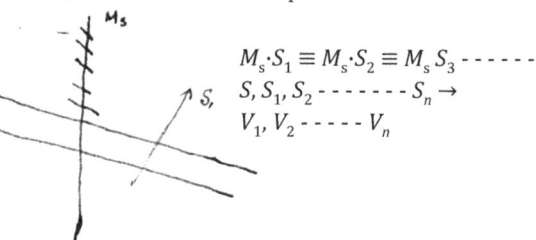

$$M_s \cdot S_1 \equiv M_s \cdot S_2 \equiv M_s S_3 \text{------}$$
$$S, S_1, S_2 \text{--------} S_n \rightarrow$$
$$V_1, V_2 \text{-----} V_n$$

system of ~~re~~presentations. Immediate experience is a subjective world. But the subjective world is also public. Creature is a subject, but from view of creative advance it is a predicate. Creativity is a condition for the creature. Subjective psychological fact enters into the occasion.

Laws of nature are expressive of facts of things in nature. The nature of the creatures in nature are laws of nature. What is objective is always for a subject. What is subjective is always V̶i̶m̶V̶partially objective.

Two theories of bifurcation:

(1) primary and secondary qualities.

(2) perceptive side and conceptual side –

It is conceptivity analyzing perceptivity. Synthesis of concept and perceptive.

Thursday, 15 April 1926

Roethlisberger's notes

|28| Process of physical world cannot be expressed in the simple-minded way of a serial advance. Not the full way in which <u>new</u> is related to <u>old</u>. Distinction even in Plato between time and becomingness. Distinction becomes important in science. Turns up in science by alternative linear time system appeared, as well as alternative space systems. The extensive relation is absolute, the temporal relation is relative. Creative advance can only be expressed by the bundle of ~~ways of~~ alternative serial-systems. Extension as an attribute – Descartes $\xrightarrow{\text{leads}}$ materialism. Extension is a relation → organism

---

1. The Yale graduate student transcribing this portion of Robinson's notes stopped here and never picked it up again. The content from the footnote above to this point seems to be for 10 April as it does not match what Roethlisberger has for 13 April.

as a key word. Creative advance has two sides: (1) organic determination – whole determines the new parts (2) in respect to creative advance, you conceive extensive community as differentiated.

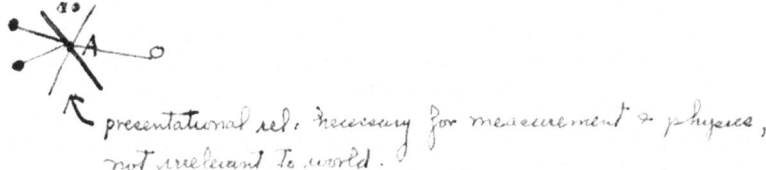

(1) extension as basis of world as a community.
(2) causality as becomingness of organic determination.
(3) presentation as the outcome – the nature of A – a perceptivity.
(4) the becomingness of A as synthesis – a unity as regards relations to past and contemporary A is a fact for its own sake and a ⟨'determinant'⟩[1] of what passes beyond it. Perceptivity is basis of physical world.

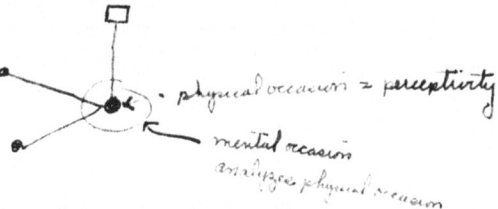

Saturday, 17 April 1926

Roethlisberger's notes

|29|

1. ⟨The?⟩ one genus of physical facts.
2. Cartesian materialism.
3. Difficulties of Cartesian subjectivism – entities which require nothing else but themselves to exist.
4. Organic Realism.
5. Fundamental organic relation.
6. Space and Time.
7. Enduring Organisms.
8. Cosmological Order.

1.

actual factors in <u>both physical</u> & <u>mental</u> occasions
eternal objects[2]

---

1. Roethlisberger clearly writes 'determinate' but it seems likely that Whitehead said or intended 'determinant'.
2. These last two lines are quite faded and written separately from the rest of the text, midway down the page on the right side. This was the last lecture before Harvard's spring break. According to his

Harvard lectures, spring semester 1926

Saturday, 1 May 1926

Roethlisberger's notes

|29|[1] Reconstruction of problem of mentality. Course ⱽtwoⱽ main points (1) ideas of physical science (2) ideas of accuracy. Now point of view of mentality. How is knowledge possible first requires description of what you mean by knowledge.

Some unity of principle required in mind and body. Cartesian dualism is a breakdown. Descartes' principle is "real fact is multiplicity in a ⱽself-containedⱽ substance."[2] Corporeal substance and cogitating substance. Why two?

Physical fact and mental fact. If you start from principle you cannot abstract anything from real world and say it exists on its own. You cannot separate things from real world and cannot be explained ⱽpartⱽ from it. Thorough doctrine of internal relations.

Relationship wants relatum. But if a thing is constituted by ⟨relatum⟩, ⟨relatum⟩[3] must be there in order to have things. There must be some element which is independent. Settled universe should involve a description of ⟨relationships⟩ which are not actual but which are passing into actuality. Any ultimate real fact must be described in terms which are not real (universals, ideas, eternal objects). Analysis requires (1) reference to other facts and (2) potentialities for actualization. You need realm of eternal objects which are relational and enter into facts. By themselves they apply not to any particular facts. How they qualify this particular fact with rest of universe. Regulate perspective of rest of universe for particular fact.

Facts only grasped under perspective forms. Some eternal objects are irrelevant.

Fusion is something for its own sake – a value – an achievement – something felt and graded. In existing it passes the creativity on to a new phase.

Another way in which these forms enter via mental concepts of bringing things together. The physical is the ground for the

---

engagement book (Whitehead, 'Pocket Engagement Book'), Whitehead embarked on an extended trip to the Midwest, leaving by train Saturday, 17 April and returning early afternoon on 30 April in time to give his Friday seminary at 7:30 p.m. He first read a paper to the Philosophical Society at McGill University in Montreal on 19 April. He did the same at the University of Michigan in Ann Arbor on 21 April. Victor Lowe notes that neither paper was ever published, and that the same paper might have been read at both locations. Finally, Whitehead stayed for six days (23–28 April) in Urbana, giving five lectures at the University of Illinois. These were also never published, but apparently were well attended. See Lowe, *Alfred North Whitehead, Vol. II*, pp. 206–7.

1. Roethlisberger repeats the number 29 in his page numbering here.
2. It is not clear that this is a direct quotation from Descartes and, if so, from which work it might come.
3. Here we have expanded the abbreviation 'rel' to 'relatum', since throughout his notes he is consistent in using the abbreviation 'R' for 'relationship', including in the instances two sentences below.

mental synthesis. Concept synthesizes by giving "how" of exemplification. Mentality is always analytic of what is physical.

Tuesday, 4 May 1926
Roethlisberger's notes

|30|

1. Final concrete fact is physical-mental occasion. Bipolar. Physical occasion = settled ground and is described by mental occasion.[1]

Mental occasion is a concretion like physical occasion. Physical occasion = blind perceptivity. How does mental occasion remove blindness from physical occasion? Only a "settled nature" from a standpoint.[2] Settled occasions pass into actual under perspective limitations. – (forms?)[3] On mental occasion you get a new ingression of forms. These new forms are concepts. Conceptual ingression. On perceptual side, the universal is irrelevant.[4] Qua concrete ingression – it enters via universal potentiality – (significant,[5] relevant) aesthetic element. Perceptual mode of ingression is particular. Mental occasion analyzes under form ⟨of⟩ associated physical occasion.[6] Every actual occasion exemplifies every form, although negligible. Not (exemplified or not).[7] But how exemplified? Concept is analytic of whole world as synthesized in immediate occasion.

Physical occasion = organization. Immediate occasion[8] = reorganization. Not actual until fused with universal potentiality. To be a creature is to be something passing beyond itself.

Consequence of this theory

1. Knowledge is always from standpoint of physical occasion. How far can you get rid of standpoint? ⟨Yo⟩[9] (Truth and falsity only apply to actual world.)

---

1. Hartshorne's notes add: 'Physical side derivative from mental occasion to idealism. Not so for Whitehead' (Hartshorne, p. 73).
2. Cf. Hartshorne: 'Nothing is settled in nature except from a definite standpoint' (Hartshorne, p. 73).
3. Cf. Hartshorne: 'Passage into new occasion under a perspective limitation, provided by eternal forms and a previous actuality' (Hartshorne, p. 73).
4. Cf. Hartshorne: 'In mental occasion a new mode of ingression of forms into an actual occasion. In physical occasion forms enter only as limited to that particular ingression. Redness only as for this occasion given. But in mental occasion forms enter as concepts, i.e. on its other side, as retaining its universality' (Hartshorne, p. 73).
5. 'Significant' may be struck out or underlined.
6. Cf. Hartshorne: 'Universal potentiality of form becomes relevant, becomes ingreded [through potentiality or creativity of subject as representative of and involving the ultimate creativity]. How is whole community in my mental |74| occasion? Via analysis of my associated physical occasion' (Hartshorne, pp. 73–4). It is not clear whether 'ingreded' is correct, or whether a variant was spoken or intended, such as 'ingressed'.
7. Cf. Hartshorne: 'How the physical occasion exemplifies the ⟨concepts?⟩. Each occasion does it somehow with respect to every form. But it may exemplify by reducing to irrelevance, i.e. negligibility' (Hartshorne, p. 74).
8. Roethlisberger often abbreviates Whitehead's different types of occasions as O_m, O_p or $O_i/O_{im}/O_{imm}$ to represent mental, physical, and immediate occasions, respectively. Here he has 'O_i', which we have rendered as 'immediate occasion', yet Hartshorne writes 'mental occasion' here (Hartshorne, p. 74).
9. The letters 'Yo' are clearly written and are not struck out by Roethlisberger, but their meaning is unclear. Our assumption, reflected here, is that Roethlisberger started the word 'You', but stopped mid-word to insert Whitehead's parenthetical comment and forgot to strike it out.

You can have a universal judgment within facts synthesized. You cannot go beyond immediate occasion but whole world is synthesized in each occasion. Can community in immediate occasion be impartially surveyed by reason? Immediate occasion necessary in order to point to[1]

Thursday, 6 May 1926

Roethlisberger's notes

<u>Omit question of freedom for present</u>
<u>Transcendental Theology</u>
 Conception of God which Kant talks about is <u>scholastic approach</u>. Logical side has new motive. Dependence of man leading to something which is ultimate. Should we talk about "universal energy" or "universal" or "unknowable"? This is about God as the "<u>ultimate</u>" and not as "father" or of ethical significance to man. Same as concept of Spinoza.
 Ideal = not a rule but archetype.[2]

Saturday, 8 May 1926

Roethlisberger's notes

|31|
 Knowledge is essentially analytic of the <u>given</u>. For Kant, the given is chaotic, and analysis is introduction of order. For Whitehead, the ultimate given is physical given ~~in~~ the world as perceptively organized. Fallacy is to put perceptivity on mental side rather than on physical side.
 The concept is mental. Both have <u>form</u> fused with facts. Aptitude for particularity is feature of ~~physica~~ perceptive side. "Red qua concept for any physical situation".
 Form is an ingredient qua potentiality = universality.

---

1. Roethlisberger's notes inexplicably end mid-sentence. The final part of this lecture as recorded by Hartshorne is significantly different from what Roethlisberger recorded in this final paragraph. Cf. Hartshorne, 'Can't treat physical occasion alone as a concrete fact. Always main point that it isn't something else. Sin = might have been otherwise. Sheer realism in art i.e. bare fact an abstraction. Fact in itself = feeling = something for its own sake. Toothache an expression of <u>my</u> individuality which is tooth-achy. What a thing is for itself = also a character of creativity. Passing by itself. Value = how of determination. Knowledge always from standpoint of physical occasion. How get knowledge from <u>universal</u> standpoint? <u>Can</u> get rid of standpoint of particular occasion, but not of community of occasions' (Hartshorne, p. 74).
2. Though Thursday, 6 May would have been a regular class meeting day, for reasons that are not clear, Roethlisberger has crossed out with a giant 'X' the entirety of his notes for this date, which appear at the bottom of a page that begins with notes for 4 May. It may be that he began writing notes for a different class here and later crossed these out to transfer them to a new page. It is also possible that there was on this day a guest lecture, such as happened with Hartshorne and Demos the previous academic year. Nothing in Whitehead's engagement book clarifies the matter.

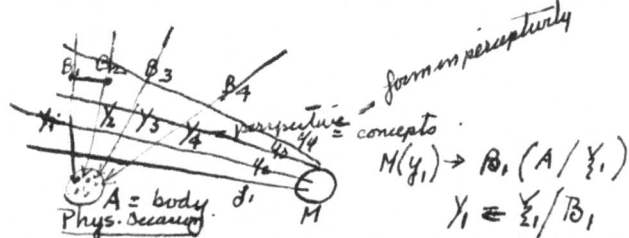

Concepts are analytic of the perspectivity of body. Mind with limitations of concept vfrom Mv analyzing perspectivity under limitation from A. Analysis mostly qua memory rather than immediacy. Voluntariness lies in bringing up of the concept.

Concept is a reference to the actual world as a possibility.

M <u>knows</u> B, but not *simplicita*, but B as exhibiting ξ_1[1] from standpoint A. A is the <u>unity of knowledge</u>. M is not conscious of itself. The unity it knows is A. The unity of self = appeal to <u>historical route</u> of <u>A</u>. Grasp of unity of body is greater than unity of <u>mental</u> <u>occasion</u>.

Saturday, 15 May 1926

Roethlisberger's notes[2]

|32|

Bradley on immediate experience:– "<u>positive</u>, <u>non-relational</u>, vnon-objectivev <u>whole of feeling</u>".[3]

Whole of feeling – value.

Non-relational – something for its own sake. – a definite fact that can be taken by itself. Epochal occasion, on other hand, is essentially <u>incomplete</u>. To treat as complete fact ⟨is⟩[4] erroneous.

---

1. It is likely that the symbol in Roethlisberger's notes is meant to be a small Greek letter xi, ξ, but it is not possible to be sure. It is likely that it corresponds to the symbol in the diagram, for example in (A/ξ_1).
2. Roethlisberger has no notes for Tuesday, 11 May or Thursday, 13 May. It is unclear whether Whitehead did not lecture these days, or whether Roethlisberger simply did not attend. Nothing in Whitehead's engagement book clarifies the matter.
3. This is in fact an exact quote from F. H. Bradley's *Essays on Truth and Reality*. For context, the following is the full paragraph in which the quote appears: 'In some manner it, however, seems possible to reach the idea of immediate experience. That experience we have seen is a positive non-relational non-objective whole of feeling. Within my immediate experience falls everything of which in any sense I am aware, so far at least as I am aware of it. But on the other side it contains distinctions which transcend its immediacy. This my world, of feeling and felt in one, is not to be called "subjective", nor is it to be identified with my self. That would be a mistake at once fundamental and disastrous. Nor is immediate experience to be taken as simply one with any "subliminal" world or any universe of the Unconscious. However continuous it may be with a larger world, my immediate experience falls, as such, strictly within the limits of my finite centre. But again to conclude from this that what falls within these limits is merely myself, would be an error entailing in the end theoretical ruin. The above idea of immediate experience is not intelligible, I would add, in the sense of being explicable; but it is necessary, I would insist, both for psychology and for metaphysics.' Bradley, *Essays on Truth and Reality*, p. 189, available at <https://archive.org/details/cu31924016877239>.
4. Roethlisberger has 'as' here; we have made the correction based on context.

"Not to be called subjective". "Contains distinctions". Not to be identified with self.

If you take epochal occasion as complete, you are tied to a static world.
1. What is ⟨immediate experience⟩¹ for itself as a creature?
2. Value is a reference of one occasion to another – Value is for ⟨blank⟩.

Truth in one sense <u>relative</u>, in <u>other</u> <u>absolute</u>. If you take <u>value</u> and <u>valuer</u> together, you have something absolute.

Fact is something definite. Immediate occasion cannot be torn out of community, but how one entity is perspective of another is what is definite. The perspective in immediate occasion is definite. What is inseparable as in itself is separable in perspective.

Fact: (1) something which is <u>definite</u>, <u>complete</u> and <u>actual</u>. (2) It <u>was</u> a fact that Caesar crossed the Rubicon, the fact for its own sake.²

Proposition: Cannot leave out this essential perspectivity. Has reference to actual world – We have the concept of "any x" which is R to A.

$$(\text{Any } X \underset{y}{\overset{D}{\leftrightarrows}} A) = \text{proposition}$$

Epochal occasions are dated from immediate occasion.

Tuesday, 18 May 1926

Roethlisberger's notes

|33|

Broad: *The Mind and its Place in Nature*, <u>p. 81</u>.³
external teleology
internal teleology

Tuesday, 25 May 1926

Roethlisberger's notes⁴

1. *Formaliter*, i.e. with its own individual form and something for its own sake. – "self enjoyment" – ∧source of value – finite truth – truths of isolation∧

---

1. We have expanded Roethlisberger's shorthand 'E_{im}' as 'immediate experience', but it is an educated guess as this particular abbreviation is not common for Roethlisberger and context permits alternatives. 'immediate occasion' and 'immediate entity' seem both to be ruled out as, elsewhere, different abbreviations are employed for these, namely O_i and O_{im} respectively.
2. For reasons that are not clear, the remaining text for this lecture, from 'Proposition' to 'occasion.' was circled by Roethlisberger.
3. Broad, *The Mind and Its Place in Nature*, available at <https://archive.org/details/minditsplaceinna00broa>. The referenced page is to a section with the heading 'Teleology, Mechanism, and Design'. See the Introduction (pp. xxviii–xxix) for more on Broad and Whitehead.
4. Roethlisberger has no notes for Thursday, 20 May or Saturday, 22 May. It is unclear whether Whitehead did not lecture these days, or whether Roethlisberger simply did not attend. Nothing in Whitehead's engagement book clarifies the matter.

2. Objective i.e. as it is for others
Both these points of view leave out something. There is no settled "the universe" – always from a standpoint – essential incompleteness. There is the event.

3. Transitive – i.e. as issuing
When you ask for (1), you come to (2).[1]
1 *Formaliter*
2. Objective[2]

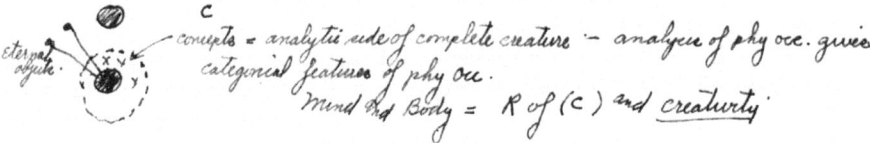

concepts = analytic side of complete creature – analysis of phy occ. gives categorical features of phy occ.
Mind and Body = R of (c) and creativity

3. Transitive
To know (1), you have to know creativity.[3]

---

1. In the figure below, for the expression 'R of (c)', 'R' means 'Relation', while '(c)' may mean 'concepts'.
2. The words 'Static view' with a bracket referring to numbers 1 and 2 appear to the left here.
3. This is the last page of notes that we have for the 1925–6 academic year. Whitehead wrote in his engagement book (Whitehead, 'Pocket Engagement Book') that examinations began on Wednesday, 2 June; it is unclear whether Whitehead lectured in the intervening days (Thursday, 27 May, Saturday, 29 May and Tuesday, 1 June). These days may well have been a period for preparation for examinations. According to his engagement book, in June Whitehead spent over a week with Henry Osborn Taylor. At the back of his engagement book there is a note that says '135 E. 66 S.t New York City and Knowles House Cobalt Connect.' His visit with Taylor was followed by a train trip to Madison, Wisconsin. It is not clear whether he delivered a paper in Madison. 'Degree Day' appears for 24 June with a note saying 'reserved seat on platform', presumably referring to the Harvard University graduation ceremony. For more on what Whitehead did during the summer of 1926, refer to the Introduction (pp. xxx–xxxi).

Harvard lectures, fall semester 1926

⟨Thursday, 30 September 1926⟩[1]

Nelson's notes[2]

|1| There is no such thing as "philosophy of science", any more than there is a Protestant Truth, a Catholic Truth, etc. There is just one truth. The ideas dealt with in a "philosophy of science" course are ideas suggested by scientific thought.

There have been three main epochs in which the scientific outlook on nature has suggested scientific ideas; viz.:

1. Time of the Greeks. The Greeks found out the habit of thinking clearly and logically. They had some advantages over us: perhaps they were abler, but however that may be, they did have more leisure and were not sophisticated by past history as we are to-day.[3] There was a certain freshness about the Greeks, perhaps it is a little analogous to that of the Americans. (It is very important for the student to get a thorough knowledge as to how the universe looked to the Greek).

2. Seventeenth Century. In the 17th century were the people who set forth the ideas that have been energizing during the past three hundred years. Descartes and Locke will never be superseded because they said things that must be taken account of by every philosophy. It is very important to read Descartes and Locke[4] on matter, mind, extension, duration, etc. (Locke's *Essay Concerning Human Understanding*,[5] and Descartes' *Meditations*.)[6]

3. Modern. Parallel to Locke's work is John Dewey's *Experience and Nature*.[7] Dewey formulates the problem much the same as Whitehead would; that is, he

---

1. There are five sets of notes available for this term: Conger's notes are used as the primary account for 34 lectures, and Nelson's for the remaining 2 lectures, while King's, Jackson's and Burch's notes are never used as the primary account. Refer to the table on p. 417 for a full list of fall semester 1926 Harvard lectures by note-taker and date, and see also the Introduction for a detailed discussion of each note-taker and their notes.
2. There is a note on the back of page 1 that reads: 'Read Hume's account of induction, experience, and causality.'
3. Jackson's notes put this a bit more aptly: '(unbound by traditional nomenclature)' (Jackson, p. 2). King notes that the Greeks were 'plastic' (King, p. 1).
4. Conger has more detail here: 'Locke probably thought he was overthrowing Descartes. Thought he could get along without metaphysics. Introduces idea of substance without using the word. Descartes not as fundamental as thinks self' (Conger, p. 1). Note that Conger's page numbers reset each lecture. Where he has not numbered the pages (as is the case here), we have provided page numbers.
5. Locke's *Essay* had not been assigned reading for the previous year. There have been many editions of it, but a likely one here is the 1894 edition edited by Alexander Campbell Fraser: Locke, *An Essay Concerning Human Understanding*, available at <https://archive.org/details/anessayconcerni00frasgoog> (Vol. I) and <https://archive.org/details/anessayconcerni17lockgoog> (Vol. II).
6. Closing parenthesis supplied. Conger (p. 1), King (p. 1) and Jackson (p. 2) all specifically list the Haldane and Ross translation of Descartes's philosophical works, which Whitehead had assigned for the previous year. See Descartes, *The Philosophical Works, Vol. I*, available at <https://archive.org/details/philosophicalwor01desc>.
7. Conger notes that Dewey and/or his *Experience and Nature* is 'profoundly wise' (Conger, p. 1). See Dewey, *Experience and Nature*, available at <https://archive.org/details/experienceandnat029343mbp>.

looks at nature in about the same way.¹ Of course the two men have a different philosophical outlook in that Dewey is a Pragmatist while Whitehead is a Rationalist.² The works of Whitehead to be read are: *The Concept of Nature, Science and the Modern World*, and *Religion in the Making*.³

The influence of mathematics and logic, although it has helped to create philosophy, has helped to mislead philosophers. It is often said that a proposition is either true or false, but it is very difficult to get a proposition that is both perfectly definite and true or false.⁴ It is not right to take a proposition out of its setting and then test it for truth or falsity. Propositions always presuppose a certain way of looking at the world. Of course, for practical purposes, there's a way that's good enough, but this is not so with first principles. Furthermore, every proposition is elliptical. We point at things. Every proposition presupposes a world as a background. How is the particular proposition wrong? With what background, meanings, etc., is it wrong?⁵ The same questions are relevant in regard to truth. Ideas that are accepted quite the world over and through long stretches of history actually are true.⁶ Descartes is wrong only if we take him out of his background. This fact is true of such a proposition as two and two make four. The "and" and the "make" are apt to be given a more concrete application than they ought to be given. Likewise, with "four". Propositions are largely formulae in action,⁷ but they're not the whole story, as Dewey contends they are.⁸ (Reading in Dewey: Chapters 1 and 2, perhaps 3 also.)⁹

|2|¹⁰ Note on Kant. Kant brought in Leibniz' train of thought. Leibniz insisted on the activity of substance. Prichard's work on Kant is very good,¹¹ but he left out the genius of Kant by his minute criticism.¹² It must be remembered that

---

1. Conger adds that 'Whitehead gets profound enlightenment from Dewey' (Conger, p. 1).
2. Conger writes here: 'Hopes to fill up ditch' (Conger, p. 1). It is unclear whether this is meant to refer to Dewey or Whitehead.
3. Conger specifies the 'metaphysical portions of *Religion in the Making*' (Conger, p. 1). That work had just been published in August.
4. King adds here: 'All we have is a form of expression. Language is an inadequate method of giving an exact proposition. Nothing can be completely and adequately defined without a complete metaphysic, (and) none of us have this' (King, p. 1). Cf. Conger: 'Each word suggests an idea. Usually very ill defined. Language inaccurate method. Shown by successive translations' (Conger, p. 1).
5. Nelson here missed the explicit point that Whitehead was trying to emphasise, namely: 'Proposition in the sense of formula is not properly defined' (Conger, p. 2).
6. Conger is more nuanced here: 'When you find propositions held by generations of clear thinkers appealing from one nation to another, you have hold of ideas which express some truth about the world' (Conger, p. 2).
7. While Nelson, Conger (p. 2) and Jackson (p. 3) have 'formulae in action' here, King (p. 2) has 'formulae and axioms'. Such errors illustrate the benefit of having multiple sets of notes to compare.
8. Conger adds here: 'A question of making our formulae more penetrating, more precise. Truth has certain grades and scales. How far can disengage from backgrounds?' (Conger, p. 3).
9. Closing parenthesis supplied. The chapters refer to the aforementioned *Experience and Nature*, as confirmed by the other note-takers.
10. Prior to the Kant note, Jackson has here: 'Hume (Berkeley) – experience and causality' (p. 3).
11. Whitehead is likely referring to Prichard, *Kant's Theory of Knowledge*, available at <https://archive.org/details/kantknowledge00pricuoft>.
12. Cf. Conger: 'ⱽEssence of Leibnizⱽ ⟨is⟩ insistence on activity of substance. Substance did its own work. Kant with Leibnizian tradition of activity behind him. Order imported into world by mind. "I can't say a word about Kant without offending somebody." Drew attention to general way of fronting

Kant was saturated with Newtonian physics and the developments of it. Kant brings together Newton's physics and Leibniz' philosophy with Hume standing there. Modern men have usually forgotten that Hegel comes between them and Kant; e.g., Caird's Commentary on Kant.[1]

Whitehead's objection to Descartes, Leibniz, Kant, and to a less extent, Locke, is that they tacitly or explicitly presuppose that the final reality is an enduring subject with adventures. ⟨Descartes⟩[2] has three types of substances.

The world is a system of occasions whose nature is that they are continually superseded.[3] They anticipate the cases in front of them and the already superseded cases are somewhat[4] in their nature. Thus, each occasion is incomplete.[5]

⟨Saturday, 2 October 1926⟩

Conger's notes

|1|[6] Science looks for general law.[7] Laws are stated in terms of concepts applicable to events, but any occasion ⟨exemplifies⟩[8] an infinite number of

---

problem which Leibniz had brought in. Showed Leibniz capable of many modifications. Showed many modifications which it ought to have. I do not look on Kant as beginning of Philosophy. Read Prichard on Kant. Kant ⟨does⟩ not hold water – meanings of his terms alter' (Conger, p. 3).

1. Conger adds here: 'Whitehead brought up in Glasgow school. Caird. Once knew Caird commentary almost by heart. Kant never vague, but not consistent. Caird vague, but consistent' (Conger, p. 3). Whitehead is referring to Scottish philosopher Edward Caird (1835–1908), likely either his 1877 book *A Critical Account of the Philosophy of Kant* or his 1889 work *The Critical Philosophy of Immanuel Kant* (in two volumes). The 'Glasgow school' refers to the 'neo-Hegelian' school of philosophy of the late 1800s and early 1900s, in which both Caird and F. H. Bradley (1846–1924) were leading figures. There is an interesting parallel to this remark in Whitehead's 'Autobiographical notes' for his Library of Living Philosophers volume *The Philosophy of Alfred North Whitehead*: 'By the time that I gained my fellowship in 1885 I nearly knew by heart parts of Kant's *Critique of Pure Reason*. Now I have forgotten it, because I was early disenchanted. I have never been able to read Hegel: I initiated my attempt by studying some remarks of his on mathematics which struck me as complete nonsense. It was foolish of me, but I am not writing to explain my good sense' (Whitehead, 'Autobiographical notes', p. 7).
2. Nelson incorrectly has 'Kant' here, where Conger and King both have 'Descartes'. Cf. Conger: 'Descartes' three types of substance: 1) plurality of extended bodies, 2) cogitating minds, 3) God has all in him. Dewey and Whitehead think an entire mistake' (Conger, p. 3).
3. Conger writes before this line: 'Ought to look on each thing as <u>epochal occasion</u>' (Conger, p. 3).
4. In Conger's notes, the superseded occasions are 'in some sense' in their nature, rather than 'somewhat' (Conger, p. 3).
5. Cf. Jackson: 'In their nature incomplete – inherent in real things. Character of passage' (Jackson, p. 3).
    Through comparison with the Lester King notes, it is clear that this is the end of the 30 September lecture.
6. Jackson (p. 4) and King (pp. 2–3) both record a reading list here that does not appear in the notes of Conger or Nelson. From King: 'Descartes, *Principles of Philosophy*. Part I. 51–64. Meditation number 6. Dewey. *Experience and Nature.* ⟨Chapters⟩ I, II. There is a very sharp contrast. Whitehead is more akin to Dewey, in one way. Like Descartes in mathematics and rationalism. |3| Whitehead. *Science and the Modern World. Religion in the Making*' (King, pp. 2–3). The '51–64' likely refers to the numbers of Descartes's principles themselves, rather than page numbers. See Descartes, *The Philosophical Works, Vol. I*, available at <https://archive.org/details/philosophicalwor01desc>, and Dewey, *Experience and Nature*, available at <https://archive.org/details/experienceandnat029343mbp>.
7. Cf. Nelson: 'The purpose of science has been stated to be the discovery of general laws exemplified in occurrences of the actual world; but this statement conceals many questions in the understanding of scientific procedure' (Nelson, p. 2).
8. Supplied from Nelson (p. 2).

concepts. Inexhaustible supply of notions. When, where, how big?¹ Universe is inexhaustible. Our thoughts attach to its mere surface. Haven't got intellectual machinery to think adequately about the world – ought to get this into head. Philosophy search for wide general notions whose special forms can give us ∨proper∨ ideas. Haven't yet framed proper general ideas.

Applicable concepts inexhaustible. Numberless characteristics ignored. Only those laws can be detected which are expressible in concepts available for ⟨our⟩ use.² Newton needed notion of mass.³ Discovery of relevant concepts is as much part of science as the framing of laws. Concepts rendered explicit control finding of the laws.

Some necessary concepts not ordinary.⁴ Historically science better described in terms of discovery of concepts. Sliding scale from concepts to laws. We want concepts of important applicability.

A taste in concepts ought to be developed. Simple, obvious, normal concepts? Such as control our instinctive action? But thoughts ⟨caught⟩⁵ by abnormal.

⟨Three classes of ⟩⁶ concepts:

(1) Universally applicable to all occurrences. Main philosophical categories.

(2) Generally but not universally applicable to all occurrences, e.g. solid body.⁷

(3) <u>Those exceptionally applicable to occurrences. Theory starts here.</u> Try to discover concepts which express important facts of these things.

⟨Excluding?⟩ numbers in arithmetic, separation between classes not sharp. History of thought passage from drama to ⟨rationalization⟩.⁸

Dramatic situations may be ⟨conceived as⟩⁹

---

1. Cf. King: 'A particular can never be exhausted by a list of universals' (King, p. 3). Cf. Nelson: 'a thing cannot be exhausted by description' (Nelson, p. 2).
2. Nelson prefaces this sentence with: 'The primitive peoples used the concepts now in ordinary use' (Nelson, p. 2).
3. Cf. King: 'Early laws were stated in familiar concepts, thought to be applicable. But too many characteristics were simply ignored. Newton's laws were inexpressible in concepts familiar to Egypt, e.g. He required concepts of space, time, and mass' (King, p. 3). Nelson also references Galileo here: 'We had measure of time and of space long ago, but the law of gravitation could not be expressed until the notion of mass was perfected, which was done by Newton (in the main) and Galileo' (Nelson, p. 2).
4. Cf. Nelson: 'Concepts control the finding of the laws. Daily life does not give explicit concepts' (Nelson, p. 2).
5. Supplied from Nelson: 'The attention of daily life is caught by the abnormal, not by the normal. We do not get a record of everyday details' (Nelson, p. 2).
6. Supplied from Nelson (p. 2) and King (p. 3).
7. Cf. Nelson: 'e.g., notion of solid, body, planet, paving stone. Life consists in regarding these things' (Nelson, p. 2).
8. Supplied from King (p. 3). Nelson has a great deal of material here that is not present in Conger: 'This classification must be kept clearly in mind in order to understand the history of science. Concepts of the first class came late in human consciousness, after the other two classes. In daily life we don't draw attention to facts that are always there; i.e., to concepts that are universal. Theory has its origin with concepts of the third class. Science grew up because of the dramatic features of the universe. Religion, terror, etc. arise from exceptions. It was necessary to discover concepts that express these abnormal occurrences. Philosophy is not a rationalization of habitual routine' (Nelson, p. 2).
9. Supplied from Nelson (p. 3). Bullets below added for clarity.

- transcendent – lightning flash from unknown. Negation of rationalism.
- immanent – Endeavor to construe dramas as unusual illustrations of what is ~~useful~~ ⟨usual⟩ in ordinary life. Bring two tuning forks together get – Enhancement, ⟨?⟩. Conversely, shows what is ordinary is capable of drama. Every scientific experiment is a prearranged drama.

(2)[1] Language in words, phrases, syntax has provided us with examples. Concepts mainly suggested by language.[2] Characteristic of Greek philosophy. Greeks knew only one language. If Aristotle had known Egyptian and Chinese.[3]

Every law is hypothetical. If (concepts) find exemplification ... then (complex concept) finds its exemplification.

This stage of rationalism is appeal to common sense. And language is child of common sense. Romance yields to homely thought.

As drama tamed into experiment, so language is ⟨tamed⟩[4] under influence of rationalistic thought.

Man concentrates in himself in a high degree the conceptual feelings inherent throughout nature and thus modifies – what he serves.[5]

|2| Notion ⟨develops?⟩ generic categories, but each finds exemplification in peculiar circumstances.

Number and velocity. No collection has bare multiplicity.

Numerosity –

W.E. Johnson.[6] Determinates incompatible; class either 6 or 10. Either this or that, but can't ⟨be⟩ both.[7] Value of universal generic concept lies in reference to incompatible species. Essence of world is incompatibility. <u>Generic</u> – Incompatible ⟨determinations⟩.[8]

Gradations even in universality: entity – diversity – incompatibility.

---

1. Referring to the second class of concepts.
2. Cf. Nelson: 'Language has given us a storehouse of concepts of the second class. Laws are complexes of concepts' (Nelson, p. 3). Cf. Jackson: 'Appeal to language characteristic ⟨of?⟩ shift from concepts of third class to second class' (Jackson, p. 5).
3. Conger does not finish this thought, and none of the other note-takers has anything like it. However, it much resembles a comment Whitehead made in the first lecture of the spring 1926 semester: 'It is obvious that philosophy started from language and a rather naive trust in grammar. It was a great calamity that Aristotle didn't know Chinese. I have no doubt that it is an equal calamity in China that the Chinese don't |2| know Greek' (p. 114).
4. Conger actually writes 'strained' here, but given the 'As, so' construction, it seems more likely that Conger misheard the second 'tamed' as 'strained'.
5. Conger marks this sentence with four vertical lines in the left margin, presumably to emphasise its importance.
6. William Ernest Johnson (1858–1931) was a British philosopher and logician who, like Whitehead, was also a Cambridge Apostle. When in 1905 Whitehead applied for a Doctor of Science degree, Johnson was one of two people (the other being H. F. Baker) who evaluated his submissions, these being his *Treatise on Universal Algebra* and papers published in the *American Journal of Mathematics*. Johnson gave Whitehead a glowing review, and he was granted the doctorate by Cambridge's Special Board for Mathematics (Lowe, *Alfred North Whitehead, Vol. I*, pp. 262–3).
7. This seems likely to be a reference to Johnson's three-volume *Logic*, published between 1921 and 1924. See Johnson, *Logic*, available at <https://archive.org/details/logicpart01johnuoft> (*Part 1*), <https://archive.org/details/logicpartiidemon00john> (*Part 2*) and <https://archive.org/details/logicpart03sparuoft> (*Part 3*).
8. Conger wrote 'situations' here, but both Nelson and King have 'determinations'. Cf. King: 'The general concept has reference to incompatibility, the basis of the world. What is this is not that. <u>Generic</u> refers to incompatible specific determinations' (King, p. 4).

Widest notions whose specific determinations are concepts to be elucidated.

Search for meaning = search for generic concepts of widest scope. Every occurrence can then be analyzed in terms of specific determinations of the general concept.

Philosophy acts as critic of current abstractions. It has passed to higher generalities and gained vision of alternative potential incompatible generalizations. Thought in blinkers[1] versus imaginative thought.

Philosophy filtering through a civilization should give it an imaginative tinge. Philosophy one way of preserving a freshness and novelty of imagination in a civilization. From that point of view, rise of a new school is not a loss. Here is a new imaginative idea burst upon the world. William James definitely refreshed the imagination of the world. Philosophy disciplines imagination – be imaginative and yet sane.

Historically philosophy like all necessary avocations sometimes a pitfall. When put philosophy in background of their particular times, and restrict to own interpretations, divest of generic amplitude. What is important in philosophy isn't Aristotle as a Greek among Greeks.[2]

Final attainment of absolute understanding must remain an ideal. But there are degrees in relatively. Philosophy scheme for comparatively abstract.

Without philosophy, rationalism in bondage to experiment. Experiments are events deliberately brought to pass. Great steps in progress can be traced back to experiments which failed. E.g., failure to devise relevant experiment.

Sometimes recourse to alternative generic concepts, but this has its limit, set by our habit of ignoring the inexplicable.

Only features receive expression.

Beat gongs when sun is eclipsed.[3]

⟨Tuesday, 5 October 1926⟩

Conger's notes

|1| Our resolute habit of ignoring the inexplicable.[4] ⟨There is⟩ bogus ~~adequacy for~~ ∨evidence for∨ final adequacy of current scientific and philosophical notions. In every epoch adequacy of notions appears overwhelming. Only those features receive expression which can be expressed in terms of them.[5]

---

1. Whitehead is using the UK term for what in American English are termed 'blinders' (used to restrict a horse's vision).
2. Cf. King: 'Scholarship in the hands of unimaginative men often brings the present under the yoke of the past' (King, p. 4).
3. This last sentence, written in the lower-right corner of the last page of the notes for that lecture, is strange because it does not seem to belong here at all, but rather to the next lecture. Cf. Jackson's notes for 5 October: 'Undisciplined excitement at mysterious instances does not get us very far (ancestors beating tom toms at eclipse)' (Jackson, p. 6). It is unclear how or why Conger ended up putting this note here instead.
4. Cf. Burch: 'Our scientific habits are set by ignoring the inexplicable' (Burch, p. 2).
5. Cf. King: 'People look down on revolutionary concepts. Our ancestors had the sense to draw attention to the fact that the universe was exhibiting inexplicable phenomena' (King, p. 4).

Observation does not consist in passive reception. Bacon defective: look at particular instances and general laws stood out of themselves.[1] In order for your physical experience to ~~enter into~~ become knowledge, must analyze physical experience.

Mind is feeling, and its mode of feeling is confrontation of physical would with a conceptual feeling – a mode of analysis –

Concept is analytic of the percept. Percept is physical fact – by conceptual feeling, issues in knowledge. You don't know beyond what you bring. Vary conceptual feelings and you will ⟨probe⟩[2] the universe in a different way.

My belief is that massive perceptivity of things is a physical nature.[3] ∧Kant ought to have∧ expanded ∨Transcendental Aesthetic∨ ⟨into a whole volume⟩.[4] Full account of perceptivity is full account of what nature is.[5]

Two senses of word experience (make for purposes of explanation a cleaner cut between body and mind than I believe in):[6]

- Complete physical experience – your body. Blind Experience.
- Then the usual sense of experience – Knowledge of physical experience, which is dependent on <u>further fact of conceptual outfit</u>.[7]

Conceptual feeling is probing something which is primarily to be conceived as physical experience – in Greek sense of word physical. In modern sense too narrow.

Search for generic concepts has to be systematized into a discipline. Have to have disciplined method of producing general concepts.[8]

Discipline. Two ⟨?⟩ ⟨sets of concepts:⟩[9]

(1) scientific

(2) philosophical

Distinction between two sets lies in relative width. Concepts which apply universally are philosophical. ⟨Concepts which are⟩ of other class, scientific, apply frequently and generally, but not universally. Solid, fairly rigid body.

Science appeals to arbitrary facts which universe exhibits as <u>there</u>, but not as inherent in its being the universe that it is. Philosophy to <u>necessary</u> relational facts, inherent |2| in very character of occasional occurrences. <u>Multiplicity</u>.

---

1. Cf. Nelson: 'Some theories of induction are very defective; e.g., Bacon said that all we have to do is to look at particular instances, and the general laws stand out by themselves. This is not true' (Nelson, p. 3).
2. Conger writes here: 'clothe(?)', but both King (p. 5) and Nelson (p. 3) agree that the word was 'probe'.
3. This sentence appears in the right margin, and has been placed here based on comparison with King's notes (p. 4).
4. Supplied from Nelson (p. 3) and King (p. 5).
5. Cf. Nelson: 'When dealing with perceptivity, we are dealing with nature; and an account of perceptivity is an account of nature' (Nelson, p. 3).
6. Parentheses and colon supplied. The parenthetical material appears in the left margin. The bullets below have been added for clarity.
7. Nelson (p. 3) has 'conceptual equipment' here, but both King (p. 5) and Jackson (p. 6) record 'conceptual outfit'.
8. Cf. Jackson: 'Undisciplined excitement at mysterious instances does not get us very far (ancestors beating tom toms at eclipse). Must bring disciplined rationalization' (Jackson, p. 6),
9. Supplied from King (p. 5).

Arithmetic of finite numbers would belong to science. What is it to have a definite number – philosophy. Genus belongs to philosophy, species to science. But can't cut up universe so neatly. Wish ~~univer~~ intellect did dispel ambiguity.

Difference between science and philosophy is how you're treating subject matter more than the subject matter itself. Science and philosophy united in explanation in broadest sense. Whitehead diverges from John Dewey here. For Dewey, goal is use⟨/action⟩.[1] For Whitehead, explanation. Consideration of use is one test as is whether you have things straight. Explanation is basis of successful action. But everything is something in itself and for its own sake, and object of science and philosophy is attempt to get explanation.

First people who studied philosophy ⟨had⟩ no idea it was any use – wanted it for explanation. Chinese took their science pragmatically. So Egyptians geometry. In Europe, got into hands of men who didn't care about action, but were well fixed. Sat down and thought about science because were interested in it.[2] Motive power to get something new is an interest in explanation. Cf. Faraday, finds principles but doesn't apply.[3] – Totemism and domestication of animals.[4] Love of explanation is ultimate motive for fundamental advances in civilization.

Philosophy pursues the route of self-evidence, clarity, distinctness / logical coherence, exemplification, adequacy. Ideas of first sort ⟨i.e., first three⟩ are put up imaginatively – fish out such ideas. Then use them, test them by

1. coherence
2. exemplification (confront ⟨them?⟩ with world of physical experience)[5]
3. adequacy

If it's philosophy – are they so general that they extend everywhere? Are there regions of your experience which can't be expressed in terms of such ideas?

Science analyzes more detailed relations – in cosmological epoch in which we are set at present – electrons, protons, etc.

|3| Laws of nature which are special to any epoch are derived from type of organism which dominate that epoch. Three dimensions of space and Clerk Maxwell's law of electron equations are metaphysical facts which have their importance ∨for∨ ages unending backwards-forward. That type of organism will gradually modify so that other than ∨Clerk Maxwell's theory∨ ⟨of⟩ three-dimensional relations of space will rise into importance. These ~~⟨?⟩~~ ∨propositions∨ ⟨will⟩ then be told to children as stories of *Arabian Nights*.[6]

---

1. Supplied from King (p. 5) and Nelson (p. 3).
2. Cf. King: 'The Chinese made great progress in science but looked on everything pragmatically – for action. Europe was |6| interested in explanation. The Egyptians were interested in geometry, but pragmatically. The Greeks looked at it for its interest' (King, pp. 5–6).
3. Cf. Jackson: 'Not a penny to Faraday. History of electricity' (Jackson, p. 7). The work of Michael Faraday (1791–1867) laid the groundwork for the practical application of electricity in technology.
4. The line 'Totemism and domestication of animals' is odd; none of the other note-takers has anything like it, and it is not clear what is has to do with what is being discussed. It is possible that this was an oblique connection that Conger himself made, rather than Whitehead.
5. Parentheses supplied.
6. A collection of Middle Eastern folk tales with a frame story in which the ruler, Shahryār, is told a series of tales by his wife, Scheherazade, that end each night with a cliffhanger designed to so engross Shahryār that he postpones her execution until the following night so that he can hear the rest of the story.

Neither science nor philosophy can demonstrate that there must be such an epoch as that which we are in now. Shouldn't adjust genetic notions merely to express what finds exemplification in science.

Philosophy ought to provide science with general ideas. Science ought to provide philosophy with mathematics for its less general notions, from which philosophy generalizes yet more penetrating generating ideas. Thus philosophy is critical of ideas of science, but in being critical it is also creative – perceives *sub specie generalitatis*.[1]

Philosophy the stimulant of scientific/∧poetic∧ imagination.[2] At basis of religion, science, poetry.

Science would discusses its muddled facts, philosophy its muddled ∧generic concepts.∧

If you find a scientific man quite clear and definite on all scientific subjects, he is ten[3] years behind the times.

ⱽWhenⱽ muddle assumes striking shape, get antirationalist school – Mankind has arrived at ultimate muddle – the mystic/∧agnostic.∧ Both place arbitrary boundaries for ~~intellec~~ (explanation).

Rationalism now arbitrarily disconnected, inadequate, vague. Rationalism not a doctrine, but a faith – that desertion of fact in interest of ideal description returns to find fact ~~embody~~ exemplifying its most delicate fancies. Faith of rationalism is procedure of all orderly thought, including science, philosophy.

Imaginations generated by congruity with way in which disciplined mind works.

Self-assertion of reason an ultimate fact.[4]

⟨Thursday, 7 October 1926⟩

Conger's notes

|1| Progress in philosophy consists largely in rendering presuppositions explicit. Differences between schools might have another aspect. Each starts with implicit assumptions. Usually presuppositions are interwoven (with background) and no practical motive to search them out.[5] This is the task of metaphysics – unending, because below each depth a deeper.

---

1. In this context, the meaning of the Latin phrase is unclear, but it would typically be translated as 'under the aspect of the general' or 'by a view of the general'.
2. Jackson adds here: 'That is why it is dangerous study, because people who are apt to take up unorthodox ideas' (Jackson, p. 8).
3. Burch's notes say 30 years (Burch, p. 2).
4. King writes after this last line: '*Science and the Modern World*, chapter 1' (King, p. 6). This may have been the assigned reading for the next class, though no one else makes any note of it.
5. Cf. Nelson: 'The philosopher must be aware of the different tempers of mind, and of different philosophical approaches. The philosophical problem is to render explicit things taken for granted in previous philosophical systems. Each school starts with implicit assumptions not quite the same as other schools. And practical needs do not require that these assumptions be rendered explicit' (Nelson, p. 4).

We do not believe because we philosophize – vice-versa. Apart from beliefs ⟨there is⟩ nothing to think about. You inherit your beliefs. Philosophy is a criticism of beliefs.[1]

Standards ⟨for rational criticism⟩:[2] Sliding Scale
1. Intensity of belief
2. Concurrence of belief
3. Clear expression of belief
4. Analysis of belief
5. Logical coherence of many beliefs
6. Exemplification of beliefs
7. Adequacy of beliefs

Previous list:[3]
- Self-evidence
- Clarity
- Distinctness
- Logical coherence
- ⟨Exemplification⟩[4]
- Adequacy

Now self-evidence has been replaced by intensity ⟨and⟩ concurrence.

vOldv ⟨idea of⟩ self-evidence refers to ideal, not to fact. No intellects with their knowledge clearly spread out before them. No such apparatus of clear thinking. Old rationalism on this fallacy.[5] At any instant some facts are luminously obvious – remainder of experience involved ⟨is⟩ in umbral shadow. When try to formulate the obvious, we have to embody a reference to penumbral[6] experience – this reference is made with a clearness entirely unwarranted by our intellectual apprehension of the time.[7]

Language itself is a series of violent metaphors. Mathematician doesn't meet with mathematical truth clearly spread out – takes intellectual holiday. Truths which he does immediately perceive lack clear and distinct formula of meaning. True nature of numbers not immediately obvious when infers 2 + 2 = 4.

---

1. Cf. Nelson: 'Philosophy is rationalistic, and does not assert ultimate standards of criticism. We philosophize because we believe; we do not get beliefs from philosophy, we inherit them. Philosophy is a criticism of belief, preserving it, deepening it, and modifying it. Therefore, philosophy is the acceptance of belief after criticism. To criticize, standards are needed; and philosophy in the past has been careless in regard to standards of criticism' (Nelson, p. 4). Rather than Nelson's 'Philosophy. . . *does not assert* ultimate standards of criticism', King writes 'Philosophy is rationalistic. Rationalism *never deserts* standards of criticism' (King, p. 7).
2. Supplied from Nelson (p. 4).
3. Bullets supplied. This is the list of standards that Whitehead presented during the last lecture, which Whitehead is now criticising and revising. See p. 177.
4. Supplied from the previous lecture (p. 177) and from King (p. 7).
5. Cf. King: 'The old rationalism was founded on the narrow field of knowledge, clearly formulated and constantly in mind' (King, p. 7).
6. The umbra and penumbra refer to different parts of a shadow: the umbra is the darkest portion, in which the light source is completely blocked, while in the penumbra it is only partially blocked.
7. Cf. Burch: 'Some facts are luminously obvious, but the rest of our experience is obscured in a deep penumbral shadow with reference to which our intellectual faculty varies from that of a savage to that of a jellyfish' (Burch, p. 3).

Danger of overstatement with respect to self-evidence. Cf. Euclid; Lobachevsky.[1] Colossal example of mistake.[2]

Belief in self-evidence does embody a great truth. Its influence immense. Reaction to it now against all rationalism – pragmatism. Don't take the extreme form of pragmatism. Thinks Dewey working backwards from extreme form. Looking backwards to modified rationalism. Real self better than superficial denial. Perhaps Dewey could accept the seven standards as touchstones of pragmatic criticism.

Controversies finally beaten out in merely a verbal quibble. When both rationalism and pragmatism have stated what they mean – it's a real controversy; each side has in mind facts about universe and human knowledge which are true, but haven't yet formulated these facts adequately. When formulate, will edge nearer and nearer to each other. But this is philosophy. Formulating these implicit things which we know so clearly and formulate so badly.

|2|

⟨1.⟩ <u>Intensity of belief</u>

Doesn't mean <u>Emotional intensity</u>. But Kant's sense of "necessary" – can't do otherwise than believe it.

ᴠThoughtᴠ necessary – continuous functions. <u>Weierstrass'</u> work on continuous functions. Taylor's theorem. Formulation wrong and proof wrong in the 30s.[3]

Must finally come back to things which are obviously there – what you do know. Can't elicit an argument except from premises. Knowledge must be on this basis – there's a certain obviousness (= intensity).

2. <u>Concurrence in belief</u>

(Social) Concurrence of immediate memory – What I saw half a second before is still there. Observation is really an integration of a succession of facts. Memory concurs with immediate fact.

(Don't give example because) overmuch precision is a way to ⟨blank⟩ your mental confusion. No good getting a sham preciseness.

3. <u>Clear expression</u>

Question of expression. May be clear expression (e.g., patriotic song) without clear analysis. Ought to have a clear "integral expression" in words which other people ⟨can⟩ accept is an additional safeguard.

---

1. Nikolai Lobachevsky (1792–1856), Russian mathematician. Lobachevsky formulated a non-Euclidean geometry in 1826, which is now called 'hyperbolic geometry' or 'Bolyai–Lobachevskian geometry'.
2. Cf. King: 'Euclid to Lobachevsky is 2,000 years. It was thought that Euclidean geometry must apply to our experience. We know this to be false' (King, p. 7).
3. Cf. Nelson: 'E.g., all mathematicians a few generations ago believed that a continuous function would have a necessary coefficient; but this has been proved wrong' (Nelson, p. 4). The Weierstrass approximation theorem states that every continuous function defined on a closed interval can be uniformly approximated as closely as desired by a polynomial function, and all polynomial functions can be developed into Taylor series.

4. <u>Analysis</u>
See what it is that you're expressing.[1]
Further
5. <u>Logical Coherence</u>
Compare with other beliefs. If contrary, figure out ⟨4?⟩. Extremely powerful. Deduction rarely wrong. If original statement wrong, gets shown up.[2]
Can take certain sections of deduced propositions, turn them into premises, and deduce your original premises from them.
Trick of deduction logic only recently found out.
Magnifying glass.
6. <u>Exemplification</u>
You're always in a new situation, and every situation is a test of all old beliefs. Beliefs verified unthinkingly. Events will do it for you.[3]
Pragmatic point is sound.
⟨7. <u>Adequacy</u>⟩[4]
Most facts can't be fitted in. Always hope we could get them there if had time and could get them there. But always something escapes. Boa constrictor in Paddington.[5] Other things about universe may not be coherent.[6]

⟨Saturday, 9 October 1926⟩

Nelson's notes

|6| A system of philosophy is the result of an attempt to express some character that is universal in nature. Competing philosophies take their peculiarity from their emphasis on different factors. Individuals, ages of individuals, countries, epochs differ in regard to the place of emphasis. The problem of philosophy is to get something more embracing in a clear-cut and definite manner. Philosophy is valuable insofar as it is clear and definite and embracing. But if it is clear cut and definite it is apt to be one-sided. For example, in regard to the contrasts,

---

1. Cf. Nelson: 'The expression of a belief should be analyzed bit by bit into clear statements. Must get something perfectly definite before one' (Nelson, p. 5).
2. Cf. Nelson: 'Logically coherent premises lead by deductive logic to many other statements; so, if the original statement was wrong, we are likely to come to some statements which we recognize as wrong or as incoherent with some of our other beliefs' (Nelson, p. 5).
3. Cf. Nelson: 'Exemplification is never ended. Events will verify beliefs for you. E.g., wrong beliefs will lead you into situations that you did not expect' (Nelson, p. 5).
4. Conger actually wrote this explanation of 'Adequacy' at the top of the page of lecture notes where it was first introduced, apparently because he had run out of room at the bottom of his second page and did not want to spill onto a third. We have moved the material back to the bottom of the page, in the place where Whitehead would have actually said it.
5. Cf. Jackson: 'Always facts which escape – The wild facts that can't be tamed. Wild boa constrictor got loose in London station' (Jackson, p. 11).
6. Cf. Nelson: 'We have a system of general beliefs, and we find that most facts fit in as examples of these ideas. But occasionally there's a "loose" fact that won't fit in, and so our beliefs have to be modified. The more adequate one's system of beliefs, the more it can be trusted' (Nelson, p. 5). Nelson's description of adequacy here is rather unlike Conger's, King's and Jackson's, who all emphasise that most facts *do not* fit our systems.

1. Permanence and flux: everlasting order – flux of confusion. The chief difference between youth and age is the view of this contrast. The young conceives of flesh as both permanent and pleasant – plastic world – nothing permanent (?). The old do not want to modify the permanent. Differences of temperament lead to differences in the emphasis on this contrast.

2. Mixed with this first contrast is the contrast of continuity and atomicity.[1] People with lazy minds like continuity. People with clear minds like atomicity. Those who emphasize flux also emphasize continuity, and conversely. Philosophical intellects in India (and China)[2] represent continuity. Semitic intellects have emphasized atomicity – self-containedness of each individual. These two sides have fought a very equal duel, e.g., electro-magnetism is based on continuity. It was formerly believed that chemistry would eventually be explained as continuous.[3] This happened about 1898 with the electromagnetic theory of matter. But this view had to surrender part of the old view of electromagnetism – atomic – electrons and protons. So it was really a victory for atomicity. The quantum theory seems to indicate atomicity, but we still have to use differential equations – introduce continuity.[4] The real problem is to show in what sense the universe is to be construed in terms of atomicity and in terms of continuity.[5]

3. Physical and Mental.

4. Known and Unknown (subject and object). The function of knowing, according to Kant, is a function of order.

5. Sensation, feeling, emotion, action – logical discernment (between mathematics and pragmatism).

Philosophy's interest leads one to put undue emphasis on one or the other. Because a philosophy is contradictory doesn't mean that it is wrong, e.g., hitching horses; zeppelin raids.[6] Every new idea when first broached looks silly and is crude. It can't explain some of the most obvious facts. It is illogical usually.[7]

DESCARTES

Descartes combined antagonistic virtues: He was a soldier, a philosopher, a skeptic, a Jesuit,[8] a mathematician. Descartes emphasizes the permanent and

---

1. Conger adds here: 'Atomicity and continuity applied to same subject-matter. Cut sheep in two and get mutton' (Conger, p. 1).
2. Supplied from Conger (p. 1), King (p. 9) and Jackson (p. 12).
3. Cf. Conger: 'In every epoch of history of thought a dissenting minority. Chemists say privately electromagnetic theory hasn't explained so much' (Conger, p. 1).
4. Cf. Conger: 'Can't do without Clerk Maxwell – differential equations – continuity. Differential equations of Einstein presuppose a certain continuity' (Conger, p. 1). Cf. Jackson: 'Energy used to be thought indivisible in atoms, but now quantum theory says hand-outs of energy in parcels' (Jackson, p. 12).
5. Conger adds here: 'In what sense is it a sheep and in what sense mutton?' (Conger, p. 1).
6. Conger also refers to 'zeppelins over London' (p. 1), undoubtedly a reference to the zeppelin raids of the First World War between 1915 and 1917.
7. Conger adds here: 'The state of imaginative muddle – must have a whole series of possibilities in mind which won't do as you have them. Stage of being formative is stage of entertaining imaginings and working at them to reduce them to logical tests' (Conger, p. 1).
8. To clarify what Whitehead intended: Descartes was educated at the Jesuit College of La Flèche between 1606 and 1614.

enduring side of the world. He sees the world as a multiplicity of substances – minds and bodies. The world should be construed in terms of body and mental sub-|7|stances. Descartes overlooked the continuity side of the universe. Descartes said the main attribute of physical bodies is extension. He denied empty space. Descartes and Newton showed the enormous importance of mass.[1] (Newton didn't believe in action at a distance).[2]

Thursday, 14 October 1926

Conger's notes[3]

|1| Very important lecture
Descartes made up a philosophy to include mathematical ⟨physics⟩.[4] Back to Plato for another such start.[5]

Plato at once faced by a reaction – Aristotle. In modern world Plato might be American ⟨and⟩ Aristotle English. Plato viewed politics with a certain Platonic detachment. ⟨Aristotle represented⟩ revolt of biologist against mathematician, interested in politics. Both lead him away from mathematical view.

Rationalism vs. Dewey. Cf. seven tests above.[6]

Emphasis on rationalism. Emphasis on importance of discursive reason in pursuit of truth. Greeks thought mathematics as they knew it and ∨Aristotelian∨ logic as they understood it exhausted rationalistic procedure. Greek language as adequate vehicle for all ∧truth∧. Strictly speaking both are wrong, ~~true~~ but enshrine much truth. Truth more important than the error.

Mathematics and logic form background of seven tests. Other tests depend on incommunicable.[7] Rationalism stands or falls ∨with view that∨ nature of things embodies in itself exemplification of finite truth. Rationalism an ideal for man because a fact in the universe.[8] Believe in it because of overwhelming

---

1. For King (p. 9), it is just Newton who showed the importance of mass; for Conger (p. 2) and Jackson (p. 13) it is Newton and Galileo.
2. Cf. King: '[Science is started – physical material bodies in space influencing each other; and minds. This was the working view of science way up into 19th century. Descartes didn't quite hold it; nor Newton, who didn't believe in action at a distance.]' (King, p. 9).
3. It appears that there was no class on Tuesday, 12 October, as none of our five note-takers for this period have anything for that day.
4. Conger has 'philosophy' here, but Nelson (p. 7), King (p. 10), Jackson (p. 14) and Burch (p. 4) all confirm that it should be 'physics'.
5. Cf. Nelson: 'Descartes is a mathematician and his philosophy was a philosophy made up by a mathematician, a philosophy that included mathematical physics. His philosophy is through and through pervaded by the mathematical type of intellect. Plato was much like him, also a mathematician of the first school of mathematical physicists' (Nelson, p. 7).
6. Referring to the seven standards for rational criticism that were outlined in the last lecture. See pp. 179–81. Cf. King: 'Dewey's revolt is not Aristotelian but it is anti-|10|rational. The gap between the two schools (pragmatists) is not so very wide. Rationalism admits pragmatism has corrected a false rationalistic method' (King, pp. 9–10). Cf. Burch: 'Aristotle revolted against the rationalism of Plato; Dewey, against that of Descartes. Whitehead's type of rationalism takes a middle course which corrects the false method of Descartes, and which is easily reconciled with the pragmatic point of view' (Burch, p. 4).
7. Cf. Jackson: 'Logic and mathematics form backbone of rationalism – Pragmatism overdosed with subjectivity – Logic and mathematics objective, universal, and communicable' (Jackson, p. 14).
8. Nelson's notes add here: 'Apart from this justification, it is a folly' (Nelson, p. 7A).

obviousness, and because conduct of life requires it in detail. Apart from it details lose their relevance. Satisfies all tests which do not presuppose it. But when thrown back on test of obviousness, we term our belief an ultimate faith.

In past domain of logic and mathematics both misapplied and exaggerated. Most cluster around fact that exemplification of abstract possibilities by particular fact crudely assumed as guarded by ~~abstract~~ ∧rational∧ certainty of logic and math. Thus the faith upon which it rests the first task.

Self-justification of rationalism merges into a self-limitation. So get popular confusion between rationalism and opposing skepticism. Cf. popular use of "rationalism" [Gauvin][1]

|2| Math has impressed on philosophy the consideration of method. Consider method of doubt. Whitehead thinks can't find Archimedean point.[2] This method is transference into ~~Greek~~ philosophy of method of Greek geometry[3] – discard complexities until you reach presuppositions which are obvious. Reduce to points, straight lines, etc. Obvious propositions emerge which are premises for deducing reasoning. Descartes' reduction to simplicity provides propositions of immediate obviousness.

Geometry first great intellectual success ~~to~~ ∨in∨ applying rationalistic method. Greeks thought geometry pushed them back to abstract certain knowledge about actual world – but in fact it suggested to mathematicians the notion of an <u>abstract scheme of purely logical relationships exhibiting possibilities of actual relationships among actual entities whose actual connections happen to conform to this scheme</u>. Rough exemplifications in geometrical diagrams.

Demonstrate certainty of the science attaches only to abstract ~~obj~~ demonstration and not to gratuitous assumption of exact physical exemplification which could be provided if men could make exact diagrams. ~~But~~ Such diagrams beyond power of men, so reduced to ~~power of~~ faith. Very meaning of geometrical elements viewed in actual world requires discussion insofar as we want to apply abstract science to physical world.

All mathematics says is ~~(point)~~ if there is any class of entity which for sake of name we will call points whose interrelationships conform to such and such abstract conditions (be classified in such and such ways), and if such and such propositions hold about such and such a classification, then such and such propositions also hold. But nothing to say about whether anything exemplifies or not.

---

1. Marshall J. Gauvin (1881–1978) was a Canadian atheist/freethinker. From 1921 to 1926, he resided in Minneapolis, Minnesota, where he wrote for the Freethought periodical *The Truth Seeker*. As an assistant professor of philosophy at the University of Minnesota, Conger would likely have known Gauvin's work well. The fact that the reference to Gauvin is in brackets, and that both Conger and Gauvin lived in the same city around this time, makes it a virtual certainty that this reference is Conger's own, rather than Whitehead's.
2. Cf. Nelson: 'Mathematics have impressed upon philosophy a method, partly good, but also partly fallacious, e.g., Descartes' method of doubt. Reference, first paragraph of Second Meditation of Descartes. Descartes' hope to find a thing indubitable is hopeless and can't be done' (Nelson, p. 7). See Descartes, *The Philosophical Works, Vol. I*, available at <https://archive.org/details/philosophicalwor01desc>.
3. Burch references Euclid specifically, though none of the others does (Burch, p. 4).

|3| Mathematics tells you about possibilities of world but not about world actually before you. Space of VinV this room has its points – Science of abstract geometry tells you nothing. Straight line in this room, geometry tells you nothing. Ancients didn't know that. Ancients were elaborating a scheme of abstract notions which they believed to apply to the room. No exact ideas, exact measurements. Appeal to mathematics for certain knowledge is a fallacy.

Notion of simplifying by discarding until we arrive at self-evident notions about world eludes us. Simplicity thus arrived at is a logical simplicity and not a simplicity of application. In applying these abstract ideas to actual world, can you find an actual entity which is a point? Logical simplicity about interrelations of things in actual world – but things thus related need not be simple.

In general the two simplicities diverge widely. Obvious things with obvious relations are not simple. and not elements whose relations are obvious VlogicallyV simple, and when get them where logical relationships are simple, it's hard to know how they're constituted and what mathematical relationships they exemplify. Nothing actual is simple. Pursuit of simple actual entity a mistake.

No notion about actual world which is not subject to revision. Contrast between Cartesian rationalism (and modern rationalism. Cartesian rationalism) proceeds by discarding complexity to arrive at simple notions, independently obvious, immediately self-evident. Modern rationalism uses Cartesian discarding as preliminary guide to imaginative construction. But essential feature apart from its psychological aids – starts with imaginative system of ideas in logical interrelations and complexities of logical structure. Thoroughly explored so far as there is any likelihood of applications in actual world. Mathematical physicist.

|4| This logical exploration will show no one set of premises from which the remainder of the system is a set of deductions. Nor is there any one set of fundamental notions in terms of which the remainder are constructions. Within system indefinite liberty of choice of fundamental propositions, is possible that choice must be made so remainder of system can be derived as logical construct.[1] Certainties of deductive logical reasoning – if such a complex notion finds exemplification in such actual occasion, then such and such other complex of notions is also finding exemplification either in same actual occasion or another actual occasion with such and such relations to other occasion. All our certainties are hypothetical propositions, certainties of logic can go no further than this.

Point to necessity of having recourse to such measure of obviousness as is inherent in direct experimental knowledge. Older rationalism conceived of premises intrinsically self-evident and intrinsic premises. The Axioms of Geometry are the axioms convenient for the occasion in hand. If such and such apply then the whole....

---

1. Cf. King: 'There is a complete liberty of choice of fundamentals, but the rest must be derivable as a logical construct' (King, p. 11).

Newer rationalism, any proposition is ∨suitable for∨ a premise, when taken in connection with a judicially selected set of other propositions of system.

Comparative clumsiness of deduction from some sets compared with elegance from others is minor aesthetic satisfaction. Mathematician impelled to find beautifully simple sets of propositions – No mathematician is merely a mathematician – also an artist when conceiving the importance of mathematics in pursuit of truth (Artistic side of no philosophical importance).[1]

So obviousness ∧of any system∧ is to be put into a common pool – tie them all together. According to old method, verifying the deduction is formally invalid as far as light is concerned.

|5| Can deduce any proposition from false proposition:
$3 = 2 \quad 3 - 1 = 2 - 1 \quad 2 = 1$

McTaggart[2] and Pope[3] are two, hence they are one.

But no system can completely pass seven tests – always contrary instances, vagueness. Measure of success – elucidation of our knowledge into greater clearness.

Exemplification merely reaches to ∨edge of∨ generic ~~verif~~ feature of concept. Also, shared by ∨concepts of∨ incompatible systems. Cf. wave motion. Theory which requires particular kind of wave motion and have found wave motion. Can't be sure you're right. Add to its probability, but not certain. Might call this conceptual vagueness.[4]

Second form, expressive vagueness. Whole theory of expression is the least explored side of philosophy. Language ⟨is⟩ a concentration of particular form of symbolism.[5]

Eaton, ⟨*Symbolism and Truth*⟩[6]

Wittgenstein's *Tractatus Logico-Philosophicus*. Brilliant, but Whitehead can't follow.

Whitehead, *Universal Algebra*,[7] *Principia Mathematica*, concerned with some aspects.

But deeper topic than any which these books touch. Gap between expressing and expressed. Most talk about language and symbolism vitiated by not going deep enough.[8] Representation of all our Knowledge and conceptual feelings in terms of presentational immediacy – the natural symbolism of knowledge – shared no doubt by animals.

---

1. Parentheses supplied. The parenthetical comment appears in the left margin.
2. See note 6, p. 54, on McTaggart.
3. It is unclear who 'Pope' is.
4. Cf. Nelson: 'Suppose we have a theory that requires that a certain kind of wave motion be present in order that it be verified. We experiment and find that there is wave motion. Then we conclude that our theory is verified. But this conclusion is not valid because there was a vagueness here in regard to waves, e.g., we did not find that the particular kind of wave was present' (Nelson, p. 7).
5. This sentence appears in the left margin; it is not completely clear where it should be placed.
6. Supplied from Jackson (p. 15), who was the only one who caught the title of Eaton's book. Ralph Monroe Eaton (1892–1932) was made an assistant professor of philosophy at Harvard and a Guggenheim Fellow in 1926. He committed suicide in 1932.
7. King (p. 11) references Chapter 1 specifically.
8. This sentence appears in the right margin; it is not completely clear where it should be placed.

Berkeley – Our knowledge of world a symbolism of our ⟨?⟩ with God. Language a conventional ⟨?⟩ narrowing of this process by which knowledge is rendered vivid, distinct, often erroneous.[1]

Saturday, 16 October 1926

Conger's notes

|1| Hoernlé, *Matter, Life, Mind, and God*.[2] Whitehead agrees with it, though Whitehead is absolute idealist.[3]

Convergence between ~~scientific~~ philosophy of scientific realism (in England, perhaps America).

Cambridge School[4]	Oxford School
C. D. Broad	A. E. Taylor,[6] fine scholar
Bertrand Russell	Norman Kemp Smith[7] (?)
G. E. Moore[5]	Hoernlé
Whitehead →	

Forming a convergence, c.f. Bosanquet's *Meeting of Extremes*.[8]

Religion in the Making, special exemplification of how to handle. Whitehead's general views as to how to handle criticism of philosophical system from point of view of old Greek rationalism.[9] Assumes philosophy of religion has been always conducted in obedience to assumption of rationalism, but according to method of old Greek rationalism. It's a continuous criticism of influence of misconceptions of that type of rationalism. Will give philosophy

---

1. Nelson (p. 7), King (p. 11) and Jackson (p. 15) all note the details of an assignment due on Thursday, 4 November (three weeks from this date). Nelson's account of it is the most detailed: 'Assignment – Reports on: 1. Pragmatism and Rationalism. 2. Contrast in their notions of truth and their methods of truth. 3. Analyze different forms of rationalism. Minimum literature: Dewey: *Nature and Experience*, chapters 1, 2. Descartes, *Meditations* 1, 2. Lectures' (Nelson, p. 7).
2. Hoernlé, *Matter, Life, Mind, and God*, available at <https://archive.org/details/matterlifemindgo00hoeriala>. Augustus Frederic Rudolf Hoernlé (1841–1918) was a German-British Orientalist.
3. Of Hoernlé's book, Nelson writes: '(Popular lectures of an absolute idealist. The early chapters are instructive on method.)' (Nelson, p. 8). Nelson's note makes Conger's line 'though Whitehead is absolute idealist' seem somewhat suspect.
4. In Rudolf Metz's famous 1938 book *A Hundred Years of British Philosophy*, available at <https://archive.org/details/hundredyearsofbr030561mbp>, Broad, Russell, Moore and Whitehead himself – all four Cambridge products – are classified as new realists, whereas A. E. Taylor and R. F. A. Hoernlé – both Oxford products – are classified as neo-idealists. The question mark after Norman Kemp Smith is justified, for he did not study at Oxford (nor at Cambridge) and he is no neo-idealist (but a new realist according to Metz). Metz's classification is appropriate, for Whitehead refers to Bernard Bosanquet's 1921 book *The Meeting of Extremes in Contemporary Philosophy*, in which Bosanquet discusses the opposition of realism and idealism.
5. George Edward Moore (1873–1958), British philosopher.
6. Alfred Edward Taylor (1869–1945), British philosopher.
7. Norman Kemp Smith (1871–1958), Scottish philosopher.
8. Bosanquet, *The Meeting of Extremes in Contemporary Philosophy*, available at <https://archive.org/details/meetingsofextrem00bosauoft>. Bernard Bosanquet (1848–1923) was an influential British idealist political philosopher.
9. Cf. Nelson: '(This is an exemplification of the use of the method of the New Rationalism.)' (Nelson, p. 8). Nelson also identifies these three listed books as '(Literature on the New Rationalism)'.

method – application of new rationalism to special example of procedure of the older.

⟨?⟩¹ apropos of logical coherence. (4th ∨5th∨ test) Recognition of importance of analysis of belief and logical coherence together form Greek gift – worked on endowment they shared with older civilizations. ~~civilization~~ Semites surpass in spiritual insight. Some Psalms – universal. Analytic touch transforms poetry into philosophy. Greek tragedians, Plato. What you don't find in Psalms. Christianity started from Semites, but received its touch of analytic clearness from the Greeks.²

Descartes was a devotee of analytic clearness. Descartes's idea of substance that needs nothing else than itself in order to exist. Conveys a half-truth – Whitehead wants to see other side. |2| Whitehead's whole course on this point. – Appealing to method of the newer rationalism.

Revolt against old rationalism started in England with revolt against metaphysics – short-circuit it, put it aside. Started concurrently in scientific world, Newton ∧(puts aside metaphysics)∧;³ in philosophy, Locke ∧(won't try to examine what essence of mind is)∧.⁴ Scientists now sooner or later must ask "What am I talking about?" – this is metaphysics. If you put it aside you end by assuming some metaphysics without saying so. Slip in misconceptions under ~~idea ideas.~~ ∧careless use of language.∧

Whenever he is thinking about Descartes, doesn't agree ∧with him∧ and joins with new rationalism, but unconsciously. Subconsciously assumes main Cartesian positions.⁵ Same with regard to Newton. All assume final actual entity is self-contained and requires nothing but itself in order to exist (⟨also⟩ in Hume).⁶ Challenged by Hegel, somewhat by Kant, recent absolute idealists, and Dewey and pragmatists. William James challenged in "Does Consciousness Exist?" – In challenge, very diverse schools agree. Hoernlé is exponent of new rationalism.

---

1. The character here looks like a large exaggerated Greek π, but its meaning and significance are unclear.
2. Cf. Nelson on the back of his page 4, which covers 5 and 7 October. It is unclear why this bit from 16 October ended up on the back of that page: 'The Greeks gave us the 4th and 5th tests. Some of the Psalms (as set forth in the Episcopal prayer book) are unsurpassable poetry, are universal, surpasses the poetry of the Greeks. The touch of analytic clearness that transforms poetry into philosophy comes from the Greek tragedians, Plato, etc. The secret of Christianity is that it started from the Semites and got a touch of analytic clearness from the Greeks' (Nelson, p. 4, back). The '4th and 5th tests' refers back to Whitehead's standards for rational criticism, that is, analysis of belief and logical coherence of belief. See the 7 October lecture, pp. 179–81.
3. Parentheses supplied.
4. There is an ambiguity here. The parenthetical comment that appears below 'Newton' has a very clear line connecting it to his name. In contrast, the words 'won't try to examine what essence of mind is' appear just below Locke's name, but there is no line specifically connecting them. Hence, in contrast to how we have rendered it, Conger may have intended: Scientists now ∧won't try to examine what essence of mind is∧. Sooner or later must ask 'What am I talking about?'
5. Both King's and Nelson's notes suggest that Whitehead is talking about Locke here rather than himself. Cf. Nelson: 'Locke hardly ever mentions Descartes in his *Treatise Concerning Human Understanding*, but it is evident in reading it that, when Locke was discussing "substance," he had Descartes constantly in mind; but when he was not thinking of Descartes, he assumed in ordinary phrases of language that the final actual entity is self-contained and requires nothing but itself to exist' (Nelson, p. 8).
6. Parentheses supplied. The parenthetical statement appears in the right margin. '⟨also⟩' is supplied from Nelson (p. 8).

Metaphysics as pursued by old rationalism. Though it created metaphysical science, had its limitations which were irking people. They looked on it as a revolt against metaphysics.¹

C.D. Broad, *Scientific Thought*,² *The Mind and its Place in Nature*.³ Critical Philosophy. Analysis and definition of fundamental concepts. ~~but~~ **A necessary and possible task. Other sciences use concepts and assume beliefs – Critical philosophy tries ⟨to⟩ analyze former and criticize the latter.**⁴ (Whitehead doesn't object to Critical philosophy)⁵ **Experimenter assumes nature obeys uniform laws. Pure mathematics like philosophy has no use for experiment. In pure mathematics, main intent to deduce remote consequences.**⁶

Broad says must have a certain kind of insight.⁷ **Speculative philosophy must presuppose critical.**⁸ Whitehead says yes. **People in philosophy have**

---

1. King seems to make Whitehead's point more clearly: 'The revolt against metaphysics is madness, for Whitehead. It usually is the revolt against the old rationalism' (King, p. 12). Also, note that the correct order of paragraphs in Conger's notes is not always clear, since Conger often created left and right columns on a page and switched back and forth without much rhyme or reason. This paragraph appears to the left of the next longer paragraph on critical philosophy. See the Introduction (p. xlviii) for more on the challenges with Conger's notes.
2. Broad, *Scientific Thought*, available at <https://archive.org/details/in.ernet.dli.2015.6694>, was assigned reading for the previous year (see p. 46). Nelson's notes provide a specific page number: 'As a modern example of this same old revolt, see Broad's *Scientific Thought*, commencing on page 18. Broad's view is a misconception of the place of speculation in the scheme of things' (Nelson, p. 8). It is clear that for the next few paragraphs Whitehead was actually reading down from the bottom of page 18 of Broad's *Scientific Thought*, and continued to read portions of Broad's book from there through to the end of page 21. It is not entirely clear if Whitehead read these pages uninterrupted (albeit with occasional interruptions for commentary), and Conger and the others simply did not record it all, or if he was instead skipping around a bit (this latter seems more likely to us). We have **bolded** the portions that are clearly being read aloud from Broad's book. (For more on bolding, see Introduction, p. xxxvi.)
3. Broad, *The Mind and Its Place in Nature*, available at <https://archive.org/details/minditsplaceinna00broa>. This book was originally delivered as the Tarner lectures at Trinity College Cambridge in 1923. Whitehead had delivered the inaugural Tarner lectures in 1919 (which were subsequently published as *The Concept of Nature*), with Broad's 1923 lectures being the second set of Tarner lectures, so Whitehead's interest is unsurprising. Incidentally, Bertrand Russell would give the third set of Tarner lectures in 1926 (*The Analysis of Matter*).
4. Here is the corresponding passage from Broad: 'These two branches of Philosophy – the analysis and definition of our fundamental concepts, and the clear statement and resolute criticism of our fundamental beliefs – I call *Critical Philosophy*. It is obviously a necessary and a possible task, and it is not performed by any other science. The other sciences *use* the concepts and *assume* the beliefs; Critical Philosophy tries to analyse the former and to criticise the latter' (Broad, *Scientific Thought*, p. 18).
5. Parentheses supplied; the parenthetical statement appears in the right margin.
6. Whitehead seems to have skipped the rest of the paragraph and to have continued reading from the middle of the first full paragraph on page 19 of Broad's *Scientific Thought*: 'The experimenter assumes that nature obeys uniform laws, and that similar results will follow always and everywhere from sufficiently similar conditions. This is one of the assumptions that Philosophy wants to consider critically. The method of Philosophy thus resembles that of pure mathematics, at least in the respect that neither has any use for experiment. There is, however, a very important difference. In pure mathematics we start either from axioms which no one questions, or from premises which are quite explicitly assumed merely as hypotheses; and our main interest is to deduce remote consequences'.
7. Whitehead has again skipped ahead a bit in Broad's *Scientific Thought* (or Conger failed to record everything), picking up near the top of page 20: 'Philosophy is mainly concerned, not with remote conclusions, but with the analysis and appraisement of the original premises. For this purpose analytical power and a certain kind of insight are necessary, and the mathematical method is not of much use'.
8. Broad, *Scientific Thought*, p. 20.

made ∨as∨ conspicuous fools of selves.¹ |3| **Best speculative philosophy only at best happy guesses. Dogmatic. More certain of** ~~any~~∨every∨**thing than had right to be of anything.**²

Whitehead: you can't get a single absolute premise.

Broad: analysis of truth and falsehood or nature of judgement not likely to be influenced by hopes and fears.³

Whitehead thinks entire misconception of place of speculation in scheme of things.⁴

Broad thinks for critical philosophy necessary analytical power and a <u>certain kind of insight</u>.

Whitehead: something which you bring to ~~physi~~ critical philosophy.

Descartes and older rationalists thought if purge mind of confusion you could see isolated self-evident truths. Definite set of axioms. Endeavor to impart a certain kind of insight – Disciplined rational insight – Misled by mathematics, ∨misapplied method∨, which better than their theory they were really following.

A properly apprehended speculative philosophy can't be sharply separated from properly apprehended critical philosophy. ⟨It is a⟩ fact that people are likely to get excited. "You cannot refuse to go up on a height and survey the scenery because some people have weak heads and will fall off."⁵

Tuesday, 19 October 1926

Conger's notes

|1| Problem of epistemology⁶ ∨⟨?⟩∨ became acute because at preceding epoch it became evident that various philosophical schools ∧schemes∧ derivative from the 17th century were all mad in one respect – that their

---

1. King records Broad's quote on page 20 that these large speculative systems are 'moonshine' (King, p. 12).
2. 'At best Speculative Philosophy can only consist of more or less happy guesses, made on a very slender basis. There is no hope of its reaching the certainty which some parts of Critical Philosophy might quite well attain. Now speculative philosophers as a class have been the most dogmatic of men. They have been more certain of everything than they had a right to be of anything' (Broad, *Scientific Thought*, p. 21).
3. King's notes (p. 12) suggest that Whitehead finished by reading the entire last paragraph of Broad's page 21, as he also mentions 'keep⟨ing⟩ half an eye on speculative philosophy': 'A large part of Critical Philosophy is almost exempt from this source of error. Our analysis of truth and falsehood, or of the nature of judgement, is not very likely to be influenced by our hopes and fears. Yet even here there is a slight danger of intellectual dishonesty. We sometimes do Critical Philosophy, with half an eye on our Speculative Philosophy, and accept or reject beliefs, or analyse concepts in a certain way, because we feel that this will fit better than any alternative with the view of Reality as a whole that we happen to like' (Broad, *Scientific Thought*, p. 21).
4. To the right of this paragraph is a mysterious roman numeral II with the letters 'a b c d e f g h i' written vertically, one above the other, between two vertical lines. The significance and meaning are unclear.
5. Closing quotation mark supplied.
6. Nelson's notes preface the lecture with: 'During the last two generations there has been a sensible method of practice, but a misconception as to the foundations of philosophy. It has been held that the foundation of philosophy is epistemology' (Nelson, p. 8). For Jackson, epistemology developed 'during past fifty or sixty years' (Jackson, p. 17).

description of what knowledge ⟨is⟩ had a gap – what was known was not an external world. Common sense resurged. Problem emerged. How is knowledge possible? Reformed rationalism must hold that knowledge, self-evident obviousness is an ultimate fact – you don't explain it but merely include it in your scheme. Obviousness not complete self-evidence nor clearly defined self-evidence. We endeavor to give analytical expression to this obviousness. Rationalism is a procedure towards a purging of beliefs and towards a gain in obviousness. No appeal beyond self-evident fact that procedure of rationalism results in deepening of obviousness and self-evidence. Complete analytical expression is ideal. What is self-evident is gain in progress towards this ideal ~~with~~ under method of rationalism. It is the culmination of this cycle of experience: action – emotion – belief – rationalization. Obvious is ∨uncertain yet∨ in a way certain. Rationalism strengthens and defines the obvious. Appeal to practice (Hume, Bertrand Russell) is appeal to action – emotion – belief. We find ourselves acting. Interweaving of action, emotion, belief. Appeal to practice an appeal to these beliefs by means of immediate obviousness in isolated occasions, then ∨subsequently∨ remembered. This appeal is ~~an~~ confession of inadequacy of philosophical scheme in question.[1] Scheme aims at being all-inclusive so far as generic concepts are concerned. ~~Oc~~ Practice is the ocean of immediate experience which lies outside the petty canals of the various sciences. ∨Two sides:∨ ⟨1.⟩ Systematized axiomatic propositions from which various sciences start. Then ⟨2.⟩ the unsystematized beliefs of practice. Science hasn't covered whole field of practice.

Science and practice when philosophy is perfect should exemplify resultant systems and not supplement them.[2] Don't appeal to practice to <u>supplement</u> philosophy. |2| Cf. how absurd if a chemist supplemented chemistry that way. We must exemplify our philosophy in everything we believe. Kant: If don't do this, some muddle.

Procedure of rationalization[3] is twofold – (a) imaginative suggestion of a scheme of ideas – eternal object functioning conceptually. Ideas mutually defined and logically coherent. (b) Comparison of this scheme with total experience as surveyed in practice and science.

~~In~~ We have no perfect philosophy – always a measure of non-exemplification and inadequacy.[4] Philosophy thereby supplies synoptic vision. By its general survey the adequate scheme is gradually approximated.

Conversely belief emerging in practice and axioms of science get ~~comb~~ connection as we gradually gain confidence in philosophical scheme.

---

1. Nelson's wording is a bit clearer: 'Appeal to practice is appeal to beliefs that are sporadically adopted because of their immediate obviousness in isolated cases and afterwards remembered. If you believe anything that is not in your philosophical scheme, your philosophy is inadequate' (Nelson, p. 9).
2. Nelson adds here: 'Science and practice are the data of philosophy' (Nelson, p. 9).
3. Conger and Jackson (p. 18) have 'rationalization' here, while Nelson (p. 9) and King (p. 13) have 'rationalism'.
4. Cf. King: 'Comparison elicits exemplification and adequacy' (King, p. 14).

Same as in any specific[1] science. – You bring your thoughts to discipline. Apart from attention in an observation you don't see anything. The imaginative scheme of ideas the basis of your mental attention. Elucidation, explanation, gain in confidence and obviousness. Philosophical scheme supplies activity of imagination to the narrower scientific procedures. C.D. Broad. Philosophy concerned with (pruning) premises. vButv philosophy produces "a certain kind of insight." Broad thinks mathematical method not of much use. Danger of producing wild ideas because look pretty.

One way to avoid ⟨this is by⟩ direct observation – Are your ideas exemplified? Other – Rigid Logicality. Ideas hang together in rigid deductive systems. Deductive reason increases your scheme by consequences. Increases area of direct exemplification, without your emotions distorting your ~~imag~~ observation. Mathematical method – Strictly logical method.[2]

Two factors of knowledge – mental production of imaginative scheme, meeting and analyzing perceptual production of physical experience, physical fact. Imagination meeting physical perception constitutes knowledge. No Knowledge of either alone.[3]

Older empiricists misconstrued this process. Didn't see we bring the conceptual |3| scheme to any analysis. Even when say this is a table. Older thought that mere perceptive activity produced inevitably the relevant conceptual functioning – Muddled ~~ph~~ conscious perception with physical ~~experience~~ perception. Conscious perception is analytic of physical perception, but not necessary result of it.

When conscious perception very partial and variable because depends on, springs from something else than physical perception. Requires the conceptual mental functioning. Only analyze the correlative physical occasion in terms of your different concepts.

Here we are coming near to Kant. Kant is saying "This man has misunderstood me." ∧Both Whitehead and Kant:∧ there is the given conceptual functioning which meets the given physical datum. Kant calls it experience of the senses, "mere experience." But Kant made perceptivity mental. The order which was knowledge was introduced in the process of knowing.[4]

⟨Whitehead:⟩[5] But process of knowing ought to be something general of which we are only particular modes. If just my knowing, the world as ordered

---

1. Conger has the abbreviation 'spec.' The proper expansion in this case is unclear.
2. Cf. Nelson: 'Broad in *Scientific Thought*, p. 20, says that the ⟨mathematical⟩ method is not of much use, but this is not true. How do we get away from specific systems? (?) 1. By observation, but this is not adequate alone; and 2. by rigid logicality – rigid deductive system. Deduction increases the scheme by all its consequences; it takes it out of the region where emotions are distorting reason. The mathematical method is the method of strict logical reasoning. It is essential to speculative philosophy' (Nelson, p. 9). See Broad, *Scientific Thought*, available at <https://archive.org/details/in.ernet.dli.2015.6694>.
3. Cf. Nelson: 'There is no knowledge without both imagination and physical perception' (Nelson, p. 9).
4. Cf. King: 'But Kant made perceptivity purely mental – in meeting the datum. And so, the physical datum was chaotic for him. The order was introduced in the process of knowing' (King, p. 14). Nelson adds to this: 'The conscious perception introduced one order (the spatial and temporal), and then the conceptual functioning introduced another, and as a result we know the empirical phenomenal world' (Nelson, p. 9).
5. Supplied from Nelson (p. 9).

is just my fake.¹ It is not what Kant meant. Kant's answer to Hume's scepticism unless in a sense process of knowing is made general.²

Philosophy starts with definite problem. Produces a scheme ~~made poss~~ Vpartially V thought out, which explains peculiar difficulties which he starts out with. Whitehead thinks Kant started with nonsense unless is talking of my knowing and your knowing as separate things; but produced a scheme of thought – which didn't produce what was wanted unless you wipe out the peculiar complex underlying his thoughts. If make Kant consistent, cease to be Kantian and ~~make~~ become absolute idealist. Same with Descartes if make him consistent.

Never understand philosophers unless realize that this is the psychology of philosophers. Dissociate what philosopher says from way in which he must be purged to make him coherent.

|4| ⟨But⟩ Whitehead thinks Kant much bigger than absolute idealism. Don't prematurely sacrifice adequacy of a scheme to its coherence.

Kant misconstruction of conceptual functioning of mind – put perceptual side into that – because supposition that datum was chaotic. Kant right in saying perception has definite form. But Whitehead thinks physical perception not mental at all. Physical perception includes what Kant called the datum, together with its form. What is knowledge is knowledge of relations of identity between conceptual functionings ~~and~~ (mental pole) and ~~(?)~~ perceptual functionings – physical pole. These diverse functionings arise from fact that same eternal objects are forming the what and the how of the perceptual functioning and conceptual functioning. Clumsy term ∧eternal object.∧ All other terms like "idea" etc. are conceptual and are taken to mean the mental side. ~~There is something~~ – These abstract forms are equally physical and mental – forms of both functionings, but have different ingressions on physical and mental side.

Proper antithesis to Kant is Francis Bacon.³ Father of old classical empiricism⁴ – Physical facts provide ideas. Go look without any idea in your mind, dispassionately. They ~~provide~~ Vforce V the ideas on you. By and by, law will stand out. Hopelessly wrong. Cohen on Bacon.⁵ ∧Whewell exaggerated

---

1. Jackson's notes are considerably more colourful here: 'because if it is just my knowledge, all that business of glacial age, dinosaur's eggs, etc. is just fake' (Jackson, p. 19).
2. Conger seems confused here. So does Nelson, who actually inserts a question mark at the end: 'Kant's answer to Hume's skepticism makes the process of knowledge of general. (?)' (Nelson, p. 9).
3. Francis Bacon (1561–1626) was an English lawyer and philosopher, often credited with the development of the scientific method.
4. Nelson adds here that 'Kant and Hume were brothers' (Nelson, p. 10).
5. Referring to Morris Raphael Cohen (1880–1947), American philosopher and legal scholar who received his PhD from Harvard in 1906 and taught at City College of New York from 1912 to 1938. His son, Felix S. Cohen, was in Whitehead's class this very term, with Whitehead awarding him an 'A' for his efforts (Whitehead, 'Student Record Book', p. 21). Whitehead would later write a recommendation letter for Felix at his father's request (Whitehead, 'Letter to Morris Raphael Cohen', 9 June 1930; Whitehead, 'Letter to Edward MacDowell', 10 June 1930). As a student at Harvard, Morris Cohen had been the roommate of Felix Frankfurter, who held a chair at Harvard Law School at the time of Whitehead's arrival and became his close friend (and in 1939 a Supreme Court justice). Cohen also reviewed Whitehead's *Principia Mathematica* in 1912 (Cohen, 'Principia Mathematica'), his *Adventures of Ideas* in 1933 (Cohen, 'An adventurous philosopher') and spoke at Whitehead's 70th birthday celebration in 1931 (Whitehead et al., *Symposium*). As to what Cohen said about Francis Bacon, Cohen did not write any books until

admirer.∧[1] But Bacon did give expression to what science is now and is going to be still more in the world. One of formative agents in making new mentality. Whitehead: ideas have to be there in order to analyze facts. Kant would say ⟨ideas have to be there in order to⟩ "constitute" ⟨facts⟩.[2]

Mind grows imaginatively as result of own activity when in contact with the facts. Mind inherits from physical world a definite occasion just as it inherits from mental. How far a real dualism between mental and physical. Physical {?} world inherits from mind. Can't really tear them apart, but must speak of them apart. Finally, what is is the process of knowledge in the immediate occasion is the mental concepts meeting physical percepts.

Newton. *Hypotheses non fingo.*[3]

Scientific repudiation of metaphysics same way. Part of imaginative equipment. When no imagination wanted, metaphysics useless to science.[4]

Thursday, 21 October 1926

Conger's notes

|1| Mind passive in English empiricism. English mind incurably lazy. Poetic reason stirs him up. Certain sluggishness about Anglo-Saxon mind which stays

---

the early 1930s, so Whitehead is likely referring to his 1916 article 'The place of logic in the law' in the *Harvard Law Review*, in which he writes: 'According to the prevailing theory – a theory for which popular philosophy is largely indebted to a famous lawyer, Francis Bacon – facts are "out there" in nature and absolutely rigid, while principles are somewhere "in the mind" under our scalps and changeable at will. According to this view scientific theories are made to fit preëxisting facts somewhat as clothes are made to fit people. A single inconsistent fact, and the whole theory is abandoned. Actually, however, facts are not so rigid and theories not so flexible; and when the two do not fit, the process of adaptation is a bilateral one. When new facts come up inconsistent with previous theories, we do not give up the latter, but modify both the facts and the theory by the introduction of new distinctions or of hypothetical elements' (p. 626). Later in the article, Cohen writes that 'The great apostle of induction was Bacon – a good lawyer, trained in the handling of cases in the Inns of Court, but one who made no contribution at all to any natural science' and adds in a sarcastic footnote: 'Harvey, the discoverer of the circulation of the blood, said of Bacon: "He writes science like a Lord Chancellor"' (p. 628). Cohen, 'The place of logic in the law', available at <https://archive.org/details/jstor-1326498>.
1. William Whewell (1794–1866) was an English scientist, philosopher and theologian who considered himself to be a follower of Bacon. Whitehead would have been familiar with Whewell's thought due to the latter being the Master of Trinity College, Cambridge, from 1841 until his death resulting from a fall from his horse in 1866 at the age of 71. He was buried in the chapel of Trinity College, which Whitehead would begin attending 14 years later, in 1880, and where he taught from 1884 until his resignation in 1910.
2. Nelson's notes end with an amusing additional comment about Kant: '(Kant's intuition without concepts = physical perception). The whole of the *Critique of Pure Reason* is sound if properly construed, but to construe it properly is to misunderstand entirely what Kant meant' (Nelson, p. 10).
3. Latin for 'I do not feign/imagine/make/frame hypotheses', first used by Newton in his 'General Scholium' (1713). Andrew Motte did the original English translation in 1729, rendering the passage as follows: 'I frame no hypotheses. For whatever is not deduc'd from the phaenomena, is to be called an hypothesis; and hypotheses, whether metaphysical or physical, whether of occult qualities or mechanical, have no place in experimental philosophy. In this philosophy particular propositions are inferr'd from the phaenomena, and afterwards render'd general by induction' (Newton, *Newton's Principia*, pp. 506–7, available at <https://archive.org/details/newtonspmathema00newtrich>).
4. Jackson's notes add at the end: 'Metaphysics essential to discipline imagination of science' (Jackson, p. 20).

in England. Lack of originative factor ⟨on?⟩ side of mind.¹ Newton's *hypotheses non fingo*. Doesn't apply to Newton's own work. Newton friend of John Locke.

~~Now~~ Another group emphasized *a priori* – What the mind does before it reaches experience. What mind does is part of its functioning in meeting experience.² No ~~⟨?⟩~~ mental functioning in pure abstraction from experience.³

When you have a metaphysics of your own, always misinterpret people with whom you agree. All ~~definitions~~ ᵛideasᵛ only defined in terms of system of ideas.

A priori school ⟨does⟩⁴ draw attention to mind's knowledge of ~~actual~~ potentiality of actual world. Can't tear actual fact apart from potentiality. But actual world is a limitation ~~upo~~ among its own potentialities. What this is can't be discerned by any consideration of conceptual functionings in abstraction from their analytical relation to actual world. *A priori* school neglected to observe proper rôle of potentialities of world – realm of eternal objects.

Conceptual functionings – discernment of some fragment of world as constituting what and how of analysis of immediate physical fact. Our minds meet physical world with a question, not with an imperative.⁵ Concepts not bare things mind is looking at – they are modes of functioning.

Philosophy must have a theory as to relation of table to color, touch, sound etc. Sense data – yet we all say it's the table. Kant: Certain kinds of knowledge leave field of all possible experience and get beyond, where experience can't supply object. Kant here thinking of Hume and causality.⁶

New rationalism depends on addition of nature of knowledge, and this depends on ᵛgeneralᵛ metaphysical conception out of which it arises. Don't start epistemology without any metaphysics. Ought to say it all at once. Notion

---

1. Cf. Nelson: 'Exactly contrary to Kant was Locke who didn't allow any activity in the mind; e.g., Locke's "white sheet of paper." This is similar to Bacon's view that the mind passively receives the facts' (Nelson, p. 10). The reference to Locke's 'white sheet of paper' is to Locke, *An Essay Concerning Human Understanding*, book 2, chapter 1, paragraph 2.
2. Cf. Nelson: 'Whitehead: the mind doesn't do anything before, but what it does is its functioning in meeting experience' (Nelson, p. 10).
3. King adds here: 'Better, what the mind is within experience' (King, p. 16).
4. Conger has 'doesn't' here, while Nelson has 'does.' Given the context, the latter seems more likely.
5. Cf. Nelson: 'Our knowledge is limited by our mind. The physical world is a fact to be known. Minds neither create the world nor give us certain knowledge about it. Kant is correct on his insistence on intellectual activities' (Nelson, p. 10).
6. Cf. Nelson: 'For Kant's great problem from which he started his *Critique of Pure Reason*, see sentence beginning, "For even if we remove from experience . . ." in Müller's translation. The relation of the table to the sense data is the problem that still remains, and is one that must be solved by every philosophy. Kant wrote, "But what is still more extraordinary is this, |11| that certain kinds of knowledge leave the field of all possible experience, and seem to enlarge the sphere of our judgments beyond the limits of experience by means of concepts to which experience can never supply any corresponding objects." (From Müller's translation, p. 2). Here Kant agrees with Hume and has in mind causality' (Nelson, pp. 10–11). Nelson's transcription of the long quote is word perfect; the other, immediately preceding sentence to which Whitehead refers is this: 'For even if we remove from experience everything that belongs to the senses, there remain nevertheless certain original concepts, and certain judgments derived from them, which must have had their origin entirely *a priori*, and independent of all experience, because it is owing to them that we are able, or imagine we are able, to predicate more of the objects than can be learnt from mere experience, and that our propositions contain real generality and strict necessity, such as mere empirical knowledge can never supply' (Kant, *Critique of Pure Reason*, p. 2, available at <https://archive.org/details/immanuelkantscr07kantgoog>).

only gets its ~~notion~~ definition in a system of notions. ⟨Alternate?⟩ between: Give general sketch and elaborate details with precision.

|2| Outward real actual entity – actual occasion ∧reminds us that time element essential∧ – something which happens – timefulness is of essence of it. ⟨It⟩ is an individualization, concrescence of the entire universe into the one real actual unity ∨~~entity~~∨ which is the self-presentation of itself to itself in its character of being that representation of the universe. A real presentation of the universe and in being that it is a real presentation of itself to itself. This self-presentation is to be looked on as self-valuation – an end for itself – but more ⟨than⟩ an end for itself, for in being an end for itself it is thereby constituted as the character of the creative concrescence which supersedes it. It is the character of what goes beyond it. You must have a world which is a passing, temporal world – must have four sides to it.

1. It is what it is – self presentation of universe.
2. In being what it is, it is an end to itself. Something there.
3. In being an end it is also, thereby constitutes that character of the universe which carries the universe beyond it.
4. ⟨?⟩ In being what you are you pass on to next phase. You condition yourself into your next phase. Complex description future in barest way.

Concrescence of entire universe – other actual occasions are in this actual occurrence. Here again if once shut self up in private world, you will never get out of it. Unless skepticism, Hume, absolute idealism – There is a private world, owner of it the absolute.[1]

Privacy not what I mean. You are constituting what I am. My activity can only be described in my relationship to you.[2]

|3| Eternal objects have ingression into actual occasions. Other actual occasions are represented or objectified in actual occasion. Modes of ingression of eternal object into any one actual occasion constitute the relations between one actual occasion and other occasions. Modes of ingression ⟨are⟩ modes of functioning of eternal objects. Any elements of actual entity are descriptions of modes of functioning – How is the actual entity in question actually itself? There is an activity which a partial description of what the concrescence of an actual entity consists in.

Objectification of other occasions in a given occasion gives others a peculiar status or relevance ~~of~~ with ⟨respect?⟩ to occasion in question. Might call this perspectives. Perspective for *b*, that complex of eternal objects needed to describe how occasion *a* is objectified for ∨occasion∨ *b*.

You are an object for me now – You are constitutive of me objectively. Objects for me. This the subject-object view. You are constitutive of subjects.

---

[1]. Cf. King: 'Descartes introduces the principle ultimately of private worlds – solipsism. The only way out is to throw up the sponge with Hume, or be an absolute idealist with "there is a private world", whose owner is the absolute' (King, p. 17).
[2]. Cf. Nelson: 'Whitehead tries to avoid both difficulties, to avoid privacy. You as elements are constituents of what I am' (Nelson, p. 11). Cf. Jackson: 'What am I – I am somebody lecturing to you people – I am explained in my relationship to you' (Jackson, p. 23).

Leibnizian point of view. Notion of perspectives. I see you under perspective from my standpoint.

Ultimately most concrete occasion is dipolar. Thinking of a magnet. Likes this. ~~so wouldn't say it has two arms~~. Can't sever poles. Whitehead wants this implication. Can't disjoin two poles of occasion. Further implication. Strength of positive pole in magnet is always equal to strength of negative pole. In concrete occasion ⟨this is not true;⟩ great variations mental and physical. May have both poles practically negligible if thinking of aspect of occasion as being an end in itself. Epochal occasion in empty space not important end in itself. Must be gradations of actuality.

Originative side – what fundamentally there is in world depends on comparative intensity of occasion as an end in itself.[1]

One pole is primary, purely synthetic side of actual occasion. Call that pole the physical – describe in purely synthetic terms, coming together, physical perceptivity.

|4| The other is the secondary, supervening, analytical side – mental occasion. Mental occasion is completion of physical occasion by self-knowledge supervening upon merely synthetic functioning being merely that outcome of self-presentation.

Physical occasion – superject – that which arises from its own ~~from~~ ...

Mental occasion – disject. Undoing of physical occasion and putting it together afresh.

Mental occasion is the entering of the process ~~how the~~ into the creature. How of physical creature becomes self-knowledge of its own creation. If have merely physical creature, how is it to know what it is? No machinery behind the scenes. Can describe machinery of creature in terms of what other creatures are – this is why metaphysics is possible.

The knowledge is the concrescence of two distinct modes of functioning of eternal object, two different modes of ingression. Both conditioned by common past, present, future, but mutually independent with respect to their own originality. ⟨certain origin which is conditioned by common world in which find selves⟩.

First mode of ingression ⟨(perceptive mode of ingression)⟩[2] produces associated physical occasion, which is the ground for knowledge.

Second ⟨mode of ingression is⟩ characteristic of supervening mental occasion whereby ground is analyzed with respect to identity or diversity of eternal objects functioning in concepts with ~~the~~ eternal object functioning in percepts.[3] ~~Percept~~ Conceptual functioning is characteristic of mental occasion.

Knowledge is concretion in one creature of recognition of identity and diversity arising from this analysis. Conceptual functionings ⟨are⟩ a hypothetical test of perceptual functionings.

---

1. Cf. King: 'Freedom depends on the ⟨comparative⟩ intensity of an occasion as an end in itself' (King, p. 18).
2. Parentheses supplied.
3. Cf. Nelson: 'The physical occasion is analyzed with respect to the identity or diversity of eternal objects functioning in consciousness with the physical percept (?)' (Nelson, p. 12).

Mind originative, brings forward what arises from own mental activity, which brings conceptual analysis to bear upon given fact. Imagination is of essence of knowledge.[1]

Saturday, 23 October 1926
Conger's notes

|1| Mental occasion is completion of physical occasion by self-knowledge, supervening upon purely synthetic functioning which physical occasion has of being merely that outcome of self-presentation. Mental occasion, disject, has its own unity. Mental occasion is entry of underlying character of the process into the creature which is the process. The how of creation becomes the knowledge of creation. ~~Physical~~. vMentalv occasion inevitable outcome of physical occasion. How much and what sort of mental occasion is outcome of physical is very different matter. But concrete fact is physico-mental. I admit no breaks. Won't admit that there are in principle different kinds of actual things.

One thing which may be described as God.[2] But same principle applies to God as to an electron as one occasion in its history or to ourselves. Such vast real differences as to put various actual entities into entirely different categories. But fact of being actual is a common fact capable of description in a common way. Not an equivocal sense to what you mean by being actual. Two or three ways which metaphysicians have of coating over the fact ~~wh~~ that can't work out theories as finely as wish – appeal to practice;[3] to equivocal meanings – (vsayv different senses in which can use a word) – ⟨?⟩ only because vofv underlying point of view of language that you don't use two. Insofar as one ~~sense~~ vmeaningv, the two senses ought to get one word for that more general meaning. Metaphysics is unexhausted topic. ⟨?⟩ thing is to be honest and know where you have failed.

Knowledge the concrescence of two modes of functioning of eternal object, conditioned by common past, common present, common future, but mutually independent in respect to independent originality. ⟨First –⟩ Physical occasion is always the ground, datum for knowledge. In all its aspects purely synthetic – Starts with nothing to analyze, so ⟨it⟩ has to be.

Second pole – characteristic of supervening mental occasion whereby the ground is analyzed with respect to resemblance or diversity of eternal objects functioning as concepts and percepts.

|2| This bringing together is the concretion, which is the mental occasion identifying specific elements in mental with specific elements in physical functioning ⟨and⟩ vperceptual functioning.v A concept is properly a mode of functioning. But you find the matter of a concept. Identity of that which makes the conceptual functioning to be first what it is is ⟨that⟩ which makes

---

1. This last paragraph is written vertically up the right side of the page, as Conger had run out of space.
2. Conger has an indecipherable symbol here that both Nelson and King confirm must mean 'God'.
3. Nelson adds to this: 'beyond metaphysics' (Nelson, p. 12).

the perceptual functioning to be first what it is. This is basis of importance of relations of identity and diversity. (Why have any eternal object?)[1]

Knowledge is the concretion in one creature the mental occasion of recognition of ~~density~~ identity and diversity. Fusion of perceptive ground with conceptual consequents.

In complete occasion you have two originative sources of activity: Perceptive functioning whereby there is the ground, conceptual functioning whereby there is the activity.

Creativity of the one fact is analyzable into two modes of functioning.[2] And therefore the conceptual functioning is to be looked on as in ⟨?⟩ essence a hypothetical test of physical[3] ground. Possible to meet the ground with ∨complex∨ bundle of conceptive functionings which disclose no identity. ~~May~~ Say then ⟨that⟩ conceptual functioning is pure fancy. Sometimes bound down as slave – does nothing but disclose identities – that is black, etc. – merely conscious perception. May be conceptual functioning is of such mild, slight character that hardly has any character at all.

Percepts and concepts both conditioned by whole past, present, and future of whole occasion.

Imagination is essential factor in knowledge. Issues in ⟨partial?⟩[4] vision of the ground in terms of those potentialities inherent in its mere abstract generic character of being a physical occasion. Insofar as specific physical occasion has generic character of being a physical occasion, it has certain potentialities which are part of itself.

|3| Potentialities cannot be omitted in the description of what it is to be actual. These potentialities may or may not have been relegated to irrelevance in ground of physical occasion as it is. Notion of attentiveness can be analyzed into imagination, and ~~partial~~ analysis and partial character of analysis.

Theory of Error. If no Error.

Primary Knowledge is ultimate fact in a sense; secondary knowledge is believed fact – functioning by which interpretation and expression arises ∧(Each presupposing the other)∧[5]

That process in virtue of which some elements in primary knowledge are taken as though they expressed elements which might have been in our primary knowledge, but owing to its partial character were not. . . .

---

1. Parentheses supplied. The parenthetical statement is circled and appears in the left margin. Presumably this is Conger himself doubting Whitehead's formulation. Cf. King: 'A concept is a mode of functioning. The identity lying behind both is an eternal object. A concept is always an element in a mental occasion' (King, p. 19).
2. King adds here: 'Dipolar' (King, p. 20).
3. Nelson has 'perceptive' here (p. 12), but King agrees with 'physical' (p. 20).
4. Supplied from King, who has here: 'The mental occasion is describable as a partial vision of the physical occasion in terms of its potentialities' (King, p. 20). King also has a question mark in the margin next to this sentence. The word Conger has here is hard to read, and in truth does not look much like 'partial'.
5. Parentheses supplied. Cf. King: 'He has been talking in terms of primary knowledge – ultimate knowledge, not secondary knowledge or belief. To make primary knowledge true, secondary knowledge or belief must be brought in' (King, p. 20).

Only possibility of having a theory of belief self-justified by own evidence. Yet a theory of error to which you are compelled ⟨blank⟩

Metaphysics incapable of gradual unfolding so that one topic is exhausted before another is brought on. Only seemingly possible when dealing with long established metaphysical system so ~~ea~~ system has become a matter of common knowledge, and suggests proleptically its proper niche. If reconstruct, must have preliminary reconstruction.

Phrase Immediate Experience. Misused phase, can prove anything by appeal if you don't define what you mean. May mean

⟨1.⟩[1] physical occasion, which is primary self-presentation arising out of the representation in itself of the entire universe. Pure perceptivity whereby an actual entity originates from limitations imposed upon the entire universe which thereby becomes one entity. Universe not properly one entity – can't ⟨become?⟩ without leaving some ⟨yet?⟩ out.[2]

|4| 2. May mean partial intellectual vision, partly imaginative, partly exemplified of physical occasion. Mental.[3]

3. May mean ultimate fully concrete occasion which is both physical and mental. One concrete entity is both perceptual and imaginative. Imaginative side is resurgence into aesthetic relevance of ~~perceptual side~~ potentialities which perceptual side may have relegated into ⟨?⟩ irrelevance. ~~May mean physical side or mental side~~[4]

Secret of progress towards higher phase of existence lies in strong and disciplined imagination, but proven of adequate physical ground.[5] Both mental and physical only to condition of favorable environment. Progress always finally progress on imaginative side. But arises out of adequate physical side.

Now back to Descartes. You never disagree with a philosopher unless you almost agree with him – otherwise you neglect him. Descartes took very long step towards coming to type of metaphysics which present state of cultural progress strongly suggests to us. Descartes father of all modern philosophy. ~~Did not~~ Just missed final simplification. All philosophy must keep in touch with general cultural state of civilization in which it arises. The first way of doing this. First stage is to analyze language.[6] vHow finest ideasv expressed. ~~of idea~~

In Greek philosophy ⟨there is⟩ a childish trust in language. Unless people believed in it, they would never have given it the investigation of Plato and

---

1. Conger has no number or paragraph break here, but all four other sets of notes (Nelson, King, Jackson, Burch) number this to indicate the first of three meanings for 'immediate experience'.
2. Nelson's notes add: 'The universe is pluralistic' (Nelson, p. 12).
3. Cf. Nelson: '2. Partial intellectual vision – partly fanciful and partly exemplified by the physical occasion. This is the mental occasion whose originative element is the imagination. (A concrete entity is perception and imagination)' (Nelson, p. 12).
4. Cf. Nelson: 'Actual fact in the immediate experience but may mean some abstraction on physical or mental side' (Nelson, p. 13).
5. Cf. King: 'Immediate experience is what an actual fact is in itself. Progress toward higher existence lies in disciplining the imagination' (King, p. 20). Cf. Nelson: 'One's metaphysical scheme depends on one's meaning of immediate experience' (Nelson, p. 13).
6. Cf. Jackson: 'Philosophy getting down to brass tacks analysis of language' (Jackson, p. 26).

Aristotle.[1] Great disaster to human race that Plato and Aristotle didn't know Chinese, etc.[2] As soon as analyze language, at once see ordinary proposition: the attributing of a subject to a predicate. Predication or attribution fundamental for metaphysics, with enormous exercise of scientific imagination. People went behind all words and said here is great fact of predication.

|5| Just there they were led to great truth that there are such fundamental ideas which underly. But also they got it in an extremely limited form – omitted that language is a very imperfect form of symbolism. So far from expressing what it does, it has general words which merely wave vaguely to context for you to know what you are doing from context. Predication ~~rarely~~ ⟨an⟩ extremely vague notion which cloaks inconsistencies of meaning.

Always an element of pointing in every sentence. Many meanings when I say "That is red." May be psychologist talking of own mentality. I am such that there is a redness for me. Maybe I'm an artist and interested in color patch. Maybe interested in wall. Maybe interested in President's house. Attribution of redness has radically different meaning in these various cases.

Notion that you have a well-defined meaning in predication highly erroneous, and as soon as abolish it in predicate, lose it in ~~pred~~ subject. Whole notion of well-defined subject – under certain circumstances perfectly definite, but has been applied to radically different situations. (See *Concept of Nature*, chapter 1)[3]

Descartes ~~tried~~ ⟨long step to⟩ get rid of it. For Descartes – a substance was an actual entity. There he wavered a bit – inconsistent, to his credit – had clearer view of what he meant than terminology to which bound himself down, allowed him to express. In some sense or other a substance is on its own – Individuality has its own separate independence.[4]

Tuesday, 26 October 1926

Conger's notes

|1| Depth of objection to subject-predicate form of proposition viewed as giving fundamental metaphysical principle. All propositions highly elliptical.

Descartes' scheme made to conform to sentences – ⟨e.g.,⟩ all men are mortal. Implication of insistence on fundamental character of these sentences is that we have here the typical exhibition of fundamental process of predication. In taking that as fundamental for fundamental type of rational thought, you are really accepting a superficial metaphysics.

---

1. Cf. Nelson: 'Language is the form of expression of ideas. In Greek philosophy there is a childish trust of language. And it is lucky that there was, for if there had not been, they wouldn't have given it the thorough-going investigation that it received in Plato and Aristotle' (Nelson, p. 13).
2. Whitehead makes this same point in the spring 1926 term. See 9 February 1926 lecture, p. 114.
3. Parentheses supplied. The parenthetical comment appears in the right margin with a circle around it. See especially Whitehead, *The Concept of Nature*, pp. 18–21.
4. Nelson adds at the end: 'Pluralistic Realism is true: there are many hard facts' (Nelson, p. 13).

Assumed that fundamental concept is real entity qualified by an attribute – Socrates is mortal. Subject-attribute concept. Supposes predication has well-defined unequivocal meaning – but Whitehead says no. Various meanings to be attached to the notion; indiscriminate substitution gives confused metaphysics. Language has made up a blank form which is really a method of pointing at things. "IS" is a way of pointing at a situation.

Assumption that there's a definite metaphysical fact underlying the "is"[1] is wrong. Solidarity of the universe requires that every proposition should include some form of reference or other to the general background constituted by every other ~~obj~~ ∨element∨ in universe. Can't get away to atomic proposition in which ⟨there is⟩ merely mortality and Socrates. Fact that if Socrates dies he must be buried should warn you there's something more.

This is in effect Bradley's doctrine when he says reality is the final subject of every proposition.[2] ~~Here~~ Can't talk of everything at once. General universe is included under some systematic relevance which includes ~~the~~ ∨all other∨ particular elements merely as contributing to this systematic character of universe ∧⟨the background⟩.∧[3] ∨Namely∨ so much of what we say presupposes systematic character of universe is spatiotemporal – You think of Socrates in a spatio-temporal world. Whole of spatio-temporal universe enters into statement "Socrates is mortal."[4] Mortality has reference to spatio-temporal universe, ~~etc.~~ Socrates too, etc., etc. This systematic relevance to the universe varies so as to fundamentally distinguish between various classes of propositions which are all linguistically expressed by "S is P."[5] You have |2| a fundamental difference. S is P is a convenient form for rousing human attention. Much more general than usual way of looking at matter, and SP point of view is misleading metaphysically. Extremely important stage in metaphysical development to see these are general metaphysical ideas. Another ellipsis in language.

Context determines particular meaning of various words – Particular meanings for which universe provides systematic background not distinguished. Every proposition extraordinarily vague. Lack of adequate analysis of proposition S is P.

Offshoot of subject-predicate notion has dominated theory of knowledge – subject-object theory. Subject qualified by <u>its</u> objects. Then there goes into the subject qualified by <u>its</u> <u>ideas</u>. Whitehead ⟨is in⟩ substantial agreement with Descartes' theory of ideas, but it had to be construed so as to feed in with this subject-predicate notion – a mind with ideas as <u>its</u> predicates, <u>its</u> modes – the privacy of the its. In some sense obvious.

The subject-predicate which drops the background and leaves subject with its predicates as final statement ~~is obliged~~ ∨goes over∨ here in this

---

1. Quotation marks supplied.
2. Bradley makes this claim in *The Principles of Logic*, first published in 1883. See Bradley, *Principles of Logic, Vol. I*, p. 42, available at <https://archive.org/details/PrinciplesOfLogicBradley>.
3. Parentheses supplied.
4. Quotation marks supplied.
5. Quotation marks supplied.

subject-object theory of knowledge into the private mentality with its private qualification of ideas as the final and adequate statement. Subject-predicate theory is ~~always~~ generally defended by arguments which hold water; it is then construed in practice ⟨?⟩ giving you \solipsist view,\[1] the subject on its own with its predicates. This subtle emphasis in philosophy has come in from logic.

Misuse of subject-predicate not in Aristotle – Aristotle wasn't typical Aristotelian.[2] Atomic view of subject-predicate came out in Middle Ages. Descartes didn't invent, but presupposed it. Aristotle liked it because groundwork of methodology of science. Must be able to neglect background and take this as a going concern. Necessity of contraction as ~~nec~~ methodology. But metaphysics should get beyond this contraction. Trap for all philosophers sooner or later – subject with its private complex of predicates. |3| There is no such privacy owing to the essential relevance of the universe. In proper sense of word, no private world of thought, no private fact at all. If once admit that privacy, then knowledge is a dream and history is concerned with one individual.[3] To reconcile must get some idea of illusionness, appearance, inferior genera of reality, etc.

This is Whitehead's fundamental objection to uncritical reliance upon subject-predicate mode of speech. Great difficulty in exposition because subject-predicate mode of speech is taking common form of language and saying this enshrines metaphysical fact. ⟨Might?⟩ act[4] metaphysics or put it in art[5], but wouldn't be distinct. Draw diagram in order to evade language. One has to insist on unfamiliar forms of language.

Language can be made more general, but ⟨this is⟩ hard. Got to start with some more general notion than predication – I call it the notion of relevance; there are scales and stages of relevance. Intensity of relevance, importance of relevance.[6] Irrelevance is the lowest stage of relevance – something you can leave out, something imbedded in system. "Socrates is mortal"[7] asserts a certain specific relevance of Socrates and mortality. Doesn't do to put naive trust in language to see what this specific relevance is.

Descartes correcting some major excesses derived from subject-predicate complex of medieval philosophy. Got rid of mysterious view of substance and said substance is actual entity. Locke still more.[8] Neither really grasped problem in completeness. Substance had been arrived at in its vagueness. ⟨They⟩[9] didn't see why philosophers inevitably drifted into ⟨the⟩ trap ⟨of⟩ \ascription of privacy to set of single notions\. Reason is subject-predicate

---

1. In King's notes, it is the '*atomic* solipsist view' (King, p. 22).
2. Cf. King: '⟨Aristotle not a typical Aristotelian because he lived with Plato⟩' (King, p. 22).
3. Nelson adds here: 'The solidarity of objects is then included in the dream of the one subject' (Nelson, p. 14).
4. It is not clear whether the letters 'act' are an abbreviation or not.
5. The word here is likely 'art', but it is possible that it is 'act'.
6. In King's notes, there are also 'styles' of relevance (King, p. 22).
7. Quotation marks supplied.
8. Cf. King: '⟨Descartes⟩ got rid ⟨of⟩ some of the mysterious notions of substance. Locke still more on his guard' (King, p. 22).
9. That is, Descartes and Locke. 'They' is supplied from Nelson's notes (p. 14).

form of proposition held to be final ~~form~~ triumph of logic and at same time as criticizing notion of substance. Whenever they aren't thinking of what they are ~~kno~~ criticizing, they fall into the trap. Descartes – substance a real entity is somehow on its own. Its individuality has its own separate independence. (Appld term held in common)¹ ⋁Whitehead – problem of metaphysics:⋁² Must construe solidarity of universe in sense which makes it consistent with individual ⋁independence⋁ of each real entity. If you forget there's a multiplicity of real entities and at same time a solidarity, which is what you mean by real world, fall into a trap.

|4| Metaphysics never going to reach final conclusion – reason is at each stage of thought. When produce metaphysical synthesis, find you have fallen into some new trap – assume something vague without proper analysis. All you can do is raise difficulty which the culture of your time hasn't been worried about. Always a depth below a depth.

Descartes overemphasized individuality of things. Whitehead try correct. For Descartes, world is composed of multiplicity of substances (God, mind, body).³ Right in <u>general</u> account of relation of God to other substances.⁴ <u>Descartes</u>: All substances require concurrence of God in order to exist. Whitehead: ought to have gone further – that proposition is not peculiar to God because all require each other in order to exist. If don't require each other, your idea of causality, theory of knowledge all going west.⁵

Don't use up your actual entity in each substance by itself and have nothing left over for relations, making them ~~exist~~ unreal. You want to get an interaction of substances. If cut relations out, always a struggle to get them back.

Descartes always better than the statement "requires nothing but itself..." Whitehead: Can't keep my thoughts straight when use ~~world~~ ⋁word⋁ "substance."⁶

World is a multiplicity of real entities. How specify the ultimate real entities so as to preserve the other equally obvious fact that there is a systematic solidarity of the world of which the real entities are elements? World no other reality than reality of its real elements. Real elements not to be considered as real on ⟨their⟩ own and merely accidental in the world. Don't say "I might be solitary" – you are by virtue of your status in the world. These two points of view are what we have got to conciliate.

---

1. Parentheses supplied. Parenthetical appeared in right margin. The proper expansion of the abbreviation 'Appld' is not clear.
2. King's notes add here: 'The one and the many' (King, p. 22).
3. Parentheses supplied. The parenthetical material appears in the right margin.
4. Cf. Jackson: 'Where ⟨Descartes⟩ was best is in God's relationship to other substances' (Jackson, p. 29).
5. King (p. 23) also has the phrase 'go west'. It is a British idiom meaning 'die, be killed', popularised during the First World War, and is also associated with the setting sun.
6. Cf. King: '[Descartes not consistent. Sometimes minds are all individual. Sometimes every entity is a separate entity ⋁substance?⋁]. Spinoza said at once that there was but one substance' (King, p. 23). Cf. Nelson: 'What can you mean by the relationships between substances? Relations cannot be realities, for all real things are substances: so Descartes would be in a tight place, but he is always better than his statement. But what is this real substantial entity? In many sentences, Descartes implies that minds are such; in many others, physical objects' (Nelson, p. 14).

Thursday, 28 October 1926

Conger's notes

|1|[1] Descartes, Spinoza, Leibniz use geometrical form. Bring out hypothetical notion not because necessarily true, but because seems to have proximate claim on truth.[2] Geometrical method presupposes there is a language in which your terms are known. How do you know the meaning of words?

Most complete unit which we can deal with is the sentence. In metaphysics you ought to not first define isolated words – words can only be defined with sufficient accuracy through the medium of sentences. You're in a vicious circle. Any other method (e.g. geometrical) is wrong: ~~means~~ You think ordinary language enables you to frame sentences such that fairly obvious and precise meaning of various words will enable you to get precise rendering of sentences. Endeavor to construe sentences as one coherent system will introduce an enlargement of thought and of your use of language, and your enlarged view of system will define words. Finally, in metaphysics the words define ⟨the⟩ system, and ⟨the⟩ system defines ⟨the⟩ words. In apprehending system of metaphysics, you gradually define the meaning of your words.[3]

Descartes' Principle 51.[4] Whitehead: God also requires other substances in order to exist.

"Catastrophe of German Idealism"[5]

---

1. Conger appears to have missed the beginning of the lecture. Cf. Nelson: 'It has been said that starting with James and Bergson there has been a revolt against Descartes, but this might just as truly be called a movement towards Descartes and away from the German schools of Idealism, on the ground that it does not satisfy the condition of taking the world as we find it. The result is towards an attitude of mind that is fundamentally Cartesian. We part company with Descartes at the point of his metaphysical twist caused by the subject-predicate point of view. Divest Descartes of this, and it will be found that pages and pages of his work will be accepted by the new movement' (Nelson, p. 15). Cf. Jackson: 'Revolt from idealism of Kant, Hegel, etc. to Cartesian point of view' (Jackson, p. 30).
2. Cf. Nelson: 'Whitehead is opposed to Descartes' always putting reason in the geometrical method. In geometry, we begin with definitions and axioms, while according to the New Rationalism we must bring forth a set of notions because they seem to have the first claim on truth, and then analyze immediate experience by reason of them' (Nelson, p. 15). Jackson calls this a 'distinction between old and new rationalism' (Jackson, p. 30).
3. King adds: 'With these words we gain an elucidation and ~~experien~~ explanation of our immediate experience. The geometrical method of building up gradually from elements, is a trap' (King, p. 23).
4. Whitehead is referring to Principle 51 from Descartes's *Principles of Philosophy*, which Whitehead cites somewhat frequently. Following is the text of Principle 51 from the 1911 Haldane and Ross translation, which is what Whitehead had assigned for this class: 'Principle LI. *What substance is, and that it is a name which we cannot attribute in the same sense to God and His creatures.* As regards these matters which we consider as being things or modes of things, it is necessary that we should examine them here one by one. And when we conceive of substance, we merely conceive an existent thing which requires nothing but itself in order to exist. To speak truth, nothing but God answers to this description as being that which is absolutely self-sustaining, for we perceive that there is no other created thing which can exist without being sustained by his power. That is why the word substance does not pertain *univoce* to God and to other things; as they say in the schools, that is, no common signification for this appellation which we apply equally to God and to them can be distinctly understood' (Descartes, *Philosophical Works, Vol. I*, pp. 239–40, available at <https://archive.org/details/philosophicalwor01desc>).
5. Cf. King: 'Principle 51. Substance what requires nothing else. God alone fulfills the requirement. The definition of being actual doesn't apply |24| to God, or else this world isn't actual. This is preparing the way for German idealism. Either we get into one substance – Spinoza. Or else God requires everything else in order to exist. Or every substance requires every other substance in order to exist. (Whitehead)

Can't have complete revolt from any great philosophy.

Knowledge is a functioning of eternal objects perceptually or conceptually ⟨whereby⟩[1] other actual entities are partly constitutive of what I am. When we perceive or conceive anything, the functioning relates me as an entity to world of actual entities. Naive realism from which Descartes starts and ~~from~~ which Whitehead holds. When think of Aladdin it's a concept of Aladdin relating him to the real world – where, can't find him. Can't conceive *Arabian Nights* as fairy tales without conceiving the real world to which they do not apply. Conceiving is a functioning whereby real world enters into my mental occasion. Agree with Descartes, only he got it in the subject-predicate form.

Descartes' doctrine of perception. ∨To give him∨ maximum consistency is ∨different∨ concern. Whitehead wants suggestions from Descartes.[2] Eternal objects are functioning in the re̲presentation of actual things, namely substances.[3] Objectification of other occasions in the concrescence, which is any one of them. In metaphysics, put your definitions at end. "A thorough exhibition of circular reasoning."[4]

Descartes's idea like Whitehead's eternal object, but Whitehead's eternal object is more a form of thought; it's a form of perceptive objectification, too. Doesn't like word "idea" ∧[universal]∧. Whitehead: ⟨there is⟩ identity of form between perceptual functioning and conceptual functioning.

|2| Descartes says actual ~~idea~~ ∨thing∨ ∧e.g. sun∧ exists in idea. Descartes' idea = Whitehead's objectification. Subject in which thought resides is mind[5] – getting towards subject-predicate idea. Idea of sun will be sun itself as it exists objectively, ∧not formally∧, in mind. Descartes – much less perfect.[6] Whitehead – concrescence under limitation. Descartes expresses concrescence, then runs away from it under subject-predicate obsession. But then went on to say my ideas are mere predicates of myself as subject. How do I know not illusory? – recourse to God. Very predicates which qualify me tell me of something beyond myself. Whitehead agrees with Descartes, but not that it applies only to God. His principle is a general ontological principle.

– be consistent and apply it to God' (King, pp. 23–4). Jackson's notes also say that Principle 51 is an 'overstatement involving certain truth of individuality' (Jackson, p. 30).

1. Conger clearly wrote 'whether by', but Nelson (p. 15) and King (p. 24) both have 'whereby'.
2. Nelson' adds here: 'See Descartes' definitions, pp. 229f' (Nelson, p. 15). He is likely referring here to Descartes, *The Philosophical Works, Vol. I*, but the page number is probably incorrect. It points to the beginning of Principle 24, but Whitehead had just been quoting from Principle 51, which appears 10 pages later in the Haldane and Ross translation, on page 239. Given context, this seems more likely to be the intended reference. Meanwhile, in what could be a similar corresponding passage of Jackson's notes (it is difficult to tell, since Jackson's notes are so sparse), Jackson (p. 31) references Descartes, *Philosophical Works, Vol. II*, pp. 52–4, available at <https://archive.org/details/philosophicalwor02descuoft>. This reference is to Descartes's 'Arguments demonstrating the existence of God and the distinction between soul and body, drawn up in geometrical fashion'.
3. Cf. King: 'The eternal objects must also be a form of physical perceptiveness. Not only a form of thought. The thing re̲presented in the idea is an entity' (King, p. 24).
4. Closing quotation mark supplied.
5. Cf. King: 'Descartes: A substance is something in which what we perceive inheres. That in which thought immediately resides he calls mind' (King, p. 24).
6. Cf. King: 'The idea of the sun is the sun existing in the mind – though not formally, and much less perfect' (King, p. 24).

Whitehead wants to force metaphysics thoroughly from subject-predicate complex – Made up 2,000 years under this complex. It isn't the simple obvious basis for metaphysics.

What is a thing which is both a growing together and an entity in itself? To something for its own sake is notion of value. What comes together has its individuality for itself, and value is that which is individual.[1]

If a growing together of all the other elements in universe, they must have something in them by which they insist on growing into other things. Actual thing is what conditions the concrescences which supersede it – conditions creativity. This is the principle of causality.

Ought to not be able to describe what you mean by "being actual"[2] until describe whole system of metaphysics. Descartes wrong here with his geometrical method. What it is to be actual is to do all things which actual things do.

Whitehead: Don't think of metaphysics as a stick with two ends – It's a wheel with spokes. vDescartes'v distinction between vrealv ideas which don't ⟨?⟩ you about external world, relational ideas which do is false principle.

You are done if you once admit that some ideas are mere predicates of a subject and others aren't. As you read *Arabian Nights*, you know it's imagination. Imagination is imagination of real world under very general systematic character ⟨such⟩ as refusing Aladdin.

|3| Events = Physical occasions gets back to Descartes. See *Principle of Relativity*.[3]

Saturday, 30 October 1926

Conger's notes

|1| Descartes tried to get a metaphysics which would fit philosophy of nature. Descartes' doctrine of independence formulated what was then limitation of ~~meth~~ scientific methodology. Don't construe Descartes as simply wrong.[4] Revisions of old ideas = second approximations.[5]

---

1. Cf. Jackson: 'Concrescence: What comes together has its individuality for itself and therefore a value for itself – The actual thing (the concretion) conditions the concrescence that supersedes it' (Jackson, p. 31).
2. Quotation marks supplied.
3. Nelson's notes (p. 15) specifically reference 'pp. 38f'. This is the final two pages of the chapter on 'The relatedness of nature', in which Whitehead writes that 'This line of thought, supplanting "stuff" by "events," and conceiving events as involving process and extension and contingent qualities and as primarily relata in the relationship of ingression, is a recurrence to Descartes – with a difference'.
4. Cf. Nelson: 'It is nonsense to criticize Descartes as simply wrong if we admit that his concepts have been sufficient for science for the past three hundred years and with the proper safeguards and a few corrections will be sufficient for the next three hundred' (Nelson, p. 16).
5. Cf. Nelson: 'New ideas include the old, reinterpret them, and add minor corrections. That is, old concepts are combined under more comprehensive ones' (Nelson, p. 16). Jackson (p. 32) mentions Newton and Einstein here.

Ten commandments are over-individualistic.[1] Must have solidarity of the universe. Communion of saints – Original sin unpopular now, but shows solidarity of universe. When overemphasize ~~solidarity~~ \independence\, fatal to ~~ethi~~ philosophy and ethics. Principle \(enunciated in?)\ unguarded way. Bradley treats temporal world largely on Whitehead's principle \(get absolute idealism)\[2]

Social Ethics the conciliation of two doctrines.[3] Thou shalt not steal – substantial independence. Property is robbery – solidarity.[4] Both <u>inconsistent</u>. If ⟨there is⟩ substantial independence, can't steal. If no substantial independence, can't have property. Aim of metaphysics. How can there be individuals which at same time form solid community?[5]

Interpretation of evolution in itself looked on insofar as evolution toward better. Endeavor to originate a society of individuals. Individuals taking their character from social environment, at same time each individual an end for itself, each with its measure of creative freedom – so whatever each individual does subject to condition of own being in environment shall not constitute robbery, but be a real contribution to welfare of all (cf. a delightful evening).[6]

Each individual doing what likes, but by reason of its own character is contribution to real freedom and depth of environment of every other \(Kingdom of Heaven)\.[7]

|2| There's no one far-off event. There are whole species of events. Any reference to a \general\ end is made irrelevant to existence by the independent substance idea. Leads to conception that conception of universe for which morals are meanings is not nonsense.[8] Might be merely a material universe, and in such a universe morals would be irrelevant. Ends are second thoughts, intruders. Thus morals are imposed on alien universe by crude device of

---

1. Cf. Nelson: 'Descartes' view of substantial independence has been the origin of many deficiencies of modern civilization and in our summary ethical codes. E.g., Descartes' view led to a thorough misapprehension of the ten commandments in over-individualizing them' (Nelson, p. 16).
2. Parentheses supplied. The parenthetical material appears in the left margin. Cf. Nelson: 'The doctrine of substantial independence as derived from Descartes has produced a fundamental inadequacy in philosophic thought of the last 300 years. This view has haunted modern philosophy even since, including the Hegelians' Absolute, Spencer's Unknowable, Bradley's Absolute' (Nelson, p. 16).
3. Nelson prefaces this sentence with: 'Whatever requires nothing but itself has a private property in its own life. Whenever a people feel this, ethics goes into the background' (Nelson, p. 16).
4. Cf. Burch: 'Social ethics is the conciliation of two doctrines: thou shalt not steal (individualistic, substantial independence), and property is robbery (socialistic, solidarity)' (Burch, p. 7).
5. Cf. Nelson: 'Both law and social ethics are engaged in conciliating these opposed statements: to show how there can be a fulfilment of private ends that is not robbery: how there can be individuals (ends in themselves) and at the same time allow a solid community. This is the problem of metaphysics' (Nelson, p. 16).
6. Parentheses supplied. The parenthetical comment appears in the left margin.
7. Parentheses supplied. The parenthetical material appears in the left margin.
8. Conger's notes seem rather confused here. Cf. Nelson: 'A view such as Descartes' substantial independence leads to a conception of the universe for which morals are meaningless. In Descartes' world, morals are irrelevancies to the world itself, but are brought into it from the outside by God' (Nelson, p. 16). Cf. King: 'Any reference to a general end is thereby (Descartes) made irrelevant to existence, for each substance is what it is. The conception of a universe for which morals are useless is |26| all nonsense' (King, pp. 25–6).

will of God. This line of development worked out by Newtonian mechanistic materialism. Cartesian God a frail bulwark against it, ontological ∧argument∧ metaphysical *tour de force* – can only be put on its feet by explaining it away.

Cartesianism finishes in mechanistic scheme of thought. Inadequate because inadequate analysis of immediate experience. Santayana, *Scepticism and Animal Faith*. Descartes, *inspectio*. Hume, Practice.

According to Descartes ⟨there are⟩ degrees of substantiality – Whitehead: relative independence or absolute independence of God is erroneous – foreign to very nature of substance. Only refers to ⟨blank⟩ in which particularities of dependence are irrelevant. ⟨Systemic?⟩[1] facts ∧of universe∧ which underly are not expressed. E.g., when Socrates is mortal. ⟨Systemic?⟩ view of universe underlying and relative to it.

|3| Whitehead: Agreement with Descartes. Identify substance with <u>actual</u> entity, not with a substratum which requires in abstraction from its qualities and modes which together with it constitute actual fact. Not substance and actual fact, but actual fact <u>is</u> substance.

⟨1.⟩ Disagreement – Dedekind expressed what <u>he</u> meant by continuity anyway. Bertrand Russell.[2]

⟨2.⟩ Disagreement – Employment of subject-predicate form of expression as expressive of any unique fundamental metaphysical relation. Leaves out expression of solidarity of universe which is relevant to each truth in some particular way – Sometimes one way, sometimes other. Three-fourths of time[3]

3. Disagreement with Descartes in substituting the notion of universal relevance of all entities (actual and non-actual). No fundamental disconnection anywhere – every entity ⟨has⟩ its status in respect to every other. Three types – (1) eternal object and (2) actual entities, (3) objectifications. (3) comes when you explain what you mean by (1) and (2). These are all universally relevant (?) ᵛwordsᵛ. Characteristic word ⟨for⟩ Whitehead is <u>actual</u>, by but not real. Existence is static. Santayana, Real is any the *res*.[4] |4| Actuality bears in itself reference to activity. Activity is creativity described from the standpoint of one element implicated in its specific form. Specific creativity is their description as activity of that element. Element active because implicated in total activity. Total result is an actuality – an actual entity. Individual creativity is the

---

1. Here and at the start of the next sentence, Conger has the abbreviation 'Systc', which could reasonably be expanded as 'Systematic' or 'Systemic'. Comparison with other notes does not provide any clarification.
2. In his *Introduction to Mathematical Philosophy*, Bertrand Russell extensively discusses the construction of real numbers by means of Dedekind cuts (pp. 67–73) and the notions of 'Dedekindian' and 'Cantorian' continuity (pp. 100–5). See Russell, *Introduction to Mathematical Philosophy*, available at <https://archive.org/details/introductiontoma00russuoft>.
3. Cf. Nelson: 'Three-fourths of the time when Descartes is thinking about substance, Whitehead agrees with him; but when he is not thinking about substance, he is misled by the subject-predicate mode of expression' (Nelson, p. 16).
4. *Res* is Latin for 'thing'. The context of Santayana here is unclear. In Whitehead's Gifford lectures, delivered June of the following year (1927), he appropriates Descartes's concept of the *res vera*: 'Descartes uses the phrase *res vera* in the same sense as that in which I have used the term "actual." It means "existence" in the fullest sense of that term, beyond which there is no other.' Whitehead, *Process and Reality*, p. 116.

individual actual entity. <u>The watchmaker is the watch.</u> Sounds like nonsense. Emerson, true shipbuilder is the ship.¹

4. Disagreement. For Descartes, God, in addition to being the only substance which has absolute independence, is only substance which is self-creative – only process for which process of creation is also the creature. But in Whitehead, this is general characteristic of all actual entities. On one hand, deny God has absolute substantial independence. On other, raise all entities to level of being self-creative. They are their own originations. Every self which is beyond them is in itself a character of the specific creative act [in them?]. Insofar as any actual entities are creatures (result of process of activity), God ought to be called creature.

∧Solidarity of creativity, but ~~not~~∧ no creative activity other than each immediate actual occasion. Fundamental supremacy ascribable to God. If desired in accordance with usage and sentiment to restrict "creature" to temporal creatures. All these words are literary words with vague meanings. Use creature for that element in the universe by which it gets on. The essential activity of getting on and having a multitude of individuals in it.

|5| Likely to lead you into ∨⟨?⟩∨ unconscious apprehensions. No metaphysician can dare to be consciously slack or vague in use of language. Every great metaphysician has been vague. Can't avoid it. Spinoza shocks public sentiment because not properly understood; absolute necessity of looking to your own technical terms and meanings and derivatives and their meanings is the first virtue of metaphysics. Don't neglect a ∨mathematical∨ symbol for public sentiment – fatal.

Alternative to Cartesian metaphysics. Analysis of meaning of being actual. Base it on rational and experiential foundations.

<u>Six ∨Main Metaphysical∨ Principles</u>.

1. Solidarity – Every actual entity requires all others actual or ideal, in order to exist.

2. Creative Individual – Every actual entity is a process which is its own result depending on own limitations.

3. Efficient Causation – Every actual entity by fact of own individuality contributes to character of process ⟨etc.?⟩ which are also actual entities superseding itself.

4. Ontological Principle – character of creativity is derived from its creatures and expressed by its creatures. Nothing behind veil.

5. Aesthetic Individuality – Every actual entity is end in itself for itself, embodying its measure of self-satisfaction and constituting the result of itself as process. |6| Process is a result and vice-versa.

6. Ideal Comparison – Every creature involves in own constitution an ideal reference to ideal creatures in ideal relationship with each other and in comparison with its own self-satisfaction and invol⟨ves comparison⟩.²

---

1. From Ralph Waldo Emerson's essay 'History': 'The true poem is the poet's mind; the true ship is the ship-builder.' Emerson, 'History', p. 15, available at <https://archive.org/details/essays20emergoog>.
2. It is not clear if 'invol' was meant to be crossed out or not, or just left unfinished. King (p. 27) has 'involves comparison' here.

Tuesday, 2 November 1926
Conger's notes

|1| Since Aristotle the implications of language read into metaphysics. Language a pragmatic success, and nothing can be a pragmatic success unless expresses some fact about universe. But sort of truth expressed has been misconstrued. Not merely words have meaning, but syntax, and this has been misconstrued. Socrates is mortal. Can be construed – there is a fact which exclusively concerns Socrates and mortality, and apart from Socrates and mortality, that fact refers to nothing. Atomic, individual proposition. No one would admit it when put barely, but that is the implication which has tinged philosophy. First expressed in logic that essential affirmation in logic is affirmation of predicate in a subject, complete in itself, beyond it might be nonentity. Secondly ~~line~~ got into substance-quality point of view, ∨meaning∨ that an ultimate metaphysical fact is substance qualified by an attribute. If world beyond, it's that substance with other attributes, or other substances with that attribute or other attributes.

Substance $\underline{A}$ ∧(little atomic fact which refers to nothing else)∧[1] with quality x. Can fatten it out or keep a herd of substances with attributes. This is the implication that comes from that point of view – derived from syntactic form of sentence. So not sufficient to say I have grave doubts with current way of looking at substance. Must go back and ask how did they come to think about it.

You object to the style of thought. When tried to express truth, used style current. Style comes from such sentences as Socrates is mortal. No such facts – Whitehead – Entire misconception of what language really means. Like a grammarian criticizing a poet. Poet can pack more into sentence than grammarian is aware of. Think what you mean by Socrates is mortal – Not Socrates among nonentity has mortality, but Socrates as in the world has mortality as in the world. ∨Possible relationship that∨ mortality can have with Socrates. But in common sense |2| there is a reference to the world. You must dive into the essences ~~of~~ ∨in∨ this way. (Bosanquet, Bradley, Royce). But mislead in construction of absolute – misled by common form of language – Something by itself [Either solipsism or Absolute Idealism].

Difficulty if I have to refer to world. World has ∨all∨ its materiality – things with no essential bearing on fact that Socrates is mortal. Not reference to world, to all its infinite particularity. Thus you have to hold that the references to the world in such a proposition is to a certain systematic character of world. Absolute ∧necessity.∧ Socrates's Athenian residence not essential to mortality. World as a whole comes in as the world bearing[2] some general aspect. Necessity of metaphysics and the general truth. Unless there is general, can't be particular. Particular refers to world under aspect of generality.

---

1. Parentheses supplied.
2. Conger also writes the word 'bearing' again in the right margin, and puts a double box around it, but it is unclear why.

Childlike trust in language – This Socrates is mortal, this ~~room~~ ∨rose∨ is red. This room is oblong. Nature is cruel. Is it same general character of world relevant in these cases? Answer is quite plainly no. Fundamental idea of quality and substance is misleading – a <u>general</u> blanket form for a whole variety of meanings which are at once supplied by common sense. Question of stating ∨verbally∨ what is the systematic character of world in any particular case would puzzle us.

Can't speak of particular without reference to the general. ∨Basis of∨ every actual entity requires every other in order to exist. But can't drop. Must have some general reference which includes in its scope every other entity.

Not ridiculous – Contained in your simplest thoughts. Things you don't ordinarily think about always appear ridiculous. <u>Ridiculousness is not one of the rational tests.</u>

Agreement with Descartes in identifying substance with actual entity. Quarrels about words foolish. Whitehead calls actual entity what Descartes calls substance. Whitehead – Subject-predicate form of expression doesn't express any fundamental metaphysical principle.

|3| <u>Whitehead</u>: universal mutual relevance of all entities, actual and non-actual – Eternal objects, actual entities, objectifications which are derivative entities. Doesn't think Platonic realm apart by itself, no such realm for non-∨actual∨ entities. Non-actual entities are only to be described and have only existence in relevance to actual. Each actual entity not only has its existence in its relevance to ∨all∨ actual entities, but to all non-actual entities. If man has not got two faces, you are saying something about him.

Lowest degree of relevance – irrelevance, ∧non-exemplification.∧ Each actual entity holds in itself a comparison of itself as actual with the ideal, the ideal is the total set of non-actual entities. This comparison is an inherent fact in each entity. Propositions not true of a man among the most important things about him. (Celestine V) made great refusal, and Dante sent him to hell.[1] Intense importance of comparison of actual and ideal.

Whitehead: my characteristic word is "actual" – ~~actuality~~ ∨activity∨, action all same root – Something happening. Every actual entity to my mind is a happening. Don't like word "real" – has a certain static notion; nor "existing."[2] What happens is the getting together of the whole universe as one individual thing – Under the aspect of this individuality.

Individualizing of whole universe – Something that happens. That happening is not to be looked on as a mere endurance. What happens is <u>new</u>. Each instant an absolute new fact, but it is a happening – has to have its time thickness, but it's essentially a happening. The idea is a creativity. Agree there with Descartes. Descartes having same view of substance. ∨Descartes says∨ substance in any portion of time requires its own (God's) creativity.

---

1. Conger has 'Celestine III', but surely Whitehead is referring to Celestine V, who abdicated the papacy in December 1294, after just five months in office. His abdication led to the election of Boniface VIII as his successor, who would become one of Dante's greatest personal and theological enemies. See Dante's *Inferno* III, 58–60.
2. To better capture Whitehead's meaning, quotation marks supplied for 'real' and 'existing'.

|4| Creativity is a general fact, a general characteristic of universe – but not one Entity which is being created – Each entity is an individualization of the character of creativity[1] – in its nature embodies all other individualizations. Solidarity of universe – a concrescence of individuals which are solid with each other. A solid universe. In trying to describe the status of any other entity, actual or non-actual, you must always refer to this entity as acting. How is that element involved in the active creatureness? In order to think of status, simplest to conceive how that other entity is functioning in makeup of actual entity in question. Every entity, every other entity is to be looked on as having its own specific activity in the makeup of any one actual entity. Can't arrive at a fact about an entity which neglects this activity of concrescence. Never can arrive at any statement of fact about an entity which neglects fact that each actual entity is something in own right. That's where isolation view comes in. Each entity is something for itself.[2] I am born. You are born as in the world. Can't neglect each actual entity is something for itself, but must refer to rest of universe. Each entity in being something for itself is thereby in some way made a character of the rest of creativity. May be referent to it in two ways – if other entity is antecedent – which your boredom confirms (?) or may be relevant to future entity as laying a confirmation (?) upon it. <u>Passes back to me.</u>

Play and interplay described in terms of high-grade entities. If you are going to deal with notion of actual entity, then you must have some sweeping meaning of term "actual." Mustn't have lot of entities actual in totally different senses. Must lay down what meant by actual and stick to it. Man, animal, vegetable, stone, electron, patch of empty space.

|5| Must bring in gradations of intensity in actuality – perfectly obvious – the ultimate basis of whole notion of intensive quantity. Intensive quantity is ultimately that which contributes to force of actuality. Agree ∧with∧ Kant ⟨that⟩ when intensive quantity is zero, zero of existence {Not with ∧Kantians∧}.

(2) If you are to have degrees of actuality, the current idea that the way to ~~describe~~ ∨get∨ proper descriptive scheme of actual entity – not to look at least intense type, but to variety of types which show various intensities. Mustn't say all you know about actual ~~sp~~ entity in terms e.g. merely of empty space. Have get thoroughgoing idea first thing to be careful about is to be adequacy. Then you may show that you've been redundant. Get descriptive scheme which is adequate, then ruthlessly carry it through. Opposite to scheme of that before Darwin. Before Darwin, all sorts of exceptions. God one entity, man with his intellectual powers actual in different sense, animals, stones, etc., etc. Merit of taking each set by itself.

Descartes ⟨was⟩ clear-headed, tried every actual entity and gave it a different meaning, but gave it meaning. Then came after Darwin a move for better and worse. World started from humble beginnings ultimately described as fundamental only what can discern in humblest specimen. Matter, but now

---

1. Cf. King: 'There is not one entity which is the creativity, but each individual has the character of creativity' (King, p. 28).
2. Conger also wrote 'assertion of something for itself' in the right margin.

a bit of ∨empty∨ space-time (though no such thing). Now describe and explain (or explain away) everything which wouldn't fit in scheme. Feats of juggling – naturalism of nineteenth century produced rabbits from up sleeve. Go back to Descartes and in pursuit of adequacy take elements – don't assert anything which he doesn't, but when I put it down as character of one thing, I say of everything. Things have a certain group of characteristics in terms of which they are adequate.

Nothing behind the veil. Character of creativity whereby there's a solid universe in each individual thing is metaphysical principle of general character which find selves. Exemplified in each individual instance. If the character is always – the general character in every form requires a general creature. God is a creature, Supreme Creature. He is not creativity, but concrescence in virtue of which all other creativity bears his character.

Thursday, 4 November 1926

Conger's notes[1]

|1| One of the main causes of misapprehension in logic, is that the logician assumes that he is dealing with something definite, clear and distinct. Example: Kant's synthetic and analytic method. He is really in the realm of the ideal.[2]

In logic we deal merely with symbols. In practice, they excite our minds to the apprehension of meaning. But this meaning is not analyzable as are words. Nor do we often get a definite steady meaning, which has possibility of analysis such as words and symbols have. A sentence is the addition of vague meaning to vague meaning. Whole sentence gives more definite meaning to words.[3] Through discourse meaning is attained. This the object of discourse.

Assumption of definite meaning made by Greeks and 17th century thinkers. Assumed their definite symbols pointed to definite meanings.

You cannot get deductive reasoning until you approach a definite proposition.[4] Deductive reasoning is not what we want anyway. We want a train of discourse leading to exact and definite meanings. Subsequent chapters or sentences must make original proposition definite. Assumption that science has done this job has had bad influence.[5] Even definite words omit relevance of universe in background. You cannot think of an electron apart from the rest of

---

1. Conger's notes for 4 November and 6 November are typed, and he writes at the top of the page for the 9 November lecture: 'two lectures out'. It seems likely that Conger borrowed someone else's notes and typed them up. We do not know whose notes he borrowed.
2. Cf. Nelson: 'Logic assumes that we're dealing with exact, definite propositions – definitely true or false. This is an ideal' (Nelson, p. 18).
3. Cf. King: 'To say true, or false, or analytic, etc, is dignifying it too much. The fluctuations of the propositions should control each other, and approach the limit of fixity (?)' (King, p. 29).
4. Jackson adds: 'In math you get an uncommonly near approach to a proposition' (Jackson, p. 39). Jackson's notes are sparse enough here that it is not clear where exactly this statement belongs, but it goes somewhere in this general area.
5. Cf. King: 'The job is assigning fixed meanings to fixed symbolism – To think language has done this is erroneous' (King, p. 29).

the universe.¹ You cannot think of a horse without thinking of him as existing in an environment. If philosophy is going to help ~~philosop~~ science, it must remember this environment.² The logical 'complex' (pseudo-psychological sense) forgets the environment.

|2| There are six main metaphysical principles:

I. There is a principle of solidarity. Every actual entity requires all other entities, actual or ideal, in order to exist.

II. The principle of creative individuality. Every actual entity is a process which in its own result, depends on its own limitations.

III. The principle of efficient causation. Every actual entity by the fact of its own individuality contributes to the character of processes which are actual entities superseding itself. An actual entity is an efficient cause.

IV. The ontological principle. Converse of III. Character of creativity is derived ⟨from⟩³ its own creatures and expressed by its creatures. Every creature is a creative character.⁴

V. The principle of aesthetic individuality. Every actual entity is an end in itself for itself involving its measure of self-satisfaction, individual to itself and constituting the result of itself-as-process.

VI. The principle of ideal comparison. Every creature involves in its own constitution an ideal reference to ideal creatures, (a) in ideal relationship to each other, and (b) in comparison with its own self-satisfaction.

Actual entities synonymous with creatures. Used indiscriminately. The creative character is to have processional character of the universe. This is actuality. Use the two words in order to lay emphasis on creativity.

Ideal entities are elements in constitution of actual. The conception of what is actual must be thorough-going with no exception. You must find in what is actual, the basis for aesthetic and moral values. The world must not be split in two. You cannot after your description of the universe say, 'O, by the way, there are values'. Fault of Descartes: he leaves values for his 'second volume'.⁵ Whitehead suspects Plato is much nearer to keeping notion of value as part of actual than Aristotle. Values cannot be fundamental unless they are necessary part of actual world. There can be no philosophy of values unless they are made part and parcel with the rest of the universe and its actuality.

The above principles are essential to actuality.

---

1. Cf. Nelson: 'The value of the background is evident in science; e.g., the electron is considered as in a field of force' (Nelson, p. 18).
2. Cf. Jackson: 'Keep things in their environment. Science always does – philosophy has not always' (Jackson, p. 39).
3. Conger has 'by' here, but clearly it should be 'from', as confirmed by all four of the other accounts.
4. Cf. King: 'We do not make a fairy tale of behind the veil. No character of creativity behind the veil. Everything is a creature, but is also creative' (King, p. 30).
5. Which of Descartes's works Whitehead had in mind as the 'second volume' is not clear. Descartes's second work was the *Meditations* (1641), but that work rather famously does not consider anything related to 'values'. Indeed, Descartes spends almost no time on ethics or aesthetics in his works, though he does discuss the overall role of ethics in the preface to the French translation of *Principles of Philosophy* (1647), where he describes the 'tree of philosophy': 'The roots are metaphysics, the trunk is physics, and the branches emerging from the trunk are all the other sciences, which may be reduced to three principal ones, namely medicine, mechanics and morals'. See Rutherford, 'Descartes' ethics'.

God is pure act, – the supreme actuality. But to be actual is to be a creature. Hence, God is the supreme creature. Alternatives: (1) God is non-actual, i.e. an ideal entity. (2) God lies beyond anything we can have conception of. Both views have been held. For many, God is an abstract thought. Dean Mansel[1] held to (2). He was the Dean Inge[2] of his time. (Whitehead did not say this last sentence with much sign of seriousness. Evidently trying to place Dean Mansel for those who might not have heard of him). Mansel held that God lay behind everything. Can't postulate anything about him.[3] Not wise or good in any sense in which we mean those words. Thus religion is one colossal failure.

|3| If notion of God has any religious value, you must steer between these two extremes. Language of philosophic theologians and popular language. So anxious to separate God from the actual world as result in falling into one or other extreme. Danger of paying metaphysical compliments to God. Nemesis: destruction of rational basis of religion.

One of the causes of this tendency is that God conceptions originated in barbaric views of universe. These barbaric deities have been elevated into metaphysical realities. Result: Conception of a God not particular⟨ly⟩ interested in truth, or afraid of ruthless intellectual honesty. Metaphysics must be made to touch life everywhere.

Doctrine of concrescence. Derived from Principles I and II, and explained by later principles. Value and solidarity essential. An entity is an individual by reason of solidarity.[4] Individuality a causal determinant of process of supersession.[5] Specific value of occasion arises from end attained individually. But this end includes relevance of ends beyond itself. Self as an end not independent of other selves as ends.[6] This is the doctrine of ⟨social⟩[7] solidarity. Communion of saints analogous to communion of electrons.[8]

Value in one occasion infectious throughout universe.[9] An actual occasion is a concrescence as individual value and a concrescence beyond itself.[10]

---

1. Henry Longueville Mansel (1820–71) was an English philosopher and theologian, and also an Anglican priest. Whitehead refers to him as 'Dean Mansel' because he was appointed Dean of St Paul's Cathedral in London in 1868.
2. William Inge (1860–1954), like Mansel, was an Anglican priest and was also appointed Dean of St Paul's Cathedral in London, in 1911. He was a prolific author and was nominated for the Nobel Prize in Literature three times.
3. Cf. Nelson: 'If He is non-actual, he is an ideal abstract thought and as non-actual as Aladdin. If he lies beyond everything, he is just postulated' (Nelson, p. 19).
4. Cf. Burch: 'The actual entity is not an individual apart from its solidarity with the whole universe; it is an individual by means of that solidarity' (Burch, p. 10).
5. Cf. Nelson: 'Individual self-satisfaction expresses the enjoyment of the how of social solidarity issuing into individualization which is thereby a causal element in the process of succession VsupersessionV' (Nelson, p. 19).
6. Cf. Nelson: 'The special value of the individual occasion arises from the end attained individually, but this end includes the relevance of ends beyond itself which are always attained or attainable by reason of its end' (Nelson, p. 19).
7. Supplied from Jackson (p. 41) and Burch (p. 10).
8. Cf. Jackson: 'Doctrine of social solidarity represented by doctrines of original sin. Original virtue (communion of saints and equally the communion of electrons)' (Jackson, p. 41).
9. Cf. King: 'What is good enters into every |31| individual and also what is evil' (King, pp. 30–1).
10. Cf. Nelson: 'An actual entity is a con-|20|crescence, and a concretion, an individual value, and a quality of concrescence beyond itself, and also a self-criticism' (Nelson, pp. 19–20).

Each of the above six metaphysical principles enters into description of all the other five.

Saturday, 6 November 1926
Conger's notes

Elucidation of Six Principles[1]
Principle I. (Solidarity)[2]

1. Ideal entities are eternal objects. Simpler to make a new form of philosophical terminology. You might call them 'ideas', universals, concepts. But none of these latter terms are exactly my meaning. When you analyze actual entities, you have a concrescence. You find something not actual – function of all other entities in an event. The "How" of the process, probably best statement of this functioning. The "how" of the perceptivity is a physical fact. The "How" is a gradation of relevance. Some characters highly relevant, others not. This the functioning of eternal objects – the "how" of my perceptivity. Their functioning constitutes the <u>relation</u> between you and me.

2. The "How" of my <u>conceptual</u> functioning. The concept is a function of my relation to the world, the total world. Concepts are always meeting the world as individualized in my perceptual functioning. Knowledge is the evaluating comparison. There is a Yes and No comparison between conceptual and perceptual functioning. My conceptual functioning is analytic of perceptual functioning.[3]

The Eternal object is not the concept of percept. It is the "How". Knowledge is the evaluation of the mental side of an actual occasion, it is the knowledge of the identity.

|4|[4] Term, idea, concept look at problem in wrong way. Cf. *Concept of Nature*, Chapter II. The only way to avoid bifurcation of nature: perceptivity must be considered as physical. Knowledge is analytic of the physical, a partial analysis. Nonsense to put sense data in physical world and not to put perceptivity there. If you don't, you will get a muddle-headed philosophy.[5]

Principle II. (Creative Individuality)

Every actual entity is a process. To be actual is to be limited. The "How" is the relation of actual to the whole background. Actuality comes from happiness

---

1. That is, the principles discussed in the previous lecture.
2. We have supplied the names of the principles from the previous lecture.
3. Cf. Nelson: 'The conceptual functioning meets the perceptual functioning with the same concept. (Correspondence theory of truth)' (Nelson, p. 20).
4. Conger's page numbers generally restart each lecture, but the typed up notes for these two lectures that he apparently missed were numbered without the pagination being reset.
5. Cf. Nelson: 'Locke, Galileo, and Descartes get around this difficulty if they say the perceptivity is physical, and the sensa are the <u>how</u> of physical relations. Then knowledge is analytic of the physical relations, but only a partial relation. If we put sensa into the physical world, we must put perception into it too' (Nelson, p. 20).

of limitation. God being the most deeply actual, is limited. Limited by His goodness. The only way to be really infinite is not to be at all, because it is a combination of incompatibles.

Principle III. ⟨Efficient Causation⟩

Principle of causation. N.B. word 'supersession'. Connected with idea of time. Universe has in some way or other – Time. (1) Creative passage of nature. (General). (2) Measured time and its relation to definite organisms, whose thronging together makes cosmological epoch.[1]

The creative passage is an essential fact. Here with Plato, who distinguished between becoming and measured time. Many more of Plato's ideas sensible – more than is often imagined. Some of the apparently most foolish are beginning to be recognized as expressing profound truths.

Principle IV. ⟨Ontological⟩

Ontological principle. Will discuss later.

Principle V. ⟨Aesthetic Individuality⟩

Principle of individuality. Notice it is a self-satisfying process.

Principle VI. ⟨Ideal Comparison⟩

Inherent in actuality is notion of potentiality. You simply cannot separate these two. Potentiality belongs to essence of actual, either in physical or value world. You cannot describe world without reference to it. Example: Idea of continuity involves idea of potentiality; also idea of 'divisibility'. Continuous not because divided but because divisible.[2] Notion of contingency involves reference to potentiality.

The world is both continuous and atomic. Actual entities atomic. Potentialities refer to the continuity of the world.[3] World is divisible in an indefinite number of ways. But 'atom' introduces an actual division.[4] Remember this is atomic actuality.

Tuesday, 9 November 1926

Conger's notes

|1| Existence of Supreme Creature
   1. Solidarity
   2. Creative Individuality
   3. ⟨Efficient⟩ Causation
   4. Ontological Principle
   5. ⟨Aesthetic⟩ Individuality

---

1. Nelson adds here that 'Creative passage is of metaphysical value' (Nelson, p. 20).
2. Nelson's notes add here: 'a field of force is such that if . . . , then . . . All physical laws are really of this hypothetical form' (Nelson, p. 20).
3. Cf. Jackson: 'World ⟨both⟩ continuous (potentialities) and atomic (blank matter-fact)' (Jackson, p. 43).
4. Cf. Nelson: 'Where the continuous side is prominent, you are dealing mainly with the potential. Where the atomic side is prominent, you are dealing mainly with the actual. The electron produces an actual division' (Nelson, p. 20).

6. Ideal Comparison[1] – Every creature involves an ideal reference to ideal creatures in ideal relationships to each other.

No exception to our metaphysical principles. If ⟨there is⟩ to be a supreme actual entity, must be in accord. So call God creature.

⟨Principle⟩ 6 is nothing more than general principle concerning the nature of an actual entity whereby it has a mental side or pole. Whole point of view of mentality – it is a conceptual functioning which is analytic of ~~the pure~~ synthesis – primarily analytic of pure physical synthesis – Also analytic of mental functioning insofar as this is synthesis.

Concept is conceptual functioning – Santayana brings out this point. If ask what the functioning is doing, it is the self-analysis of the creature in question, whereby the creature in question heightens its own prerogative of individuality, being an end in itself, something for itself – In heightening own individuality, it turns the pure blind physical perceptivity into consciousness by fact that the conceptual functioning is another ingression of the eternal objects into the actual occasion, and this is the ingression of the eternal objects as entering (within?)[2] the concept of ideal possibility and as analyzing the actual occasion. Its self-analysis of itself as enshrining all ideals. It confronts its ideal creatures with its actual creatures. The very nature of conscious perception – it's the concept meeting physical percept and yielding in that synthesis the yes form – the identity relation – the what of the blind intuition ~~is the~~ meets the redness of the conceptual functioning, and the result is conscious perception of a red brick.[3] Consciousness is provided by conceptual functioning, but conceptual functioning has own origination. The perceptual and conceptual both imaginative, both arise from the one past of the ~~historical~~ occasion, and both vary in intensity of achievement of actuality. Conceptual functioning may be merest ripple, almost a non-entity, analogous to the ripple almost nonentity which constitutes ~~em~~ occasion in emptiest portion of empty space.

|2| Origination obediently takes the ⱽsameⱽ conformation as the perceptual. ~~Get fancy~~ Always meets the physical fact of the physical percept with the yes form. As it grows, its originative intensity grows, and you have fancy. Meets with no form, ~~these~~ diversity. ⱽ~~Error~~ Illusion isⱽ genuine perception, but inferences with respect to universe ~~wouldn't~~ based on it wouldn't go.[4]

Principle of ideal comparison is principle of mentality, of mental background. ~~Whole~~ Embraces theory of knowledge as well as of morals. Knowledge is always the ideal and meeting the actual. Actual may not come to you as particularity of this entity or that – or may be ⱽexploringⱽ blank possibility afforded by general

---

1. Conger is here listing Whitehead's six principles again from the last two lectures that he missed, but getting a few things wrong: he had 'sufficient causation' for principle 3 and a blank before 'individuality' for principle 5. None of the other students relist the principles here; Conger may well have been quickly getting them from a classmate.
2. Instead of 'as entering within', Nelson has 'entering as' (Nelson, p. 21).
3. Cf. Nelson: 'The redness of the perceptual functioning meets the redness of the conceptual functioning, resulting in the conscious perception of the red object (e.g., a brick)' (Nelson, p. 21).
4. Cf. Nelson: 'Originative image gives no form – if I imagine you in scarlet coats. If drunk, I get a genuine percept, but the mistake is concerning ~~with~~ the universe referred to' (Nelson, p. 21).

systematic form of universe. When think of Aladdin, think of universe of ⟨space-time⟩.¹ generalization as being patient of the drama of Aladdin. But independent originative function of ~~the~~ mental, of mentality.

Deduction of supreme creature – six principles express general character of creativity.

⟨1.⟩² There is a creature in virtue of which creativity bears this character.³ Nothing behind the veil. Character of creativity derived from and expressed by its creatures. ⟨Take⟩ creativity away from creatures and you get nothing. Therefore ~~have~~ there is a creature in virtue of which you have a ~~ch~~ science of metaphysics.⁴ No matter if put out other principle or not. If admit ontological principle, nothing behind the veil, science of metaphysics means a creature whose character is such that there is a science of metaphysics.

2. There is a creature with a general relation to all creatures, including itself. Never make an exception. Run through principles, affirming them all of this general creature and see what can make.

3. This creature requires all other creatures in order to exist, yet is in a sense ontologically antecedent to them, since its character determines metaphysical principles, and is determined by them. Reminiscent of Stoic view of God – lays down law he obeys. |3| Cf. Seneca.

4. This creature is a process which is its own result – Like all other creatures, in a sense self-creating. Depends for its actuality on its own limitationsᵥ whereby subordination of relevance.ᵥ To be actual is to be an individualization of the universe, and to be an individualization is to be exclusive as much as inclusive. Can't think of individualization as merely inclusive. Excludes into the minimum of relevance which I term irrelevance. General gradations of relevance issue in comparative intensity of actuality. Creatures who haven't excluded cross-reference of incompatibles have minimum of actuality. Those which have individualized universe in maximum of harmony have maximum of actual intensity. That subordination of relevance is the goodness of God. ~~5.~~ God is limited by his goodness.

5. This creature contributes to character of all other actual entities ~~creatures~~ in superseding itself. Passes out into all other creatures. Extreme generality of its relations to others is what constitutes this creature as supreme being. Supersession ᵥwill beᵥ haunting us all session.

6. This creature is an end in itself –

7. This creature involves in own constitution an ideal reference to ideal creatures in ideal relationships to each other. Here ᵥdealing withᵥ the omniscience and the valuations – conceiving all creatures in ideal relationship

---

1. This is an expansion of the abbreviation 'spt.', which normally means 'space-time', though its proper expansion here is not completely clear.
2. Conger and Nelson have no '1', but Jackson's notes (p. 45) suggest that this is the first point.
3. Cf. King: 'By the ontological principle, there is a principle whose creativity bears this character' (King, p. 32). Cf. Burch: 'By the ontological principle, there is a creature by virtue of which creativity bears its character' (Burch, p. 10).
4. Cf. Nelson: 'There is nothing behind the veil: the character of creativity is derived from its creatures, is in its creatures. Therefore, by virtue of the creativity, there is a metaphysics' (Nelson, p. 21).

to each other.¹ V̶i̶s̶i̶ Conceptual vision is unlimited and complete, yet depends on own limitations – on self-originated harmony of relevance which is its goodness. There is an intellectual completeness of intellectual vision of conceptual functioning – is what issues in goodness. There you have ∨since there is completeness∨ the immediate disclosure of the possibility of harmony, what possibility of harmonious relation any creature has with respect to any other ideal creature – complete intellectual vision of harmonies and disharmonies.

|4| These steps come entirely and immediately out of the general principles I've laid down. Can't be many proofs. Either general metaphysical principles involve an ontological principle, and therefore a supreme creature will fall out at once. According as you handle your metaphysical principle, you'll arrive at different conceptions y̶o̶u̶'̶l̶l̶ ̶a̶r̶r̶i̶v̶e̶ of character to be ascribed to your creature.

Each ∨actual∨ entity enters into every other entity under some limitation which call objectification. It is an objectification the other entity. (Descartes +).² That principle applies to God. God in world or any entity is God as objectified for that entity – that aspect of God which it stands in the nature of that entity to find relevant to itself. ⟨So⟩ true to say that God has a history in the world. Going to general static conception, under substance-quality view, there is a tendency to misconceive time statement of God in world. Always stated as if he had one purpose – Poor view of omniscience ∨of God∨ and resourcefulness of universe. That purpose of God is always relevant to actual state of the world. Always that of eliciting that issue from the world which i̶t̶ stands in his vision as deeper harmony, deeper actuality. Purpose i̶n̶ ̶a̶ ∨varies in a∨ sense from day to day. God in world always objectified with relevance to actual world. Complete unchanging intellectual vision. But relevance of that to actual state of world varies. There is a history of the temporal world in God and vice-versa.

Last ten pages of *Religion in the Making*.³

Laski's o̶r̶i̶g̶i̶n̶a̶l̶ inaugural. Past never dead – capable of recreation.⁴ Each moment of time is a recreation embodying its objectification of the past.

Purpose of God in world road to deeper to actuality, but also ⟨practicable?⟩⁵ road which changes from day to day.

---

1. Cf. Jackson: 'Involves in its own character a reference to ideal creatures in ideal relationship, but since is God is aboriginal and not conditioned by particularities of others, etc' (Jackson, p. 46).
2. None of the other note-takers mentions Descartes here. The meaning is unclear. It could mean 'Descartes also', or 'Descartes adds to this' or 'Descartes plus something else'.
3. The reference is to the section 'The nature of God' and the final conclusion. Much of the discussion of God in this lecture is a recapitulation of ideas from *Religion in the Making*, and the final part of the lecture is Whitehead reading directly from its pages.
4. Harold Laski (1893–1950) was a British political theorist and economist. He taught at Harvard from 1916 to 1920 and maintained a circle of American friends there for the rest of his life, including Whitehead's friend Felix Frankfurter, later a Supreme Court justice. He returned to England in 1920 and in 1926 accepted a post at the London School of Economics, where he taught for the rest of his life. Nelson notes that the quote comes from 'Professor Laski's inaugural address upon accepting the appointment at the University of London succeeding Graham Wallace as Professor of Political Science' (Nelson, p. 22); that address was on 22 October 1926. The exact quote is: 'The past is never dead, because it is capable of re-creation at each moment' (Laski, *On the Study of Politics*).
5. Here Conger uses the contraction 'practble', the correct expansion of which is not entirely clear.

Don't make immediate need the eternal good. Make principle you adopt with necessary foundations of society. |5| Eternal good is eternal purpose (principle of concretion) of meeting ⟨immediate⟩ need.¹ H.J. Laski: Separate from facts of history the abstract truth that interpenetrates them.²

∨Whitehead:∨ Abstract truth which interpenetrates universe is eternal purpose founded upon omniscient valuation of all possibilities.

"To be an actual thing is to be limited"...³

A measure of harmony in the ground is necessary for ~~percep~~ future. A Unlimited possibility and abstract ~~cont~~ ∨creativity∨ pure nothing.

Definite entity necessary as antecedent ground for entry ∨of ideal form∨ into actual world.

Aboriginal – God must include all possibility of physical value conceptually. Thus as concepts they are grasped together. God gains depth of actuality in . . .

Unlimited fusion of evil with good would mean mere nothing.

Ideal world of conceptual harmonization is a description of **God himself. Ideal forms are in God's vision as contributing to his complete experience. Kingdom of heaven is overcoming of evil by good, transmuting. God as factor saving world from evil by providing of himself as the ideal. Transcends temporal world because actual fact in nature of things.**

Thursday, 11 November 1926

Conger's notes

|1| Only two metaphysical principles in virtue of which the existence of an actual entity can be inferred as distinct from immediate knowledge.

(1) Principle of efficient causation ∨by virtue of which∨ every actual entity includes in itself principle of own supersession. Consider what actual entity is, it's thereby the reason for another entity beyond itself. Every actual entity is a character conditioning creativity and thereby involving its own supersession because it adds a reason for creation beyond itself.

---

1. Conger has 'eternal' again here, but, per King, it was probably meant to be 'immediate'. Cf. King: 'Prevent making the immediate need the eternal good. The immediate need changes daily. The eternal good is the eternal purpose of meeting the immediate need' (King, p. 34).
2. Most of this paragraph is an extended quote from Laski: 'For the study of ideas in their historical context is a source of political illumination as valuable as any that lies in our hand. Not only does it serve to correct, more truly than any other discipline, that tendency to over-estimate the originality and significance of our own ideas. It prevents, as no other study can, that vicious habit of making the immediate need the eternal good, which is the source of some of the worst evils in contemporary politics; for we seek, wherever possible, to confound the principles we adopt with the necessary foundations of society. And by the study of ideas it becomes, I think, possible to separate from the facts of history the abstract truth that interpenetrates them' (Laski, *On the Study of Politics*).
3. Portions in **bold** are from *Religion in the Making*, specifically from the section Whitehead had already referenced on 'The nature of God'. In fact, from this point on Whitehead is simply reading bits from this section to end the lecture, with no breaks for commentary. See Whitehead, *Religion in the Making*, pp. 150–6. (For more on bolding, see the Introduction, p. xxxvi.)

(2) vOntologicalv principle in virtue of which any generality of character as shared among entities – that presupposes the character of generality. Entities immediately known have a character which itself possesses an intrinsic generality. This character of generality requires an entity ⟨with⟩ the corresponding character of generality. It's not a character merely of this entity or that entity – The ontological principle requires a corresponding entity exhibiting this character whereby the creativity acquires this character – that is the ontological principle. Ontological principle merges in with what is true with main principle in the experiential school of philosophy – nothing to be known which can't be found in some actual entity, matter of fact. The denial that there is a pure reason in abstraction from actual fact, which in abstraction from any actual fact can intuit truth.

There is a further doctrine in naturalistic experiential school of 19th century – which Whitehead disagrees with – that is, that actual matter of fact is merely presentational immediacy of sense data. Bradley, *Essays* II – purely arbitrary to limit experience to mere sense data.[1] ~~Something~~ vWhitehead: But nothingv to be known which is not character of creature.

If nothing general, no basis for any reasoning beyond the immediate solipsist moment. Only by reason of generality of character that have any rational justification for going beyond. No experience which can be described as merely a knowledge of solipsist moment.

Direct Knowledge. Can't infer yellowness – either immediate knowledge or it is unknown.[2] Growth in concept is the extension of imaginative self-origination of immediate knowledge of eternal object whereby more delicate self-analysis of actual entity is obtained.[3]

|2| Knowledge I am seeing yellow depends on two facts. Yellow is the what of one of my blind perceptual relationships, and also yellow is the form of my conceptual functionings. This arises in the self-origination in my mental side.

Knowledge of the world has two independent origins. Concept is never concept in abstraction – always whatever functioning there is is in the unity of the one actual entity. Perceptual functioning is functioning in unity which elicits the actual entity as an end in itself. Conceptual functioning. ~~Total~~ Completes itself by its own self-analysis. Always dealing with fact. ~~This~~ Two originative principles correspond to two poles. Knowledge is the synthesis of these two poles ~~which~~ described from the point of view of what mentality contributes to the actual entity. Contributes its self-analysis.

You don't know yellow vis therev merely because of blind perception – lots of things have entered into your perceptive side which you don't attend to. We

---

1. Nelson's notes refer to 'Bradley's last book' (Nelson, p. 22). This can only be a reference to Bradley's *Essays on Truth and Reality*, which Whitehead had referenced in the 15 May 1926 lecture (p. 193), but the exact passage is unclear. See Bradley, *Essays on Truth and Reality*, available at <https://archive.org/details/cu31924016877239>.
2. Cf. King: 'No inference of eternal objects. We either know it or don't know it. Either immediate knowledge, or it is unknown' (King, p. 34).
3. Cf. Jackson: 'growth of knowledge is extension of imagination vextendingv propelling immediate fact of eternal objects' (Jackson, p. 49).

are apt to meet the percept with the concept, but ⟨also⟩ apt not to – mental pole is a selection from the other pole. We are apt also to have concept not met with percept. ∧There is the yes form and the no form.∧ When the two do meet, call it conscious perception – imagination or fancy.[1]

The particular objectification of occasion A in or for occasion B so occasion A is an objectification for B is a demonstration of A for B. It is demonstrated under limitation of its particular objectification. How in a way we get beyond the relativity – A knows B not as mere object, but as something in itself and for itself with its own relevance of gradation, though limited by particular objectification. Yet A is demonstrated to be a something for its own sake. In knowing A as an object, we also know A in ⟨?⟩ subject to B, still A is a subject for its own sake, an end in itself. That is the force of that idea of demonstration. Objectification puts emphasis on how A is limited by its relativity to B; demonstration points out limitation is yet disclosed in this limited way, but discloses A's own position and point of view, A is something for itself and ∨for∨ own sake. Otherwise get solipsism, B with its own dream. Must admit that objectification, though limits A with reference to B, still includes a demonstration.

|3A|[2] Objectification includes a presentation of A as itself having its own individuality.

Particular ingression of an eternal entity α in occasion β is a demonstration in same sense of α for β. Though there is the limitation of that particular ingression, what α is in itself is still constitutive of β. Otherwise it wouldn't be α which makes ingression in β, but something else. It is

Limitation is a limitation of its relational essence. All sorts of possibilities with respect to its functioning and its relational essence. Conditioned by yet more subtle and abstract eternal objects of more tenuous grade. And all the possibility of α with respect to its functioning constitute what I call its relational essence. α must be limited in accordance with some limitation of its relational essence. Always going to some higher, more tenuous eternal object – greenness of green – ∨green and how it can be in universe∨

Idea of demonstration – asserts realism as opposed to solipsism of actual entity. ⟨Also⟩ as opposed to nominalism, that there is the actual entity, the eternal object α is demonstrated under limitation and yet with its individual essence intact. Just as A is demonstration for B with subjective individuality intact. –[3]

---

1. Cf. Jackson: 'We are also very apt to have a concept not met by a percept. "They are not chained together." There is the "yes" form and the "no" form in comparison – when percept met by concept it is "yes" form – when not it is the "no" form – this is what we call imagination, fancy, etc.' (Jackson, p. 50). Nelson's notes cite an example: 'Also, we are apt to have a concept that is not met with the percept, e.g., I imagine you are clothed in red coats' (Nelson, p. 22A).
2. There is a numbering error here. This unnumbered page appears after three numbered pages, but through comparison with the other sets of student notes, we know that this unnumbered page is actually the third page of notes, while the page marked '3' is the fourth page. We have thus reversed the order of these pages and renumbered them '3A' and '3B'.
3. Cf. Nelson: '1. The demonstration of an actual entity is an assertion of realism as opposed to solipsism and as opposed to the idea that there is only one entity. 2. The assertion of realism as opposed to nominalism:

Asserts two forms of realism. Something which has own being apart from particular occasion A has demonstrated that there are entities which preserve their self-identity in other occasions, have their identity in other point of view. Idea of identity bound up in demonstration. If no demonstration, identity is nonsense. Hold of something which will survive ⟨?⟩ when pass from A to diversity. Amid diversity there is identity. Demonstration means within your knowledge, can't know anything without knowing that what you know can have its identity within a diversity.[1] When I have A demonstrated, I know that A has another life. A is for itself, A is given to its possibility of another life. When an eternal object α is demonstrated, there is α with its possibility of another life.[2]

|3B| ⟨?⟩ example of demonstration need not go beyond B ∨(Ego)∨[3] itself. Because I have ground here and ground there. One event which know by touch and by sight. There are The objectification of an entity is analyzable into many objectifications. In unity of one entity, may be many objectifications.

An eternal object such as a color may have diverse modes of ingression into same actual entity.

Apart Demonstration that elt is the patience of the relationship of ∧identity∧. That demonstrates an actual bit of space time. Two objectifications which are diverse are connected by relationship of identical space time or actual entity.

Any one of those objectifications has the possibility of identity (with) another objectification. Possibility of identical relationship with another objectification with respect to another entity is demonstration. There is an actual entity which is greater than the mere objectification of it.

No matter of fact can be wholly diverse from ∨devoid of∨ possibility; potentiality. Demonstration is the possibility, potentiality in the objectification. It de Objectification demonstrates actual entity with potentiality beyond itself – it doesn't say what they are – some will be realized, some not. This is why an objectification is to be termed a limitation. A limitation because can't divest objectification from what it is and from what it isn't – from other life of that piece of ⟨space-time?⟩ which is there.

Can't apprehend an eternal object without a reference to potentialities. That is ⟨brown?⟩ – has potentiality of other ingressions. Might find it anywhere. Logical nominalism was endeavor to divest actual fact from its potentiality. Solipsism is endeavor to do it. People won't admit they're solipsists after have driven selves into that corner.

'The eternal object a is demonstrated under a limit, but yet with its individual essence intact' (Nelson, p. 22A).
1. Cf. Nelson: 'The particular occasion A has demonstrated that there are entities that preserve their self-identity in other occasions. The concept of identity is wrapped up in "demonstration". Identity requires diversity and diversity requires identity. Demonstration = can't know without knowing that what you know can have its identity in a diversity. Beyond the immediate there is an identity' (Nelson, p. 22A).
2. Nelson (p. 22A), King (p. 36) and Jackson (p. 52) all reference a 'patch' here, presumably a patch of colour: 'When an eternal object a is demonstrated it is demonstrated with its possibility of another life – demonstration not merely as ending itself in this particular patch' (Nelson, p. 22A).
3. Parentheses supplied.

Harvard lectures, fall semester 1926

~~Always really there is a reference to the~~ ∧Whatever you know has∧ patience for otherness. Otherness is potentiality. ∨Application to Continuity in lecture out.∨[1]

Tuesday, 16 November 1926

Conger's notes

|1|[2] Demonstration is that character of the concrescence in virtue of which the objectification is not purely a dependence on the concrescence, but is an objectification of a world on equal terms. Demonstration is how the relativity of objectification is transcended. Demonstration in virtue of which perceptivity is perceptive of ourselves in a common world. There is another point – any particular actual entity which is for me an actual entity[3] is an actual experience.[4] Actual experiencing of entire universe.

Definite concrescence B. How α ∧(eternal object)∧ has ingression.

(1) α <u>may</u> have ingression into B as constituting a physical relationship between B and some other particular occasion ⟨A⟩. α is how of objectification of A for B. Particular special physical fact depends on this sort of ingression.

(2), (3), (4) are mental, conceptual. Generality brought in by what you may term potential mentality.[5]

⟨(2)⟩[6] α A does enter into B as constituting a conceptual relationship between B and each particular occasion X, whereby the patience of X for its physical relationship ~~for~~ ∨to∨ B is objectified for B. ∨Showing up X as∨ possibly related to big B via α. This mode of ingression involves the yes form and no form of comparison.[7]

This mode of ingression may be quite irrelevant to aesthetic individuality of B. May be such a faint subconsciousness as to be irrelevant. A mental potentiality in B. When it ⟨wakes⟩[8] up into relevance in B, it is what we call imagination. It is all the ∨possible∨ imagination – what you are remains irrelevant. Another

---

1. This last addition is very likely Conger noting that he sees a connection between this point and a point from the two lectures that he missed, those on 4 and 6 November.
2. Whitehead apparently recommended some of Conger's work to the class, though unsurprisingly, Conger himself did not write this down. The references appear in both Nelson's notes (p. 23) and Jackson's notes (p. 54), but Nelson's references are more detailed. They refer to an article that appeared in print on 28 October 1926, which would have to be Conger, 'What are the criteria of levels?', and a book, which is probably Conger, *A Course in Philosophy*; the Nelson notes specifically refer to Appendix A of the latter, which is 'The Implicit Duality of Thinking and Its Consequences for Philosophy'.
3. Conger's notes duplicate the text 'is for me an actual entity'; we have deleted the duplication.
4. Cf. Nelson: 'Any actual occasion ⟨B⟩ will be both mental and physical, which is for me an actual entity in an act for experience' (Nelson, p. 23).
5. Cf. Nelson: 'Generality is brought in by a potentiality or passive mentality' (Nelson, p. 23).
6. Conger's notes do not have a '(2)', but Nelson (p. 23), King (p. 36), Jackson (p. 54) and Burch (p. 11) all agree that (2) begins here.
7. King's notes add here: 'X objectified for β under form α' (King, p. 37).
8. Conger has 'works' but both Nelson (p. 23) and King (p. 37) have 'wakes'.

226

(3) α does enter into B as constituting a conceptual relationship between B and universe as systematically patient of the relationship between B and any of its occasions. |2| Draw distinction between B and this occasion and total systematic fact. This mode may be irrelevant.

(4) α does enter into B as constituting a conceptual relationship between B and environmental universe as systematically patient or impatient of α by reason of its environmental character. <u>Now</u> think of the occasions with an environmental relationship. This mode may or may not be irrelevant.

(2), (3), and (4) constitute necessary ingression of α into B via the mental functioning, but 2, 3, and 4 may be irrelevant in B so far as concerns this eternal object α. Then α is not ⟨effective⟩[1] within the mentality of B. That idea of ineffectiveness is no mentality. Every eternal object is ineffective.[2] Then the environment of B consists of these occasions whose objectifications for B, physical or mental, constitute some degree of effectiveness to the eternal objects which qualify the objectifications. The environment of B is those occasions which really matter, add something distinctive and individual, are individually valuable for B, and then they are individually valuable – note specific character of objectifications. Incompatible that they should have other specific characters.

Science and the Modern World.[3] Can't have induction from immediate occasion to what is true for all occasions, but only for a community of occasions in some special relation to B. But beyond that can't make any induction. Power of making induction gradually fades off.

|3| Whatever you talk of has being.[4]

~~Theory of Time~~

Few general remarks:

1. Distinction between being and its various genera. To be an entity is the most general fact of having logical stability, of having potentiality, of being unequivocal identical entity discernible as constituting form of some relationship between diverse modes of functioning. Logical stability, you find it as constituting the what of diverse modes of functioning. It constitutes identity of various modes of functioning, those modes of functioning are characterized by identity. Define it this way – any other defines a special type of entity. Any type constitutes the form of some mode of concrescence.

An entity can be the unequivocal denotation of different demonstrative phrases. Something which can be pointed at. When you point at an entity, it is given in one mode of functioning as the operative form of another mode of

---

1. Conger and King (p. 37) both have 'affected' here, while Nelson (p. 23) and Jackson (p. 55) have 'effective'. The latter makes more sense, as Whitehead never speaks of eternal objects being 'affected' by anything.
2. Conger seems a bit confused here. Cf. Nelson: 'If every eternal entity is ineffective in B, B has an ineffective mentality; but if some are effective, then B has an effective mentality' (Nelson, p. 23).
3. The reference in Nelson's notes is to 'treatment of induction in *Science and the Modern World*' (Nelson, p. 24). He is probably referring to the discussion of induction in the chapter 'The century of genius', in which Whitehead criticises Francis Bacon, much as his friend Morris Cohen had done years earlier (see the 19 October lecture, note 5, p. 193).
4. This line appears in the upper-right corner of the page. It is unclear where it should be inserted.

functioning. My pointing ∧at house∧ is one functioning, then you see it, which is other mode. Identity is demonstrated independently of either mode of functioning.

Whenever in two occurrences of a demonstrative phrase there is ∨in any sense∨ diversity between "it" of one phrase and another phrase. Two are not demonstrating same entity. Every entity has possibility of being demonstrated in diverse ways.

~~Every "it" has the potentiality of (?)~~

This is the fundamental doctrine of pluralism. If can't really get same entity twice, knowledge collapses. No good having "very like" without identity.

|4| Two types ⟨of entities⟩:
1) Actual entities or actual occasions
2) Eternal objects

Actual entity is only ideally describable in terms of its particular relevance to each among all other entities, actual or non-actual and including itself. Can't describe actual entity without describing relation to every other entity. So description of actual entity can never be completed; every stage involves introduction of new types of relevance which are themselves entities. Cf. Bradley.

An eternal object is an entity which is only describable in terms of its general relevance to various species of other entities. An actual entity is particular in its relevance to other entity, whereas an eternal object is connective or general in its relevance to other entities.

Can't understand what I am without settling fact whether have or have not on a red coat. An eternal object is different from actual object – it is what characterizes actual entity – color, shape, how good I ∧am,∧ badness, anything that expresses what or how I am. It is not actual – turns up again as exactly same thing without any limitation of itself in any ∨⟨other?⟩∨ entities. Nothing for itself but a necessary element in description of what other things are in themselves. These non-actual things which you must bring in in order to describe.

|5| If you take redness, can't describe redness – can say all you can say, but without any relation to particular objects. Redness is what it is, quite irrelevant to how it is ingredient to what is going on here. Eternal object described in terms of its relational essence, type of way in which it can be related. Now all description is in terms of relationship and omits the final individual element in each entity. This formal element is unique individuality of that entity in its relevance to direct experience. It may be itself an act of direct experience. It may be an eternal object such as redness. ∨In describing redness∨ must leave out the redness of redness – you'll describe it merely in terms of possible relations. What is indescribable is individual essence of each entity.

Fundamental doctrine of solid universe. Each entity has a status in the universe which is describable in terms of other entities. Each entity is its individual self, and this is not describable. Each description presupposes demonstration of its various terms of description.[1] Thus description

---

1. Conger wrote this sentence twice, though the first time it lacks the word 'each'; we have deleted the duplicate sentence.

presupposes some demonstration in order to construct a machinery which leads to another demonstration. vYou haven't seen red – I say so and so's tie is red.v All the various terms <u>presuppose</u> other entities. That being presupposed constitutes a description of a particular relation which redness has to use.

Get immediate demonstration via a description which presupposes other immediate ~~description~~ ∧demonstrations.∧[1] When deal with concrete entity, you have always particularity. You can only describe a concrete entity by means of a reference to other concrete entities.

|6| Can describe general status of eternal object, and then if you want to demonstrate it, can only demonstrate it in terms of immediate relationship between you and some other concrete entity.

~~Creativity~~[2]

Thursday, 18 November 1926

Conger's notes

|1| ⟨There is⟩[3] an actual world which is a multiplicity of actual entities. An actual entity is to be looked on as an act of percipience, an ~~per~~ act of percipience of the universe. Therefore each actual entity is an act of percipience of[4] universe of actual entities, but each has own individual limited mode of the percipience, and if ask "what about these perceptions of other actual entities?",[5] can only describe it in terms of other entities which are not actual entities. The what, the form of perception of various other entities is supplied by and expressed by other entities not actual, which I call eternal objects. These are in a sense the specific character of specific perceptions.[6]

One entity as an object of perception for another. The what supplied by eternal object α. Perception by B of another entity X. Under limitation that X exemplifies α[7] for B. Not a string of perceptions, but one.

B is merely the coming together, concrescence of all actual entities. The percipience is the entity. X is demonstrated under guise of α.

---

1. Cf. Nelson: 'To have any knowledge we cannot get away from immediate demonstrations' (Nelson, p. 24).
2. Interestingly, Conger is not the only one who has a hanging 'creativity' right at the end of the lecture. King's notes end with '~~Creativity gen~~' (p. 39) and Jackson's with 'Creativity –' (p. 58). Whitehead apparently started to make some point about creativity and then ran out of time or thought better of it.
3. Supplied from Nelson (p. 24) and Burch (p. 11).
4. Jackson agrees with 'of' (p. 59), while Nelson has 'in' (p. 24).
5. Quotation marks and question mark supplied.
6. We have replaced Conger's drawing of the figure below with the one from Nelson (p. 25), who had a much cleaner rendering of it.
7. Conger actually has 'A' here, but it seems more likely that he intended 'α'. Note, however, that in the previous lecture (16 November 1926) he uses both A and α.

α-ness of X doesn't obscure the fact that X is actual entity for own sake objectified for B under guise of α. Otherwise solipsism.

Because objectification includes demonstration, you have B knowing itself as in a world.

Concrescence is a complex process. First pure percipience, then on top of that as datum and procedure, a self-percipience of B which is reflective percipience,[1] and that involves an origination of its own which can be called an imaginative origination. If I ⟨consciously?⟩ know X, a conceptual ingression of α, which is then the mental pole or side of B. When B is consciously perceiving X as illustrating α, is really the unification synthesis of conceptual ingression of α with pure perceptual ingression. That comparison either has yes form or no form – that again is a synthesis.

|2| In a way the ordinary correspondence theory of truth. In some way the conceptual function is analytic of the perceptual ingression. A new origination and a comparison.

If γ different from α, "no" form of comparison – pure imagination might have world merely patient of α. Might have been yes form, but is no form. When shift emphasis on patience of yes form, you have the imagination.

Then – always using word creativity – this is essentially an act of percipience which leads in to other acts. The activity of it leads to concrescence other than itself, and creativity is the most general conception of this activity. It is the form of the form. Every entity ∨non-∨actual (α) or actual (B) is only to be understood in connection with this creative action, dynamic view of the world. No dead entities. Must always ask how does any ∨actual∨ entity supply a character for creativity in a different way from which a non-actual entity supplies a character.

Every entity expresses some way in which activity of world is characterized or qualified. E.g. activity of α in objectifying X for B, or activity of X as being an element constitutive of B. Creativity is most general form which acquires its specific character in each individual instance of an actual entity. That's why it's so general that you can hardly call it an entity at all. Only reason is because it anyhow has certain general characteristics, qualifications, which can make into metaphysical principles. There are general principles – those principles may be looked on as general character of creativity. But creativity is never acting under general character – that only assigns creativity to a genus.

|3| Don't think of creativity as an entity. Creativity has general relation to whole creative process, and ⟨is⟩ itself an example of that process. Stoic doctrine of God. ~~Stoic~~ Lecky. God obeys laws he fixes.[2] [How would this square with the doctrine of types?][3]

---

1. Cf. Nelson: 'B is as a matter of fact a complex process: 1. There is pure percipience, and 2. (not temporally related) On top of this is a self-percipience of B' (Nelson, p. 25).
2. Lecky, *History of European Morals, Vol. I*, available at <https://archive.org/details/historyofeuropea00leck>. The first note on page 163 reads: 'Seneca maintains that the Divinity has determined all things by an inexorable law of destiny, which He has decreed, but which he Himself obeys'. Whitehead references the same quote in the first chapter of *Science and the Modern World*.
3. Brackets supplied. This sentence appears in the right margin with a box around it.

B by being an act of percipience has added a character to creativity which gives it *C*. Philosophy with pragmatic bias or rationalistic bias. Pragmatism interested in *B* as to how it passes on to *C*. But can't be quite pragmatic. [Stevenson – Inhabitants gained living by taking in each other's washing.]¹ Further question about *C*. What is interest of each actual entity for its own sake, for itself?²

Essence of actual entity is that it has individuality for own sake, expressed in character of creature by its reflective side, its analytic ᵛmentalᵛ pole. What is it for itself – squeezes all it can out of this. This side overemphasized by Descartes. ᵛOught to sayᵛ requires nothing but itself for its own self-satisfaction, but what it is in itself ⟨requires⟩³ the whole world. Its self-satisfaction is something which is individual, but never can get away from social character of world. Whatever is individual in *X* enters into *B* under some objectified form of relevance. So *B* in being something for itself also includes an objectified apprehension, percipience of *X*, *Y*, and *Z* as something for themselves. Essence of point of view of demonstration. It is not merely a ⟨bare?⟩ demonstration of an unknown being, something for itself, but very individuality of *X*, *Y*, and *Z* are objectified for *B*.

|4| Always a measure of percipience – foundation of question where when you ask where can get fullest type of individuality, not of individual entity, but one whose individuality embraces in most complete ~~way the~~ relevance the individual ~~self~~ character of its environment. So you get being yourself in most complete way comes from most complete embracing a ⟨sympathy?⟩ with environmental fact.

Essence of religion – not because it's right – can't be all right. All religions ~~gives~~ have one extraordinary value – they ~~ar~~ represent mentality of on whole the most developed types of mankind working at white heat of general insight. The emotional side on the whole detracts from the scientific accuracy of the phraseology – this is why religions are so hopelessly at variance – get very poor expression of very deep insight. Therefore viewed as systematic ∧complete∧ statement of metaphysics, don't get much help. But explain as much as you like, never explain away the deep insight which all the great religions give.

Must lose life in order to gain it – to be deepest instance of percipience you must have the deepest objectification of what *X*, *Y*, and *Z* are in themselves. *B* insofar as exclusive of ⟨sympathetic?⟩ apprehension of its environment has least actuality. ~~individ~~ Obvious that in order that such ⟨an?⟩ insight should give possibility of harmonious result, must be a certain harmony in *X*, *Y*, and *Z* so they shan't cut each other out. Harmony in environment necessary for depth

---

1. Brackets supplied. This sentence appears in the right margin with a box around it. It is unclear which 'Stevenson' is intended. The saying 'They eked out a precarious livelihood by taking in each other's washing' is of unclear provenance. It seems to have been a common saying in the UK in the 19th century: see O'Toole, 'They eked out a precarious livelihood'.
2. Cf. Jackson: 'Essential difference, pragmatist is simply interested in *B* as to how it passes on to *C*. Rationalist would |60| ask, "what about *C*?" *C* passing on to *D*, *D* to *E*, etc. – Rationalist considers *B* for what it is for its own sake' (Jackson, pp. 59–60).
3. Conger has 'acquires' but Nelson has 'requires', which seems more likely (Nelson, p. 25).

of actuality. Just as pragmatism emphasizes as to how passes, rationalism emphasizes what is that. |5| Can't be leading on to nothing.

First burst of pragmatism ∨tended to∨ forget that B is something for own sake. There is ⟨not⟩ creativity and its creatures, but ⟨rather⟩ creativity in its creatures.[1] Creativity endeavors to express pure activity, pure act; but no such thing as pure act, always specific act. Thus can only look on it as an entity by considering it in some specific form. So transitory universe is one ambiguous creature – always changing, yet one multiplicity in solidarity which is always different, as from the differing standpoints of the different creatures. There is a creature creating the universe. So this view of mutual relevance is the solidarity of the world in its process of attainment. What is immediate, now is in a sense an integration of the past. What X, Y, and Z are in themselves enter into what B is. B is an integration of the world out of which it comes. View of variation, relevance, intensity shows have enduring creature –[2]

B, B' B_{1000} ⟨It⟩ is really a succession, a historic route of actual entities, but of such a character that there is peculiar congruence of these successive entities. Relevance of B_{1000} to what ~~B1 B2 is in itself to~~ B is peculiarly intense[3] objectification. Integration of B_{1000} ∨out of past of B∨ is of peculiar ~~importance~~ intensity, but is the same in principle. My integration of ~~what~~ your past – same in principle as of me – but quantitative difference of intensity so great that amount practically to difference of kind. Basis ∨of∨ sympathetic relations of humans, but need this principle in order there shall be demonstration at all. Descartes' lump of wax. Only a barren X which we know by *inspectio*.

|6| Get idea of knowledge which doesn't penetrate, ~~etc. you~~ it isn't knowledge. There is a real knowledge, real percipience, but faint, fluctuating, vague. But real demonstration of what other elements in world are in themselves and for themselves comes out ~~of~~ in memory. My perception of sense data gives precision and definition of my vague perception fluctuating apart from perception. This entity has issued from past. I applied it in vague way – if have presentational immediacy of it that gives distinctness and definition of what would otherwise be too vague. Now something for own sake entering from past. Sense data has ⟨definite?⟩ spatial-temporal relations for me to rest of world. Definiteness of that lifts faintness of historic route into apprehension of it. Because there is a faint ∧not∧ distinct apprehension, the presentation picks it out.[4]

In metaphysics must remember can't have anything outside the universe conditioning ⟨?⟩ it.[5] Given this the universe is so and so. Whatever there is to say

---

1. To capture the intended meaning, the two bracketed words have been supplied. Cf. Jackson: 'Creativity in its creatures, not and its creatures' (Jackson, p. 60).
2. Nelson's notes add here: 'The past is alive in B' (Nelson, p. 25).
3. There is a duplication of the phrase 'peculiarly intense' here, which we have deleted.
4. Conger marks this sentence with a double vertical line in the left margin with the letters 'ID' below the line, but their meaning is unclear.
5. An orphaned quotation mark appears here, and it is not clear whether it is opening or closing.

about the universe is part of it and must be included in it. Everything has got to be an example of your metaphysical principles, including the metaphysical principles themselves. You are brought up against an ultimate irrationality. Can't give a reason beyond your entity. Finally can only arrive at something which is self-explanatory, hangs together, lays down laws which itself obeys. Anything else is merely shirking problem. Why concept of God has deserved bad reputation in metaphysics. Metaphysics starts with telling you what is true about actual entities – then gets into muddle and presupposes another actual entity beyond, makes exception of that entity which somehow decrees them.[1]

Saturday, 20 November 1926

Conger's notes

|1| Two hinges of whole point of view:
- Pluralistic – a multiplicity of actual entities.
- Solidarity of actual entities.
    - their monistic side

Actual entity = Cartesian notion of substance. Can't confine notion of entity to actual entity. Come across fundamental entities not actual – eternal objects ∧detachable∧. In asking about the what and the how the complex character of ~~eternal~~ actual entity – have to state in eternal objects.[2]

Eternal objects essentially _for_ actual entities. When ask about particular actual entity, you then arrive at the endeavor to pick a particular pattern of eternal objects. ~~This expresses how all actual object~~[3]

Infinite pattern of eternal objects never can be exhausted by finite description. Expressive of relationship of rest of actual world to one actual entity.

B – X: Can analyze out the contribution of X to particular impression – particular way in which solidarity of world is actualized in B.

---

1. Nelson (p. 25) and Jackson (p. 61) both have a reference at the end to R. B. Braithwaite's review of *Science and the Modern World* in the journal *Mind*. Braithwaite is quite critical. The review ends thusly: '*Science and the Modern World*, regarded as the exposition of a metaphysic, is a disappointment. I was the more disappointed in that I am a sincere admirer of Dr. Whitehead's philosophy of nature, and am convinced that the truth about the natural world lies somewhere along its lines. For the philosophy expounded in this book Dr. Whitehead gives hardly any reasons, nor for the connexion of his *Metaphysik* with his *Naturphilosophie*, so that the reader is continually asking plaintively "Why?" "Why?" "Why?". The "philosophy of organic mechanism" appears here as an intuition of Dr. Whitehead's, which may, of course, be as correct as is his reasoning about the Method of Extensive Abstraction. But the reasoning is lacking: we are given the answer to the sum, we want the working out. Will not Dr. Whitehead give us this in a still "more complete metaphysical study"?' (Braithwaite, 'Science and the Modern World').
2. Cf. Nelson: 'An actual entity is a complex and is analyzable and we come as a result of analysis to eternal objects (entities that are not spatial-temporal, and are detachable from particular actual entities). The what and the how of the actual entity must be stated in terms of eternal objects' (Nelson, p. 26).
3. Cf. Nelson: 'When you put your mind on a particular actual entity, and ask about it, you are then arriving at the endeavor to pick a particular pattern of eternal objects, and this pattern is expressive of the relation of the rest of the actual world to the one actual entity you are dealing with. The pattern expresses the form that the solidarity of the world takes in regard to the particular actual object (?)' (Nelson, p. 26).

Particular pattern of eternal object: $X\alpha$ is an element in $B\wedge?\wedge$. It's the objectification of the X (form of) B.[1]

Thus you get derivative entities expressive of how the eternal objects perform their functioning in being constitutive of solidarity of world.

$X\alpha$ is a fact for B. All ~~other~~ actual entities are fundamental because all other entities can be expressed as being for the sake of actual entities – as being in some way elements contributing to actual constitution of some one actual entity. Actual entities contribute to each other.

|2| Can start consideration by thinking of definite eternal object α – ∧red, happiness.∧ If entity can be considered in itself.

α as an entity essentially refers to the solidarity of the actual universe – not thinking necessarily of a particular actual entity, but of ⟨?⟩ world of actual entities as the field for the exemplification of α. As matter of fact any eternal object as being considered refers to the world under a certain uniform systematic aspect, the world as systemically capable of exemplifying α. May be particular circumstances in this or that actual entity so α is irrelevant, but world systematically capable of exemplifying α.

... Relational essences of various eternal objects. Insofar as B has in itself exemplifications $X\alpha$, $Y\langle\alpha?\rangle$[2] etc., the systematic character of world which is expressed for each expression $X\alpha^1$ etc., shows any other actual entity which has important relationships to B insofar as what B is in itself ⟨is?⟩ predominantly good by $X\alpha_1$. $Y\alpha_2$, must express in an important manner that systematic character of the world expressed by combination of α_1 α_2 etc.[2] That's why an entity B determines an environment of other actual entities whose important relationships to each other must in some important way express a certain definite character. Real basis which makes induction possible. Point not to make induction easy, but some glimmer of ⟨justification⟩. Indicates why there should be induction and why limited to environment. These environmental actual entities whose relationship to b ~~is~~ in important in objectification of B. ... √Importance of√ objectification in B in Y |3| arises because B is constituted by concrescence of objectifications. So Y must bear in itself a certain systematic character derived from α_1 α_2.

Exemplification of B in Z may be very faint, unimportant. In that case know very little. Unless get point of view that when you know the self-knowledge of B as to what it is in itself gives some induction information which characterizes a society of events, of actual entities environmental to B but can't give you much about all possible societies – gradually shades off as you get beyond the environment.[3]

---

1. Cf. Nelson: 'The objectification of X for B is "X exemplifies for B the complex eternal object "α"' (Nelson, p. 26).
2. Cf. Nelson: 'So far as B has a certain objectification the systematic character of the world which is exposed by its patience for a_1, a_2, etc., shows that any other actual entity that has a relation to B, must be such as to express in an important manner that systematic character of the world expressed by the combination of a_1, a_2, etc.' (Nelson, p. 26).
3. Conger marks this paragraph with a vertical line in the left margin with what appears to be the underlined letters 'ID' next to it.

On road to enable us to see how induction gives new information. Ought to be able to give some ground or else irrational. May glory in irrationality of it – Santayana's artistic spirit here triumphs over his metaphysical. Can get magnificent ⟨literary?⟩[1] contrast between *Scepticism and Animal Faith* that doesn't try to make rationality penetrate *Animal Faith*. Whitehead says first part of book magnificent, sceptical dialectic irrefutable on certain assumptions. Second part gets out aesthetic effect of contrast of animal faith with intelligence. Second part is a drama. *Animal Faith* comes in as Laertes and solves for Skeptic Hamlet.[2]

$X\alpha$ is a fact for B. I call an objectification a fact, but a fact always has the particularity of the actual entity for which it is or of the group of ~~group~~ actual entities.

Caesar crossing Rubicon is a fact for me – was not for Alexander the Great. ~~Have~~ Limited objectifications always have particularly – either particular actual entity or group of actual entities.

|4| Whitehead objects to great deal of philosophy.

Cambridge realists[3] – begin to talk and do not in their philosophical statements do not discriminate between actual entity or of ~~universe~~ eternal object or of objectification for actual entity. More than these three types, too. Don't discriminate what they are talking about, and get into false metaphysical principle where you shift your meaning. Logical truths are true for any ~~logical~~ entities.

Solidarity of universe comes out with respect to whatever sort of entity you deal. If start to think about B, comes out from particular way in which there is a concrescence of other actual entities in B via these objectifications. If start by thinking of eternal object α, solidarity of universe comes out in systematic character of universe in respect of which it is patient of α.

E.g. Grins ∨without∨ cats (Lewis Carroll).[4] Actual entity ∨(universe)∨[5] patient of being objectified as example of grinningness. Universe as capable of grinningness. You are never without a background.

Principle of Relativity. Has been trying to reverse ever since between metaphysics and mathematics.

II. Relatedness of nature[6]

Hume threw out, Kant, Hegel, Caird tried to put back. If once conceive fundamental fact as subject qualified by predicates, disjunction of

---

1. The abbreviation here and again several classes later (27 November) is 'lit', which could plausibly be expanded in other ways.
2. Laertes kills Hamlet at the end of Shakespeare's *Hamlet*.
3. See the discussion of Cambridge realists on 16 October 1926 (p. 187).
4. "'Well! I've often seen a cat without a grin,' thought Alice; "but a grin without a cat! It's the most curious thing I ever saw in all my life!'" Carroll, *Alice's Adventures in Wonderland*, p. 94, available at <https://archive.org/details/alicesadventur00carr>.
5. Parentheses supplied.
6. This is the title of the second chapter of Whitehead's *The Principle of Relativity*, available at <https://archive.org/details/theprincipleofre00whituoft>, which he originally delivered to the Royal Society of Edinburgh when it made him the first recipient of the James Scott Prize. The ensuing notes follow portions of the first five pages of this chapter closely enough that it seems safe to assume that Whitehead was reading bits of it aloud with breaks for commentary. **Bold** portions correspond directly

subjects is presupposition from which you start, and can only account for conjunctive relations by some sleight of hand. Whole idea of subject qualified by predicate is trap.[1]

Can discern in nature example[2] of uniformity. Fact is a relationship of factors. vFact belongs to universe.v Every factor of fact essentially refers to a vitsv relationships within fact. |5| Apart from this reference it is not itself. Every factor of fact has fact for its background, and first fact peculiar to itself.[3] ~~No~~ Idea of background.

Use term <u>awareness</u> – as consciousness of fact. *Principle of Relativity* doesn't make distinction between physical concrescence and conceptual analyses. **A converse mode of statement ⟨is that⟩ awareness is conscious fact as involving factors.** *B* is consciousness of solid universe as involving details.

Use term "cogitation" for consciousness of factors prescinded from their background of fact. Can't take away background, but can get to higher abstraction for which background has more tenuous ~~ind~~ uniformity.

Consciousness of individuality of factors – each factor itself and not another. Blue requires a ⟨certain?⟩ patience of universe for it. Now when you get blue, not merely patience of universe, but the particular blueness. Relational patience of the universe may be same for all colors – but now have blueness of blue – ~~it is~~. its individuality – Not red ~~but~~. Blueness of blue has a certain relational essence only expressible via blue – on higher stage of abstraction but keeping individuality. ~~Where~~ Consider a ~~more~~ still more abstract eternal object with same individual essence, but more abstract relational essence.

It is really product of mental activity, but ought to say demonstration ⟨greater/more⟩[4] than cogitation.

|6| Analytical mentality analyzing out more abstract eternal object. Might say abstraction consciousness of individuality of factors in which each factor is itself and not another. Many different factors like blue and red might impose or imply same patience of universe. **Essence of cogitation is consciousness of diversity.** vConcentrate onv blueness of blue – how blue is essentially different.

---

to passages in the text, with the rest likely added extemporaneously in class. (For more on bolding, see the Introduction, p. xxxvi.)

1. Assuming that Whitehead was indeed reading aloud here, we can say that Conger caught some phrases almost exactly, but summarises others. A comparison of this paragraph with the corresponding text in *The Principle of Relativity* may help to give the reader a better sense of how closely Conger was capturing Whitehead's words: 'It is hardly too much to say that the course of subsequent philosophy, including even Hume's own later writings and the British Empiricist School, but still more in the stream which descends through Kant, Hegel and Caird, has been an endeavor to restore some theory of relatedness to replace the one demolished by Hume's youthful skepticism. If you once conceive fundamental fact as a multiplicity of subjects qualified by predicates, you must fail to give a coherent account of experience. The disjunction of subjects is the presupposition from which you start, and you can only account for conjunctive relations by some fallacious sleight of hand, such as Leibniz's metaphor of his monads engaged in mirroring. The alternative philosophic position must commence with denouncing the whole idea of "subject qualified by predicate" as a trap set for philosophers by the syntax of language' (Whitehead, *The Principle of Relativity*, pp. 13–14).
2. In *Principle of Relativity*, it is a 'ground' of uniformity (p. 14).
3. '... and refers to fact in a way peculiar to itself' (Whitehead, *The Principle of Relativity*, p. 14).
4. Conger here and below uses the mathematical symbol >.

When go to high enough abstraction, the relational essence of the background is merely diversity. Most abstract eternal object has merely that relationship of diversity.

Cogitation presupposes awareness and limited by limitation of awareness, is refinement of awareness. Fact in its totality is not an entity for cogitation – has no individuality with its reference to anything other than itself. Might say totality ⟨greater/more⟩ than fact. but ∧to actuality best.∧[1] **Fact enters into consciousness not as sum of factors, but as concreteness of inexhaustible relatedness among inexhaustible relata.**

One fact among others = factor. Totality suggests definiteness. actuality But no one entity which is the actual universe. Any totality which you say is actual universe always implies an entity beyond itself. When admit it, get all sorts of detail practically all ∧wrong∧. Might give particular meaning from my point of view or yours.

|7| Inexhaustibleness.

Use limitation as most general description of finitude.

Bergson – canalisation. $B - X$: X not objectified for B simpliciter in B, but it's $X\alpha_1$ which is (?) which is in B. X as exemplified in α_1. **That a factor is a limitation of fact refers to whole universe as canalised into the system of relata to itself.**

α means whole universe capable of α. But no such thing as an entity apart from universe, ridiculous. Can't get rid of it – but reason why, always there is reason why it has dropped out of language. Language met bad for metaphysics. Metaphysics general. Language particular. Language essentially antimetaphysical. Reason why

Metaphysics can only be expressed in forms of expression grotesquely unsuited. If try to write metaphysics, realize how metaphorical language is.[2] In accepted metaphysics[3] You get used to the metaphors – e.g. substance. Standing under is to stand on the ground. Only try to put metaphysics freshly by employing new metaphors and try avoid old erroneous point of view.

|8| Get from *Principle of Relativity*:

Red refers to facts as canalised by other factors.

Three is aspect of fact to factors grouped in triplets.

An entity is an abstraction from concretion which in its fullest sense means totality.

Start with something violently silly and crude. Struggle back to commonplace, but purge it of subject-predicate fallacy. Deductive reasoning on account of (?) induction bares in it possibility of some little error, ∨at first no great good effect,∨ but by and by your erroneous conception important.

---

1. Cf. Whitehead, *The Principle of Relativity*, p. 15: 'I might have used the term "totality" instead of "fact"; but "fact" is shorter and gives rise to the convenient term "factor"'.
2. Cf. Nelson: 'Language wants to talk of things that are not always there, while that is just what metaphysics talks about. All language is metaphorical' (Nelson, p. 26).
3. It is unclear if this is part of the preceding sentence, the start of the next sentence, or an incomplete fragment on its own.

Harvard lectures, fall semester 1926

Tuesday, 23 November 1926
Conger's notes

|1| System of ideas with which we have been working define each other. You start with a series of statements and got meaning gradually sharpened. Two tendencies in philosophy, sometimes emphasize one, sometimes other. ⟨1.⟩ Have general descriptive system which gets before you vividly by literary presentation what you mean (but language inadequate). Likely to end in fluffy metaphysics. ⟨2.⟩ Other point of view ⟨to⟩ make everything sharp and distinct. Owing to inadequacy of language and properly delimited word from previous systems, can't get beyond inadequate kind of thought of your predecessors – little logical game over abstractions already made. Until metaphysics reduced to definiteness, has lost half its value. ~~Incr.~~ Definitely increases your confidence, be bolder reasoner, (not more timid).[1]

Idea of potentiality. May now try ⟨to⟩ pull together. Potentiality of a creature is the range of alternative characters of that creature which are compatible with the efficient causation whereby concrescence of that creature is derived from other creatures. Potentiality is definite with respect to genus ∧(sort of thing)∧,[2] and ambiguous with respect to specific mode. Potentiality can be limited – to be defined in reference to definite set of other creatures whose efficient causation has to be taken into account.

There is the unrealized potentiality in respect to these alternative characters, the creature realized one of them. How about the others? Instance ~~of~~ usually treated as unfortunate habit ⟨of⟩ insisting on mind outside universe. ~~Putting mind~~ We are thinking of inclusive mental-physical actual world.[3] One wants to see how ambiguity of antecedent potentialities can actually enter into creature; Potentiality is a genus – one specific mode is realized. The creature in itself ∨in its aesthetic integration in its own self satisfaction∨ not only realizes the mode which it is, but also realizes the genus of modes which it might be. I am realizing not merely colors, but the genus color, the ambiguity, my own patience of colorful experience, as well as actual physical color experience.

Realization – We are here on one of the prime functions of mentality – In the mentality of the occasion that the genus is realized. It's on the mental side where we can primarily discern the genus in being conscious, ~~of~~ ∨there is∨ physical realization of ∨specific∨ color – the mental realization of dark where might be light and vice-versa. Concrete actual fact cannot be torn away, for

---

1. Cf. Nelson: '2. Endeavor to make everything sharp and distinct. If this side is overemphasized, owing to the inadequacies of language, one will be bound down to the inadequate lines of thought of his predecessors. Hence, an overemphasis on this logical presentation will bind one down to the metaphysics of the past and will make metaphysics lose half its value. The value of logic is to make one a bolder reasoner' (Nelson, p. 27).
2. Parentheses supplied.
3. Cf. Jackson: '(obstacle of putting mind outside the universe – something we're thinking about – but world inclusive of mental and physical)' (Jackson, p. 62).

it would mean determination of the genus ∨primarily on mental side∨.¹ The mental side adds its tone to mental, and physical is different by reason of the mental. One has to talk as if oversharp cutting – but concrete occasion has a realization of the might-have-beens which are then realized as potentialities, though in some sense unrealized.²

|2| The unrealized potentiality is really part of the realized fact – only a different form. Thereby pledged to different ways of realization – whether realize it or not. If it's actual question, this is relevant or this is not – then whole idea of realization of potentialities falls to ground. Because can discern different stages of realization (pure physical, conceptual analysis, ∧etc.∧) which does not find self realized in physical datum. Actual occasion adds to itself layers of diverse modes of realization. What is unrealized in one mode is realized in potentiality in original mode and actually in the superimposed mode. The mental influences the physical so the physical is different.

Best analogy – field of force of a dynamo ∨(way it builds itself up)∨³ – generates itself. If go and disjoin body and mind as Descartes does, this falls to ground. If go and put mind in nature and don't have division of substances, then this point of view – no sheer blank matter of fact apart from potentiality.

19th century praiseworthy, to get mind into world.⁴ ⟨Blank⟩ of mind is part of physical fact. No real physical fact, mental fact – but mental-physical, but not really of inseparable poles.⁵

Notion of probability

Point of view of potentiality is necessary to give any meaning to obvious and immediate self criticism, which is essential in the realization of any actual entity.

So much of difficulty of philosophy comes from giving inadequate account of matter of fact, and having given this account, then wresting it all away by saying you don't quite mean it.

Notion of probability derived from potentiality. Character α is probability character of ⟨creature⟩ A having regard to creatures $x_1 x_2 \ldots x_n$ if $A\,\alpha$ is included in the potentiality which is relevant to⁶ ⟨....?⟩ creatures, to $x_1 x_2 x_3$. Estimation of degree of probability depends on degree of relevance of objectifications of creatures $x_1 x_2 \ldots x_n$, for ⟨?⟩ ⟨creature⟩ A. |3| This mode of thought gives some sense to notion of probability – though doesn't work out all the difficulties.

J. M. Keynes⁷ did formal logic. J. M. Keynes' theory is most clever. ⟨His⟩ *Treatise*

---

1. The proper placement of this interlineation is somewhat ambiguous. It could belong at the beginning of the next sentence, or earlier in the sentence in which we have placed it.
2. Conger marks the passage from 'Concrete actual fact' up to this point with a line and the letters 'ID' in the left margin.
3. Parentheses supplied.
4. Cf. Nelson: 'This point of view depends on the view that mind and body are not independent substances: it puts mind back into the world' (Nelson, p. 27).
5. Cf. Nelson: 'There is no mere physical or mere mental fact, but a physical-mental fact, of which either pole may be emphasized' (Nelson, p. 27).
6. Instead of 'relevant to', Nelson has 'derivate (?) from' (Nelson, p. 27).
7. John Maynard Keynes (1883–1946) was one of the most influential economists of the 20th century. The relationship between Whitehead and Keynes is an interesting one. Keynes submitted his *Treatise on Probability* as a dissertation for a fellowship at King's College, Cambridge, in 1908. It was reviewed by

on *Probability* just starts with statement that there is a notion of probability. If matter of fact world, what is, is. What isn't, isn't. Why should there be induction? If go into world of blank matter of fact, you are brought up to that. Keynes shows it isn't statistical probability.[1] Convinced Whitehead. Probability carries with it induction.

– Another idea which seems closely mixed with whole idea of potentiality – notion of <u>endurance</u>. Almost any philosophy (⟨e.g.⟩ Descartes') distinguishes between endurance and measured time. ⟨Descartes:⟩[2] Endurance an attribute or mode – practically only way ⟨anything⟩ can be real – Whitehead agrees there. Measured time is only our way of thinking of the universe. Doesn't elucidate the matter happily. Bergson – durée, definitely one fact, and measured time is taken in segments.[3]

Whitehead: Obviously something in that. Here is your definite act of being alive, perceptivity, yourself in specious present. People talk as though that act were an instantaneous act with no thickness to it, but can't be yourself without endurance, and some motion. Watch trolley car go round – A certain thickness of the trolley car as coming along. There is a definite endurance, tenth of a ⟨second⟩.[4] There's one fact of actuality for you, an epochal fact. As a real entity, it's one.

What is the endurance of it?

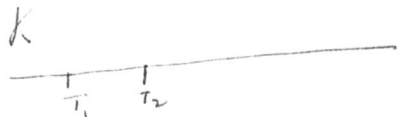

All say before one thing happened, something else must have happened. But before T_2, $T_{1\frac{1}{2}}$, $T_{1\frac{3}{4}}$. How do you get beyond T_1? What happens? What is your next phase? What do you pass on to? Vicious regression back to infinity with no beginning. Whitehead in *Science and the Modern World*: only old Zeno.

|4| Suppose say there is no thickness, it's all at an instant. Jamming together of spatialized entity gives dynamic suggestion. But before one point a preceding one must be done. Infinite number between any two. Same vicious regression.

Whitehead and W. E. Johnson. Whitehead's review was decidedly negative, while Johnson's was more positive. In the end, Keynes did not get the fellowship in 1908. After revising based on the comments of Whitehead, Bertrand Russell and Johnson, Keynes submitted the dissertation again in 1909. The reviews were much more positive, with Whitehead writing: 'The dissertation of this year appears to me to be a great improvement upon that of last year. This is probably due to three causes, (a) the dissertation has been improved in respect to the substantial ideas contained in it, (b) the mode of presentation of some of the ideas has been improved, (c) as the result of a second study of it after a year's interval, I have understood it much better' (Whitehead, 'The principles of probability'). This time, Keynes got his fellowship, but the dissertation was not published until 1921. In the preface, Keynes notes that he was much influenced by Johnson, G. E. Moore and Russell, but makes no mention of Whitehead.

1. Cf. Nelson: 'J. M. Keynes, in his *Treatise on Probability*, does not tell why there is a notion of probability, why there is such a notion in the world of matter of fact. In a world in which things are either true or false, why is there probability at all? Probability |28| is not a statistical problem' (Nelson, pp. 27–8).
2. Conger draws a line connecting 'Descartes' to the beginning of this sentence, making clear that this is supposed to be his theory.
3. Cf. Nelson: 'Another idea mixed with the idea of potentiality is <u>endurance</u>. In Descartes we find an explicit distinction between endurance and measured time. By endurance he means an attribute or mode: the only way to be real is to endure. Bergson too makes the distinction: ⟨durée⟩ is one fact, and measured time is another' (Nelson, p. 28).
4. Conger wrote '2nd' here, but Whitehead clearly intended 'second' as in a measure of time.

Suppose you say must drop idea of being a dense series, that points do come one after another. Point 1 is real ∧fact∧, point 2 is real ∧fact∧, but relation between them is left out of reality as a <u>superreal</u> fact and set of superreal facts.

Must always have an all-embracing totality when say all. You have an epochal occasion realized as a totality, but the endurance of it consists in the unrealized potentiality of subdivision. It might have been twenty epochal occasions, and it was one. That is the endurance – its complex character is such that its own unity is a definite mode which is being actualized and contains in itself the potentiality of the actual fact having been otherwise.

A further This is the basis of the extensive relation. Every epochal entity which is that actual entity contains within itself of a fraction, breaking up into many actual entities, only they are merely potentialities so far as certain formal relationships are concerned.[1] Also realizing in itself a genus, a possibility of alternatives – which would have allowed it to be many. Endurance is the potentiality of many in the actuality of one. Potentiality of many is an indeterminate many – Where idea of continuity comes in. |5| Basis of endurance. Of course that {?} character of having that sort of potentialities gets confused with various feelings and other characters.[2] Endurance is an instance of unrealized potentialities.

General Consideration of Time

Epoch = Specious present has in it a potential multiplicity. Whitehead wouldn't put past and future out of specious present, but see <u>supersession</u>.

Saturday, 27 November 1926

Conger's notes[3]

|1| Up to now has been abstract – doesn't hook in to concrete question of how philosophical questions arise. Take more general ∨popular∨ point of view and show bearing. This is the old and the new. Contrast between novelty of immediate present and settled facts of the past. How does one's philosophy arise from this sort of thing? Metaphysics has reference to everything – colors every thought. If youth would be quiet, preachers could forecast future. Both sides embody invoke religion – God adventure, ∧God prohibitions∧.

What is there in the nature of universe which causes this concept to arise? Start with most general. What mean by actual world – Our immediate complex activity of perceptive reflective experience – immediate tenth of second. One's self now. *Cogito ergo sum*. Can know nothing beyond the self revelation of this immediate fact, actual occasion. Final example of individual thing in actual world. Actual world a community of occasions. In ∨this∨ self-revelation an element of demonstration – the inclusion in our actual occasion of what other

---

1. Cf. Nelson: 'Every epochal entity contains within itself the potentiality of a breaking up into many entities' (Nelson, p. 28).
2. Nelson adds here: 'e.g., tedium' (Nelson, p. 28). Jackson's cited example is 'duty' (Jackson, p. 64).
3. Thursday, 25 November was Thanksgiving, hence there was no lecture.

actual occasions are from own point of view. Demonstration of other things as real in own right. Unless admit, solipsism. Demonstration = animal faith. No answer to Santayana's arguments that apart from it must relapse into skepticism. Animal faith implies irrationality of belief to which Whitehead doesn't assent. Descartes' Sixth Meditation, *Inspectio* for experience beyond selves.¹ If no demonstration, can't talk of ⟨the⟩ practical. ~~Then~~ Mere knowledge that these are youth and age etc. presupposes this demonstration. Each actual occasion includes demonstration of others. ~~Demonstration means~~ Passing from past through present into future means demonstration.

Santayana's *Scepticism and Animal Faith* ⟨has⟩ too much ⟨literary?⟩² contrast. High light on both skepticism and animal faith. Our minds include ideas which represent to us other actual occasions, but these ideas not mere adjustment of our mental state.

Must include direct intrusion of world beyond into your immediate occasion. Representative perception not an adequate account of demonstration. Essence of demonstration is inclusive of demonstrated occasion in constitution of demonstrating occasion. B is ⟨in some way⟩ an element in constitution of A. A ⟨as immediate occasion⟩ as constituted by the composition of its perceptions. Perception is not a mere adjective of the perceiver. Only way to escape is to be so voluminous that your readers are in such a muddle that your readers will accept anything.³ Whitehead construes good deal of philosophy this way.

|2| Every actual occasion must be in some way ⟨be⟩ an epitomé of the whole universe.

Apprehension. Reflective consciousness. Actual occasion is compound of prehension and apprehension. Inclusion of another occasion under limitation that some elements are very relevant, others practically irrelevant. Gradation of elements is objectification of occasion for perceiving occasion.

Qualities which occasions exemplify are detachable elements in experience – Elements which constitute identities in respect to which actual occasions are compble.⁴ They are the universals. Function of universals is to effect objectifications.⁵

Each occasion is just what it is by reason of way rest of world is epitomized for it.

Question: what universals will emerge in prominence in objectification of B ~~by~~ ⟨for⟩ A? Universals are relational between A and B. Choice depends partly on what B is in itself and ~~which~~ under which A enters into existence. Insofar as A's – allows internal spring of self-objectification.

---

1. Cf. Nelson: 'Whitehead prefers the notion of demonstration rather than "animal faith". Santayana implies something irrational. Descartes calls it "inspectio"' (Nelson, p. 28).
2. See note 1, p. 235.
3. Cf. Nelson: 'We must not explain perception as a mere adjective of the perceiver: if ⟨we do⟩ so, we cannot escape from radical skepticism' (Nelson, p. 28). Cf. King: 'This challenges the sensationalist, that what we have is the immediate sense data – merely the mind and its adjectival qualities' (King, p. 42).
4. The appropriate expansion of this abbreviation is not entirely clear.
5. Cf. Nelson: 'The function of universal (eternal entities) is to effect objectifications of actual occasions for one another' (Nelson, p. 28). Cf. King: 'An occasion is perceived as an awareness of qualities. Qualities exemplified by occasions are universals, which are to objectify the occasions to each other' (King, p. 42).

Also, the mental side of actual occasion may be negligible or dominant.[1]

pqr^2 v(universals)v[3] enter as forming character of conceptual function of A, whereby A is reflectively analyzing itself so as to secure partial consciousness of its perceptivity. Consciousness of prehension constitutes apprehension. This mental side vin turnv moulds physical side – thus physical and mental are intertwined. Both ~~matter~~ vphysicalv and mental has a measure of independence. ⟨?⟩

Independent origination of universals in perceptual functioning is imagination. In prehension the self-originating order of the physical universe.

|3| Can't treat imaginative order of mind and physical order of nature in isolation.

World evolves by reason of new characters which it gains from its own creatures. Each occasion can be treated pragmatically, but something must have the satisfaction vand dissatisfactionv of self-enjoyment. Otherwise no pragmatic standpoint. Each occasion unless were arbitrary, has to have its own self-satisfaction and dissatisfaction. World is bound in bonds of sympathy. Prehension, apprehension.[4] Individual self-enjoyment is most individual fact about individual actual entities.

Gradations in intensity are gradations in individual actuality. Trivial – occasion in empty space. Important – (consciousness?) in life of man. Conditions for depth of individual actuality are those of aesthetic intensity. Vividness – ~~relative importance in~~ arises from synthesis of generic identity and vvividv specific difference of detail (secret of art).[5] Color and sound do not yield vgoodv contrast.

(In objectification, if occasion A universals arise partly from other occasions, partly from physical and mental of A. A must constitute own vividness by meeting ⟨(?)⟩ universals by own contribution with effective contrast as above).[6] Contribution from past in generic, vividness in working out. Revolt of youth ought to preserve generic character of social organism.

Reversion in ⟨physics?⟩[7] – Vibration. Reversion assumes form of multitude of minor rhythms issuing in average stability. Sometimes reversion emerges as definite oscillatory changes. Double reversion doesn't restore original state.

|4| Codes can only be understood in light of this. Justification of code not in prescribed details. Utility of code depends on fact that vividness of details preserves certain generic identity through stages of social evolution.

---

1. Cf. Nelson: 'A molecule on its physical side is blind perceptivity. It also has a mental side; every actual occasion has' (Nelson, p. 28).
2. 'p.q.r.' also appears in King's notes, where they are said to be 'qualities'. It is unclear what is being referred to, though perhaps it is to terms in a diagram that no student copied down.
3. Parentheses supplied.
4. Cf. King: 'The world is bound by bonds of sympathy, partly analyzed in mental apprehensions' (King, p. 42). Jackson adds here: 'Self-enjoyment = bringing together diverse elements in one occasion' (Jackson, p. 65).
5. Parentheses added. The parenthetical comment appears in the left margin with an arrow pointing to this sentence.
6. Opening parenthesis supplied. Note that its proper placement is ambiguous.
7. The abbreviation here is 'phys', which usually means 'physical' but sometimes 'physics'.

Background favorable for contrast ⱽwhichⱽ provides real opportunity for self realization which epoch provides. Generic identity necessary for widespread social self-realization.

Rôle of imagination. Untamed almost always useless. Ignorant genius such a bore. No generic unity with thoughts of today. Great man at a tea party, but useless. Anything <u>may be</u>. Imagination with some immediate relevance is required.¹

Trained mind acquires generic habits, subject to those habits retains ~~altern~~ ⱽimaginativeⱽ freedom with respect to alternative details. Mind with generic habit needed. But must teach details. ∧If only details wooly minded.∧ How produce with generic habit by means of details and still keep it imaginative? Initiative – long ⟨word?⟩², but it has pep. Details tend to be destructive of originality.³

Difference in epochs depends on difference in education. Cf. Erasmus – magnificent teacher – Interested in classics – Elizabeth⟨an?⟩ ⟨?⟩ between magnificent teachers and pedantry. Pedantry creeps over classicism, but saved by science, then unpedantic. Some new ⟨?⟩ upsets pedantry.

In imaginative constructions, the genus itself undergoes slow variation. Slow secret change in scientific mentality.

The life of a man is a society of successive occasions closely bound by generic unity. Slow secular change. Quick imaginative construction of hypothetical species.

Thought and scientific activity are themselves elements in nature. A certain plasticity of environment to self-development of organism, but effect microscopic. Behind all our thought stands nature accepting or rejecting the creative activity of her children. Can't get any brilliance of imagination which somehow fails to conform. Some deep truth, conformity to general nature of things.⁴

Saturday, 4 December 1926

Conger's notes⁵

|1| Whitehead revolts from extreme claims of mathematical analysis. But this is a method which promotes meticulous analysis of ideas which hasn't been

---

1. Cf. Nelson: 'Untamed imagination is useless; it is great at a tea party, but useless in the evolution of civilized thought. Detached imagination never helps. To be valuable, imagination must have some immediate relevancy' (Nelson, p. 28).
2. The abbreviation here is 'wd', which for Conger usually means 'would'.
3. Cf. Nelson: 'We must teach details; if not, we will get a fuzzy minded individual; but details tend to be destructive of originality. So the problem is: How can we produce a generically trained mind by means of details. We must keep initiative and imagination' (Nelson, p. 28).
4. Cf. Jackson: '"Back of all this welter of imaginative activity stands nature herself" – accepting or rejecting by test of conformity to ultimate fact –' (Jackson, p. 66).
5. We have omitted the lectures of 30 November and 2 December since they were given by Charles Hartshorne rather than Whitehead. See the Introduction (pp. xlvi–xlvii).

adequately ⟨performed?⟩ in philosophy when philosophy starts from literary standpoint.

Time not one simple notion, but ∨those∨ extremely complex facts of universe are capable of analysis. If don't analyze, sometimes talk of one factor, sometimes of another.

Disservice of Hegel to make philosophers satisfied with contradictions. Thought higher region of thought, instead of which they were in a muddle. This has checked patient going back. (cf. <u>intuition</u>)[1]

Philosophy has to learn from science – No science sets out from complete set of relations taken as a whole. Looks on its presuppositions as incomplete speculative formulations to be always in state of flux, always made more precise. In philosophy, shouldn't read ⟨?⟩ man with dogmatic system. Bundle of notions ∨which would be∨ coherent, clear, distinct in perfect world. Question of combining – making more precise.[2]

- Distinction between actual occasion as itself enduring ∧("internal time")∧ and time as relation between actual occasions ∧("external time")∧.[3]
- Distinction between time and measured time
- Relation between time and space – mixed up in modern science –
- ⟨Distinction⟩[4] between time and novelty. 1234 – nothing very novel when ∧go from 4 to 5.∧
- Causal element in time – future issuing from past.
- Future somehow there, though doesn't seem to exist.[5]
- Time and Creativity.
- Time as Serial. Mixture of time and space ~~seems to~~ means seriality of time ~~dist~~ forgotten.
- Continuous nature of time

Paper?[6] ⟨?⟩

Same ideas now, but show how time comes in.[7]

I. Supersession

II. Prehension

---

1. Parentheses supplied. The parenthetical comment appears in the right margin next to this paragraph.
2. The bullets below are supplied. Nelson's notes render it as a numbered list (Nelson, p. 29).
3. Parentheses supplied.
4. Conger oddly has 'question' here, while Nelson has 'distinction' (Nelson, p. 29).
5. Nelson adds here: 'e.g., time tables (optimism in a sense)' (Nelson, p. 29). Whitehead is referring to something like 'time tables' for scheduled public transportation, such as trains.
6. This is a reference to Whitehead's paper 'Time', which he had read at the Sixth International Congress of Philosophy (13–17 September) about three months earlier, and was subsequently published in the *Proceedings of the Sixth International Congress of Philosophy*. It is clear that Whitehead was taking that paper as his starting point here; Conger's question mark is probably meant to convey that he was not sure how much of the following material was from that paper. In fact, very little of it is (the few lines which are clearly direct quotations have been **bolded**). Whitehead's lecture here might be considered an extended introduction to that paper; in subsequent lectures, he dives more deeply into the six individual sections.
7. Roman numerals have been supplied for the following six items. These match the six sections of Whitehead's 'Time' essay. Jackson's notes preface the list with 'Six separate ideas involved in time' (Jackson, p. 75).

III. Incompleteness
IV. Objective Immortality
V. Simultaneity
VI. Time as Epochal

If don't take time seriously,[1] look on universe as definite fact.[2] If look on universe as definite totality,[3] time falls out – Everything already there. Time an illusion which one part has of another. When get notion of something definite, "real fact" definite subject for experience – nothing to be got new. Time then an illusion. Get it when get subject-predicate point of view – ∨as soon as say∨ there is the definite actuality with its adjectives. |2| If really have a multitude of actual entities which form a completed class, then your class is completed; one or many, same result for time.[4]

If time be ~~not~~ ∨not∨ taken seriously, no actual ~~no~~ concrete entity can change – only be superseded. An actual entity doesn't change, it is superseded – if take Descartes' actual entity, change of adjective has inferior degree of actuality – change of form as inferior actuality playing on surface of substance.[5] But therefore if going to make ~~change in~~ world of change the actual fact – make that which changes not of superior but inferior reality.

What changes is universal, which finds itself embodied in succession of concrete facts. ∨In any one person∨, one universal formula has been exemplified in a certain society of actual entities which form a historic route which have peculiarly important relation to one another in that each one is derived from and integrates and epitomizes the "predeceased" route. The route of occasions is the final ⟨thing⟩[6] –

You are the multiplicity in which the antecedent route is of peculiar importance. Not in principle different from relation to others. Relevance ∧Intensity∧ much greater – bind yourself together as that whole. Your past is the past of rest of world – in enormously greater relevance.

Two types of unity ~~(?)~~ in each one – one formula which is exemplified in each of your occasions. For few minutes now to very large extent same formula. Back to your birth – ~~first~~ ∨same∨ formula is rather a thin abstract formula. Still something.

There is the change of formulae and the continuity of the route. If

But each point or route inherits from its immediate past. Formula as take small portions of route – there is gradual generic change in formula. |3| That

---

1. Both Nelson (p. 29) and Jackson (p. 76) reference Alexander here, whom Whitehead does in fact mention at the start of his paper on time. Cf. Nelson: 'Alexander implores philosophers to take time seriously'.
2. Cf. Jackson: 'Unless you ⟨take time seriously⟩, there is a complete, definite totality' (Jackson, p. 76).
3. The exact quote from Whitehead's paper is: 'No philosopher takes time seriously who *either* conceives of a complete totality of all existence, *or* conceives of a multiplicity of actual entities such that each of them is a complete fact, "requiring nothing but itself in order to exist, God only excepted"' (Whitehead, 'Time', p. 59). (For more on bolding, see the Introduction, p. xxxvi.)
4. Cf. Nelson: 'We won't be helped if we say that there is a multiplicity of entities that form a completed class' (Nelson, p. 29).
5. Cf. Nelson: 'If we take the idea of a final subject, of an independent substance that is the real entity, then the change of adjectives has an inferior degree of actuality' (Nelson, p. 30).
6. Supplied from Nelson (p. 30).

continuity of change, with a changing formula – but always a formula which will hold through any portion of ~~it~~ route. A formula finding itself in different occasions.

In what sense are you to describing the derivation of one entity from another? (Standard?)¹

Question of relevance. Why does point 2 ⟨spring?⟩ from ⟨point⟩ 1 more than from ⟨point⟩ 3? ⸲ ⸲ . .. (Formula is an ideal formula.)²

~~Wont get~~ Complete formula for one point is different from other, but will be a partial ⟨?⟩ formula for the 2. And that partial formula is very penetrating. Three minutes back will be more partial than one. (Sock)³

The intensity of transmission is one element. Unity of formula is other. Intensity of transmission ⟨?⟩ rises because there is a penetrating formula which is shared.⁴ Creativity dominated by united congruence of objectifications. Intensity of transmission and existence of formula practically same thing. Anything from a side route looked on as casual oddity – main ⟨trend?⟩.⁵

Transmission notion at basis of modern physics and science. More important than that of a subject enduring. Trying to avoid different and detached principles. Antecedent life of molecule is equally part of its past environment – here use endurance – but Whitehead says no – use transmission notion on route as well as on side lines.⁶

Actual entity just that at one point, not same ego extending over more. What does change is something more abstract than concrete entity. Formula is in different exemplifications from moment to moment. |4| Formula means same as pattern.

There is an endurance which has to be attributed to actual entity, but distinction of that and analogy of that to successive relations of historical route has to be brought out. Descartes failed to make sufficient analysis. Prefers Locke's phraseology to talk about time "perpetually perishing."

Supersession ought to be disengaged from creation in time – Supersession much more general. Much more idea of presupposition – ground v(datum)v and consequen⟨ts⟩,⁷ that by reason of one point ~~have~~ supersession. When by reason of one there is the other.

When A presupposes B – When to define B must define A, but in defining A are led to definition of B. Not necessarily pass from one to another in time. ~~but~~ Each requires the other. Can take A as datum and B as requiring A. Supersession

---

1. Parentheses supplied. The parenthetical material appears in the left margin.
2. Parentheses supplied. The parenthetical statement appears in the left margin.
3. Cf. Nelson: 'E.g., the sock that is darned and darned: is it still the same sock?' (Nelson, p. 29). 'Darning' is the process of repairing a hole in a sock using needle and thread.
4. Cf. Nelson: 'The intensity of the transmission arises because there is a penetrating formula that leads on' (Nelson, p. 30).
5. Cf. Nelson: 'The existence of a formula is nearly the same thing as the intensity of transmission. What comes from another route is an oddity: e.g., moving arms, temper' (Nelson, p. 30).
6. Conger marks this paragraph with a line in the right margin and writes 'Levels?'
7. Conger has 'consequence' here, but we think 'consequents' is more likely what Whitehead said. Nelson has 'ground and consequence' (p. 36), while Jackson has 'Ground and datums' (p. 77).

needn't go only one way. Can exhaust each as superseding the other. Idea of *A* involving *B*, *B* involving *A*.

When divest of idea of creative novelty, you can have many exemplifications of it. Physical and mental pole – internal supersession.

Entity is complex, one part is superseded by other – one part is ground for another part. One occasion ~~is~~, but internal supersession. Might say potential division into more than one entity. Potentiality of alternative subdivision instead of total unity.

|5| You must allow for superorganisms.[1] Each individual, each electron as organism – Body as whole.[2] Electron can't be adequately ⟨treated?⟩ except as element in body – body can't be adequately treated except as element comprising that electron.

Get mutual supersession. Each organism has occasions which are something for own sake, yet with peculiar intimacy they supersede each other. Not merely one mode of supersession, but an indefinite number of modes.

Most general idea of ground and consequent by which you get ~~most~~ organic relation of entities to each other in universe. Some more and some less-organized. Minor entity presupposing major, ∨major entity presupposing minor.∨

Must have some general idea or get into great difficulty in explaining any organic character of universe.

If don't analyze time, must ask which is first, body or mind. Can't get grip on mutual relation between one and other.

This diagram (......)[3] is idea of most strung out notion of supersession into future. Most obvious case.

|6|[4] <u>Individuality</u> – In a stone no epochal occasion adding anything to universe.

Space – Transmission in <u>general</u>.

Individuality apparently in intensity.

---

1. This appears to be the first time that Whitehead uses the term 'superorganism'. The likely source of the term for Whitehead is William Morton Wheeler, whom Whitehead met upon arriving at Harvard in 1924. For more on the relationship between Wheeler and Whitehead, as well as the term 'superorganism', see Sölch, 'Wheeler and Whitehead'.
2. Cf. Jackson: 'Electron and body (organism and super-organism – major and minor entities)' (Jackson, p. 77).
3. Parentheses supplied.
4. This page appears in the same folder as the first five pages, but it is not clear that it belongs here. There is enough space at the bottom of the fifth page to suggest that the lecture notes finish at the end of Conger's fifth page.

Tuesday, 7 December 1926

Conger's notes

|1| ⟨I.⟩ <u>Supersession</u>.[1]
Soon as you get hold of actual entity, lose it.[2] Cf. Pragmatism. All demonstration is an instance.[3]

(1) The demonstrating entity takes you on beyond yourself. In dealing with demonstrating entity, find self dealing with demonstrated entity.

(2) Body and mind. In completing actuality, get supersession of perception by conceptual analysis.[4]

(3) Extensive connection of entities – Extended physical universe – internal relationships of this room p̶v̶ demonstrate a space outside it. If know what room is in itself, there's a spatial relation outside it.

(4) Your bodily spatial relations demonstrate a world outside it. Extensive connections.[5] Spatial relationships of brain and retina demonstrate actual world outside – this is why we see things outside. Doesn't matter how g̶e̶t̶ ̶i̶n̶t̶o̶ light gets into eye. Light from mirror demonstrates space behind mirror.

(5) Creative passage into future.[6] Locke, perpetual perishing. If more general, try to get rid of time side. Correlative to passage beyond itself, there is passage within self which we call endurance, one part of itself conceived as potentiality, actual with a creative passage into another part of itself.[7] A difference there which stands out between actual thing as itself, an enduring entity, and temporally related to other enduring entities (perhaps levels in time).[8] Creative passage and endurance are obviously interconnected.

⟨II.⟩ <u>Prehension</u> (converse of supersession – how each entity is complex)[9]
Other side of same. Original entity as complex, and complexity arising from inclusion of other entities.[10] Same fact dealing with.

---

1. Nelson, King and Jackson all have a similar definition of 'supersession' here that Conger missed. Cf. King: 'Supersession is that character of an actual entity whereby it gives place to an entity other than itself' (King, p. 46). Whitehead is here clearly taking the basic structure of his 'Time' paper as the starting point for this lecture, beginning to discuss each of the six sections of that paper in their turn, though he covers only the first three in this lecture (Supersession, Prehension, and Incompleteness). This first part of the lecture on supersession does not follow his original paper closely at all, but rather seems mostly original to this lecture.
2. Cf. Jackson: '"you always find yourself somewhere else"' (Jackson, p. 79).
3. Cf. Nelson: 'All demonstration (pointing out) is an instance of supersession' (Nelson, p. 30).
4. Cf. Jackson: 'Body and mind within one actual entity you describe as purely perception vit isv supersession of conceptual functioning – a complex –' (Jackson, p. 79).
5. Conger draws a vertical line in the left margin next to these previous few sentences with the letters 'ID' next to it.
6. Cf. Nelson: 'Creative passage into the future – into something that was not and now is' (Nelson, p. 30).
7. Cf. Nelson: 'Correlative to the creative passage beyond itself is the passage within itself, endurance. These two views are muddled in Descartes. Endurance represents a potentiality of the complex actual entity' (Nelson, p. 30).
8. Parentheses supplied. The parenthetical text appears in the left margin.
9. Parentheses supplied. The parenthetical text appears in the left margin.
10. Cf. Jackson: 'Factor of prehension – your original entity as complex and inclusive of potentialities' (Jackson, p. 80). Nelson (p. 31) and King (p. 47) agree with Conger's 'inclusion of other *entities*' rather than 'potentialities'.

In analyzing one entity, find it includes other entities – if concentrate on an element in it, in considering one entity you're considering another. Original entity included or prehended in itself the demonstrated entity. Every entity is the unity of being actual impressed on a multiplicity of other entities. The one fact ⟨?⟩ which comes out of a multiplicity.

⟨Problem of⟩[1] solidarity of world and multiplicity of actual entities. Keep realistic – don't say it's mere appearance. Produce concepts which will enable us to avoid this difficulty. Difficulty and obscurity here.

Complexity of the universe enters into time. Naive view ⟨that⟩ time is to be considered as serial succession is not as obvious when consider how time emerges from complexity (though there are serial successions related to time).[2]

Philosopher ought to be shocked by scientist, not vice-versa. Only way to get ideas is to look at facts. Philosophy should be more imaginative than science. Philosophy should be more general than science. |2| If can get to genus concept of indefinite number of alternative species, philosophy ought to have most general notion of possibility. Philosophy ought not to be compilation of first chapters of various science – get general idea of which first chapters are various exemplifications.[3]

When try analyze an actual occasion as complex, it has many elements – fall into two classes – other actual occasions and universals[4] – ⟨?⟩

Eternal object the means by which an actual entity is a complex issue out of multiplicity of other actual entities. ⟨**Eternal objects are the**⟩ **media of actuality. They** ~~are~~ **constitute the forms or definite ways in which ∨unity and∨ organization of any one occasion *A* is achieved out of rest of world. That's why call world a system.** How do you get rest of world? – must express how other actual occasions enter this actual occasion as examples of eternal objects. Eternal objects make other actual occasions this and this and this.

Definite way in which any occasion includes others modes of prehension.[5] Physical world a system of organisms, arising out of concrescence of blind intuitions of other organisms. Includes eternal objects as defining elements as to how it's related to other organisms. But insofar as merely physical, doesn't include them conceptually.

Further element of value by holding apart the eternal objects and that which they exemplify bare that.[6] Other occasions are exemplifications of that.

---

1. Supplied from King (p. 47).
2. Parentheses supplied. The parenthetical phrase appears in the right margin.
3. Cf. King: 'Philosophy should aim at generalizations – at ∨some∨ new idea superseding "the first chapters of scientific text-books"' (King, p. 47).
4. **Bolded** portions correspond directly to quotations/paraphrases from Whitehead's 'Time' paper. In these instances he was clearly repeating the paper verbatim.
5. Cf. Jackson: 'The definite way in which *A* includes other actual entities is blind physical perceptivity (prehension)' (Jackson, p. 82). Cf. King: 'Mode of prehension ∨(?)∨ – the way one includes another. This is the blind (Kantian) physical perceptivity' (King, p. 47). The original passage from Whitehead's paper is: 'The definite way in which A includes other occasions in its concretion is here called "Prehension." By this term, blind physical perceptivity is meant. We recall Kant's doctrine that "Intuitions without concepts are blind"' (Whitehead, 'Time', p. 60).
6. This word and the same word at the end of the following sentence may be 'thot' for 'thought.'

Thought holds apart bare entity from what it exemplifies – *Concept of Nature*, ⟨chapter⟩ I. **Mentality is analytic, but it does exhibit an originality.**[1] Two foci of original creation in the one actual entity: ⟨1.⟩ Physical perceptive origination, ⟨2.⟩ Mental conceptive origination. Though the two are born(e) apart,[2] nourish each other. Concept doesn't always find its part in the percept. Yes and No Forms.[3] Concept synthesizing itself and analyzing percept. Imagination sometimes suggests what isn't to be found. Ingression of eternal objects, prehension of other actual occasions into given occasion.[4]

⟨III.⟩ **Time requires incompleteness**. vCf. William James.v Physical universe with time is not a pure spatial universe as might be implied up to now – not a whole of many entity of which each entity interpenetrates the others. If run subject-predicate point of view too hard, are bound to get on to view that actual world is complete.

In mathematics may make mistake of thinking of everything ⟨as⟩ given. Mistake entered from very beginning.

When Hegelians find tendency to make mistake, call it deep seated tendency of universe. Older rationalism spatialized.[5]

|3| If treat not time series, but timeful world series – nothing more real than actual timeful world – incompleteness enters very nature of actual entity. Enter into nature of God, too.

In any actual entity something which in a sense is and is not – essence of incompleteness. Broad, with great logical thoroughness – future is without qualification nothing, non-entity – awkward because can't poke about in it.[6] If pure nothing, can't talk of it in any sense whatever. Fact that we do speak of future.[7]

vGreek view.v Think of process of becoming as in some sense a union of being and not being.[8] Here must have potentiality as an actual element,

---

1. Cf. Nelson: 'Pure perception has been wrongly assigned to mentality' (Nelson, p. 31). Cf. Whitehead's paper: 'But pure perception is the fundamental relationship of physical occasions in the physical world. It has wrongly been assigned to mentality, which is merely analytic; though this analysis, being partial and also having regard to the exclusions as well as the inclusions, can exhibit a contingent originality, in the forms "attention" and "imagination"' (Whitehead, 'Time', p. 60).
2. King (p. 48) and Jackson (p. 82) both have 'born separately'.
3. Cf. King: 'The concept doesn't always find its mark in the percept. An originative searching of the world by concepts is possible (Whitehead can think of us as dressed in red coats.) (The no-form of comparison is imagination.)' (King, p. 48).
4. Cf. Nelson: 'Ingression = how an eternal object enters into an actual occasion. Prehension = how one actual entity enters into another' (Nelson, p. 31). Cf. King: 'Prehension is practically perceptivity' (King, p. 48).
5. Cf. Nelson: 'James insisted that the older rationalism spatializes, and believes that it finds everything finished up somewhere or other' (Nelson, p. 31). Jackson's notes (p. 83) additionally reference Bergson here.
6. Conger draws a vertical line in the left margin next to these previous two sentences with the letters 'ID' next to it.
7. Cf. Nelson: 'Railway companies issues quite a large literature about the future. Is it talking about nothing?' (Nelson, p. 31). Cf. Whitehead's paper: 'A calendar of next year, and a railway time-table, render this truth about our physical occasions intellectually explicit in our mental occasions.' Whitehead, 'Time', p. 61.
8. Nelson (p. 31) identifies this as Whitehead's view, rather than the Greek view.

something which is <u>actually realized in actual element</u> (possibility).¹ Refer to endurance. Future has its potentiality already objectified in present. Future as in free actual present is incomplete – not the actual element. Highly incomplete. Potentialities partially determinate. Incompleteness of ~~present~~ future makes present also incomplete. Future ~~is~~ already has its partial determination in present. Can't finish it out adequately.² Not yet and yet something.

Attempt to express all our knowledge in terms of spatialized portion ~~yet~~ we know of a defense in which future – then try to express it in terms of something already there – words or spatial images already there with immediate presentational value ∨in∨ which ~~is~~ everything is clear and distinct.³ Sometimes these elements express others badly. Tend to distort our thought.

⟨?⟩ (thinking) a beastly habit. **Everything incomplete because holds in itself own future. Anticipation is blind physical fact – only mental by means of ⟨the partial⟩ analysis characteristic of** ~~sp perceptual~~ ∨**conceptual**∨ **mentality.**

Kant has to bring in time as form of perception with no reason.⁴ Form of perception is what perception is. **Physical anticipation – Character of creature found in analysis of creativity and vice-versa.**⁵

To be not yet actual is to be something. The not yet actual is included in the actual. Hegel's point – you must get on.

Thursday, 9 December 1926

Conger's notes

|1|⁶ Sheldon:⁷ why take time seriously? Can take any order you wish – No definite order. Whitehead: paradox, but untrue. Sheldon rigorously brought out consequences. Whitehead thought his statements therefore inadequate.

---

1. Parentheses supplied. The word appears in the left margin.
2. Cf. Nelson: 'Time as merely a serial fact is an incomplete way of looking at time. The future is not a non-entity. As an actual fact, it is presupposed, though incomplete' (Nelson, p. 31).
3. Cf. King: 'Endeavor to express all our knowledge in terms of its spatialized portions is the essence of expression. The spatialization has an immediate value of presentation' (King, p. 49).
4. Cf. Nelson: 'Kant says the datum is the immediately complete fact' (Nelson, p. 31).
5. Cf. Whitehead's paper: 'Physical anticipation illustrates the truth that the creativity, whereby there is supersession, cannot be disjoined from the creature which is superseded. The character of the creativity is found in the analysis of the creature. The creativity *for* the creature has become the creativity *with* the creature; and the creature is thereby superseded' (Whitehead, 'Time', p. 61).
6. At the start of the lecture, King records what is apparently Whitehead giving an assignment to write a paper. Neither Conger nor Nelson records this assignment. Cf. King: '<u>Paper</u>. January 11. Getting hold of point of view. "Influence of Subject-Predicate Analysis of Propositions." Influence on Scientific concepts of Natural Science. Philosophy, Attempt to Define the notion of an Actual Entity. (Notion of Absolute; Bodies-Minds; Atoms; Flux). How an actual entity is influenced by subject-predicate analysis. Illustrate from our reading, the problem of Ontology' (King, p. 49).
7. Whitehead seems here to be referring to Wilmon Henry Sheldon (1875–1980), whom he had earlier referenced in the Radcliffe lecture of 5 January (p. 44). The 1 October seminary notes of Sinclair Kerby-Miller make clear that Whitehead is here thinking of the Sheldon's 1926 article 'The spirituality of time'. See p. 345.

Whitehead's only answer to Sheldon is some sort of theory of objective immortality.[1]

⟨IV.⟩ **Objective immortality**[2]
Physical memory is example of incompleteness and prehension together. Occasion $A \rightarrow B$

In occasion B, there is a physical memory of each antecedent occasion. B prehends A into itself as contributing a measure of determinate ⟨completion⟩.[3] Prehension adds to determination. **This prehension is a relational functioning with own individual character. Expressible in terms of eternal objects and individuals which A gives to B.**

Eternal objects determine objectification of A whereby it becomes a constitutive element in the occasion of B. Past incident – bundle of universals. Universals as exemplifying those particular incidents in my life.

My past life limited by those universals as constitutive element in what I am now.[4] ***A* is relatively determinate v in the objectification**,[5] the universals v ~~compared to~~ finish it up and give it relatively determinate character. But I now have the indetermination of my hurrying on to the future. Except there is still the determination. There is the anticipatory objectification of *B* in *A* reflected back into *B* as incompleteness of *A* by reason of fact that *B* is not yet there.

Have two poles in a linkage – that is the full transaction between *A* and *B*. |2| ***A* in that linkage is more complete than in A abstraction from that linkage.** It is in *A* with anticipatory objectification of *B*. But take *A* by itself, it is *A* with the incompleteness of a future which ~~is mere in~~ has not yet been determined.[6]

~~Determination of B in A~~.

In community of *A* and *B*, incompleteness of *A* by *B* is rectified by completion of *B*, and *A* has thereby an added meaning.[7] Crossing Rubicon when crossed; but now has added significance of completed series of events. As a matter of fact the only thing which changes in a way is the past. But "changing" used so loosely that it's difficult to get clear. **Each occasion A is immortal throughout its future** – future can never get rid of fact that Caesar crossed Rubicon or that we are here. Sometimes fact is minor, but there it *is*.

---

1. Neither Nelson nor King has anything about Sheldon. In Conger's notes, this paragraph appears on the right-hand side of the page, while the rest of his notes for this page occupy the left half. Placement is thus somewhat ambiguous; we have placed it here since it seems to lead in to the discussion of objective immortality.
2. Whitehead is once again reading portions of his paper 'Time', with breaks for commentary. We have **bolded** the portions where he is clearly reading directly from the paper.
3. Conger has '(prehension?)' here, while Nelson (p. 32) has 'completeness'. We have supplied 'completion' from Whitehead's original 'Time' paper (p. 61).
4. Cf. King: 'But there is an element of demonstration, which is the particular actual entity' (King, p. 49).
5. Cf. Whitehead's paper: 'This transaction exhibits *A* as relatively determinate, except for its indetermination arising from the indetermination of *B* in the converse anticipatory objectification of *B* in *A*' (Whitehead, 'Time', pp. 61–2).
6. Conger draws a vertical line in the left margin next to this paragraph with the letters 'ID' next to it.
7. Conger draws a box in the right margin near this sentence and has in it: 'Could use all this with subject-predicate!'

Any later event *B* enshrines memory of *A* in its own concretion, and this has to conform to its memories. When I start a sentence, the latter half has to conform to the earlier part. In case of memory of your past you have a conscious knowledge of how what you are now is conforming to your past. **Thus physical memory is causation, and causation is objective immortality** – No distinction. Trying to get general ideas. Not have all special ideas.

|3| **Also conscious memory is that partial analysis of causation which is affected by the associate mental occasion.**[1] **Hume, when asks for direct consciousness of causation, should be directed to memory.** Consciousness is always incomplete. Where you have memory, these have direct consciousness of causation. Why remember beginning of lecture? Because it happened in the past. When you remember, you have knowledge of how past is now affecting your present. What you have knowledge of is present ~~past~~. You haven't a queer little thing called mind which remembers back, inspects past, and comes and tells you.

In physiology certain accounts of memory can't be right. Memory – Previous history of brain gets your brain in particular state so it's likely to repeat itself. Then you have images and experiences of past. Much exact physiology very little relevance. Molecules of brain are waggling somehow. But waggling is fact in present. Insofar as has a mental accpt[2] (is used in mental achievement, namely that you have definite images) those images are images now. You say, yes, but they're copies – but that isn't an account of how you know they're copies; that's an account of ~~how~~ ∨why∨ they should be like the past, and you bring in your memory to give ∧account of why∧ they should be like the past. (Your ordinary account of ~~your knowledge~~ minds waggling.)[3] Leaves out entirely the throw back – that knowledge that it's a memory.

Thinks when you have true memory, have faint image conjoined with it.[4] Memory gets vivid when the image meets the memory. Can get images of all sorts which aren't memory and which have little to do with what is going on outside. Pink rats.

Physiology simply tells you what's happening now – Can't be any physiological account of memory.

Irreversibility of time follows from doctrine of objective immortality.

|4| Never can repeat an earlier event without the objectification of the early event. If Declaration of Independence signed again, it would be a second instance.

---

1. Cf. King: 'Conscious memory is when mental occasion seizes the event and holds it up to the high light of ⟨?⟩ conceptual analysis' (King, p. 50).
2. The proper expansion of 'accpt' is unclear. Below he uses 'acct', which is properly expanded as 'account'. It is possible that is intended here, but it is not possible to be sure.
3. Parentheses supplied. The parenthetical phrase appears in the left margin. Its placement is somewhat ambiguous.
4. Whitehead's 'Time' paper (p. 62) reads: 'According to the doctrine which is now being developed, the image in the present is the outcome of the gathering up of the true memory into the creativity of the present. Hume's "faint copy" is the image in the present, but its equally present character of being a copy arises from its comparison with the objectification of the past which is the true memory.'

ᵛA sense in whichᵛ an actual entity has no history – Its objectification has a history, the history of its objective immortality. No history of Caesar crossing Rubicon – it's an event in history; there is the history in which Caesar crossing Rubicon is an element. If actual event could occur second time, would have history of its occurrences. History of its influence, its objective immortality is really the history of other events – how they were influenced by their conformation to event in question.[1]

Time depends on Causation – Causation on Time. Both abstractions of same event as how one entity is in the other. Time can't be disjoined from notion of causation and notion of incompleteness. If think of time as ordinal series, all that is lost. But not all of time. Whole notion of simultaneity and present comes in.

⟨**V. Simultaneity**⟩ **Can explain past and future as referring to causal relationships. There are occasions not prehended in *A* in any causal sense, except as conforming to general systematic character of universe.**

You depend now on what I have been a few moments ago – but not on what I am now. Simultaneous events happen in what call causal independence of one another.

Special characters are independent of each other. At this definite moment you are independent of what I say because sound takes time. Sound and sight of me comes from my past. My immediate present takes time to get over to you anyhow on its physical side.

Time is really primarily concerned with physical relationships. Penetration of mental side not properly to be conceived in time – really comes from physical side.

Saturday, 11 December 1926

Conger's notes

|1| Time as[2] depends on <u>relative</u> completeness of entities with respect to each other. If from standpoint of *A*, a direct incompleteness of *B*. Objectification of *B* for *A* leads to incompleteness of *B*.[3] *B* has no individual independence from *A*, but is object found for *A* on its confessedly incomplete side. *A* is not the end of the story – there is a passage in it.

B has to conform to what *A* is in itself. What *A* is in itself as thus objectified is an element in objectification of *B*. ᵛHere is causal relation.ᵛ So *A* is causal element partially determining *B*. Essential character of antecedent and succession which you have in time arises from that. *B* is determined as a form of entity-not-yet. Formal systematic relationship of *B* to *A* is determinate,

---

1. Conger draws a vertical line in the left margin next to this paragraph with the letters 'ID' next to it.
2. The letters 'as' are clear, but the sentence seems to be a fragment. It is possible that a word between 'as' and 'depends' was unintentionally omitted by Conger.
3. Cf. Nelson: 'If *B* is not yet an actual entity, its objectification for *A* leaves an incompleteness in *A*' (Nelson, p. 32). King's notes (p. 51) also record that the incompleteness is in *A*, not *B*.

but not B in itself. Essential character of incompleteness is antecedents and consequents.[1] Nor can you, if you take this account of causation, can you first look on A as given fact, and secondly look on B in isolation, know all about B, and then say, by the bye there is an additional queer fact that A has a causal relation to B. Causal relation of A to B is part of makeup of B. No causal relation between A and B in addition to what A is and B is. Causal relation therefore is essentially internal relationship. ~~Always~~ Think of it as internal – anything is what it is by reason of the cause. Difficulty by forgetting that cause enters what a thing is. External point of view has arisen from idea of substance as something complete in itself.

Only putting into words what is commonplace of science.

Electron has oval shape by reason of field of force which is inherited from pos(ition?).[2] Don't consider electrons by selves, know all about them, then put them into each other's fields of force. Can answer question what is an electron only by way it enters into other electrons.

|2| Science drops notion to large extent as to what things are in themselves, and largely considers them as how they affect space and motion of other things.

Science (?) ~~You~~ doesn't consider creature in itself, but creature as ∨a∨ character of creativity.

Whitehead – Whatever anything is in itself turns up by determining its creative character. Only reason why look on at ellipsoid is because its creative character is explicable as being an ellipsoid.

Character of field beyond ∨electron∨ can be expressed as character of definite creature. Cf. ontological argument of existence of supreme non-temporal creature is paralleled in every work of physics which exists. Presuppose character of field of force is to be found in the character of creature. This is the meaning of explanation. If simply stating the sequence of things, why feel that you have explained? Orbit of Saturn. No difficulty in stating sequence of phenomena. If merely take description point of view, wouldn't know anything about it. Everyone said this is unsatisfactory. ~~Thereby a~~ Thereby a description of field of force affecting orbit of Saturn. Must be a creature to which this creative character can be assigned. Looked for it. Then they calculated.[3]

Creature not exhausted even by universals, certainly not by orbits of Saturn. Can deduce lots of other consequences. Enormous importance of going from creature to all its creative objectifications. Creature is ∨a∨ much more general character of the creativity. To be a creature is to be a concrescence of the objectifications of other creatures. To be a creature is to be objectified – What

---

1. Cf. Nelson: 'We cannot tear the relation of antecedent-consequence apart from cause-effect' (Nelson, p. 32).
2. Given its position, this sentence is intended to reference the diagram on its left. Cf. Nelson: '. . . inherited from others' (Nelson, p. 33).
3. Cf. Nelson: 'Explanation: usually we say science gives the sequence of things. Take the case of the discovery of Neptune through observation of the orbit of Saturn. Description alone was not satisfactory. It was concluded that there must be a creature to which this creative character could be assigned. If science were merely descriptive, scientists would have been satisfied with reporting the changes in the orbit of Saturn without explaining what causes the changes' (Nelson, p. 33).

Harvard lectures, fall semester 1926

it is in itself is thereby a character of the future beyond itself. If you know about creative character of creature, may be able to solve *A*.

|3| Simultaneity. Here there is a relationship of entities to each other. Objectification of entities for each other which does not conform to notion of more complete and less complete. Conformation of simultaneous events is different. *A* ⟨?⟩ certain of its personal peculiarities ᴠas an elementᴠ superadded to ᴠsomeᴠ systematic character of universe as whole.

(Gestalt psychology)[1] *A* for *B* is a figure with the universe as background.

(Figure and Background)[2] *A* has systematic character which it shares with rest of universe, and expresses its solidarity with universe. At same time has individual character to which under some limitation (objectification) *B* must conform.

Simultaneity

• ↔ • Antecedent and consequence has gone. Relationship of relative incompleteness has gone. That side has gone.

Objectification of *B* for *A* still makes *B* a sharing in the systematic background.... But the universals which complete the demonstration of *B* for *A*, which give the particular character of how *B* is for *A*, now depend not on *B*, but on *A*. *A* out of its own originality supplies the physical bond. ᴠᴠizᴠ content of physical bond by which *B* enters into *A*. But *B* is demonstrated as complete – not incomplete. No incompleteness in *B* except as to future. *B* and *A* are on same level of completeness, but *B* is demonstrated to *A* according to an originality which depends on *A*. This is the plain fact of sense perception – reason why whole tale about secondary qualities arose.

|4| Cf. seeing double, mirror. Whole point is the presentational immediacy of space over there depends on state of my body here – normal or abnormal. 17th century – because what we see is a mental addition. But ᴠasᴠ matter of fact, body is in a certain state of excitement. Red coats outside nature – Bond between us is a physical bond as much as anything is – a function of the universe which is always to be construed as relational. But a physical fact. Analysis of nature is partial.

Simultaneous events happen independently, so far anyhow as physical causation is concerned. Simply doctrine of physics – ~~look up~~ e.g. when look at stars. Cf. star may be blown to pieces. What is going on ~~now~~ ᴠat this instantᴠ is quite independent of me and I of it.

~~If make general principle of~~

Personal peculiarities are independent of

---

1. Parentheses supplied. The parenthetical text appears in the left margin with vertical lines on either side of it. Neither Nelson nor King records anything about Gestalt psychology, hence it is not entirely clear whether it was Whitehead himself or Conger who makes this reference. However, Whitehead seems the more likely choice, given that Wolfgang Köhler (1887–1967) visited Harvard in early May 1925, with Whitehead referencing him in his 7 May lecture that year for Philosophy 3b. See HL1, pp. 365, 368, 368 n.1, 370 n.2.
2. Parentheses supplied. The parenthetical material appears in the left margin.

each other. My present no consequence to you, but my immediate past has consequence for you. A historic route with unity of pattern. Each point in my past comes in and tells practically same story. Unification of objectification. That is why ~~I am~~ ∨you are∨ so insistent that there is something there to which you must conform. Thus what might be vague background becomes an individuality.

And you act[1] as though that story were going to be prolonged.[2] ~~My~~ ∨Result, under normal circumstances A's∨ objectification which arises from what ~~I am~~ ∨A is∨ via universals which A ~~(have)~~ ∨has∨ supplied will have a <u>relevance</u> to what B is in itself. Objectification of B for A not derived from what B is in itself, but from antecedent.

|5| Result, anything which gives abnormality which masks relationship to B's past transmitted by minor routes of creative transmission. Will get objectification which is irrelevant to B, or may have something odd at prolongation of B, some new sudden influence coming in.[3] Result is we use the objectification drawn from our own nature as giving us intelligence ⟨of?⟩ what [B] is – it may or may not be right. How we do see that element demonstrated is how we do. Might by looking into a mirror see ⟨your?⟩ ∧⟨spt?⟩[4]∧ objectified as radiator, and may make wrong est⟨imation?⟩ that there is a radiator there.

All our judgements depend on assumptions of normalities. If normalities disturbed, judgements will be wrong. Real independence of simultaneous entities.

Thursday, 16 December 1926

Conger's notes[5]

|1| Organic realism. Real world a multiplicity of actual entities. Actual entities all involve each other – so solidarity. Each entity <u>an organism</u>. Organisms can be analyzed as complexes of many elements, some entities <u>actual</u>, others not actual, but involved in actual entities.[6]

What becomes? Must be an actual entity. Therefore you are at once brought up against Zeno's argument.[7]

---

1. There is a line drawn from here with an arrow pointing to the dots in the lower-right portion of the above diagram.
2. There is a line drawn from here with an arrow pointing to the 'B' in the above diagram, with the words 'B, e.g.' next to it.
3. Cf. Nelson: 'Anything that disturbs the transmission will give an object that is irrelevant' (Nelson, p. 33).
4. It is possible that this is 'sp t', which could be expanded as 'space and time', but it is not possible to be sure.
5. We have omitted the lecture of 14 December, since it was given by Raphael Demos rather than Whitehead. See the Introduction (pp. xlvi–xlvii).
6. Cf. Nelson: 'Pluralistic system. The involution of one entity by another is the organic side' (Nelson, p. 33).
7. Cf. Nelson: 'Time becomes an actual entity if we look on it as a becoming. Thus, we are brought up against Zeno's argument. We view time as a continuous flow' (Nelson, p. 33).

Harvard lectures, fall semester 1926

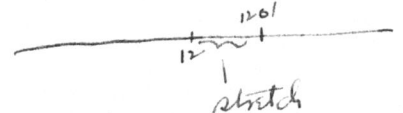

What happens to get beyond 12 ⟨o'clock⟩? Not so in the arrow moving as the universe getting on. Idea of time leads you into a difficulty of supposing something happening in time.¹ Until here you are at 12 wanting something to happen. The very definition of a vicious regress.² Might say happening is an adjective which differentiates the character of the real. Then find your actual entity lies below time, the subject of time. Time not the becoming of the actual, but what the actual finds itself to be enjoying. Time is an adjective expressing what is the timeless enjoyment of the actual entity.

⟨Come?⟩ at once to world as phenomenon of appearance which is the outcome of the nature of actual entity. Not the becoming of actual entity, but it is what constitutes the life, being of actual entity. So phenomenal world is play of appearances, not interplay of actualities – come down to underlying abstractions and a world not real in sense in which actual entity is real. Come down to monistic system.

Alexander ⟨took time⟩ seriously = the becoming of what is actual. But then the continuity leads to Zeno's difficulty.³

McTaggart⁴ – pluralist, but didn't take time seriously. "Solidarity of many entities, but they were all there and time was an adjective."⁵ If ~~get~~ v⟨?⟩v pluralistic system, must preserve continuity in some sense and get rid of the Zeno business. Pythagoreans, Irrational ~~⟨?⟩~~ numbers – Something you'd better not talk about, sit on the scandal.⁶

Might say actual entity not to be looked on as ⟨a point but a stretch⟩⁷ – then must knock anything like motion out of the character of actual entity. Organic relationship of motion which is so essential.

---

1. Conger wrote 'backward' in the left margin here.
2. Cf. Nelson: 'The essence of extensive quantity is such that the second half presupposes that the first half has already happened. How does the arrow get out of its position? When anything happens, it must presuppose an infinite number of happenings. So, if time is the happening of an actual entity, there is something wrong about this' (Nelson, p. 34).
3. Cf. Nelson: 'If we take time as the becoming of what is actual, we ask what becomes, and apparently the continuity of time leads to Zeno's difficulty' (Nelson, p. 34).
4. Whitehead is likely referring to the famous 1908 essay by McTaggart, 'The unreality of time'. For more on McTaggart and Whitehead, see the 10 October 1925 lecture, note 6, p. 54.
5. Closing quotation mark supplied.
6. It seems likely that here Whitehead is drawing from Heath, *A History of Greek Mathematics, Vol. I*, available at <https://archive.org/details/historyofgreekm01heat>. Heath wrote of a Pythagorean named 'Hippasus, about whom the different stories ran (1) that he was expelled from the school because he published doctrines of Pythagoras, and (2) that he was drowned at sea for revealing the construction of the dodecahedron in the sphere and claiming it as his own, or (as others have it) for making known the discovery of the irrational or incommensurable' (65). He later notes that 'The evidence suggests the conclusion that geometry developed itself for some time on the basis of the numerical theory of proportion which was inapplicable to any but commensurable magnitudes, and that it received an unexpected blow later by reason of the discovery of the irrational. The inconvenience of this state of things, which involved the restriction or abandonment of the use of proportions as a method pending the discovery of the generalized theory by Eudoxus, may account for the idea of the existence of the irrational having been kept secret, and of punishment having overtaken the first person who divulged it' (p. 155).
7. Conger has the words 'stretch' and 'point' inverted, but this does not appear to be the correct order, as confirmed by Nelson's notes: 'We might say that an actual entity is not a point but a stretch, but then we have the difficulty of getting motion out of the actual entity (?)' (Nelson, p. 34).

259

|2| If look on series as everywhere dense, haven't helped yourself because between one instant and another an indefinite number of instants. Don't get rid of vicious regression.

Must get discretion ~~insta~~ in some sort.

If discrete instants, nothing to say about relations between them. Milton's half-created lion.[1]

Any ~~(?)~~ leads you into difficulty, <u>but this raises</u> every one it can without solving.

Anyhow you must hold that what becomes is to be looked on as having in itself duration, one second or $1/_{1,000,000}$ second. Motions are elements ∧or functionings of∧ in actual entity. To this extent, monistic. Therefore have what is to be looked on as succession of entities becoming. Each with its duration, but each enters into composition of other entities, and peculiarly close relationship to immediately succeeding entities. Discreteness wrong. One presupposes another in peculiarly intense way.[2]

Subdivision which is possible of one entity means ∨may have intermediate ~~entity~~ ∨⟨meaning?⟩∨ but (organic point of view)∨[3] this entity as one is analyzable, and its complexity is such that it represents the potentiality of an antecedent and subsequent part with this relationship of succession. Possibility is actual complexity in the actual entity which we can represent of the possibility of two entities antecedent and subsequent (possibility wiped out by actuality).[4] There was one entity, but that is left as factor in character of actual entity. One of innumerable cases in which you can't disjoin actuality from possibility.

Must describe actuality in terms of possibility. There is nothing but actual facts, actual entities, but we do talk of possibilities, the might-have-beens. If there's nothing but actual fact, must find possibility in actual fact.

|3| Possibility – which is an inherent character of ∨actual∨ fact which constitutes the continuity. Relationship of one epoch to another shows there was converse possibility of a whole which is two. If the alternatives had been realized, it would have been a different world. Because however you describe an actual entity in its terms as a composition, complex entity "[5] arising out of other actual entity, there is some final individual realization which is just that entity.

Demos on contingency.[6]

---

1. Referring to Milton's *Paradise Lost*, book VII: 'now half appeared / The tawny lion, pawing to get free / His hinder parts, then springs as broke from bonds, / And rampant shakes his brinded mane' (lines 463–6).
2. Cf. Nelson: 'Discreetness is avoided because each entity is connected with the others' (Nelson, p. 34).
3. Parentheses supplied. The proper placement of this interlineation is ambiguous; it may not belong here.
4. Parentheses supplied. The parenthetical phrase appears in the right margin.
5. The intended meaning of the marks rendered here as quote marks is not clear. They could be ditto marks, but the spacing and positioning relative to the sentence above do not make this likely.
6. Contingency was Raphael Demos's main topic in his guest lecture of the previous session (14 December), which Conger did not record, though King (pp. 53–5) and Burch (pp. 19–20) did. Conger wrote 'IVc' in the left margin next to the following paragraph, which may refer to section IV of Demos's lecture as recorded by Burch.

Look for contingency of universe ∧if there is any∧ in final individual fact, in how presupposing the elements out of which it is composed and which attain a real togetherness in that actual entity "[1] how that actual entity as just itself has an individual character which in a sense can be abstracted from rest of universe. Way in which a thing self-creates itself into that individual is where you get ~~the~~ what contingency there is.

Strength of Cartesian position that actual entity requires nothing but itself in order to exist. But this goes too far. Whitehead: Every entity requires itself in order to exist. There is an individual element added in the actuality. That goes with whole point of view that not going to make any distinction between actual entity. Something can be said of all, including God. There you have a general entity. Extra-temporal but which therefore has ~~itself~~ self-created[2] aspect. Its character is a character which presupposes, requires an actual world, but not the actual world.

An aboriginal element. This self-create⟨d⟩[3] element has thereby in its character assumed a more dominant aspect. That conceptual valuation of all possibility which is the self-create⟨d⟩ element giving the sole order which is the aboriginal order out of which the very possibility of actual world arises.

|4| One division of complexity shows elements which as possibility could arise from half being actual and other being actual, but actual fact was whole epoch, and that whole epoch adds its peculiar ∨element of∨ self-created unity to the world.

Works out in effect of attention.

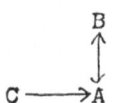

Actual entities in same present presuppose each other. A[4] presupposes B, but ∨is∨ B only formally. Content of relationship between B and A only for B itself. A has to conform to what C has been, but A merely has to conform to extensive spatial-temporal character perspective which B has for A. Particular form of that relationship (might say matter) arises from character of A in itself. How A is itself having regard to fact that it must conform not merely to its antecedent history, but also to B's antecedent history – and still the contingent fact that A is just itself.

If you're going to assimilate all creatures ⟨to?⟩ each other, you'll be inclined to think a self-creating tendency in ~~all~~ ∨every∨ creature.

Past (if look on what is added by self-creating of each entity, the past has a continuity).[5] "Becoming of continuity, but not continuity of becoming."[6] There

---

1. Again, the intended meaning of these marks is not clear. They could be ditto marks, which would correspond to the word 'attain'.
2. Nelson (p. 34) has 'self-creative'.
3. Conger has just 'self-create' here; we have changed it to 'self-created' to make it consistent with his earlier use. Nelson has 'self-creative' here instead (p. 34).
4. Conger's original diagram here is confused, since the 'A' in this sentence appear to be doing double duty as part of the diagram and as the first item in a normal line of notes. We have instead inserted Nelson's diagram (p. 35).
5. Closing parenthesis supplied.
6. Whitehead would later use the same formulation of this phrase in his Gifford lectures that became *Process and Reality*. It had first appeared in a slightly different form in his paper 'Time': 'Thus there is no continuity of becoming, but there is a becoming of continuity' (Whitehead, 'Time', p. 64).

are all these possibilities which are explanatory in the character of whole – What is explanatory can be found in the antecedent. Unless hold this view, Bradley.[1]

|5| Don't have a realism which fails to take account
Question of Extensive Relationship. Formal condition of organism.[2]
Entities presupposing each other hitherto discussed too simply.

Saturday, 18 December 1926

Conger's notes

|1| Presupposition, Anticipation. Dealing with A and B, actual entities in actual world. B presupposes A.

B presupposes A when what I am ∨B∨ presupposes myself at breakfast A. When A is objectified for B as an entity with a determinate or settled ∧(prefers determinate because settled is in past tense)∧[3] character with respect to its actuality. as with Definitely A is objectified for B as being definitely actual – slightly different from causal point of view. What A is for B, way A is prehended into B ∨is∨ as being definitely actual.

A anticipates B when B is objectified for A as an entity with determinate relationships to A, but with no definite actualized character, though with a potentiality for actualization. Trying to define what a <u>future</u> is. There are determinate relationships not yet actualized – promise to go out to lunch. No actualized determinate character of that lunch.

B presupposes A when A is settled. A anticipates B when B not settled. Not direct contradiction, nor even contrary view.

Define what mean by A precedes B when B presupposes A and A anticipates B. A and B are compresent ∧(sense different from Alexander)∧[4] when each presupposes the other. Then must hold that of two ∨actual∨ entities, past, present, or future, deal with either one precedes other, or they are compresent.

Now analyze <u>compresence</u>: Presupposition is not quite that How A is objectified for B is as settled or definite. Objectification may have one of two characters – ∨objectification∨ effected by universals which limit what A is for B. Two ways in which can have those universals. {?}

|2| Universals may be partly determined by what A is in itself, or may depend on what B is in itself. If depend on what A is – causal relationship. If depend on what B is, you have presentational immediacy of the sense data. If

---

1. Cf. Nelson: 'The proper alternative to this view of time is Bradley's' (Nelson, p. 35).
2. Cf. Nelson: 'Extensive relationship is the formal condition of organism' (Nelson, p. 35).
3. Parentheses supplied.
4. Parentheses supplied. For Alexander, 'compresence' means 'togetherness': 'As an example which presents the least difficult take the perception of a tree or table. This situation consists of the act of mind which is the perceiving; the object which is so much of the thing called tree as is perceived, the aspect of it which peculiar to that perception, let us say the appearance of the tree under these circumstances of the perception; and the togetherness or compresence which connects these two distinct existences (the act of mind and the object) into the total situation called the experience' (Alexander, *Space, Time, and Deity*, pp. 11–12, available at <https://archive.org/details/spacetimedeitygi01alexuoft>).

~~dependence on~~ B has to conform to objectification for A, B is causal. ~~If~~ B may lay down condition, in which case get presentational immediacy. But always have <u>formal</u> <u>condition</u> of extension, and always get determinate relationship. Cf. railway timetable. (Connection is extensional connection?)[1]

What A is in itself beyond that doesn't come in when have presentational immediacy. When A precedes B you have a causal relationship; whatever varied form it takes. When A and B are compresent, each presupposes the other, but may have three possibilities –

- May have A objectified for B with presentational immediacy via sense data which ~~ex~~ depends on B.
- My sensa now depends on state of my body.
- State of my body (?) me the universals which demonstrate certain element of space-time for me.

When have B, have another set of entities demonstrated.[2] ~~by~~

Because ~~B presupposes A, no reason why A shouldn't presuppose B~~ ~~B~~ A causally related to B, no reason why B shouldn't be causally related to A. Get essential organic connection of entities. Take superorganism like body. Physical side of me as this occasion of my bodily life.

|3| When one is included in the other, the body is what it is by reason partly of what the electron is. Can't explain about body without explain electron.

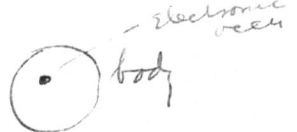

But <u>reciprocal</u> – electron equally depends on what body immediately is. You get interlocked compresence in which each causally depends on the other; this is the essence of the organic connection. Each has to adjust itself to the other in that immediate present. That is the problem of superorganisms in relation to lower included organisms. Brings out that extension. Whole idea of extension is really the formal side of the organic relationship.

Question how they ∧electron and body∧ are conditioning each other may be special characters, but fact that they should be organically interlocked is expressed by whole-part relationship which comes out in extension.

Quite agrees with Kant. Time and space are forms of ~~prehension~~ perception. But Whitehead: perception is general fact of internality of physical relationships. Kant didn't see he was there dealing with physical world.

Still another possibility. Objectification always. Grades of relevance. Every entity includes everything, towards individualized one fact of self-realization. Grades of intensity. Various elements in complex unity which have various grades of intensity.

All universals ~~which~~ affect objectification of A for B, but only certain of them have any important relevance, but only some contribute to intensity – only some are intensively effective.

---

1. Parentheses supplied. The parenthetical material appears to be Conger's question rather than Whitehead's, but it is impossible to be certain.
2. Given its position, this sentence is intended to reference the diagram on its left.

|4| There may be two ⟨?⟩ settled for the other\/ entities which no universals are intensively affecting. Those belong practically to the blind spot. Represent a blind spot to each other.[1]

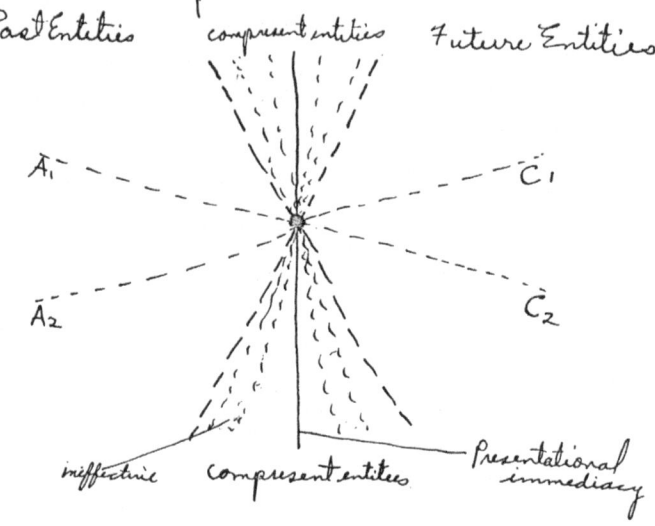

Then the compresent entities. Among them the entities with presentational immediacy. There are entities inside B. And there are those which although compresent are neither ~~causal, anticipated~~ in presentational immediacy, mutually causal, or \/organically\/ inside, and yet they are compresent but ineffective.

Ask whether should say

According to modern view of relativity, construed realistically – the entity with presentational immediacy and the entity inside, are not all the compresent entity $\begin{smallmatrix}+&+&+\\+&+&+\end{smallmatrix}$

Vertical line – set of presentational immediacy

All within ⟨...?⟩ are compresent + + +

Other ⟨four⟩[2] dim⟨ensions⟩

This is what is wanted from modern physical point of view. View of time is so far perfectly compatible with it. Provides various classes absolutely.

View of time as linear succession has to go – but in a sense there is a succession.

Historical routes.

---

1. We have replaced Conger's figure here with the one from Nelson (p. 36), below, which is considerably cleaner and clearer. Conger points out in his diagram that B is a 'complex entity', and he notes that A_1 and A_2 are 'entities in past which anticipate B', while C_1 and C_2 are 'entities which B anticipates'.
2. This appears to be a '4', but could be a '+', as in the line above.

 How are we to define an immediate successor? As possibility. Haven't provided that there must be an ineffective one, but no reason why couldn't have if science wants.

Question of immediate succession. B immediately succeeds A ⟨when:⟩[1]

1. B presupposes A, and A anticipates B.
2. B presupposes every entity which A presupposes.
3. Every entity which B presupposes is presupposed by A, either compresent with A or in A's past.

|5| Nothing in between. But haven't secured that if you have A, not secured only one entity which A immediately precedes. A∴[2]

B – haven't secured that it has not more than one immediately predecessor. ∴B

A presupposes every entity which is compresent with it. May be entity C compresent with A and with B. Modern science requires this possibility.

Have put down conditions which are common sense conditions with respect to time.

Satisfies common sense pl claims as regard to time, but doesn't secure it as one necessary linear series. Have alternative routes. Linear series within spatial-temporal continuum, but no one such series which is the time series. Science wants. Philosophy ought to have seen by analysis.

Life[3] of an enduring organism. Actual occasions owing to analogy of their character. Each by its congruence inherits from its immediate past with peculiar intensity. Sums up and integrates its past with peculiar intensity.

Organisms of that sort have field of presentational immediacy.[4]

Tuesday, 21 December 1926

Conger's notes

|1|[5] Two levels of generality:
1. 'Brass tacks'.
2. Earth on which ∨stand is∨ relevant and all details.

Higher level controls common sense and imagination. A general knowledge of the chess board. Not always formulated easily. What is worth thinking about is within the general rules of the game. Ought to have generic notion as to what ∨sort of thing∨ you're trying to get through.

---

1. Supplied from Nelson, p. 36.
2. Both here and below, Conger draws three dots that resemble a 'therefore' sign, but from context it is clear that the dots are intended to represent multiple other actual occasions which succeed A or precede B.
3. This word is connected to the figure on the left.
4. Given its position, this sentence is intended to reference the diagram on its left.
5. King wrote at the start of his notes for this lecture: 'Last lecture in course before Winter recess. Very rotten lecture' (King, p. 58).

Philosophy of 17th century in touch with science and provided the general notions at that time. ⟨?⟩ ~~De~~ Science kept on line taken by Newton – gives mechanistic point of view. General feeling that too many difficulties philosophic and scientific for us to look on that as final point of view. Scientific idea of matter, stuff, electrons – <u>material</u>. Space, time must be considered (way to new point of view).[1]

– Go back to Descartes and see how he does it. Individual substance and attributes working it in with notion of space, time. 2. A Whole presupposition which comes in –

– Subject-predicate point of view leads to atomism.
– Linguistic sentence enunciates a complete fact taken by itself and enunciates it fully.
– Subject-predicate not the general notion of fact.
– Sentence really omits background of the universe. Can't take extension in little bits.
– Really have certain systematic aspect of universe spread out before you.
– A Descartes ~~nearly~~ vsometimesv concedes all this, but comes back to subject-predicate point of view. Then when he gets to individual minds, thinks he gets something which is just on its own. Can't understand mind without ⟨God⟩ in background. ~~ANW~~ A little misunderstanding of Descartes would have given a different development of modern science.

|2| Descartes presupposes vsomev things with astonishing naivete.
– e.g., <u>Extension</u>, <u>Endurance</u>.
– Measured space has extension.
– Endurance has something like extension.
– vSuggestsv something common to endurance and space, namely extensiveness. Hard to specify just what mean.
– Notion of measured quantity.
– This is how we think about (Descartes).

vWhy howv think about things vuselessv unless has some relevance. This is a naïve dismissal of problem.

Notion of quantity is not unanalyzable notion. Aristotle did harm by his categories. Philosophy took categories naïvely when couldn't get over.

Quantity. Elucidate properties of number to elucidate properties of things, because the actual world has properties which are elucidated by considering some relationship between them and numbers.

Quantity, which can be dealt with by number, really spells structure ~~whose~~
– structural relationships in universe which can be understood. Internal relationships of the structure are identical with internal relationships to be discerned in number field. Can transfer relationships from number field to structure.

What can you say of the structure of things which leads them to be numerically measured as quantity? Get behind time and space to a certain

---

1. Parentheses supplied.

community which we will call extensive character, and a more sharp questioning with regard to structural relationships which can be discovered with respect to them and which are the basis of their being measured.

|3| Now ask what are the things in nature. Descartes says they have endurance and spatial extension. Are they not two different entities? Extension of endurance and spatial extension ∨have∨ not same extension underlying them? Shows we are ~~dealing~~ near modern scientific view of relativity – closer connection between time and space.

Then Newtonian insistence on bit of matter with its empty space. This seems to cut across the Cartesian view, Descartes seems to be a little wobbly on it.

Enormous success of Newtonian point of view, which fixed attention on matter, then secondarily forces. Forces in background and got motions. Then Clerk Maxwell, ∧Faraday∧ emphasized field of force going on in empty space. What is going on in empty space not quite clean cut between that and your bit of matter. Proton and electron radiating away as radiant energy.

Descartes had nice difference between real entities, which were minds, and extended entities. These went back ∧on St. Thomas Aquinas∧{Gilson}.[1] The clean cut now is not at all so obvious. Notion of having two genera of actual entities not so attractive.

Ether as substratum for something going on, obvious point of view of scientific men was we know all about matter – continuous stuff, the real entity to which things happen. Things happen in so-called empty space – must be something continuous, some stuff, the real entity. Scientific notion of ether based on mistaken notion of matter. Subject-predicate point of view is common basis on which both are derived. ~~Predicate~~ Ether a kind of ~~passage~~ passive substance for the predicate of the entity.

|4| Suggests ought to go back and do what Descartes tried do. Ask what real entity is. An event with its spatial-temporal extension, but it is something going on, a happening which is an actual fact. The actual fact is of the nature of action. Can't disjoin that happening from all other happenings. Don't say extensive relation within happenings, and extensive relation between Descartes – fundamental fact from which we start is immediate act of experience which each of us is (Whitehead thinks rightly).[2]

Fundamental concrete fact. Fact of ultimate relationships of an actual entity is how one entity is constituted by way in {?} which it draws other entities into itself. Constituted out of its perspective of other entities ∨together with∨ other entities forming it. Internal self generating character of that experience – reflexiveness of it.

---

1. This sentence appears to record an interjection by Gilson in Whitehead's lecture. Étienne Gilson (1884–1978) was a French medievalist philosopher and philosopher of history. He was a visiting professor at Harvard in the autumn of 1926, 1927 and 1928, and became fast friends with Whitehead, with the two frequently attending one another's courses. See Petek, 'Whitehead and Étienne Gilson', and Shook, *Étienne Gilson*.
2. Parentheses supplied.

Locke talking about mind was really talking about complete occasion,[1] but misconstruing it because was thinking of it as purely [subjective vs.?] mental.

|5| Find Descartes talking of actual entity in terms of thoroughgoing internal relationship. So get that point of view.

(1) What has become of your continuity? – Continuity side of universe.

(2) What make of future?

(3) Continuity of becoming. James Ward,[2] William James, continuity in psychology.

(4) Neither actual, nor merely nothing?

Must have something very like the Spinozistic extended God. Prefers to call it φύσις.[3] Have to have this as locus of possibility which has its character φύσις, which is always changing according to the actual creatures because its character is determined by them. But also with certain characters which maintain themselves.

The potentiality of the universe as limited by what is already actual. Take the creativity as having a character, and in its character an extension, because the future must have certain determinate relationships with the past. Cf. Day after tomorrow already settled by what is already going on.

Determinate relationships of actual entity constitute the underlying φύσις. φύσις is locus of possibility and character of the creativity as determined by its creatures.

That φύσις is extensionally extended and continuous, but that actual entities, what is actualized is discrete and but is one actual entity, though as a mere extended φύσις, it might have been many entities.

|6|[4] There is always among actual entities the relationships which they have as actualized elements of φύσις, which is locus of actualized ∨limited∨ potentiality.

Continuity comes from φύσις, doesn't tell you what is to be actual, but merely the conditions which are to hold between entity if to be est continuous.

Might have been one, but actually two.[5]

Sane[6] relations. What might have been ∧controls∧ ∨(internal?)∨ relations of one entity, then turn into perspective relations whereby one entity enters into other. General φύσις which is not actual. Cf. *Natura Naturans* and *Natura Naturata*.

---

1. The figure to the right appears here.
2. James Ward (1843–1925) was an English psychologist and philosopher who for many years was a colleague of Whitehead at Trinity College, Cambridge.
3. Greek, *phusis*, usually translated as 'nature'.
4. There are notes on the reverse side of the final page of this lecture that are for another course; they have been omitted.
5. Given its position, this sentence is intended to reference the diagram on its left.
6. The word 'sane' appears clearly, but what it means or whether another word, such as 'same', is intended, is not clear.

Tuesday, 4 January 1927

Conger's notes

|1|[1] Extension
Logic Measurement – Why is the universe logical? Kant's answer in essence right, but muddled up and in presentation defective.[2]

We are in midst of dealing with time.

Ontology, how it is that the universe is community, solidarity, incompleteness.

Time viewed as measurable is a special exemplification of a more general fact – essential transience of the universe. No entity can be apart from a supersession beyond itself.

You cannot disjoin the individuality of an entity as being for itself from the fact that thereby there is a fresh creative determination of an entity which will supersede it. Every entity is a creative character in being an entity.[3] Not a paradox, but a philosophical paradox as Bergson says, because philosophy spatializes and holds up universe as though it were a complete collection of complete entities.

Can look on solidarity of universe apart from its supersession. Arises from fact that each entity is really a creative determination of the totality of entities. It is a creativity of real togetherness on the part of the whole universe, but it is the universe as objectified, under grades of self-illustration, under a limited form of eternal self-realization – eliciting a reality, a real unity completing its multiplicity.[4]

The ultimate complex entity is an actual entity. It is that real unity of what is complex which is an actual entity. Actual entities of the universe contribute to each other in four different ways. These give you distinction between past, present, and future.

ABCD(E)5: Nature

Actual entity

Different species of objectification, (α), (β), (γ), (δ). Four different ways jam together over different ways of looking at present.[6] Whole question of modern relativity whether or not the two distinct ways of looking at present come to

---

1. Nelson has marked the start of his notes here with the word 'Review'. As this was the first lecture after the winter recess (yet still the fall semester), it is not clear if he meant that this lecture is supposed to be a 'review' of recent material before the break, or 'review' of the course in general in preparation for an exam.
2. This first portion of the lecture notes appear in a box at the top right of Conger's first page. It is not clear if this is actually what Whitehead said first, or whether Conger wrote the text in later.
3. Cf. Nelson: 'There is no such thing as a complete actual entity' (Nelson, p. 37). This seems likely to be the 'paradox' that Whitehead discusses in the next sentence of Conger's notes.
4. Cf. King: 'A limited form of self-limitation. A real unity transcending and limiting the multiplicity' (King, p. 58).
5. The 'E' is supplied from King (p. 59), and also from the 'E's which Conger wrote in below. Conger replaced a number of 'D's with 'E's (King did the same thing, p. 59).
6. Whitehead appears to discuss only three species of objectification in this lecture, (α), (β) and (γ).

same thing or not, temporality ⟨then?⟩ as one series. (Time is serial. Question whether uniquely serial.)[1] ⟨If?⟩ do, classical theory of time. Don't ⟨have?⟩ certain complexity with respect to serial theory of time.

|2| Time a fact of ⱽthisⱽ cosmological epoch. When dealing with Nature, referring ⱽtoⱽ the determinate possibility as from the standpoint of some definite actual event or group of events with certain presuppositions about what is already actual.

(α) A (as determinately actual) is objectified for B in terms of ⱽrelevantⱽ universals derived from A's individual experience.

The character of creativity is its creatures. B is actual entity, A is objectification of B.

A's individual experience is simply A. Its individual experience is what it is. A is an act of being something for its own sake (go into this when come to whole notion of extension).

B has to take account of the ~~universals~~ predicates of A as relevant to B, as exemplifying certain predicates. B has to be what it is subject to that relevance. A is to be taken as determinate, and predicates are determined by what A is. That is <u>causation</u>. Consciousness of it is <u>memory</u>.

Memory ⟨almost?⟩ always of past. Remembering what the world   .... ⟨.. x⟩ was.[2] If I didn't remember it, I have to be what I am subject to what the past is for me. Thinks there is an immediacy of knowledge – if isn't, how can you know you are issuing from a past?

A is in B's past. When A is determinate for B, and when universals derived from A's individual experience, then A is B's past. Not in <u>the</u> past. The past initially is an ⟨individual?⟩ fact.

|3| (β) Future has its own difficulties – So bring in Nature. If hadn't talked about future, wouldn't have brought in nature. Must bring in something which hangs between being and not being.

E ~~D~~ [as undetermined, but demonstrated by systematic predicates] (D in future)[3] is objectified for B in terms of relevant universals which demonstrate ~~D~~ E as having to include in itself a determinate objectification of B.

It is determinate in its definite systematic relations, and also as having to include universals derived from B itself. It has definite systematic spatio-temporal relations.

Thus ~~D~~ ⱽEⱽ is determined <u>via</u> natural relations, but is not determined <u>qua</u> actual entity. It is determined via the possibilities which it must fulfill, and why it must from point of view of B is that B has added a character of the creativity. The definiteness of the future is expressive of the definite character we have added to the creativity.

Railway ⟨?⟩ timetable. I and my past constitute the character of the creative activity, and this timetable is an analysis of that character.

---

1. Parentheses supplied. The parenthetical text appears in the right margin.
2. Given its position, this sentence is intended to reference the diagram on its right.
3. Parentheses supplied. The parenthetical phrase appears in the left margin.

|4| If, ~~ea~~ as C.D. Broad says, future is nothing, can't talk about. Often ~~a book~~ nothing in a book.

~~D~~ v*E*v waiting for predicates from *B*. ~~but D is no~~ *E* D is in *B*'s future.

(γ) *C* (as determinate) is objectified for *B* in terms of relevant universals of two characters.

(1) ~~Demonstrating~~ Exemplifying systematic element in relationship between entities peculiarly relevant here. Spatial v temporal v relationship.[1]

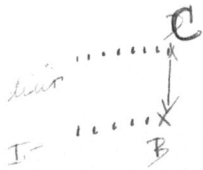

B as actual for its own sake with certain systematic relationship to *C*, but (2) illustrated also, ~~objectify~~ exemplifying predicates which are relevant ~~to (?) only~~ to, derivative from *B* only.[2]

Chair is demonstrated for me partly ~~from~~ as having a certain standpoint in systematic complex of entities, as determinately actual, but as illustrated purely by predicates which are drawn from what I am and have nothing to do with what ~~D~~ v*C*v is.

(1) Only information about ~~D~~ *C* (avoiding solipsistic universe).[3] *C* ~~D~~ is determinate with reference to systematic relationships. But illustration of it is drawn from *B*.

To demonstrate means ~~D~~ v*C*v is actual for itself, but there are predicates ~~from~~ drawn from |5| *C* as actual entity is in *B* with presentational immediacy.

When we have experience through our senses, stars may vhave gonev out of existence. Space beyond there demonstrated vaguely by spots of light. You see space immediately illustrated out there in the distance. I'm not seeing a star 300 years ago – have presentational immediacy of elements of space-time now. What it is conjecturally due to is star 300 years ago. Which is important? If painter, important to see heavens now.[4] Poet Shelley, worlds like bubbles on river.[5] Star 300 years ago.

Question what you're really seeing is a muddle, what you're really thinking about.

Same with man who looks in mirror. Fire ten feet behind mirror, in front of mirror. You see space behind mirror illustrated by universals of color. What that behind space is is its systematic relations – illustrated by universals which merely come to my state at that moment as determined by my past.

But can get past so distinct that universals by which I illustrate *C* is irrelevant to what that space is. |6| Cf. Nova Persei[6] – What we saw illustrated space in terms of something quite irrelevant to what was there now. Cf. sound.

---

1. Nelson adds here: 'This is presentational immediacy' (Nelson, p. 37).
2. Cf. King: 'but objectified exemplifying predicates (universals) which are (relevant to A only) derivative from B only' (King, p. 59).
3. Parentheses supplied. The parenthetical text appears in the left margin.
4. Cf. Nelson: '(The painter deals with presentational immediacy.)' (Nelson, p. 37).
5. Percy Bysshe Shelley (1792–1822), 'Worlds on worlds are rolling ever'.
6. Nova Persei, discovered in 1901 by Thomas David Anderson (1853–1932), was the brightest recorded nova since 1604, but it was surpassed 17 years later by Nova Aquilae.

Harvard lectures, fall semester 1926

In γ, particular universals spring from B. It's B as realizing itself in spatial relatedness to other elements – determinate actual elements. In determinate world spatially related, but illustrated according to the nature of B itself.
© ~~There are 2 elements~~

Thursday, 6 January 1927

Conger's notes

|1| Various ways in which another entity enters into the makeup of B. Can be properly causal.[1] May be in the future – B discloses itself as requiring a systematic character in the actual universe, not yet determined, indeterminate, but must be occasions with certain definite systematic relevance to B. B as objectified for E under that relevance must enter into makeup of E. B objectifies E as a partially determinate element which expresses the character of creativity, but creativity hasn't yet obtained that character. E not yet actual – an indeterminate event in the future.

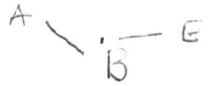

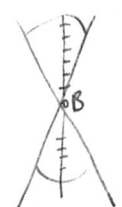

Can consider occasions which are concurrent with B – May look on as sense presentation – World as now for my senses immediately presented to me. Occasions which are exhibited for is under presentational immediacy[2] – systematically, exhaust themselves for B as part of the system required by the universe, but not having any further relational presentation.

All concurrent events because not passing in, not ⟨coming?⟩ from.[3] ~~All~~ Are concurrent events the same as events for the presentational immediacy?

If identify the two.

Being concurrent ~~is~~ a mutual relationship.

If have C as concurrent with B, have presentational immediacy. Get just one locus for whole lot. If you don't Videntify the ⟨<?⟩V, might get an event C, may be concurrent, but locus of presentational immediacy may come down at [parallel to B].[4]

|2| And will get into considerable muddle in speaking about time and space, because you haven't same meaning of simultaneity.

What is there which is absolutely systematic with respect to time and space which we can say about nature? If everything you can say about time and space depends on what has happened (events), then you can't from your own self-knowledge base your self-consciousness, analysis of what is immediate, get to know anything about what goes on beyond – can't know what are the

---

1. Cf. King: 'How another entity can enter into the makeup of B – if in the past – causally' (King, p. 60).
2. King adds '– compresent' after 'presentational immediacy' (p. 60). 'Compresent' is a term which Whitehead made much of in his 18 December lecture (p. 262).
3. Cf. King: 'Concurrent events, not entering into or issuing out of B' (King, p. 60).
4. There is what looks to be an illegible diagram in this vicinity, at the bottom of the page. Cf. King: 'The locus of presentational immediacy of C may fall outside of B' (King, p. 60).

272

characters which exist beyond. Must be something systematic, given, required of the universe by every actual entity in it. Every actual entity requires some systematic character of universe in order that entity may be what it is. Principle of solidarity. Does that systematic requirement apply to notions of space and time? Mathematicians covertly always do presuppose they are dealing with something which has a uniform systematic character.

Any measurements which happen to take will do – rectangular coordinates, polar coordinates, areas, curves, etc., but what do you mean by a method of measurement? Can measure point P from O by infinity of procedures. Use same methods of measurement and use different numerical quantities to get to Q.

In your process of measuring P, you were in a series of particulars. Then you go through another series of particulars and land at Q. Why are methods the same? Because there is a systematic structure and a homology with respect to the elements of that structure. There is something systematic throughout the structure.

|3| If not something systematic, why say system of coordinates? Coordinate system is a way of cataloging homologous systematic elements. Can get one-to-one correlation, but steps to get to P and steps to Q. If nothing systematic, can't talk about a system of coordinates.

Commonly told – all measurement is coincidence. Obvious that there is such an appeal. But if that is all, it simply says coincident things are coincident. Something beyond coincidence – Refers to something that holds apart from coincidence.

In physics dealing essentially with an extensive magnitude.

Between two point events according to Einstein, a quantitative relation.

ds ds'

Physics, relativity[1] founded on idea that between two point events near enough together can observe quantitative relation there and there, and any entity which passes from P to Q that total sum of all those quantities has a certain sta⟨tic?⟩ magnitude – But won't get any increase or decrease ⟨of?⟩ quantity realized. No matter if do have slight variations.

Like at top of a pass – always keeps ~~at~~ on level, neither gains nor loses.[2]

What do you mean by saying ds is a quantity? Quantity not fundamental category, therefore depends on idea of structure.

If is proper description of physical universe, how compare ⟨elements?⟩? Can't take up ⟨?⟩ events and carry ~~them~~ it to another.[3]

---

1. To the right of the diagram above and below the words 'Physics, relativity' appears the phrase 'Then add up'. Its meaning and proper placement are not clear.
2. Conger set off this sentence from those around it. Its proper placement relative to the sentences around it is unclear.
3. Starting from the beginning of this sentence at the word 'If', Conger draws a line vertically up the left margin and an arrow that appears to point to the diagram above.

|4| Coincidence is nonsense if get universe down to extension, what happens here happens here, not there.

Then if you ask how it's done, take any system of coordinates which you like.

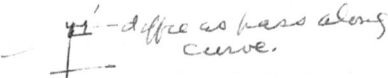

You can express *ds* <u>in terms of</u>[1] = $ds = f(x, y, dx, dy)$. Analogously, $ds' = f(x' y', dx' dy')$. In order to work that point of view, you must know what you mean by saying x and y are coordinate of point <u>in same sense</u> that $x + dx$ and y and dy are coordinate.

Habitually stated as if you were dealing with a <u>particular</u> fact, but ∨by what right∨ use same <u>method</u> for different points? In presupposing coordinates, you presuppose a systematic structure in accordance with which measurements are made. Coordinates are logically prior to the physical law which is expressed in terms of them. Something systematic logically prior to the particular ∨physical∨ facts. That is inherent. Mathematicians would disagree – Whitehead wants to see arguments answered, not ignored.

That fundamentally alters explanations as given ~~which~~ of what Einstein ⟨?⟩ means. Is there anything in our immediate knowledge ∨of the universe as demonstrated∨ which is prior to the particular systematic intrinsic character of the facts? How ⟨?⟩ facts are bound together. How B^2 has to adapt itself to A depends on what A is in itself. Past is not our strong suit. Relationship of causation is bound up with particular fact A affecting what B is in itself.

|5| Because science is primarily interested in causal relations, has led to wrong est⟨imation?⟩.

But when come to presentational immediacy ~~it is~~ (or future)[3] B from what it is in itself thereby determining a systematic relationship with D and E. ⟨?⟩ D as definitely actual, exhibited merely as objectified ~~from~~ ∨by∨ universals drawn from B and not what B is in itself.

E is only systematic relationship which must find its niche in actuality. Unless systematic character finally enters into actuality, everything about future is nonsense.

B obtains information with respect to universe which is irrelevant to what is ∨actually∨ at D or E, yet enters also into actuality. Also, systematic character lends its perspective to what A is (in past).

So demand for system also comes out when try to analyze ∨ontological∨ relationship to each other. Especially true with respect to future – no specification of future – can't measure. There is really an appeal to some system. Science requires it. Systematic character glaring with respect to <u>future</u>. Might say confuses physical and private psychological space.

---

1. This phrase is circled; we have replaced the circle with an underline.
2. There is an 'A' in the margin with a line connecting it to this 'B', but the meaning is unclear.
3. Parentheses supplied.

Harvard lectures, fall semester 1926

Saturday, 8 January 1927

Conger's notes[1]

|1| Consider where physical science joins general ontological concepts which have been developing.

If begin to talk about private psychological space of immediate sense data, if once admit that that is part of my psyche, everything in that immediate presentation is to be reckoned as private. Something withdrawn from common world. If not demonstrating a common world, is <u>properly</u> to be called private and have this difficulty – all our scientific measurements concern this immediate, presented psychic private world. You are saying something <u>about</u> the immediate presentation of sense data – and all scientific observation is observation of that. If put aside immediate presentation as not demonstrating a world, your scientific observations is nothing to do with anything concerning a common world. Must look elsewhere for it. Holding that our experience demonstrates a common world; it's what we presuppose as demonstrating a common world.

We have therefore this locus of presentational immediacy in ⟨which?⟩ according to all the evidence of our experience, the common world is demonstrated by its systematic character and by other universals proper to the occasion, but occasion for which they are proper is the immediate ⟨person?⟩ for whom there is this presentation. Since this presentation is a presentation of world beyond ourselves, is drawn from systematic character of world required by the fact that we are in it. If are going to make the demonstration depend on what happens ⟨there?⟩, it is inexplicable how.

World patient of actual occasions – so have natural assumption that sp⟨atial?⟩ relations represent ⟨systematic world?⟩.

A general system of coordinates requires a general systematic <u>structure</u> in terms of which the ~~trans~~ measurements relating to different particulars can be correlated one to the other.

Correspondence of particulars which involve [particular numbers arise from analogy of systematic structure.]

|2| Physical space is a logical construct.

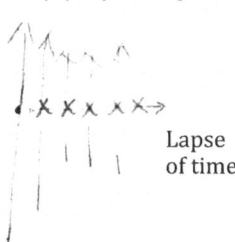

Lapse of time

Let this be route of separate occasions of life history (<u>Diagram in metaphysics is a Platonic myth</u>).[2] Then this is the locus of presentational immediacy.[3] Three dimensions. Its set of immediate occasions. Body x is at rest [in one time system?]. <u>Later</u> occasions parallel ~~to~~ y coordinates.

We will neglect the thickness of endurance and what you see is that there is ⟨<u>a</u>?⟩ succession

---

1. Unusually, Conger circles a large number of words in this lecture. The circles have been replaced with underlines.
2. Parentheses supplied. The parenthetical phrase appears in a circle in the right margin.
3. An arrow points to the left-most line in the accompanying figure.

of instantaneous three-dimensional spaces which are the locus of these other actual occasions demonstrated for the occasion under presentational immediacy. Past what is antecedent to presentational immediacy subsequent.

Idea of motion in instantaneous space is nonsense. Everything is where it is. What you mean by space without thickness as a limit. (vSeev Extensiveness and Abstraction).

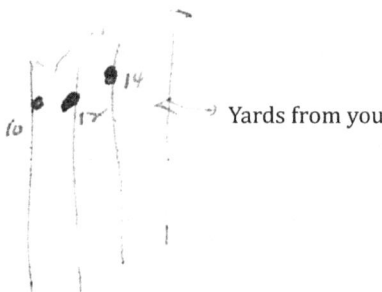

Yards from you

Can take some other enduring object and say it has got from that to that. But, what do you mean by a yard? Settle it up for one instantaneous space, then for another. But how correlate the two? If you believe there is a correlation, don't have a theory of the universe which denies it. Ought to be some real method of correlating if you believe there is a real correlation of standards.

|3| Fundamental axiom. If two entities remain at rest relatively to each other, distance won't alter.

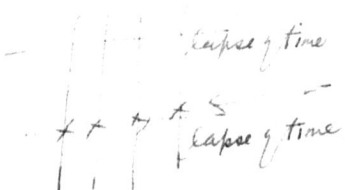

This series all takes place at same point in physical space.[1] The locus of occasions which can be looked on as at rest. Giving another locus at rest in same sense will give you a correlation. Right angle-ness has nothing to do with rest or motion. Angle is of no importance; rate of change is important.

Physical point so far from being simple is a succession of point occasions. Simple point only pertains to instantaneous space.

Suppose something at rest in a different sense. Anything moving uniformly to us.

On classical theory enduring object ⟨?⟩ different occasion.[2] Those have their are all at same distance from each other. Both uniformly increasing with velocity v. On classical theory that would ⟨represent?⟩ the correlation of the different instantaneous spaces.

Time length intervals must always like equal.

Space is like ⟨?⟩ So vthree dimensions ofv space like surface of sphere, all radii equal.

---

1. Given its position, this sentence is intended to reference the diagram on its left.
2. The text in the upper left of the diagram appears to be '3 dim⟨ensions⟩ packed here'.

Harvard lectures, fall semester 1926

|4| If you hold that the presentational immediacy gives you three-dimensional space, your knowledge contains an instantaneous space. And the common space V[of instantaneous presentational immediacy]V is a make up taking lapse of time and getting a correlation of various instantaneous spaces which is done by fundamental notion of rest. (Having split up into instantaneous spaces, put them together again)[1] That apprehension of rest is not a unique state – there are modes of rest.

Relative motion is <u>comparison</u> of different modes of rest. And different modes of rest really give you different physical spaces.

If you are going to deal with common space for world according to one or other mode of rest, you are really appealing to different common spaces.

Sun or Sirius. Either has as much right to be called at rest. The one you put down first number get rest of diagram. If the sun is at rest, always at same point. If Sirius <u>etc</u>. According to Sun, Sirius is moving ⟨from?⟩ point to point, and vice-versa.

|5| Even if you stick to the classical theory – notion of a common space to the universe in which all motions take place must be wrong. Argue against Newton's view of common space as receptacle. Neither Newton nor Einstein would agree.

⟨Newton⟩ wouldn't agree with real actual entity being an actual occasion. Nor will it work if you start by appeal to immediate experience. Endeavor to meet criticism of people who say immediate experience is inst<u>antaneous</u> fact. There is a privacy to this extent – Immediate occasion has private relation to *A* and *B*.

Newton said immediate presentation is of receptacle. Whitehead: is of other actual entity in an ordered relation strictly peculiar to those actual entities.

A measure of privacy you have a sorting out of the universe. Newton said there is a receptacle always same, could be disengaged from things received in it, would be there whether things in it or not.

Status of this receptacle. Newtonian receptacle not view of Descartes or Leibniz. Newton had to say one of these entities is really at rest, and all others only apparently at rest.

|6| Newton Vwould have to confessV no physical means of discriminating between this mysterious <u>proposition</u> ⟨of?⟩ being actually at rest.

Whitehead – None of the sets more at rest than others. Rest is a generic term for a relation of historic route to the universe – generic term with different species of rest.

How about this crosscut of presentational immediacy? Do different entities always <u>have</u> the same crosscut of presentational immediate? If don't, under what circumstances do they differ? Is there any metaphysical prime which tells you about that?

---

1. Parentheses supplied. The parenthetical text appears in the right margin.

Classical theory assumes crosscuts always the same. We have a
Continuum is differentiated by given structure of ⟨possible?⟩ loci
of sense presentation.

Idea of one common space which is a logical construct is nonsense. There is physical space for one definition of rest, another for another. Points of space from point of view of sun. Are different entities from point of view of Sirius. You are talking of different things. If take different type of ~~space~~ rest, have different meanings for space. Importance of ~~rep~~ recognizing difference of meaning is blurred because formulae so simple.

$$x_0 = vt + x$$

|7| If want to go back to ord⟨inary?⟩ theory and run a realistic view of universe so as to get rid of that mysterious receptacle ~~and simply take his view of~~. What is immediately given is an instantaneous space, physical space is complex construct, different for different modes of rest.

Chief differences of theory of relativity are really inherent in classical theory if try to make any sense of it ~~with regard to~~ for realistic view of universe. Presentations of occasions.

Next question – Why believe in Whitehead's theory that locus of presentation is same for all entities? Challenge next time.

Tuesday, 11 January 1927

Conger's notes

|1| Put aside notion of space as receptacle. There are three other points of view.

Descartes: World of nature made up of corporeal entities and an entity is its extension. Space is derivative from analysis of what an actual corporeal entity is.[2] ~~Whitehead rash~~

A philosopher is a man who is troubled about what he means.

Newton (=) Space logically prior to actual entities which are in it.

Whitehead with Descartes; but difficulty that the relationship between actual corporeal entities is spatial, so can't discover from one corporeal entity, but from relationships. Descartes didn't put his whole weight up against the difficulty – writes with hopeless ambiguity. Sometimes speaks as if multiplication of minds were balanced by multiplication of actual entities.[3]

Leibniz' monads extended and mirror extended universe.

Whitehead: Each actual entity is made up of its relationships; is its act of experience which is to be looked on as concrescence into a real unity of relationships ~~it~~ with the other actual entities. In these relationships you ought

---

1. Given its position, this sentence is intended to reference the diagram on its right.
2. King adds here: 'Space is an essential plenum. Actual entities are spatial. Apart from actual entities, there would be no space' (King, p. 61).
3. Cf. King: 'Descartes didn't say, unity of substance, but he must be construed as such. Spinoza did have the unity' (King, p. 61).

to look on each <u>actual entity as relegating the community</u> into an ordered relationship which is the objectification of the community into the one entity. <u>Each entity is in parts</u> and is <u>in its parts a self-object</u>, one part [for another] and therefore <u>each entity has its own extension</u> – has whole world including itself mirrored among other things in an extensive relationship, perceived as such ~~by~~ from own standpoint. But extensive relationships of various entities have in common that impartial scheme of relationships by means of which extensive relationships of whole community as mirrored in any one entity – the impartial scheme which is the least common multiple vin itv – Every standpoint finds its niche.

|2| Then must ask what we ⟨conceive?⟩ the actual experience to be.

(1) Causal

(2) Anticipatory

(3) Merely in systematic relationship – Compresent

(4) Presentational immediacy

That presentational immediacy very rashly and narrowly ~~h~~ some have tended to confine our whole experience of an external world. If do, get into difficulties.[1]

All our scientific representation arises via succession of instantaneous presentational immediacies.

Schemes of presentational immediacy

$\left. \begin{array}{c} A_1 \\ B_1 \end{array} \right\}$ Events as presentationally immediate.

Life history of organism embodied in different actual occasions.[2]

Universe from point of view of A is sorted out as antecedent or succeeding.

~~Are~~ vDoV these modes of translating the universe agree with one another so that loci are identical?[3] Always assumed that they were. Now think though under certain circumstances may be same, under other circumstances not. Have here a definite structural fact – universe divided off, sorted out, arranged into a structure. Universe after millions of years pretty well structured out.

Is there any ~~⟨?⟩~~ wider significance than private minds and private worlds? Based on notion of self-existent, self-sufficient entities – which happens to nothing but mind. Knowingness disjoined from actual things. Somehow this entity has arisen from a past and is passed on. If essentially in A's nature that for A there is that structural relation, then it's a fact which to some extent enters into makeup of every other entity.

---

1. Conger marks this paragraph with a line in the left margin with the letters 'ID' next to it.
2. Given its position, this sentence is intended to reference the diagram on its left. King adds: 'A presentationally immediate to B, B need not be for A' (King, p. 61).
3. Cf. King: 'Are the loci of the two routes identical - Or are there alternate schemes of presentational immediacy. Else there are knowingnesses going on outside the universe' (King, p. 61).

|3| If concurrence of entity all with same mode of presentation, may expect with sufficient weight of such entity that that structural relation is an important physical fact. If only comparatively few, though it might be important problem for general laws of nature, it isn't.

Perhaps for some laws of nature physical relationship has to be taken account of, for other laws not. Purely a question for observation.

Sound empirical way of looking at matter. But heretical now.

Einstein orthodox way – immediate presentation; is obviously of no relevance in the formula of any law of physics. Crept in as obvious dogma from theory of private worlds. That the structure is simply product of our idle mentality. Against all anal⟨ysis?⟩ – that anything could happen to these disconnected entities.

Since it appears in what A is, the structure is not idle. Idle mentality leads to dogma.

If you make your world too private, then ~~your~~ whole of your scientific observations take place in solipsism.

Three possibilities. ⟨(1)⟩ Only one such structure; any other organism which endures through a succession is parallel to first (classical).

⟨(2)⟩ Many structures, but coordinated with each other. Special Theory of Relativity. Whitehead holds to be proper theory ⟨to?⟩ stick to.

Coordinated series of structures are important – Indefinite number, coordinated. This coordinated structure fact of different structure open to organism is of physical importance.

|4| (3) Might hold an indefinite number of such structure all non-related – very unlikely that any one structure would be of any importance whatever. Relationships competing more than reinforcing.

Mustn't fall into Newtonian fallacy – first thinking that our spatial relationships ~~re~~ made for us, then we come in.

Possibility of there being coordinated subcommunities of actual entities which call life of an electron or man – Possibility of one point inheriting intensity from predecessor. Intense inheritance so that that is practically a reproduction of that. Obviously depends on an environment which is permissive of the dominance of this historic route in its successive members.

~~What any one has to be in order to~~

You require for actual entities of importance with a depth, which sum up and integrate a past in this intense way, a favorable environment. You must be in an environment of definite species and genera whose concurrent effects are favorable to (continuation of historic route).

Only get such organisms among throngs of other organisms of same species. Electrons and protons.

Must be an organism of such a character that way you affect environment is favorable to existence of other organisms of same species. Mutually helpful. And environment must be favorable to production and origination of such entities.

Then these will be perhaps associated ~~energies~~ VspeciesV. Other ~~energies~~ VspeciesV mutually helpful.

|5| This is what we find in the world. Existence means mutual advantage. Can have bad and wicked entities. One which kills off its environment. Whitehead working up to.

This structure presentation is the evolution of that in coordination. Wasn't first the necessity of such a coordination.

The organism evolved with coordinated immediacies of presentation. <u>We are passing through a cosmological epoch</u> VinV which the organisms have evolved as part of the favorable environment [and] concurrent presentational[1] ways of stratifying the universe. <u>Coordinated ways not all same, but all very nearly same. Each entity must take account of this fact of evolution</u>. Been going on for uncounted billions of years. Spatiality of presentation and structural coordination is not an abstract metaphysical necessity, but a fact of evolution, but one of the first physical facts in the universe and is there and practically dominates the universe as we know ⟨it⟩.

{?} Has been trying to get imaginations right. <u>Spatial facts have been evolved</u>. Otherwise dull.

Thursday, 13 January 1927

Conger's notes

|1| Classical theory: every entity only one VlocusV ofV immediate presentation.

A structural system which sorts out in its structure every event in the universe – classical view of time – an infinity of instantaneous three-dimensional spaces.[2]

If ask what is a moment of time – the line is a moment of time. The objective entity is instantaneous locus. <u>Nothing to correlate one position Von a lineV with another – nor is there any principle or relationship indicated whereby you can get any differentiation with respect to moment of time</u>. Principle by which geometry of any system of entities is established.

Notion of straight line is simply correlated with nothing else. Notion of motion from this point of view nothing so far as we've gone. In an instantaneous space you are where you are. Series of atomic static universes.

Bergson's complaint. Philosophers hold up ⟨space⟩ [time into ∧space?∧]. First place, presentation is not instantaneous space without time thickness – always a time thickness and the possibility of division which is not <u>actual</u>.[3]

---

1. Two marks appear before the word 'presentational' which could either be an orphaned quotation mark or a ditto mark that could conceivably refer to 'evolved', which appears directly above it. Neither seem likely.
2. In King's notes (p. 62), the diagram on the left represents 'simultaneity of three-dimensional space'.
3. Given its position, the second half of this sentence is intended to reference the diagram on its left.

281

Define instantaneous space at the limit – *Concept of Nature*.[1] {Consider accuracy next semester}

Besides new presentation, each time have another experience of rest and motion.

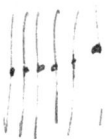
Life history of an entity.[2] There is the experience of a uniformity of condition. Its general relationship, structural system of the universe is unchanged. Uniformity of condition in the structural scheme as thus exhibited gives <u>rest</u>. ∧Motion a case of rest∧.

So soon as you admit that system then ∨(Are there?)∨ Alternative system of moments – first hypothesis (classical assumption) only one. But are there alternative renderings of the idea of rest? Have idea there are modes of rest of same species and no change of general relationship.

|2| But can have a mode of rest of another species ∨in that case∨.[3]

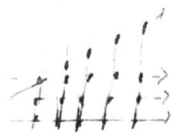
On classical system, if one entity has mode of rest of one species and another of another, then relatively to each other they have uniform velocity.

A mode of rest gives you a mode of correlated different points in successive instantaneous spaces. <u>Apart from some experience relating one to the other then, you would have no correlation.</u>

These instantaneous spaces are limits.

Experience of universe as within epochal occasion is rest.

One act objectified for another – not detached experience ∨(Look out for world of detached bits like Descartes)∨.[4] We have straight lines in time, but not any in space. Must think of all time lines as same. Shows how inadequate a myth (diagram) is likely to be.

When we say anything is at rest, we can say at one point, but then think of common space acting, which has <u>impartial</u> connection with every moment of time. Or might say physical space – space of physical science. Space in which you say planets have an orbit.

---

1. Conger clearly writes 'Concepn' for 'Conception', but this would appear to be a reference to *Concept of Nature*. Whitehead discusses instantaneous space a great deal therein, especially in the fourth chapter, 'The method of extensive abstraction'.
2. See the figure on the left.
3. 'in that case' actually appears before or above the rest of this sentence, but we are place it here under the assumption that it was a later interlineation.
4. Parentheses supplied. The parenthetical text appears in the right margin.
Cf. King: 'The antecedent experience is demonstrated in the next, and is the demonstration, in one unity. Otherwise, the real world is in detached bits, and the relations are of inferior reality. (Leibniz)' (King, p. 62).

Then must say is one point. So a point in the impartial space must be a row, route from entity which is at rest in the general structural system.

All the points in an impartial space must be the points of bodies at rest according to same species of rest. Each species of rest[1] has own impartial relative space. Every motion relative. No such thing as rest.[2] There are different species of rest, and every species has own special ⟨impartial⟩[3] space.

|3| Take a body with another species of rest. What is that doing in our space? Moving in straight line with uniform velocity.

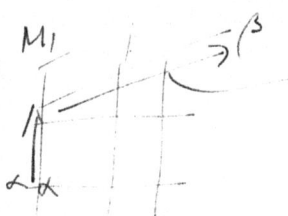

From every point event which ~~calls~~ forms β point, draw an α point – you have projected. Track in μ, which is projection of β point. α points have projected β points onto μ_1. A track with a whole system of other tracks.[4] Two entities at rest in same system never meet, but go on. Perfectly obvious that projection of tracks is straight line:

M_1 is instantaneous straight line. Definition of straight line – vEuclid:v a straight line lies evenly between its two points. Straightness of straight line comes from fact that when you stand and look down track, what you see is not what the lorry is going down, you see M_1.

Road M_1 is immediate diagram representation of what the lorry is going to do.

and say that's the road the lorry is going down

but lorry actually goes down this track

A straight line in α v⟨impartial?⟩v space is a locus of points which intercept[5] a point in some other (β) space. All diagrams instantaneous.

Existence of straight lines – Not first the straight line and then thing moving uniformly in it. Thing moving has uniform relation to whole, and by interplay of those relations have straight lines. |4| That is why notion of rest or uniform motion is so fundamental. No difference between rest and uniform motion.

Get congruence. ∧All∧ α points will project β points into parallel straight lines. Congruence really comes from opposite sides of square equal. Further difficulty – this merely tells you how to get square equal. Will have difficulty in saying what you mean by congruence of lines

---

1. King (p. 63) has 'system at rest'.
2. Cf. King: 'No absolute rest' (King, p. 63).
3. Conger has 'important' here, but King's 'impartial' (p. 63) seems rather more likely.
4. Cf. King: 'Each β point can be projected into the α system – projected on to another track. . . . The instantaneous straight lines are the projection of the tracks' (King, p. 63).
5. King (p. 63) has 'intersect'.

which aren't parallel. Congruence comes from having structure and saying two stretches have analogous functionings in same systematic structure.

There will be a characteristic velocity which will express difference between the times.

No principle which gives you relation of these lengths.[1]

You can get a space congruence, but can't state what time congruence is. Must be some principle because do measure pp time. Glimmer of how to run a theory of congruence.

If once assume rest or uniform motion, get reason why should be kind of geometry there is. Reason why straight lines are of such importance stands out. Ought to have relation between α system of rest and β system should correspond to a velocity V. Vαβ

Now ask where a modern relativity theory would differ. Modern relativity theory: if say there are alternative rest points and meanings of rest, but alternative species of these instantaneous moments[2]

|5| Alternative systems of spatial specification. Now what say? Have to ask about different species of rest. Each species of rest ⟨is⟩ correlated with the species of presentation.[3]

α rest system which has a peculiar correlation with α presentational system – ~~In (?)~~ An entity at rest in α-rest has α presentation moments for its immediately presented universe. β system – come up against α system scissorwise. α and β have different presentation system.

Physical spaces ⟨and times⟩[4] will differ very much more from each other.[5]

In the new system the instantaneous presentation lines differ – special theory of relativity.

One entity looking on its instantaneous spaces coming one way, other the other.[6]

Special relativity not very greater paradoxes than classical theory of relativity.

Even on ordinary theory, must say different impartial spaces according to different systems of rest.

---

1. Given its position, this sentence is intended to reference the diagram on its right.
2. It is unclear if the first sentence on the page following is intended to be a continuation of this sentence.
3. King (p. 64) has 'presentation system'.
4. Supplied from King (p. 64).
5. There is an odd mark that may be a question mark here, but it is unclear.
6. Cf. King: 'For each entity, time is successive, but the spaces come down on each differently' (King, p. 64).

Saturday, 15 January 1927

Conger's notes

|1| According to Newton's laws, no physical way of judging what is at rest and what isn't. Motion is essentially relative.[1]

Question whether ⟨?⟩ the entity α is at rest or not is being argued by a and b.[2]

According to A B has moved upwards.[3]

$QA = X_\alpha$
$QB = X_\beta$

Q is man's position at time T.

$X_\alpha - X_\beta = AB$
$\qquad\qquad = Vt$

Alternative way[4]

Different presentations. Immediate present to one may be different from other – X_α would say one is immediate, one would say other – ~~So differences~~ So antecedence would depend on what was present.

Whitehead – two meanings of "present". In one meaning a number of other entities compresent with it in sense of not being antecedently causal. α and β differ as to which of the compresent entities they select for presentational immediacy.

Now to get coherent theory of time which agrees with physical science.

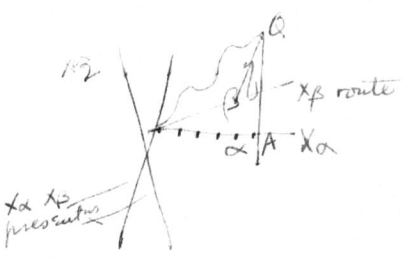

Two species of rest, one associated is mode of presentation X_α, other with X_β. If ask what entities use one, what the other – An organism propagating itself along historic route at rest with regard to X_α will have so adapted self as to use X_α presentation. X_β ~~mode~~ route will use X_β presentation. If use one for your space, corresponding one for time, etc.

Both α and β will have say about specifying Q, and also time at which he arrived at Q.[5]

---

1. King (p. 64) labels the vertical axis 'x' and origin 'o'. He then writes that 'Q moving more slowly to B by virtue of the relation AB with which he pursues it. xo = one-dimensional space. A system of rest in respect to xo.'
2. Given its position, this sentence is intended to reference the diagram on its right.
3. It is not clear whether this is meant to be segment 'AB' or points 'A, B', that is, A relative to B.
4. In the diagram below, 'Sp' means 'space-time'.
5. King's notes (p. 64) spell out that 'X here stands for space and the 't' below for time.

$OA = t_\alpha$

$QA = X_\alpha$

β is looking along the road (in one-dimensional space). β according to A has yet different dates on road, not a one-dated road. Can't get different immediate occasions under same date.

β must use time t_β and $t_\alpha \neq t_\beta$ $QB = X_B$

|2| Not only are a and b in first diagram at odds as to what is to be called rest point (in different meanings of rest), but agreed on common one of time and agreed about one dated presentation of universe. Second set disagree about one dated presentation of universe, and that leads them to differ as to their time.

Must have some principle according to which get these relationships. What relationships are there between t_α and X_α, t_β and X_β? Each pair corresponds to same Q. Might say no relationship; but if whole thing were haphazard, obvious that your measurements will have no relation to the universe.

Mathematical physics is possible. There is a science of measurement which will give you important information about what is going on in the universe are implicated according to some general systematic fashion.

Einstein laid down <u>space-time principle</u>. Newton got at it for particular case, but no one realized what fundamental principle it was. Einstein made it fundamental.

Einstein: no reason for taking α form of rest and presentation as preeminent to other or vice-versa.[1]

Take some idea which has haunted thought like a ghost. Man of genius takes it by neck and makes something of it.

A law of nature expressed in terms of ~~those~~ ∨one set of∨ two measurements ought to be expressed exactly same in other – ought to be expressed according to an invariant mode.[2]

Newton: $f = ma$. ∨ $\underline{X_\alpha \text{ is distance}}$ ∨ $\underline{X_\alpha \text{ on road is moving with rate } \dot{X}_\alpha}$ (acceleration velocity), and acceleration is rate of change of velocity $\ddot{X}_\alpha$.

Also have X_β $\dot{X}_\beta$ $\ddot{X}_\beta$

In first diagram, one man will think Q is going faster by reason of own ~~rate~~ ∧velocity∧.[3]

$\dot{X}_\alpha - \dot{X}_\beta = V$

$\ddot{X}_\alpha - \ddot{X}_\beta = 0$

|3| If your laws of motion had to deal with ~~laws of motion~~ ∧velocity∧ only, come out with expression for force in different forms. Velocity doesn't govern force, but acceleration. And ~~{?}~~ no difference of accelerations, so you have an invariant law.

mass $x \ddot{x} \alpha$ = force

mass $x \ddot{x} \beta$ = force

---

1. There are lines here pointing back to '$t\alpha$ and $X\alpha$, $t\beta$ and $X\beta$'. This sentence was clearly added later in pencil.
2. Cf. King: 'In transferring from one set of coordinates to another, the laws would be the same if we merely substitute the different values' (King, p. 65).
3. King's notes (p. 65) label the first expression below as 'velocity', and the second as 'acceleration'. Conger has an odd line here somewhat below and to the right of the 'V' which could conceivably be a subscript '1', but may instead be a line connecting the 'V' and '0'.

Modern mathematical physicist trying to get laws into invariant form which does not depend on mode of measurement.[1] In second case the time is not the same. Can't make this form[2] invariant if t alters as well as x.

Electromagnetism between Newton and Einstein. ~~These~~ Clerk Maxwell's equations not invariant for old classical theory V(when put in connection between α and β).[3] β man has different equations from α.

People said in addition to space there is ether of space – there is a predominant system of rest, rest relatively to ether.[4] Clerk Maxwell's laws ⟨hold?⟩ for the system at rest relatively to ether. So ~~on assumption that~~ laws will ~~get~~ take different form for man moving relatively to ether. Might say α in first diagram at rest in ether, β at rest on earth. Wouldn't get same laws because V would turn up – Laws different, phenomenon would be different.

But Michelson–Morley experiment[5] (~~many~~ others ∧too∧). Evidence is no velocity of Earth ⟨relative to ether⟩[6] (though evidence a little wavering). Might say sun is practically at rest in ether – but then ~~relation~~ velocity of Earth in its orbit altered, and variation with direction of Earth six months apart. Always possibility of velocity of sun taking whole thing along.

Miller – you do observe a velocity at top of Mt. Wilson. Someone else recently more careful experiment and doesn't observe it.[7]

Mass of experiments of others show in some way or other you must neglect fact of Earth moving through ether. What you ought to observe isn't observed.

Einstein – <u>These electromagnetic equations are fundamental equations and not mass · acceleration = force</u>. Electromagnetic equations ought to be invariant.

|4| What relation between $t_\alpha \cdot X_\alpha$ and $t_\beta X_\beta$ will make Einstein's equations invariant,[8] so get same laws either way? – Bring in a velocity which is practically ~~etc~~ velocity of light *in vacuo*. Only practically, because gravitation will interfere. c ⟨= velocity of light⟩.[9]

$$\sigma = \frac{1}{\sqrt{1 - \left(\frac{V}{c}\right)^2}} \qquad t_\beta = \sigma \left(t_\alpha - \frac{V x_\alpha}{c^2} \right)$$

$$X_\beta = \sigma (X_\alpha - V t_\alpha)$$

---

1. Cf. King: 'In reference to relativity, science tries to make its laws invariable' (King, p. 65).
2. A line points back to the expression 'mass $x \ddot{x} \alpha$ = force'.
3. Parentheses supplied.
4. Cf. King: 'After Maxwell's electromagnetic equations, it was said there was one predominant system of rest relative to the ether' (King, p. 65).
5. An 1887 experiment by Albert A. Michelson (1852–1931) and Edward W. Morley (1838–1923) that attempted to detect the existence of ether by comparing the speed of light in perpendicular directions.
6. Supplied from King (p. 65).
7. Dayton Clarence Miller (1866–1941) conducted more experiments with Morley from 1902 to 1904, and more again at the Mount Wilson Observatory in 1921 and 1925–6. Whitehead discussed Miller's findings in the final lecture of his first year. See HL1, p. 403. The 'someone else' here may refer to the 1926 experiment of Roy J. Kennedy (1897–1986) at Pasadena and Mount Wilson. See Kennedy, 'A refinement of the Michelson–Morley experiment', available at <https://www.ncbi.nlm.nih.gov/pmc/articles/PMC1084733/pdf/pnas01848-0007.pdf>.
8. King (p. 65) has '$t_\alpha v_\alpha$ and $t_\beta v_\beta$'.
9. Supplied from King (p. 65).

These relations chosen because make electro-magnetic equations invariant.

If c is very large, σ nearly ⟨unity?⟩ and in ordinary motions come down to $(X_\alpha - X_\beta = AB = Vt)$ of first diagram.[1]

But in refinements, modern physicists must take something else.

For small velocities fraction ~~large~~ small, square of fraction smaller. Little taken from one, square almost one, quotient almost one.

$$\frac{2}{4} + \frac{2}{5} = \frac{10}{20} + \frac{8}{20}$$

$$t = \frac{l}{c+v} + \frac{l}{c-v} = \frac{2lc}{c^2 - v^2} \quad \frac{-lc-vc+lc+vc}{c^2+v^2}$$

$$\frac{2lc}{c^2-v^2} = \frac{2l}{c} \frac{1}{1-v^2/c^2}$$

---

1. Parentheses supplied. Cf. King (pp. 64, 65).

Philosophy 3b Mid-Year Exam 1926-7

HARVARD UNIVERSITY

PHILOSOPHY 3b

At least four of these questions are to be answered.

1. Discuss the method of the establishment of truth by the rational coördination of propositions. Contrast the influence of mathematics in Greek philosophy with that of natural science in the modern epoch. Consider the following statement:— "A self-satisfied rationalism is in effect a form of anti-rationalism. It means an arbitrary halt at a particular set of abstractions."
2. Discuss the influence on philosophy arising from the importance assigned to the subject-predicate form of proposition in Aristotelian logic.
3. All actual entities in space and time can be demonstrated, relatively to each other, by analogous processes of spatial measurement:—Discuss whether or no such a claim [implicit in the use of coördinates in mathematical physics] presupposes that space and time possess some uniform structural character.
4. State and discuss the lecturer's theory as to the relationships between events which constitute the notions of past, present, and future.
5. Discuss the theory that the general space of physical science is a logical construct from more primary elements in experience:— namely, 'rest, i.e., uniformity of condition' and the succession of instantaneous spatial presentations of concurrent events. Explain also the further doctrine that 'rest' is a generic notion with diverse specific exemplifications, and that there are a corresponding diversity of 'physical' spaces. Further point out where, on this theory, the divergence between the 'classical' notion and the modern 'relativity' notion of space-time arises.
6. Explain, with your own comments, the lecturer's doctrine that an 'actual entity' is an act of experience, and that the universals [i.e. 'eternal objects'] are relational elements whereby each such act is both a perceptual consequence of the community of acts and a conceptual analysis of its own concrescence.[1]

---

1. Unlike the previous year's mid-term exam, this exam was marked at the bottom of the first page as 'Nº 25', perhaps to make sure that all exams were returned.

|2|
7. Discuss, with your own critical comments, the notion of 'experience' which is explicit or implicit in the system of any one philosopher.
8. Explain the difficulties arising in connection with the justification of Inductive Reasoning. Consider what conditions the datum for observational knowledge must satisfy in order that there can be any such justification. Consider the doctrine of any one philosopher on this topic.
9. Perception is the fundamental physical relation; mental functioning supervenes in the form of conceptual analysis:—explain this doctrine of the lecturer's, point out its bearing on the doctrine of primary and secondary qualities, and give your own comments.
10. Potency refers to the continuum of nature, Act to community of atomic creatures. Potency is the character of the creativity due to the creatures. Explain this doctrine pointing out its bearing (a) on the logical inconsistency in the notion of a continuous becoming of an extended continuity of creatures, (b) on the doctrine of an evolution of laws of nature, (c) on the meaning of 'future.'

Mid-Year. 1927.

Harvard lectures, spring semester 1927

Thursday, 24 February 1927

Conger's notes[1]

|1| Most general ideas wanted in science, and investigate those ideas and try to get on same plane, show identity with ultimate metaphysical ideas.

(⟨Eccentric?⟩, ⟨concentric?⟩, geometry, algebra, logic, complete treatment of pragmatism later.)[2]

Will find in philosophy that there have been many schools of divergence from Cartesian, Newtonian school of thought which depends on notion of stuff or extension. Of course there have been midway schools. Characteristic of German schools – had to bolt its science whole. Their entity no reference to science.[3] Bosanquet. Science dealing with ~~empirical~~ something lower.

Now try develop some system ⟨to⟩ avoid difficulties on which old naïve materialism split, and at same time find self with that close contact with fundamental notions of science. ~~As soon as~~ Criticism turned edge of philosophy away from particular ideas which you find at beginning of ~~meta~~physics.[4] Descartes' metaphysics and physics continuous.[5] Bradley looks through from wrong end of telescope – ∨I seeV very diminutive little thing which you people call science.

Ideas on philosophy method now in different form – Two ways of getting general ideas on universe. When you come to apply them to every topic – you can't adequately analyze every topic of your experience and find general ideas fall out.[6] Bacon way.[7]

At some stage you must make an imaginative leap. You must say, "By Jove, I believe it's this"[8] – imaginative leap beyond your evidence, and that elucidates the whole of your experience.

---

1. There are four sets of notes available for this term: Conger's notes are used as the primary account for 11 lectures, King's for 3 lectures and Weiss's for the remaining 13 lectures, while Burch's notes are never used as the primary account. Refer to the table on p. 418 for a full list of spring semester 1927 Harvard lectures by note-taker and date, and see also the Introduction for a detailed discussion of each note-taker and their notes.
2. Parentheses supplied. This sentence was originally written in the top right corner of the notes with a line around it.
3. Cf. King: 'Characteristic of German idealism is, it had to bolt its science. Its entities had little to do with what the men of science talk' (King, p. 66).
4. Cf. King: 'Berkeley and following edged away from the primary data of science' (King, p. 66).
5. Cf. King: 'For Descartes his metaphysics began where his physics ended' (King, p. 66).
6. Cf. Weiss: 'Two ways to approach the universe – Analyze particular cases and get the general law' (Weiss, p. 50).
7. Whitehead had harshly criticised Baconian induction during the fall semester. See the 19 October 1926 lecture, note 5, p. 193.
8. Quotation marks supplied.

Two ways in which imagination works. *Science and the Modern World*,¹ imaginative makeup of modern science was very akin to the imaginative makeup of great Athenian tragedians.² Tragic method: inevitable premises which govern the universe. Then you combine those premises in law v(motion {?} moral law)v,³ then given matter of fact, and then there is the necessary development which issues from that particular initial matter of fact under sway of inevitable premises {This is the tragedy of the universe}. Essence of tragedy is inevitableness.

In all forms of religion.
    Augustine's doctrine of grace⁴
    Calvin
    Catholic Controversy
    Jansenism,⁵ Jesuits
    Pascal an Augustinian, tragic view.

Jesuits had the <u>epic</u> view of the universe. A few great epics and <u>half-epics</u>. Homeric epics standard. By Plato and Aristotle's time, epic influence superseded by tragic. Aristotelian philosophy made up under influence of drama. Everything had its final end and was in great hurry to get there. |2| It also had its fixed beginnings – categories, premises. Also (in Plato) the influence of mathematics. Aristotle was a tragic philosopher. Plato not to same extent. Every religion likely to wither unless revise morals of its gods, which are likely to be the morals of a barbaric people. Plato unduly swayed by mathematical method.

In view of myth, had ~~in~~ epic point of view. For epic begins in <u>medias res</u>. Tragedy is unfolding of inevitableness inherent in a given situation. Epic is adventure in ~~unknown~~ partially unknown. *Pilgrim's Progress* is half epic. Intensity of imagination with regard to the adventure. Faerie Queene. Essence of epic – don't know where you are.⁶

There are categories which we can approximate to, but it's difficult to get them straight. Material on which they must be tested and from which they are to be elicited is overwhelming. From a partial survey of the material, have to make imaginative leap which even then can't see has given us final and necessary truth, but "adventurous truth" which works out as far as you can see, but which probably leaves some rough edges.⁷ The philosophy of adventure must start from some particular topic and endeavor to elicit categories which then it hopes will be elucidatory throughout the whole of the truth. Tending towards the truth.

---

1. The discussion of tragedy here at times tracks quite closely with Whitehead's discussion in the first chapter of *Science and the Modern World*, entitled 'The origins of modern science'.
2. King's notes (p. 66) add: 'Fate there, gravitation here'.
3. Parentheses supplied.
4. Cf. King: 'Augustinian view – inevitable, irresistible grace' (King, p. 66).
5. Jansenism was a 17th- and 18th-century French theological movement arising from the work of Cornelius Jansen (1585–1638) which emphasised human depravity and the necessity of divine grace, including Augustinian predestination.
6. Cf. Weiss: 'The essence of tragedy is inevitableness – has beginning and end. Epic is adventurous, begins in middle – goes to the unknown' (Weiss, p. 50).
7. Weiss's notes (p. 50) make clear that Whitehead is still discussing the 'epic view of philosophy' here.

Last term started in medias res with categories not very {?} precisely defined. Give metaphysical description which would work best over all the fields of thought. This time start with scientific ideas and analyze with some care. See how they fit on to categories with which dealing. Science deals with extensive magnitude and ∨we∨ must start with topic of extension, with certain definite notions about number.[1]

Lloyd Morgan, Aristotelian Society 1926–7, preface to *Science and the Modern World*, acknowledge indebtedness to Lloyd Morgan. "Objects under reference," accepts formulation of extension – gives his working out of way in which must get point of view of *Science and the Modern World*.[2]

Reading
Hy(?)
Broad, chapters I–II[3]
Concept of Nature, ⟨chapter⟩ III
|3| Lloyd Morgan is admirable summary of what Whitehead was lecturing last session.

Whitehead,[4] *Introduction to Mathematics*, chapters I–VI, XII, XV.
Concept of Nature – pp. 47–48, Chapters III–IV, p. 197 note on Greek concept of a point.

Broad's *Scientific Thought*, read some of beginning, then read ~~Par~~ some of Part II.

Another very excellent book.
Metaphysical Foundations of Modern Science, E.A. Burtt.[5] He deals with people like Newton, Descartes, Galileo. A very excellent book and quite easy reading.

Meanwhile going to start with notion of extension with rather the scientific point of view. One evil of older ∧tragic∧ view of philosophy was that in dealing with topic of extension, thought when you had {?} uttered space geometry-extension, you were dealing with something which had to be all – the axioms of <u>extension</u> the axioms of <u>geometry</u>.

---

1. King has 'definite notions of number, pure math' (p. 66), while Weiss has 'pure number' (p. 50).
2. C. Lloyd Morgan (1852–1936) was a British ethologist, psychologist and philosopher who served as the President of the Aristotelian Society 1926–7 and was highly sympathetic to Whitehead's work. Weiss's notes (p. 50) confirm that Whitehead is referring to Morgan's presidential address to the Society delivered on 1 November 1926, 'Objects under reference', in which he explicitly discusses and adapts some of Whitehead's ideas from *Science and the Modern World*. For his part, Whitehead had noted in the preface to that book that 'There has been no occasion in the text to make detailed reference to Lloyd Morgan's *Emergent Evolution* or to Alexander's *Space, Time and Deity*. It will be obvious to readers that I have found them very suggestive' (p. xi). Morgan published another article, 'A concept of the organism, emergent and resultant', in the same issue of the *Proceedings of the Aristotelian Society* that featured his address, in which he again explicitly discusses Whitehead's ideas from *Science and the Modern World*; it was originally delivered on 14 February 1927, just 10 days before this lecture.
3. Conger does not write the name of the book here, but he has it as *Scientific Thought* below, which is surely what he is referencing here. See Broad, *Scientific Thought*, available at <https://archive.org/details/in.ernet.dli.2015.6694>.
4. The words '10 more' appear below 'Whitehead' and to the left of '*Concept of Nature*'. Its meaning and proper placement are not clear.
5. Edwin Arthur Burtt (1892–1989) was an American philosopher. See Burtt, *The Metaphysical Foundations of Modern Physical Science*, available at <https://archive.org/details/metaphysicalfoun00burtuoft>.

ⱽThere areⱽ several layers of ideas and independent of each other. Most general view genus extension, special type which in science we are interested might still be extensive universe in another cosmical epoch.

Organisms arise out of environment in which they maintain their existence, but by their very existence they impose a character on the environment, so environment and organism evolve together. Only thing is, if you devote your attention to a few thousand million, they perhaps may be not enough to sway. Must look on it from big point of view.

Mankind alien intrusive organism having hard struggle in protons and electrons.

Perhaps when enough the type of extensiveness of this world will gradually alter.

At present we are in that type which arises from electromagnetic organisms of protons and electrons. A special type of extensiveness. First more general, then specific.

|4| Present epoch for us as individuals is given. As a sufficient ⟨?⟩ throng of organisms might change.

Explain what we mean by accuracy. No good saying if had practical training, you'd know no experiment is accurate. But how can an experiment be inaccurate unless there is an <u>ideal of accuracy</u> to which can approximate.

In dealing with extension and measurement, we always haunted by idea that measurements are inaccurate and might be more accurate.

Saturday, 26 February 1927

Conger's notes

|1| Type of transformation of an alternative way of putting things which best suits modern science and set it against 16th and 17th ⟨century⟩ ∧(admirably described by E.A. Burtt)∧.[1] I agree at many points.

(Take up 19th century of an aether.)[2]

Descartes' vortices something like a plenum.[3] Newton – receptacle notion in which there were casually bits of matter. Had matter and then ⟨?⟩ forces between them. <u>Simple location</u>.

(19th century view of light as bombardment helped empty space point of view.)[4]

---

1. Whitehead is likely referring to Burtt's *The Metaphysical Foundations of Modern Physical Science*, which he had assigned during the previous lecture.
2. Parentheses supplied.
3. Cf. King: 'Whitehead agrees with Descartes in making space an essential plenum' (King, p. 66).
4. Parentheses supplied.

Newton himself doubted about mere empty space. Cotes[1] too, Clarke[2] too. Newton also had the push-pull theory.

Boscovich [SJ.(?)][3] Gravitation due to little corpuscles lying about. Phenomenon of interference and diffraction made corpuscular theory apparently unable to explain finer experiments.[4]

Wave theory of light, if take view of wanting stuff seemed to require an ether. Ether brought in to provide noun[5] for verb to "undulate."

Theory of elastic solid. <u>Clerk Maxwell</u>. Strains and stresses in all-pervading stuff set up and maintained in elastic solid. Couldn't prove exactly what matter was, and was correlated with ether in such a way as to maintain strains and stresses. Clerk Maxwell showed strains and stresses which would be required for electro-magnetic phenomenon, if had anything vibratory would send a vibration through the ether. Proved by taking electro-magnetic vibrations that these waves would follow through matter with velocity of light. Therefore waves of light are waves of electro-magnetic vibration of the ether and of the electro-magnetic stresses. Had been explaining universe in terms of ideas which are matters of brought under your perception, e.g. elastic rod.

Fundamental Newtonian idea, the constancy of mass. Energy began to be constant. Apparently as much or little ∧fundamental as constitution of mass.∧ Potential energy – Kinetic energy. Desperate attempt to express energy in terms of mass. Kelvin. Ether frictionless, continuous medium with vortices (bits of matter).[6] |2| vKelvinv failed to get in touch with facts of nature.

Idea of essential continuity of things got knocked on head by electrons and protons, apparently little bundles. ⟨Essential⟩[7] atomicity.

Little billiard balls with bands between them for chemical affinity – gave way to molecule – scene of intense electro-magnetic activity. Electricity dissolved into something atomic, scene of intense activity.[8] {?} Then have belief – final result – the table as <u>continuous</u> physical entity is a sheer fake.

Not an interaction of definite quantums. Never get down to a pure nominative case, but an interaction of functionings. Always functioning going on. That being the case, the ether as continuous stuff (as nominative case) so

---

1. Conger wrote 'Coates' here, but it is likely Whitehead was referring to Roger Cotes (1682–1716), an English mathematician known for working closely with Newton by proofreading the second edition of the *Principia*. This is confirmed by reference to Cotes in Burtt's *Metaphysical Foundations* (p. 287). See note 5, p. 293.
2. Burtt's book (p. 21) references 'Newton's theological champion, Samuel Clarke'. Clarke (1675–1729) was an English philosopher and Anglican priest who famously conversed with Leibniz about Newtonian physics during the years 1715 and 1716.
3. Roger Joseph Boscovich (1711–87) was a Jesuit physicist and philosopher.
4. Cf. King: 'The corpuscular theory left empty space between the little corpuscles' (King, p. 66).
5. Cf. King: 'subject' (King, p. 67).
6. William Thomson, 1st Baron Kelvin (1824–1907), was an Irish mathematical physicist. Whitehead may be referring to the lecture he gave on 27 April 1900 entitled 'Nineteenth century clouds over the dynamical theory of heat and light', available at <https://books.google.com/books?id=YvoAAAAAYAAJ&pg=PA363> (last accessed 2 September 2020).
7. Conger wrote 'especial atomicity', but King's notes have the altogether more likely 'essential atomicity' (p. 67).
8. Cf. King: 'Matter dissolved into electricity, which is dissolved into atoms – internal activity' (King, p. 67).

far from being a transcript of immediate experience is now something very different.

~~Hasn't the color~~ Color depends on state of my body.[1] That which we see as continuous depends on state of body. Only ⟨prereq?⟩[2] of light is normal way in which sensa of sight comes. As long as light enters, I see you – no matter whether you're there.

Idea of continuous ether as peculiarly sane explanation based on immediate experience has gone to pieces. Probably partly arose as interpretation of immediate experience.

Don't quite sympathize with animal faith. vWhiteheadv objects to view of unknown x which is merely nominative case.

Can define what we mean by things going on without reference to blank bare stuff, but require notion of actual entity which emerges from a potentiality.

Can define an ether of events as an alternative to an ether of stuff. No mere blank x underlying it. No blank sheer substance underlying attributes. There is an actual entity which is only to be described in terms of activity. Activity of actual entity both produces self as actual entity – produces itself out of vpastv conditions. Activity of synthesis out of which actual entity arises. In realizing potentialities it inherits from the past. |3| Produces something out of which next actual entity arises.

In that way you can provide both for continuum and atomic quantum, both of which appear to be absolutely inherent in nature.

~~The~~ From a given standpoint looking on world as having advanced these conditions of immediate future, potentiality only to be described in form of continuum, but group of actual entities which thereby arise are definite quanta determined by ⟨the conditions of the past⟩[3] and also what is added to potential conditions out of which they arise in the act of self-creation.

If going to hold to strict determinism. Water arises according to these conditions and is fully determined according to those conditions. If hold freedom or contingency, will hold there is a self creation – Act of arising, being a final entity has a reflexive knowledge of self, of what it is coming to, and add to own determination in forming itself. Not in time but really a ⟨past?⟩[4]...

Potentiality determined by how organism takes self, judges itself in this non-temporal process as being itself. Organism always highly complex. Added another creative determination to world, and potentiality immediately beyond itself is complete as a potentiality, and a new actual entity thereby arises.[5]

So have possibility of there being a certain self-judgment as to what you are.

Actual entity is just a limited occasion, and then when have low-grade actual entity, its self-judgment or self-feeling is negligible, and thereby

---

1. Cf. King: 'What we perceive depends on the state of our body' (King, p. 67).
2. This might conceivably by 'prerog', though that seems less likely.
3. Conger has 'and conditioned upon' here, which appears to be somewhat confused. The supply is from Burch (p. 65), and is corroborated by Weiss (p. 50), who did not have 'conditions of', but did have 'determined by the past'.
4. This might be 'part', though that seems less likely.
5. Conger places a line and a roman number 'III' in the left margin next to this paragraph.

perhaps nothing is added to potentiality which arises. If high-grade, may have something else.

|4| Finally the potentiality handed on to next act is strictly determined by the past, and potentiality which stretches into future always to be looked on under guise of continuum, and actual entity is always to be looked on under guise of a quantum.

Always find quanta, atoms, and always find aspect of nature which is just to be looked on as continuous. It is for science to disentangle where quantum is relevant and important, and where potentiality stretching into future is important.[1]

Self building up of actual entity as ⟨of?⟩[2] energy of dynamo or judgment, and control by reason, freedom, etc. Whichever of these two alternatives take will be landed in difficulty.

Mathematician great difficulty to put into words.

1. The one genus of physical facts with like materialists and ether people – only one genus of physical facts.[3] May be characteristics of that genus which are negligible for certain purposes and stages, but fundamentally, all facts are same genus.

Descartes starts that way. vPracticallyv all physical facts about corporeal substance. Folly to quibble about words – if you call corporeal substance what I call objectification, the ⟨?⟩ which has arisen (ox).

Actual entity itself emerges from creative activity which has welded together its characteristics into a unity. Substance arises from activity which is synthesizing the attributes, not attributes emerging from substance.

Tuesday, 1 March 1927

Conger's notes

|1| Table seat of violent activity of minute organisms.[4] Far as we can penetrate there is always functioning. Sweet simplicity of starting from what hard-boiled man has to admit has been lost. In approaching metaphysics from point of view of science, ought to take hold at start and generalize something which is part of ordinary experience and which hasn't been explained away by science. Try avoid telling a fairy tale. We Fundamental idea which we have is that of an actual entity. vE.g.v Ourselves as actual entity in a community of actual entities. When get down to what Santayana calls vulgar experience.

---

1. Conger writes '(actual entity)' in the left margin next to this sentence.
2. Two words appear above 'entity as ⟨of?⟩' and to the right and end of the preceding sentence. They could be 'look on', 'hook on' or even 'book on'. The proper placement and meaning are unclear.
3. Cf. Burch: 'Whitehead agrees with the principle upheld by nineteenth century materialists, that there is only one genus of physical facts' (Burch, p. 65).
4. Burch begins the lecture with some material which none of the others has: 'The seventeenth century metaphysical foundation of science was good for 300 years – proof of its great merit. They attempted to start from something which is in our immediate knowledge. But now we look on a physical object not as a continuous corporeal reality only relatively at rest, but as a violent activity of infinitesimal organisms' (Burch, p. 65). Meanwhile, the first line in Weiss's notes is: 'Body not continuous' (Weiss, p. 51).

When ask what you mean by actual entity since any actual entity which manifests self to us in physical world, ought primarily to have recourse to ourselves. There I am with Descartes. When Descartes had recourse to self only found a mind; later he did find a body, but wasn't so certain of it as mind – anyhow he said he wasn't. I think it was.

What we know of ourselves isn't a mysterious substratum with enormous and very doubtfully remembered life history, an *x* which is decorated with transient qualities, but which gets its character and principal[1] attribute from something, it always comes with it – <u>but</u> what we find is what Descartes managed to maintain, a happy ambiguity. [necessary for system].

What Descartes ⟨ought to ⟨have⟩⟩ found is an act of experience vaguely delimited from predecessors and successors. I am now conscious of an act of experience – that is an actual entity. ⟨?⟩ Descartes as living ~~ought to have~~ from a baby to an elderly man has to be explained as a particularly linked succession of acts of experience, such that each act with a succeeding act in peculiar degree integrates and issues from the antecedents. Actual entity is a succession of acts of experience.

Then when ask what act of experience is, having regard to knowledge of physical world, what we find is primarily it's a taking account of other actual entities. It's consciousness of our taking account of other actual entities. Analyzable into many ~~act~~ parts, but a certain unification and togetherness which issues in a certain vivid intensity, |2| a certain self ⟨?⟩ realization of value. A value is that which contributes to an intensity – ~~an element~~. A value is an element contributing to an intensity. There is a certain real togetherness of that which can be analyzed ⟨but?⟩ which issues in one entity. The entity arises out of a constitutive activity and issues from a type of element which are ~~not~~ themselves entities. Actual world is constituted by solidarity of actual entity. Solidarity is that each actual entity arises as an intensity for its own sake which comes from its taking account of other actual entities, and in so taking account, the creativity or activity of synthesis which created it thereby receives a new character from its own existence. Every actual entity adds creative character to world and passes on to entities beyond ⟨?⟩ itself. If take that view, you look on the notion of perception –

Ultimate character of perception doesn't involve consciousness necessarily at all, but involves the taking account of, and ~~the very being~~ it rises into being an entity by reason of its being a synthesis of perceptual relatedness.[2]

Quarrel with word substance in historical and etymological sense. Superject arises out of synthesis of its relationships. substance | circumstance | superstance.

Sympathy with those people who say in approaching metaphysics should never desert a first-hand knowledge of own experience. Consciousness

---

1. Burch's notes have 'some simple' in place of 'principal' here: '. . . decorated with transient qualities, but getting its character from some simple attribute which it always carries around with it' (Burch, p. 66).
2. Conger marks this paragraph with a line in the left margin with what appear to be the letters 'IVc' next to it.

arises when there's a conceptual analysis of the perceptivity. Not complete – Perceptivity comes with it physical relations.¹

Conceptual must be held to have in some extent an independent origin – throws <u>high light</u> on perceptual relationship. Consciousness of our perceptivity is different from perceptivity itself.

|3| We are constructing action of actual entity from something which we all vulgarly assume is in our direct experience. There we are taking same line as men of 17th century. ~~Then~~ This though ~~the~~ knocks materialistic view of nature which Descartes first introduced by his idea of corporeal substance. Corporeal substance didn't do any thinking.² Whitehead – actual entity is dipolar – a perceptivity which <u>turns on itself</u>³ into conceptual analysis.

Intensity of being doesn't necessarily or equally lie in various occasions or equally between two parts⁴ of an occasion, and therefore can have one side or other perhaps negligible. There agree with Lloyd Morgan and Alexander in ~~a~~ emergent evolution.⁵ What ⟨?⟩ is negligible in one type of entity may emerge in another type of entity into importance.

Each actual entity arises from its taking account of whole past – if it does that it can't have any great intensity of being unless anyhow that portion of the past which has greatest importance in its formation is favorable to existence of actual entity of some peculiar intensity.

If environment merely one of cross currents and chops, can never get something great – a faint ripple of being ∧arising from nonentity∧. Insofar as environment conspires and doesn't check itself, you get stronger intensity of being. Like chops in Strait of Dover. My idea of unfavorable environment.

Further type of favorable environment when there is the antecedent historic route in a favorable environment which is such that each entity so peculiarly play into one another's hands by congruity that main description of any one entity is a summary of its antecedents and peculiarly aware of them.⁶ This is an enduring entity.⁷

|4| Hope to have a conception of a physical fact as one which applies throughout all nature – ⟨even⟩⁸ to empty space, which is a physical fact of minor

---

1. Cf. King: 'Perceptivity has the completeness of the physical relationships. A completeness of relationships we are not always conscious of' (King, p. 68).
2. Cf. King: 'Descartes had two substances – corporeal and mental' (King, p. 68).
3. King (p. 68) and Burch (p. 66) both have 'turns of itself'.
4. Burch's notes (p. 66) have 'poles' instead of 'parts'.
5. C. Lloyd Morgan originated the term 'emergent evolution' in his 1922 Gifford lectures at St Andrews, which were later published as *Emergent Evolution* in 1923. In the book, he references Alexander frequently, noting that 'The most resolute attempt to give a philosophic interpretation of nature as a whole, with adequate stress on the concept of emergence, is that of Professor S. Alexander in *Space, Time, and Deity*'. Morgan, *Emergent Evolution*, p. 9, available at <https://archive.org/details/emergentevolutio00morg_0>. See also the 24 February lecture, note 2, p. 293.
6. Cf. King: 'An entity is the summary of its antecedents – If conscious, it is aware of its antecedents' (King, p. 69).
7. Cf. Weiss: 'Where the result is merely aware of its antecedents and doesn't consolidate them we have enduring entities – like electrons' (Weiss, p. 52).
8. Supplied from King (p. 69).

importance, but owing to regulants of enduring organisms like electrons ... has just one general conception – an actual occasion.

Look on conceptual side as vfor your purposesv negligible – then get the physical world. Physical world is primarily to be conceived in terms of extension. vNotion ofv extension[1] is primarily descriptive of how one actual entity is in itself a complex organism – it is itself extended and also of how it takes account of all other actual entities. A complex actual entity is internally complex – takes account of its own complexity ~~how it takes account of own~~ and also how it takes account of the rest of the world also to be described in terms of extension.[2]

Extension is extremely ⟨abstract⟩.[3] Don't say there is extension and a table in it. ⟨Extension is⟩ what expresses my relationship with table, but only partially; it is an abstract statement of certain characteristics of that relationship.

Feeling of touch – of sight – of color marking out certain space-time – table being an element which is a determinative or causal influence in the world around it. All make up experience of table (Cf. Kant.).

It's the primary fact with regard to that complete relationship. When I want to describe that relation which is of a particularly complex kind, must describe that abstraction from relationship which I |5| call extension. Extension is fundamental organic relationship.

Here make distinction. ~~In~~ Descartes looked on extension as attribute of the extended things. Corporeal substance essentially extended. I look on extension as one very abstract side, one element in relationship of things, and even a relationship vof any one thingv to its own components in relation between any one thing in analysis. Extension ∧in first ... [realities⟨/⟩∧instances∧]∧[4] a relation and not an attribute.

Descartes thought of extension purely in terms of geometry. Thought whole property of geometry. Another principle attribute which was endurance, insofar as it existed, endured.[5] Never clearly cleans up idea as to why existence would want endurance. Brings it in ⟨Meditation⟩ II. Now a certain extension in time. That is an extensive quantity.[6]

If they are extensive quantities, something common to both. What is common to both is just extension – very general characteristic of this organic relationship between actual entity or within actual entity – something very abstract.[7] Then further determinations which are the result of more particular experiences, and furthermore nat⟨urally⟩ hold vmeasuredv space and vmeasuredv time are not so sharply distinguished as Descartes, though

---

1. Weiss (p. 52) has 'space' here, while Conger, King and Burch all have 'extension'.
2. Conger marked this passage with a vertical line in the left margin, to the left of which are three illegible words.
3. Conger has 'complex' here, but the notes of King (p. 69), Burch (p. 67) and Weiss (p. 52) all suggest that it should be 'abstract'. Cf. Burch: 'Extension is extremely abstract, because extension only partly represents my relation to the physical object'.
4. The proper placement of this interlineation is not clear.
5. Cf. King: 'Everything mental or physical, so far as it existed, endures' (King, p. 69).
6. Cf. King: 'He never cleared up why existence and endurance went together. An extension in time – extensive quantities with space' (King, p. 69).
7. Cf. Weiss: 'Endurance is extension in time' (Weiss, p. 52).

Whitehead holds ~~these~~ that (another point).¹ That element in the universe which gives some distinction between time and space, and yet some connection between them. First element in connection between time and space is this primary and abstract organic relationship of being extended. Therefore that ~~relationship~~ characteristic relationship would be compatible with having a purely static universe.

Difference between morphology and functioning of universe. Universe not mere morphological structure in which notion of time |6| is an absurdity or one of these partial mistakes which the Absolute seems to fall into when it indulges itself. With: Bergson and William James Whitehead believes in unfinished universe. Whatever stage you have arrived at, your actual entities as soon as have built selves up, get fresh creative element so pass beyond. We only know ourselves in our extensive parts, our analysis. But as <u>final</u> <u>entity</u> we are creative determinations. We can look back in next embodiment. We are always a little behind hand in our knowledge of ourselves because we are creative. Using word "know" where it is merely an unconscious being something. Final entity is creative, realizing its many partial intensities² which have had part in its unity, but its unity immediately passes into creativity beyond itself.

~~These~~ This incompleteness supervenes upon morphological extensiveness. I'm lecturing from point of view of where they're taken to pieces. The temporal aspect of the world arises from differentiation of modes in which the other entities taken account of, enter into being of actual entity in question. Insofar as actual entities enter as entities which have arrived at their unity and therefore have passed over as creative determinants into the entity in question, they are in the past. Insofar as all entities are happening together with a certain common past, then in certain sense independent of each other with a peculiarly vivid consciousness of each other. I am causally ~~independent of~~ vonv you in past,³ but you are held up to me vividly by presentational immediacy of the sense data. So I get peculiarly vivid presentation of space vrelationsv of you under guidance⁴ of eternal objects – essences. Environment being favorable, my past has something to do with yours. Past enters into determination of what I am. How the organisms find a structure in space as enduring organisms from which the greatest intensity arises and relation between space and time depends on peculiar character of favorable unity of organisms⁵ which now dominates physical world. vSpecial measurable property of space and timev are of much more superficial character than general organic relationship.⁶

---

1. Here the word 'time' appears alone, nearly centred on the page, equidistant between the lines of text before and after it. Its intended relation to the surrounding text is not clear.
2. King (p. 70) has 'entities' instead of 'intensities' here.
3. Cf. King: 'I in the present am independent of you in the present, but am dependent on you of the past' (King, p. 70).
4. This page is rather convoluted in that it has text written along every edge: up the right side, upside down at the top, and down the left side. The next few lines are written vertically up the right side of the page.
5. This is the end of the text written vertically up the right side of the page. The notes appear to continue with a number of lines written upside down at the top of the page.
6. This marks the end of the text written upside down at the top of the page. The remainder of the text on this page is written vertically down the left side. We are assuming that it belongs at the end of the page,

They supervene upon them. Complete relationship has elements in it analyzable and sep⟨arable?⟩¹ from each other. Some deeper than others. More <u>superficial</u> aspect now imposed by electro-magnetic organism and related to those principles.

|7| Can't persuade self that that is an ultimately necessary character of world for all eternity. (⟨Hendrik⟩ Lorentz)²

    Cf. flat plain
    – flat world
    – solar system
        astr⟨onomical⟩ system
    – must enlarge still more.

If consider fundamental questions of actual world, can't stop at such trivialities as three dimensions, four of space? Why not <u>49,449</u>?

Same with ultimate laws of physics – obvious characters of an epoch which has arisen ∧and which may ⟨pass?⟩ in form in which we know.∧ Ought to be able find deeper elements which suggest more permanent, yet much more abstract. Inclined to think laws of arithmetic of that sort.³

Might become unimportant.⁴

Eternal Essences, that element which is the source of all its possibility.⁵ Positively unbounded – not a few noble ideas, but every idea you can think of.

~~Som~~ Realizing under some form of order of possibilities. In actual world as unrealized factor.⁶

Factor in background which might have been but not.⁷

Seems to be an element in experience ∨may∨ become prominent in our conceptual functioning. Something which is our perceptual functioning is unimportant and is not there.⁸ ⟨No?⟩ man in red coat. Unrealized elements in background.⁹

---

but this is not entirely certain. All or part of it may have been intended to be inserted in some earlier portion of the text.
1. Conger has just 'sep' here, which could mean either 'separate' or 'separable'.
2. Parentheses supplied. Visually it appears that the name goes between the two 'that's of the previous sentence, but as this makes little sense, we have treated it as a parenthetical to the sentence instead. What Conger actually writes is '*Max* Lorentz', but the intended reference seems more likely to be to Hendrik Lorentz (1853–1928), a Dutch physicist who won the 1902 Nobel Prize in Physics.
3. Cf. Weiss: 'Perhaps the laws of arithmetic are the basic laws of the earth' (Weiss, p. 53).
4. Immediately following this line are a few paragraphs of text written upside down and crossed out by a thick, wavy, blue line. The material does not appear to be related to Whitehead's lecture. It seems likely that these were notes from another class, and Conger decided to cross them out and use the page for Whitehead notes. The struck-out material is not reproduced here.
5. Cf. Weiss: 'That element which is beyond all its possibilities is an eternal object' (Weiss, p. 53).
6. Cf. Weiss: 'It is ~~related~~ ∨realizing∨, but keeps an original possibility as an ⟨?⟩ ∨unrealized∨ factor' (Weiss, p. 53).
7. The remainder of the text for this lecture is written vertically up the right side of the page.
8. Cf. Weiss: '⟨Possibility⟩ is an element in experience which may become prominent in our perceptive functioning (?)' (Weiss, p. 53).
9. There is a final page bundled together with this lecture that is marked as 'ANW, March 1st, 1927' with a page number of '1' written in the top right corner. The rest of the page is mostly blank, containing fewer than 20 words, which seem unrelated to Whitehead's lecture, but similar to the struck-out material from the previous page. This material has been omitted.

Thursday, 3 March 1927

Conger's notes

|1| Sensa values, not prefig⟨ured?⟩, but patterns of organization are, and acquire this as they filter through to us.[1]

Primary relationship underlying physical universe is extensive relationship between entities. One is likely to have allusion in way of thinking. Don't look on ~~different~~ VasV whole <u>series</u> of different relations between actual entities. A B VhaveV concrete actual fact what B is for A and vice-versa. That is primal fact. That concrete fact is analyzable into $A \rightleftarrows B$ that pair of facts – and each one is analyzable into a set of abstractions which as a matter of fact – get abstract characteristics of concrete relationships. Notice board is green is an abstraction of what that is for me – What $A \rightleftarrows B$ is for me is a unity, but a synthetic unity. Deal with it as a complex of abstractions which we still call relationships. Among those abstract characteristics is what is termed extensive relationships. When dealing with extension, call an entity extensive when it has some rendering of this fact if analyzable into components which are also ~~co~~ extensive and also analyzable in same way and of same genus.[2] One characteristic of extension. ~~Relationship~~ Extensive relationship Vof me to notice boardV is really composed of how that notice board is separated for me from other elements of space and time – Perspective made up of continuum of entities of the same sort. Obvious that you cannot consider ~~as~~ extensive relationship of notice board as if there were merely the notice board and myself. Others in between the situation in extensive continuum constitutes relationship.

Whole point is – what it is for me starts from a relativistic point of view – Always the "for me" in it, but owing to complexity of relationship. As a matter of fact VrelationshipV can be described in an impartial manner in which the particular entity only enters as a possible standpoint.[3] How it will be for all possible standpoints – that idea of intervening, whole and part.

I have extensive relationship to part of my body. Idea of contact someway or overlapping which is another way of looking – contact with some other extensive entity which shields it – shading and contact.

|2| Here the literary tradition of philosophy has erred ~~Take this~~ by taking extensive relationship, saying few vague things about it, and passing on as if that was the end. We know extensive relationship, hardly ever think of it in purity – muddle it with others fused with it – the particular spatio-temporal relationships which presuppose (extensive) relationship but are something more.[4] Not one characteristic of pure extensive relationships, but have to make

---

1. This first sentence appears in the upper-right corner of the page, separate from the rest of the text. Its correct placement in the flow of Whitehead's lecture is unclear.
2. There is a marginal note next to this sentence that reads: 'I should say ⟨?⟩'.
3. Cf. King: 'Can be described in a partial manner – the particular entities enter as a partial standpoint' (King, p. 70).
4. Cf. Weiss: 'Extendedness has many independent characters. Inquiry ignores simultaneity and time' (Weiss, p. 53).

it into a bundle of characteristics – independent propositions. One may be true, another false – can't prove one from another.

Principles of Natural Knowledge – method of extensive abstraction. These based on conception of whole and part – this is really the important fact about it. Obviously left out something – then wanted to define what we should mean by a point. Couldn't define it properly – without ~~som~~ bringing in further question of ~~how~~ measured time, idea of a duration (Alm⟨ost⟩)[1] took in Bertrand Russell and one or two others).[2] Fairly obvious that that was because I left out some element. Starting point from whole and part.

De Laguna[3] ~~⟨?⟩~~ – Whitehead would have done better to have had a more general notion of extensive connection, not that of whole and part.[4] In that way you could define point. Illustrates care necessary to reason accurately and from your premises. Hard especially in philosophy.

It is a habit – always see whether if you said cause means this – always substitute in future your definition and see if still writing sense. Ordinary language supplies all sorts of obviousness.

Best way to be quite certain that you are reasoning from definitions is to make up a symbolism.

Analyze extensive connection to get root characteristic of relationship between physical objects.

Bertrand Russell sharpest reasoning in symbols since Aristotle, but he's also a literary man – not quite so careful. ~~From p~~ E.g. when he reasons about cause, slips in something.

|3| Philosophy carried on by men who ought to know more. Methuselah[5] should have made self a philosopher.

Relationship of Extensive connection

  1.0 Q. = Df. Relationship of extensive connection

Here ~~have~~ √Whitehead has√ already diverged from Descartes and whole tradition of philosophy. Extension always primarily described as an attribute – Primarily extensiveness √has to do√ with a relationship between entities.

Always use big letters for relations[6] –

---

1. The letters here could be 'alm', which is expanded as 'almost', or 'alw', which is expanded as 'always'. The former seems more likely here.
2. Parentheses supplied. The parenthetical text appears to the left of the main paragraph. Its correct placement is not completely clear.
3. Weiss's notes (p. 53) reference the *Journal of Philosophy* specifically. Whitehead is likely referring to Theodore de Laguna's 1922 article 'Point, line, and surface, as sets of solids'. From the article: 'In the course of the development, a modified form of Professor Whitehead's method of "extensive abstraction" is introduced. The modification consists in the use, not of the relation of "extending-over" (the relation of whole to part), but the relation of "containing," in the sense of not simply including as a part but completely enveloping. Through this modification the method is greatly simplified and strengthened. It is, I believe, impossible by means of the method in its original form to give a definition of the point in terms of the solid' (p. 451).
4. Cf. Weiss: 'Whole and part starting point is too narrow. Extensive connection is more basic than whole-part' (Weiss, p. 53).
5. Methuselah lived longest (969 years) of all people mentioned in the Bible.
6. The correct flow of notes on this page is extraordinarily difficult to discern. It is loosely organised into two columns, with text on the left and logic symbols and explanations on the right, but with some things crossed out and moved around with arrows, and circled text boxes in a number of places. We

xRy, x has relation R to y.
Field of relations – any entity, x or y.[1]
$C'R$ is field of R.[2]
Greek letters for classes α.
~~$x \in \alpha$~~ x is a member ⟨of⟩ the class α: $x \in \alpha$.
$x, y \in \alpha$
$x \in C'R$

$C'Q$ set of entities[3] which enter into extensive relations with other entities – call these extensive entities.

Don't say quantity – measurable quantity never comes in from additional notions to mere extensive entities.

Essence of reasoning is always to get it in its most general form.
Generalization carries along ⟨imitatively?⟩. ⟨Compounding?⟩ of words.
Field of relations, domain of relations.[4]
Symbolism always introduced to make things easier.
Must keep on with exact thinking ~~of~~ $\lor$on$\lor$ simple things in philosophy (symbolically) before trust selves in words.

~~In~~ Math's gift is that you can dare trust your argument to the foot of the letter and come to paradox and say it's true. When can't, you're always connecting yourself by common sense.

|4| Difference with common sense is that its shocked by anything new – so man who is always connecting reason by common sense ends by being ~~cosmo~~ common sense.

Math phys⟨ics⟩[5] reasons boldly through acres of mathematics – and says you'll find this to be true.

Can know when come to startling conclusion that an experiment can give you valuable information [cf. Einstein]. Refraction of light through crystals.

Matter of convenience whether say an entity is part of itself. ~~Class cannot be member of it.~~

Convention – ~~never have~~ $\lor 1 \cdot 1 \lor \sim (xQx)$ Pp. Primitive Propositions

You don't find Q because the extensive relationship is just an abstraction. It's a relationship Q with such abstract characteristics. Tells you what you are assuming. Really it's a mere convention. It's a symmetrical relationship.[6]

---

have ordered everything as carefully and clearly as we are able, but the reader should regard the ordering of the remaining elements for this third page with a healthy dose of scepticism.
1. Cf. Weiss: 'The field of an entity is the entity x which has the relation R to y or the y which has the relation R to x' (Weiss, p. 54).
2. 'Field' is a non-standard term, but in this instance Whitehead means 'domain', that is, the collection of all x, y (with indices, if necessary) such that xRy.
3. Cf. Weiss: '$C'q$ are those relations which enter into other relations with other entities – they are extensive entities' (Weiss, p. 54). Whitehead had earlier spoken of an entity being the member of the 'class' alpha; here, he speaks of the 'set' of extensive entities. Whitehead is using these two terms as synonyms, though later work in set theory would tend to treat them as different things.
4. Conger has a note in the right margin here that seems to be to himself: 'Bring in propositional functions in your paper'.
5. There is a superscript 'l' here, which may have been a later addition. Normally such a construction would be expanded as 'physical', but that makes less sense in this context than 'physics'.
6. To the right of the two lines below, Conger has written 'Take my body – notice board'.

If xQy, yQx

1.2. $xQy \supset yQx$ Pp

1.3. $x.y \in C'Q. \supset .xQ^zy$. Pp ∧(true with regard to extensive connection)∧

   $xRy \cdot yRz$
   {transitive}
   xR^2z

Whether or not x, y are connected ∨or∨ not, there is sure to be some third member connected with both.

Whole nerve of an investigation depends on your definitions. |5| Underlying assumption that definitions are important. Express what you want to talk about.

Now bring in idea of shielding, shading, whole and part.

Various ways of being in contact

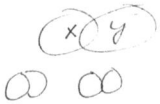 

Possibility of <u>tangency</u>.

Saturday, 5 March 1927

Conger's notes

|1| When you deal with symbolic work, the enormous importance of keeping in mind the ideas behind the symbolism. Immerse self three months in symbolic investigation and forget why you undertook it. – Importance of presupposition with which you start, sometimes not expressed at all, sometimes in briefest possible statement.

Euclid's first sentence always thought ⟨to?⟩ be the very beginning of geometry of the physical world.[1] "A point is that of which there is no part." Written as pri⟨mary?⟩ fact that you could say about pri⟨mary?⟩ entity. σημεῖον ἐστιν οὗ μέρος οὐθέν ∧(280 BC)∧.[2] Expresses idea you have got to look for world in undifferentiated simplicity and space made up of external relations of points. All math assumed that the starting point of all geometric thought.

Extension to be explained in terms of relationships between points. ~~Lines in~~ motion by philosophers of 17th century all had theories which tended to make that an unbelievable statement – but people's ideas were fixed by that

---

1. Cf. King: 'One of the most important sentences influencing Western thought' (King, p. 71).
2. Parentheses supplied. The sentence 'A point is that of which there is no part' is the translation of this Greek sentence. It is the first definition in Euclid's *Elements* (https://farside.ph.utexas.edu/Books/Euclid/Elements.pdf).

time. Never any effort to deal with geometry except from Euclidean standpoint. Descartes talks about extension and endurance as fundamental, ~~Descartes~~ not about points. Ought to have asked how are you going to define a point in terms of an extended entity.

Leibniz. Relational theory of space. He ought to have asked, if that is the case, what happens to your point? Ought to have considered point as complex idea which arises in dealing with the related thing.

Whitehead is to certain extent combining Descartes and Leibniz. Extended entities are extensive because all share in type of relationship which constitute them an interconnected manifold.

|2| This ∨Euclidean∨ sentence is deathblow to organic theory[1] of nature if taken as fundamental to geometry – Nature must then seek simple entities in external relationships to each other. Deathblow to organic theory. Voluminous character of extensiveness thereby derivative from relationships of the points. This voluminous entity is constituted by its relationships to other voluminous entities. It is constituted by reason of its relationship to own parts. External voluminous entities ~~by~~ with which indirectly extensively connected.

– Now we want to invert that whole point of view and say the foundation of the physical geometry has got to start with voluminous entity which is complex and made up of its relations to other voluminous entities.[2]

Take a particular exemplification of such relationships – areas on blackboard.[3]

From i–vi consider Q as being such a relationship which in this particular exemplification of {?} with entities[4]

    i–vi, xQy
            yQx
    vii $\sim xQy$
            $\sim yQx$

But vii in many ways interrelated by extension.

Anyway have

    i–vii xQ^2y.

First point to notice, we are as yet ascribing to Q no quality whatever.

|3| Remember what the thing is meant to express – bare fact of extensiveness. Any extensive entity has an inside and an outside.

How to express iv, v, vi being inside.
Whitehead took relation of whole and part to be fundamental – de Laguna's improvement[5] – start with <u>connection</u>.

---

1. King (p. 71) uses the word 'character' rather than 'theory'.
2. Somewhere in this vicinity, King writes: 'There is a high correlation between common sense and the common place' (King, p. 72).
3. The numbering for the below diagrams appears to match up with Weiss's diagrams on p. 53. For Weiss, i–iii represent 'contact', iv–vi represent 'shielding' and vii represents 'not in contact except as relation'.
4. Cf. King: 'In the examples, 1–6 are xQy. 7 is an example of $\sim(xQy)$ xQ^2y' (King, p. 72).
5. See note 3, p. 304.

What characterizes y as a part of x? x shades y.[1] No entity can be extensively connected with y without being connected with x. Whole and part is x shading y. Very intimate relation. I think my instinct was right, it's the most important relation. Relations to insides more important than to external world.

$Q_s = q$ shading
$xQ_s y =$ Df $x \neq y$ $\vec{Q^c} y \subset \vec{Q^c} x$ (nerve is here)[2]
$x, y \in C^c Q$ (Simply brought in to deal with extreme cases. x and y must belong.)[3]

Must make up mind as to whether a thing can shade itself. More convenient to begin with proper part.

$x \neq y$ ~~$\Pi Q y = \Pi Q x$~~

Want to express class of things extensively connected with $\langle y? \rangle$.[4]

$\vec{Q^c} x \quad z \in \vec{Q^c} x$
$\vec{Q^c} y \quad = z \cdot z Q^x$

β part of α $\quad \beta \subset \alpha$ ($\subset$ means "lies in")[5]

Suppose x and y weren't extensive quantities at all – then $x \neq y$, no members of y class ⟨is?⟩ x class.

Look out for extreme cases – likely to get wonderful results based on them if you don't.

|4| Important to be able to discriminate iv from v, vi because possibilities of tangency are so intricate they upset your simple statement.[6]

ii, iii are external connections.

i, ii, iii characteristic peculiarity

In two cases i, i_a, iv, v, vi can find extensive entity in the two.[7]

ii Though x and y are connected with each other, no entity inside both.

What perf⟨ectly⟩ general characteristic you want ⟨and?⟩ see how going to define it.[8]

~~$x Q_s y$~~ Pp ~~Relationship here unsymmetrical~~[9]
$x Q_\varepsilon y =$ Df. $\quad xQy : xQ_s z \supset_z \sim y Q_s z : y Q_s z \supset_z \sim x Q_s z$
{⟨Now then?⟩, they shade nothing in common}

---

1. Cf. King: 'Relation of whole and part is to be considered as a shading ~~including~~ relation. What is in relation to y must be in relation to x' (King, p. 72).
2. Parentheses supplied. The parenthetical comment appears to refer only to the right-most expression on this line.
3. Parentheses supplied. There is a line connecting the expression on the line with '$x \neq y$', above. Both expressions have been circled, presumably to make what the line is connecting more clear. Also, the '$\neq$' has a double underline, which has been removed to make the expression clearer.
4. In King's notes (p. 72), this character looks like either a 'y' written over an 'x', or vice versa. Conger's notes are unclear in much the same way. Meanwhile, for the below expressions, King has the same two expressions on the left, but then has: '$Z \in \vec{Q^c} x = Df ZQx$'.
5. Parentheses and quotation marks supplied. The parenthetical text uses the word 'this' and has a line drawn to the '$\subset$'; we have replaced 'this' with '$\subset$' for clarity.
6. Cf. King: 'Shading doesn't discriminate between 4, 5, 6., which are all internal connections = shading' (King, p. 72).
7. Cf. King: 'In 1, 4, 5, 6, there can be an entity inside both, but not so in 2, 3' (King, p. 72).
8. Conger adds a number of clarifications underneath the expression below defining various parts of it. The epsilon in 'Q_ε' is 'external shading'. '$\supset_z$' means 'for every value of x' (King: 'for every value of z'). He also adds the following below '$xQ_s z$': 'shaded by x'.
9. Cf. King: '$xQ_s y$ is insymmetrical – by postulation ∨assumption∨' (King, p 72).

No particular area z is an apparent value.
So have notion of external connection.
Symmetrical relationship – same statement for x and y as for y and x.
Now iv distinct from v and vi.

v, vi, external entity, both externally connected with y and with x. But now anything connected with y in iv has to penetrate inside x and has to have entity lying inside both x and y. Anything connected with y can't be [merely] externally connected with x.

|5| iv x shades y in interior.[1] Nothing externally connected with both. Anything connected with y shades something in common with x.[2]

$xQ_iy = \text{Df} : xQ_iy \cdot \sim \exists! \{\vec{Q}_E^c x \cap \vec{Q}_e^c y\}$

Existence – There exists a member of class α.[3]

$\exists!\alpha$

$\sim \exists!\alpha$

{⟨incomplete?⟩ intersection} [Logical addition] (are you right in your paper?)[4]

Not all definitions given. Would need more Primitive propositions.
Polish up your logic – get as few premises as can select.
Simple – ⟨?⟩ not redundant.
When you're at grips trying to express something, all that is put behind you.
Like haircut for pioneers.
Logical elegancies.
Next time consider ⟨how to⟩ define a point ⟨?⟩.

Tuesday, 8 March 1927

Conger's notes

|1| Couldn't get any entity which touched both externally.[5]
Q any extensive connection

   xQ_sy Shading
   xQ_ey External connection
   xQ_iy Purely internal connection

Essence of definition – what you hold to be true about q makes xQ_sy etc. important.

1. King (p. 72) has a figure here which does not appear in the notes of Conger or Weiss:
2. In the expression below, Conger has noted that the 'i' in 'Q_i' stands for 'interior shading'. In the expression two lines down, Conger adds that '∩' stands for 'nothing in common with', then crosses this out and writes 'common part of'. King has further clarifications: '$\exists:\alpha$ There exists a member of class α. $\neg\exists$ – the negation. ∩ = the relation in common. ∩: common part' (King, p. 72). Also, Conger has a closing right bracket below, but both King (p. 72) and Weiss (p. 54) do not, so we have removed it.
3. There is some illegible text to the right of the expressions below. Note that the existential quantifier followed by the exclamation mark is Russell's 'E-shriek'. This is stronger than the normal existential quantifier, in that it asserts the existence of a *unique* something.
4. Parentheses supplied.
5. Given its position, this sentence is intended to reference the diagram on its right.

xQ_oy overlapping or having a common part includes Q_s and Q_i.[1]

xQ_oy = Df · (∃z) · xQ_sz, yQ_sz

If you're to have the relationship Q, Q in xQy, means either xQ_ey or xQ_oy

When writing things for yourself symbolism a question. Symbols for ideas instead of sounds. Cf. Chinese ⌵written⌵ language different from spoken.

What beliefs about q do we want for continuity and unboundedness? Don't expect to come to boundary of extension. A sort of continuity.

Idea of divisibility $Q_s = Q_s^2$
More special $Q_i = Q_i^2$

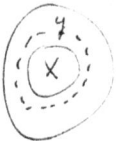

$xQ_iy ⊃ xQ_i^2y$

$∃z · xQ_iz, zQ_iy$

$xQ_iz · zQ_iy ⊃ · xQ_iz$

If not obvious and trivial, it wouldn't be a primitive proposition.[2]

But suppose start with xQ_iz, zQ_iy

Idea of infinite[3] divisibility.

$x ∈ CQ$.

This is inf⟨inite?⟩ divis⟨iblity?⟩:

$X_eCQ. ⊃ .(∃y)xQ_iy$

Can always get another, smaller and smaller.

|2| [Whitehead didn't write formula][4]

<u>Unboundedness</u>   ~~eq q~~   x and y   C'Q

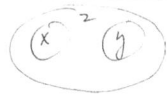

Can find a bigger volume in which the two belong.[5]

$x · y \, C'Q : ⊃ [∃z] · x · yQ_iz$

Idea of ~~content~~ ∧Extensiveness∧

Containedness. Completely divide it up in ⌵indefinite⌵ number of ways into a non-overlapping set of bits. Can we get a definition for it?

---

1. For the below expression, King (p. 73) has an 'i' instead of an 's' in the penultimate term: xQ_oy = Df · (∃z) · xQ_iz, yQ_iz. Additionally, King has the following figure to illustrate overlapping:
2. King (p. 73) writes here: '(Something intermediate can be put in)'. For the second line of the above, Weiss (p. 54) has an 'x' in place of a 'z' for the final term: (∃z) · $xQ_iz · xQ_iy$. Meanwhile, the final term of the third line seems to be an error, since the last term is simply a reiteration of the first, and tells us nothing. In order to say anything non-trivial, the line should probably be: $xQ_iz · zQ_iy ⊃ · xQ_iy$.
3. Conger wrote next to this word: 'no not⟨ion?⟩ of inf⟨inite?⟩'.
4. Closing bracket supplied.
5. Cf. King (p. 73), '(something within x)', and Weiss (p. 6), 'A part of class Diss 'x'. For the expression that follows, both King and Weiss have: $x ∈ C'Q ⊃ (∃y)xQ_iy$.

Harvard lectures, spring semester 1927

This is the way to know whether you're bringing in a new idea.

Can't define any <u>one</u>, but can define what we mean by the class of such subordinate entities.

x – ~~Intersection~~ ∨Dissection∨ of x.

Call whole class   Diss 'x

A class whose numbers are classes.

Every member of α is shaded by x.

$\alpha \in$ Diss 'x = Df:$y \in \alpha \cdot \underset{y}{\supset} \cdot xQ_s y$: Every y is shaded ∧by x∧.[1]

But might leave out one member.

Could find μ which could lie in omitted one and doesn't overlap any remainder.

But ~~want to show anything~~ can't find anything which doesn't overlap at least one member of α.[2]

$xQ_s\mu \cdot \underset{\mu}{\supset} |\exists y| \cdot y \in \alpha \cdot yQ_o\mu$

y is an α, y overlaps μ.

|3| Can define. Q might be grandfather, grandson. Definition would hold, but no exemplification. No dissection of grandfather would yield anything of that sort.

Must have a belief or primitive proposition if Q is to fit idea of extension.

$x \in C'Q \cdot \underset{x}{\supset} \cdot |\exists \alpha| \cdot \alpha \in$ Diss 'x

~~When have~~ x is idea of dissection as an analysis of the content. Analyze extensive quantities up into subord⟨inate?⟩ extensive quantities. One way of getting complete set of components.[3] If there exists an α ~~whi~~ such that $\alpha \in$ Diss'x and $\alpha \cdot \in$ Diss'y

$(\exists \alpha) \cdot \alpha \in$ Diss '$x \cdot \alpha \in$ Diss '$y \supset . x = y$.

An entity q is determined by any one of its dissections. Notion of analysis of an extensive quantity in terms of content.

Can't get idea of straight line, line lying evenly. Notion of geometry founded on extension without bringing new ideas, other than Q, which can be defined in purely logical terms.

How far our notions of space bring in new ideas. Question is that it shall be important. Your beliefs, primitive propositions make your definitions to be of importance.

Unity of an event or extensive quantity.

x and y ~~form~~ are a dissection of z.[4] But if have ⓧ ⓨ, why not say one extensive quantity? Lack continuity, therefore numerically two.

|4| A certain continuity is required in order one area should be unity with another.[5]

---

1. An arrow in both Conger and King (p. 73) indicates that the expression picks up after the colon with the below '$xQ_s\mu \cdot \underset{\mu}{\supset} |\exists y| \cdot y \in \alpha \cdot yQ_o\mu$'. King has an '$s$' in place of an '$o$' for the final term: $yQ_s\mu$.
2. For the expression below, Conger notes that '$\underset{\mu}{\supset}$ implies for every μ'.
3. Cf. King: 'One way of getting a complete set of non-overlapping components' (King, p. 74). Also, for the below expression, King has '$(\exists x)$' where Conger and Weiss have '$(\exists \alpha)$'.
4. In fact, King's figure (p. 74) shows a 'z' outside the circle at the top.
5. Cf. King: 'There is no continuity required for ~~one~~ two entities to form one entity' (King, p. 74).

311

[Cf. possibility as valence]
Not true ⓧ q ⓨ. So can't make one continuous entity.
$x \in C'Q \supset \sim (\exists y \cdot z) \cdot y \neq z \ (\sim yQz)$. Class formed by y and z is a dissection of $'x$

Can't get a dissection of any external entity which has only two members and which are not in extensive connection.[1]

Might have:

Thinks ought to exclude this.[2] Ought to define an area – would take too long. [Must define point]

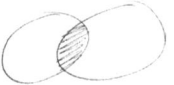

Quite natural to think 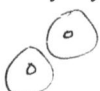 is common part. But haven't said so. Have said only both have entities which shade in common.[3]

Might have: Would have to have a primitive proposition to state if two entities overlap at least a class of entities which are shaded by both, which do not overlap each other (might touch) and such that any other entity which is shaded by both is shaded by one and only one ∧(not sure about this)∧.

Always draw tame animals.

Find after months some infernal little dodge you haven't thought out.

|5| Now come to idea of analyzing extensive continuum with more and more accuracy. If you want to express relationship of:

It's a complex business.

Insofar as geometrical relationship Take smaller part – smaller still ... get more and more accurate. Ideal of a point in Boston and point in New Haven. Our senses never allow us to get to that ideal. You can't really say senses are inaccurate unless your material is such that it presents you with an ideal of accuracy. Couldn't try make instrument more accurate unless material is such that greater accuracy has a meaning.

Certain sorts of materials which don't ⟨?⟩ admit of this method's considerations. E.g. sheep. Can't dissect. Sometimes greater simplicity as dim⟨ensional?⟩ extent. When cut sheep in half, get mutton.[4] You get one sort of knowledge more accurate by diminishing, but possibility of another sort gone

---

1. To the right of this sentence are the struck-out words 'mere point'.
2. There is an arrow pointing to the right-most figure above.
3. King (p. 74) adds here: 'For Whitehead, a point contact gives duality'.
4. This is a classic puzzle of mereology/mereotopology and remains an active issue. See for instance Simon, *Parts: A Study in Ontology*.

all together. Whole ⋁of it⋀ connected with idea of organism. At certain stages analysis leaves out something which can't be done by reconstructing notion of morphology of sheep.

Something else turns up. Cells. There are the various methods of study. Take that sort of size for certain sort of study. How organism is functioning refuses to disclose itself by merely putting together your knowledge acquired with regard to various entities in isolation. Stands out more and more.

Absolute ideals first geometry – get down ⟨until?⟩ practically lose dimension. Can we define a point without geometry and state use of definition?

Thursday, 10 March 1927

Conger's notes

|1| Methods of Extensive Abstraction
The Concept of Nature, 79ff. ***A* and *B*. Two events in extensive entity. In many respects relations between parts simpler than *a* and *b*. Principle which presides over all attempts at exact observation.**[1]

Get idea of approximating to ideal simplicity of relationship. As you approximate, you lose sight of facts of nature which are only apparent when you have a certain extension.

Define what you mean by idea of limit. Traditional answer you find a point – which Whitehead challenging. Point not ultimate ⋁definitive⋀ element of an extensive manifold, and that manifold is made up of points in external relations. Area is most concrete fact – don't see points; you see area.

That dispute not new. Aristotle takes one side, Plato the other. Thomas Heath, *Greek Mathematics, Euclid in Greek.*[2] **Euclid means a point is that of which no part or has no part: a point is indivisible. Other writers have** ~~ext~~ **added point has no magnitude.** Greek word used for point really means a mark, dot to mark where point is: but dot is not the point. Can always divide

---

1. Per the citation, this paragraph comes from page 79 of *The Concept of Nature*, in the chapter 'The method of extensive abstraction': 'If *A* and *B* are two events, and *A'* is part of *A* and *B'* is part of *B*, then in many respects the relations between parts *A'* and *B'* will be simpler than the relations between *A* and *B*. This is the principle which presides over all attempts at exact observation' (Whitehead, *The Concept of Nature*, available at <https://archive.org/details/cu31924012068593>).
2. The referenced books would appear to be the two-volume *A History of Greek Mathematics* (1921) and *Euclid in Greek* (1920) by Thomas Little Heath (1861–1940). In his 'Note on the Greek concept of a point' at the end of *The Concept of Nature*, Whitehead remarks that Heath's latter book was 'a classic from the moment of its issue' (p. 197). Despite these explicit citations, Whitehead may actually have been reading from *The Thirteen Books of Euclid's Elements*, translated by Heath, for the first half of this lecture, particularly pages 155–6 (although some similar material on the definition of points also appear on page 293 of *A History of Greek Mathematics, Vol. I*). **Bolded** portions following this note are places where Whitehead appears to have been reading from the text. See Heath, *The Thirteen Books of Euclid's Elements, Vol. I*, available at <https://archive.org/details/thirteenbookseu02heibgoog>; also Heath, *A History of Greek Mathematics, Vol. I*, available at <https://archive.org/details/historyofgreekm01heat>, and Heath, *Euclid in Greek*.

any such mark. Process of division wouldn't come to end – must get from dot which has size and position to point which has position but no size. Mentally disregard magnitude of dot and regard point as indivisible and having position but possessed of no other attributes.

This had been stated before Euclid's time by Aristotle. **Aristotelian point indivisible in respect to quantity and has position. No distinction between point and place where it is.**

|2|[1] **No accumulation can give us anything continuous such as a line.**[2] **Only by motion in space can a point generate a line.** If cut line into part, or two lines cut one another, cut is at a point which is where the line is cut. Position or place determined by division or intersection (Aristotle, Heath summary ~~Eucl.~~ Greek position generally).[3]

Cutting is at a point, which is where the line is cut: position or place determined by ⟨division?⟩ or intersection. Think of lines as mathematical lines – have no breadth. Any line which has an end or ends, ends in point, which is simply where it ends.

Before Euclid's time, ᵥGreeks saidᵥ στιγμα,[4] prick. But puncture gives indentation of some size. Not nearer abstract mathematics than dot.

Heath: Objection to Euclid's definition that states what point is not more than what it is. Really have to get our conception of a point by other means before can understand Euclid's definition. If think of area as whole, what are you left with? Abstract from notion of area.

Whitehead – Don't find notion of an area allows self to be, thereby a notion of another ultimate area which call point.

Heath: Other ancient writers preferred other definitions. Plato objected with recognition of points as separate class of things and regarded them as geometrical fictions. Preferred to consider a point as mere beginning of a line; Plato puts up {geometrical fiction, beginning of line, indivisible line}.

As Aristotle says, even indivisible lines must have extremities, hence an indivisible line must contain at least two points, and so can't be same thing as a point.

Pythagoras said a point is a monad having position.

|3| Curious Plato here diverges from Pythagorean tradition and ~~Plato~~ Aristotle retains it. Monad or unit being regarded as indivisible.

Whitehead: Plato's statement of beginning of a line leaves out of question what is the beginning of a line. Indivisible line – Aristotle bowled over. So brought back to his ᵥPlato'sᵥ statement a geometrical fiction. Whitehead thinks Plato embodies a great truth in imperfect statement. Idea of a fiction is still going strong. At least half ⟨of⟩ physicists here would say electron a convenient fiction, ᵥif mean byᵥ fiction haven't got down to completely adequate analysis.

---

1. There are notes on the back of page 1 of this set of lecture notes that are crossed out, and appear to be for another class. They have not been reproduced here.
2. Cf. King: 'A sum of points does not have magnitude' (King, p. 75).
3. Parentheses supplied. The parenthetical text appears in the left margin.
4. Conger clearly writes 'στιγμα', but Heath (p. 156) has 'στιγμή (a puncture)'.

If has merely meaning of half-truth, I do not mind, because practically all our statements have some elements which we adequately analyze and only vaguely see. Never reach properly defined proposition in which there was nothing indefinite. Statements of formal logicians inadequate and appear so far off when you're engaged in actual discussion of ~~concrete~~ \actual\ bits of concrete truths.

But if meant on face value that it is a fiction – this is on face of it nonsense. Must be some true relevance; must be making some statement which is true about actual facts under discussion. If no relevance of that sort, starting from a fiction without any real validity cannot help you arrive at truths which have any validity. Fiction of man in moon not entering adequate proof of any statement which really has validity. |4| When you have a notion like a point which you can see has some sense, this is throwing up intellectual sponge.[1] Has some relevance, you don't know what. If you think that everything actual has its full extension and that we are talking of actual world as extended and actual world not made up of fundamentally unextended things which are actual entities. It's your business to state what is the actual character of your extensive manifold which you are talking about when you are talking about a point.

All these geometrical elements – points, lines, surfaces ⟨–⟩ are really references to routes of approximation toward greater and greater accuracy. May have route of approximation towards maximum ideal of accuracy.

That such a set of events. Any two members of such a set – Either a or a' or vice-versa. One lies inside the other.

You have gone on approximating and approximating so no solid core left.[2] When you get to one of these geometrical elements, you have {?} lost dimensions but not extension. Dimensions have meaning, but here you're below the level. What are you approximating to? – Answer is "nothing." If two sets – compare their relations. You are getting entities which have more and more simple relations. But both are routes of unending approximation. |5| False idea from differential calculus that any route of approximation has a limit – quite untrue. Think of set of fractions. Put them out in order of magnitude.

0 $1/2$ $T/1$ $3/1$ Approximate to that fraction whose square is 2. Root 2. But there is no fraction which is root 2.[3] So go on ideal of approximating – get nearer and nearer, get more and more accurately the square = 2. Always \too\ small – You're approximating to nothing because no fraction whose square is equal to 2. Horrible scandal of traditional position – The Greeks treated it in exactly same way as Tennessee treated evolution – Ought not to be talked about.[4]

---

1. That is, give up, or 'throw in the towel'.
2. King (p. 75) adds here: 'Like Chinese Boxes, there is no least box'.
3. With the series of fractions at the beginning of this paragraph, Whitehead is likely trying to convey that the root of 2 cannot be expressed as a fraction, but this number sequence does not show this. It is possible that Conger made an error in how he recorded what was on the board.
4. Whitehead is referring to the 1925 Scopes trial in Tennessee, in which high school teacher John Scopes was prosecuted for violating a new state law banning the teaching of evolution. The trial was much discussed at the time, by Whitehead as much as anyone else. He wrote about it in at least three separate letters to his son, North, between May and July 1925 (see Lowe, *Alfred North Whitehead, Vol.* II, pp.

This waited for theoretical solution for 2,000 years [Weierstrass, Cantor].¹

|6|² Bertrand Russell, *Introduction to Mathematical Philosophy*, Math 82.3.7

Phil 192.28.5, ~~the~~ Bertrand Russell, *Philosophical Essays*

Broad –⟨?⟩'7'–³

Saturday, 12 March 1927

Conger's notes

|1| View of extension – you don't ~~stop~~ start from these peculiarly simple entities which are actual and then build up from external relations – but have extended entities with relationship of extensive connection with each other. Simpler elements, lines, ~~points,~~ surfaces, all represent routes of approximation. Point of such a route of approximation, in some respects as you descend the various relationships ~~between~~ become simpler and simpler. As you get smaller and smaller you may get below the magnitude at which certain important characteristics can be found. ~~When~~ It is not wholly gain, but you do gain whenever physical relationships are to be expressed in simplicity, in geometrical relationships.⁴

No point there. You approximate to nothing. $e_1 e_2 e_3 \to$ nothing. Same if approximating to straight line or surface.

(1) What is the use of such approximation? Obvious use in all physics.

(2) Show there are different kinds of such series. Different species of such series all approximating to nothing. Show you can define intrinsically different types of such series. Lines, points, surfaces still capable of definition.

313, 315, 317). Whitehead opined that 'The remote simplicity of these distant states is extraordinary' (Lowe, *Alfred North Whitehead*, Vol. II, p. 317).

1. Karl Weierstrass (1815–97), along with Augustin-Louis Cauchy (1789–1857), developed the 'epsilon/delta' method of taking limits which formally eliminated any need for, or talk about, 'infinitesimals' in the differential calculus, and is the mathematical basis for Whitehead's discussion about 'routes of approximation'. Georg Cantor (1845–1918) gave the first successful formal treatment of set theory, and in the process established the different 'cardinalities' ('size', if you prefer) of different levels of infinite sets, thus demonstrating that 'infinite' was not a single thing. Taken together, they for the first time rendered fully intelligible the idea of numbers that were neither integers nor fractions of integers. A very readable history of the period of Weierstrass/Cantor mathematics can be found in Cassirer, *The Problem of Knowledge, Vol. IV*. Whitehead's sanguine reference to routes of approximation that have no limits considerably oversimplifies matters, and his example is far from satisfactory, but he is ultimately correct. His own mereology (later, mereotopology) has no limits at either the large or the small scale, and falls under the heading of what contemporary mereology calls 'atomless gunk'.
2. This page was unnumbered. It seems possible that the numbers accompanying the book titles were library catalogue numbers.
3. No title is given and most of the numbers are too faded to read, but it seems likely that the reference would have been either to Broad, *Scientific Thought*, available at <https://archive.org/details/in.ernet.dli.2015.6694>, or Broad, *The Mind and Its Place in Nature*, available at <https://archive.org/details/minditsplaceinna00broa>, both of which Whitehead discussed in class.
4. Cf. Weiss: 'Man, insects, microbes fade away as you go down. Qualitatively you get nothing, quantitatively some value' (Weiss, p. 55).

Pestilent heresy in ordinary explanations of mathematics. Series of fractions in order of magnitude forms series. This series approximates to nothing – very large propositions of mathematics and philosophy – by conceptual activity we postulate an entity as the entity to which we are approximating. Whitehead thinks a derivative of Kantian conceptual activity which enables us to get whole physical world out of conceptual activity. $\sqrt{2}$ Whitehead doesn't believe in this creative activity – *habeas corpus* act; if ex talk of $\sqrt{2}$, must explain what you talk about. If no such entity, all the postulation in world won't bring it into existence. An abstract ⟨?⟩ entity is something. It is our business to say what it is. A very important step in philosophy that mathematicians succeeded in stat⟨ing⟩ what they mean without this. If mathematicians couldn't state what they meant, fact that common sense makes us use $\sqrt{2}$. If we hadn't succeeded in stating, though it would have considerable general |2| philosophical effect – math would be caught in act of depending on postulational activity of mind. Necessary for those who reject view of mind as creative of entity to explain what is meant. Analogous fact with regard to geometry when felt geometry was certain, and to be got by interrogating inner consciousness. Certainty of geometry taken as evidence that intellect could *a priori* discover physical conditions which actual world satisfied. That was in sense *a priori* to experience. Kantian question ∨different∨: how can everything given in experience be universal for all experience?

Older rationalistic idea *a priori* to experience there are conditions. Reject whole fictional idea. Plato of enormous surface[1] – mistaken bulwark against Aristotelian idea that there was a point there. By explaining the word fiction so it doesn't mean fiction, Plato may have pointed way to something important. False objection and false answer, Cf. Copernicus – celestial mechanics different from terrestrial.[2]

(1) What use will be series of quantitative measurements connected with e?

		$s = (e_1\ e_2\ e_3) \to$ nothing		
very	$q(e_1)$	physical measurements of	$e_1 \to$	
⟨analogous?⟩[3]	$q(e_2)$		$e_2 \to$	Each
measurements				converges
(quantity)	$q(e_3)$		$e_3 \to$	

Any one measurement has analogue all along.[4]

---

1. The word Conger writes here is clearly 'surface', though that seems to make little sense. It is possible that he intended another word, like 'significance'.
2. While Copernicus had offered a hypothesis that dethroned Aristotle and Pythagoras, his reliance on circles still left no connection between heaven and earth. It required Tycho Brahe's meticulous observations, Kepler's imaginative leap to ellipses rather than circles, and the mechanics of first Galileo and then Newton to bring the two together, all of which took place over a span of some 200 years.
3. This is an expansion of Conger's abbreviation 'analgs'. The exact expansion is not clear.
4. Cf. Weiss: 'Each q has analogue in others – external or internal' (Weiss, p. 55).

Harvard lectures, spring semester 1927

As matter of fact

	$q(e_1)$ $q(e_2)$ $q(e_3)$	$\rightarrow$	$q(s)$	Converges to a class of limits.
any measurement	μ_1 μ_2 μ_3			~~the~~ ("Each represented by ~~a~~ numbers...?)
	ratio of one set to another	may converge to $\rightarrow$	μ_s	The ~~limit~~ number which is the limit of that

Series converging to nothing guides your physical measurements to a series which converges to set of limits. Get a peculiar simplicity of physical relationships if deal with limits of such series.

Never can measure down and down and down. Take something as small as we can – Either take measurements connected with it as good enough, true within limits of accuracy, |3| and may take something near or the limit or see an approximation, ~~and~~ take leap, and say it's that exactly.

Newton had never dealt with m_1-m_2, but with moon planets. Made a jump toward an exact law. If these particles exactly true, and m_1 and m_2 were there the masses, attraction between them

$\gamma \frac{m_1 \times m_2}{PQL}$.[1] Then verified inductively.

This which converges to nothing but which has various members of it, all satisfying some condition.

You have your physical measurements which do converge to something. Some measurements become negligible – that is converging to zero. More complicated measurements which concern two such series.

Why a point, surface, straight line is important, and why we had to go into it.

$q(e_1)$ $q(e_2)$ etc. measurements muddled up with limits of accuracy which converge to $\neq 0$.

$\mu_s \neq \eta_1$ $\mu_s + \eta_1$ $\mu_s \neq 0$
η_1 η_2 ⟨errors?⟩

– Get down to peculiar simplicity.[2]

This is simply a general description of what is done in physics.

All the talk about the actual point has been lugged in by mathematicians and philosophers.

Discuss how going discriminate different types of series and how going to find such a series.

When dealing with points – here only one sort of approximation –

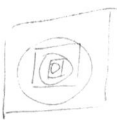

Someone says squares just as well as method of approximation. Explain how different series can approximate to different points. |4| When have explained, you have evaded necessity of stealing with Kant as creative. Takes away one prevalent philosophical way of explaining mathematics.

---

1. This may be some form of Newton's law of universal gravitation.
2. Conger writes 'converge to' above the expression '$\mu_s \neq 0$'.

Harvard lectures, spring semester 1927

Define notion of route of approximation.[1] Sweep away absurd case of class with no members.

When any two members are taken, one is inside other.
Another pestilential method of approximation – if let self in for you're worried by all subtleties of tangency.
Might go like this.[2] Must secure not merely inside other, but completely inside. This is why great care to exclude internal content. You can't exclude a thing you haven't defined. Mere excluding shows you are using the idea. Cf $xQ_t y$, $xQ_s y$, with tangency excluded. Relationship of being inside without any internal content. If start with central core, can start outside and go on approximating to that.

Go on until practically got below any extension whatsoever. Whatever extension you go on you've got to exclude.

E, lying inside every one of series. So have got to say no event which lies inside every one of my set. When do that can't be a last member. Suppose one were i since I have said every extensive quantity shades others there will be an extensive quantity which is inside. Such a series unless has inner core must go relentlessly on and on and can't stop.

|5| Write down your symbols. What call this series? Always tell you you get a point by abstraction. Take hint. Call ~~set~~ such a series an abstractive class. It's the class which performs that operation which I think is wrongly called abstraction. Perhaps not.

The sort of abstraction which only applies to notion of extensive continuum – call it all the theory of extensive abstraction.

As soon as start from conception of what you want to do and why do it[3]

$\alpha \in \text{AbsCls} \therefore = \text{Df} \therefore \exists! \alpha \therefore$

$x, y \in \alpha . x \neq y . \supset_{x,y} : xQ_s y . v . y Q_s x \therefore$

No z which every member of α holds.

$\sim (\exists z) : x \in \alpha . \supset_x . x Q_s z$

Has drawn abstractive classes as if went up to points. How define abstractive classes which have same convergence or different sort of convergence.

Class of all methods of approximation.

Don't ⟨hook?⟩ ⟨upon?⟩ with statement

point is either ~~geom or~~ squares or ⟨?⟩.

Same point must be neutral with respect to any way of getting at it.

In important respects get to same physical quantities. Not always, Cf. magnetism.[4]

---

1. Cf. Weiss: 'There are different methods of approximation to the same point' (Weiss, p. 56).
2. Given its position, this sentence is intended to reference the diagram on its left.
3. Conger gives some explanations for the two expressions below. He notes that 'AbsCls' is 'Symbol for whole set of abstractive class'. Under '∃', he has written 'There are some members' and goes on to say: 'Merely get rid of silly nugatory ~~wor~~ case which we needn't bother about'. For the second expression, he notes that it 'presupposes x and y different, might have two symbols meaning same thing'. He also notes that 'v' means 'or' and that this with the terms '$x Q_s y$' and '$xQ_s x$' has 'excluded tangency'. Here, Weiss (p. 55) has instead '$xQ_t y$' and '$yQ_t x$'.
4. The text below is written vertically up the right of the page.

319

Harvard lectures, spring semester 1927

Difference between magnetic force and magnetic induction. Converge to different plates or little walking sticks.

Magnetic density at a point. Shape of convergence is irrelevant. Shape of convergence is here relevant. Magnetic induction like walking stick.

|6|[1] *Science and the Modern World*, 177

Divisibility arises from character of spatial-temporal extension.[2]
Science and the Modern World, 223

Meaning of term possibility as applied to A – there stands in the essence of A a patience for relationships to actual occasions –[3]

Tuesday, 15 March 1927

Conger's notes

|1| (Both sides) What's the use of routes of convergence which propose to substitute for abstract elements of points? Inverted notion of point as concrete entity. How did ideas of points and surfaces arise and why useful? See whether can give route ① of approximation a meaning and get idea of equivalent routes of approximation.

Different routes of approximation to same point; if not would wreck theory. Careful sort of analysis required. Philosophy is vitally concerned with notions which can only be treated in this accurate analytical manner. Protest against treatment of in literary manner. Elaborate theory in a haze. New accurate methods introduced by (mythical) Pythagoras. Particular subject. How consider, analyze out interconnections of different routes of approximations. Only one way.

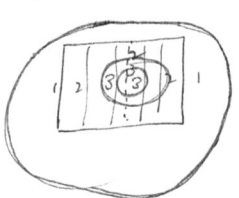

May have two routes getting to zero.[4] Now take another route which approximates to a point in that area. What must be interconnection between the two? The big end doesn't matter.

Sooner or later must find a #4 which lies inside. . . . Call first conve abstractive set α; call other β. First thing to do is to make up phraseology. Say α covers β. This doesn't mean every member of α set covers every member of β set. Means whatever number of α set I like to set take [say 3] by going far enough down the β set I can find a v at least one v member which lies inside 3. Since all small end

---

1. This page is unnumbered; it is the reverse side of the final page of these lecture notes. The quotes from *Science and the Modern World* seem unlikely to be derived directly from Whitehead's lecture.
2. The pagination of course refers to the original printing. This quotation comes near the end of chapter 7, 'Relativity': 'In this account "time" has been separated from "extension" and from the "divisibility" which arises from the character of spatio-temporal extension'.
3. This quotation comes from near the beginning of chapter 10, 'Abstraction': 'The meaning of the term "possibility" as applied to A is simply that there stands in the essence of A a patience for relationships to actual occasions'.
4. 'May have two routes' appears to the left of the figure, and the rest of the paragraph appears on the right. Given its physical location on the page, it is not completely clear whether 'getting to zero' is supposed to be the continuation of 'Only one way' or 'May have two routes'.

320

of β set lie inside any member you like to take, ~~any~~ must lie inside 3.... Could find smaller β which lies inside 4. Representing symbolically – may neglect the symbolism $\alpha Q_c\beta.[=\alpha \text{covers}\beta]$. Symbolism here better than language because "covers" suggests no reference to particular extensive relation Q, which is basis of whole theory we are talking about. [See *Revue de Métaphysique*, 1920][1]

$\alpha Q_c\beta.$ = Df:$\alpha,\beta \in$ Abstr Cl:$x \in \alpha. \supset_x .(\exists y)\vee y \in \beta \vee .xQ_iy$

Can find a y such that x shades y. If had said Q_x, would have been worry of internal tangency. Being able to define something which excludes tangency. Suggestion of de Laguna.[2]

Might say why not have a general definition of covering without the limitation to abstractive classes. A technical question. If writing a longish book on symbolism, continually finding ⟨bad?⟩[3] shots. Bound to have more general questions turn up – then can knock out <u>$\alpha, \beta \in$ Abstractive class</u>. When want special case, must drag in as more general statement. Don't be too general at beginning. If too specific, some propositions depend on your restriction and some do not. Restrict selves to abstractive class when talking of covering.

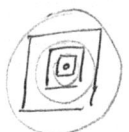
This is fundamental relationship, but when draw figure, may have very different modes. Might have them covering each other. Squares and circles converging to point. Since both converging to same point, you're ⟨to?⟩ have since you take any entity must be one of other set which is closer approximation and ~~simul~~ conversely. Must cover each other – No end, to infinite series, but down and down to nothing. If covering each other, let us call them equal, equal in their sharpness of convergency and |2| what then converging to. Though both converge to nothing, there's a kind of equality of convergence. $\alpha = \beta$. Symbolism? ⟨?⟩ $\alpha Q_c\beta.\beta Q_c\alpha$. Here again just as use word equal to cover each other – but this idea of equality is going to be so perpetually used we must have a symbol for it. Use symbol $\alpha Q_{eq}\beta$ = Def. $\alpha Q_c\beta.\beta Q_c\alpha$.

---

1. Assuming that Whitehead is referencing his own work, then the 1920 date seems to be an error. There is a one-page review of Whitehead's *Enquiry Concerning the Principles of Natural Knowledge* in volume 27, number 2 (April 1920), p. 5, but the more likely reference is Whitehead, 'La theorie relationniste de l'espace', which appeared in the *Revue* in May 1916.
2. This paragraph is written on the right side of the page, and appears as though it may refer to the interlineation near the end of the above expression, i.e. '$y \in \beta$'. Note also that Conger writes '"any" comes in here' next to the subscript x in '$\supset_x$'. As for the reference to Theodore de Laguna, this is likely a reference to his note 'Extensive abstraction: a suggestion' in *Philosophical Review* in 1921. In it, he writes: 'The method of extensive abstraction, employed by Mr. Whitehead in his *Principles of Natural Knowledge* and in his *Concept of Nature*, can be greatly simplified and strengthened, if, instead of the indefinable relation of whole and part, or "extending over," we assume the relation of "containing – in the sense of not only including as a part but completely enveloping. In this sense, one geometric solid would contain another solid, when the second was a part of the first, and no solid external to the first could touch the second. Using "containing" as an indefinable, we can at once define the expression, "The event A extends over the event B" as meaning: "There is no event which is contained by B and not contained by A; and there is an event contained by A and not contained by B"' (de Laguna, 'Extensive abstraction', pp. 216–17).
3. Conger's handwriting here is unclear. It could plausibly be 'had' instead of 'bad'.

Now if want to define a geometrical element like point, surface, straight line – ~~de~~ in way which is abs⟨olutely?⟩ =[1] neutral as between indefinite number of routes of approximation and abstractive classes. Any one may be taken to represent it. One might say nest of spheres for which point is common center. Only objection – if bring in sphere, bring in new notions – distance. If cube, rectangle and straight line. No way of discriminating particular propositions. So ask whether instead of getting habitual one, must go to opposite extreme and take whole bundle of equal abstractive classes with equal right to say they abstract to point. Therefore the point is the whole bundle of these abstractive classes. A geometrical element represents these routes of approximation which are all equal to each other and which

Only entity ⟨open?⟩ to us is notion of logical entity. It's to be a class.

Geometrical Element[2]

$\kappa \in \text{GeomEl} = Df:: \exists!\kappa:.\overset{}{\cancel{(\exists(?))}}:\zeta \in \kappa: \overset{}{\cancel{\zeta Q\epsilon\eta Q}} \supset_\zeta.$

$\zeta \in \text{Abstr Cl}: \zeta Q_{eq} \eta \equiv_\eta .\eta \in \kappa$

To be equal to ζ is equivalent to saying you're a kappa and vice-versa.

In that way have said geometrical element is a bundle of abstractive classes which are equal to each other, and any abstractive class equal to one is to the other and belongs to it.

~~Which~~ How far we are from Euclid's utmost simplicity! Element without parts or magnitude. If with these geometrical elements you can do everything which points lines surfaces are wanted to perform in geometry. Defined geometrical element all right, turning whole idea on its head. Curious that subject like that can be stood on its head.

∨Son of Darwin∨[3] When you design an instrument, must think ~~whether~~ what is to move and what is to be fixed. Try it ~~sam~~ vice-versa, if can see if – get instrument which will do same job that way.

|3| Has moral with regard to thought. Real way to get new slant is always to try to turn it topsy turvy. Most efforts will result in dead failure. Things in which you're most likely to get new idea are in those which have been taken for granted for longest period. Still see if can discriminate between different ~~types.~~ ∧geometrical entities.∧ Easy to do it if define by a point. See *Concept of Nature*.[4]

---

1. Conger frequently uses the '=' sign as a shorthand, which would normally be expanded as the word 'equal' or 'equals', as in two sentences above. In this instance it has been left as it is, as the proper expansion is not clear.
2. Conger makes numerous explanatory annotations for the below expression. For '∃', he adds: 'Class has some members. Not be fogged off with nugatory cases'. Above the exclamation point, he adds 'shriek', which is another term for an exclamation mark. Under '∃!κ', he has 'Class of all routes of approximation which are equal to each other'. For the 'ζ in '$\supset_\zeta$'', he adds 'for every value'. For the '$\equiv_\eta$' on the second line, he notes 'Equivalent for every value of η'. Here kappa is a unique element, such that anything that is a part of it is Q-equal to anything else that is a part of it. Kappa in this case is a 'geometrical primitive', which Whitehead views as a construct.
3. Charles Darwin had five sons who survived infancy, but the ensuing discussion of scientific instruments means that the most likely referent is Horace Darwin (1851–1928), who co-founded the Cambridge Scientific Instrument Company in 1881. Like Whitehead, he was a Fellow of Trinity College, Cambridge, as well as a Fellow of the Royal Society.
4. It seems likely that Whitehead is referring to pages 86–7 of *The Concept of Nature*, which de Laguna quoted in his 'Extensive abstraction'. See the note earlier in this lecture.

Bring in notion of time, durations to do it. Whitehead there hadn't seen how to get rid of difficulties of tangency. Obvious method didn't seem to work. Want to define point by saying you've got the sharpest kind of approximation you can. Nothing has sharper type of approximation. Can't cover any other element with a sharper type of approximation. Abstractive element converges to a point of every abstractive class which it covers. ~~really~~ Also covers it so really the two are equal to it. That ⟨?⟩ shows you've got down to the utmost sharpness of convergence there is.

Since have Q_i without internal tangency, it works here. Can't exclude anything which you can't define.

Thing would work perfectly – there are elements of that sort.

$\kappa \in$ GeomEl.

$\kappa \in$ Pt. = Df: $_\lambda \zeta \in \kappa \cdot \zeta Q_c \eta. \supset. \eta Q_c \zeta$

This will work as notion of point.

Presupposed dealing with abstractive classes.

Difficult if hadn't been able to get rid of internal tangency. Whitehead got rid of it in book by invoking notion of time, simultaneity. Can now get rid without fresh notion.

Would have been in difficulty among abstractive classes, should have had classes of this sort.[1]

Then should have had[2]

Red and white classes both converging to point – All have common tangency. Red covers white, but no white covers any red. Can't define your point in that way. Deceitfulness of riches nothing to the deceitfulness of tangency.

Real difficulty – can prove by this instance[3] in the extensive continuum of sort which you want nothing which corresponds to[4]

Thursday, 17 March 1927

Conger's notes

|1| Point represents bundle of equivalent or equal modes of convergence which are the sharpest routes of convergence. Can't deal with geometry merely from point of view of points, must also consider idea of lines. Question is how define line. Every definition corresponds ⟨to⟩ a primitive proposition that the entity which corresponds to that definition are important. There is always a reference to importance.

First considered notion of the sharpest convergence – but another notion, the sharpest possible type of convergence under such and such circumstances. So must consider ~~what~~ ∨how∨ we define that. Can define it in same way as

---

1. There is an arrow from this sentence pointing to the figure on the right.
2. There is an arrow from this sentence fragment to the sentence above it.
3. There is an arrow here pointing to the figure on the right.
4. There is an arrow here pointing to 'Pt.' in the above expression, i.e. $\kappa \in$ Pt. = Df: $_\lambda\zeta \in \kappa \cdot \zeta Q_c \eta. \supset. \eta Q_c \zeta$.

point only. Must put in the general notion in addition that all convergence satisfy assigned conditions – May not be any sharp convergence. Can't force a thing into existence by defining it. Only Descartes' ontological proof manages that.

If ξ is abstractive class, might write σ(ξ) for definite conditions. Make definition hold for any conditions which you like to put. Let us call the ∨abstractive classes which have∨ sharpest ~~definition~~ convergence under these conditions primes – can't get ⟨subject?⟩ to these conditions any sharper condition.

Prime (σ) is class of sharpest convergence. Any abstractive class ~~is~~ ξ is a prime with respect to condition σ means –

(1) that ∨condition∨ σ(ξ) holds: ξ satisfies condition ∧σ∧.

(2) ξ is an abstractive class, a convergence which satisfies condition σ.

(3) ~~If each~~ ∧Fact of∧ η also satisfying σ(η) and ξ "covering" η ~~then~~ ⟨?⟩ is equivalent to saying ξ is equal to η. Namely, ξ covers η and η covers ξ.

Cover each other, and therefore both belong to same geometrical elements with equivalent convergence. |2| Converse way is if η does satisfy and ξ covers η, can't...

Here you have a geometrical element such that every member satisfies σ(η) – and ξ ⟨?⟩ ~~∨covers∨~~ ∧is equal to∧ η. That's a definition if the sharpest condition you can get under certain circumstances – Don't say what circumstances because want to consider a variety later. ~~Next point~~

Another concept the least sharp convergence – the fattest geometrical element. Anti-primes.

See what want to get hold of – define segment ~~of line~~ between two points, then can define line. Do it without new idea.

No point to talk about the order of ∨⟨exact?⟩∨[1] points yet.

Define a line between the two. The logical savage naturally says it's a series of points which connect; but how going to define – you haven't got the idea of points in series yet – notion of order. Propose to define it by reference to a line. What do you mean by these things being in order – This is the advantage of dealing with symbols. What is important is you should know what you're doing. True safety of philosophy when considering extension is really to take nothing for granted.

– Habit of writing literature when ought to write mathematics very deleterious in philosophy.

 Do it by areas, general idea of extended entity. What we want is notion of sharpest convergence of abstractive class of entities which give sharpest convergence subject to fact that every |3| member covers every abstractive class which belongs to class 1 and class 2.

---

1. Conger has the interlineation 'exc' above the word 'of'. The proper expansion and location of the interlineation are not clear. It could be 'order of exact points yet', 'order exclusive of points yet' or some other variant.

Want notion of sharpest abstractive class which is prime in respect to fact that it satisfies the condition and every abstractive class which is a member of π_2. Will then converge to some line drawing π_1 and π_2. π_1 and π_2 and will be end points of line. Sharpest type of convergence which can get under those conditions. Condition $\sigma(\varepsilon)$ now means ξ covers every member, i.e. every abstractive class of π_1 and every member of π_2.

Any abstractive class converges to a line of which π_1 and π_2 are the end points.

An inf number of lines joining π_1, π_2.

If had ⟨sketch⟩ If converging down to this – the π_1–π_2 would be a sharper convergence than the one which went beyond it. ~~Yellow se~~

Or suppose x – find ξ covers x, but x doesn't cover ξ ⟨?⟩. π_1–π_2 include something which x doesn't

η is red class – big outside. Although ξ covers it, doesn't cover ξ.

Would call $\pi_1 \pi_2$ the end points.

Then take whole set if equal abstractive classes and can see condition σ is such that if equal, π_1 and π_2 are still contained in them and will be the end points of the whole lot.

Doesn't in any way presuppose that there is any 1 line in point 2. Not every line has an end point, suppose just knocked out.

|4| Can think of all the points which are covered by the line. Any abstractive class ν which converges to πν is covered by any abstractive class which converges to that line – idea of incidence. Can think of line as class of points – our familiar geometrical way of doing it.

Can make these notions do work of point. Can define segment as one and only one [set] ...

Doesn't matter what suppositions – Pool ⟨together?⟩ the ⟨shaky?⟩ obviousnesses. Each ⟨?⟩[1]

Idea of a line going on and on. Nowhere a complete line.

Original line λ

How say can't go any farther?

Any point νπν lying outside line can't find ⟨?⟩ a finite line νμν which includes ⟨?⟩ original line and also includes π.

Question as to whether notion has any application within the ⟨space-time?⟩ of our experience – Don't think have defined fundamental relation of physical universe into existence –

Closed line, which returns on itself such that if take any two points π_1 and π_2, there are exactly two segments of points with π_1 and π_2 as end points, and the two segments include all the points in the line.

---

1. There is a sizable gap on the page between this point and the next line of text, in which Conger switches from pen to pencil. It seems likely that his pen ran out of ink, and that in switching over to pencil he missed some material.

|5| Now get on to surfaces.

Point on surface is half in and half out – a set of entities on surface of this entity *a* such that it has all abstractive classes belonging to that point such that every member of these abstractive classes overlaps *a*, but is neither shaded by *a* nor does it shade *a* – therefore get notion of surface of *a*.

Points in volume. Then axioms enable you to say ~~in~~ complete surface to *a* and shared by nothing else –

Can define area, define straight line – without reference to any line. Euclid says lies evenly between its points. Can say shortest distance, which presupposes measurement. Can ⟨give?⟩ in terms of extension. First – define ~~complex~~ \/completely convex\/ ⟨sided?⟩ in terms of intersection.

Then ~~when~~ can

If have curved line when you get near enough down in a close enough approximation in volume will have some points concave and some convex. |6| If can apply approximation purely by convex solids, you'd have a straight line.

Saturday, 19 March 1927

Conger's notes

|1| Actual instruments of thought – something much earlier than geometry – that is underline{number}. Chapter 2, *Science and the Modern World*.[1] Extraordinarily high grade abstraction. Cf. catches of fish. Could be compared – But couldn't compare multiplicities of class of underline{different} objects. Notion of correlation. Multiplicity of a class abstracted from question. Then cf. . . .

Then idea of multiplicity ~~ab~~ as abstract quantity. Simply concerned with what can be looked on as one entity. That's abstract. Must take enormous time to elaborate. Get idea numbers as antecedent to classes. Did Plato and Pythagoras think there were numbers somewhere tucked away in peculiarly perfect world of abstractions and in some way ventured into this dusty world of empirical experience, but that number was before the world?

Question – What is number? Hard-headed view of empiricists, number depends on counting. Objection to that, like all these explanations. If no one to count, no number. Question: How many ichthyosauri[2] existed is perfectly definite, and surely the answer was definite before there were any men. Whitehead can't understand position which requires operations of an adequate mentality in order that definite facts of that sort should be.

Then another objection – counting if only you have time to count long enough can elicit relationships of any number. There is [realistic view]. Anyhow you would have polished up a good many. Ideally possible to get to any number – not to get to all numbers. If read the literature written in middle of last

---

1. Chapter 2 of *Science and the Modern World* is entitled 'Mathematics as an element in the history of thought'.
2. Ichthyosaurs are an extinct species of marine reptile.

century 1850 Weierstrass. Another question. Assuming number depends on counting, you say 1st 2nd 3rd 4th 5th. Ordinal number is prior to cardinal.

|2| Number entirely depends on fact that every class of number can be arranged in a serial order, not merely a serial order, but a particular serial order. 1st 2nd 3rd   A first term which has one next door neighbor. If go on
 ·   ·   ·   forever – no end to it – every other term will have two next door neighbors. If only getting up to finite number, class has last term which has only one next door neighbor. Can find a particular way.

Arriving at a final term, the nth, is peculiar of number.

vN^{th}v Fundamental proposition of number – however you rearrange that class, you will always find correlate your names and find arrive at nth in other series.

The right way is really derivative from the way Clifford marked out – and embodies it as highly particular case.

See W. K. Clifford ⟨?⟩ *Common Sense of the (Physical) Sciences*.[1] Anticipated Einstein by about 50 years. {Clifford said one day he shouldn't be surprised if matter was nothing else but a kink in space.} Somebody lacked the still small voice which whispers "Fiddlesticks". Best thought of 1870's. Too little known. {Compares somewhat to Charles Peirce.[2] Very great ill luck.}

{Clerk Maxwell died early. Clifford in his 40's. Peirce out of action.} Biggest since Newton.[3] All died early. Sufficient genius to turn world topsy-turvy.

|3| It was always held that when you got to infinity, that if tried to treat infinity as a number, you arrived at contradictions, and infinite number was mysterious self-contradictory notion which delighted people who were speculative and didn't know much mathematics. [Probably driving here at new infinity].

Another point. Notion of order types. A line can be looked at as class of points. Question of order type – serial order of points in line. One peculiarity of type of order of line – Between any two points an infinite number of other points.

Another peculiarity – Suppose two cut each other.

We hold they cut at a point. You deny that all the points on line *AB* can be divided into two classes – all those to left and to the right. Deny that that is exhaustive of all the points on the

---

1. It is unclear why 'physical' is in parentheses, but this is the wrong title for the referenced book by William Kingdon Clifford (1845–79), which was actually called *The Common Sense of the Exact Sciences*, available at <https://archive.org/details/commonsenseexac02clifgoog>, published posthumously by Karl Pearson.
2. Charles Sanders Peirce (1839–1914) was an American philosopher and mathematician, probably best known as the founding father of the philosophical school of pragmatism. Charles Hartshorne, who attended many of Whitehead's Philosophy 3b lectures in 1925–6 and would later develop Whitehead's process philosophy into a process theology, was much enamoured with Peirce's work, and would co-edit his collected papers with Paul Weiss in the 1930s. Whitehead had agreed to write a preface to the collected papers, but for reasons unknown that did not come to pass. In the previous semester of this academic year, Whitehead invited Hartshorne to deliver guest lectures on Peirce's philosophy, on 30 November and 2 December. See the Introduction (pp. xlvi–xlvii).
3. It is not clear whether this statement is supposed to refer to Maxwell, Clifford, Peirce or all three.

line because there is a point *C* left out. Can't divide points up all to left and all to right. Could you derive the extra dense property from mere fact of being dense?

Take *Al* ~~to~~ as one inch. Mark down all points whose distance from *A* is some fraction (proper or ᵛimproperᵛ integral) of an inch. Can always find fraction between any two fractions so those points will be everywhere dense. But not all the points because have proved by geometry that a line $\sqrt{2}$ can be drawn, and point for $\sqrt{2}$ doesn't lie in the dense series.

For rational numbers can find line which cuts *AB* where no such point. Proves existence of everywhere dense series which hasn't extra density which we assume ⟨as?⟩ property of straight lines.

|4| Extra dense property now called continuity. Distinction between mere density and continuity – Dedekind.[1]

That awoke a notion – here different types of order. Dense type of serial order. Continuous type of serial order.

What sorts of types of order can you have? That awakens the notion – When you have a class, what types of order can you put its members into?

1 2 3 4
. . . .

Can put into ᵛorder byᵛ² number ᵛof ~~order~~ waysᵛ by permutations. Can't put into type of order which goes off to infinity, because aren't enough terms.

Suppose an infinite class.[3] Take stand and example class of numbers 1.2.3.4. . . . $\sqrt{2}$ $\sqrt{2}$ There is a class which is confessedly dense but has no continuity – class of fractions[4]

$1/_T, 1/_3, \ldots 1/_2 \ldots 4/_5 \ldots 2/_1 \ldots 3/_2$

Two peculiarities

(1) dense

(2)

Some difficulty about being logically consistent (No difficulty about in physical space).

Can correlate this up with rational points of line, and between any two rationals an infinite number of irrationals. And rational and irrational together make up a continuous series.

Lowest type of dense series. Rational numbers. Least erected type.

First type of infinity – 1 2 3 4. Everyone has next door neighbor. Wherever stop, have a finite class; can only get to infinity by going on and on. Not infinite series until to bitter end and is no end to go to. Must consider it as totality before get infinite series.

---

1. Whitehead is likely referring to the 1872 work 'Continuity and irrational numbers' by German mathematician Richard Dedekind (1831–1916), which first appeared in English translation in 1901. See Dedekind, *Stetigkeit und irrationale Zahlen*, and Beman, *Essays on the Theory of Numbers* (Chicago: Open Court Publishing Company, 1901), pp. 1–27. Wooster Woodruff Beman translated Dedekind's book.
2. The proper positioning of this interlineation is unclear.
3. There is a struck-out figure below this text which we have not included here. It is possible that the '$\sqrt{2}\sqrt{2}$' was also intended to be scratched out.
4. In the series below there seems to be an error. $2/_1$ and $3/_2$ should be reversed, as they are in a later series in this same lecture.

Can select other infinite series |5| in dense series of fractions. Wherever you stop you have an infinite number.

$0 .. 1/3 .. 1/2 .. 4/5 .... 1/1 .. 3/2 .... 2/1$

Looks as if type of infinity here different from that of integers. You can prove that you can arrange the fractions in the form of a progression, in that type of order. Thus two types of infinity – these two are the same. When get to continuity, can prove can't arrange series of fractions in continuous series. Can prove not enough fractions.

Momentous discovery. Look back to references to infinity in 1870's to see what an advance. Get proposition as soon as get to infinity the human mind staggers.

Something sensible had been proved now – definite proposition, discriminating between types of infinity. No philosophy interested in it when it was made. Begin to see differentiate between cardinal and ordinal number. Obviously an ordinal number is to be looked on as reference to order type. If order types same, can get one to one correlation without disturbing the order. Arrows never cross. So the correlations don't disturb the order type. (The notion of cardinal number?)[1]

Clifford in particular case of finite number

When come to ⟨prove?⟩ – can you put same class into variety of order if order types can only do it if members of class have it sort of multiplicity? Sometimes don't have enough entities to do it. Some propositions antecedent to any particular ∨order∨ type which a class has which has to be right. Namely – If same class can go into two order types, these types must both show the same multiplicity. So cardinal number primary. Simpler and presupposed. (Cantor. The power of a number)[2]

|6| Independent of particular type of order as long as has same multiplicity.

In ⟨proving?⟩ different sorts of infinity – <u>different infinite cardinal numbers</u>. Then define a cardinal number so as not to assume you are dealing with a finite class. See how far can go in arithmetic without presupposing finite or infinite. See how in arithmetic holds for infinite numbers.

Reason why contradictions turned up, assumed arithmetic for infinity must be same. In many respects same, many respects different. But had to prove first in particular cases different infinite cardinal numbers.

Tuesday, 22 March 1927

Weiss's notes

|56| 12345 ... continuous $1/1$ $1/2$ etc ⟨?⟩ $1/2 .. 1/\sqrt{2}$ etc. continuous.
Between any two fractions you can find as many fractions as you like.
Between them there are an infinite # of irrationals making discontinuous gaps in the fractional series.

---

1. Parentheses supplied. The parenthetical text appears in the right margin.
2. Parentheses supplied. The parenthetical text appears in the left margin.

|57| There are an infinite number of classes, each having a finite number of members.[1]

$\frac{N}{D}$, $N + d = m$ = index

Class Index	1	2	3	4	n
	0,1	1,1	~~0,3~~	~~0,4~~	~~0,n~~
		~~0,2~~	1,2	1,3	1, n − 1
			2,1	3,1	2, n − 2
					n − 1, 1
	$\frac{0}{1}$	$\frac{1}{1}$	$\frac{1}{2}\ \frac{2}{1}$	$\frac{1}{3}\ \frac{3}{1}$	$\frac{1}{n-1}\ldots\frac{n-1}{1}$ −

The fractions are now in a continuous series.

$2/3$ is the relation of integer m to integer n by virtue of fact that $3 \times m = 2 \times n$ $n(n-1)(n-2)$, all at a time.[2]

The number of subclasses is always greater than the class. The subclasses can be correlated to the class ⟨?⟩ $\vee \beta$ − some at a time∨ but not exhausted

$\beta +$ subclass of β

xyz   y y + z

One-to-one correspondence

If every y contains x, among the x's is the class of only one member not taken care of. All the β are ⟨?⟩ in the correlation of unit classes ⟨...?⟩ $\pi(xyz) - \eta$ ⟨...?⟩.

Thursday, 24 March 1927

Weiss's notes[3]

Bernstein-Schroeder Theorem: Zermelo[4]

One-to-one correlation β to δ. But δ is part of γ. Number $'\beta \leq N'\gamma$

One-to-one correlation γ to M. But M is part of β. Number $'\gamma \leq N'\beta$.

---

1. The rest of this lecture is giving a construction of the 'Cantor set'. The set of all subsets of a given set always comprises a new set (the power set) that is larger than the original. This is how Cantor showed that the set of reals/irrationals is larger than the set of all fractions, even though the latter is infinite.
2. This line of text appears in the left margin, and its correct placement is not entirely clear. There is also some indecipherable text in the left margin in the same vicinity.
3. Weiss's handwriting makes it very difficult to have confidence in accurately rendering his symbolic notation, Greek letters in particular. This is especially difficult with the letters phi (Φ) and psi (Ψ). See the Introduction (p. lii).
4. The Bernstein–Schroeder theorem states that if there exists injective functions $f: A \to B$ and $g: B \to A$ between the sets A and B, there exists a bijective function $h: A \to B$, and hence A and B have the same number. This theorem should be called the Cantor–Bernstein theorem, as Cantor first formulated and proved it, and as Bernstein's 1887 alternative proof was correct, but Schroeder's 1886 one was flawed. Yet another proof was found by Zermelo in 1906, which may be why Whitehead mentions him in this context.

Therefore Number 'β = Number γ. An infinite class can be correlated to a proper part of itself.

⟨?⟩ – Smallest infinites $X_0 + X_0 = X_0$. $X_0 \times X_0 = X_0$

$n \times m$ = the number of couples in the two classes; $n + m$ is the class containing both.

Proof there are an infinite number of primes $(1 \times 2 \times 3 \times \therefore n)+1$ – prime

3, 5, 7, 11 ... p – primes

6 10 14 22   2q   ⟨?⟩ $z \times p \times q = X_0$

There will be a member corresponding ⟨with?⟩ each but different from both.

|58| There will be 2 classes $2p \times q$ & $2q \times p - \frac{1}{2}$ ⟨...?⟩

$F(\alpha_\psi)$ there exists a predicate ϕ which ① is equivalent in truth value to Ψ ② exemplifies F i.e. for which $\neq ((\phi?))$ is true. Number could be defined as a relation between predicates but it is a class of predicates $\alpha_\psi \alpha_\phi$.

Tuesday, 29 March 1927

King's notes[1]

|76| The notion of numbers $\alpha, \beta, \gamma ....$

Numbers deal with the – is an attribute of the class by reason of the multiplicity. The same multiplicity $\alpha \overset{1-1}{\leftrightarrow}$ one to one correlation between two classes.[2] They have the same multiplicity. The definite number is the whole class of classes with a one-to-one correlation – a unique relation to the multiplicity.

The notion of cardinal numbers. Within it there are especial sets of cardinal numbers. 0, 1, 2 ... ∨and so on∨ always by adding one. But this "and so on" – is it a primary notion? And, can we always add one? We will have to bring in the axiom of infinity.

The <u>inductive</u> numbers. 0, 1, 2, 3 etc.

The arithmetical operations $m +_c n = p-, m \times_c n = q$

Fractions – m has the relation $\frac{N}{D}$ of n which means $m \times_c D = n \times_c N$.

A fraction is a relation between two numbers.

$\frac{N}{D} +_f \frac{N'}{D'}$ $\frac{N}{D} \times_f \frac{N'}{D'}$

$\frac{(N \times C') +_c (N' \times D)}{D \times_c D'}$ $\frac{N \times N'}{D \times_c D'}$

⟨?⟩ $x, n = m$. What must x be? Sometimes I can answer it, sometimes not. When dealing with fractions we have left the inductive numbers behind. Finding the gap, the cut in a series is like the Greeks finding a point.

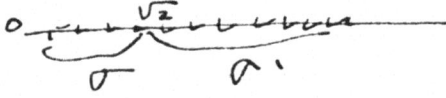

---

1. Neither King nor Weiss has any notes for Saturday, 26 March. It is unclear whether the class did not take place, or we simply do not have any notes from any student who attended it.
2. Cf. Weiss: 'One is $a \leftrightarrow B \leftrightarrow C$ ∧(one-to-one relation)∧. Fractions are relations ⟨?⟩ vectors' (Weiss, p. 58).

σ has no end point.
σ' has no beginning.
|77|

σ is a <u>real</u> number(?), $\sigma_1 + \sigma_2$ where $f_1 + f_2$ – any <u>fraction</u> of one <u>segment</u> with[1]

Thursday, 31 March 1927

Weiss's notes

|58| Hereditary Class – if $m\varepsilon y + mRv$ then $v\varepsilon m$ – ⟨?⟩
$xR_*y \equiv y$ belongs to every hereditary class and ⟨...?⟩
$n(+_c 1) m = m = n + 1$
$n(+_c 1)_* m * - ⟨?⟩$
$1(+_c)_* n =$ inductive ⟨numbers?⟩.
Axiom of Infinity ⟨...?⟩
Reflexive Class – ⟨...?⟩[2]

Tuesday, 5 April 1927

Weiss's notes[3]

The universal element in judgment arises from the conformation of thought to the universal forms constitutive of human beings: Thought arises as a functioning in connection with actual things. You think by determining the actual against a background of pure potentiality. Without potentiality, no error. Actuality involves real synthesis of that common to thought and nature ⟨?⟩. That ⟨?⟩ correspondence of thought and object is an identity or diversity in eternal objects. The what and how of thought is identical with nature. An act of thought |59| or nature is each an activity gaining a real unity out of the indefinite multiplicity of eternal objects by primary inclusion – relevance. The content is constituted by the relevant elements which are abstracted out of the background or pure potentials. Two kinds of content of thought: ① Its own

---

1. Weiss (p. 58) has additional material about imaginary numbers that King does not seem to have: 'An imaginary number is an ordered couple of numbers.
   $(a,b)+(x,y) \subseteq (a+x),(b+y)$.
   $(a,b)\times(x,y)=(a\times x)-(b\times y),(a\times y)-(b\times x)$
   $(0,1)\times(0,1)=(-1,0).$'
2. This line of text appears in the left margin. It is unclear if it is intended to go with this lecture or the 5 April lecture, which also appears immediately adjacent on the same page.
3. Neither King nor Weiss has any notes for Saturday, 2 April. It is unclear whether the class did not take place, or that we simply do not have any notes from any student who attended it. Note also that there is some indecipherable text in the left margin.

proper content of relevant potentialities or eternal objects, ② an associated act of nature:– To understand thought ⟨?⟩ must understand ②. Thought is analytic of nature. Correspondence is identity of ① ⟨and?⟩ ②. No clean cut between thought and nature. Nothing like pure abstract thought. Any set is the abstraction of some elements of everything else. "Some" and "all" are relevant to such abstraction ⟨...?⟩.

Thursday, 7 April 1927
King's notes

|78| Induction
We start with actual fact, something particular now, and then we generalize.

We must ask, how does the particular involve what is beyond itself, the universal. How does the experience of the present carry a relevance to the future and the past.

Possibly we have only a private world of our own ideas. Perception is of immediate facts of our mind. If so, we are deprived of the comfort of an external world. If all knowledge of perception is a component of my experience, we have the difficulty with an external world. How can my experience give us knowledge of an immediate external world?

Analyze what we mean by experience. Analysis is not passive. Start with a hypothetical metaphysical construction.

The first test of such a system is a theory of knowledge, theory of perception. But we do not start with it.

We must start with pure potentiality – complete abstraction. No knowledge unless there are elements which can be transferred from one field to another. There is a multiplicity of pure potentialities – of every grade, with interconnections of potentialities.[1] This realm ∨of potentiality∨ is not self-subsistent, but a reference of where it is to be found. The potential entities cannot be understood by themselves. Essential in the character of an actual entity that it exhibits the whole realm of potentialities – either relegating them as pure potentialities, unfulfilled, or promoting them to the status of potentialities fulfilled.

|79| These potentialities are called eternal objects. Describing what is actual in terms of how what is actual exemplifies what is potential. What is actual is a selected activity, which is also achieved – At once the act and the activity.

The fact of being actual is an activity of abstraction in respect to sheer potentialities. It divides into a foreground and a background.

"Universals" are implicated in an activity. The community of a common world. There are settled acts. ⟨?⟩ As we are in the present, the past is defined relatively to us. There is essentially a standpoint of immediate activity and a settled past. Each immediate entity has a settled past.

---

1. Cf. Weiss: 'There are potentialities of potentialities ∨eternal objects∨ and connections between them' (Weiss, p. 59).

Pure potentiality is imagination. The present rises out of the past (but not determined by it.) Not merely my own past, which is enormously relevant, however, but the whole past of the world. Keep the world together.¹

Natural potentiality, which is ⟨open?⟩ to me by the nature of things. The less relevant past has a settled relationship to which the present must conform.

S under abstraction (another selection) from its ⟨former?⟩ completeness, is, in that abstract sense, present in *I*.

To be actual is to effect a real synthesis among potentialities (eternal objects) and settled actual entities. Actuality comes in in contrast between real and potential.

That synthesis is of two parts.

Synthesizing the whole actual world under |80| abstraction from its former completeness. That gives natural potentiality.

The natural ground from which any entity must arise. In conceiving its synthesis, conceive it as arising from something settled.

Unless we have self-building, we throw over morals altogether.

Saturday, 9 April 1927

Weiss's notes

|59| Relations between entities in particular, which are "objectifications"² of an object for a given ⟨object⟩ subject. As a world of activities it is atomic. The superject is an ideal outside of everything and is really nothing. You explain a thing only in terms of what it is to something else. There are some aspects that must be taken as continuous and some as one vquestionv. Each life cycle or portion of it is a quanta.

Tuesday, 12 April 1927

King's notes

|81| Perception as appropriating a disembodied universal is not a proper analysis of Phil. is ⟨...?⟩.

Logic doesn't consider differences of right or wrongness. The category of right or wrong is not primary for the discovery of truth. Scientific method is a state of imaginative muddled suspense.

Immediate obviousness of sens our experience. There is learned tradition, isolating topics and stating them with precision.

Another learned tradition – of philosophers.

---

1. Cf. Weiss: 'The pasts of different events are largely identical' (Weiss, p. 59).
2. Closing quotation mark supplied. It is unclear whether it should appear here, at the end of the sentence, or somewhere in between.

Third, the ineradicable habit of popular thought.
Three appeals of philosophy.
Disagreement is ① Lack of coherence (internal) ② Lack of correspondence (with facts.)[1]

Thursday, 14 April 1927

Weiss's notes

|59| Complexity of actual reduced to publicity of individual. An entity may be considered objectively – what it is for another or as what it is for itself – formally. |60| Objectivity means abstraction from formal completeness. Nature of universe in itself is interconnection by abstraction, not from entity as individual, but from its formal ⟨?⟩ – Do not see yellowness and squareness disembodied, but that yellow and that square in that perspective, etc. I arise out of a real context of diverse percepts which develop into further phases. Thought is abstract, but so is nature, which abstracts from formal completeness. Private ground of actuality vsubstancev cannot be eliminated. You arise from an actual ground into something which is you with-ground.[2] Process of self-creativeness ⟨?⟩.

Saturday, 16 April 1927

Weiss's notes[3]

An actual entity is something by itself. The ground is the natural potentiality of relationship which arises from the past. Ground continuous, though what arises out of it not.

#2
... Natural potentiality
-- settled past – ground

There is principle of most possible actuality permitting best synthesis. Ground is first v#1v substantial and perceptual phase. Second phase is #1 plus ⟨aesthetic?⟩ satisfaction and criticism of #1. Whitehead is #2 plus mentality.

---

1. Weiss (p. 59) has only a few lines of notes for the 12 April lecture. They do not match up with anything in King's notes at all: 'The percept is one of particular shape, not of universal shape. No shapiness. Element of particularity which cannot be got rid of.'
2. It is not clear whether the hyphen after 'with' is in fact a hyphen or an 'a'.
3. This was Whitehead's last lecture prior to his departure to Virginia to give the Barbour-Page lectures, which would be published as *Symbolism: Its Meaning and Effect*. We know from a letter of Whitehead's to his son, North, dated 25 March 1927, that he was gone from 17 April to 30 April, during Harvard's spring break (Whitehead, 'Letter to T. North Whitehead', 25 March 1927). Apparently not all of the trip was devoted to delivering the lectures, as Whitehead wrote that 'Our visit to Virginia has been extended by four days, at Lowell's request, to enable us to be present at some celebration in Philadelphia'.

#1 has added nothing to potentiality but that it is real. This is process of acquiring attributes which have an individual character. The first phase or formal content of the settled past in part constitutes the natural potentiality of the new event. The individual issues from the potential ground of the settled past. Sense data are given by past and ⟨?⟩ the present.[1]

Tuesday, 3 May 1927

Weiss's notes[2]

|61|[3] Synthesis is most fundamental character of an object. It is first category. Not ⟨disjoined?⟩ from analysis. Perception involves a symbolism. We go from the perception of a colored object to a colored chair. Sense presentation is a quality of higher organisms. Direct experience is infallible. Symbolism is not direct experience or pure abstraction only approximated to. Mind acts symbolically when some components ∨symbols∨ of its experience elicit emotions, beliefs, etc. of other components of experience ∨meaning∨. Symbolic reference is a going from symbol to meaning. It is the active synthetic element contributed by the nature of the percipient, requiring a ground founded on the community between symbols and meaning. Perception is a phase of self-production of an organism arising out of some primary given phase. Activity is self-production, which is synthesis. Percipient has perception and thing perceived is internal relationship. No way of determining which is symbol and which is meaning. Nothing which is only one. Most primitive is always meaning-realism. Symbolic reference holds between two components in an experience which is capable of analytical recognition. To fail to recognize it means you are low-grade percipient.

Percipient must connect the two components of symbolic reference. The act of experience determines which shall be the symbol.

You see a star as a space there illuminated now by a ⟨?⟩. We perceive only particulars. Error is primarily a fact of symbolic reference and not of conceptual analysis. No sharp line between mental and physical. Absence of perceptual immediacy and not absence of thought that makes error. Symbolic reference is one form of perceptual immediacy by which what is actual arises out of what is potential actuality.

---

1. There is some indecipherable text in the left margin.
2. Whitehead was gone for two weeks while he delivered the Barbour-Page lectures in Virginia (see note at end of previous lecture). Given what we have from Weiss's notes, it appears that at least over the next four course days (3, 5, 7 and 10 May) he is sharing what is now the first two chapters of *Symbolism*. It is likely that Whitehead finished presenting chapter 3 in the subsequent lectures, but Weiss was absent or did not take notes on those days (12, 14 and 17 May) and we do not have notes from other sources for those dates.
3. Note that there is some indecipherable text in the left margin.

Thursday, 5 May 1927

Weiss's notes[1]

Truth and error are in the world because of synthesis. Every |62| actual thing is a synthesis whereby what is actual arises from its given potentiality – symbolic reference. Presentational immediacy is sense perception. The quantum always involves a specific entity and not a society of them. Present conforms to the past. Mere succession abstraction from time.

Saturday, 7 May 1927

Weiss's notes[2]

Time is not mere succession. Involves conformation to the past. Causal efficacy is known prior to concepts – ⟨stones?⟩ etc. Conformation is a mask of primitive experience. Present issues from the past and is conditioned by it. Sense data and locality are two elements which intersect in causal efficacy and presentation. Two sides of one act. Sense data are the given. The sense data common to both is referred to a localization. Color is referred to external space and to the eyes as an organ of vision.

Tuesday, 10 May 1927

Weiss's notes[3]

Causal efficacy first; presentational immediacy second – Hume reversed it. No different species for sight, hearing, etc.

Thursday, 19 May 1927

Weiss's notes[4]

Euclid. Thing equal to same thing, equal to each other. ac & Bc ergo AB.
Equality means transitivity ab, bc, ac – but implies ~~simplicity~~ symmetry – ab & ba, bc & cb, from which deduce reflexivity.
Matching involves $\gamma(c_1 c_2 \ldots c_n)$ class of colors.
P matches $Q \to \gamma$ – symmetrical; does not imply transitivity.
P matches $Q \to \gamma(c_1)$ and $Q =$ matches $R \to \gamma(c_2)$.
If we limit c's to mutually exclusive entities, transitivity and reflexivity follow.

---

1. Here again Whitehead is drawing from his Barbour-Page lectures.
2. Here again Whitehead is drawing from his Barbour-Page lectures.
3. Here again Whitehead is drawing from his Barbour-Page lectures.
4. We have no notes from Weiss for 12, 14 or 17 May. For more on this, see 3 May 1927 lecture, note 2, p. 336.

Congruence requires justification of transportation via congruence of opposite side of ▱.

Equals added to equals, the wholes are equals.

Addition of $P + Q$ determines R

$R \to c_3 = c_1 \oplus c_2$

⟨Saturday, 21 May 1927⟩

Weiss's notes[1]

Whole greater than parts.

Magnitude and quantities must be correlated one-to-one.

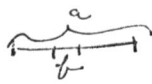 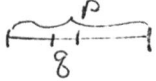

$A = P \to \gamma$
$B = q \to \gamma$
B is part of A
q is part of P
We ⟨?⟩ $A = q \to \gamma$
        $P = B \to \gamma$

This holds of infinite classes.

We assume possibility of infinite subdivision. $\frac{1}{n} c - a$ can be ⟨derived?⟩ Archimedes. Any ⱽgivenⱽ distance is finite ⟨and?⟩ can be excluded. Axiom of Archimedes. Peano's curve filling all ⟨?⟩.[2]

We can define #1 as all fractions ⟨?⟩ 0 to 1 – 1 not included.

---

1. Weiss marks the date as 'May 20', but since this was a Friday, the correct date is probably 21 May.
2. This line of text appears in the left margin. Its correct placement is unclear. In 1890, the Italian mathematician Giuseppe Peano (1858–1932) showed that it is possible to define a one-dimensional curve that completely fills a two-dimensional region. This is one of many counter-intuitive results that prompted mathematicians to have their intuition guided by logic.

Seminaries and guest lectures for 1926–7

Philosophy 20h: Seminary in Metaphysics, fall semester 1926

⟨Friday, 1 October 1926⟩[1]

Conger's notes[2]

|1| Dewey's book reminds of Locke. Locke {?} almost said what John Dewey and Whitehead say.[3]
1 – Descartes' <u>substance</u>. Leave out his scholastic background, etc.
2 – Mental <u>substance</u> –
3 – <u>Bodily</u> <u>substance</u>. Extension, duration, body, space, time.[4]
~~Locke~~
Descartes
    Meditation 2, 150–154, 160–169
    Principles, <u>20–21</u>
    Principles 61, 62, 63
{?} Descartes doesn't say God is a mental substance – evidently a third kind of substance.[5]

John Dewey, *Experience and Nature* 144.[6] **Preoccupation with elementary units is marked in logic, physical biology. Instrumental character of**

---

1. Date supplied from the notes of Kerby-Miller.
2. All the notes presented here are those taken by George Conger, though Kerby-Miller also had notes for the 1 October and 8 October sessions. Refer to the table on p. 419 for a full list of seminary sessions by date, and see also the Introduction for a detailed discussion of each note-taker and their notes.
   It is important to remember that Whitehead's seminaries were more discussion-based than his Philosophy 3b lectures, and hence the person speaking may not always be Whitehead.
3. Conger has a great deal more notes than Kerby-Miller in total, but the latter is considerably more thorough at the beginning of the session. Cf. Kerby-Miller: '⟨Whitehead⟩ identifies his point of view with that of Dewey, and opposes it to Descartes and Locke. Yet Dewey's *Experience and Nature* like Locke's *Essay*. Both men have broad humanity. ⟨Are?⟩ wise' (Kerby-Miller, p. 1).
4. Kerby-Miller's notes make clear that these three numbered points are things in Descartes that should be investigated: 'Read *Concept of Nature* and his later book. Report on. Investigate points in Descartes. The *Meditations* and *Principles*. (1) Doctrine of Substance, 'what he said exactly' ⟨and?⟩ views. (2) Doctrine of Mental Substance, especially as regards understanding, conceiving, perception, etc. How we come to know or infer the existence of particular substances. (3) Bodily substance, space, ⟨place?⟩, position, duration and time' (Kerby-Miller, p. 1).
5. The page numbers here refer to Descartes, *Philosophical Works, Vol. I*, available at <https://archive.org/details/philosophicalwor01desc>. There is some disagreement about page numbers between Conger and Kerby-Miller. Cf. Kerby-Miller: 'References: 1. Meditation. 2. p. 153–4. (Haldane and Ross translation). Meditation III 166, 168, 169. Principles 20 and 21 (p 227). 61 (p 239), 62–3 (p 240). 2. Meditations I, II (God mental substance? He does not say), p. 157. Meditation VI (p 185–6 and ⟨196?⟩) 3. Principle 32 (p. 232), 58 (p. 247). 3. Bodily substance, ⟨extension place, space ⟨(?) duration of time⟩ (*Principles* in above translation, *expurgatis*)' (Kerby-Miller, p. 1).
6. Dewey, *Experience and Nature*, 1929 reprint available at <https://archive.org/details/experienceandnat029343mbp>. Kerby-Miller notes that the following are 'Extracts from Dewey, ⟨charming?⟩ similarity with Whitehead' (Kerby-Miller, p. 1). In looking at the notes of both Conger and Kerby-Miller, it is clear that pages 144–5 were read aloud. As in other instances, passages in bold are places where Whitehead is reading directly from a text. In this case he is at times reading from Dewey's *Experience and Nature* and at other times from his own essay 'Time'.

elements. If treat as independent entities, insoluble epistemological problems. What are designated as elements depend on existence of immediate qualitative objects. Sensory data products of analysis. Elements of.[1] Terms must have a significance. Propositions have implications. A purely unitary physical element would have no efficacy. Large momentous facts of human life just as we find it.[2]

148 Empirically individual objects, unique affairs exist but unstable. Tremble on verge of disappearance. – Eternal ought not to be perduring absolute being.[3]

Math objects are instruments applicable (∨Whitehead:∨ applied to) to [real situation]

⟨I.⟩ Supersession ⟨II.⟩ Prehension ⟨III.⟩ Incompleteness ⟨IV.⟩ Objective Immortality ⟨V.⟩ Simultaneity ⟨VI.⟩ Time as Epochal[4]

⟨I. Supersession⟩ Can't conceive of pluralistic multiplicity of independent entities and take time seriously.[5]

Temporal – ⟨deficiency?⟩ in actuality.

If time be taken seriously, no concrete entity can change – it must be superseded.

Occasion with supersession as part of real essence –

(Bodies/Minds) **Each occasion is dipolar. One is physical, one is mental – Either as conceived in abstraction ⟨is⟩ devoid of full concreteness of**

---

1. Cf. Dewey: 'Unless macroscopic things are recognized, cells, electrons, logical elements become meaningless. The latter have meaning only as elements *of* (Dewey, *Experience and Nature*, p. 144).
2. This last sentence comes from a page-long quote that Dewey pulled from an address by psychiatrist Adolf Meyer (1866–1950) in the book *A Psychiatric Milestone* (1921). Cf. Dewey's book: 'There is always a place for elements, but there is certainly also a place for the large momentous facts of human life just as we find it' (Dewey, *Experience and Nature*, p. 145).
3. Cf. Dewey: 'But individually qualified things have some qualities which are pervasive, common, stable. They are out of time in the sense that a particular temporal quality is irrelevant to them. If anybody feels relieved by calling them eternal, let them be called eternal. But let not "eternal" be then conceived as a kind of absolute perduring existence or Being. It denotes just what it denotes: irrelevance to existence in its temporal quality. These non-temporal, mathematical or logical qualities are capable of abstraction, and of conversion into relations, into temporal, numerical and spatial *order*' (Dewey, *Experience and Nature*, p. 148). Kerby-Miller also notes that 'Eternal etc. refers to Whitehead' (Kerby-Miller, p. 1). It is not clear if this note of Kerby-Miller's is supposed to mean that Dewey's statements merely *apply* to Whitehead, or that Dewey was here actually *referencing* Whitehead's work without naming him. On the one hand, the latter seems unlikely, since Whitehead did not use the phrase 'eternal objects' in print until *Science and the Modern World*, which was published in late October 1925; Dewey's book was published the same year. On the other hand, in a letter to Whitehead dated 6 April 1926, Dewey wrote: 'I have learned, in spite of my limitations, a great deal from your previous writings, and I should have acknowledged them definitely in my *Experience and Nature*' (Dewey, 'Letter to Whitehead', 6 April 1926).
4. Note that bolding now indicates Whitehead reading from his paper 'Time', which he had read at the Sixth International Congress of Philosophy (13–17 September) about three months earlier, and which was subsequently published in the *Proceedings of the Sixth International Congress of Philosophy*. He also discusses his 'Time' paper in his Philosophy 3b in early December 1926. The rest of the seminary seems to be Whitehead re-presenting this paper to the seminary group, albeit with a few additions, including references to Dewey, Bergson and Zeno. Readers are encouraged to refer to Whitehead's original 'Time' paper; we footnote the full version only when Conger's notes are particularly unclear or inadequate.
5. Cf. Whitehead: 'No philosopher takes time seriously who either conceives of a complete totality of all existence, or conceives of a multiplicity of actual entities such that each of them is a complete fact, "requiring nothing but itself in order to exist, God only excepted"' (Whitehead, 'Time', p. 59).

dipolar occasion. **Contrast of importance between the two poles. Mental pole may be negligible.**

Each occasion supersedes others, is superseded by others, is internally a ~~part of~~ process of supersession.

|2| Paper

Potential and actual.

Potential – to Descartes

    Bergson, *durée*

Mental supersedes physical. Physical must be explained first.

Linkage between physical and mental poles illustrates truth that category of supersession transcends time – Linkage is extratemporal, yet supersession.

{Event as physical pole, mentality as functioning as a mental pole}
v(Working toward)v[1]

⟨**II. Prehension**⟩ **Time: Supersession, prehension, incompleteness.**[2]

Trying to describe same thing as Dewey.

Prehension. How world is a system of organisms.

Occasion is a concretion of diverse elements.

Elements as organized fall into two classes.

(1) The other occasions {Dewey really takes each occasion on its own}.
Otherwise *deus ex machina*

(2) Universals. Eternal objects.

World can't be a system unless get ----[3]

Definite way in which *a* includes other occasions is here called prehension. Blind physical perceptivity.

Kant: intuitions without concepts are blind. Suggest Kant – missed way.

Physical world includes eternal objects as its defining elements, but only intuitively.

Trick of organization of world into a system and of {?} physical world each physical occasion as organization of whole world from one point of view implementing concrete individuality upon organization as done by this blind perceptivity.[4]

Pure perception is the fundamental relationship of physical occasions in physical world.

Occasion *a* prehends *b* under limitation of objectification (an object for something else) – Same as Leibnizian perspectives.

Subject is prehending occasion.

Objectification is provided by eternal objects – *b* is prehended into *a* as example of these objects.

Universals are functioning.

---

1. Parentheses supplied.
2. Cf. Whitehead: 'The concept of time is complex, and arises from the interplay of three fundamental categories, namely, *Supersession, Prehension,* and *Incompleteness*' (Whitehead, 'Time', p. 60).
3. Conger seems to have misheard here. Cf. Whitehead: 'Because the other occasions are each in a definite way required for the organization of any one occasion A, the world is called a system' (Whitehead, 'Time', p. 60).
4. This entire paragraph appears as a kind of marginal note on the right of the preceding paragraph.

Creativity.
The activity of eternal objects as characterizing the creativity.
John Dewey and Whitehead emphasize activity.
Every entity involved in an activity whereby something beyond itself is being produced and every occasion in what it is producing.

|3| Eternal object has its activity in two forms. Either <u>conceptual</u> – activity being a concept where has to deal with mental analyzing of physical world. Or <u>physical</u> – blind perceptivity. Wants a neutral term between mental and physical activity – eternal object.

Relation of identity very important. Only holds between diverse things – diverse functionings of the same eternal object or of the same occasion. Always diversity when apply relation of identity.

***B* is objectified for *a*. Eternal objects are relational elements which affect the objectification.**

Eternal objects have modes of ingression which define the objectivity – the prehended occasion – define concepts by which associated mental occasion analyzes physical occasion and effects new synthesis – consciousness.

Eternal <u>objects</u> are active entities ˅because they˅ ⟨are⟩ in the <u>objectification</u>.

⟨III. Incompleteness⟩ Time requires incompleteness.

No system of occasions which is completed. No one well-defined entity which is the actual world. Past, present, future occasion defined from some present – He, she, it, tomorrow, yesterday. Meaning defined by context.

A prehends in its concretion objectifications which must supersede *a*, but haven't in a reality of ˅fully˅ concrete occasions.[1]

Every occasion holds in itself its own future.

Anticipation is primarily a blind physical fact, and is only a mental fact by reason of mind's partial analysis.

Physical anticipation – creativity whereby there is supersession can't be separated from creature. ~~Form~~ **Then there will be individualization of creativity. As soon as you have the creature, there is creativity with a new character. Creature is thereby superseded.**[2] **Always when talk of future – Process of becoming is union of being with not being.**

⟨IV.⟩ **Objective Immortality – Physical memory is example of incompleteness. In occasion *B*, occasion *b* prehends *a* into itself as contributing a measure of determinate completion.**

---

[1]. Cf. Whitehead: 'The incompleteness of an actual occasion A means that A prehends in its concretion objectification of occasions X, Y, Z, . . . which must supersede A but, as in A, have not the actuality of determinate concretions' (Whitehead, 'Time', p. 61).

[2]. Cf. Whitehead: 'The character of the creativity is found in the analysis of the creature. The creativity *for* the creature has become the creativity *with* the creature; and the creature is thereby superseded' (Whitehead, 'Time', p. 61).

A is relatively determined except from indetermination arising from incompleteness of *b*. *a* which *b* prehends has already an anticipation of *b* as incomplete.¹

So full prehension² constitutes *A* and *B* as poles in a linkage. Don't abstract from linkage. Incompleteness of *a* by reason of *b* is rectified by ~~its~~ the ⟨completion⟩³ of *b*.

Hence each occasion is immortal.

B enshrines *a* in its own concretion.

Physical memory is causation – causation is objective immortality.

|3b|⁴ Also conscious memory is that partial analysis of causation – Hume should have been directed to memory.

Image in present is not ~~memory~~ image of memory in past.⁵

Image in present is outcome of gathering up of ∨⟨?⟩∨ creativity into present.

Objectification of past is true memory.

Irreversibility of time follows from this ~~cause~~ doctrine of causation.⁶

Sheldon.⁷ Time is Reversible, etc. etc. (Exact merit of Hume's philosophy – takes assumptions and shows what leads to).

Whitehead – Must have past in some sense with you so you're definitely different from past.

5. Simultaneity

Occasions not prehended in *A* except as conforming to the general systematic character of universe.

Only really simultaneous events independent of each other.

A prehends these occasions in mode of presentational immediacy – Eternal objects turned up in this functioning are the sense data.

Laying foundations of theory of truth, identity – same eternal object in differing functioning.

Self-creative character of *a* in its concretion constitutes *a*'s peculiar originality.

Character of physical imagination in generalized sense of word. Has normally to conform to physical memory of immediate past – sense perception.

---

1. Cf. Whitehead: 'This transaction exhibits A as relatively determinate, except for its indetermination arising from the indetermination of B in the converse anticipatory objectification of B in A' (Whitehead, 'Time', pp. 61–2).
2. Whitehead's original paper has 'transaction' rather than 'prehension' here (p. 62).
3. Conger has 'completeness' here.
4. This page is unnumbered and had been placed in the folder of notes after the five numbered pages. However, it is very clear through a comparison with Whitehead's 'Time' paper that it belongs here.
5. Unclear if the strikeout was Whitehead's or Conger's. The original essay has: 'But the image in the present is not the *memory* of the image in the past' (Whitehead, 'Time', p. 62).
6. Whitehead's original paper has 'doctrine of objective immortality' rather than 'doctrine of causation' (Whitehead, 'Time', p. 62).
7. Kerby-Miller's notes (p. 1) specifically reference a 1926 paper in the *Journal of Philosophy*, which can only be Sheldon, 'The spirituality of time'. Whitehead also references Sheldon in his Philosophy 3b lecture of 9 December 1926 (pp. 252–3).

If VtoV remote past, image.[1]
If to some intrusive element in immediate past, illusion, ecstatic vision, imagination.[2]

All have common past. I see you because your past leads you to be there and leads me to see you.

{?} **Two meanings of simultaneity:**
– non-causal, or
– presentational immediacy.

If identify these two meanings – reduced to classical view of time.
Individual perceptivity is the ultimate physical fact.

6 ⟨Time as Epochal⟩ – Supersession not a continuous process of becoming – can't combine supersession and continuity without vicious infinite regress.

Some earlier portion must have superseded.

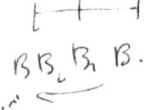

Don't know what supersedes A.
Avoid attempt to begin at infinite end – there is no infinite end. All vicious regresses the tacit supposition you begin at infinite end.

|4| "... If you live long enough, no cardinal number that won't be counted"
Same point about <u>ending</u>.

Supersession of *a* has to commence at infinite end.

Supersession can't be regarded as continuous unfolding of a continuum.

Time is epochal.

~~Go~~ If go back to moment.

Series being dense and continuous, no next door neighbors.

Idea of something becoming. It is inconsistent with idea of a continuity of becoming.

Zeno had fine point, but mixed up – Some right, some wrong.

Arrow – Zeno thought difficulty of motion, space. If had asked how arrow get into a portion of <u>time</u>. Zeno thought something wrong with infinite series as such.

Achilles and tortoise just other way round – you begin nicely from the beginning half.

He has needed continuous refutation ⟨for⟩ 2,000 years.

Define quantum of time. Epochal character. Foundation of atomic organisms and quantum theory.

Bergson's *durée*.

Not all quanta are equal.

Can't even discuss relative sizes unless divisible and comparable.

A continuity of time arising from indefinite divisibility – potentiality an essential element in actual world.

---

1. Cf. Whitehead: 'It may conform to the physical memories of the more remote past: it is then called the image associated with memory' (Whitehead, 'Time', p. 63).
2. Cf. Whitehead: 'It may conform to some special intrusive element in the immediate past such as, in the case of human beings, drugs, emotions, or conceptual relationships in antecedent mental occasions: it is then variously called delusion, or ecstatic vision, or imagination' (Whitehead, 'Time', p. 63).

Potential supersession internal to each actual occasion. Continuity depends not on fact things are divided, but divisible. Might have been potentially other epochal occasions, units.

No continuity of becoming, but a becoming of continuity.

|5| Divisibility presupposes potentiality.

Question of extensive character of time relations of temporal and spatial entities, measurements of space-time.[1]

Resemblance is in respect to a certain identity.

Eternal objects only exposed in the how of the relation.

Concept and percept have an identity between them – an eternal object.

Relation of identity is an generic relationship.

Each relationship is a relationship between different functionings.

What of the relation is just the eternal object which forms character of this functioning and that?

Resemblance has explicit reference to other differences. Two men resemble each other.

Identity relation simply an explicit relation to sameness of element in make up of one to the other.

x is x is relation between the functionings which have the x.[2]

That x at beginning vendv of sentence is the α at beginning.

Any identity ⟨?⟩ is a relation between functionings of one and same eternal object. This gives idea of identity as relation.[3] But can't say $α$ is $α$ without different functionings. (Functionings of x as object is functioning of x as subject). ⟨If?⟩ take resemblance would mean same thing.

⟨Friday, 8 October 1926⟩[4]

Conger's notes

|1|[5] Make idea of time fundamental.[6]

Descartes. Start from the permanent not vorv Heraclitian. After Descartes, exaggeration of emphasis on matter.

Might start from flux of things or continuity of things. Continual creativity and passing on.[7]

---

1. Cf. the final paragraph of Whitehead's paper: 'The question of the extensive relation whereby time acquires its extensive character, termed "duration," and the question of the connection between temporal and spatial relations, and the question of the measurement of space-time, cannot be considered without extending this communication beyond its assigned limits' (Whitehead, 'Time', p. 64).
2. Cf. Kerby-Miller: 'x is x. Two functions, subject and object, but same x functioning. x = analogous to eternal object' (Kerby-Miller, p. 2).
3. Kerby-Miller's notes add here: 'Identity as a relation in *Principia Mathematica* is cooked-up' (Kerby-Miller, p. 2).
4. Date supplied from the notes of Kerby-Miller.
5. The pages of Conger's notes for this session are unnumbered, except for the final, seventh page, which has been numbered '6'. We have numbered them from 1 to 7, changing the number for the final page.
6. Kerby-Miller has a line at the top of the lecture that Conger missed: 'Conciseness, clarity, definiteness philosophical virtues. e.g. Descartes, Spinoza, Leibniz' (Kerby-Miller, p. 3).
7. Kerby-Miller has a great deal of material here that is not present in Conger: 'Descartes started on one hand with the permanent and lasting. The other possible starting point is from flux. Both then

Philosophy 20h: Seminary in Metaphysics, fall semester 1926

Most <u>fundamental</u>[1] start is with fluid events in some definite region of space-time.

Corporeal matter, extension with endurance (Descartes), space-time! Descartes handled it differently. When philosophers say the things they see most clearly, they get beyond their system. Can't pin a man down to his system. Occasion must be essentially passing on – Essentially supersession.[2]

⟨?⟩[3] Primary character of entities. Every entity by being itself it adds a novel character to essential creativity of the universe.

Every fully concrete occasion has two poles, physical and mental. Physical side prehensive. Mental side analytic. Mental occasion supersedes physical occasion. Fully concrete fact is prehension, perceptivity, thereby superseded by the analysis of itself, which is its mental side – its knowledge.

Each occasion an organism – \by its/ prehension of all other occasions in itself. Frightful difficulties as soon as try to make final actual entity self-contained. Object to Cartesian idea of stuff is attributes – self-contained. Can't describe this social world in terms of self-contained entities. Difficulties of causation; how can it know beyond itself: Unless world as social enters into makeup of each entity. Each entity is a social view of the world, a social drawing together of the world. Otherwise can't get the essential togetherness of it. Each entity one exemplification of the social side of the world. Each occasion draws whole world under limitations of ~~own~~ \the/ occasion into itself.

---

explain intermediary facts and relation. Table is real but also is air and events in space. Matter is not the fundamental material or prime make up of the material universe. Subsequent to Descartes there was an exaggeration of matter. Gilson said Descartes in reaction against St. Thomas to Plato in emphasis on mind. But mind in Plato for Descartes substantial while for Plato, according to Woods, a complex of relations. Descartes looked at Plato from as one trained in Aristotle' (Kerby-Miller, p. 3). The two people mentioned were Whitehead's colleagues in the Harvard philosophy department, Étienne Gilson (1884–1978) and James Haughton Woods (1864–1935). Gilson had first met Whitehead at the Oxford Congress of Philosophy in 1921, and would later teach courses in philosophy at Harvard in the autumn of 1926, 1927 and 1928, where he and Whitehead were frequently visitors in one another's classes. See Petek, 'Whitehead and Étienne Gilson', available at <http://whiteheadresearch.org/2018/05/10/whitehead-and-etienne-gilson/> (last accessed 2 September 2020). Woods was the current chair of the Philosophy Department and had helped recruit Whitehead to Harvard; it also appears that Whitehead may have been attending one of Woods's classes in the autumn of 1925. See Petek, 'Whitehead and James Haughton Woods', available at <http://whiteheadresearch.org/2018/10/08/whitehead-and-james-haughton-woods/> (last accessed 2 September 2020).

1. The words 'primary actual entity. But' appear below the word 'fundamental'. The intended meaning and proper placement are unclear. It could be a sentence fragment intended to appear after the sentence concluding in 'some definite region of space-time' or it could reasonably have been intended to be an insertion after the word 'fundamental'. In the latter case, the text would read, 'Most <u>fundamental</u> primary actual entity. But start is with fluid events in some definite region of space-time.' Finally, it is also possible that 'fundamental' is actually crossed out, rather than underlined.
2. Cf. Kerby-Miller: 'World (?) allows itself to be discriminated in many ways, but finally it comes down on events finally. Descartes on the other hand said matter was extension + duration. He did not mean of it (?) in modern sense. Substance (in some senses) taken to be there. There is the same bit of stuff which "has adventures"' (Kerby-Miller, p. 3).
3. The symbols here are illegible, though the first may be a Roman numeral IV. From this point, it appears that Whitehead's paper on time is being discussed. Here, Whitehead (or someone else) is explaining or unpacking the paper rather than reading it. Kerby-Miller has a marginal note that reads either 'Sec⟨tion⟩ Abstract' or 'See Abstract', referring to a one-page summary of the paper that Whitehead seems to have handed out to the class (p. 3).

|2| Physical world is intuition without concepts. It is being something for its own sake but not reflecting upon what it is. Perceptivity always referred to mind. Perceptivity is primarily a physical fact.

But all this doesn't give you time. Might have occasions very socially prehending each other. Get rid of idea that ultimate entity is complete. vEach occasionv not only requires social relations, but there's an essential incompleteness about it. Must pass beyond it and make more complete what is incomplete in it. As soon as complete reality, time illusory. Can't describe ordinary life apart from time and we are in inferior type of reality.[1]

Can distinguish completeness from totality – but how can incomplete thing have any creative force – it's complete, shut up in itself. If it's complete, the future must be complete for it. Our knowledge of the future is of something which in a way is and is not. It's undetermined.

Can't have social relations with the incomplete unless you are incomplete. Blind physical anticipation of undetermined future.

Potentialities are partly settled – yet things are in themselves indeterminate.

Past is immortal in every entity – not *simpliciter*, but the past as objectified for A. Past under certain limitations for *a*, only certain sides of itself there. Linkage A and B. B is future for A. B is in A as incomplete, unrealized, not actual, but there so far as it is incomplete marked out by the conditions it has to fulfil and which there has to be an entity fulfilling. Conditions it has to fulfill, as yet unfulfilled potentialities – incomplete in *a*. When get to B have A as relatively complete. There is also a relative incompleteness. Linkage A and B more concrete than either by itself. A by itself is incomplete because B is incomplete from standpoint of A.

|3| B has point of view of A with incomplete of B in it. A and B are further incomplete. Can only get relatively more complete by being more adequate. General sketch of social character of the universe.

Physical memory is causation. Causation one aspect – the present is an integration of past. Past is alive in present. Conscious memory is a partial mental analysis of physical memory. To trace memory to molecules in brain waggle[2] – nonsense.

Why do you know at ⟨age⟩ twelve about your experience at ⟨age⟩ ten, and know it as an experience in the past? How do you know now what you experienced before?

Eternal objects flow out of bifurcation of nature.

Presentational immediacy seems to depend on bodies, not on world, vgetv secondary qualities.

Mongoose to catch snakes,[3] space to catch colors. Not real.

Alcoholic ward.

---

1. Cf. Kerby-Miller: 'Once admit completeness and time becomes illusory. Als Appearance and Reality follows' (Kerby-Miller, p. 3). This last would seem to be a reference to the 1893 book by F. H. Bradley, *Appearance and Reality*.
2. Whitehead uses this same odd word in the 10 November 1925 lecture, p. 76.
3. Kerby-Miller references Hume here (p. 4).

You must give account of presentational immediacy which dodges difficulty of giving sense data in a private psychological world – you'll never get an external physical world going.

Time Epochal. Bound to has run up against Zeno difficulty. Event superseded by another event – must be definite event which supersedes back to infinite regress. Difficulty arises however you take time. If time is becoming, ever something becomes. If instants of time are everywhere <u>dense</u> you have the difficulty. Epochal theory means a definite event – continuity of time has got to be disjoined from becoming of reality. Becoming isn't continuous, but what becomes, it's continuous.

Danger – get fluid (mush?) but universe is obstinately atomic. History – warfare between continuity and atomicity. Clerk Maxwell, ether, {atoms, electrons, quanta}.

If you want (reasonable?) logical view of universe, advantage to limit your knowledge.

|4| Definite quanta turn up. Zeno argument insists time quanta. In heart of continuity itself you've got to interweave continuity with quanta. An atom not complete. Each epochal occasion primarily real. The atom as same all through is more abstract.

Each occasion inherits whole universe.[1]

 Owing to character of the route, there is a congruence of objectifications of that group and that group dominates inheritance of itself and reproduce its own character. Inheritance from other events more superficial modifications.

You inherit from whole world, but owing to the character of environment which favors dominance of the congruent set, you are practically integrate the b all (into yourself).

Real atom: abstract congruity, between definite pattern, complexity, substantial form ········

Abstraction, Eternal object.[2]

Not real atom, but substantial form gives important (analogous?) set of epochal organisms is what we call the life of the atom. vCf. original sinv[3]

Inheritance from environment must be permissive – the basis for the dominant integration – vsuchv organism can only exist when you have an environment which favors that type. Have families of organisms which provide by their inheritance from each other, provide an environment favorable for each other.

|5| Would expect throngs of simple organisms of few species. Cf. Electrons and protons.

---

1. Given its position, this sentence is intended to reference the diagram on its left.
2. The correct placement of this sentence is unclear. It appears near the left margin, below 'Real atom' and to the lower left of the series following 'Real atom'. Also, there is a lack of clarity regarding the comma between 'Abstraction' and 'Eternal'. Two marks appear as horizontal lines next to the letters 'abstrac^n'. They could be '=' or 'abstrac^n'.
3. This is written in the right margin next to the two preceding sentences. The correct placement is unclear.

Laws of nature not eternal. Describe character of environment produced by such organisms. We are running through a period of electrons and protons. Laws of nature not eternal, necessary.

(Clerk Maxwell equations most ~~ production of human intellect)

Might have four, 555 dimensions, no dimensions at all. Three dimensions the relationships among events which are important in expressing mutual inheritance of organism from organism.

What is complete is not actual; it's the pattern, the eternal form. There is a life history of

An eternal form is not actual. Anything actual is incomplete.

Diagram – A Platonic myth.[1]

An event is physical occasion; event rather more as regards potentiality of universe. Any past epochal occasion might have been something else.

Might be superpo(sitio)n of epochal occasions. Event rather broader term (includes potentiality?) Potentiality with regard to past.[2]

<u>Epochal physical occasion</u> – becomes as one divisible but not divided in its becoming.[3]

In *The Concept of Nature*, no epochal view, nor of relationship of physical and mental, but clear on supersession and eternal objects having to have more complex relationship to world than usually given – to avoid bifurcation.

Nature can be thought of as closed system.

Physical occasion is an abstraction. Complete concrete fact physico mental.[4]

Occasion prehends or blindly intuits all universe. Partial knowledge of perception is sense awareness.

Now sees sense awareness not to be assigned to mental.

Sense awareness is ⟨very?⟩ stuff.

Each occasion is simply concretion of its complete sense awareness of all the rest of the universe (not in sense of presentational immediacy).[5] A social concrescence of the rest of the universe into the one limited individualization's ⟨point?⟩.

|6| <u>Eternal object</u> whereby that [table] as an object for me is limited – It's primarily a physical fact. My knowledge of it is partial analysis of physical fact.

⟨This⟩ not in *The Concept of Nature*. Chapter II is right, but at end real difficulty – how are you to conceive things really?

Actual occasion {physical, mental}

---

1. This is written in the right margin.
2. Cf. Kerby-Miller: 'Use of term <u>events</u> broad, includes all <u>occasion</u> and epochal occasion as involving some being for self or sel measure of definiteness' (Kerby-Miller, p. 4).
3. The text from here to the bottom of the page is very difficult to place in sequence. Sentences are written in blocks all around the bottom of the page rather than one after another. Hence the reader should be leery of the sentence order.
4. Somewhere in this vicinity of the lecture, Kerby-Miller has the following: '<u>Entity</u> kinds. (1) actual, phys-mental. (2) physical pure perceptivity, (3) conceptual analysis' (Kerby-Miller, 4). He also makes a reference to *Concept of Nature*, 'p. 3 ff', but it is unclear if this reference and the list are connected.
5. Parentheses supplied.

Physical side – blind perceptivity, concrescence of perceptivities.

Analysis of it via concepts. The what of the objectification expressed in terms of eternal objects. The how of the analysis – conceptual functioning, objectification. Eternal object functioning as analytic concept, conceptual modes of analysis. Eternal object expresses the how of concrescence, how of analysis.[1]

Historic route of enduring object – a pattern ∧(an eternal object)∧[2] is a dominant inheritance, congruity (baby and man of 50).[3] Peculiar intensity of inheritance.

Future concreted in too but peculiarly incomplete. Present anticipating potentialities ⟨?⟩ limited.

An entity must be something for itself, must have an inside to it as well as an outside. The subjective side – self enjoyment of being a concrescence.

Individuality of past event is only relatively complete. Objectivity of past conditioning because of relative completeness – Past and future refers to causal relations of events.

Simultaneous or Present ⟨vs.⟩ Presentational immediacy, neither Caused nor Causing. Do they come to same thing? Relativist says no.

Presentational immediacy would also be a cone, but let the specious present drop.

|7| Every philosophy ought to give its proper weight to pluralistic realism. Winning card in physical science now. Individual hard facts there whether we know them or not.

Friday, 15 October 1926
Conger's notes

|1|
Body Mind
Descartes thought of substance as the real underlying thing, but said something else about it which colored Newtonian variation of Descartes – Substance requires nothing but itself in order to exist. God only answers to it.

Other things apart from God satisfy the definition – Substances don't depend on each other. Thoroughgoing system of external relations. Heading toward Leibniz.

Get real independent substances with anticipation for relations.

Science left the question where Descartes did.

Must bring in God as Leibniz or take Spinoza's view. Going to bother about causation, induction, etc.

---

1. Cf. Kerby-Miller: 'Eternal objects should not be called concepts because concepts are functions' (Kerby-Miller, p 4).
2. Parentheses supplied.
3. Parentheses supplied.

Cogitating mind will be independent of others, substances too.

Descartes: Sun gets into mind/"objective." Body requires nothing but self to exist. Mind, too. Then ~~distinction~~ \connection/ between body and mind becomes problem.

Thing requires nothing but itself to exist.

Locke is good Cartesian except when thinking about Descartes.

When say won't discuss metaphysics, means stick in metaphysics without discussion.

Locke: one state of mind (doesn't) depend on another's state of mind. (Hume).

Newton: get your bit of matter, then discuss forces acting on it – forces half real.

Describe the formula which gives you the motion.

Say just opposite – Actual entity is essentially social. No independent real entity. In order to be itself, it's an assemblage of other entities.

Descartes' relation of substance to God is left indeterminate.

Substance is socialization of whole actual world into one individuality which is one actual entity.

Entities not socialized simpliciter, but under some limitations as in certain relationship.

Each \actual/ entity being complex, you[1] require other type of entities to be arrived at by analysis of other entities which provide the ⟨how?⟩ of the prehension of other entities into each actual substance.

Each actual entity is an occasion of perceptivity. Each other entity comes to it. \(The ⟨how?⟩)/[2]

Each actual entity is concretion of perceptivities. Physical perception.

Not peculiarly mental to get hold of things outside you – this is the physical side.

~~He~~ \Kant/ has conceived of intuition without concepts.

Whitehead: Physical entit(ies) in being themselves create the relationships by reason of which physical occasions are possible.

That organization ought to be considered on intuitive more than mental side. You have organized world on physical side because each physical entity being itself is creative of its relationships with all others.

|2| Don't have entity first and then relations. Because entities are what they are because of their relations. But other entities you want to express those relations. Eternal objects – entities which are elements or factors in actual world. Not existing on their own. These factors by reason of which entities prehend each other each into its own concretion, under a limitation – not simpliciter, but as qualified by eternal objects; these ⟨?⟩ are relational – they operate relationally.

Grass as occasion is prehended in certain other occasions by the limiting ~~occasion~~ operation of green, \⟨or?⟩/ there is greenness qualifying my

---

1. Duplicate 'you' deleted.
2. Parentheses supplied.

apprehension of grass. Both ways of speaking elliptically. Forget concretions for which grass is green. True fact is the relational working of green in objectifying the grass, and thereby being a relational element [by, which those]

May say a relation between grass and some other physical occasion and grass is the what of this relationship.

Actual entities objectified by eternal objects.

How account for error? J.A. Smith.[1] I have nothing to do with the pathology of mind.

The physical entity subject is what it is – includes every eternal object and every actual entity, only some are so objectified are practically irrelevant. Some only slightly relevant.

Can't say ∨only∨ some among eternal object are operative – how about those left over? Get into hopeless situation of realm of eternal object waiting. Eternal objects always operative.

Mind another way in which eternal objects operate.

Can talk of evil in physical world, but not error. Social object which is real togetherness has its self enjoyment. Self-satisfaction which is its own individuality – may have comparative depth of actuality which may be thwarted. When it's superseded, it ought to be superseded by what follows from it. Individual creative supersession may be thwarted by prehension of other eternal object.

Evil in sense of descent toward nothingness ∧(towards slighter and slighter occasion)∧. Physical world depends for its depth of actuality on a favorable order.

No error because physical world is what it is.

Mental occasion is analytic of its associated physical occasion.

Supersession not merely ⟨more/greater than⟩[2] time (supersession of physical by physical), but also creativity turning on and analyzing itself.

Mental occasion a creature which is analytic by reason of eternal objects now functioning as engines of analysis. A concept is a functioning. Mental occasion includes whole world, but via association ∨to∨ physical occasion, and analyzes it by its conceptual functioning.

|3| Mental occasion may have a greater or lesser depth of actuality. Analysis may be more or less partial. According to strength of conceptual functioning there is a new concretion which is the concepts functioning as analytical. The concretion being together is the enjoyment of knowledge.

Ingression of eternal object functioning as concepts.

Concepts are relational functionings between physical occasion and mental occasion.

Eternal object determines both what of physical occasion prehension of another occasion – how that occasion is objectified – and how a concept is more

---

1. Whitehead is likely referring to John Alexander Smith (1863–1939), a British idealist philosopher who worked on a 12-volume translation of the works of Aristotle with William David Ross. Smith delivered the Gifford lectures in Glasgow for 1929–31, entitling them 'The heritage of idealism', but the lectures were never published.
2. Conger has '>' here, which could mean 'more than' or 'greater than'.

than a bare functioning. It has a specific form of functioning, and the specific form of its functioning is the eternal object.

Conscious perception ~~of~~ or intuition seems to be identical with judgment. Disjunction of judgment for conscious perception is a sheer fallacy. The concepts are the conceptual relationships.

Concrescence of total functioning into one occasion is the mental occasion.

Physical occasion by self or mental occasion by self are abstractions. In separation, each suffer.

~~Eternal object specify~~ Eternal objects constitutive of differtia between diverse prehensive relationships of the physical occasion to diverse other occasions in the system of the world.

Eternal object constitutes what is different in different prehensions in physical occasion.

Eternal object also constitutive of difference between diverse conceptual relations which connect physical and mental pole of occasion in question.

Peculiar way in which mental occasion prehends physical occasion and <u>via</u> physical occasion gets whole world into itself.

Prehension the general category of relationship between ~~physical~~ occasions.

Concretion which constitutes mental pole is enjoyment of one or other of two contrasts which can be yielded by conceptual functioning.

How this conceptual functioning analyzes world – forms a contrast with a prehensive functioning in the physical occasion. V(correspondence theory)V[1]

The way of being analytic is it separates out a particular prehensive functioning of physical occasion whereby some other physical occasion has been prehended and contrasts itself with that. Two forms of contrast – yes form and no form.

Yes – when contrasted relationships yield relation of identity with respect to eternal object functioning conceptually in mind and prehensively in physical occasion.

Mind doesn't find the concept verified. Concept isn't in physical occasion. Concept is mind analyzing. The <u>how</u> of it. (There isn't bare |4| analyzing – but analyzing this way or that way.)[2] Eternal object as constituting the what of the analyzing, giving its specific character to the ~~ph~~ analyzing is contrasted with physical prehension – get identity or diversity.

Question of originality of mental functioning – derived from fact of inheritance etc. – is conditioned – but partly real originality. What freedom in the world is in the mental functioning which is inherited into the physical.

Would have to use coherence criterion as everyone does – but coherence criterion only comes because mind operates so dimly. Actual correspondence may be very irrelevant. Mind not always clear – partial analysis – a tendency of the machinery of creation to occur in the creature. In knowing about the mind you can know about the creativity.

Universe is always issuing into its own creatures.

---

1. Parentheses supplied.
2. Closing parenthesis supplied.

When a concept has the no-contrast, mind acts first imaginatively. Knowledge is <u>first</u> imagination, then comparison of imaginations with world.

The analytic functioning – analytic of physical occasion – the what of the contrast is via a determination of the mind that I should be looking for blue and not red. Imaginative activity of mind, otherwise would have appallingly matter of fact mind.

Wrong about conscious judgment identical with perceptivity.

Truth is correspondence – verification is pragmatic. Only a subsequent correspondence. Corresponds to concept of prehension.

Physical pole abstract in absence of mental. Either may be faint. Degrees of intensity of actuality.

Total individuality of the thing is physical-mental, but begin your explanation on physical side

<u>Question</u>. Physical pole complete, reduplicated in mental. Physical pole doesn't demand completion?

<u>Answer</u>. Whatever there is issues in a creature. No character behind it. Character can always be described as creature or as character of a creativity. Creature undoing itself into a creature which is exhibiting creativity.

Start from your own little patch of immediacy. Its knowledge of a world which exhibits its undefined potentialities. Room is patient of being different (all objects prehended in it), but it is <u>this</u> room.

Divisibility of world really comes from potentiality.

|5| An image is presentational immediacy produced by mentality, but is physical.

Distinction between presentational immediacy and memory.

Body no special kind of physical object.

Any bit of empty space would be physical object.

Body has been led up to by a route of physical objects which have a certain unity of systematic character, general systematic character of whole environment of occasions.

Inherit from our whole previous life with a very peculiar systematic character.

We integrate our previous history and previous history of world.

Actual occasion – is just the occasion in this actual occasion. ~~must~~

Sometimes by odd trick of congruence one inherits a slice of other mind.[1] Believes in ⟨?⟩[2] v(Four dimensions a systematic character of an epoch, but must have something systematic to have depth of actuality).v[3]

Physical and mental only take in under gradations of relevance.

Physical more systematic. Mental somewhat arbitrary. Same principle of relegating to irrelevance.

---

1. An opening square bracket appearing before the word 'slice' has been removed.
2. The letters here appear to be 'telep', which could plausibly be shorthand for 'telepathy'. However, the handwriting it is too unclear to be sure and we are loath to guess because of its possible significance for the sentence.
3. Parentheses supplied.

Don't get ⱽeffectiveⱽ action at distance unless systematic historic route leading up to it systematically so you get effective action.

Unless transmission your action is at cross purposes.

Things all objectified telling a harmonious tale. Concurrence, congruity along a historic route.

Occasion have any characteristics in own right? Always some freedom – but ~~infinitely~~ in physical occasion infinitely less freedom than mental.

Universe as self conditioned issues in its creatures.

Universe not an exhibition of all it might be – It exhibits self under limitation which is not from outside. Exhibits itself as something partial. It's that course; might have been some other. In a sense having some determinative originality. The price of being anything.

Anything which was an infinite would be nothing because of crosscurrents.

Anything infinite – limited by goodness.

Incompatibility in eternal objects. To state metaphysics, a library ought to be simultaneously before you. Take each factor in universe and make it central.

Large harmony of world requires a principle. God as savior more than ⟨creator?⟩.

|6| Can't take eternal objects merely by themselves and not look on them as potentialities as creativity.

Actual objects have impress of all their potentialities.

Question. Eternal objects are principles of individuation –

Answer. Essential limitation that each actual entity.

Eternal objects are not the principles whereby these are individuals – they're the potentialities.

Creativity is principle of individuation.

⟨Undated 1926 seminaries, circa 22 October to 17 December⟩
Conger's notes

|1|[1] N. K. Smith[2] good case for Locke rationalist more than empiricist.[3]
Locke: Power as constitutive relation.
Normal subject-predicate form of sentence always turning up in hostility to relation
Relation won't work with simple notion. Suspect that in "clearheaded" philosophers always first deny it and then run away with it.
⟨?⟩ Reflexion – Empirical Self
Leibniz: Every creature involving ~~universe~~ ∨the infinite∨ expressing ∨the∨ universe (is durable as universe).[4]
New System. Hypothesis of harmony.
Extension a relational complex of things, ~~It is is~~ not a resolvable attribute.
These relations satisfy many conditions, then get extensive relational complex.
Only one way to be actual, but many intensities ⟨so?⟩ always be some degree of consciousness. But Leibniz brings in subject-predicate view.
Gilson says Locke innate ideas against schoolmen.
Bertrand Russel's view of substance – a class of sense data.
C.f. ⟨Whitehead?⟩[5] J. S. Mill. Permanent possibility of sensa.
Gilson: Descartes' substance is actual entity, not medieval view of substance.

---

1. These seminary notes are undated, and likely come from multiple seminary sessions. However, since we have dated seminary notes for the first three October sessions, and all 1927 sessions up until Conger's departure in mid-March, we can say that these notes must belong to seminaries that took place between 22 October and 17 December 1926.
   This first page (the page numbers here have been added by the editors; they are not Conger's) was bundled together with the 20 November Philosophy 3b lecture, but clearly does not belong there; that the notes are written in multiple columns also suggests they are for a seminary.
   Pages 2–5 were bundled together with the 27 November Philosophy 3b lecture, but likewise do not belong there. These four pages may be notes for multiple sessions, or may constitute two or three different presentations in the same session.
   It is possible that these undated notes were taken on seminary dates near to the Philosophy 3b notes with which they were bundled, i.e. 19 November and 26 November. Two pages that are clearly a presentation by Charles Hartshorne have been omitted; Hartshorne also delivered lectures in Whitehead's Philosophy 3b around this time, on 30 November and 2 December 1926.
2. Norman Kemp Smith (1871–1958) was a Scottish philosopher. Whitehead reads aloud from Smith's commentary on Kant's *Critique of Pure Reason* during his 8 October 1925 lecture (see p. 52), and identifies him as a member of the 'Oxford School' of philosophy in his 16 October 1926 lectures, i.e. British idealism, neo-Hegelianism (see p. 187). A fellow member of the Aristotelian Society, Smith was an admirer of Whitehead's work, and was one of the people principally responsible for his invitation to deliver the Gifford lectures in Edinburgh. In response to the invitation, Whitehead wrote to Smith that 'The honour is one which I greatly appreciate, and it gives me an opportunity to put out a systematic work on the metaphysical notions which are occupying my mind. Also, no small part of the attraction is the prospect of having some conversations with you, and A. E. Taylor, and ⟨E. T.⟩ Whittaker. As to the subject and title – I am inclined to think that "The Concept of Organism" expresses what I want to lecture about and is a reasonable title' (Whitehead, 'Letter to Norman Kemp Smith', 6 April 1927).
3. See Smith, *A Commentary to Kant's 'Critique of Pure Reason'*, pp. 591–2, available at <https://archive.org/details/commentarytokant00smituoft>.
4. Parentheses supplied.
5. What appears in the text is 'w.h.'; 'wh' would normally mean 'which' and 'W' would normally mean Whitehead, though 'ANW' is more common.

Whitehead: Locke's <u>use</u> of ˅word˅ substance is medieval, though has another idea. – ˅when not thinking about his views,˅ presupposes it as much as Descartes does.

Derivation of <u>inherent</u>.

Locke's *nescio quid*.[1]

Kant's *Ding an Sich*,[2] Spencer's unknowable[3] implicit in much modern realism.

Does ⟨ID?⟩ indicate bare substance? – No: open, <u>bare or not bare</u>.

|2|

Descartes, Locke, and Hume[4]

Descartes muddles the immediate act of experiencing with the I which persists.

Descartes says when I stop thinking I should cease to be. Perhaps it would happen.

In last analysis, obvious.

Criteria purge the wavering obviousness.

Bind together the ˅more wavering things by their˅ obvious relations.

Locke's reflection, physical sensibility parallels Whitehead's conceptual activity, perception. Knock out ⟨Locke's⟩ treatment of <u>mind</u>.

    A A'
    B B'

A and A' can be described on own.

~~Hume: What is the tie?~~

B and B' on own complete in itself.

Whitehead: of course don't find anything complete in itself, and if do, fall prey to Hume.

Descartes ⟨Meditation⟩ 3 for God, duration requires conservation, which needs something outside as much as creation.[5]

Hume influenced by Descartes

impression	clear experience
logic – contradiction	logic contradiction
cause ✓	cause goes to God

---

1. This refers to Locke's definition of substance as 'something, I know not what'. See Locke, *An Essay Concerning Human Understanding*, available at <https://archive.org/details/anessayconcerni00frasgoog> (Vol. I) and <https://archive.org/details/anessayconcerni17lockgoog> (Vol. II).
2. This refers to Kant's concept of the noumena, the *Ding an Sich* or the thing in itself. See Kant, *Critique of Pure Reason*, available at <https://archive.org/details/immanuelkantscr07kantgoog>.
3. This refers to Herbert Spencer (1820–1903), an English philosopher and biologist who is best known for having popularised the phrase 'survival of the fittest'. Spencer's theory of the unknowable is that science and religion must recognise as the 'most certain of all facts – that the Power which the Universe manifests to us is utterly inscrutable'. Spencer, *First Principles*, p. 46, available at <https://archive.org/details/firstprinciples19spengoog>.
4. The handwritten text here is extremely difficult to follow, with the various paragraphs divided into small blocks and spread around the page. Readers should be aware that some text may not be in its intended order.
5. 'It is as a matter of fact perfectly clear and evident to all those who consider with attention the nature of time, that, in order to be conserved in each moment in which it endures, a substance has need of the same power and action as would be necessary to produce and create it anew' (Descartes, *Philosophical Works, Vol. I*, p. 168, available at <https://archive.org/details/philosophicalwor01desc>).

After Book I,[1] Hume doesn't build up ideas like Locke, but criticizes them, like Descartes, before he synthesizes to show error arose. Is not psychological atomist.

|3| Descartes' modes – this universal square. Clear and distinct ideas are all universals.

External is only another word for saying "Something real on its own." Descartes would have had this if had got quite free from medieval point of view.

Math never tells you <u>what</u> things are.

When Descartes talks about wax, ~~doesn't~~ ought to talk about extension, but he doesn't hold to his doctrine of substance – Imagination is dominated by other point of view.

I am unity of my experiences. An element of my experience is piece of wax introduced to me by the yellowness.

But Descartes takes sensa as mere adjectives of mentality. Takes view of knowledge as detached survey on part of one entity which requires nothing but itself in order to exist.

. . . .

Percep(tion?) concrescence. If metaphysical principles apply to God, he requires only self to exist.

God is that entity by respect to which you need not explain how it happened. ~~Descartes~~ God the ⟨pod?⟩ into which all uncertainties are put. God is Perfect Substance. But same difficulty as between other substances.[2]

<u>Problem</u> of attribute. Class and parallel ⟨?⟩.

Can get a purely relational knowledge may have non-relational elements. Line connecting two points with relative coordinates in analy⟨sis?⟩.

Descartes alternates common sense discussion with metaphysical discussion, which would show him they were quite valueless.

|4| Problem made vague by bringing in idea of substance and not speaking of expression.

One part of knowledge which gives relations of entities to each other and to ourselves with perfect distinctness. Lifts knowledge about entity with same sort of qualities into distinctness. This is why use it as expression.

If the historical route of book had no spatio-temporal relationships, then what is expressed is bogus. If no relationships, there is nothing there.

Don't try to solve the problem without philosophy. ~~by~~ What is meant by one part of experience expressing another is hopeless. Sense data are expressing something not themselves.

What is the perceptive knowledge which is being expressed and yet is too indistinct to be lifted out apart from the symbol.

Use words to express something which when expressed you don't need words for.

---

1. It is likely that this refers to book 1 of Hume, *A Treatise of Human Nature*, available at <https://archive.org/details/treatiseofhumann00hume_0>.
2. The final three paragraphs on this page of Conger's notes appear to the right of the main column, and may be intended to be insertions at different points in the main text.

But essence of sense data they are useful all along line. Thing apart from sense data always tends to lapse back into unconsciousness. Must have something insistent but indistinct, why people use idea of books, tables, chairs with congruence to each other and unity of type.

Lifted into distinctness my apprehension of efficient causation.

That immediate entity as last term in life history of book is delimited and sheds light on immediate past of the book and how I am conforming to the causal relations of the world or objectifications of the past out of which I arise.

Lifted into particularity. So get intersection of two forms of knowledge and one form of it ∨sense data and external reference∨ used as expression of other – spatio-temporal relatedness. . . .

Own knowledge of own past is same character only very much more intense. Practical difference in quality.

Language takes sense data, gives artificial, sophisticated external reference, but make it do same sort of work which the sight of Boston does. If no knowledge of past – self as entering into or issuing out of it – then we have no knowledge. In making it precise, we are often misled by functioning in wrong way. Likely to have concept first of causal efficacy of past and from concept presuming that we have a definite knowledge of it. Unless have some perceptual knowledge, have no knowledge, and whole talk of past and present is fictitious.

|5| Classification so elaborate. Why not talk about patches of color? Sense data give last term of historic route of that book – but book with its past more abstract than any one occasion. The universal which it has in common with its antecedents – ∨congruity and∨ why there was this instance. Viewed apart from its routes, is merely the characteristics which it ~~ends~~ has. A bundle of entities.

⟨Personality?⟩ of a society is same kind ~~of~~ as yours or mine in principle – but each of us more important examples.

Space-time together gives you endurance – or something going on.

Endurance being an attribute is internal characteristic (durée).[1]

But time relations between actual entities are not characteristic of any one. Duration is characteristic of entities. Time is relationship between actual entities.

Descartes ought to write of epochal occasions. That is an actual entity – it has its own endurance (internal spatial-temporal relations which represent potentialities of ⟨?⟩ – its relations of objectification to other entities which give it spatial-temporal relationships with other entities).

Descartes – piece of wax. Extension and endurance the formal characteristics of something going on, always there in terms of which you can define its relations to other entities.

But Descartes has medieval notion of substance as something which gets out of one occasion into another. Mixed the two notions. Presupposed medieval substance.

Whitehead – Sameness of wax is only sameness of universals which apply.

---

1. Parentheses supplied.

Book inherits from last occasion with such dominance that community of its occasions has a peculiar bond, but its unity as one is identity with respect to the universals.

Objectification in causal efficacy of one occasion in another so one takes its characteristics from antecedent route with differences (man from child).

Character of each age always such that passed itself on ... Cf. Irishman's sock.[1]

Actual entity at beginning from end: Whitehead ⟨says⟩ wax different, Descartes ⟨says⟩ wax same.

Difficulty now that chair is a community of things going on.

ⱽWhiteheadⱽ thinks Descartes medieval in thinking of chair as continuous substance, but his idea of extension ought to have led him differently.

Gilson says Descartes looked on extension as one substance.

Spinoza's monads = Whitehead actual entities.

Friday, 7 January 1927

Conger's notes[2]

|1| In predication, distinguish attribute from identity. Actual entity has predicate of actualizing such and such a possibility. Complexity of organism is a predicate. Common element in all subject-predicate propositions. Can't express it as solipsist relation of predicate to subject.

Jones is mortal. Jones at a moment is just himself. Statement that he is mortal refers to future without Jones, to events which don't include Jones. Jones being mortal is nonsense apart from the universe and an expression of his relation to the universe. Predicate is absolute nonsense without Jones and the universe, and universe with a time extension.

---

1. It seems likely that Whitehead's meaning here is the same as in his 4 December 1926 lecture (p. 247): that a sock could be repaired so often that one wonders if it is the same sock if it has little or none of the original material. This is a famous question within the metaphysics of identity that is usually put in terms of the ship of Theseus.
2. These notes by Conger, labelled as pertaining to Whitehead's 7 January 1927 seminary, were probably the most difficult to edit of all the notes in this volume. They consist of eight manuscript pages with content on both sides of each page. The content for the 'front' sides of the pages appears (loosely) to all go together (note that there are several different sets of numbering which could indicate different sessions), while the content for the 'back' sides of the pages also appears to go together. However, it is not clear if the notes on the 'front' sides of the pages are for this same session, or are even Whitehead notes at all – they may be for another class entirely, or may record what is being said by another student in the seminary, or may be something else again. Some of the content sounds consistent with Whitehead, while other portions clash somewhat with what we might expect from him; for example, at one point the Upanishads are mentioned, and at another 'neuronic conduction'. Owing to these uncertainties and after a close inspection, we have decided not to include any of the content from the 'front' sides of the pages. (Our best guess is that Conger was using the back sides of pages of notes he no longer cared about, perhaps to save paper.)

    Note also that the page order for these notes is unclear (they were not numbered; we have supplied numbers). For instance, the page that has the date and class heading at the top appears last in the folder. What seems most likely is that someone inadvertently flipped all eight pages in the folder, reversing their intended order. Hence, we present them here in the reverse order of how they were placed in the archival folder.

~~That is an~~ The rose is red. Primary and secondary qualities raised by it. Universe must be such as to provide percipients for whom the rose is red. ⟨Validity?⟩⟨[1]

This drop of water is spherical. Sphericity involves reference to ⟨?⟩ space with geometrical properties. ⟨?⟩ Solipsist sphericity is absurd.

Universe isn't the ultimate subject. ~~There~~ Has its solipsist predicates. Subject dealing with reference beyond itself.

Bradley doctrine presupposes
  (1) Subject-predicate form, solipsist meaning. And he runs it to the absolute.
  (2) There is an unambiguous entity.
If (1), ⟨?⟩ there must be (2).
If solipsist predicates, must be an absolute other entities ⟨...?⟩.
Grass is grass. False or tautologous. ~~or false~~[2]

Sentence neglected in logic. Aristotle – multiple relations, logic of classes. Sentence form elliptical.

I should say universe must be such as to supply predicates. Different types of propositions bring out the reference either more or less ⟨obviously?⟩. Couldn't ⟨?⟩ keep questions of <u>validity</u> out of it.

Bradley: the absolute is the ultimate subject. Identity is limit of attributes. Universe isn't ultimate subject.

What Whitehead means, universe as background.[3]

All reference to universe form of general statements, but these are not really presupposing a complete entity ⟨requires some general reference to all entities⟩.⟨[4] Wh⟨itehead?⟩[5] has got attracted into this idea of the universe. Really thinking of limited portion of it.

|2| <u>Notion of abstraction</u>

Abstraction from the universe the notion of the universe as a background. Universe in its indefinite variety of detail is irrelevant. Only some general characteristics that we have as making up the solidarity of things.

Systematic character pervading relationships of things in respect to which Jones is mortal expresses a particular proposition. A kink in a system – There is a system which admits of this particular fact.

Cf. Significance and patience. Entity patient[6] of universe and universe patient of entity. Any proposition refers to a universe which is patient of that particular proposition.

---

1. Parentheses supplied.
2. There is a sizable gap between this text and the rest of the text on this page; the text following may have been added later. Also, the correct order of the following text is not always clear, as it is written in a number of 'blocks' with ambiguous structure.
3. The words 'subject-predicate ⟨requiring?⟩' look to be an insertion by Conger and are placed below the first word of the sentence 'Universe isn't ultimate subject', and to the left of 'What Whitehead means...'. Their proper placement is not clear.
4. Parentheses supplied.
5. When Conger writes just 'wh', he normally means 'which'. Here it appears to refer to Whitehead.
6. Conger used a ditto mark below 'significance', but from context it seems clear that he meant the mark to signify 'patient'.

The patience of the universe is a systematic character. But particular differentiations within system are irrelevant.

Thus a proposition is a characteristic detail in the universe. Proposition abstracts from infinite variousness of the universe. Relegates everything except general ontological character and relegates to irrelevance the details which must be there but are irrelevant for its purposes.

In propositions the exact character which find in actual entity – the actual entity relegates to irrelevance the propositions which it doesn't want.

|3| Abstraction. Abstractive ~~proposition~~ functioning of a proposition comes in everywhere – Jones as a man is infinitely various – real essence can't be exhausted. Only in mortality does he turn up, and fact that he can be indicated by the word Jones.

Mortality has a status in the universe which transcends Jones. You don't require real essence of Jones in order to indicate him – "Jones" is means of pointing. Language is so elliptical. This uniquely indicated entity is mortal.

Unique indication requires systematic interconnections in the universe. Never get away from presupposing some systematic generality.

Complex subject-predicate propositions. Even Caesar is mortal, conjunction of two predicates. Caesarity and mortality as strangely in same entity.

That Jones is mortal is that the entity as demonstrated by Jones – vhavingv definite status in ~~universe~~ – ⟨?⟩ system of universe under the perspective of mortality. Jones really objectified – under the limitation of mortality. Subject-predicate proposition is merely an expression of what I have called the fact of objectification. Every entity is a concrescence and that what an entity is for another entity is not that entity simpliciter, but *A* under some limitation.

|4| Subject-predicate proposition merely expresses how an entity can enter into an objectification. How Jones can be something for you under the guise of his mortality.

Always Jones as demonstrated – Jones as with a status in the systematic universe, the rose as demonstrated that rose over there.

Subject of the subject-predicate proposition is conceived as objectified is that which is for objectification by the predicate. That therefore the situation which find in the rose is red is essential character of subject-predicate proposition – the objectification of Jones as mortal for a percipient, Jones as capable of this objectification.

If you make it an assertion you are stating it, always referring to certain percipients.

Really ⟨?⟩ subject to a proposition. Primary and ultimate subject. Ultimate subject or group of subjects is plurality of minds.

Whole group of percipient entities into whose concrescence rose enters under perspective of redness. Rose is subject of proposition but rose is objectified entity. Proposition is merely the concept of what is done in the objectification of an actual entity.

Predicate is simply the consideration of the limitation under which entity which is the subject will enter into certain assigned other actual entities.

|5| Sometimes you get a proposition addressed to universe. Usually only a particular portion.

A proposition is an intermediate universal. Doesn't specify its primary subject, but does specify actual universe (sometimes particular entities in it) – ᵛactual entityᵛ in respect to general reference to universe as a whole.

Caesar crossed Rubicon specifies ~~in~~ perspective in which Caesar and the Rubicon are causally relevant to all entities which succeed and also in respect to which they lay in the possible future under limitations of conditions laid down by all preceding entities. Refers somehow to the percipience of all the actual entities in the universe. Secondary qualities raising special difficulty vanishes altogether and becomes perfectly general. Approaching Bradley with different result.

There is so to speak what one is for one's self – Must bring in the endurance, the extension of an actual entity. Can't look on concrescence as a simple fact – simple ⟨?⟩.

Actual entity is essentially a unity which yet has stages which supersede each other, not stages in time, but stages of completeness.

Have therefore the higher or superseding stage. Has in itself the objectification of antecedent stage.

|6| Actual entity is to be looked on as extended in time, although its concrescence is one fact – but holds within itself, is analyzable into what might have been many concrescences but are one – they are superseding concrescences in one objectification and therefore there is a self objectification of part by superseding part. Here get fullness of experience. One part is objectified in the higher part.

Also the new form of objectification via knowledge and concepts which might be irrelevant on the perceptive side.

An entity insofar as complete concrescence has no predicates for itself, doesn't objectify itself – it only objectifies a stage of itself.

My mentality gives me a knowledge of myself as perceiving a reddish colored bowl. That is my analytic side. I am not merely the perceiving of ash bowl.[1] ᵛThere areᵛ stages and parts in what is actually one.

Entity as finished with real essence is not an object for itself. Entity as unfinished is an object for the entity as finished. This is the essential meaning of endurance.

|7| This entity is immediate object of the next one, but not to itself. An entity is not a fact for itself. All fact is statement about objectification. This is why get dominance of subject-predicate form. Subject-predicate form really conveys the doctrine of objectification.

Percipience only a word for relationships of entities. Mentality is analysis of percipience.

---

1. That is, an ash tray for cigars. Conger had noted in his diary that during the seminaries, almost everyone except he himself and Whitehead smoked. See Conger, 'Notes from the diary of George P. Conger on his friendship with Whitehead'. These 'Notes from the diary' had been bundled together with the Whitehead notes that appear in the University of Minnesota archives, and are reproduced as Appendix 3 to the present volume (pp. 435–7).

One comes back to something not very different, their atomic propositions – except secondary qualities ought to be taken in broad sense and avoid bifurcation of nature.

Reference to universe means reference to general metaphysical principles relevant to that proposition and which holds

No truly particular proposition.

No self-subsistent actual entity, all bound together in that way.

Any proposition can only be understood by dealing with all other entities.

|8| Making definite (~~entity~~ ∨(?)∨) in ~~stage in~~ continuity, there self creation turns up – what freedom there is is in what is actual arising out of that ground. How it takes itself.

Nature as potential side determined for it except for indefiniteness of demarcation.

As soon as have a definite region which is together there is a new situation which arises.

Continuity in nature. Atomicity is what actuality imposes on nature. How it treats by itself its new situations as it passes to completion is the opportunity for contingence. Maximum at self analytic stage – taking first that percipience ~~which~~ and how ⟨well?⟩ you analyze it into knowledge. Nature always reformed by new creatures which arise. All entities arise out of fully determined nature except insofar as continuity is concerned.[1]

A creature is a potential process which is in fact one. Potentially many, and in fact one.

Zeno argument makes idea of its becoming nonsense if admit there is something which becomes. Then can't be a continuity of becoming. Actual entity has temporal endurance.

Throughout physics atomicity and continuity. ∨Potential∨ ground for becoming is continuous. What becomes is atomic. Atomic character achieved in its potentiality.

Want to describe distinction between potential ground undefined and one which is ultimate ground of actuality ~~now~~, left in indefiniteness. Indefiniteness in the ground is the continuity. First stage of actuality is achievement of real unity.

Friday, 14 January 1927

Conger's notes

|1| Difficulty. Class with pure extension is just a multiplicity of entities. Can have a predicate which applies to these and no other. Won't be merely one, but can make others. If want to get hold of class as one, reduced to arbitrary selection among these predicates.

---

1. This marks the end of the left-hand column for this page; the right-hand column follows. In this case it is not clear which column should come first; for other sessions Conger typically numbers his columns and switches between starting on the right or left, depending on the side of the page he was writing on, but here he does not number his columns.

But extension is just these entities – no question of arbitrary selection. How point to entity, not one of arbitrary number of predicates, but which is in some unique manner that multiplicity of things.

Molecules of chair have definite binding relation. They hang together – definite interconnected mode of behavior to each other. Code of behavior is such that it... unity. A synthetic scheme of relations between them. Chair actually a class of molecules. It's a chair of molecules. If think of molecules merely a class, the chairness has gone. Want in dealing with class to find some relationship not as particular predicate, yet has binding property to evolve one entity out of it.

Predicate as marking out class is a false light. Molecules synthetically one as a chair not because molecules have individually a predicate ~~Its~~ of chairness. It's an interrelation of whole. Physical connection. Geometrical form brings about a unity.

Not true that every predicate marks out a class which can be taken as one entity. Can get predicates which mark out entities, and if you suppose there is a class of these entities – there must be some entities outside the class. Ordinal numbers. 1·2·3·· infinite ordinals. Class of ordinal numbers well-ordered. That class will correspond to ordinal number which is greater than any ordinal number in the class, and therefore unequal to it. vClass ofv ordinal types. Ordinal number is a type of order. Think of class of all ordinal types, then ~~that~~ the number of ordinal types in that class has an ordinal type which is greater than any in the class.

So notion of class as one, which is in some sense outcome or representative of the many, breaks down. Same applies to cardinal number. Same applies to all propositions. Say every proposition is false or true – another which doesn't belong to that class.

You can get many such. Shows notion of predicate and notion of class, while obviously have interconnections, are not in such a fundamental connection. Theory of logical extension sadly mixed by muddling it up.

Principia Mathematica tried to run close connection of idea of predicate and idea of class by method which didn't presuppose there was such an entity in pure extension at all. Whenever you talked of a class, you were talking of a predicate in a certain complicated way so any predicate with same extension would do. Suppose affirming a predicate A vav of x; *Principia Mathematica* says ~~if~~ all you need when dealing with classes is a predicate ϕ such that ϕ is equivalent to a, and ϕx. ~~That is~~ vItv simply depends there on what you may term its extension – you are really talking about ϕx any predicate equivalent to a, so you get rid of your dependence on particular predicate a.

|2| In propositions which deal with classes, can always conceive them as talking neutrally about any one of the predicates of the same extension. vShowedv could count classes and treat them as if they were entities.

To get rid of paradoxes, must run elaborate theory of types. Say e.g. teaspoon and number 2 being of essentially different ~~class~~ vtypev can't form ~~type~~ class. Class must be homogenous. Whitehead thinks can class teaspoon and deadly sin. Thinks can get class of disparate entities.

Obviously is one collection – four bowls as one – perfectly definite unity in which you have got rid of the predicate.

Theory of types – of different types of proposition and must have theory that can't talk of all the types. But we do.

Different sorts of propositions. Negation has different meaning for different ~~propositions~~ types – ⟨?⟩ $p \cdot q$ p or q – different meanings for different types – Systematic ambiguity. More thinks about it, less believes it. Gave reason for not drawing conclusions which would have landed in self contradiction.

Rule of safety. ⟨Probably?⟩ tied up too much more than too little. Now thinks it's untrue.

What is a class? Difficulty of saying it's that and that and that and that. Sheer and does not really have any synthetic form, to give it a unity. If only the unity of thot in your mind private to that mind. When that act of mind has gone, class has ⟨gone?⟩.

⟨Mere?⟩ grammatical and doesn't seem to give anything.

New theory. Gives two types of classes. A class is a certain form of proposition. Real difficulty about defining is you want to get hold of notion of class before you have dealt with particular predicates.

You want to define class before you have got to material facts. Find something in pure logic whereby the multiplicity receives the synthetic bond which achieves unity. In logic only one set of complex unities – propositions.

A proposition is a complex entity and it is one. As a proposition has a unity. Hook up unity of class and of proposition. A class is a certain kind of proposition. Two ways of thinking about proposition – Moral uplift – desire to know whether its true or false, has dominated logic. Another way – ask what sort of complexity they've got.

A class is a proposition not considered in respect to its truth or falsehood (Whitehead thinks all classes are true propositions), but all classes of propositions of a certain sort of propositional complexity.

Complexity of propositions has two origins – may arise from content of a proposition, if analyze it. This rose is red – When analyze it. Elements aren't propositions. But a logical complexity in a proposition which has nothing to do with particular content except insofar as particular content will come in as to whether believe or not. Conjunction of propositions. And, or disjunction or represent peculiar complexities of formal logic.

|3| p and q. Peculiar property that when you analyze it into p and q – the two parts you find are themselves both propositions. Same for p or q. That type of complexity which on analysis gives you elements of same genus as whole entity – the synthetic connection or type of complexity is properly what is called extensive.

Technical words you take one which has more or less proper meaning.

Instinct which has led people to take space as extensive and talk of logical extension is sound. Cf. Euler's diagram.[1]

---

1. Euler diagrams are used to represent sets and their relationships.

Essence of extension – you have synthetic wholes with bond of synthesis such that its elements are also of same genus. You have an infinitely divisible extension if elements itself are ~~concerned~~ complex. Cf space. Divide room into two parts – still get volumes. *p* and *q*. *p* or *q* – properly to be called an <u>extensive complexity</u>.

<u>What</u> propositions are conjoined so as to make a complex element? Quite obvious – must be as many propositions as there are members of extension.

Predicate point of view would say that's an ash tray.....

You may take a conjunctive complex or disjunctive complex – in doing that you have brought in a particular predicate. Might as well have taken ashtray on ~~pre~~ table as predicate.

No difficulty getting an ~~entity~~ Vlogical∨ proposition with synthetic unity corresponding to that proposition (?) (?).

Proposition has advantage that is a unity of a multiplicity. A multiplicity of propositions. Unity of propositions taken conjunctively or disjunctively. Can find a unity of exactly the – you want except it is hooked up to a particular predicate.

Cannot you get a proposition which indicates the definite entity without hooking yourself to one definite predicate? Make use of something of much more nebulous character. Assertion there is an adequate description of every entity. There is a description φ which applies to <u>that</u> ash tray and only that. That is a proposition about the ash tray which is practically the general logical equivalent of ⟨Lo?⟩ the ashtray there it is, the entity is determinate in the universe. It is really fixing in the mind the proposition which is simply saying there's an entity. Instead of merely <u>an</u> entity it is the apprehension of an entity put into a general proposition. If take propositions conjunctively or disjunctively, which have to do with members you have a propositional unity.[1] That proposition has properties which you want a class to have. If you deny there is such a thing as a class, can only do it by denying there is such a unity as the proposition.

Either conjunctive or disjunctive type will give you just the unity or multiplicity which you want.

|4| Class is defined independently of appealing to any common predicate. Question of whether there is a proposition corresponding to members of extension remains for determination in each case. Obvious if you have a finite extension – If can get inductively in orderly manner, ~~to~~ thinks can define such a proposition. Otherwise with infinite not clear.

Also don't have to bother about ~~def~~ difficulties of type.

Difficulty about many making one is reduced to logical difficulty of many propositions ~~taking~~ making one is a logical.

Algebra insists on being two-dimensional. Two types of classes which at once arise corresponding to two dimensions of algebra. Thinks can get a reason why should get two dimensions, the real and the ~~alg~~ imaginary in algebra

---

1. Two small vertical strokes appear after the word 'members' and before 'you'. They do not appear to be ditto marks. Their significance is unclear.

corresponding to two types of classes. Reason why number and logic apply so admirably to space is they both share extension, being extensive complexes.

Aristotelian logic a muddle of two things. (1) discussion of formal relations whereby propositions arise, complex forms and relations of truth values of wholes and some of parts to remainder of the parts. If you're interested in truth and falsehood (2) Under what circumstances do you hold that such a proposition is true? Can you make inferences? In order to do that he analyzed content of propositions. Doesn't belong in formal logic – study of extensive complexes. Then study content of elementary propositions to truth value of ~~whole~~. Complex proposition as whole.

The "and" 1 and 1 and 1. . . . Is the "and" of a mental act? The four ash trays are obviously many. And there is not a unity which is a one unit, the class.

Difficulty of the class can be reduced to the proposition. Might deny proposition is one – Might say my proposition is essentially different from yours. Conjunctive and [Propositional and of conjunctive complex] is different from enumerative and which is mental. Assume there is a description which will describe that entity uniquely. To every entity there is a proposition asserting its demonstratable character. If some entities aren't demonstratable, ~~why~~ vhowv do we know anything about them. Can't stop Plato's ideas –

That is a class of <u>ashtrays</u>. <u>Ashtrays</u> are the many. Need class as one in <u>math</u> – Unity is always abstraction in mind. First have unity of spatial synthesis. Can then abstract into more general type, which can call class.

|5| What has been left to give you synthetic unity when you are through with spatial unity. Conjunction of four propositions asserting demonstrable objects – Still leaves you that form of unity which gives you a proposition.

Can't think of all entities – because then the class of all would be another. Can think of all below a certain type.

There are different types of things – Virtue and ash tray, but theory of types doesn't depend on it. Avoid trouble of types. Now don't have to hold every predicate corresponds to a class. If you have contradiction in finite classes, would be fatal, but only when get to odd ~~types~~ infinite classes. There is the predicate of being a ~~All~~ class.

But the extension of that predicate is itself a class. There is not the class of all classes – Can always point to another which doesn't belong to it.

Notion of class not an entity, but an essential multiplicity. Can't represent the extension of that multiplicity by any form of unity. If there's a <u>class</u>, there is.

Class with only one member and distinction between class and member.

Math begins with classes, not Logic.

Proposition is wider term than class – is bringing down class to be particular type of proposition.

Proposition is an intermediate type of universal. May have on it elements which aren't universals, but particulars.

Philosophy 20i: Seminary in Logic, spring semester 1927

Friday, 25 February 1927

Conger's notes[1]

|1| Logic can't be treated apart from metaphysics.

What is a proposition? Can't answer without putting in form – World being what it is, how are these propositions in it? vOtherwisev explain what you mean in terms of ideas not criticized.

Dislikes muddling judgment with proposition. A proposition is judgable, but act of judgment is much more psychological. A proposition may never have been judged as to whether it's right or wrong.

Proposition is a complex unity analyzable into components which aren't propositions. Can't deal with question of complex unity without asking how there are such.

Can make proposition psychological – but if you have privacy – ⟨?⟩ how can you get solidarity?

Absolute skeptic always taken too easily. ⟨Noneqns?⟩ is absolute solipsist – business of philosophy to touch common sense. Don't say "of course we don't believe that" – but so describe our experience as to justify whole bundle of vulgar beliefs. They prune them, adjust them, but finally after adjustment, finally philosophy has got to accept them.

Hume pestiferous habit ⟨of⟩ appeal⟨ing⟩ beyond philosophy to practice. vLikev Bertrand Russell. In practice we may assume. What you can't order your life without assuming is somehow a valid element in your experience. No way of getting validity other than that.

Give coherent account of what you assume in practice. Practice comes in at beginning and has got to emerge at end with feathers a little pruned down. All these purgations lead to more penetrating knowledge of experience at end. You can't get away from practice. If you dodge autos, can't have philosophy that there aren't any.

Hume ought to say, in practice, I don't abide by these conclusions, therefore I must have left something out

I – What is a Proposition?

II – What is Logic?[2]

---

1. All the notes presented here are those taken by George Conger, though Paul Weiss also had notes for the 4 March and 11 March sessions. Refer to the table on page 419 for a full list of seminary sessions by date, and see also the Introduction for a detailed discussion of each note-taker and their notes.
   It is important to remember that Whitehead's seminaries were more discussion based than his Philosophy 3b lectures, and hence the person speaking may not always be Whitehead.
2. Conger writes in the margin that these first two items are 'two things that ought to be separated'. Slightly below this, roughly next to 'Logic', he adds 'Inference'.

(III) –

(IV) – Men were emitting propositions in form of grunts long before had logic.[1]

Wittgenstein, Hamelin,[2] French Hegelian.

Logic probably not theology, but may be anything else.

W. E. Johnson uses proposition as description of a fact.

|2| Objection to Wittgenstein, which is skeptical view.

Whitehead. What the universe is before can tell what proposition is.

Lloyd Morgan and Alexander have influence Whitehead.[3] Lloyd Morgan's Presidential address not far from what Whitehead says. Whitehead more convinced as to general approach than to details. Agrees with Lloyd Morgan to very large extent.

Whitehead: objectification ∨(object under reference)∨.[4] Actual entity, though it includes everything, includes it under a limitation.

Crystal, amoeba, molecule are organisms.[5] Events go together in kinds of relatedness in such a way as to constitute an organism that organism. Atomic molecule living, etc. in accordance with its status in an (extended) natural hierarchy.

Lloyd Morgan welcomes organic view of nature.

Believe there is a cluster of events out there. That which is correlated with object of reference use the word thing.

Whitehead: three objects

1 – Percipient organism object under references a component.

2 – Immediate portion of space which is out there shining th at you demonstrated to you.

3 – Other obs ∨object vaguely demonstrated∨ 43 seconds[6] earlier. No use interpreting unless some knowledge.

Thing – the as was – second ago.

Object the immediate here and there (planet, book).

Connection with some schema of reflex under reference.

Between any two organisms seems to be fundamental kind of relatedness. What are these fundamental kinds?[7]

(1) temporal

(2) spatial

(3) physical

---

1. To the right Conger writes four dates which correspond to the final four seminary sessions he would be able to attend before his departure back to Minnesota: 25 February, 4 March, 11 March and 18 March. The final date is circled.
2. Likely referring to Octave Hamelin (1856–1907), a French philosopher.
3. See the 24 February 1927 lecture, note 2, p. 293.
4. Parentheses supplied.
5. The bolded portions correspond to Whitehead reading from Morgan, 'Objects under reference'.
6. Morgan uses the example of light waves taking 43 *minutes* to reach our eyes from Jupiter (Morgan, 'Objects under reference', pp. 9–10).
7. Parentheses supplied. The numbers for the list following have been supplied to match Morgan's list on p. 3 of 'Objects under reference'.

(4) referential ↔ Demonstration (Whitehead)[1]
Discuss *tsp* in abstraction from *r*.[2]
Common to all organisms ∨(none derivative from other kind).∨[3] ***t-s-p-r* intrinsic to any organism are these *tspr* and extrinsic *tspr*.**[4] **Relatedness within any organism is of same nature as relatedness between.**

Whitehead doesn't agree about <u>duration</u>.

Accept *tspr* as given in correlated whole of nature. Emergence not ~~given~~.[5] **Emergence applies to different modes within same kind. Molecular cell – different modes of physical.**[6]

If abstract *tsp* from *r*, get human body which is *tspr* system – to this in entirety emergence is applicable.

|3| *r* abstracted and called <u>mind</u>.

In a man, items of mind.[7]

Planet and I as concrete organisms are *tsp* and *r* too. Might say one-sided. No evidence of reference from Jupiter to observer.

Lloyd Morgan: influence of retina on planet is negligible but [let's not say not existent].

Reference ⟨of⟩ observer to planet is high level of emergence. Planet to observer only taking note of – for all practical purposes negligible.

Outcome of *tsp* influence by organism is change of *tsp* relatedness in organism. Relative importance may be altered.

Physicist can fill in *tsp*[8] relatedness with events.

Whitehead – a thing is past because it's in physical relationships.

Could <u>past</u> be <u>persistence</u>?

Physical relationships constitute fact of being past. Things in same present happen independently so far as physical relations are concerned.

Can't carry much farther without bringing in what Whitehead calls eternal objects and what Santayana calls essences.

Eternal objects constitute the <u>what</u> of *tspr* correlations. If ask what ~~it~~ ∨*tspr*∨ is, must express in terms of ∨correlation∨. Eternal objects, essences, universals.

---

1. Parentheses supplied.
2. 'Now we may, and habitually do, discuss TSP in abstraction from R. Why not, so long as we clearly realize what we are doing? We then get highly emergent TSP-system and, in the case of the human organism, speak of this as the body. But the human organism in its concrete entirety is not a TSP-system only. It is a TSPR-system' (Morgan, 'Objects under reference', p. 4).
3. Parentheses supplied.
4. Whitehead has skipped around from the fourth page back to the third page: 'Intrinsic to any organism is TSPR in intimate correlation as I use this word. And extrinsic to any organism – linking it up with other organisms – is TSPR' (Morgan, 'Objects under reference', p. 3).
5. 'But if the concept of emergence does not apply to these or other kinds of relatedness, to what does this concept apply?' (Morgan, 'Objects under reference', p. 4).
6. 'Thus in the atomic organism, the molecular organism, the living organism, there are different modes of that which we commonly speak of as physical (TSP) relatedness' (Morgan, 'Objects under reference', p. 4).
7. 'In a man as a concrete organism there are items of mind*ing*, such as sens*ing*, perceiv*ing*, remember*ing*, think*ing*, and so forth, which go together in the substantial unity of what Professor Alexander and I call enjoyment' (Morgan, 'Objects under reference', pp. 4–5).
8. Conger actually writes '*pst*' here, but we have changed it to '*tsp*' for consistency; this matches Morgan's usage on p. 7 of 'Objects under reference'.

Jupiter objectified. <u>Whitehead</u>: Object referred to under limitation of reference is component of immediate unit, actual entity which

Lloyd Morgan, he is there. Reference is here at emergent level of perception and backed up by conceptual reference.

Whitehead – A double relatedness.

A precise reference to the bright spot in the sky, and then lifts into a definite demonstration of something which is more than immediate bit of space time which I see now gives a demonstrative ⟨?⟩ to the previous history of the table from billionth of a second ago backwards as being a physical influence on my experience.

Whitehead thinks reference isn't conceptual apprehension of yourself as under physical influence, lacks demonstrative force.

Table cloth as physical thing suddenly becomes obvious to one. What I see depends on my own body, but its outcome of physical influence with a past.

|4| That's why immediate data gives me element of space there, and has functioning of rendering evident my physical relatedness influence from the tablecloth.

~~Unce~~ It picks out a physical influence for other reasons too. Where error comes in. If I see the table, I do see it – Error in <u>double</u> reference. One must be true, other false.

Catastrophe not to be able to constitute truth or error. Experience is leaky. Sensible ∨data∨ influence demonstrates a portion of space-time immediate – blueness there the what of a certain relationship which is that portion of space as something contemporary with me and sensitizes me to really demonstrative force of physical influence on me as also demonstrating the historic route of the existence of the tablecloth. ~~But~~

Both references include <u>what</u> – First gives <u>blue</u>. Second more complicated. Elicits into distinctness an element of experience, is not distinct but swamped in general feeling of physical relatedness.

Hallucination picks out space, time, but error in getting to the physical.

Might say influence – <u>reference</u> is <u>inter</u>action to environment. Looking at is ∨something∨ like acting on.

Get <u>something</u> without reflective reference. And behavior shows reference – dog snaps at you.

Whitehead thinks everything is *tspr*.

Error – Aesop's fable of dog with leg of mutton. Sees dog ∨reflection∨ in stream.[1]

Correlation called concomitance.

Elliptical ~~from~~ expressions. For beginnings in philosophy, common speech was best way to get at man's experience – cf. analysis of it in early philosophy. Plato, Aristotle – but very fallacious if you take it too far. All phraseology is elliptical.

Influence ⇆ reference

---

1. Whitehead also uses this example in his Barbour-Page lectures of 1927, which were later published as *Symbolism*. At this point, he had not yet delivered the lectures (he did so in mid-April).

|5| **Time interval in influence. No time interval between reference from and reference to.**

Lloyd Morgan's reference parallels Whitehead's presentational immediacy. Position is <u>receptacle view</u> of space.

But nobody reflects on future – ∨Future and∨ past go into non-entity. **Future and past have being under reflective reference.**

Necessary possibility, connection with <u>past</u>

He says it's through the interpretive schema.

"Now"[1] (is) a slab of *tsp* events where relations before and after are <u>less</u> than some assigned value.

If that is an account of what the universe is, where do propositions come in? Start from that sort of thing. Your actual entity is an organism which builds itself up.

To deal with the job of logic properly, must take some general view of universe and show how what you call a proposition, what it is.

If you don't go into metaphysics, you assume an uncritical metaphysics. Spatial-temporal matter point of view always assumed and expressed in those terms. Every scientific man in order to preserve his reputation has to say he dislikes metaphysics. What he means is he dislikes having his metaphysics criticized.

Friday, 4 March 1927

Conger's notes[2]

|1| Sidgwick's *Methods of Ethics* can't find sanction.[3]

Metaphysics ought not to be neglected because can't find agreement. Must ask how do these first principles fit into the universe. How, the universe being what it is, are you to explain there are such things as propositions? If don't do that, so much reasoning presupposes crude Cartesian metaphysics. Mental world, physical world. Some say if assume know physical world, needn't assume mind. Nor for minds on their side need you assume matter. Crude metaphysics (bifurcation). Comes from not really putting minds up to metaphysics.

1. A proposition is a complex unity. One entity analyzable into many component elements. Extended and not extended propositions.

---

1. Quotation marks supplied.
2. Lewis Ford published a version of these 4 March 1927 seminary notes in Ford, *The Emergence of Whitehead's Metaphysics*, pp. 317–22. He prefaces these notes (p. 317) with the following: '(These propositions were dictated to Whitehead's "Seminary in Logic 20" on March 4, 1927. This version is collated from the notes of Paul Weiss and George P. Conger.)'. Ford used the same two sources that we are using to do his collation. Weiss's 'notes' were in fact four typed pages seemingly pasted into a pre-numbered notebook. At first Ford thought that this was a 'handout' given in class (Ford, 'Letter to Paul Weiss', 14 July 1978), but the presence of question marks in parentheses in the document seems to indicate otherwise. Given the usual brevity of Weiss's notes for this term, it seems likely that these typed notes were taken by another student and given to Weiss. See the Introduction (p. lvii).
3. Henry Sidgwick (1838–1900) was an English philosopher and economist. *The Methods of Ethics* (1874) was his best-known work, laying out a utilitarian philosophy. See Sidgwick, *The Methods of Ethics*, available at <https://archive.org/details/methodsofethics00sidg>.

2. Extended is one which is analyzable into component propositions logically antecedent to given propositions and with a bond of unity.[1] Also Whitehead and ⟨...?⟩

3. Non-extended proposition not capable of such an analysis. There may be propositions among its components, there are also non-propositional elements among the components and they are not capable of such analysis.

Man whom I saw yesterday has gone away.[2]

⟨4.⟩[3] Kind of basic proposition – Non-extended is not analyzable into components, including other propositions.[4]

"That is red." Natural to call it atomic proposition, but slightly different sense.

How do these come to be complex entities in the universe? Propositions as particular sort. How what is many can also be one. Requires some general assertion which lies outside logic altogether.

5. Source of all types of complex units to be sought ~~from~~ in derivation of individual ~~activity~~ ⱽunificationⱽ of the universe in each actual entity – nothing is left out but relevance. You can find every entity in each actual entity. Character of universe as actual is this progressive individualization of itself.

⟨6.⟩ Every other type of complex unit is derivate from that type. Possibility of derivation. Complex unity of actual entity discloses among its components subordinate types of complex unity. In abstracting certain components from finished actual entity, or abstracting finished entity from components, you leave ⟨out?⟩ the individual ~~entity~~ unity of the actual entity. These more abstract types of unity are derivate types.

|2| ⟨7.⟩ Actual entity ~~⟨?⟩~~ is fundamentally to be looked on as an act of experience. The rest of your life by its peculiar relevance to that antecedent portion. You are always new, only integrating your past.

Descartes: God sustains universe by perpetually creating it.[5]

Nothing in the universe which can't be found in sufficiently adequate analysis of immediate act of experience. Nothing to be known beyond that, or anyhow don't know it.

Real crux of metaphysics – great difficulty – Enormous difficulty of stating with actual precision all the elements that make up an act of experience. All – must oversimplify.

Our own knowledge of what our experience is always dim, fitful. Not maintained that every entity includes own adequate self analysis.[6]

---

1. Weiss follows this with '(I am here and the chair is there)' (Weiss, p. 80).
2. Cf. Weiss: '3. A non-extended proposition in a proposition which is not capable of such an analysis, though there may be propositions among the components which are bound together in one proposition. (The man I saw yesterday went away – The man I saw yesterday is a subordinate proposition)' (Weiss, p. 80).
3. Conger's numbering is incomplete, while Weiss's notes contain uninterrupted numbering from 1 to 22. We have supplied Weiss's numbers in angle brackets in places where Conger is missing them.
4. Cf. Weiss: 'A basic proposition is a particular sort of non-extended proposition, which is not analyzable into components which include other propositions' (Weiss, p. 80).
5. Weiss's notes add here: 'You are numerically different in different times' (Weiss, p. 80).
6. Cf. Weiss: 'Every act of experience – every actual entity – includes its own act of analysis' (Weiss, p. 80).

Such self analysis – never can observe accurately, can know what you are unless you have thought of it before. What is new is dimly and inaccurately observed. Practically it is the imagination which disciplines observation.[1]

⟨8. Analysis⟩[2] Requires imaginative leap towards scheme of sorts of components to be found in experience. Discipline it by

(1) antecedent knowledge

(2) logical coherence

(3) aesthetic congruence (dim, vague (1))[3]

(4) partial verification

Appeal is to future acts of experience rendered more adequate by their inheritance of this conceptual hypothesis.

Not one-tenth of scientific hypotheses ever get printed.[4] Imaginative leap.

9. Act of experience or actual entity, actual occasion in temporal world v and only v is

(1) a synthesis of perception of other acts of experience, together forming the actual universe.

It's perception how the other acts of experience, rest of actual universe is synthesized into the one entity which is the act of experience of question.

(2)[5] Emotional or int esthetic intensity which is the primordial may call it the enjoyment of being synthetic constituting the outcome of the synthetic unity.[6]

(3) Conceptual functioning whereby what might be enters into synthesis with what is and is analytic of it by reason of yes and no type. Concept meets percept – if yes type, unity and identity of relationship to percept. If of no type, a certain diversity.[7]

(4) Additional self creative action of the self judgment of the act of experience upon the complex stages of non-temporal constitution[8] of the actual entity.[9] New element is self-judgment upon what is logically antecedent in entity.

|3| In this way control and adjustment – what is put forward or led back. Begins as emotional intensity reconstituted by act of self-judgment.[10]

---

1. Cf. Weiss: 'But you must think of it before you try to observe. Imagination disciplines observation. You must know what to look for' (Weiss, p. 80).
2. Supplied from Weiss (p. 81).
3. Parentheses supplied.
4. Cf. Weiss: 'This is the method of science' (Weiss, p. 81).
5. Parentheses supplied for numbers 2–5 below, for consistency's sake.
6. Cf. Weiss: '2. The emotional aesthetic intensity which is the primordial, unit, individual fact constituting the meaning or outcome of this unity. It is an aesthetic intensity which is an enjoyment of that synthesis' (Weiss, p. 81).
7. Weiss's notes have 'divergency' instead of 'diversity' (Weiss, p. 81).
8. Weiss's notes have 'evolution' instead of 'constitution' (Weiss, p. 81).
9. Weiss adds here: 'The entity is analyzable into layers each of which presuppose one another logically' (Weiss, p. 80).
10. The content of the main list of points (1–22) diverges here somewhat between Conger and Weiss: Weiss's point number 10 starts immediately below, where Conger has '(5)'. We have moved the '10' one paragraph further down, past Conger's (1)–(5) numbering, as Conger clearly intended (5) to go with (1)–(4). But the correct placement of '10' is very ambiguous.

(5) Emergence of final actual occasion.[1] This doesn't sit in judgment on itself or know itself, providing a new creative character for the universe whereby creative passage is conditioned for the (next?) act in question.

⟨10.⟩ What is it to be actual? Always creative passage beyond itself. Perceptivity is not the inclusion of other acts simpliciter, but their inclusion under limitations of certain predicates and exclusion of other predicates.

⟨11.⟩ Some acts included merely as exemplifying certain predicates.[2] "Predicate" used here because logical. Santayana calls them "essences". Platonic ideas. "First cousin to Platonic ideas." Aristotelian qualities. <u>Eternal objects</u>. These predicates as functioning in perceptivity are relational between the perceived and the percipient.

⟨12.⟩ The perceived is objectified for the percipient. Perceived enters into constitution of percipient as exemplifying those predicates for the percipient. Perceived acts are many and are complex. Objectified as exhibiting their interdependence[3] in unity of solidarity of world.

Synthesis of many objectified acts into an objectified unity.[4] <u>That</u> is objectified for me under <u>predicate</u> of a cylindrical box. Ingression, prehension.

~~Thus a~~ Two types of perceptual functioning:
(1) Relation between perceived and percipient.
(2) Relation between diverse ~~acts~~ other perceived acts of experience whereby they are objectified in the unity of a complex entity.[5] Millions of molecules in box given to me under one predicate.

13. When consciousness supervenes, yet another synthesis of various objective unit entities with predicates which might have been theirs or may be theirs, and this synthesis of conceptual functioning with perceptual functioning issues in yes or no form –

14. In rudimentary stages of conceptual functioning the yes-form dominates.[6] No form emerges when the imagination which produces the conceptual functioning arrives at an independent activity whereby predicates irrelevant[7] in perception become relevant for conception. Practical absence of no form is stage of unconscious instinct.[8] Consciousness emerges with emergence of unverified propositions. ∨(trial and error)∨[9]

---

1. Cf. Weiss: 'The contribution of the synthetic or perceptivity to the emotional or aesthetic intensity is reconstituted by an act of self consciousness which may not be conscious' (Weiss, p. 81).
2. Cf. Weiss: 'The act of perceptivity or act of experience includes other acts merely as exemplifying certain predicates and as excluding others which they might exemplify for that experience, but don't' (Weiss, p. 81).
3. Weiss's notes instead have 'independence' (p. 81); given the context, this seems unlikely.
4. Cf. Weiss: 'By the relation of the predicate the objectification includes the synthesis of many objectified acts into an objective unity, for the predicates bind the one with the many' (Weiss, p. 81).
5. Weiss adds here: 'That is done by the bond of the predicate which extends over the whole, for they express the union of many entities' (Weiss, p. 82).
6. Weiss adds here: 'You vaguely know that you are perceiving' (Weiss, p. 82).
7. Weiss's notes have 'relevant' instead of 'irrelevant' (p. 82); given the context, this seems unlikely.
8. Weis adds here: 'Only a high grade intelligence can make errors' (Weiss, p. 82).
9. Parentheses supplied.

|4| ⟨15.⟩ Consciousness is the enjoyment of the distinction between the verified and the non-verified. If haven't the distinction in your mind, how can you be conscious it is red?

Predicates are non-actual elements in universe whereby factual or hypothetical objectification is effected. Predicates not good term.

⟨16.⟩ Eternal object.[1] Those objects in the universe whereby objectification and its conceptual analysis are effected. Eternal because in each entity, but impartially with respect to various entities. Each one in its abstract nature doesn't tell you about the how of its relation to the various entities.

⟨17.⟩ A finished objectification passes beyond itself.[2]

⟨18.⟩ Never is self objectified in state of being finished <u>qua</u> finished – always passes beyond self. As a ~~complete~~ ∧finished∧ entity it thereby passes beyond itself and only to be found in the objectifications of itself in other entities.

19. A proposition is an intermediate universal. ⟨(1)⟩ Not a pure essence which is neither true nor false. No eternal objects in isolation from actual world. Every eternal object has a meaning with respect to its possible functioning in actual world.

Eternal object gives no information about itself. ⟨?⟩ Pure rational consideration of ideas, you can't construct the actual world.

A pure essence is merely <u>for</u> the universe in its various modes of functioning. Doesn't tell how it functions in particular instance.

(2). A proposition is not a particular since it's not an element in the conceptual functioning of just one particular ~~element~~ functioning. My belief in a proposition is a particular belief, and my act of judging is a particular. The proposition itself is not a particular – has an impartial relevance to all of us. ~~Proposition~~ A certain type of universal relevance.

(3) When you analyze a proposition it includes acts of experience among its components. It's about the actual world. It includes acts of experience among its components. It's the universal which objectifies hypothetical objectification of any set of acts for any one act of another set.

|5| ⟨20.⟩ ~~Caesar c~~ Hypothetical object form of act of objectification.[3]

Certain predicates which bind together that set of acts of experience as one object, one fact for us. An objectification of that set for us by a certain complex predicate. Then ~~that~~ those predicates objectify the Caesar set of acts as an element in the perceptive synthesis of any subsequent act of experience. Particular relevance of set of objectifications left undetermined – depends on whether you're Italian etc. as to what perspective you add on.

Does determine and condition the perspective of the Caesar crossing Rubicon set condition which limits objectification of that act in any subsequent act of experience. May be so trivially relevant that it's in background for any

---

1. Weiss's notes do not say just 'eternal object,' but instead: 'Universals, essence, eternal objects, qualities, or ideas are . . .' (Weiss, p. 82).
2. Cf. Weiss: 'The finished act of experience passes into objectification in acts beyond itself. It is never objectified for itself' (Weiss, p. 82).
3. Cf. Weiss: 'Caesar crossed the Rubicon is a proposition which expresses the hypothetical particular form of objectification of one set of acts or experience – that set implicated in Caesar crossing' (Weiss, p. 82).

definite physical analysis. Sufficiently accurate self-analysis can find effect of shower of meteors on Andromeda.

Must allow fantastic differences in degree of objectification by new scientific measurements.

21. A proposition contains two subjects which have different functions.

(α) logical subject whose possible objectification is topic proposed – that should be verified in perception. That particular set of actual entities. Topic proposed in the conceptual functioning of the proposition lies behind it.[1]

(β) Percipient subject for whom the objectification is or is not a valid element in its experience with due addition of perspective and relevance depending on the subject.

Always for whom or for what the proposition is is valid if it happens in its conceptual functioning to bring it forward.

Also the other question as to what the proposition is about.

That[2] is a hypothetical objectification of a certain set of actual entities and only valid for subsequent entities.

⟨22.⟩ Percipient subject is any one of a set of acts of experience.

Part of content of a logical proposition is identification of logical subject from standpoint of any one of perceptual subjects.[3] Proposition written out from standpoint of where we are now to bring out. Get you to state of mind where you point.

A proposition is <u>for</u> any one of its percipient subjects,[4] and it is about its logical subject.

|6| That Caesar crossed Rubicon not <u>for</u> Romulus and Remus. Balk this by divesting a proposition of its temporal relevance.

Is it <u>modality</u> of propositions (?)

If have propositions about a particular act of experience, makes difference whether there is any or not. How past is an object for its successors.

The blue is the relationship of identity between by concept and percipient.

It's any one of a set of percipient subjects.[5]

Whitehead wouldn't have different <u>proposition</u>, but would have different perspective.[6]

Perspectives demonstrate something which isn't perspectives, else no external world.

Caesar crossing Rubicon an impartial fact which has its history in each of us at this moment, and for our successors. Rustic on bank looking at Caesar didn't see the proposition.

Fictional propositions – *Alice in Wonderland*. ∨In fictional (?)∨ You are

---

1. Cf. Weiss: 'The proposition is that which lies behind the conceptual functioning' (Weiss, p. 83).
2. Weiss has 'Caesar crossed the Rubicon' in place of 'That' (p. 83).
3. Cf. Weiss: 'Part of the act of experience consists in the identification of the logical subjects from the standpoint of any one of the percipient subjects' (Weiss, p. 83).
4. Weiss adds here: '. . . and they perceive it whether they see it or not' (Weiss, p. 83).
5. Cf. Weiss: 'Some propositions, like that of arithmetic are for all subjects because they are about any act of experience and for all acts of experience' (Weiss, p. 83).
6. There is some illegible marginal text to the right of this sentence.

dealing with ᵛcomplicatedᵛ imaginative history of many individuals who have seen printed pages. Otherwise there is no Alice.

Proposition about Caesar the objectification of these molecules which made up Caesar for the percipient subject.

Unless you specify for whom your proposition is dealing, you run into a contradiction in terms between the future and the past.

Proposition only for those who come after. Only effectively <u>for</u> those who think of it consciously.

Perhaps time not only condition which limits percipients. <u>Large number of logical subjects</u> – molecules in Caesar and have passive totality of universe in background.

Prehension more general than ingression – the <u>general</u> way in which ~~ingression~~ things come together. Objectified for entity.

Must get a perspective of ~~that~~ enjoyment in order to contemplate it.

⟨Friday, 11 March 1927⟩[1]

Conger's notes

|1| Paper on Hume.[2]
Mill don't identify a proposition with a judgment.
Proposition refers to things, not ideas.
2. Hobbes belief of speaker is predicate is name of same thing as subject.
3. Proposition not reference of something to a class. Class is nothing but indefinite number of individuals denoted by general name. Things not found in nature in classes. Propositions assert connections not between names, but what terms ~~(?)~~ ⟨connected?⟩, i.e. connections between <u>phenomena</u>.

    Classification of existences:
    States consciousness
    Minds
    Bodies
    Succession and Coexistence, Likeness or Unlikeness
    ⟨?⟩ these nameable things facts made up.
    <u>Existence</u>, <u>Coexistence</u>, <u>Sequence</u>, <u>Causation</u>, <u>Likeness</u> | <u>Connection</u>[3]
    II Configuration seems to be defective.
    Analytic, Synthetic
    II 2 <u>synthetic</u>[4]

---

1. Conger misdated this seminary 12 March.
2. Conger may here be noting that a student presented a paper on Hume for which he did not take notes, since the notes for this session are mainly about John Stuart Mill (though Hume is mentioned). It is also possible that the Conger's notes on Mill record the presentation of a paper given by a student, rather than Whitehead – since Whitehead usually mentions Mill only in passing in his published writings – but this is not clear.
3. The following six lines are written between the two columns of Conger's page of notes; it is unclear where exactly they belong within the larger sequence.
4. It is not clear what this and the two subsequent sets of Roman and Arabic numbers refer to. In the transcendental analytic of Kant's *Critique of Pure Reason*, book II discusses the analytic/synthetic distinction.

II 5 <u>analytic</u>
Whitehead: <u>extension</u> in print?
Assimilation in ⟨psy?⟩ II 4

Real or synthetic propositions, the propositions of logic. Analytic propositions don't relate to any matter of fact.

Copula marks assertion and connotes existence.

Mill's theory of matter can as well be considered his theory of perception.

Minor differences between laws of perception in Logical Examination.

<u>Possibility</u>. of <u>sensation</u>. Possibility like substratum to that spread over it. Groups of possibility as permanent reality in nature.

<u>Perception</u> – Explain what external world is.

Class ought to refer to things

Existence for Logic is Phenomenal Existence.

Mill. Mathematical truths not necessary and not exact.

Asserts connection between what is connoted by the terms – i.e. phenomena.

Hume by comparison <u>rationalistic</u>, but Mill <u>inductive</u>.

Hume: Passages which suggest <u>pure</u> <u>mathematics</u>. Mill didn't know difference between pure math and applied math.

Applied mathematics has to depend on some observation. John Stuart Mill well behind the mathematical knowledge of his day. <u>Gauss</u>,[1] for example. Mill might have taken ⟨?⟩ view mathematics the form of mental operations.

Analytic proposition not worth bothering about.

Mill says there's a psychological element, but common public fact is the other things. Relationship between things is ∧public∧[2] fact. But what then the fake propositions.

|2| Doesn't face up question what ~~is~~ a proposition is.

Synthetic proposition has to imply existence.

Inductive Reasoning. Reasoning on analysis – throws out deduction and Mill is thus in difficulty.

Propositions ~~ex~~ nothing to do with existence – it's over the question of names. Meaning settled as soon as name centaur. Words mean something – when say centaurs have settled sense. Each word means something – Words together in unity of proposition. Can't by the proposition in which the word centaur appears add to meaning.

Centaur a method of pointing at an entity.

Complex meaning arises from that pattern of pointing which is the proposition. Entities are these before the proposition.

Actual entities which form bones of proposition must have their type of existence settled.

Whitehead: Don't have truth or falsehood ~~by~~ except with reference to actual world.

– Mill in 1st chapter, meaning of language. Language one of the helps of thought. Mere complication beats us.

---

1. Carl Friedrich Gauss (1777–1855) was a German mathematician and physicist.
2. The proper insertion point is not completely clear.

Chapter <u>Mill</u> <u>When put into words, it gets to be a proposition.</u>
Object of all enquiry, express selves in proposition.
A proposition according to simple proposition discourse in which something is affirmed or denied of something.
Predicate is name denoting what is affirmed or denied. Quality yellow affirmed of subject gold. Subject is ⟨personal?⟩ thing.
Names must be names of something.
This is rotted by desire to put everything simply.
–Is a name a sound which I make once start by talking about gold being yellow? Then name gold and name yellow.
|3| Why go to language? Convenient for symbolism, but get same difficulty in talking about words.
Why linguistic in one portion in order to be acquainted with another portion? Have to practically, but where is the theoretical advantage?
Why linguistic in sensa which is name yellow in order to talk about thing yellow?
Why is <u>linguistic</u> <u>sensa</u> a <u>sentence</u>, and why is a <u>color</u> <u>pattern</u> not a <u>sentence</u>? Insects mit might deal with color pattern. Whole dealing with words, deal dealing with them in superstitious way. If know name you can do all sorts of things.
Stanly[1]
Words – sure you have those in common. Can do things by ⟨martial?⟩ music too.
Mill never realize separated logic from psychology.
Propositions have to do with objectifications of entities. Entertaining subject better than percipient subject.
Mill. A general name truly affirmed of indefinite number of things. Relation of a thing to its meaning as an affirmation. Every name is a proposition.
No <u>firmness</u> ⟨?⟩ there – too loose, easy, popular.

Friday, 18 March 1927

Conger's notes

|1| (Miss Brown's[2] paper)
Wittgenstein, *Tractatus Logico-Philosophicus* and Bertrand Russell *Principia Mathematica*[(2)]
{Introduction: founded partly on Wittgenstein, partly on Sheffer}[3]

---

1. This may be a reference to Philip Edwin Stanley, a student in the seminary. See 17 November 1925 lecture, note 6, p. 80.
2. From Whitehead's grading notebook, we know this to be Sarah H. Brown (Whitehead, 'Student Record Book', p. 31). Brown taught at Wells College, New York state, from at least 1931 until her death in an automobile accident in 1938, and possibly also at the University of Washington around 1929. As she died young, she published little. See Brown, 'The right and the good'. It is not always clear whether it is Brown or Whitehead talking, though Conger does seem to have done his best to provide the speaker's name when he could.
3. Henry Maurice Sheffer (1882–1964) was an American logician, and Whitehead's colleague in the Harvard philosophy department. Russell's introduction to the English translation of the *Tractatus* mentions that

Philosophy 20i: Seminary in Logic, spring semester 1927

Method of formulating problems ∨rests on∨ misunderstanding of logic of language. What can be said can be said clearly. (Whitehead protests – actual state of any language not such.)[1] **What the form is that makes it a language can't be expressed in that language. Proposition can't expressed, that which makes it a proposition.**[2]

(1) Wittgenstein skepticism – Opp⟨oses?⟩ validity of expressing propositions or stating propositions, all the forms of proposition. Validity of reflection on structure of proposition.

Second point, can some other proposition express something?

(2) Wittgenstein separates propositions as regards structure or truth of elementary propositions – makes

(3) Nature of truth functions, or rather secondary proposition. Wittgenstein – Confines to truth function.

First part.

World is everything that is the case.[3] **Picture is a model of reality. Most propositions about philosophy senseless. We make to ourselves pictures of facts.**

Gramophone record, logical structure.[4]

If central problem of book, what relation must one fact have to another in order to be a symbol? Can't express that relation which makes one fact symbol of another. Picture (– elementary proposition). This is red. Socrates is wise.

Skepticism, solipsism, mysticism.

Philosophy can only show impossibility of philosophy. Ultimate truth shown, but not expressed. View probably has roots in *Principia*'s theory of types.

Propositional function can't be contained in itself. Function can't be own argument.

– Problem of language – **compare linguistic expression to projection in geometry ∨Can be projected in many ways∨ – Projective proposition of equ original language are ~~much same~~. ∧unchanged∧. To proposition belongs everything which belongs to projection.**

Same position restated with regard to propositions. Propositions can represent whole reality, but can't represent. What have in common with reality – i.e. logical form. Propositions show logical form, but what can't be shown can't be said. Final submersion in mysticism.

 Wittgenstein was clearly familiar with Sheffer's work (Wittgenstein, *Tractatus*, pp. 13–14, available at <https://archive.org/details/tractatuslogicop1971witt>). Bolded portions are clearly being read from the *Tractatus*, sometimes from the text proper, and sometimes from Russell's introduction.
1. Parentheses supplied.
2. Our certainty that this is being read directly from the *Tractatus* is less sure here, but Russell's introduction has something very similar: 'Everything, therefore, which is involved in the very idea of the expressiveness of language must remain incapable of being expressed in language, and is, therefore, inexpressible in a perfectly precise sense' (Wittgenstein, *Tractatus*, p. 21).
3. This is the first sentence of the *Tractatus*, following Wittgenstein's Preface.
4. '4.014 The gramophone record, the musical thought, the score, the waves of sound, all stand to one another in that pictorial internal relation, which holds between language and the world. To all of them the logical structure is common' (Wittgenstein, *Tractatus*, p. 65).

Philosophy 20i: Seminary in Logic, spring semester 1927

|2| Ramsey review, *Mind* 1923.[1] Can't talk about what makes a fact a fact. Every proposition is about nothing. Every proposition about a proposition....

Wittgenstein. **In analysis of proposition, must come to elementary proposition which consists of names in combination. Simplest asserts atomic \existence of\ fact. Even if world infinitely complex, must be objects and atomic facts.**

This is red elementary. This is red is true secondarily. Proposition this is red can be analyzed is secondary. This is red is believed is secondary proposition.

Wittgenstein – **Elementary is combination of names and objects.**

Proposition which has rel⟨ational?⟩ cl⟨ass?⟩ for Russell molecular.[2]

Whitehead. If changed by change of subsidiary proposition – provided new subsidiary proposition, either true or false.

If alter the truth value. If give this another content. Either this is true or not true.

Complex propositions which include subsidiary propositions which are not changed are called truth functions.

Miss Brown. If Ramsey were true – All propositions would be nonsense, since no proposition would have an object. Wittgenstein emphasizes not constituents of facts, but form of representation which the sentence \proposition\ facts have in common with reality facts and make them representative of it.

Russell – obvious interpretation of Wittgenstein. **Wittgenstein's His attitude on this grows out of doctrine of logic. Logical proposition is a picture true or false of the fact. Structure can't be put into words since it is a structure of words. Everything about language is inexpressible. In this inexpressible is hides all philosophy.**

Mr. Wittgenstein manages to say a good deal which can't be said.

Russell: **Every language has a structure concerning which in the language nothing can be said – but ma in some other language.**

Wittgenstein – totality of such languages. Russell – Is no totality.[3]

|3| Mr. Russell's terminology should be changed from language to proposition. No proposition can express own structure, but can be expressed by new proposition – so on *ad infinitum*. This proposition – that all propositions are of infinite form – is a proposition about all propositions. Miss Brown – reject \Wittgenstein's premise\ all propositions are by nature statements in non-reflexive extension. A proposition refers to an object. This \is\ red

---

1. Ramsey, 'Critical notice of L. Wittgenstein's *Tractatus*'. Ramsey also assisted with the translation of the book into English.
2. This sentence is set off to the right of the sentences starting with 'This is red' and ending with 'names of objects', which are written in a narrow column.
3. Russell's introduction reads: 'These difficulties suggest to my mind some such possibility as this: that every language has, as Mr Wittgenstein says, a structure concerning which, in the language, nothing can be said, but that there may be another language dealing with the structure of the first language, and having itself a new structure, and that to this hierarchy of languages there may be not limit. Mr Wittgenstein would of course reply that his whole theory is applicable unchanged to the totality of such languages. There only retort would be to deny that there is any such totality' (Wittgenstein, *Tractatus*, p. 23).

demonstrates an object. This red is a significance. Non-reflective extension means ~~an~~ statement about an object which is not itself.

Possibly Wittgenstein creates dilemma by statement of problem – What relation must one fact have to another in order to be a symbol of it? This is red. Sound waves, musical score, gramophone record, all symbolic structure of one and same thing.

<u>Three Chinese boxes</u>. Internal propositions same in all three. Though the three are different boxes, *a* can be taken to be a model of *b*, *b* a model of *c*.

All these three through association can be related to same sound patterns. Three language systems: English, German, French. Projections of a principle of construction $\phi(x)$. In three boxes, mathematical projection. In ~~second~~ sound waves, etc. No principle of projection which would make one a projection of other – through association. In language you have the two combine: logical projection of form ϕx, also some associated element of sign with fact.

Boxes and sentences exemplify their principle of construction and do not express it. Shows principle and doesn't express it.

Wittgenstein. **If I can think of an object, in ∨context of∨ an atomic fact, can't think of it apart from the possibility of <u>this</u> ⟨context⟩.**[1]

Whitehead: Any entity imposes or discloses in universe a patience of that entity.

<u>Wittgenstein</u>. **A new possibility cannot subsequently be found. Everything is in a space of possible atomic facts.**

|4| Whitehead – If our picture can be a picture of other entity, it has in it the possibility of the universe. Wittgenstein shows through logical dilemma that couldn't express that. But Wittgenstein has metaphysics and ethics and has truth functions.

Every proposition which he puts down is about ultimate nature. Wittgenstein ~~does w~~ says he does what all ∧do∧. When you understand the situation you see they're all senseless. ∨(Wittgenstein gets out)∨[2]

Wittgenstein – **Picture can't represent its form of representation – It shows it forth.**

Whitehead – Here he is deluded by sensationalist doctrine. Has at back of mind simple sense data.

Red, green, blue, etc. – then brought up against fact that there's a pattern which he says is on different level from sense data. ~~Giv~~ Gets to mystical form underneath the sense data.

Wittgenstein identifies language with concrete thing. (This is red.)[3] It's a sound – a pattern of ⟨?⟩. A psychological process – it is not the significance which goes into forming concrete thing – it is the concrete thing. ~~If you have an~~

---

1. What Conger writes looks more like 'contact', but this is clearly a quote from 2.0121 of the *Tractatus* (Wittgenstein, *Tractatus*, p. 33).
2. Parentheses supplied.
3. Parentheses supplied. This sentence appears somewhat set off to the right of the sentence that precedes it.

Miss Brown. Don't get significance, this is red is identical with the object. ~~Miss Brown Principle~~ Wittgenstein: **Picture refers to fact which is a combination of objects.**

He[1] has both principle of projection and the thing. Significance made up of the two – If ∨say∨ only one, create a dilemma which isn't true.

Formal structure is not itself a concrete object.

Wittgenstein: **In the proposition the thought is expressed perceptibly through the senses. The method of projection is the thinking of the sense of the proposition. The proposition is the propositional sign in its projective relation to the world. To the proposition belongs everything which belongs to the projection** (∨Miss Brown =∨ sound) **but not what is projected** (principle of construction).

Whitehead ~~projection is relationship between the sound and the meaning~~.

Method of projection is the <u>thinking</u> of the <u>sense of the proposition</u> (Whitehead)

(Miss Brown) Think of form and put concrete elements ⟨in?⟩ this pattern.

|5| Miss Brown. Wittgenstein gets concrete and abstract separated. Sense is just <u>form</u> of representation; and you put the concrete [content] in.

Form in common is fact that ⟨sometimes?⟩ have same structure as fact. Sentence has structure that fact has.

Wittgenstein. **In the proposition the thought is expressed perceptibly through the senses. We use the sensibly projected sign of proposition.** ~~Method~~ **In propositions thoughts can be so expressed** (so correlated to pattern of sense data) **that to objects of thoughts correspond the elements of propositional signs.**

∨Whitehead∨ Wittgenstein gets one to one correspondence and pattern between two sets of things is same. Whitehead: I have one difficulty here – The world is the totality of facts, not of things – total reality is the world. Picture presents the facts in logical space. The picture is a fact. What facts are to be pictures and what not? ⟨?⟩ ~~What fa~~ ⟨Any?⟩ fact which has same structure as another?

Whitehead – Then Wittgenstein slips in sense data as only facts. Wittgenstein: Language started hieroglyph – pictures in logical pattern.[2] A proposition is a picture of sense data. Only element in experience of which we can be directly conscious are sense data. Wittgenstein – Frege had just names. Wittgenstein has names in definite order.[3]

Whitehead says Wittgenstein started out by having more, then limited it, then found dilemma and had to crawl out. All Wittgenstein's truth functions are nonsensical. Each case is a sample of the meaning, but not identical with meaning. Language can't be identified with projective geometry, or with name signs for concrete experience. Anything can be or become the sign of anything

---

1. What appears to be a ditto mark precedes 'He' and likely refers to the word above, which is 'Wittgenstein'. We have omitted it to avoid redundancy.
2. This does not seem to be an exact quote, but Wittgenstein mentions hieroglyphic writing in 4.016 (Wittgenstein, *Tractatus*, p. 67).
3. See *Tractatus* 5.02, 5.1 (Wittgenstein, *Tractatus*, pp. 103–5).

else. No structure represents its principle of construction. Thought is out of this scheme of Wittgenstein. Thought is the principle and the structure, and reality is significant. Don't have system of concrete facts without anything abstract.

|6| Any one fact can either be the case or not the case, and everything else remain the same. No relation between atomic facts. All relationship between abstracted propositions. An atomic fact is a combination of objects, entities, things – Absolute independence.

Should have logical relations between atomic facts. Existences have no logical relations as existences.

Weiss: Perhaps Principle third proposition. Whitehead: If so, this third ⟨principle⟩ is wrong.[1]

Entities in question not exhausted by representation. Mind grasps object and representation ⟨?⟩. One can't introduce concept of number and definite numbers.

Miss Brown – when introduce principle, you introduce its examples. As soon as you introduce principle of number, you have √infinite number of√ numbers. Can't have principle $\phi(x)$ without propositions. Language is unique case, in every other case the principle and its application. The principle of a proposition comes with it – so can know about principle from proposition. Sense in which a proposition can be about itself. A principle can't be its own exemplification.

See McTaggart, *Mind* 1923.[2] McTaggart – A proposition may be taken in intension. Sometimes paradox if not in non-reflexive extension.

– Proposition I am now asserting is known to God –

– What proposition asserted . . .? Proposition itself. Which? . . . infinity.

~~Being a proposition asserted by me~~

Miss Brown: If McTaggart is right, Wittgenstein is wrong about not being able to make assertions about totality of proposition. Possession of principle of proposition is like principle of number. Miss Brown – In Wittgenstein can always find another statement. Insofar as proposition is a formal entity.

|7| – Logical constants not represented by signs but themselves present in the principles.

– Inside any ultimate situation, inside and outside.

– The description of the most general form.

Propositions with regard to structure

World consists of facts. Facts may be atomic. Atomic fact contains no constituents which are themselves facts. A fact can be infinitely complex. To say infinitely divisible and parts always ~~infinite~~ have finite parts. Infinite process never ceases. How can infinite number be ~~definite~~ divided again?

~~To say~~ If process is infinite, you should never reach stage where can't divide again – but infinity can't be divided.

Whitehead: Don't see how if you go on and on you should come to anything.

---

1. These two sentences appear somewhat set off and to the right of the preceding sentence. We cannot be sure, but they appear to be recording a comment from Paul Weiss and Whitehead's response to it. The exchange could be referring to Proposition 3 from the *Tractatus*, 'The logical picture of the facts is the thought' (Wittgenstein, *Tractatus*, p. 43).
2. McTaggart, 'Propositions applicable to themselves'.

I don't know what you mean by infinite quantity. Whitehead should have thought divisible. Any definite space is a finite space. When you've divided, ~~your~~ it's a different sort of ~~infinity~~ unboundedness you're thinking of.

Miss Brown – not divisible in same sense.

There are different sorts of infinite. Take unbounded class of finite numbers – can divide into even and odd.

~~Make~~ Subtract first ten numbers from infinity – but depends on what you mean by infinity.

|8| Naming of simples is fundamental. Either p is a proposition ~~(?)~~ or not. Has no sense.

In atomic fact members like chain. ϕ and x incomplete symbols, symmetrical and asymmetrical.

ϕ and x are symmetrical. ϕ complete, x incomplete. One of positions held by R.[1]

x unifying element and ϕ independent. Might be one of Platonic positions. Universals real, existences unreal.

In Wittgenstein no intermediary which links two facts together, so don't get into difficulty of Bradley.

From an elementary proposition, no ~~els~~ other can be inferred.

All propositions of logic say same thing – i.e. nothing. Elementary facts are in nature unknowable.

Can't give number of names with ~~other~~ different meanings.

(Ramsey interprets) can't know anything about forms.

Wittgenstein gives general form of all propositions. For every ⟨blank⟩ some x ⟨blank⟩ ϕ ⟨blank⟩ ϕx.

All inference takes place *a priori*. From elementary proposition no other can be inferred. Superstition is the belief in the causal nexus. Freedom consists in fact future actions can't be known now.

Whitehead: How can he know anything on that? Wittgenstein asserts what Santayana asserts. Has brought self down to sense data.

Miss Brown: Has separated two parts and stated natures in isolation, and if do so, then that's what you get.

|9| No proposition states own truth or formal structure. In terms of themselves, tautologies.

In strict sense truth relevant only to primary propositions. Elementary proposition possesses form, secondary proposition states form. Interrelation of two, get inference and sense.

Part III

Nature of truth functions. **Truth functions of the elementary propositions. All propositions ∨(special sense)∨[2] are ~~results of~~ truth operations and on elementary propositions.**

Application of finite number of truth operations.

---

1. The proper expansion of 'R', if in fact it is an abbreviation and not some sort of variable, is not clear. Some candidates include 'relativity' and 'Ramsey'.
2. Parentheses supplied.

Symbol of a truth proposition Every σ Every one. p is elementary proposition. Take every elementary proposition. Any σ – Any selection from totality of elementary propositions like $p.q$. 2. Negate this selection simultaneously, not p or not q. Neither p nor q = p stroke q.

Since symbol of operations is totality of operations, p stroke p, large stroke q. Each p = p stroke p. Every negation of q = q stroke q. Infinity of negating processes would give you all propositions.

Whole of mathematical logic means treating propositions as q functions.

Wittgenstein originality – denies propositions have any other function than truth. Miss Brown – he considers proposition only in extension. Three kinds of propositions about propositions.

Russell in Introduction shows difficulty of that. A function can only occur. ϕx x is green through its values – this tablecloth is green, etc. – No other reference. Since a function can only attain through its values, can only occur through occurrence of ϕa ϕb ϕc.

Bothers Whitehead that in this sentence ϕ occurs otherwise.[1]

|10| Should have liked to ask Russell what he meant by it.

Could he say this mark ϕ has only meaning when there is ϕa ϕb ϕc?

Can't be the mere marking. You couldn't recognize it as values. It's merely that smudge on the paper.

Wittgenstein detachedly says good things.

This doesn't do him justice. Can't get him into definite system. Ramsey feels he has a system. ((?))

Whitehead: Wittgenstein overestimates the picture element in language.

Cf. Home they brought her warrior dead.[2]

Russell, Appendix C, Second Edition.[3] Wittgenstein contradicts self. Russell doesn't. Show Bertie an extreme position, and show ⟨him⟩[4] the fun of running it, and carries him off his feet at once.[5]

---

1. This statement appears to apply to the beginning of the previous paragraph, as there is an arrow pointing to it.
2. This is a line from a long poem by Alfred, Lord Tennyson, 'The Princess' (1847).
3. This seems to be referring to Appendix C in the second edition of *Principia Mathematica*, vol. I: 'Truth-functions and others'. See Whitehead and Russell, *Principia mathematica*, available at <https://archive.org/details/PrincipiaMathematicaVolumeI>.
4. Conger writes 'showing', but 'show him' seems more likely.
5. There are some notes on the back of this final page which are almost assuredly not for a Whitehead class, so we have omitted them.

Social Ethics 20a: Fundamentals Underlying the Social Sciences, fall semester 1926

Monday, 18 October 1926

Stenographer's notes[1]

|1| DR. CABOT: I do not know anybody that I would rather hear than Professor Whitehead. As I read in his books, the thing that strikes me is that whereas most of us come to any subject with a certain body of knowledge on one side of human life and study, he comes with a fund of knowledge from so many sides. I said two weeks ago that I thought one of the necessities for anyone who tried to approach the social sciences was to be interested in all the different sides of life of a human being, in the side that deals with beauty, in the side that works in science, in the side that reflects philosophically, in the side that is interested in the state. As we know from Prof. Whitehead's writings, he has distinguished himself not only in mathematics and the natural sciences, but of late years in philosophy (blank). Most philosophers are a little shy about physical sciences, and most men who know physical science are distinctly shy about philosophy. But Prof. Whitehead, like our own Prof. Lawrence Henderson, is one of the few people perfectly at home on each side of that unfortunate division. I am sure he feels it as much as anyone would an unfortunate division, this one of the philosophers and the men of science.

PROF. WHITEHEAD: I should like to start by disclaiming the impertinence of thinking that one could come to a seminary in a department that is concerned with social ethics and with social sciences, as a special department of thought, and contribute anything on that specialized side, which wants not only study, but which also requires that expert formation by years of quiet prosecution of that study. I have not the slightest belief that I am qualified in any way to give advice or any suggestions. I hope nothing that I say will be construed in that sense.

But of course there are general relations which are in philosophy and all other regions of systematic thought, and that general type of relation, though it varies in emphasis and aims in regard to its various sides, yet has a common aspect for all |2| sides, all topics of thought. But in addition there are certain more special relations I think between philosophy and social ethics. But in dealing with the fundamentals, which is, I see, the topic we are to discuss, I do not conceive them as the fundamentals as they look from the point of view of this department,[2] but the fundamentals as they look from the point of view of

---

1. The notes presented here are those of a stenographer, though Cabot took his own notes as well. See the Introduction for a detailed discussion of each note-taker and their notes.
2. That is, the Department of Social Ethics, which was housed on the *second* floor of Emerson Hall. It was established thanks to the gifts of a private donor, Alfred T. White, and began offering courses beginning in 1905 with the opening of Emerson Hall. Cabot took over the chair of the department in 1919. See Harvard Alumni Association, 'Social ethics', and Cabot, 'A. T. White and the Department of Social Ethics'.

the department on the first floor of Emerson Hall.[1] And just to give the point which I shall work up to first, so that it will be thoroughly understood, the two allied formulations that I want to work up to are:

(1) I think that Social Ethics is founded on two great doctrines, one the doctrine of original sin, and the other the correlative doctrine of original virtue, both in the theological sense.

(2) Then there is another two aphorisms, both of which I think are partly true and both of them partly false, and they are antagonistic aphorisms in a way, yet they have to be conciliated: one is the commandment "Thou shalt not steal", which is the great proclamation of individualism, and the other is the statement that "property is robbery". And I think they are equally true and equally false, and that the conciliation between them is where law and the lawyers and social ethics and social sciences meet.

Now I have gone to the middle of my talk that it will be seen how I am gradually working up to the sort of light that philosophy has to bestow. In talking of philosophy one must be a little careful because everybody knows that philosophy is the one subject in which there is no authoritative ⟨blank⟩ The voice of philosophy is the voice ⟨blank⟩ but every philosopher has his own voice. So I do not put it down as the statement of philosophy, but what appears to me to be a natural and true outcome of philosophy in this statement.

What is the scope of philosophy? It deals with the generic concepts of the widest scope, those concepts which have universal application; and then it endeavors to elucidate thought in every particular science, in every region of thought, by the |3| production of a harmonious, logical scheme of such wide generic concepts. So that the special notions, the special concepts of each special topic of human thought, can be expressed in terms of specializations of these generic concepts, so that philosophy is what we may term the discovery of the ultimate meanings, seeing what we can say ultimately, and in terms of which all special meanings find their place.

It follows from this view that philosophy should start, is really a survey of human interests, just as the physicist has all the nice little elements in bottles all around the laboratory, so philosophy must start by a survey of human interests, and its accrued data are the formulations of belief which are found and held to in respect to these topics of interest. Then having got hold of them, its next pursuit is imaginatively to formulate a scheme of generic concepts which performs the function which I have described above, of enabling the beliefs, the formulations, the special formulations of the special interests, to find their meanings in terms of these broader concepts.

So the tests which philosophy applies should be in the first place, the clear definition of its ideas, and that definition is promoted by their mutual interconnection and then also it appeals to their obvious exemplification as an interpretation of the immediate experience apart from the ⟨blank⟩ by this scheme. Again there is the logical coherence of the scheme and there are logical

---

1. Whitehead is of course referring to the Philosophy Department.

deductions which are also applied. And finally, having had all this, it then proceeds to conceive, to go back to its source in a more particular comparison with the accepted principles of the various systematic sciences. I think it gets its starting ground from one or more of these sciences. Usually when we speak of any particular philosophy it is to repudiate ⟨blank⟩ but I think then we have to consider whether we can interpret under this common system of ideas or accepted principles. Then we never get perfect success, and any such scheme will suggest some paradoxes, and the conclusion is that either the philosophic scheme of thought requires modification or the principles of the special science in question require modification – probably both.

So I look on philosophy as endeavoring to get a general notion of universal |4| applicability, by generalizing from special sciences, by modifying it so as to suit all the special sciences, and then having their special notions in that way. In the first place it is a critic of the notions of any one science, by pointing out where its special ideas fail to fit into what seems to be the best generalization. But it is not only a critic. It is also a stimulus to the imagination, because the special ideas of any one science will turn out to be a certain specialization of these philosophic generic notions, and philosophy would provide also the vision of possible alternative modes of specialization. So philosophy should not only be a critic, but an aid to the imagination. It should act really as a stimulus, what we may term the ⟨poetry⟩[1] of thought in that way. It is not a neat little cast-iron view, but a view of general potentialities which are suggested by ideas common and generalized from all the special sciences. And then finally, there is the final and supreme test for all philosophic thought, of adequacy; namely, are there whole regions of immediate experience which escape from any exemplification, whatever of our philosophic scheme?

Now when we appeal to practice as Hume does, for Hume has in a sense demolished causation – he says practically what the gentleman did in the eighteenth century, "I am not such a fool as to think that nothing follows from anything – that unless you think there are fixed and definite consequences, you will be knocked down before you live many hours." Now the appeal to practice, to what we believe in practice is supplementary philosophy, as supplementing philosophy is nothing but a confession of the inadequacy of your philosophic ideas, because whatever you believe ought to find its place as interpreting, as a specialization of these general notions. Practice ought to exemplify these principles and not to supplement them. Now practice as distinct from the special formulations of special sciences, practice is the ocean of immediate experience which lies outside the petty canals which are the various sciences. ⟨blank⟩ is not really countenanced by any of the great leaders.

Newton's statement that we are like a child picking up shells by the ocean.[2] ⟨blank⟩

---

1. The stenographer left a blank here, but Cabot's own notes have 'Stimulus to poetry of thought' (p. 2).
2. This quote appears in the first American edition of Newton's *Principia* (1846), in a section on the life of Newton by N. W. Chittenden: 'I do not know what I may appear to the world, but to myself I seem to have been only like a boy playing on the sea-shore, and diverting myself in now and then finding a smoother pebble or a prettier shell than ordinary, whilst the great ocean of truth lay all

The importance of philosophy to any particular science varies. When a set of principles |5| have been elaborated for a particular science which are working well, which are finding their exemplification in all the topics of the special science, and whose consequences require further elaboration and further concentration of experience, the job of scientists ⟨is⟩ to stick to those principles and work them out. They may be adequate or they may not be adequate. But you cannot move a step until you work out and see how far those principles will apply, and where they begin to break down. And that is only found by scientists sticking to those principles and elaborating them. And when a science, as it often does, gets into that state, it may say goodbye to philosophy, at least its particular workers need not bother about philosophy during their lifetime.

For example, when Galileo had adopted the Copernican hypothesis and had got his telescope and observed how it simplified the orbits of the planets, and looked at the planets and saw the mountains of the moon and the moons of Jupiter and the horns of Venus and all that, he did not want to be looking to the right or to the left. It was perfectly obvious that the Copernican hypothesis was the job of scientists. Astronomy was ⟨blank⟩ It so happened that the Copernican hypothesis in the sense of Galileo was just as wrong as the ⟨heliocentric⟩[1] hypothesis. The physicists said that the earth was at rest and Galileo said that the sun was at rest. Both in our modern sense had as much right to say so, and yet ⟨blank⟩. But there was not the slightest doubt as to what was the way of looking at things which was going to elicit progress. Then we got the next great formulation, which turned out to be the Newtonian materialistic mechanism.[2] That in a sense formulates to perfection certain aspects of the universe which ⟨blank⟩. As a matter of fact – and how often this is so – for a couple of centuries or more it was the job of scientists to stick to it. Then we got Darwin's theory of natural selection. The way in which all biologists until quite recently raged against the inheritance of acquired characteristics was a perfectly legitimate characteristic, namely how far natural selection and the theory of evolution based on the idea of natural selection would be carried, how far the facts would be truthfully interpreted |6| in that way. And we could not know whether that point was inadequate until about two generations of scientists had worked on it from that point of view.

Then we come to a more definite social science. The economic man was a godsend to political economy, because we wanted to know what would happen insofar as mankind was simply and absolutely swayed by the economic motive. And until you had worked that out theoretically and compared it with practice, you do not know, have no way of knowing, how far the economic motive was dominant, how greatly important, or whether it was simply absent. And there again when you have once got the economic man, the economists had to live with him for about a couple of generations, and then he becomes

---

undiscovered before me' (p. 58). See Newton, *Newton's Principia*, available at <https://archive.org/details/newtonspmathema00newtrich>.
1. The original has 'idiocentric' but, from context, Whitehead must have said 'heliocentric', which seems to have been a word with which the stenographer was unfamiliar.
2. Cabot's notes have 'mechanistic materialism' (p. 2).

a fearful nuisance. But scientists – I am using <u>science</u> in a general sense in which philosophy is a science – I think if you look at the history of science it is practically the mistakes made by the scientists as to what is their immediate job, how almost naked they are. But they are always and habitually overstating the scope or the validity of the line of thought in which they are engaged.[1] I think the history of science is really a most melancholy example of the overstatements of mankind. Why people cannot moderate their statements according to the evidence – if people would only stick to that idea of what may be perfectly sound ⟨methodological⟩[2] device is not thereby a final and adequate principle –

Now as soon as you have come in a science to the limit of some very fruitful principles, or if you are dissatisfied with the scope of the work which your existing principles suggested, philosophy provides the imaginative background for the reformulations of general principles, and it is a point that cannot be too often brought home – I am always repeating it, that whosoever goes out to despise metaphysics always ends by adopting the metaphysical nostrums that were prevalent in his nursery. And they had often very good metaphysical nostrums in the nursery. But the point is, in all that they have an imaginative idea of the general principles ⟨?⟩ which you are seeking. The specialization due to your particular science is really congruous to metaphysics, and the beauty of metaphysics is that is should stimulate imagination over the whole realm of physical science. If it does not do that it is not doing its job – and I think very |7| often it is not doing its job. It has shrunken into a pitiful science which has no interest beyond itself.

Now so far as social science is concerned, its principles will always reflect and in turn influence philosophy in a peculiarly intimate way. I think it is peculiarly intimate because our conceptions of social ethics necessarily depend upon the conceptions of ethics generally and our conception of the end towards which the organization of society is to be directed. And you cannot discuss ends without asking yourself, what is the world anyway? We have to come down to a general metaphysical question.

At this point I ⟨most⟩[3] specialize in dealing with philosophy, and I am interested in that type of philosophy which is peculiarly a continuation of the physical sciences. These great adaptations of philosophical ideas to the physical sciences were made by Descartes, and though nobody says they are Cartesians now, everybody who is both a physicist and a philosopher is much more a Cartesian than they like to admit. I shall start from Descartes. I think he has many merits. He is extraordinarily clear because he is French, and he is short. He has not that appalling volubility of some philosophers. He is short and clear and definite and has the supreme merit that where he is wrong, he is clearly wrong. And so, provided we dare to differ from Descartes, I shall start with him.

---

1. Cf. Cabot's notes: 'Scientist nearly infallible as to their immediate job, but habitually overstate the scope of the validity of their method' (Cabot, p. 2).
2. The original has 'mythological'; 'methodological' seems more likely.
3. The stenographer has 'must' here, but that seems likely to have been an error.

He commenced by asking what we have to say about the substances composing the world. Now a substance to Descartes – not to the antecedent scholastics – means the entities ⟨blank⟩ which in the fullest, simplest sense are the real, actual things which compose, by reason of their own reality and actuality, the real world. What are the things whose reality is the reality of the real world. Then there are the other entities in terms of which substances must be described. They are not real in the same sense as a substance is. There are various ways of talking about them. They are called attributes, forms, qualities.[1] Each word we use has a long history which usually suggests a philosophy which you want to repudiate. For that reason I have called them eternal objects. But anyhow, however we call these attributes, such entities express |8| the how and the what of the diversities of the identities which are involved in the ⟨blank⟩ of the real entity. Thus they are essentially inherent in the real entities and cannot be conceived without reference to them. It is for that reason that in my own works I have said that it is in their nature that they have ingression to the real entities. Descartes takes as the distinguishing mark of the substance the fact that in some sense or other the substance – I use here the slang phrase – is "on its own". The real entity is something of its own, it is individual, has its own spirit and independence. It is real on its own account, and for Descartes the world is composed of a multiplicity of substances of various kinds, and each substance is an individual with its own independence. Each one of us – I am in a certain sense just what I am. In fact he had three kinds of substances, God, Mind, Bodies, and so far I think any realistic philosophy must agree with him there. But now, and this is the important point for science in general and for social ethics in particular, he formulates more particularly what he means by the independence of each individual substance. He says in the first book of his *Principles of Philosophy*, in Principle 51 we find this statement: "And when we conceive of substance we merely conceive an existent thing which requires nothing but itself in order to exist."[2]

That is the great program of individualism and substantivism. I think it is in that a substance is merely, insofar as it is real entity, an existent thing which requires nothing but itself in order to exist. There are two points to notice:

(1) That it requires nothing but itself in order to exist.

(2) That its substantial character is merely that.

I think this view of substance is absolutely fatal to any adequate understanding of the world, and of thinking of it. Embodying that view of substance in a philosophic scheme means an inadequacy which I think really embodies all the divisions. I put it here under ⟨Protestant civilization⟩[3] and in the Ten Commandments, namely all the individualism which is destroyed by sound ethics. It is fatal to those two twin doctrines which I wish to impress, namely, the doctrines of original sin and of original |9| virtue, which I look on

---

1. Cabot adds 'predicates' (Cabot, p. 3).
2. This principle appears on pp. 239–40 of the Haldane and Ross translation, which is what Whitehead assigned to his Philosophy 3b students. See Descartes, *Philosophical Works, Vol. I*, available at <https://archive.org/details/philosophicalwor01desc>.
3. The original has '⟨blank⟩ specialization', while Cabot has 'Protestant civilization' (p. 3).

as the foundation stones: namely, the doctrine that whatever you are infects the world, so that the world derives from you an original sin and an original virtue, because whatever you are infects the world. Now that is exactly what is denied by Descartes, because he says each real agency requires nothing but itself in order to exist.

Still, as I read Descartes I feel what an admirably clear way that is, the idea that the real being is in some sense on its own. You then go and over-emphasize it, put it in an unbalanced way as a philosophic principle, and you thereby rule out its correlative supplementary truth. You manage to rule that out, and instead of making it antithetical, you make it ⟨blank⟩. And when you have done that you very often, in that small divergence, ruin a whole century of effort.

Now this Cartesian view, remembering what Descartes means by substance, namely that he means the real entity, has haunted modern philosophy ever since, including those philosophers who are explicitly anti-Cartesian. For example, I think it is responsible for ⟨blank⟩[1] looking for something that requires nothing but itself in order to exist, and it is fatal to ethics for two reasons. If you look at various real things as requiring nothing but themselves in order to exist:

(1) Whatever requires nothing but itself in order to exist has a private property in its own life, to please itself. You thus get privacy of what you are ⟨blank⟩ I look on as social ethics as a conciliation of the two diverse expressions by the statement "Thou shalt not steal", which is the assertion of a measured privacy, and "property is robbery", which is an assertion of the complete socialism. And both law and social ethics are engaged in conciliating these opposed statements. They are considering what principles there can be which should regulate society, in which there can be a fulfilment of private ends which do not constitute robbery. How you can have private ends in a society without robbery is really, I hold, the topic of social ethics.

|10| (2) Where I think that this formulation of Descartes is fatal to ethics is that according to it any reference to an end is made to be irrelevant to real existence. The only thing is that it requires nothing but itself in order to exist. It is a universe in which morals are meaningless. Its conceivable ends, according to this the attainment to ends are intruders in what would be adequate apart from them. We all know in saying this I am only pointing out that Descartes was merely emphasizing as an absolute philosophical principle the great method of logical discovery of the natural science of his time, namely that final ends are a nuisance in the discoveries of physical law.

Aristotle constructed his ethical science on the basis of explaining it by the final end, and Galileo and the whole of the modern scientists of the 16th and 17th centuries extruded the final ends from physics. And the result is you get a definition of what it is to be real in terms by which final ends are extruded. Philosophy was made to conform to the methodology of physics, and in doing so it parted company I think with morals and ethics. So morals in that point of view are imposed on an alien universe by the crude device of the will of

---

1. Cabot has two names here: 'Spencer's unknowable. Hegel's absolute' (Cabot, p. 3).

God. Now of course it is a crude device, because you see, if morals simply arise from the universe and the will of God, you are precluded ⟨blank⟩. You first have to know God before you get your morals. You can't go the other way round. And you cut off your main source ⟨of⟩ getting your notion of God. And we all know that Descartes came down extrinsically on the ⟨ontological⟩[1] view, which neo-scholastic theology rejects. And this development of ⟨blank⟩ in a universe without any did not remain a curious possibility, but it was the idea that was actually worked out by Newton's successors, and its responsibility to a conscienceless, meaningless nature, a nature without conscience,[2] engaged in moving itself about. And the Cartesian God is a frail bulwark against it since it depends on ⟨ontological⟩ truth, which is a <u>tour de force</u>. It is manifestly inadequate by reason of the inadequacy of its analysis of our immediate experience.

|11| I am discussing the relationship of philosophy to what I conceive to be social ethics, and I have pointed out how a philosophy which has exclusively taken its starting point from science in one of its phases has had a ⟨blank⟩. The difficulty is that it has created for all the other great topics of man's thought ⟨blank⟩. I conceive the alternative to Cartesian doctrine, if you are to put it on realistic lines and on Cartesian lines at that, to be that to say what an actual entity is we require four headings:

(a) It requires all other entities, all other actual agencies, in order to exist. It is exactly the opposite of what Descartes says, the assertion of solidarity.

(b) It is an end in itself, for itself. I think that is a characteristic of being actual, that it is an end in itself for itself, namely every actual entity is an achievement for itself. It has an inside to it.

(c) It is a process terminating in itself as the result, and

(d) It is also a character testing for processes which terminate in other actual entities beyond itself and other than itself.

So here we have a notion of value and of process and of sociability, society, essential to the actuality of an entity. So the specific value of the individual occasion arises from the ends attained, and also from the ends beyond itself which are attainable by reason of itself. It arises from the ends antecedently attained by the other processes and the ends beyond itself which are attainable by reason of the character which it is imposing on what we may term the creative process. So an actual entity is an attainment for itself, individualized attainment, not only by reason of its own originality, but by reason of what it inherits or makes possible beyond itself. For you cannot dissociate the actual entity even on the side of its own individual attainments to the total society. And this is the doctrine of social solidarity which I express by the two doctrines of original virtue and original sin. The value of any one is infectious throughout

---

1. The original has 'entological', which makes no sense here, and is contradicted by Cabot's 'ontological' (p. 4). Again, it seems clear that the stenographer did not have any advanced training in philosophy, making the recording of technical terms challenging.
2. Cabot (p. 4) has 'without consciousness'.

the universe. An actual occasion thus is a concrescence. |12| It is an attained individual value and also a qualification and concrescence beyond itself. It has a four-fold ⟨blank⟩: it grasps other occasions into itself, and the how of its grasping it determined by the eternal objects, and an occasion as grasped into another one is what we may call objectified. Thus "property is robbery" asserts the essential solidarity of individual values. "Thou shalt not steal" asserts the individual value of each occasion over its own. So right to existence is the ultimate right that there can be, the ultimate foundation of all rights, provided that in this specific embodiment ⟨blank⟩ also the intensity of attainment in the universe, including its own intensity of attainment.

And then it can be further held as the foundation of morals. So that there may be a mutual aid, a mutual intensification throughout the universe as equivalent to the intensity of attainment in the individual parts that it leads thereby. It includes therefore the summation into each entity of a harmonious past and in particular the particularization of this harmonious past. It leads to historical ⟨routes⟩[1] of successive occasions, all in that harmony with each other and each summing up all its with a particular ⟨blank⟩ What we call an individual object, a human being, an electron, from its life to its death is such a historically ⟨routed⟩ occasion. Each as it stands in its immediate presence is a summation ⟨blank⟩ of the past by reason of the peculiar harmony, its peculiar reproduction of the character of its antecedents. So that the particular occasion of its past is the dominant element in its own presence. But in principle every being, an electron or a man, inherits from the whole world not his immediate presence, but it inherits its own past as that past in the world of which in a peculiarly intensive sense it is the summation, and that is the doctrine of what I call original sin and of original virtue.

DR. CABOT: Will you say a little more about original sin?

PROF. WHITEHEAD: Sin is the worst part of it. The point being that I conceive evil not as something negative but as something destructive. Insofar as it is productive of intense self-satisfaction, in its own immediate occasion, insofar as it has a measure of self-satisfaction, in that respect it is a good. But that peculiar, that |13| special actual entity attaining that particular end may be attaining a less formal self-satisfaction than was open to it for itself; or what is even still worse, may be by its qualification of the entities that succeed, may be ⟨blank⟩ to the world in general of a more intense actuality, a more intense self realization which would otherwise be open to it, and that is evil. So evil is really plunging the world in the direction of nothingness. It is tending to destroy it by destroying the order. I hold that the order in the world – that there is an actual world of some peculiar intensity because there is a remarkable order, and if there was no order there would be the cross-purposes which would be wiping out the world. It would be sinking to a pit of empty space – it would be sinking to a ripple of non-entity.

And I hold that the intensity of realization depends on the favorable environment and on the order, and insofar as there is order, there is both in

---

1. The original has 'roots'. We have also made this substitution in several places later on.

order, there is both in reality. And evil is that which is destructive of order and is destructive of reality. So far as it ministers to immediate intensity it is so far good. And the world being not wholly a good world, and owing to the fact of original sin, even the best that is open, the ideal, has also always its side of destructiveness. And insofar as it is destructive, insofar it has been put to do the work of evil. But insofar as it tends towards the greatest reality which is open from the standpoint of the present, insofar as it is that, it is good.

The pain in the world I hold in every sense, mental and physical, insofar as it is rightly used, is the destruction of the incongruous element on behalf of the wider order.

And of course the doctrine of original virtue is just the opposite of that, namely, that the virtue has exactly the opposite effect.

DR. CABOT: What becomes of causation?

PROF. WHITEHEAD: Causation is memory. There is no distinction. The past is in you as a formative element, is in an electron as a formative element. And the memory is perceptive. It is the past and the present as conforming to the aspect of |14| the past which is objectified. And this doctrine takes fundamental perceptivity out of the mental sphere and puts it into the physical sphere, because the fundamental relationship on the physical side is the taking account of the past, and there it is fundamental as you term blind perceptivity. It is not reflective, but it is the unthoughtful achievement, the self-satisfaction when ⟨blank⟩ ideas have sunk below ... the sheer self-satisfaction arising from this concretion of the past.

I hold that when Hume asked where was causation he ought to have been told to look at memory. Then I hold that that mentality v?v is the analysis, is a further development in the immediate occasion in which it is, a partial analytic by means of concepts of the same eternal objects which function in determining the objective occasion, the physical objectification of the antecedent occasions. These same eternal objects function as concepts, and that the concept is analytic and correlative, thereby disclosing the identity of the eternal object in the ⟨blank⟩ with the identical object on the objective concrescences of the external world. And the end attained there is the satisfaction arising from knowledge, from the agreement or disagreement of a concept with the analysis of the particular occasion of the external world in the given occasion. So perceptivity is properly physical perceptivity and it is in causation and the certain eternally systematic characters of this objectification of the rest of the world in our immediate physical occasion are the characters, the ⟨spatial-⟩temporal[1] relations, and the change of the temporal relations which are investigated in physical science. We know ⟨blank⟩. Other sides are definitely new to us. We know in the past, and the general sense of power, and see the world around us – all that is our knowledge of the objectification of the world in us.

DR. CABOT: What did the Newtonian physics do with time?

---

1. The original has 'special temporal'.

PROF. WHITEHEAD: The Newtonian physics took time as a going concern. It testified VtoV the formal relations that it gains by time and said, there are the successive relations which we call time relations, which we are going to examine. But time did not enter really very fundamentally in, though it is very convenient to us, a very clear and beautiful machinery. The point is that there is no actual occasion. Any |15| actual occasion is essentially a transitional process. It is arising as a concretion, and in being what it is, it thereby becomes the character of a concretion beyond itself. It passes itself on and remains a character and a concretion beyond itself. So any actual entity can be looked on as complete. You then have the world as collection of complete entities. Then you have no use for time. Then the next step you take is to say that time is a ⟨blank⟩. Then our whole world is essentially transitional. Then you get the whole world of appearance as illusionary and having a lower reality, that is something behind the veil, and then you have recourse to the Absolute. If you are to have a reality of time, you must take hold of the actual process, which is not stopped by the occasion, but passes beyond it. It seems to me you have to preserve for the actual occasion its own individuality.
It must be something in itself, however trivial. If you take an immediate occasion, one immediate occasion of an electron trivial as you like though it has its importance in the whole scheme of things, but as a thing in itself trivial. But when you get to the deeper realities like the people here, then you get a certain intensity of importance.

DR. CABOT: Would you apply the fundamentals that you have been stating to particular classes of the social sciences, such as education? What difference would be made in the way that education should be formed if one thought as you do rather than as Descartes did?

PROF. WHITEHEAD: I hold that knowledge, for example, and character arises in the process. The enduring object is the historical ⟨route⟩, the idea of man as enduring, that the concrete idea is myself, now, as a summation of antecedent occasions which have a practical congruity to each other, harmony, and therefore in a peculiar way we enforce each other and produce an intensity of actuality by reason of their derivation. And the conclusion from that is that if you ⟨blank⟩ has implanted a static character, the static entity is arising in the occasion, in the transition of a process from occasion to occasion, so as to strengthen and intensify the achievements, to intensify the reality of the succeeding occasions. And thus I hold that all knowledge does not arise primarily from a static entity surveying the world, but that it is |16| an outcome, that knowledge always grows in this way, in a race or in a man or out of any small occasions there is always the cycle, action, emotion, belief, rationalization. That you always have that cycle. That there is the entity in its transition, gaining in its emotional value, generating beliefs and attaining to a deeper morality in which there is a purging of belief. And that, I think, can be applied to the whole stretch of human history or to the human being, or as I say to any particular situation. Each day we go through little cycles.

And I hold that education, when you come to it in this way, there is the first discipline to very early stages of action and emotion which have to be got to harmony. Then you get detached beliefs. That I call, taking it up at that last point, where you have action and emotion and belief in the young child, there is a stage I call the stage of romance, and that in dealing with any topic at first there is always the stage of romance, when you are trying to see what it means. You have your detached beliefs, your actions and emotions in regard to it. And that the mistake of the older type of the 17th, 18th and 19th century education, was that it entirely forgot that stage, and looked on education purely from its later age. Then when you got to romance – and I believe for a child there is a great epoch of romance extending more or less to somewhere between ten and thirteen, and is particularly vivid, (it varies with different children – I should have thought it was somewhere between eight and twelve when it was in its height) and then it is rapidly going off in a desire to clear its ideas. We get the age of precision, when we learn things clearly, and I think that with a properly taught child there is real love in knowing things exactly. And I think very often, especially in the newer education which has in the most praiseworthy way emphasized the necessity of romance, I think very often they have forgotten that romance is only one stage, and keep the child in the romantic stage when it really would welcome the discipline of precision, and what is more, it won't be able to face life until it has it. Luckily nature provides a child of any ability with a real desire to know exactly what it is. And when you have romance and precision you get your further rationalization, namely, you get really that stage of disciplined |17| experimentation and a disciplined power of yourself forming general ideas, testing them, and that is the stage of what I term rational power. There is that other stage in which the young man can think for himself and has his reason and his precision and his knowledge, and I think that it is a great mistake to think that all subjects run through those epochs, those various stages, together. Of course it differs in different children, but some subjects starting when other beliefs are well on towards the rational or have some glimmer of the last stage. And I hold that that point of view has arisen out of the idea of the essential process of development from entity to entity along the historical ⟨route⟩ of transition.

DR. CABOT: Do you care to take the questions suggested for discussion?[1]

PROF. WHITEHEAD: To tell you the truth, I should think it rather impertinent to answer those. They are just the questions I should ask you rather than to state myself.

---

1. Cabot is referring to a list of six questions listed in his syllabus, which Whitehead had presumably seen before he gave his lecture:
   (a) What are the fundamentals of the social sciences, in your view and from the standpoint of the body of knowledge which you represent?
   (b) Define: power, authority, responsibility, loyalty, equality, freedom, representation, conflict.
   (c) What is the central word around which your views arrange themselves?
   (d) In view of your theory, how do you deal with the problem of evil?
   (e) From the point of view of your philosophy of the social sciences, what should be the reconstruction of Harvard University and the education it offers [or some other educational experiment]?
   (f) What change should be made in our criminal law and in our treatment of offenders?

Social Ethics 20a: Fundamentals Underlying the Social Sciences, fall semester 1926

PROF. YOUNG:[1] There is one very obvious application of the present philosophical attitude, and that is some of the old problems of sociology, such difficulties as that of universal society, the reality of the state, the institutional society. Those things seem to be resolved by some such scheme of relation.

PROF. WHITEHEAD: Of course I want to free that general scheme more as an actual relation. What I would suggest is that it is a philosophical point of view which makes solution in the hands of experts possible, whereas to my mind the Cartesians would throw it up at once. It is by the nature of the case impossible, unless you start with some view of the inherent solidarity. That is the line I should take. I should not claim that anything I had said thereby finished up the problem. I should only say that it made the solution possible.

PROF. YOUNG: The lines on which it does make the solution possible suggest themselves.

PROF. HOOTEN:[2] The question I have in mind is perhaps off the main point, but I wonder what you think are the limits of achievement of the social sciences?

|18| PROF. WHITEHEAD: I am rather shy of putting any limits to them. I do not think, to speak frankly, that they have got very far yet. I do not know whether that is a heresy. But I do think that they are enormously important. I think all those have been thought of for over 2000 years, and probably entered into Egyptian speculation. But the fact that they have not got far is no reason why they should not quite surely make good progress. Because nothing to my mind is more fallacious than the idea that some particular difficulty has beaten mankind for a long time that it finally won't be resolved. In the history of mathematics, so many perplexities which were perplexities from the beginning, during the 19th century, from 1850 onwards, were in the most extraordinary way cleared up. When mathematicians finally got their principles up to the mark, suddenly a whole lot of things became perfectly easy. And in the realm of practice, take the problem of flying. It started with the ⟨blank⟩. Of course they had the birds to show them it was possible, but nobody solved it. It wanted just the general discovery of engine and motor power, then the petrol, then the internal combustion engines, then the enormous amount of experimentation, and finally a convergence of ideas from all sorts of places comes in, the thing is done. By the time you get it, it is done in a very short time. And the problems which revolve about astronomy. Mankind had made very little progress from the earliest Mesopotamians to the time of Galileo; Galileo died as Newton was born, and in about two generations.... So I do not see why the slight progress which has been made – now that the psychologist has come on the scene (and he is apt to be a little hasty in his applications) and now that we know so much more about physics – I do not see why social science should not make really rapid progress. I am sure that in one social science – that is education – I am sure there is more to be learned in education than ever has been found out, and that we are on the eve of learning it, because we have just begun to think about it from the point of view of psychology, etc.

---

1. Allyn Abbott Young (1876–1929) was an American economist.
2. Earnest Hooton (1887–1954) was an American anthropologist.

PROF. FORD:[1] I wish Prof. Whitehead would explain somewhat more his statement that an entity is an end in itself. Just what does that mean?

PROF. WHITEHEAD: What I mean is, there is a measure of self-satisfaction or |19| self-dissatisfaction, and that that, insofar as there is no reflective memory gained of it, no knowledge – that is perhaps a very minor thing that is something – it gets highly intensified in particular entities like ourselves. It is a joy to be alive, and that is so even when there is no reflection. It is creative fact that the self-satisfaction when it is positive passes into a character of reproduction in the next occasion; the superseding occasion when it is self-dissatisfaction it passes into an occasion when it is a measure of avoidance of what is past. And if it is purely dissatisfaction that is a plunge towards nonentity. It has really got self confidence before it and that arising out of the elements. What the world is for that entity is represented in that entity; what the world is arises out of the conditions. Usually it arises out of the environment, out of its inheritance of the whole world, its creative formation, unity of individuals arising out of how the past is for it, and also characterized by the fact that in being itself it is also in character what is going before. That is also an element in it. If it has its dissatisfaction, its inception of avoidance is an element in its dissatisfaction, you see. I do not think you can separate the various functions. There is the one entity which in being one side of itself is also the other side of itself. It must pass on because it is a passing on, and I think that it is pragmatically creative action, and I think the pragmatists are so far right, but wrong in not making everything an end in itself, because if you have really a passing on there is no test of whether a thing is working or not. It is the ends which are the test.

DR. HEXTER:[2] ⟨blank⟩

PROF. WHITEHEAD: I look on that as first arising from the concept of "Thou shalt not steal", the concept that every entity has a right is defeated and thereby there is loss in the world, unless it has an environment and an inheritance generally which, if the environment is such as to defeat the inheritance which it has from its own historical past. I look on the antecedent of an entity, of an enduring entity – I am thinking of a somewhat developed entity, the antecedents of which have divided into two parts, the inheritance from its own past ⟨blank⟩ |20| what would be taking the enduring entity as summed up in the existing one. And the existing entity has its earning just as capital does. But it also on exactly the same principle has the great universe behind it as a background for various intensity of objectification. That is, its environment and insofar as the environment is unfavorable and checks the achievement it might have from its own historical ⟨route⟩, it is being robbed. Insofar as the environment enables it – in a favorable environment – insofar as the entity checks the development of the environment, it is robbing it. An entity may itself

---

1. James Ford (1885–1944) was an associate professor in Harvard's Department of Social Ethics. During this semester, he was also teaching a course entitled 'Social Problems and Social Policy: Treatment and Prevention of Poverty, Defectiveness and Crime' (Social Ethics 1a).
2. Maurice Beck Hexter (1891–1990) was a professor in Harvard's Department of Social Ethics. During this semester, he was also teaching a course entitled 'Unemployment and Other Interruptions of Working-Class Income' (Social Ethics 6).

be destroyed, but after it the deluge. And I can see that the primary doctrine of social ethics is the question of environment as predominantly due to the society of social entities in which any one entity is ⟨blank⟩.

And I hold that the laws of nature are really the laws of the ⟨blank⟩ which dominate the environment, because a domination ⟨blank⟩ of entities of the same kind, all with historical ⟨routes⟩ succeeding each other, thereby typifying themselves in a congruous way in every occasion of the environment, and thus every occasion of the environment takes a definite congruity because of the congruity of all these antecedent occasions. And the enduring organisms and that congruity is really the laws of nature.... And then the Creator put in electrons! But it is the development of electrons, their gradual development, developing an environment which bears the character of an electro-mechanic ⟨blank⟩.

The environment grows with society, and that a society has to be a society of like entities which create an environment favorable to each other, and there you get a stable and successful society. And you may have a society of dissimilar entities which you get favorable to each other.

The electrons and the protons are most elemental ⟨blank⟩ which exist in such throngs that there are no entities of the same aboriginal type other than those, and we are living in an electronic, protonic stage as it were. And it is exactly true that we create environments favorable to each other, and also we see to it that the associating organisms are favorable to us, and we have the sense to build the world and to bring up domestic animals which are favorable to us, and we have the sense |21| to be favorable to them. I simply take the obvious facts of the social sciences and generalize. And why indeed that is that the bigger organisms are the organisms we can observe and the smaller organisms which we cannot observe individually have as a matter of fact exactly the same attributes or existing in throngs with allied species, and in a general environment formed by ⟨blank⟩ just as the American nation. It is exactly the same principle.

DR. CABOT: The animals form a society and each gives a favorable environment to the rest?

PROF. WHITEHEAD: Yes. And now we have the theory of the electron ⟨blank⟩. The sun radiates its messages. A certain number of them go to pieces.

DR. CABOT: Is that original sin in the ⟨blank⟩.

PROF. WHITEHEAD: I do not know. I think that the world is going on to a very different state of affairs, so far as I know immortality, prolonged existence. Some animals may be transforming themselves to a higher side, to a side which has a ⟨blank⟩ from the lower side. I do not think that philosophic doctrine and the pointing out that possibility has anything to say for or against. You cannot expect it to because some organisms go to pieces, some live a very long time, and some develop into higher forms. That is the general theory of organisms. We cannot decide on those subjects. General philosophy can have no opinion whatever.

DR. CABOT: I should like to know what would constitute the authority of the State.

PROF. WHITEHEAD: The social authority, you mean, the justification for it?

DR. CABOT: Yes. The State orders me to go to war, and I do not believe in war. What am I to think of it?[1]

PROF. WHITEHEAD: I think you have to obey your conscience. If you think war is wrong and the state tells you to do it, I think you have to obey your conscience. On the other hand, I think you have to have a certain modesty in regard to the authority of your fellow countrymen influencing the state. But if after having given all the weight you can to the necessity of maintaining the state and the evil therefore of resisting it, and as to whether that is not a greater evil than participation in war – |22| having given all authority to that, if still you think that you are right, I think you have to resist. I may say that in entering this great country I had to strain my conscience to sign a statement. The statement of belief that I had to sign justified George III, and made the fathers of the American Constitution robbers. But I strained my conscience.

DR. CABOT: I want to get at the idea whether the larger entities, the larger organisms like the state, had by virtue of their larger bulk any authority over the smaller organisms?

PROF. WHITEHEAD: No, I do not think so. I think by virtue of asserting integration of thought, I think there is a necessity of maintaining a general organization, a harmoniously organized group. Man is essentially social, and therefore a primary duty is to maintain society, and I think you have to weigh that. You are ultimately brought back to the individual conscience. It may be wrong, but you have to do it. But I think the other people gain in feeling that society has to be maintained. I do not think a nation ought to go to war ever unless it thinks that the crisis is sufficiently great to justify itself in restraining forcibly if necessary those of its citizens who believe that they ought not to go to war. I believe that is one of the evils of going to war. To go to war for frivolous reasons comes to mean logically that you shall be prepared to do that, and if you are not prepared, what are you to do? I do not think you should do it merely because there is a man living there who says you ought to. But if you go to men in the army and ask them to mutiny, I think the state has ⟨blank⟩ just as I think the state ought not to go to war unless conscription would be necessary. It is reason not to go to war unless the evil to be averted is greater than that evil. You might say no evil can be greater than that.

DR. GLUECK:[2] I was wondering what some of the criteria would be whereby the state could fix responsibility in case of any particular act of any of these

---

1. This question would have had a particular resonance for Whitehead, whose son, Eric, died in 1918 in action in the First World War, while his close friend Bertrand Russell would protest against the war and conscription. A letter from Whitehead to Russell dated 16 April 1916 makes clear his contempt for conscripted men who 'produce their conscientious objections *ad hoc* . . . I am not greatly impressed by men who ask me to be shocked that they are going to prison, while ten thousand men are daily being carried to field hospitals, women and children have been raped and mutilated, and whole populations are living in agony' (Whitehead, 'Letter to Bertrand Russell, 16 April 1916).
2. Sheldon Glueck (1896–1980) was an American criminologist and a professor in Harvard's Department of Social Ethics. During this semester, he was teaching a course entitled 'Criminology and Penology' (Social Ethics 3).

entities called human beings, as a practical problem, take the case of the violation of ⟨blank⟩.

PROF. WHITEHEAD: I think that is a special problem of social science and of the lawyers. I think it is where you meet the lawyers, and both have something to say. |23| But I am afraid I have not thought out anything of that. I do not think either it could be got without the appeal to further principles than any that I have stated, the principles that I have stated have been so general. I think they are principles which would come in, but would require to be enforced by more special principles applicable to the especial type of society.

Philosophy A: History of Philosophy, spring semester 1927

Monday, 7 March 1927[1]

|87|[2] Progressive civilization of modern times due to (1) interest in most detailed facts, and (2) ⟨interest⟩ in most general principles. Dangers of a defect in either. – But high civilizations are not necessarily progressive. E.g. China. The Chinese, though, having invented the compass, did not think to connect it with general principles otherwise manifested in nature; whereas the same invention in Europe was soon followed by Gilbert's treatise on magnetism,[3] and then by the whole science of electromagnetism – i.e. a series of detached, curious facts stimulated thought on general principles. – In studying the Renaissance we are studying what principles underlie the progressive character of all modern times, what must be conserved if progress to continue.

|94|[4] Recommended reading:

Burtt, *Metaphysical Foundations of Modern Physical Science*, 1925.[5]

Science and Civilizations, Oxford, 1923.[6] (Medieval science). Especially Singer's essay, Dark Ages and the Dawn.

Whitehead, *Science and the Modern World*, chapter 1.

Dialogues of Galileo.[7] Translation published by the Open Court Publishing Company. Very good reading!

Period ends about 1700. Newton's *Principia*, 1687, completed the foundation of modern science. (A new period now beginning, since 1900). Much more doubt regarding period's beginning. Sporadic signs as early as 1000

---

1. All the notes presented here are those of the 'official notebook' for the class maintained by Winthrop Bell, Sinclair Kerby-Miller and Robert Underhill, though Conger also had notes for the 14 March session. Refer to the table on page 420 for a full list of Philosophy A notes by date, and see also the Introduction for a detailed discussion of each note-taker and their notes.
2. These page numbers come from the pre-numbered, bound volume of the 'official notebook' for the course. For some reason, the beginning of Whitehead's lecture was recorded on page 87, then continued on page 94. A note at the bottom of this page reads: '(continued on p. 94)'. The notebook is the primary account, supplemented with notes from George Conger for the lecture on 14 March.
3. William Gilbert (1544–1603) was and English physicist and philosopher best remembered for his 1600 book *De Magnete, Magneticisque Corporibus, et de Magno Magnete Tellure* (On the Magnet and Magnetic Bodies, and on That Great Magnet the Earth).
4. A note at the top of this page reads: 'For first paragraph see above, p. 87'.
5. Burtt, *The Metaphysical Foundations of Modern Physical Science*, available at <https://archive.org/details/metaphysicalfoun00burtuoft>. Whitehead assigned this book to his Philosophy 3b students for the spring 1927 semester. It is unclear whether Whitehead recommended this book for Philosophy A, or instead discovered it himself from the Philosophy A syllabus and decided to assign it to his Philosophy 3b students as well. See the 24 February lecture, note 5, p. 293.
6. This essay by Charles Singer (1876–1960) – a historian of science, technology and medicine – is chapter 5 of this 1923 anthology edited by F. S. Marvin. Whitehead's 'The first physical synthesis' was the chapter following. See Marvin, *Science and Civilization*, available at <https://archive.org/details/sciencecivilizat00marvuoft>.
7. Whitehead is referring to Galileo's *Dialogue Concerning the Two Chief World Systems*, but we have been unable to find the referenced edition.

or even 800. But from 1000–1400, science did not share in the progress (such men as Roger Bacon great exceptions). From 1400 on {?} great preoccupation with classical writings. Still literary rather than scientific. Modern |95| science dates from 1543, date of publication of (1) Vesalius' *On the Structure of the Human Body*,[1] maintaining necessity of knowing the detailed facts instead of merely general ideas derived from the ancients, and (2) Copernicus' *On the Revolution of the Celestial Bodies*.[2] (At first, curiously, more emphatically rejected by the Lutherans, while Vatican authorities unsuspectingly accepted it!) Heliocentric theory important first, in the technical scientific sense, in giving hypothesis and not dogmatic statement, and secondly, in enlarging the scale of the universe, reducing the significance of the earth. We have now lost all commonsense notions regarding scale in physics – the vast distances of the nebulae, and smallness of the electron. – Also, importance of accuracy in detailed measurements, and in statement of general fundamental notions, began now to be emphasized. Too much pedantry here impossible. Difference of science from common sense. A condition of boldness and originality.

Wednesday, 9 March 1927

|96| Necessary balance of general ideas and specific facts for a progressive civilization. Human mind does not spontaneously produce all its general ideas, but these are suggested by the facts; and on other hand, our observation of facts is governed by our stock of general ideas – we seldom observe anything absolutely new –

A great age never constituted by men of genius alone; a social background of lesser men also needed. Among the latter: Tycho Brahe,[3] Danish astronomer, – Francis Bacon. Bacon got the general idea of a change of thought, but his particular ideas not very useful. E.g. got notion of induction but did not carry out accurately. Gave a great stimulus to the age – something between Emerson[4] and H. L. Mencken![5] – Giordano Bruno.[6] Discovered no new fact, but realized discoveries of the age involved a new |97| world view. Imaginative and stimulating – too stimulating for most people, and Bruno burned. – William Gilbert, investigator of magnetism. – William Harvey, discoverer of circulation

---

1. Andreas Vesalius (1514–64) was a Flemish physician who published *De humani corporis fabrica libri septem* (On the Fabric of the Human Body in Seven Books) in 1543, a hugely influential book on human anatomy.
2. Nicolaus Copernicus (1473–1543) published his *De revolutionibus orbium coelestium* (On the Revolutions of the Heavenly Spheres) in 1543.
3. Tycho Brahe (1546–1601) was assisted in his work by Johannes Kepler (1571–1630), who later built on Tycho's work to develop his three laws of planetary motion, the first two of which he published in 1609.
4. Ralph Waldo Emerson (1803–82) was an American essayist and a leader of the transcendentalist movement of the 1800s.
5. H. L. Mencken (1880–1956) was an American journalist and essayist, and one of the most influential literary critics of the 1920s.
6. Giordano Bruno (1548–1600) was an Italian philosopher and mathematician best known for expanding the cosmological theories of Copernicus.

of the blood.¹ Thought little of Francis Bacon – actual scientific discover(er)s and thinkers on scientific method are thus apt to be at odds. Said Bacon "wrote on science like a lord chancellor."² – Stevinus,³ of the Low Countries, formulated triangle of forces, in mechanics.

Three much greater men were: Kepler, Galileo, and Descartes. Kepler, after 30 years meditation, using observations of Tycho Brahe, gave up old ideas that planets must move in circles (with if necessary epicycles), owing to simplicity of this figure, and considered what other curves might do; he settled upon the ellipse, with sun at one of the foci. Worked out law of motion: equal areas swept out by radius vectors in equal times. This greatly simplified the theoretical assumptions necessary |98| to explain the data. Important (1) for disposing of notion that a concept of perfection (the circle) must lie at root of nature;⁴ (2) showing a piece of math (conic sections), long since studied in the abstract, might after all find a use – thus indicating that no study should ever be suppressed for its apparent uselessness.

Galileo, really the central figure in starting of modern physics, owing to his rejection of ancient ideas. Threw over Aristotle and went to the facts, experimented. And he hit on the right conception of motion. Aristotle held objects naturally at rest in their proper places; if move, is to regain these – i.e. under influence of ends. Galileo substituted notion of seeking explanation of present state of physical universe in past instead of future, efficient not final causation. Question |99| of relative validity of these two types of causation still raging.⁵

Monday, 14 March 1927

A century of people in revolt. Hadn't got their new way of thought straight. In some periods the scheme of things fits people's experience perfectly, otherwise they start by being in a muddle. The 17th century inherited from a great century, and made a synthesis which lasted for 250 years. Due to Galileo, Descartes, Newton.⁶

Don't think of these as absolutely detached from their predecessors and contemporaries. It was the shadowy people who produced the general temper

---

1. William Harvey (1578–1657) was an English physician. His *Exercitatio Anatomica de Motu Cordis et Sanguinis in Animalibus* (An Anatomical Exercise on the Motion of the Heart and Blood in Living Beings) was published in 1628.
2. Whitehead also uses this quote about Bacon in his *Science and the Modern World*. It is possible that he saw it first in a 1916 article by his friend Morris Cohen. See the 19 October 1926 lecture, note 5, p. 193.
3. Simon Stevin (1548–1620), sometimes called 'Stevinus', was a Flemish mathematician and physicist.
4. We have removed an extra closing parenthesis that seems to have been mistakenly added here to the right of 'nature'.
5. The handwriting changes for the next lecture. This 'official notebook' was maintained by several different people, and it appears that a different person took over the note-taking on 14 March.
6. Conger's notes add here: 'Galileo always in argument. Primarily a physicist. Knew enough math and philosophy for what he wanted. Descartes primarily a mathematician. Thought out philosophy when fighting. Newton hit on formulation – Knowing what Galileo did and Descartes' (Conger, p. 1).

of the age; history of science not a succession of ∨discontinuous∨ giants.¹ Have sympathy for those who went up blind alleys and discovered "No thoroughfare".

The subject of dynamics was that in which they produced their clear ideas. All engineering ⟨to?⟩-day and nine-tenths of dynamic astronomy based on them. They break down in regard to modern speculations concerning radiation, ~~of~~ light, and the nature of molecule.

Three laws of motion.

First Law: <u>Every body</u> continues in its state of rest <u>or of motion in a straight line</u> except insofar as it may be compelled by applied forces to change its state.

|100| Seemingly innocent statement ⟨?⟩ expresses Galileo's discovery. The two most shocking phrases underlined.² ⓐ The feudal view of the universe challenged here; every bit of matter is as good as every other bit. All bits of matter are free and equal. Democratic view. Arose through Galileo's discovery of mountains of moon and phases of Venus.³ ⓑ Uniform motion required no reference to anything beyond the entity itself. Not an *a priori* dogma, introduced because in this way a scientific account of the facts could alone be given. Rest becomes merely a case of uniform motion in a straight line.⁴

Aristotle had started with change in <u>general</u> and demanded reasons for it. Now what is ascribed [by virtue of assumption of law of inertia] is a specific <u>kind</u> of change. Aristotle, faced by a series of bodies moving in straight lines (like the stars) would confine himself ~~the~~ to their relative changes of configuration; Newton would assign these changes of configuration to their relative interaction.⁵

Second Law: Change of motion [momentum] is proportional to the moving force applied, and takes place in the direction of the straight line in which the force acts.

Aristotle would have said it was the amount of <u>motion</u> which was proportional, Newton says it is the amount of <u>change</u> of motion. |101| The rate of ~~motion~~ momentum = mass × acceleration. What are forces? How observable? All you can observe is the change of motion, and this law states that we are going to measure forces and directions in which a thing acts by looking for the changes of momentum that occur. This seems to reduce dynamics to the tautology, the change of motion = the change of motion. Its utility is that this ~~law~~ ∨assumption∨ permits an expression of law of force without reference to change of motion at all.

---

1. Cf. Conger: 'Nameless or shadowy people who produced state of mind so clearheaded bold genius could come and see what answer is. Sometimes final man by no means the greatest' (Conger, p. 1).
2. Conger adds here: 'Every body was the repudiation of scholastic rendering of Aristotelian point of view. World constructed for attainment of ends. Every body its peculiar end. End of stick to get near to center of Earth. End of flame is to get upwards. No general uniform type of action, but had a whole articulated according to various ends' (Conger, pp. 1–2).
3. Conger adds here: 'Even Copernicus said celestial mechanics different from terrestrial mechanics' (Conger, p. 2).
4. Cf. Conger: 'Aristotle would have said continues in its state of rest except insofar as compelled. But uniform motion in a straight line was making rest a particular case of uniform motion in straight line' (Conger, p. 2).
5. Cf. Conger: 'Aristotle's change requires a reason due to interrelations to each other. <u>Applied force</u> brings to <u>Newton's point of view</u>' (Conger, p. 2).

 Kepler looked out for a tangential force because he thought the planet had to be kept moving. For Newton the planet looks after its own motion, and looked for something to deflect it. In the sun he saw the likely agent of this force. If this was all that he had said, however, there would not have been much point to it. But if, further, when mass of S and P are equal, the force is proportional to their product of their masses divided by the square of their distance apart, then the question of the rate of motion is eliminated, and we get a statement of forces in terms of stresses between various configurations of matter.

Wednesday, 16 March 1927

|102|[1] Newton's *Principia*: lays down principles, and argues with ⟨no one?⟩. The nearest he gets to controversy is his "*hypotheses non fingo*".[2] Success of his laws started men in a new direction of thought that has remade mankind. All modern technology due to this.

Third Law: To every action there is always an equal and opposite reaction; or the universal actions of any two bodies are always equal and oppositely directed.

To us a somewhat different ring to this law. The first two laws deal with a body plus a force. Here it is forces that he talks of, though does not use the word. What he meant was that even a greater principle that of reciprocal influence. Two actual entities must be considered as being part of a greater organism ⟨?⟩.

The notion of stress – between any two bodies in universe. A further notion presupposed but not made explicit. – That wherever you find a force, a change of motion you can find bodies such that force on A is one member of a stress between them. Total force on A can be described as pairs of stresses. E.g. orbit of Neptune couldn't be explained as due to stresses with the sun and other planets. Leverrier and Adams.[3] |103| Question of stress suggests that A and B are enmeshed in a universe where something happens. Newton believed in this organic view of nature: not ⟨till?⟩ 19th century did either turn up – would complete the total organism in which you should think of A and B as embedded.

Finally, law of gravitation: Every particle of matter attracts every other with a force whose ⟨attraction?⟩ is that of the line joining them, and whose magnitude is directly as the product of their masses, and inversely as the square of their distance apart.

After Galileo, people had thought of earth as attracting the apple, but they thought of some mysterious property of earth as a whole, which Newton swept aside: it exists between all bits of matter.

You can look on moon and sun as particles, but rather harder to do in case

---

1. The handwriting seems to change again for this lecture.
2. See the 19 October 1926 lecture, note 3, p. 194.
3. Both Urbain Le Verrier (1811–77) and John Couch Adams (1819–92) hypothesised the existence of Neptune at around the same time, 1845–6.

of apple and earth. So Newton saw he would have to break the earth up into particles. What would total action of earth? Supposing earth to be distributed symmetrically around its centre, this would be centre of attraction. Held him up 15 years to express this total attraction.

|104| Can now be proved from Gauss's theorem,[1] in three lines. It took Newton 15 years to work out a very much more elaborate proof. Science is just as much a growth in simplification as in complication. Comes from finding out the relevant generalities.

Force is proportional to Mm/D^2 a general principle guiding discovery. Force related to mass. What function of distance would it be?

Not an absolutely complete statement. You are dealing with continuous bodies. The particles hang together because of the stress between them: Then that we can explain these stresses between particles not in contact as carried over an ether. We have as a matter of direct experience continuous bodies. Now that basis has gone. No more continuous bodies. First idea was that of (?) billiard-ball atoms. Now we know that this too is composed of further constituents in intense activity. And now matter has disappeared. This activity is to be conceived of as electromagnetic. And the behaviour of these atoms etc doesn't conform to Newton's laws. Newton's laws only apply to molar masses. (A parallel in human interaction).

|105| We have ref reverted to stage of early 17th century. Modern physical notions is yet coherent. Scientists have no longer the tone of authority they had in 19th century. No one has the right to say there is a complete consistent mechanistic account of the universe.

What is the general aim of science is to elaborate a concept of nature of things and their interconnections so as to elucidate our experience as exemplifications of that general nature of things. The question is what we mean by experience –

---

1. Whitehead is referring to Carl Friedrich Gauss's flux theorem for gravity, which is equivalent to Newton's law of gravity, but in many situations offers a more convenient and simple way to do the necessary calculations. This theorem is mathematically similar to Gauss's flux theorem for electrostatics, as Newton's law of gravity is mathematically similar to Coulomb's law of electrostatics. Notice that Maxwell's generalisation of Coulomb's electrostatics to an electrodynamics has been the paradigm for Whitehead's generalisation of Newton's law of gravitation (Newton's gravitostatics) to Whitehead's law of gravitation (a gravitodynamics).

Appendix 1
Tables of student notes by date

The tables on the following pages summarise which note-takers had notes for which lectures for the given class in the given semester. Refer to the Introduction for detailed discussions of the state of each set of notes.

Dark shading indicates that the note-taker's record of this lecture has been chosen as the primary account and acts as the base text for that lecture. The white numbers in these boxes refer to the page numbers in this volume on which the text of the lecture can be found.

Gray shading indicates that the note-taker had notes for the corresponding date, but that these were not chosen as the primary account, and are not included in the text. In cases where these notes contain material that our chosen primary account does not, or contain significantly different or significantly clearer phrasing, we have included a footnote at the appropriate place in the lecture. The alternative accounts can be found online at whiteheadresearch.org, so far as this is possible under copyright restrictions.

Empty cells indicate that no known notes from that note-taker exist for the given day.

Some dates were not provided by the note-takers themselves, but have been extrapolated through comparison with other notes. See the Introduction, p. xxxv, for a discussion of this issue.

Appendices

Philosophy 3b, fall semester 1925

Lecture date	Radcliffe[1] Heath	Harvard[1] Roethlisberger	Hartshorne
1 October 1925 (Thursday)	pp. 3–5	pp. 46–8	
3 October 1925 (Saturday)	pp. 5–6	pp. 48–9	
6 October 1925 (Tuesday)	pp. 6–7	pp. 50–1	
8 October 1925 (Thursday)	pp. 7–9	pp. 51–3	
10 October 1925 (Saturday)		pp. 53–4	
13 October 1925 (Tuesday)	pp. 9–11	pp. 55–6	
15 October 1925 (Thursday)	pp. 11–12	pp. 57–8	
17 October 1925 (Saturday)	pp. 12–13	pp. 58–60	
20 October 1925 (Tuesday)	pp. 13–15		pp. 60–2
22 October 1925 (Thursday)	pp. 15–17	pp. 62–4	
24 October 1925 (Saturday)	pp. 17–18	pp. 64–6	
27 October 1925 (Tuesday)	pp. 18–21		pp. 67–8
29 October 1925 (Thursday)	pp. 21–2		pp. 68–9
31 October 1925 (Saturday)	pp. 22–4	pp. 70–1	
3 November 1925 (Tuesday)	pp. 24–6	pp. 71–2	
5 November 1925 (Thursday)	pp. 26–8	pp. 72–4	
7 November 1925 (Saturday)	pp. 28–30		pp. 74–5
10 November 1925 (Tuesday)		pp. 76–7	
12 November 1925 (Thursday)	pp. 30–2	pp. 77–8	
14 November 1925 (Saturday)		pp. 79–80	
17 November 1925 (Tuesday)	pp. 32–3	pp. 80–2	
19 November 1925 (Thursday)	pp. 33–4	pp. 82–3	
21 November 1925 (Saturday)	pp. 34–5	pp. 84–5	
24 November 1925 (Tuesday)	pp. 36–7	pp. 86–6	
26 November 1925 (Thursday)	**Thanksgiving holiday**		
28 November 1925 (Saturday)	pp. 37–8	pp. 86–7	
1 December 1925 (Tuesday)		pp. 87–9	
3 December 1925 (Thursday)		pp. 87–9	
5 December 1925 (Saturday)	pp. 38–9	pp. 89–91	
8 December 1925 (Tuesday)	pp. 39–40	pp. 91–2	
10 December 1925 (Thursday)	pp. 40–1	pp. 92–3	
12 December 1925 (Saturday)		pp. 93–4	
15 December 1925 (Tuesday)	p. 42	pp. 94–6	
17 December 1925 (Thursday)		pp. 96–7	
19 December 1925 (Saturday)	p. 43	pp. 97–9	
Winter break			
5 January 1926 (Tuesday)	p. 44		pp. 99–101
7 January 1926 (Thursday)		pp. 101–2	
9 January 1926 (Saturday)	p. 45	pp. 102–4	
12 January 1926 (Tuesday)		pp. 104–7	
14 January 1926 (Thursday)		pp. 107–8	
16 January 1926 (Saturday)		pp. 108–9	
19 January 1926 (Tuesday)		pp. 110–11	

1. The Harvard and Radcliffe lectures took place on the same days at separate times, from 9 to 10 a.m. at Radcliffe, and noon to 1 p.m. at Harvard. While their content does not always match, it is usually broadly similar.

Appendices

Philosophy 3b, spring semester 1926

Lecture date	Robinson	Roethlisberger	Hartshorne
9 February 1926 (Tuesday)	pp. 113–15		
11 February 1926 (Thursday)	pp. 115–17		
13 February 1926 (Saturday)	pp. 117–20		
16 February 1926 (Tuesday)	pp. 120–2		
18 February 1926 (Thursday)	pp. 122–4		
20 February 1926 (Saturday)		pp. 124–6	
23 February 1926 (Tuesday)	pp. 126–8		
25 February 1926 (Thursday)		pp. 128–30	
27 February 1926 (Saturday)	pp. 130–2		
2 March 1926 (Tuesday)	pp. 132–4		
4 March 1926 (Thursday)	pp. 134–7		
6 March 1926 (Saturday)	pp. 137–9		
9 March 1926 (Tuesday)	pp. 139–41		
11 March 1926 (Thursday)		pp. 141–2	
13 March 1926 (Saturday)		pp. 142–3	
16 March 1926 (Tuesday)		pp. 143–4	
18 March 1926 (Thursday)		p. 145	
20 March 1926 (Saturday)		p. 146	
23 March 1926 (Tuesday)		p. 147	
25 March 1926 (Thursday)		p. 148	
27 March 1926 (Saturday)		p. 149	
30 March 1926 (Tuesday)		pp. 149–51	
1 April 1926 (Thursday)	pp. 151–3		
3 April 1926 (Saturday)	pp. 153–5		
6 April 1926 (Tuesday)	pp. 155–7		
8 April 1926 (Thursday)	pp. 158–60		
10 April 1926 (Saturday)	pp. 160–2		
13 April 1926 (Tuesday)		p. 162	
15 April 1926 (Thursday)		pp. 162–3	
17 April 1926 (Saturday)		p. 163	
Spring break[1]			
1 May 1926 (Saturday)		pp. 164–5	
4 May 1926 (Tuesday)		pp. 165–6	
6 May 1926 (Thursday)		p. 166	
8 May 1926 (Saturday)		pp. 166–7	
11 May 1926 (Tuesday)[2]			
13 May 1926 (Thursday)[2]			
15 May 1926 (Saturday)		pp. 167–8	
18 May 1926 (Tuesday)		p. 168	
20 May 1926 (Thursday)[2]			
22 May 1926 (Saturday)[2]			
25 May 1926 (Tuesday)		pp. 168–9	

1. During Harvard's spring break, Whitehead delivered lectures at McGill University (Montreal, Canada), the University of Michigan (Ann Arbor, Michigan, United States), and the University of Illinois (Urbana, Illinois, United States). Refer to the Introduction (p. xxx) for further discussion of this.
2. It is unclear if Whitehead did not lecture on these days, or all note-takers were simply absent or did not take notes.

Appendices

Philosophy 3b, fall semester 1926

Lecture date	Conger	Nelson	King	Jackson	Burch
30 September 1926 (Thursday)		pp. 170–2			
2 October 1926 (Saturday)	pp. 172–5				
5 October 1926 (Tuesday)	pp. 175–8				
7 October 1926 (Thursday)	pp. 178–81				
9 October 1926 (Saturday)		pp. 181–3			
12 October 1926 (Tuesday)[1]					
14 October 1926 (Thursday)	pp. 183–7				
16 October 1926 (Saturday)	pp. 187–9				
19 October 1926 (Tuesday)	pp. 190–4				
21 October 1926 (Thursday)	pp. 194–8				
23 October 1926 (Saturday)	pp. 198–201				
26 October 1926 (Tuesday)	pp. 201–4				
28 October 1926 (Thursday)	pp. 205–7				
30 October 1926 (Saturday)	pp. 207–10				
2 November 1926 (Tuesday)	pp. 211–14				
4 November 1926 (Thursday)	pp. 214–17				
6 November 1926 (Saturday)	pp. 217–18				
9 November 1926 (Tuesday)	pp. 218–22				
11 November 1926 (Thursday)	pp. 222–6				
13 November 1926 (Saturday)[1]					
16 November 1926 (Tuesday)	pp. 226–9				
18 November 1926 (Thursday)	pp. 229–33				
20 November 1926 (Saturday)	pp. 233–7				
23 November 1926 (Tuesday)	pp. 238–41				
25 November 1926 (Thursday)	**Thanksgiving holiday**				
27 November 1926 (Saturday)	pp. 241–4				
30 November 1926 (Tuesday)			Hartshorne[2]	Hartshorne[2]	Hartshorne[2]
2 December 1926 (Thursday)			Hartshorne[2]	Hartshorne[2]	Hartshorne[2]
4 December 1926 (Saturday)	pp. 244–8				
7 December 1926 (Tuesday)	pp. 249–52				
9 December 1926 (Thursday)	pp. 252–5				
11 December 1926 (Saturday)	pp. 255–8				
14 December 1926 (Tuesday)			Demos[2]		Demos[2]
16 December 1926 (Thursday)	pp. 258–62				
18 December 1926 (Saturday)	pp. 262–5				
21 December 1926 (Tuesday)	pp. 265–8				
Winter break					
4 January 1927 (Tuesday)	pp. 269–72				
6 January 1927 (Thursday)	pp. 272–4				
8 January 1927 (Saturday)	pp. 275–8				
11 January 1927 (Tuesday)	pp. 278–81				
13 January 1927 (Thursday)	pp. 281–4				
15 January 1927 (Saturday)	pp. 285–8				

1. Since all five note-takers have notes on the lecture dates directly before and after 12 October and 13 November 1926, it seems evident that Whitehead did not lecture on these days, for reasons unknown.
2. It was Charles Hartshorne and Raphael Demos, and not Whitehead, who lectured during these class sessions. These lectures have not been included in the volume.

Philosophy 3b, spring semester 1927

Lecture date	Conger	King	Weiss	Burch
24 February 1927 (Thursday)	pp. 291–4			
26 February 1927 (Saturday)	pp. 294–7			
1 March 1927 (Tuesday)	pp. 297–302			
3 March 1927 (Thursday)	pp. 303–6			
5 March 1927 (Saturday)	pp. 306–9			
8 March 1927 (Tuesday)	pp. 309–13			
10 March 1927 (Thursday)	pp. 313–16			
12 March 1927 (Saturday)	pp. 316–20			
15 March 1927 (Tuesday)	pp. 320–23			
17 March 1927 (Thursday)	pp. 323–26			
19 March 1927 (Saturday)	pp. 326–9			
22 March 1927 (Tuesday)			pp. 329–30	
24 March 1927 (Thursday)			pp. 330–1	
26 March 1927 (Saturday)[1]				
29 March 1927 (Tuesday)		pp. 331–2		
31 March 1927 (Thursday)			p. 332	
2 April 1927 (Saturday)[1]				
5 April 1927 (Tuesday)			pp. 332–3	
7 April 1927 (Thursday)		pp. 333–4		
9 April 1927 (Saturday)			p. 334	
12 April 1927 (Tuesday)		pp. 334–5		
14 April 1927 (Thursday)			p. 335	
16 April 1927 (Saturday)			pp. 335–6	
Spring break[2]				
3 May 1927 (Tuesday)			p. 336	
5 May 1927 (Thursday)			p. 337	
7 May 1927 (Saturday)			p. 337	
10 May 1927 (Tuesday)			p. 337	
12 May 1927 (Thursday)[1]				
14 May 1927 (Saturday)[1]				
17 May 1927 (Tuesday)[1]				
19 May 1927 (Thursday)			pp. 337–8	
21 May 1927 (Saturday)			p. 338	
24 May 1927 (Tuesday)[1]				
26 May 1927 (Thursday)[1]				

1. It is unclear if Whitehead did not lecture on these days, or all note-takers were simply absent or did not take notes.
2. During Harvard's spring break, Whitehead delivered the Barbour-Page lectures at the University of Virginia (Charlottesville, Virginia, United States) that would later be published as *Symbolism: Its Meaning and Effect*.

Philosophy 20h, fall semester 1926

Lecture date	Conger	Kerby-Miller
1 October 1926 (Friday)	pp. 341–7	
8 October 1926 (Friday)	pp. 347–52	
15 October 1926 (Friday)	pp. 352–7	
22 October 1926 (Friday)		
29 October 1926 (Friday)		
5 November 1926 (Friday)		
12 November 1926 (Friday)		
19 November 1926 (Friday)	pp. 358–62[1]	
26 November 1926 (Friday)		
3 December 1926 (Friday)		
10 December 1926 (Friday)		
17 December 1926 (Friday)		
Winter break		
7 January 1927 (Friday)	pp. 362–6	
14 January 1927 (Friday)	pp. 366–70	

1. Some of Conger's seminary notes are undated, and likely come from multiple seminary sessions. However, since we have dated seminary notes for the first three October sessions, and all 1927 sessions up through Conger's departure in mid-March, we can say that these notes must belong to seminaries that took place between 22 October and 17 December 1926. Refer to note 1, p. 358, for a detailed discussion of this issue.

Philosophy 20i, spring semester 1927

Lecture date	Conger	Weiss
25 February 1927 (Friday)	pp. 371–5	
4 March 1927 (Friday)	pp. 375–81	
11 March 1927 (Friday)	pp. 381–3	
18 March 1927 (Friday)	pp. 383–90	
25 March 1927 (Friday)		
1 April 1927 (Friday)		
8 April 1927 (Friday)		
15 April 1927 (Friday)		
Spring break[1]		
6 May 1927 (Friday)		
13 May 1927 (Friday)		
20 May 1927 (Friday)		
27 May 1927 (Friday)		

1. During Harvard's spring break, Whitehead delivered the Barbour-Page lectures at the University of Virginia (Charlottesville, Virginia, United States) that would later be published as *Symbolism: Its Meaning and Effect*.

Appendices

Social Ethics 20a, fall semester 1926

Lecture date	Stenographer	Cabot
18 October 1926 (Monday)	pp. 391–407	

Philosophy A, spring semester 1927

Lecture date	Bell, Kerby-Miller, Underhill	Conger
7 March 1927 (Monday)	pp. 408–9	
9 March 1927 (Wednesday)	pp. 409–10	
14 March 1927 (Monday)	pp. 410–12	
16 March 1927 (Wednesday)	pp. 412–13	

Appendix 2
Samples of original notes

Louise Robinson Heath, Philosophy 3b lecture notes for 1 October 1925

Appendices

Fritz Jules Roethlisberger, Philosophy 3b lecture notes for 6 October 1925

4

and final causes. Admit both. To be brought together.
Hume's solution only expressable in terms of knowing-process.
Induction — Empiricism must find in occasions something that is not in occasion.
Kant broadens Hume. Just as difficult to find something universal in one occasion. Kant assumes a multiplicity of occasions. "to which Univ. must apply"
Can we reduce all judgements to the prin. of analysis. I more generally Concepts are true
are analyzable into subordinate concepts. which are true Assert detail complete.

Hume — does convey nothing about other occasions — Kant, Descartes, Hume do not convey information about other occasions.
There are synthetic judgements not to be obtained by analysis.
Whitehead: All universal know arises from analysis but deny
the isolation of occasions — You must have a prin. of multiplicity —
find in this occasion all other occasions. Aristotle analyzed
occasion into "union of being and not-being". — "Not being" is Whitehead's
"beyondness". Logic use occasion as substantive & predicates.

IV. **Kant's Answer to Problem**
Kant asks: "how are univ. synthetic propositions possible" — To analyze
immediate occasion there is "the given" on one side and function of k on other.
Given elements are chaotic. Order is introduced in the function of
knowing. Chaotic elements expressed as sense-data. Unity
of knowing — "F of knowing" introduces the "relations" and you
obtain the organized occasion. Relational elements are universals.
Perceptual object arises from organizing faculty of knowing. For
if organizing process only introduces universals, multiplicity of
occasions vanishes into phenomenal. e.g. your f of k relating Given as a process
only introduces rel. elements because but organization only – not a multiplic
introduces relations suitable to . ("Something or other"
cannot be identified with yesterday or tomorrow"). Theory
makes world a function of mind. Kant left with Hume in shear solipsism

Only one occasion of knowing introducing universals among data — as no new data are introduced op senses from and it's something nothing but not data

Kant's is in same predicament as Hume. Bradley point of view —
monistic — a system of appearance into a phen. world. — Does not explain
the multiplicity of reals and multiplicity of occasions — (Objective idealist)

422

Charles Hartshorne, Philosophy 3b lecture notes for 13 October 1925

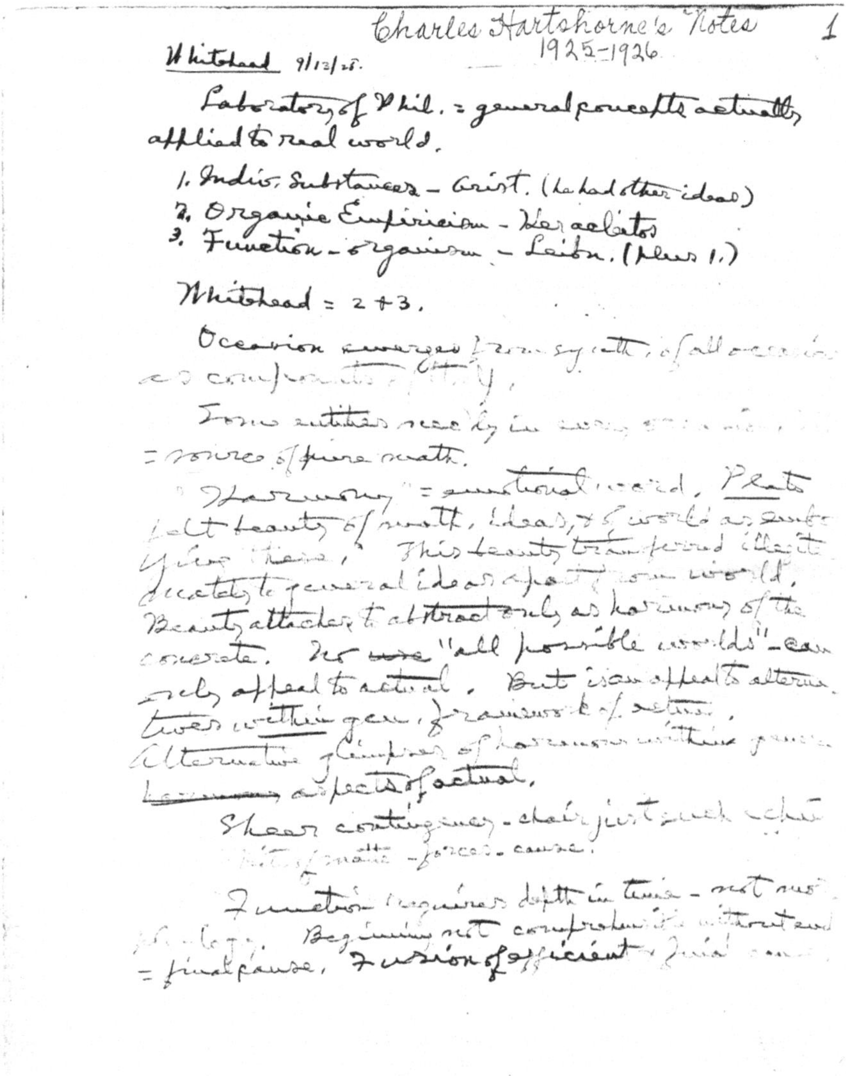

Charles Hartshorne's Notes 1
1925–1926

Whitehead 9/13/25.

Laboratory of Phil. = general concepts actually applied to real world.

1. Indiv. Substances – Arist. (he had other ideas)
2. Organic Empiricism – Heraclitus
3. Function – organism – Leibn. (plus 1.)

Whitehead = 2+3.

Occasion ~~emerges~~ from synth. of all occasions as components of it [illegible].

Form entities ready in every occasion [illegible] = source of pure math.

"Harmony" = ~~emotional~~ word. Plato felt beauty of math, Ideas, & of world as embodying these. This beauty transferred illegitimately to general ideas apart from world. Beauty attaches to abstract only as harmony of the concrete. No ~~use~~ "all possible worlds" – can only appeal to actual. But can appeal to alternatives within gen. framework of actual. Alternative glimpses of harmony within general ~~harmony~~ aspects of actual.

Sheer contingency – chair just such a chair [illegible] of matter – forces – cause.

Function requires depth in time – not mere [illegible]. Beginning not comprehensible without end = final cause. Fusion of efficient & final cause.

Edward Schouten Robinson, Philosophy 3b lecture notes for 9 February 1926

Page 1

[MS p 227]

Whitehead-- 2nd half.— 1926

How is accuracy possible?

This is it.

The idea of scientific and accurate determination of the synthesis--and. This leads you to the one and the many.

The question of comparison--matching--classification. So we get back to the <u>and</u> again.

Measure--definite determination in respect to how much: number and quantity--which refers to number but all the same is beyond it.

Gradation--inter   eness. Order. Then you have to have some concreteness. What do you mean by the actual world? I run the <u>Platonic point of view, for I am a mathematician.</u>

Confusion and harmony: things that extrude each other--contrariness, and things which supplement and intensify each other in a way. Order and God as a principle of order. The idea of progress--of an end.

Of course I am entirely incapable of carrying out this programme. Accuracy-- the ideas which we import into nature and practically find there.

How can you be not precise unless there is a precision which there might be? If there is a meaning, it is that it might be precise but always. God is an ideal which we can't think of nature without importing into nature. We can't talk of nature--there's no such thing as nature. Unless it has this in it. I usually diverge from Kant; but here I am waving friendly signals to him.

IT. Obviously an it is an abstraction. You don't see a bare <u>it</u>; you see a watch. There is not a watch and then specific determinations--you can't separate the what of the watch from the watch.

It is obvious that philosophy started from language and a rather naive trust in grammar. It was a great calamity that Aristotle didn't know Chinese. I have no doubt that it is an equal calamity in China that the Chinese don't

George Perrigo Conger, Philosophy 3b lecture notes for 1 March 1927

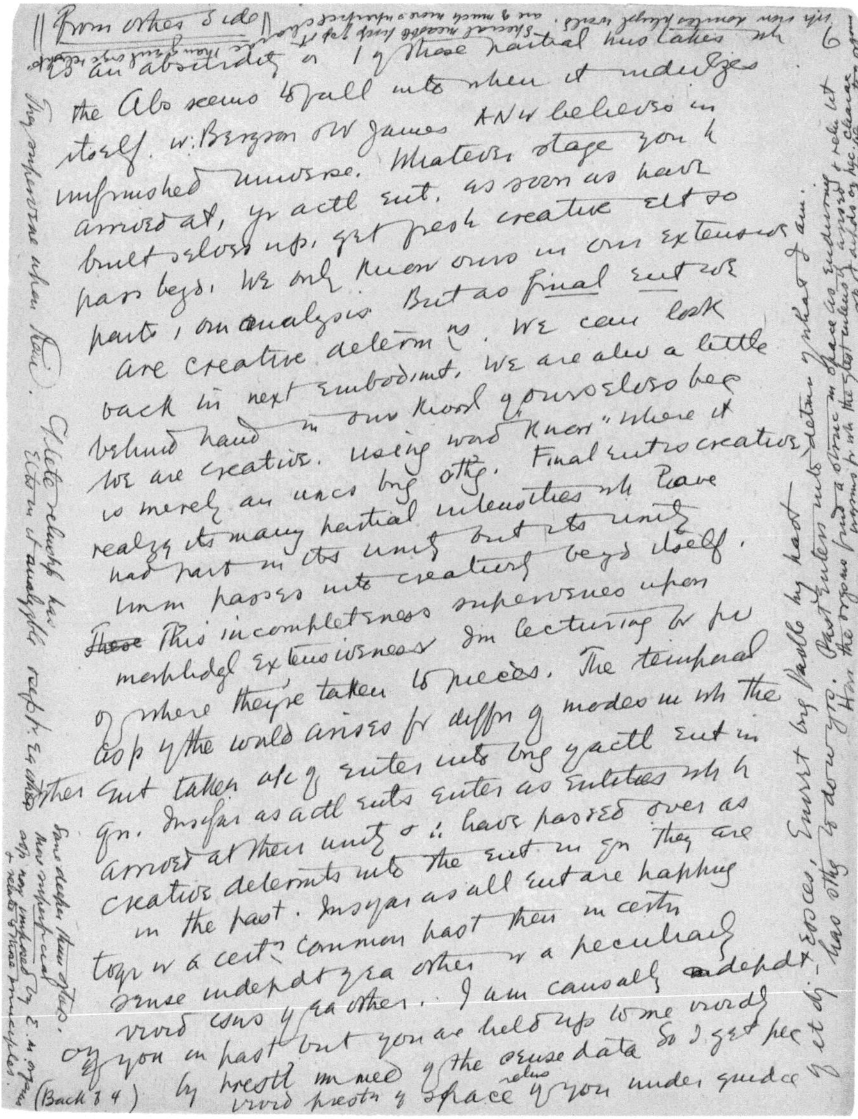

Everett John Nelson, Philosophy 3b lecture notes for 30 September 1926

PHILOSOPHY OF SCIENCE

Lectures by A. N. Whitehead

INTRODUCTORY LECTURE — The Study of Ph[...]

There is no such thing as "philosophy of science", any more than there is a Protestant Truth, a Catholic Truth, etc. There is just one truth. The ideas dealt with in a "philosophy of science" course are ideas suggested by scientific thought.

There have been three main epochs in which the scientific outlook on nature has suggested scientific ideas; viz.:

1. Time of the Greeks. The Greeks found out the habit of thinking clearly and logically. They had some advantages over us: perhaps they were abler, but however that may be, they did have more leisure and were not sophisticated by past history as we are to-day. There was a certain freshness about the Greeks, perhaps it is a little analogous to that of the Americans. (It is very important for the student to get a thorough knowledge as to how the universe looked to the Greek).

2. Seventeenth Century. In the 17th century were the people who set forth the ideas that have been energizing during the past three hundred years. Descartes and Locke will never be superceded because they said things that must be taken account of by every philosophy. It is very important to read Descartes and Locke on matter, mind, extension, duration, etc. (Locke's Essay concerning the Human Understanding, and Descartes' Meditations.

3. Modern. Parallel to Locke's work is John Dewey's Experience and Nature. Dewey formulates the problem much the same as Whitehead would; that is, he looks at nature in about the same way. Of course the two men have a different philosophical outlook in that Dewey is a Pragmatist while Whitehead is a Rationalist. The works of Whitehead to be read are: The Concept of Nature, Science in the Modern World, and Religion in the Making.

The influence of mathematics and logic, although it has helped to create philosophy, has helped to mislead philosophers. It is often said that a proposition is either true or false, but it is very difficult to get a proposition that is both perfectly definite and true or false. It is not right to take a proposition out of its setting and then test it for truth or falsity. Propositions always presuppose a certain way of looking at the world. Of course, for practical purposes, there's a way that's good enough, but this is not so with first principles. Furthermore, every proposition is elliptical. We point at things. Every proposition presupposes a world as a background. How is the particular proposition wrong? With what background, meanings, etc, is it wrong? The same questions are relevant in regard to truth. Ideas that are accepted quite the world over and through long stretches of history actually are true. Descartes is wrong only if we take him out of his background. This fact is true of such a proposition as two and two make four. The "and" and the "make" are apt to be given a more concrete application than they ought be given. Likewise, with "four". Propositions are largely formulae in action, but they're not the whole story, as Dewey contends they are. (Reading in Dewey: Chapters 1 and 2, perhaps 3 also.

Paul Weiss, Philosophy 3b lecture notes for 24 and 26 February 1927

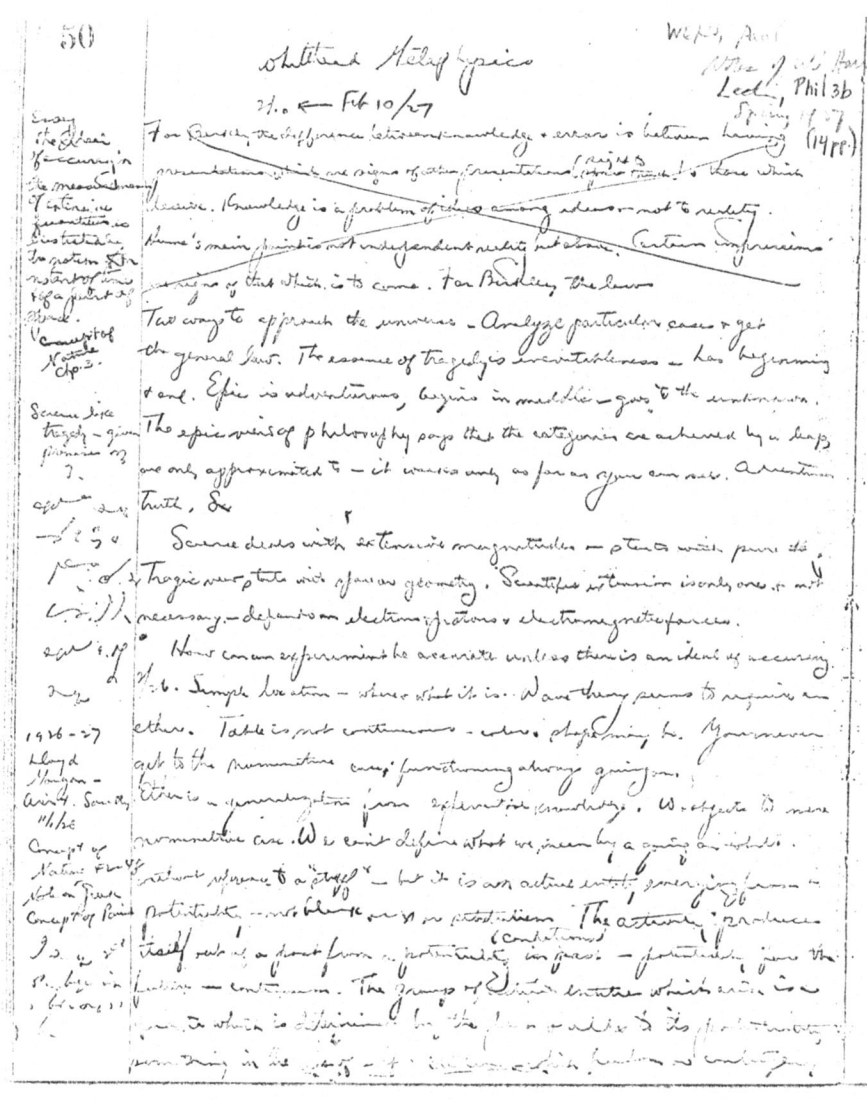

Lester Snow King, Philosophy 3b lecture notes for 30 September 1926

Philosophy 3b   Prof. Whitehead   Sept. 30 1926

Three important epochs – 1) Greek. They had more ability, and more leisure. They were not sophisticated by a traditional nomenclature. There is a freshness in their thought, analogous to the freshness of America. – plastic.

2) The Seventeenth Century. Presupposing medieval thought and neo Platonism. We study the how they emitted energizing thoughts. Descartes and Locke must be studied. They never will be superseded. D's teaching on matter, mind, extension, duration

※ D's phil. works, by Haldane and Ross.
※ Locke Essay Concerning Human Understanding.
He has an implied metaph. which he denounces

3) Modern Times.
   Experience and Nature   I, II (III)   John Dewey.
   The Concept of Nature   } Whitehead.
   Science and the Modern World

Truth and Error: meth. has created phil. and also misled philosophers. Logic says a thing is right or wrong. This, says W, was misunderstood. Analogous to math, it was thought easy to find propositions as such. They took them divorced from their particularity. It is very rare to get such a prop. All we have is a form of expression. Language is an inadequate method of giving an exact proposition. Nothing can be completely and adequately defined without a complete metaphysic, nor do we have this. So in every prop. there is implied a way of looking at the world. When this changes, the meaning changes. Also, every prop. is elliptical. We are presupposing the world as a background. Saying a prop. as a formula is wrong, we must ask, how is it wrong,

Gardner Jackson, Philosophy 3b lecture notes for 30 September 1926

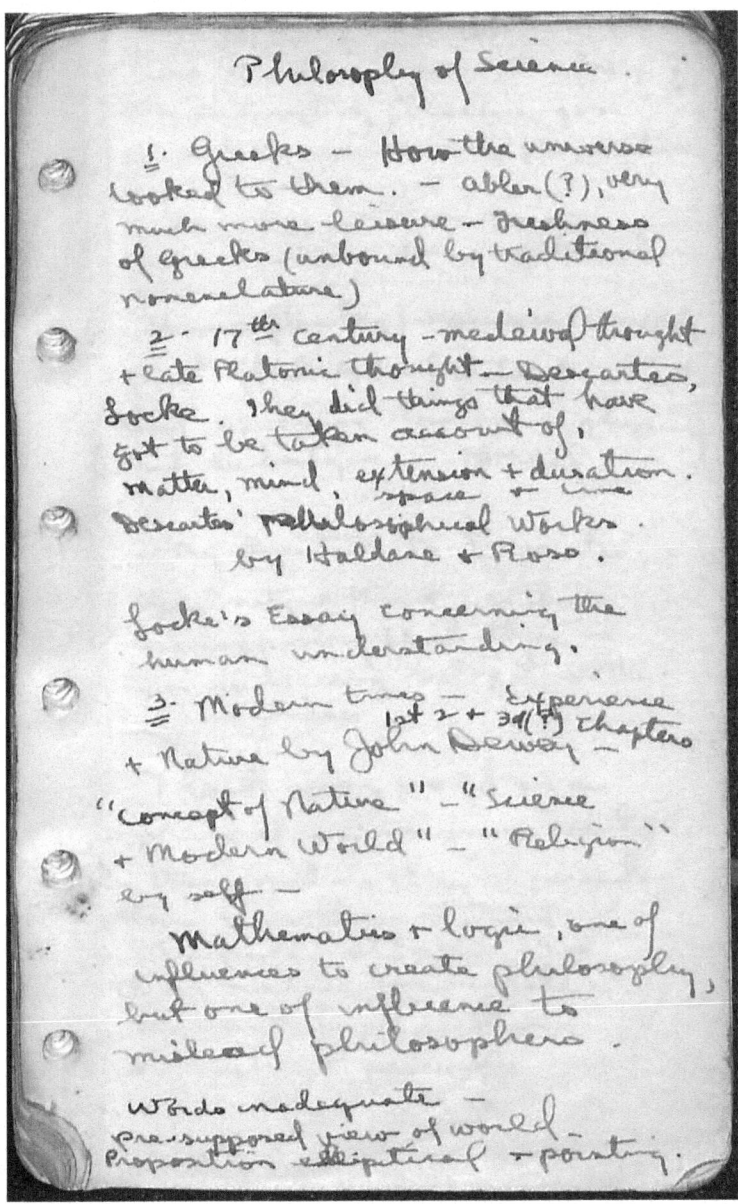

Philosophy of Science.

1. Greeks — How the universe looked to them. — abler (?), very much more leisure — freshness of greeks (unbound by traditional nomenclature.)

2. 17th century — medieval thought + late Platonic thought — Descartes, Locke. They did things that have got to be taken account of, matter, mind, extension + duration.

    Descartes' philosophical Works. by Haldane + Ross.

    Locke's Essay concerning the human understanding.

3. Modern times — Experience + Nature by John Dewey — 1st 2 + 3rd (?) chapters "Concept of Nature" — "Science + Modern World" — "Religion" by self —

    Mathematics + logic, one of influences to create philosophy, but one of influence to mislead philosophers.

    Words inadequate — pre-supposed view of world — Proposition elliptical — pointing.

George Bosworth Burch, Philosophy 3b lecture notes for 30 September and 5 and 7 October 1926

LECTURES BY PROFESSOR WHITEHEAD --- INTRODUCTION

There is no philosophy of science ; we are concerned with those parts of philosophy which are suggested by science . In three epochs science has suggested philosophical ideas : the Greek period , the seventeenth century , and the twentieth century .

Descartes , Leibniz , Locke , and Kant assume that the underlying reality of the world is a permanent substance which has adventures .

Our scientific habits are set by ignoring the inexplicable. In every intellectual epoch the adequacy of the evidence for the prevailing beliefs seems overwhelming . We must not ignore the inexplicable ; we should imitate our ancestors who beat gongs when the moon was eclipsed . But mere notice of unusual phenomena is not sufficient ; we must give them rational attention . Science and philosophy are united in a common goal , explanation . (Dewey says the goal is action.) Action and use are a test of explanation , and explanation is the basis of action , but explanation is an end in itself and is the chief end of science and philosophy . Scientists who are clear in their concepts are at least thirty years behind their times .

Progress in philosophy involves the explicit statement of assumptions implicit in previous philosophers . Rationalism never deserts standards of criticism . We philosophize because we believe ; we do not believe because we philosophize . Philosophy is a criticism of belief --- preserving , deepening , and modifying it . Standards of criticism are (1) intensity of belief , (2) concurrence in belief , (3) clear expression of belief , (4) analysis of belief , (5) logical coherence of belief , (6) exemplification of belief , (7) adequacy of belief .

Sinclair Kerby-Miller, Philosophy 20h notes for 8 October 1926

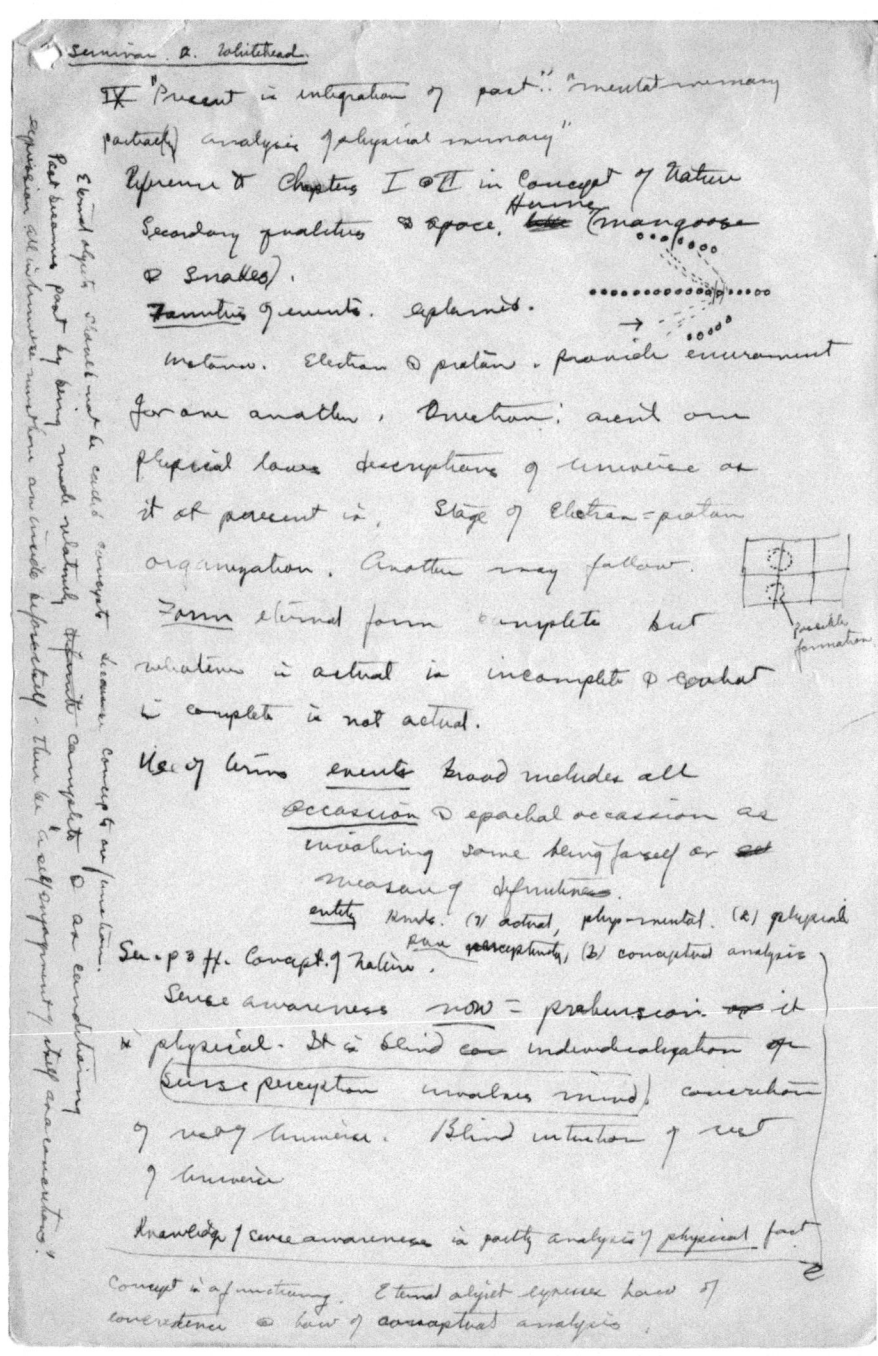

Seminar a. Whitehead.

IX "Present is integration of past." "mental memory particular analysis of physical memory."

Reference to Chapters I & II in Concept of Nature Secondary qualities & space. Hume (mangoose & snakes).

Entities of events. explained.

Nature. Electron & proton. provide environment for one another. Question: aren't our physical laws descriptions of universe as it at present is. Stage of Electron–proton organization. Another may follow.

Form eternal form complete but whatever is actual is incomplete & what is complete is not actual.

Use of terms events broad includes all Occasion & epochal occasion as involving some being itself or measure of definiteness.

See p & ff. Concept of Nature. entity kinds. (1) actual, phys-mental. (2) physical pure perceptivity, (3) conceptual analysis.

Sense awareness now = prehension. is physical. It is blind individualization of (sense perception involves mind) conception of very universe. Blind intuition of rest of universe.

Knowledge of sense awareness is partly analysis of physical fact. Concept is a function. Eternal object expresses laws of coexistence & laws of conceptual analysis.

[margin notes:] Eternal object need not be called concept because concept is a function. Past becomes part by being made relevant opposite complete & as constituting experience all inclusive nature an inside referentially. Thus is a self supporting self conscious!

Appendices

Stenographer, Social Ethics 20a notes for 18 October 1926

SOCIAL ETHICS SEMINARY

October 18th,   1926

Prof. A. N. Whitehead.

DR. CABOT: I do not know anybody that I would rather hear than Prof. Whitehead. As I read in his books the thing that strikes me is that whereas most of us come to any subject with a certain body of knowledge on one side of human life and study, he comes with a fund of knowledge from so many sides. I said two weeks ago that I thought one of the necessities for anyone who tried to approach the social sciences was to be interested in all the different sides of life of a human being,— in the side that deals with beauty, in the side that works in science, in the side that reflects philosophically, in the side that is interested in the state. As we know from Prof. Whitehead's writings he has distinguished himself not only in mathematics and the natural sciences but of late years in philosophy

Most philosophers are a little shy about physical science, and most men who know physical science are distinctly shy about philosophy. But Prof. Whitehead, like our own Prof. Lawrence Henderson, is one of the few people perfectly at home on each side of that unfortunate division. I am sure he feels it as much as anyone would an unfortunate division, this one of the philosophers and the men of science.

PROF. WHITEHEAD: I should like to start by disclaiming the impertinence of thinking that one could come to a seminary in a department that is concerned with social ethics and with social sciences, as a special department of thought, and contribute anything on that specialized side, which wants not only study but which also requires that expert formation by years of quiet prosecution of that study. I have not the slightest belief that I am qualified in any way to give advice or any suggestions. I hope nothing that I say will be construed in that sense.

But of course there are general relations which are in philosophy and all other regions of systematic thought, and that general type of relation, though it varies in emphasis and aims in regard to its various sides, yet has a common aspect for all

Richard Clarke Cabot, Social Ethics 20a notes for 18 October 1926

Oct. 8 1926

Prof. Whitehead

Phil & all other regions of thought
Fundamentals as they look [in] Phil
Two allied formulations: 1. Soc. Eth. — founded on
  original sin
  Also on " virtue
2. Thou shalt not steal (individualism) } equally true &
  Property is robbery } equally false

Here jurisprudence & soc. ethics meet

Phil. deals c̄ generic concepts [of] widest scope —
of universal application. To elucidate thought in all
science by getting a harmonious scheme so that each special
field can be related to the generic concepts.
Discovery of ultimate meaning & Survey of human
interests (as elements stand in bodies) & the formulation of
belief as they exist. With that imaginatively [to] formulate
of generic conceptions wh. will harmonize & place the special
interests. Immediate experience sh'd be interpreted by these.
Logical coherence & logical deduction.

Paradoxes will arise & either the scheme or else
the special sciences' principles need modification. Criticizing
where its special ideas fail & [try] to best generalization.
Also stimulus to the imagination so that new sciences

Official notebook for Philosophy A, notes for 7 March 1927.
Notes collectively by Winthrop Pickard Bell, Sinclair Kerby Miller and Robert L. M. Underhill

87

is founded in thinking; so long as think, something is going on. Thinking is the absolute existence; all else inferred from this.

Prof. Whitehead.   Mar. 7, '27.

Progressive civilization of modern times due to (1) interest in most detailed facts + (2) that in most general principles. Dangers of a defect in either. — But high civilizations are not necessarily progressive. Eg. China. The Chinese, tho having invented the compass, did not think to connect it with general principles otherwise manifested in nature; whereas the same invention in Europe was soon followed by Gilbert's treatise on magnetism, & then by the whole science of electro-magnetism. i.e. a series of detached curious facts stimulated thought on general principles. — In studying the Renaissance we are studying what principles underlie the progressive character of all modern times, & what must be conserved if progress to continue. (Continued on p. 94).

Appendix 3
Diary entry of George Conger on Whitehead[1]

|1| Professor Woods,[2] the chairman ⟨of⟩[3] the philosophy department, ⟨did not⟩ know quite what to do with a wandering ⟨professor about⟩; he asked ⟨me to make⟩ sure that I was not working for a degree. I told him ⟨no⟩ – all I had to do ⟨was to keep⟩ Columbia from taking away the Ph.D. she had given ⟨me⟩.[4] So he said – ⟨"You are⟩ our guest; go anywhere you like".

Whitehead continued to be very friendly and in the succeeding months afforded me what I prize as my finest professional-personal memory. I fairly haunted him – went to all his lectures, to his seminars, to the famous Sunday evening gatherings at his house, and usually about once a week for a personal conference and tea. My over-all impression of him was that here ⟨is a man⟩ whose mind is <u>ripe</u>: if I ever had any leaning to the "discussion method" in ~~so-called~~ education, ~~I I was cured in my contacts~~ as a substitute for instruction, Whitehead unconsciously cured me. ~~His lectures were~~ ⟨It was⟩ not that his lectures were organized – he rambled, ⟨repeated⟩ and seemed to pay little heed to his subject, ⟨least of⟩ all to the formidable mathematical machinery of *Principia*. One day, referring to his treatment of some ⟨abstruse⟩ subject, one of the students said "I'm <u>glad</u> Whitehead said that over <u>four</u> times; the first three times, I didn't get it."

His panpsychism (he told me once that he didn't object to being called a panpsychist) made him confuse the physical and the psychical. One day in his lecture he jumped ~~from~~ or skidded from something physical into a statement about value. ~~In~~ Before the next lecture someone – it may have been I, I have forgotten – asked him about it. In the next lecture he said, calmly – "last time when I used the word 'value', I should have said 'intensity'". ~~He was~~ In conferences he was especially patient of questions and even of criticism, though one day when someone said ~~he wasn't~~ some statement was not clear he replied "I think there are some things which are not meant to be clear."

---

1. The date of this diary entry is not known. It was given to the Yale Philosophy Club together with Conger's Whitehead lecture notes by his wife, Agnes, who also provided a typed transcription of the entry. See Conger, 'Notes from the diary of George P. Conger'.
2. James Haughton Woods (1864–1935) was one of Whitehead's closest friends in the Harvard Philosophy Department. See the Introduction(p. xxix), as well as Joseph Petek, 'Whitehead and James Haughton Woods', <http://whiteheadresearch.org/2018/10/08/whitehead-and-james-haughton-woods>.
3. The original of this diary entry is very faded and indecipherable in places, especially on the first page. At times we referred to the typescript provided by Conger's wife, Agnes, to fill in gaps. Words in angle brackets are generally from this typescript.
4. Conger received his PhD from Columbia University in 1922.

|2| His seminar met at his house in the evening. Usually it was around the dining room table. On the table was a red cigar holder, well stocked, above it usually a thick cloud of smoke, sent up by about everyone except Whitehead and me. The discussions often went up at least as high as the smoke, and Whitehead again and again asserting his empiricism ~~would say~~ – ⟨?⟩ pointing to the cigar holder while it could still be seen would say "I have to come back to 'this is red.'" I used to tell my students that Whitehead's philosophy is like a captive balloon; without discussing the question of what fills it, it goes up very high and stays up very long – but it is always tied down to the "perception ⟨of⟩ the apparent". "This is red."

We used to try slyly to get Whitehead to comment on Bertrand Russell, who in those middle years had diverged from him and was not above making snippy remarks about him ("he comes from a long line of bishops."). ⟨?⟩ Usually every trap we laid for Whitehead failed to spring, ~~except that once~~ but one night it worked. "The trouble with Bertie is" he said, "all you have to do ~~to~~ is to show him a ~~new~~ wild idea and he will take it for the fun of running it." Some ~~other~~ interviewer, not I, ~~heard~~ first heard the famous remark "Bertie thinks I'm muddleheaded, but I think Bertie's simple minded." I heard him say to ~~an~~ luncheon audience that Russell was the ablest logical mind since Aristotle.[1] When ~~I quoted~~ one day I quoted something about mathematics from Wildon Carr,[2] Whitehead said, gently, "I think anything that Wildon Carr writes about mathematics you may safely neglect." Even more gentle was the comment he made to someone concerning Alexander's *Space, Time and Deity* – "I'm afraid the dear man ~~didn't~~ doesn't know enough mathematics." He said he had come to think that much in *Principia* about the doctrine of types was wrong.[3]

My personal conferences with him were most helpful, though he took issue with my mathematical realism and its attempt to derive the earliest physical ⟨energies?⟩[4] from the mathematical field. ⟨?⟩ He looked over an outline of what I called and still call the monadic characteristics of the physical world and said he thought I had chosen the right ones. Of *A Course in Philosophy*,[5] he said "An original spring of thought."

|3| His Sunday evening "At Homes" were extraordinary. They have since been written up in Lucien Price's *Dialogues of Alfred North Whitehead* – a book which, while it brings back many things and much atmosphere to me, leaves me ⟨?⟩ with mixed feelings as regards its taste, if not ~~its~~ sometimes its accuracy. At all events, in the time Agnes and I spent in Cambridge, the Sunday evenings were delightful. There were I should say always about 15 or 20 there, sometimes more.

---

1. This sentence is inserted from the right margin.
2. Herbert Wildon Carr (1857–1931) was a British philosopher. Whitehead participated in at least four Aristotelian Society symposiums with Carr between 1919 and 1924, including one he chaired on 12 July 1924, about a month before his departure to America. See Nicholson et al., 'Symposium: The quantum theory'.
3. This sentence is inserted from the left margin.
4. The Yale transcription has 'emergence'.
5. Whitehead recommended Conger's book to his students at the beginning of his 16 November 1926 lecture. See note 2, p. 226. See Conger, *A Course in Philosophy*.

One evening I met Felix Frankfurter,[1] later a Supreme Court Justice. Any evening there would be a group ~~around~~ \shifting (gradually?) from\ Whitehead, who said "I like to talk irresponsibly", to Mrs. Whitehead and Miss Whitehead (an accomplished ⟨Orientalist⟩ on the staff of the Harvard Library).[2] On the dining room table, <u>sans</u> cigar smoke, would be a plate of cookies, and on the kitchen stove a ~~pot~~ kettle of chocolate. One night out in the kitchen warming it up, Mrs. Whitehead told me what has since become well known, that her husband's ~~inf~~ interest in philosophy ⟨dated⟩ from early in his career, ⟨?⟩ before he ⟨?⟩ began to teach the subject.

As the time drew near for us to leave, Whitehead said at one of ⟨my⟩ last interviews, "When you go I shall be quite bereft."[3] Mr. and Mrs. Whitehead had us at the house for lunch, and Mrs. Whitehead sent us a farewell telegram. After the last seminar which I was to attend,[4] when the others had left, Whitehead sat down with note paper before him. "Now what letters of introduction did you ~~want~~ \wish\?" he asked. I told him, and he wrote out one after another notes to Sir J. J. Thomson,[5] – addressing him as "Dear Master" (Master of Trinity College, Cambridge), Bertrand Russell,[6] and ~~Santa~~ George Santayana.[7]

---

1. Felix Frankfurter (1882–1965) held a chair at Harvard Law School and became one of Whitehead's closest friends after his arrival in America. For more on the relationship between Frankfurter and Whitehead, see Petek, 'Whitehead and Felix Frankfurter', <http://whiteheadresearch.org/2019/11/13/whitehead-and-felix-frankfurter/>.
2. For more on Jessie Whitehead, see Henning, 'Whitehead's daughter, Jessie', <http://whiteheadresearch.org/2020/01/15/jessie-marie-whitehead>.
3. Quotation marks supplied.
4. This would have been Friday, 18 March, though Conger also attended Whitehead's Philosophy 3b lecture on the next day, a Saturday.
5. This letter is held by Cambridge University Library (Whitehead, 'Letter to J. J. Thomson', 18 March 1927). Whitehead knew Thomson well; he was named a Fellow of Trinity College in 1881, three years before Whitehead, and became Master of the College in 1918. When Whitehead's son, Eric, was killed in World War I in 1918, Thomson sent him a letter of condolence; Whitehead's response is held by Cambridge University Library (Whitehead, 'Letter to J. J. Thomson', 24 March 1918).
6. The Bertrand Russell Archives holds this letter (Whitehead, 'Letter to Bertrand Russell', 18 March 1927).
7. Santayana's letter of response to Conger can be found in *The Letters of George Santayana, Book Three, 1921–1927* (p. 329), part of which reads: 'I expect to be here about a fortnight longer, after which I shall be in Paris. In either place I shall be glad to see you. You might have introduced yourself without the intervention of Prof. Whitehead, but I am glad to have a word from him for other reasons.'

List of primary sources

The following is a list of the archival sources that make up the text of this volume. All URLs were last accessed 18 August 2020.

Bell, Winthrop P., 'Philosophy A 1926–7 Official Note-book', Winthrop Bell Fonds, Series L, 6501-11-2, No. 3.8, Mount Allison University Archives.

Burch, George B., 'Philosophy 3b. Philosophy of Science. General Metaphysical Problems', Permanent notes of George Bosworth Burch, Volume 15, George Bosworth Burch personal archive, 1919–1943, HUC 8919.300.10, Box 5, Unit 1, Harvard University Archives, <https://id.lib.harvard.edu/ead/c/hua03013c00016/catalog>.

Cabot, Richard Clarke, 'The Fundamentals of Social Science, 1926–1927', Papers of Richard Clarke Cabot, HUG 4255, Box 90, Harvard University Archives, <https://id.lib.harvard.edu/ead/c/hua02998c00424/catalog>.

Conger, George P., 'Notes on Whitehead's class lectures at Harvard University, 1926–1927', George Perrigo Conger autographs and papers, Mss020, Box 4, University of Minnesota Library, <https://archives.lib.umn.edu/repositories/16/archival_objects/81029>.

Hartshorne, Charles, 'Whitehead Lecture Notes: Hartshorne's Notes on Whitehead's Lectures', STU112, Whitehead Research Library, <http://wrl.whiteheadresearch.org/items/show/1228>.

Heath, Louise R., 'Whitehead, Fall 1925', MS 284, Victor Lowe Papers, Box 2.9, Special Collections, Sheridan Libraries, Johns Hopkins University, <https://catalyst.library.jhu.edu/catalog/bib_556595>.

Jackson, Gardner, 'Philosophy 3b: Philosophy of Science', Gardner Jackson Papers, 1912–1965, Series 6: Bibliographical Materials, Box 96, Notebooks (3): History, Philosophy, etc., Franklin D. Roosevelt Presidential Library, US National Archives <http://www.fdrlibrary.marist.edu/archives/collections/franklin/index.php?p=collections/findingaid&id=461>.

Kerby-Miller, Sinclair, 'Whitehead Lecture Notes: A. N. Whitehead Seminaries', STU116, Whitehead Research Library, <http://wrl.whiteheadresearch.org/items/show/1432>.

King, Lester S., Student Papers, 1923–1928, HUC 8923.45, Box 2, Folder Philosophy 3B: Notes – 1926–1927, Harvard University Archives, <http://id.lib.harvard.edu/alma/990100059270203941/catalog>.

Nelson, Everett J., 'Philosophy of Science: Lectures by A. N. Whitehead', MS 284, Victor Lowe Papers, Box 2.9, Special Collections, Sheridan Libraries, Johns Hopkins University, <https://catalyst.library.jhu.edu/catalog/bib_556595>.

Robinson, Edward S., 'Spring 1926: 3b. Philosophy of science. General metaphysical problems', in Graduate Philosophy Club of Yale University, 'Notes from the Lectures of Alfred North Whitehead at Harvard University, 1926–1937', Philosophy and Social Science Manuscripts Collection, MS 644, Box 10, Folder 98, Manuscripts and Archives, Yale University, <https://archives.yale.edu/repositories/12/archival_objects/1262622>, pp. 1–45.

Roethlisberger, Fritz J., 'Philosophy of Science (Whitehead, A.N.)'. Fritz J. Roethlisberger papers, Arch GA 76, Carton 9, Folder 14, Baker Library Special Collections, Harvard Business School, <https://id.lib.harvard.edu/ead/c/bak00040c00396/catalog>.

Weiss, Paul, 'Whitehead Lecture Notes: Whitehead on Metaphysics', STU063, Whitehead Research Library, <http://wrl.whiteheadresearch.org/items/show/590>.

Weiss, Paul, 'Whitehead Lecture Notes: Seminary in Logic 20', STU064, Whitehead Research Library, <http://wrl.whiteheadresearch.org/items/show/591>.

Bibliography

All URLs were last accessed 18 August 2020.

Alexander, Samuel, *Space, Time, and Deity* (London: Macmillan, 1920).
Beman, W. W. (ed. and trans.), *Essays on the Theory of Numbers* (Chicago: Open Court Publishing Company, 1901), pp. 1–27.
Bergson, Henri, *Creative Evolution*, trans. Arthur Mitchell (London: Macmillan, 1922).
Bergson, Henri, *Time and Free Will*, trans. F. L. Pogson (London: George Allen and Co., 1913).
Berkeley, George, *Alciphron, or the Minute Philosopher* (Increase, Cooke and Co., 1732).
Berkeley, George, *Siris: A Chain of Philosophical Reflexions and Inquiries Concerning the Virtues of Tarwater, And divers other Subjects connected together and arising one from another* (London: W. Innys and C. Hitch, 1744).
Berkeley, George, *Three Dialogues Between Hylas and Philonous* (London: G. James, 1713).
Bogaard, Paul A. and Jason Bell (eds), *The Harvard Lectures of Alfred North Whitehead, 1924–1925: Philosophical Presuppositions of Science* (Edinburgh: Edinburgh University Press, 2017). [This source is referred to as HL1 throughout the present volume.]
Bosanquet, Bernard, *The Meeting of Extremes in Contemporary Philosophy* (London: Macmillan, 1921).
Bradley, Francis Herbert, *Appearance and Reality* (London: S. Sonnenschein, 1893).
Bradley, Francis Herbert, *Essays on Truth and Reality* (Oxford: Clarendon Press, 1914).
Bradley, Francis Herbert, *The Principles of Logic, Volume I*, 2nd edn (London: Oxford University Press, 1922).
Braithwaite, R. B., 'Science and the Modern World', *Mind*, vol. 35(140) (October 1926), pp. 489–500.
Broad, C. D., *Scientific Thought* (London: Kegan Paul, Trench, Trübner and Co., 1923).
Broad, C. D., *The Mind and Its Place in Nature* (New York: Harcourt, Brace and Co., 1925).
Brown, Sarah H., 'The right and the good: methodology in ethics', *Journal of Philosophy*, vol. 30 (July 1933), pp. 393–9.
Burtt, E.A., *The Metaphysical Foundations of Modern Physical Science: A Historical and Critical Essay* (London: Kegan Paul, Trench, Trübner and Co., 1925).
Cabot, Richard C., 'A. T. White and the Department of Social Ethics', *Harvard Alumni Bulletin*, vol. 23(30) (5 May 1921), pp. 700–2.
Caird, Edward, *A Critical Account of the Philosophy of Kant* (Glasgow: James Maclehose, 1877).
Caird, Edward, *The Critical Philosophy of Immanuel Kant* (Glasgow: James Maclehose and Sons, 1889).
Carroll, Lewis, *Alice's Adventures in Wonderland* (London: Macmillan and Co., 1865).
Cassirer, Ernst, *The Problem of Knowledge, Volume IV*, trans. William H. Woglom and Charles W. Hendel (New Haven: Yale University Press, 1950).
Clifford, W. K., *The Common Sense of the Exact Sciences* (New York: D. Appleton and Company, 1885).
Cohen, Morris R., 'An adventurous philosopher', *Yale Review*, vol. 23 (1933), pp. 173–7.
Cohen, Morris R., 'Principia Mathematica', *Philosophical Review*, vol. 21 (1912), pp. 87–91.
Cohen, Morris R., 'The place of logic in the law', *Harvard Law Review*, vol. 29(6) (April 1916), pp. 622–39.
Conger, George P., *A Course in Philosophy* (New York: Harcourt, Brace, and Co., 1924).
Conger, George P., 'Notes from the diary of George P. Conger on his friendship with Whitehead', in Graduate Philosophy Club of Yale University, 'Notes from the Lectures of Alfred North Whitehead at Harvard University, 1926–1937', Philosophy and Social Science Manuscripts Collection, MS 644, Box 10, Folder 98, Manuscripts and Archives, Yale University, <https://archives.yale.edu/repositories/12/archival_objects/1262622> (accessed 2 September 2020), pp. 473–5.
Conger, George P., 'What are the criteria of levels?', *Journal of Philosophy*, vol. 23(22) (28 October 1926), pp. 589–98.
De Laguna, Theodore, 'Extensive abstraction: a suggestion', *Philosophical Review*, vol. 30(2) (1921), pp. 216–18.
De Laguna, Theodore, 'Point, line, and surface, as sets of solids', *Journal of Philosophy*, vol. 19(17) (1922), pp. 449–61.
Dedekind, Richard, *Stetigkeit und irrationale Zahlen* (Braunschweig: Friedrich Vieweg, 1872).
Descartes, René, *The Philosophical Works of Descartes, Volume I*, trans. Elizabeth S. Haldane and G. R. T. Ross (Cambridge: Cambridge University Press, 1911).

Bibliography

Descartes, René, *The Philosophical Works of Descartes, Volume II*, trans. Elizabeth S. Haldane and G. R. T. Ross (Cambridge: Cambridge University Press, 1911).
Desmet, Ronny, 'The Gestalt Whitehead', *Process Studies*, vol. 44(2) (fall/winter 2015), pp. 190–223.
Dewey, John, *Experience and Nature* (Chicago: Open Court, 1925).
Dewey, John, Letter to Whitehead, 6 April 1926, LET1073, Whitehead Research Library, <http://wrl.whiteheadresearch.org/items/show/1434>.
Dewey, John, *Reconstruction in Philosophy* (New York: Henry Holt and Co., 1920).
Dickens, Charles, *The Life and Adventures of Nicholas Nickleby* (London: Chapman and Hall, 1839).
Edwards, Jr, Mark U. *Luther's Last Battles: Politics and Polemics 1531–46* (Minneapolis: Fortress Press, 2004).
Emerson, Ralph Waldo, 'History', in Ralph Waldo Emerson, *Essays* (Boston: James Munroe and Co., 1841), pp. 1–33.
Ford, Lewis, Letter to Paul Weiss, 14 July 1978, LET636, Whitehead Research Library, <http://wrl.whiteheadresearch.org/items/show/1085>.
Ford, Lewis, *The Emergence of Whitehead's Metaphysics, 1925–1929* (Albany: State University of New York Press, 1984).
Hartshorne, Charles, 'Some causes of my intellectual growth', in Lewis Edwin Hahn (ed.), *The Philosophy of Charles Hartshorne* (La Salle: Open Court, 1991), pp. 3–45.
Harvard Alumni Association, 'Social ethics', *Harvard Alumni Bulletin*, vol. 23(30) (5 May 1921), pp. 688–9.
Heath, Thomas Little, *A History of Greek Mathematics, Volume I: From Thales to Euclid* (Oxford: Clarendon Press, 1921).
Heath, Thomas Little, *Apollonius of Perga: Treatise on Conic Sections* (Cambridge: Cambridge University Press, 1896).
Heath, Thomas Little, *Euclid in Greek* (Cambridge: Cambridge University Press, 1920).
Heath, Thomas Little (trans.), *The Thirteen Books of Euclid's Elements* (Cambridge: Cambridge University Press, 1908).
Henning, Brian G., 'Whitehead in class: do the Harvard-Radcliffe course notes change how we understand Whitehead's thought?', in Brian G. Henning and Joseph Petek (eds), *Whitehead at Harvard, 1924–1925* (Edinburgh: Edinburgh University Press, 2020), pp. 337–56.
Henning, Brian G., 'Whitehead's daughter, Jessie', Whitehead Research Project website, 15 January 2020, <http://whiteheadresearch.org/2020/01/15/jessie-marie-whitehead/>.
Hillar, Marian, 'Philo of Alexandria', *Internet Encyclopedia of Philosophy*, <https://www.iep.utm.edu/philo/#H11>.
Hitchcock, Curtice N., Letter to Alfred North Whitehead, 4 November 1925, MssCol 1830, Macmillan Company records, Series 1 (Author Files), Whitehead, Alfred North, Archives and Manuscripts, New York Public Library, <http://archives.nypl.org/mss/1830#c1048570>.
HL1 *see* Bogaard and Bell, *The Harvard Lectures of Alfred North Whitehead, 1924–1925.*
Hoernlé, Augustus Frederic Rudolf, *Matter, Life, Mind, and God: Five Lectures on Contemporary Tendencies of Thought* (New York: Harcourt, Brace, and Co., 1922).
Hume, David, *A Treatise of Human Nature*, ed. L. A. Selby-Bigge (Oxford: Clarendon Press, [1738] 1896).
Hume, David, *An Enquiry Concerning the Human Understanding, and an Enquiry Concerning the Principles of Morals*, ed. L. A. Selby-Bigge (Oxford: Clarendon Press, [1748] 1894).
James, William, 'Does consciousness exist?', *Journal of Philosophy, Psychology, and Scientific Methods*, vol. 1(18) (1904): pp. 477–91.
James, William, *Essays in Radical Empiricism* (London: Longmans, Green, and Co., 1912).
Johnson, William Ernest, *Logic, Part 1* (Cambridge: Cambridge University Press, 1921).
Johnson, William Ernest, *Logic, Part 2: Demonstrative Inference, Deductive and Inductive* (Cambridge: Cambridge University Press, 1922).
Johnson, William Ernest, *Logic, Part 3: The Logical Foundations of Science* (Cambridge: Cambridge University Press, 1924).
Joule, James Prescott, 'On the mechanical equivalent of heat', *Philosophical Transactions of the Royal Society of London*, vol. 140 (1850), pp. 61–82.
Kant, Immanuel, *Critique of Pure Reason*, trans. F. Max Müeller (London: Macmillan, 1881).
Kennedy, Roy J., 'A refinement of the Michelson–Morley experiment', *Proceedings of the National Academy of Sciences*, vol. 12(11) (1926), pp. 621–9.
Keynes, John Maynard, *Treatise on Probability* (London: Macmillan & Co., 1921).
Langmuir, Irving, 'The arrangement of electrons in atoms and molecules', *Journal of the American Chemical Society*, vol. 41(6) (June 1919), pp. 868–934.
Langmuir, Irving, 'The constitution and fundamental properties of solids and liquids. II. Liquids', *Journal of the American Chemical Society*, vol. 39(9) (September 1917), p. 1848–906.
Laski, Harold J., *On the Study of Politics: An Inaugural Lecture* (London: Humphrey Milford/Oxford University Press, 1926).

Lecky, William Edward Hartpole, *History of European Morals from Augustus to Charlemagne, Volume I*, 3rd edn (New York: D. Appleton and Company, 1895).
Locke, John, *An Essay Concerning Human Understanding*, ed. Alexander Campell Fraser (Oxford: Clarendon Press, 1894).
Lowe, Victor, *Alfred North Whitehead: The Man and His Work, Volume I: 1861–1910* (Baltimore: Johns Hopkins University Press, 1985).
Lowe, Victor, *Alfred North Whitehead: The Man and His Work, Volume II: 1910–1947* (Baltimore: Johns Hopkins University Press, 1990).
Marvin, F.S. (ed.), *Science and Civilization* (London: Humphrey Milford/Oxford University Press, 1923).
Maxwell, James Clerk, *A Treatise on Electricity and Magnetism* (Oxford: Clarendon Press, 1873).
Maxwell, James Clerk, 'Illustrations of the dynamical theory of gases. Part I. On the motions and collisions of perfectly elastic spheres', *Philosophical Magazine*, 4th series, vol. 19(124) (1860), pp. 19–32.
Maxwell, James Clerk, 'Illustrations of the dynamical theory of gases. Part II. On the process of diffusion of two or more kinds of moving particles among one another', *Philosophical Magazine*, 4th series, vol. 20(130) (1860), pp. 21–37.
McDougall, William, *Body and Mind: A History and a Defense of Animism* (New York: Macmillan, 1911).
McDougall, William, *Modern Materialism and Emergent Evolution* (London: Methuen and Co., 1929).
McTaggart, J. M. E., 'Propositions applicable to themselves', *Mind*, vol. 32 (128) (1923), pp. 462–4.
McTaggart, J. M. E., *The Nature of Existence* (Cambridge: Cambridge University Press, 1921).
McTaggart, J. M. E., 'The unreality of time', *Mind*, vol. 68(17) (1908), pp. 457–74.
Metz, Rudolf, *A Hundred Years of British Philosophy* (London: George Allen and Unwin, 1938).
Montague, William P., *The Ways of Knowing or the Methods of Philosophy* (London: George Allen and Unwin, 1925).
Morgan, C. Lloyd, 'A concept of the organism, emergent and resultant', *Proceedings of the Aristotelian Society*, New Series, vol. 27 (1926–7), pp. 141–76.
Morgan, C. Lloyd, *Emergent Evolution* (New York: Henry Holt and Co., 1923).
Morgan, C. Lloyd, 'Objects under reference: the presidential address', *Proceedings of the Aristotelian Society*, New Series, vol. 27 (1926–7), pp. 1–20.
Muirhead, J. H. (ed.), *Bernard Bosanquet and His Friends: Letters Illustrating the Sources and the Development of His Philosophical Opinions* (London: George Allen and Unwin, 1935).
Müller, Max, *Lectures on the Science of Language*, 6th edn, vol. I (London: Longmans, Green, and Co., 1885).
Newton, Isaac, *Newton's Principia: The Mathematical Principles of Natural Philosophy*, trans. Andrew Motte (New York: Daniel Adee, 1846).
Nicholson, J. W., Dorothy Wrinch, F. A. Lindemann and H. Wildon Carr, 'Symposium. The quantum theory: how far does it modify the mathematical, the physical and the psychological concepts of continuity?', *Aristotelian Society Supplementary Volume*, vol. 4(1) (July 1924), pp. 19–49.
O'Toole, Garson, 'They eked out a precarious livelihood by taking in each other's washing', *Quote Investigator*, 5 November 2018, <https://quoteinvestigator.com/2018/11/05/washing/>.
Petek, Joseph, 'Whitehead and Étienne Gilson', Whitehead Research Project website, 10 May 2018, <http://whiteheadresearch.org/2018/05/10/whitehead-and-etienne-gilson/>.
Petek, Joseph, 'Whitehead and Felix Frankfurter', Whitehead Research Project website, 13 November 2019, <http://whiteheadresearch.org/2019/11/13/whitehead-and-felix-frankfurter/>.
Petek, Joseph, 'Whitehead and James Haughton Woods', Whitehead Research Project website, 8 October 2018, <http://whiteheadresearch.org/2018/10/08/whitehead-and-james-haughton-woods/>.
Prichard, Harold Arthur, *Kant's Theory of Knowledge* (Oxford: Clarendon Press, 1909).
Ramsey, F. P., 'Critical notice of L. Wittgenstein's *Tractatus*', *Mind*, vol. 32(128) (October 1923), pp. 465–78.
Robinson, Forrest Glen, *Love's Story Told: A Life of Henry A. Murray* (Cambridge, MA: Harvard University Press, 1992).
Ross, W. D. (ed. and trans.), *Aristotle* (London: Methuen and Co., 1923).
Russell, Bertrand, *Introduction to Mathematical Philosophy* (London: George Allen and Unwin, 1920).
Russell, Bertrand, *Our Knowledge of the External World as a Field for Scientific Method in Philosophy* (London: George Allen and Unwin, 1915).
Russell, Bertrand, *The Analysis of Matter* (London: Kegan Paul, Trench, Trubner, 1927).
Russell, Bertrand, *The Analysis of Mind* (New York: Macmillan, 1921).
Russell, Bertrand, 'The free man's worship', *Independent Review*, vol. 1 (December 1903), 415–24.
Rutherford, Donald, 'Descartes' ethics', *Stanford Encyclopedia of Philosophy* (autumn 2017 edn), ed. Edward N. Zalta, <https://plato.stanford.edu/archives/fall2017/entries/descartes-ethics/>.
Santayana, George, *The Letters of George Santayana, Book Three, 1921–1927*, ed. William G. Holzberger (Cambridge, MA: MIT Press, 2002).
Sheldon, Wilmon Henry, *Strife of Systems and Productive Duality: An Essay in Philosophy* (Cambridge, MA: Harvard University Press, 1918).

Sheldon, Wilmon Henry, 'The spirituality of time', *Journal of Philosophy*, vol. 6(23) (1926), pp. 141–54.
Shook, Lawrence K., *Étienne Gilson* (Toronto: Pontifical Institute of Mediaeval Studies, 1984).
Sidgwick, Henry, *The Methods of Ethics* (London: Macmillan and Co., 1874).
Simon, Peter, *Parts: A Study in Ontology* (Oxford: Clarendon Press, 1987).
Smith, N. K., *A Commentary to Kant's 'Critique of Pure Reason'* (London: Macmillan, 1918).
Smith, Preserved, *Erasmus: A Study of His Life, Ideals, and Place in History* (New York: Frederick Ungar Publishing, 1923).
Smith, W. Robertson, 'Hegel and the metaphysics of the fluxional calculus', *Transactions of the Royal Society of Edinburgh*, vol. 25 (1869), pp. 491–511.
Sölch, Dennis, 'Wheeler and Whitehead: process biology and process philosophy in the early twentieth century,' *Journal of History of Ideas*, vol. 77(3) (2016), pp. 489–507.
Somers, Wayne, *Encyclopedia of Union College History* (Schenectady: Union College Press, 2003).
Spencer, Herbert, *First Principles* (London: Williams and Norgate, 1862).
Thomson, William, 'Nineteenth century clouds over the dynamical theory of heat and light', *Notices of the Proceedings at the Meetings of the Members of the Royal Institution of Great Britain*, vol. 16 (1902), pp. 363–97.
Tyndall, John, 'Scientific materialism', *Fragments of Science: A Series of Detached Essays, Addresses, and Reviews, Volume II*, 6th edn (London: Longman, Greens, and Co., 1879), pp. 75–90.
Weierstrass, Karl, 'Theorie der Abelschen Funktionen', *Journal für die reine und angewandte Mathematik*, vol. 52 (1856), pp. 285–339.
Weierstrass, Karl, 'Zur Theorie der Abelschen Funktionen', *Journal für die reine und angewandte Mathematik*, vol. 47 (1854), pp. 289–306.
Weisstein, Eric W., 'Archimedes' axiom', Wolfram MathWorld, <http://mathworld.wolfram.com/ArchimedesAxiom.html>.
Whitehead, Alfred North, *A Treatise on Universal Algebra* (Cambridge: Cambridge University Press, 1898).
Whitehead, Alfred North, *An Enquiry Concerning the Principles of Natural Knowledge* (Cambridge: Cambridge University Press, 1919).
Whitehead, Alfred North, 'Autobiographical notes', in Paul Schilpp (ed.), *The Philosophy of Alfred North Whitehead* (New York: Tudor, 1941), pp. 3–14.
Whitehead, Alfred North, 'La theorie relationniste de l'espace', *Revue de Métaphysique*, vol. 23(3) (1916), pp. 423–54.
Whitehead, Alfred North, Letter to Bertrand Russell, 16 April 1916, Bertrand Russell Archives, Box 5.54, 710.057471, McMaster University Library, <http://bracers.mcmaster.ca/81695>.
Whitehead, Alfred North, Letter to Bertrand Russell, 18 March 1927, Bertrand Russell Archives, Box 5.54, 710.057486, McMaster University Library, <http://bracers.mcmaster.ca/81738>.
Whitehead, Alfred North, Letter to Edward MacDowell, 10 June 1930, Morris Raphael Cohen Papers 1898–1981, Box 13, Folder 1, University of Chicago Library, <https://www.lib.uchicago.edu/e/scrc/findingaids/view.php?eadid=ICU.SPCL.MRCOHEN>
Whitehead, Alfred North, Letter to J. J. Thomson, 24 March 1918, Sir Joseph John Thomson: Correspondence and Papers, MS Add.7654, W26, Department of Manuscripts and University Archives, Cambridge University Library, <https://janus.lib.cam.ac.uk/db/node.xsp?id=EAD%2FGBR%2F0012%2FMS%20Add.7654>.
Whitehead, Alfred North, Letter to J. J. Thomson, 18 March 1927, Sir Joseph John Thomson: Correspondence and Papers, MS Add.7654, W27, Department of Manuscripts and University Archives, Cambridge University Library, <https://janus.lib.cam.ac.uk/db/node.xsp?id=EAD%2FGBR%2F0012%2FMS%20Add.7654>.
Whitehead, Alfred North, Letter to Macmillan Company, 9 July 1925, MssCol 1830, Macmillan Company records, Series 1 (Author Files), Whitehead, Alfred North, Archives and Manuscripts, New York Public Library, <http://archives.nypl.org/mss/1830#c1048570>.
Whitehead, Alfred North, Letter to Morris Raphael Cohen, 9 June 1930, Morris Raphael Cohen Papers 1898-1981, Box 13, Folder 1, University of Chicago Library, <https://www.lib.uchicago.edu/e/scrc/findingaids/view.php?eadid=ICU.SPCL.MRCOHEN>
Whitehead, Alfred North, Letter to Norman Kemp Smith, 6 April 1927, Papers of Professor Norman Kemp Smith, Coll-1038 Gen.1416.5 ff128–129, Special Collections, University of Edinburgh Library, <http://lac-archives-live.is.ed.ac.uk:8081/repositories/2/resources/416>.
Whitehead, Alfred North, Letter to T. North Whitehead, 25 March 1927, MS 282, Alfred North Whitehead Collection, Box 2, Folder 21, Special Collections, Sheridan Libraries, Johns Hopkins University, <https://catalyst.library.jhu.edu/catalog/bib_505857>.
Whitehead, Alfred North, 'Pocket Engagement Book, 1925–26', MS 282, Alfred North Whitehead Collection, Box 7, Folder 3, Special Collections, Sheridan Libraries, Johns Hopkins University <https://catalyst.library.jhu.edu/catalog/bib_505857>.

Whitehead, Alfred North, *Process and Reality: An Essay in Cosmology*, corrected edn (New York: Free Press, [1929] 1978).
Whitehead, Alfred North, *Religion in the Making* (Cambridge: Cambridge University Press, 1926).
Whitehead, Alfred North, *Science and the Modern World* (New York: Macmillan, 1925).
Whitehead, Alfred North, 'Student Record Book for Harvard and Radcliffe Classes', HUG 4877.10, Papers of Alfred North Whitehead, 1924–1947, Harvard University Archives, <https://id.lib.harvard.edu/ead/c/hua10017c00002/catalog>.
Whitehead, Alfred North, *Symbolism: Its Meaning and Effect* (New York: Macmillan, 1927).
Whitehead, Alfred North, *The Concept of Nature* (Cambridge: Cambridge University Press, 1920).
Whitehead, Alfred North, *The Interpretation of Science: Selected Essays*, ed. A. H. Johnson (Indianapolis: Bobbs-Merrill, 1961).
Whitehead, Alfred North, *The Principle of Relativity with Applications to Physical Science.* (Cambridge: Cambridge University Press, 1922).
Whitehead, Alfred North, 'The principles of probability: Dr Whitehead's report', Papers of John Maynard Keynes, JMK/TP/4, King's College Cambridge Archives, <https://janus.lib.cam.ac.uk/db/node.xsp?id=EAD%2FGBR%2F0272%2FPP%2FJMK%2FTP%2F4>.
Whitehead, Alfred North, 'Time', in Edgar Sheffield Brightman (ed.), *Proceedings of the Sixth International Congress of Philosophy* (New York: Longmans, Green and Co., 1927), pp. 59–64.
Whitehead, Alfred North, and Bertrand Russell, *Principia mathematica*, 2nd edn (Cambridge: Cambridge University Press, 1925).
Whitehead, Alfred North, et al., *Symposium in Honor of the Seventieth Birthday of Alfred North Whitehead* (Cambridge, MA: Harvard University Press, 1932).
Wittgenstein, Ludwig, *Tractatus Logico-Philosophicus* (London: Routledge and Kegan Paul, 1922).

Index

Note. Greek words and letters are alphabetised as if spelled in English (e.g., φύσις as phusis, σ as sigma). Note-takers' unconventional spellings are indexed under conventional spellings, e.g. σ' (notes) is indexed as σ-prime (as in Whitehead's published work).

A Course in Philosophy (Conger) (1924), xlvii, 436
'A Free Man's Worship' (Russell) (1903), 66n8
A Hundred Years of British Philosophy (Metz) (1938), 187n4
a priori
  criteria of, 8, 52
  and critical philosophy, 52
  and necessity, 8
  and rationalism, 52
  and sceptical empiricism, 52
  and universality, 8
a priori see also antecedent, 8
abnormality, as cause of error, 152
absolute, 397n1
  of Hegel, 208n2
  versus relativity, 134
absolute determinism, 113n4
abstract
  community as, 93
  characteristics, of concrete relationships, 303
  and concrete, 43, 127, 127n4, 387
  demonstration, and certainty in science, 184
  entity *see* entity, abstract
  and experient occasion, 43
  extension as, 300
  forms, and perceptual versus conceptual functioning, 193
  fitting particular to, 132
  and future, 33
  ideas, relations of, 160
  abstract identity, 102, 102n10
  and knowledge, 43
  multiplicity as, 326
  sets, 149
  space as, 127
  thought, 6, 335
  universals as, 18

abstraction, 126
  and activity, 44
  and actual, 333
  and actual occasion, 112
  from actuality, 44
  blindness to, 126
  complex of, 303
  and concretion, 104, 105
  criticism of, 175
  versus datum, 96
  defined, 31, 104
  in Dewey, 342n3
  as difficulty, 58
  and diversity, 237
  and entity, 78, 149, 237
  versus example, 134
  and eternal objects, 44
  extensive, 148, 304
  and extensive continuum, 319
  extensive relationship as, 305
  fact as, 166 n1
  as factor in concrete, 151n1
  from ground, 114
  importance of, 123n1
  it as, 114
  justification of, 10
  knowledge as, 45
  and lack of interest, 126
  of language, 126
  levels of, 116
  limitation by, 33
  love of, 126
  mathematics as, 326
  notion of, 363–6
  and number, 124, 134–5
  and occasion, 10, 66n3
  and philosophy, 126, 175
  and Plato, 10
  and possibility, 18
  progress of, 126
  and proposition, 363–4
  and relation, 98
  relational character of, 43
  and some and all, 333
  space and time as, 127
  as starting point, 125
  and types of order, 134–5
  and universe, 335
  of value, 135, 135n3
  and *what* and *how,* 114–15
  versus world, 99
'Abstraction', in *Science and the Modern World,* 6, 6n4
abstractive class, 150
  and π, 148

  converging to a line, 325
  and covering, 321, 321*fig,* 323, 324, 325
  defined, 148, 148*fig,* 319
  equal, 325, 325*fig*
  and geometrical element, 148, 322
  locus of, 157
  in moment, 157
  overlapping, 326
  and physics, 148
  of point, 326
  as prime, 324
  and route of approximation, 148, 322
  shading, 326
  sharpest, 325
abstractive geometrical class, defined, 157
abstractness, and concreteness, 11n8
acceleration
  and Einstein, 154
  and *natura naturata,* 87 n1
  and relative motion, 154
  and rest, 154, 154n3
accelerative state, 154
accuracy
  and actual things, 116
  as art of life, 116
  and convergence to nothing, 148
  defined, 117
  and definite fact, 125
  as definite truth, 120
  of definitions, 205
  and extension, 294
  and extensiveness, 113n6
  goal of, 312
  and Greeks, 117, 117n1
  idea of, 147
  ideal of, 294, 312
  importance of, 127
  and individual versus community, 115–16
  limits of, 318
  and logic, 171n4
  and measurement, 113n3, 294, 409
  and nature, 113
  and omission, 129, 129n2
  and order of points, 130
  possibility of, 113, 113n3
  and relationships to entities, 116

Index

routes of approximation to, 315
and simplicity, 147
and space and time, 127
achievement
  and achieving, 83
  and actual, 82
  character evolved in, 83
  defined, 34
  and graduality, 101n3
  and limitation, 34, 103
  and occasion, 34, 101
  synthesis as, 31
act
  and atomic creatures, 290
  of being alive, thickness of, 240
  creativity as, 94
  pure, 232
  specific, 232
action
  appeal to, 191
  in atom, 40
  atomicity of, 93
  versus explanation, 177
  by historic route, 357
  in Kant, 12
  quantum of *(h)*, 91, 93, 93n1
  and rationalism, 191
  and science, 177
action, and emotion and belief, 191
action, emotion, belief, rationalisation cycle, 401–2
action at a distance, 38, 87, 88, 88*fig*, 183, 183n2, 357
activity
  and abstraction, 44
  and actual, 34, 333
  and actuality, 209
  attributes of, 18
  conceptual, defined, 344
  creation as process of, 210
  creative, 210, 297
  as creativity, 209
  and creature, 100n4
  data of, and eternal objects, 100
  of element, 209
  and energy, 89, 91
  and entity, 196, 296, 230, 344
  immediate, 36, 333
  knowing of, 31
  and mass, 89, 90
  and metaphysics, 18, 44
  and motion, 89
  in occasion, 62
  physical, as blind perceptivity, 344
  process as, 146
  and relationship, 196, 196n2
  and Spinoza, 18
  and substance, 297
  substantial, and occasion, 34
  through time, 93
  ultimate achievement as, 30

and ultimate entity, 30, 78
and universals, 333
world of, as atomic, 334
acts, objectified for other acts, 282
actual
  and abstraction, 333
  and accuracy, 116
  and activity, 34, 333
  analysis of, 82
  complexity of, 335
  consequent as, 105
  in creative achievement, 102
  as creative passage, 378
  creature as, 216
  defined, 30, 36, 85, 207, 209n4, 220
  as enjoying time, 259
  and epoch, 102n3
  versus essential, 62
  exemplification of potential by, 333
  future as not, 33
  how of, 217–18
  and ideal, 62, 212, 215
  importance of, 209
  and incompleteness, 125
  and individuality, 112
  and knowledge, 42, 219–20
  and limitation, 222
  and metaphysics, 18–19, 207
  necessity of defining, 213
  not yet actual included in, 252
  and past, 34
  and possibility, 18–19
  and possible, 19, 32
  and potential, 332, 334, 336, 337
  there and then as, 59
  time not becoming of, 259
  and value, 215
  as Whitehead's characteristic word, 212
actuality
  abstraction from, 44
  and activity, 209
  becomingness of, 37
  conditions for, 243
  and contrast and unity, 101
  and creativity, 110
  defined, 101, 215
  degrees of, 100, 213, 246, 246n5
  depth of, 73, 99, 104, 231–2
  and function, 36
  and future, 84
  gradations of, 104, 197
  gradations of intensity in, 213, 243
  versus indeterminations, 18
  and intensive quantity, 98
  and limitation, 116, 217–18
  of past, 33
  and *percipiens*, 30–1
  and possibility, 9, 66, 260

potential, actual from, 336
and potentiality, 218, 218n4
private ground of, 335
of substance, 246n5
and synthesis, 335
and systematic character, 274
undifferentiated, 101n1
and unity, 366
Adams, John Couch, 412, 412n3
addition, 338, 338*fig*
  defined, 139
  and equality, problem of, 125
  idea of, 132, 132n5
adequacy
  as test of belief, 181
  of ideas, 177, 179, 181
adjunction, 144
adventure
  and philosophy, 292
  and substance, 348n2
  as semi-reality, 125
  and truth, 292
Adventures of Ideas (Whitehead) (1933), viii
Aesop's fable of dog with leg of mutton, 374
aesthetic congruence, and analysis, 377
aesthetic individuality
  and ingression, 226
  as principle of metaphysics, 210
  as self-satisfying process, 218
  defined, 210
  principle of, 215, 218, 220
aesthetic intensity
  and individual actuality, 243
  and self-consciousness, 378n1
  and synthesis, 377, 377n6
aesthetic value, 215
aesthetics
  of logic, 118n2, 119n1
  of mathematics, 186
  in philosophy, 192
  and psychology, 118
  of Santayana, 235
  and science, 118, 124, 124n3
  transcendental, 176
  and types of order, 135
after
  and now, 70, 375
  versus before, 22, 70
Against the [Character] Assassin at Dresden (Luther) (1531), 73n7
age, versus youth, 182
agency, requiring nothing but itself, 397
Aims of Education (Whitehead) (1929), viii
Aladdin, 206, 207, 220
Alciphron, or the Minute Philosopher (Berkeley) (1732), as assigned reading, 4, 47

445

Index

alcoholic ward, 349
Alexander the Great, 118, 118n5
Alexander, Samuel, 124, 246, 246n1, 436
   assigned reading from, xxviii, 3
   biographical note on, 3n6, 46–7n7
   compresence in, 262n4
   disagreement with, 125
   and emergent evolution, 299
   Gifford Lectures of, 46–7n7
   influence of, on Whitehead, xxxii, 124n8, 372
   and space and time, 159
   time taken seriously by, 259
algebra, as two-dimensional, 369–70
Alice's Adventures in Wonderland (Carroll) (1865), 235n4, 380–1
all and none, principle of, 6, 6n3
American Philosophical Association, meeting of, xxix–xxx
analysis
   and actual entity, 376, 376n6
   and concepts, 354
   conceptual, and conscious memory, 254n1
   by conceptual functioning, 355
   of creature, 43
   and experience, 376n6
   of fact, 198
   and genus, 90
   how of, and eternal object, 352
   how to discipline, 377
   as introduction of order, 166
   knowledge from, 50–1
   mathematical, versus literary approach, 244–5
   and occasion, 19, 354
   of primary substance, 146
   principle of, and judgement, 50
   of proposition, 379
   sensory data as products of, 342
   as test of belief, 181
   and universal, 58
Analysis of Matter (Russell) (1927), 189n3
Analysis of Mind (Russell) (1921), as assigned reading, 3, 47
analytic, and synthetic, 381–2
analytical expression, as ideal, 191
and, as abstract entity, 113, 114
and, propositional, 370
animal faith, 242, 242n1, 296
animals, always draw tame, 312
animals, domestic, 405, 177, 177n4
animals, transformation of, 405
Anschauung (intuition)
   as blind, 108
   in Kant, 114n2

antecedent, 8
   and consequent, 11, 256
   and endurance, 74
   and entity, 299, 299n6
   eternal object as, 34
   explanatory found in, 262
   history, conformation of entity to, 261
   and incompleteness, 256
   versus present, 285
   life, primary knowledge of, 79–80, 80n1
   as limitation, 34
   versus sequent, 156
   and simultaneity, 257
   and time, 255
   see also a priori
anti-intellectualism, 4n5
anticipation
   as blind fact, 344
   of entity, 262
   versus repetition, 107
antiprime, as convergence, 156
any, as mathematical concept, 137
Apollonius of Perga, 118, 118n5
Apollonius of Perga (Heath) (1896), 118n5
Apollonius of Perga: Treatise on Conic Sections (Heath) (1896), 7, 118n5
appearance, world as phenomenon of, 259
apprehension
   blind, 108
   and cognition, 62
   of object, 68
   and occasion, 242
   and physical influence, 374
   and prehension, 62n5, 243
   of presentational relationships, 153
approximation
   and community of durations, 157
   and extension, 319
   methods of, 318, 318*fig*, 319
   proposition for, 323
   route of, 145, 147, 148, 315
approximation theorem, 180n3
Aquinas, Thomas, 267, 347–8n7
Arabian Nights, 33, 33n3, 177, 206, 207
Archimedes
   axiom of, 122, 122n6, 338
   and philosophy of science, 4
   and scientific state of mind, 4
architecture
   and environment, 16
   Gothic, 16, 20
   and religious art, 64n1
   and selection, 63, 63n6
   and volume, 16, 63n6

area
   as most concrete fact, 313
   measurement of, 134, 134*fig*
   versus point, 313
Aristotelians, and philosophy of science, 9
Aristotle
   actual and value in, 215
   assigned reading from, xxviii
   and being, 6
   and being and not-being, 81, 101n7
   and categories, 15, 123, 123n2, 266
   and Chinese language, 201
   and concrete entity, 13
   and Descartes, 114
   and drama, 292
   and enduring entity, 13, 63n2
   and ethics, 60, 63, 397
   and facts, 124
   and final cause, 5
   and final ends, 397
   and general versus specific, 81
   and language, 114, 174, 174n3, 200–1, 201n1
   and laws of motion, 411, 411n4, 411n5
   and logic, 5, 6, 60, 63n2, 149, 363, 370
   and mathematical philosophy, 183
   and mathematics, 81
   in medieval philosophy, 87
   and metaphysics, 6, 60, 94
   not typical Aristotelian, 203, 203n2
   and object of perception, 80
   and occasion, 55, 61
   and one versus many, 13
   and philosophy of science, 4
   physics of, 7, 52, 410, 411, 411n2, 411n4, 411n5
   and Plato, 114, 183
   and point, 313, 314, 317
   and politics, 183
   presentational point of view of, 32
   and process, 6, 86
   qualities in, 378
   and quantity, 140
   and reality, 125
   and relation, 98, 98n8
   and science, 81
   and scientific state of mind, 4
   and spatial relationship, 144
   and subject–predicate form, 203, 289
   subjectivism in, 53
   and substance, 86, 125, 146
   time and creativity in, 100
   and universals, 43
   and unmusical man, 98–9n10
   and view of universe, 292

Index

Aristotle (Ross) (1923), 98–99n10
  as assigned reading, 4, 47
arithmetic, and science, 177
arithmetical operations, 331
art
  and actual occasion, 16
  Chinese, 16
  and context, 16
  defined, 62
  and end in itself
  endurance of 16, 63
  versus ethics, 15–16, 60
  as exclusion, 44
  and extrusion, 62
  and God, 60
  and immediate prehension, 15
  and immediate value, 15
  impress of, 63
  individuality of, 63
  Italian Renaissance, 16
  and limitation, 62–4
  and limiting occasions, 16
  and metaphysics, 62
  motive and responsibility in, 63
  nature of, 16
  philosophical implications of, 15
  realism in, 66n8, 166n1
  religious, 16, 64, 64n1
  as selection, 63
  as succession, 15
  and value, 16, 63, 63n8
  and vividness of contrast, 243
  vitality of, 16
artist
  and entities, 18
  and eternal objects, 66
assigned reading
  Alexander, 3, 46, 124, 246, 246n1, 436
  Aristotle, xxviii
  Bergson, xxviii, 4, 47
  Berkeley, xxviii, 4, 47
  Broad, xxviii, xxix, 3, 46, 168, 189n2, 293, 293In3
  Burtt, 293
  Descartes, xxviii, 4, 47, 170, 172n6, 187n1
  Dewey, John, viii, xxviii, 46, 46n6, 171, 171n9, 172n6, 187n1
  Hume, xxviii, 4, 47
  James, xxviii, 4
  Locke, 170
  Morgan, 293
  Ross, 4, 47
  Russell, xxviii, 3, 46, 47, 47n1, 126
  Whitehead, xxviii, 3, 46, 121, 171, 171n3, 172n6, 178n4, 293
astronomy
  and Galileo, 394, 403, 411
  and Kepler, 410, 412, 412fig
  and Newton, 403, 412
  and physics, 411
  progress in, 403
atom
  and action, 41, 91
  behaviour of, 39
  and creative act, 41
  defined, 91
  density in, 91
  energy of, 92, 92n7
  and ether, 92, 92n3
  as electricity, 90
  functioning of, 39, 40
  how to study, 92
  as incomplete, 350
  life of, 350
  mass of, 90, 90eq
  as material, 90
  and matter, 39
  nucleus of, 90
  as organism, 90
  part of, 89
  partial, 90
  periodicity of, 91, 92fig
  primates of, 40, 91
  quantum character of, 41, 41n2, 92, 92fig
  real, 350
  relations between species of, 91
  size of, 90, 91–92, 92eq
  size of, equations for, 90, 92
  species of, 91
  structure of, 39, 41, 41fig, 91, 91fig, 295
atomic
  actual entities as, 218
  conceptions, in physical science, 112
  versus continuous, 149
  entity, time as, 11
  world of activities as, 334
atomic theory, 39, 91–2
  biology in, 90–1
  chemistry in, 90
  and Dalton, 39, 39n1
  physics in, 90
  rise of, 90–1
atomicity
  and becoming, 366
  and continuity, 147, 182, 295–6, 350
  and electromagnetism, 182
  and nature, 366
  and science, 11, 35, 35n5, 182, 366
  in Semitic philosophy, 182
atomism
  versus continuity, 153
  and extension, 88
  and subject–predicate view, 266
  in science, 90
atomless gunk, 316n1

attention, effect of, 261
attentiveness, and imagination, 199
attribute
  as entity, 396
  versus identity, 362
  and substance, 211
Augustine, and grace, 292
average, fallacy of, 149
awareness, 236, 237
axioms
  of Archimedes, 122, 122n6
  discovery of, by Pythagoreans, 131
  of divisibility, 121
  of Euclid, 120
  versus belief, 191
  and extension, 293
  of infinity, 332
  method for discovering, 184, 185
  in mathematics, 189n6
  as specific to occasion, 185

background
  and figure, 257
  systematic, and objectification, 257
  universe as, 363
Bacon, Francis, 409, 410
  approach of, to universe, 291
  and Cohen, 193, 193n5
  and efficient cause, 5
  and final cause, 5
  versus Kant, 193
  and observation, 176, 176n1
  and science, 5, 193–4, 193n3, 193–4n5
Bacon, Roger, as scientist, 409
Barbour-Page lectures, xxxii, 335n1
becoming
  atomic, 153, 366
  and being and not being, 251, 344
  and continuity, 268, 346, 347, 350, 366
  of creatures, 290
  defined, 344
  and duration, 260
  as epoch, 84
  epochal theory of, 153
  and graduality, 101n3
  of relationships of future of past, 34
  and supersession, 346
  and time, 84, 88, 94, 350
  of unit, 44
becomingness
  of actuality, 37
  and continuity, 85, 86
  and enduring substances, 36
  epochal, 85n4
  as gradual, 36, 85n4

447

Index

versus realisation, 11
versus time, 162
time depth in, 85
and ultimate entities, 86
before
  and after, 22, 70
  and now, 70, 375
beginning
  absence of, in time, 240
  versus end, 11, 56
behaviour
  expression of, of mass, 37
  and final datum, 33
  and nature, 87
being
  of actual occasion, 82
  and Aristotle, 101n7
  as being actual, 86
  dimension of, and measurability, 103n4
  versus genera, 227
  modal limitation of, 61
  and not being, 6, 32, 51, 81, 251, 344
  and occasion, 299
  as perception, 41, 41n1
  thought as dimension of, 103, 103n3
Being and Time (Heidegger) (1927), xliii
belief
  and action and emotion, 191
  versus axiom, 191
  concurrence in, 180
  belief, defined, 147
  formulation of, 180
  intensity of, 180
  irrationality of, 242
  and morality, cycle of, 401
  necessary, 180
  versus obviousness, 191
  as a particular, 379
  and philosophy, 179, 179n1
  versus practice, 191–2
  and rationalism, 191
  tests for, 179–181
belief, analysis of
  and Christianity, 188, 188n2
  and Greeks, 188, 188n2
  and logical coherence, 188, 188n2
Bell, Winthrop Pickard, lx
Beman, Wooster Wodruff, 328n1
Bergson, Henri, 251n5, 269, 281
  assigned reading from, xxviii, 4
  biographical note on, 4n5, 47n7
  canalisation in, 237
  versus Descartes, 205n1
  durée in, 11, 11–12n2, 240, 240n3, 343, 346
  and flow, 57
  influence of, on Whitehead, 47n7

and morphological view, 76
and space, 150
and time, 57
and universe, 301
Berkeley, George (Bishop)
  assigned reading from, xxviii, 4
  and Hume, 171n10
  and immediately given, 6
  and knowing, 30, 31, 78, 78n2
  and knowledge of world as symbolism, 187
  and perception as being, 41, 41n1
  and science, 291
  as well-rounded, 126n5
Bernstein–Schroeder theorem, 330, 330n4
Bernstein, Felix, 330n4
beyond
  as contrast of parts, 125
  and events, 147
  of future occasion, 82
  and here, 132
  knowledge of, 132
  limitation on, 12
  and time and space, 272–3
beyondness, 6; *see also* not-being
  and community, 59
  of immediate instance, 49
  nature as, 64
  not-being as, 6, 51
  and particular occasion, 6
  and past, 64
  self in, 13
  and synthesis, 59
bifurcation
  in Descartes, 74
  in Galileo, 74, 110n2
  and metaphysics, 375
  of nature, 79n5, 110, 217, 349, 361, 366
  in Newton, 87
  theories of, 162
billiard ball atoms, 295, 413
billiard ball theory, 37, 87
binding relation, 367
biology
  cell theory in, 39
  elements in, 341–2, 342n1
  and functional view, 30, 77–78
  and morphology, 76
  as science, 75
Birkhoff, Garrett, xxx
blind apprehension, 108
blind conation, metaphysical basis of, 106
blind intention, 114n2
blind intuition, 108, 219, 250n5, 343
  concrescence of 250
  and conceptual functioning, 219, 219n3
  defined, 343
  and occasion, 351

blind perceptivity, 45, 108n1, 110, 165, 219, 223–4, 352
  defined, 250n5, 400
  and entities, 250n5
  and objects, 344
  molecule as, 243n1
  and objectification, 400
  and occasions, 250n5, 343, 351, 352
  and organisation, 343
blind perceptual relationships, 223
blind prehension, 108
boa constrictor in Paddington station, 181n5
Body and Mind: A History and a Defense of Animism (McDougall) (1915), 97n2
body, 381
  and Descartes, 99, 353
  and electron, 247, 263
  versus event, 160
  and knowing, 76n3
  and mind, 164, 248, 249n4, 352-7
  and self, 298
  in space, motion of, 283
  and substance, 172n2, 204, 396
  state of, 263, 296, 296n1
  unity of, and unity of mental occasion, 167
bodies, continuous, 413
Boniface VIII, 212n1
Bosanquet, Bernard, 15, 15n1, 187, 187n4, 211, 291
  and finite truth, 99n1
  and individuality, 15
  Whitehead's evaluation of, 15n1
Boscovich, Roger Joseph, 295, 295n3
bounded *see also* unbounded, 64
Bradley, F. H., 83, 144, 172n1, 211, 262, 365, 389
  and absolute idealism, 208, 208n2
  and appearance versus reality, 51
  and finite truth, 99n1
  and function of knowing, 52
  and immediate experience, 167, 167n3
  and proposition, 202
  and science, 291
  and sense data, 223
brain
  and consciousness, 96n3
  memory in, 76, 349
  and perception, 76
  and sense data, 76
  waggling of, 76, 254, 349
Braithwaite, Richard Bevan, 232n1

brass tacks, 265
British empiricists, and relatedness, 235, 236n1
Broad, C. D.
  assigned reading from, xxviii, 3, 168
  biographical sketch of, xxviii–xxix, 3n4, 46n5
  as foil for Whitehead, 46n5
  and future, 80, 271
  importance of, to Whitehead, xxviii–xxix
  and mathematical method, 192, 192n2
  as new realist, 187n4
  qualification of future in, 251
  as realist, 187
  versus Russell, 74
  substance in, 86
  Tarner lectures of, 189n3
Brown, Sarah H., 383, 383n2
Bruno, Giordano, 409n6
Burch, George Bosworth, lv
Burtt, Edwin Arthur, 293n5, 294, 294n1, 408

c (velocity of light in a vacuum), 91, 92
Cabot, Richard Clark, lvi, lvii, lviii–lix
  biographical sketch of, lviii
  introduction by, of Whitehead, 391
  wealth of, lviii, lix, lixn1
  Whitehead's attendance at lectures of, xxxi
Caesar, crossing Rubicon, 161, 168, 253, 365, 379n3, 380n2, 381
  as event, 255
  as fact, 235
Caird, Edward
  biographical sketch of, 172n1
  and Kant, 172
  and relatedness, 235, 236n1
  and Whitehead, 172n1
calculus
  limit of route of approximation in, 315
  limits in, 316n1
  and Newton, 88
  and time, 12
calculus, differential
  and physics, 88
  problems in, 137n1
Calvin, John, 292
Cambridge Apostles, vii
Cambridge realists, mistakes of, 235
Cambridge, University of, vii
canalisation, 237
Cantor, Georg, 316, 316n1, 329, 330n4
  and continuity, 209n2

and irrational numbers, 124
and theory of order types, 129, 129n6
Cantor set, 330n1
Cantor–Bernstein–Schroeder theorem, 330n4
Carr, Herbert Wildon, 436, 436n2
Cartesian dualism, 18–19, 31, 42, 164, 194, 239
Cartesian geometry, 124
Cartesian materialism, 163
Cartesian metaphysics, alternative to, 210
Cartesian philosophy
  and spatial relationship, 144
  collapse of, 42
  versus process, 146
Cartesian rationalism, versus modern rationalism, 185
Cartesian subjectivism, 163
Cartesian substance, actual entity as, 233
Cartesian system
  arbitrariness of, 88
  importance of, 87
categories
  and Aristotle, 15, 266
  exemplified in circumstances, 174
Catholic Controversy, 292
Cauchy, Augustin-Louis, 316n1
causal efficacy
  and locality, 337
  and occasion, 362
  before presentational immediacy, 337
  as prior to concepts, 337
  and sense data, 337
causal independence, and simultaneous events, 255
causal mode, 109
causal relations
  of events, 352
  of entity, 272, 272n1
  as internal relationship, 256
  mutual, defined, 22
  and past and future, 352
  of past and present, 107
  and science, 274
causality
  as becomingness of organic determination, 163
  and ground, 110
  and Hume, 108
  as inspectional relationship, 73n8
  and morphological view, 77
  physical, 155
  principle of, 207
  and relation of substances, 204
  and relative future, 156n5
  in science, 112

causation
  analysis of, memory as, 254
  consciousness of, and memory, 254
  defined, 270
  efficient versus final, 410
  and entity, 348
  and Hume, 107, 393, 400
  and memory, 270, 345, 349, 400
  as objective immortality, 254, 345
  physical, 257
  physical memory as, 254
  and proposition, 381, 382
  and supersession, 218
  theory of, and imaginal occasion, 69
  and time, 255
cause, efficient
  and Bacon, 5
  and final cause, 5
  and immediate occasion, 59–60
  as synthesis, 59–60
cause, final
  and Aristotle, 5
  and Bacon, 5
  defined, 5
  doctrine of, 80
  and efficient cause, 5
  and immediate occasion, 59–60
  as value, 59–60
cause and effect, 48–9
  and antecedent and consequent, 256
  and anti-rationalistic bias, 49
  medieval view of, 48
Celestine V, 212
cell theory, 39
cell, 90
centaur, 382
change
  in Aristotle, 98–9n10
  in concrete entity, 246
  continuity of, 246–7
  and identity, 247n3
  pattern in, 247
  and succession of facts, 246
character
  and creation, 34
  as creature or creativity, 356
  determined, and future, 34
  and extension, 268
  in occasions, 112
  and process, 401
  special, independence of, 255
character, general
  and creativity, 230
  and general creature, 214
character, internal, inspection of, 80

449

Index

characteristic
  endurance as, 361
  extension as, 361
  general, how to define, 308
Charles I, 69
chemistry, as continuous, 182
China
  civilisation of, 408
  philosophy in, 182
  science as pragmatic pursuit in, 177, 177n2
  scientific state of mind in, 5
Chinese art, 16
Chinese boxes, and proposition, 386
Chinese grammar, 114
Chinese language
  and philosophy, 114, 174, 174n3, 201
  symbols for ideas in, 310
Chinese literature, and selection, 63
Christianity
  and analysis of belief, 188, 188n2
  and Descartes, 63
  in medieval philosophy, 87
  and substance, 146
Church, and science, 5
cigar holder, 436
civilisation, progressive, 408, 409
clarity
  and Greeks, 127
  importance of, 435
  of ideas, 179, 180
Clarke, Samuel, 295, 295n2
class
  completed, 246
  connections in, 367
  defined, 368, 381
  defining, 311
  of disparate entities, 367–8
  diversity and similarity in, 121, 121fig
  entity as member of, 120–121, 120fig, 121
  and extensive connection, 308
  hereditary, 332
  how to define, 368, 369
  infinite, and correlation, 129–30, 141, 331
  and multiplicity, 326, 370
  number as antecedent to, 326
  numbers in, 331
  of ordinal types, 367
  point defined by, 149
  and predicate, 367, 370
  as proposition, 368
  reflexive, 332
  subclasses in, 330
  and unity, 368
class index, 330
class theory, 74

classes
  comparison of different, 326
  correlation of parts of, 141, 142
  correlation of parts of, proof for, 142–3
  covering by, 145
  as entities, 367
  infinite number of, 330
  and mathematics, 370
  and propositions, 367
  separation between, 173
classification
  in Aristotle, 123, 123n2
  and extension, 113, 113n5
  and measurement, 124, 124n4
Clerk Maxwell, James see Maxwell, James Clerk
Clifford, William Kingdon, 327n1
  and finite number, 329
Cobb, John B., Jr, xli
code
  and social evolution, 243–4
  utility of, 243–4
cogitation
  and awareness, 237
  as consciousness of diversity, 236–7
  and Descartes, 53, 57
  and fact, 237
  and Hume, 57
  and substance, 94
cogito ergo sum, 30, 53, 74241
cognisance see also knowing, 52
  and actual occasion, 52
  and experiential occasion, 53
  and imaginal occasion, 53
  particular occasion of, 6
cognita
  and actual entity, 31
  inspection of, 32
  knowing, 30
  and one, 31–2
  versus percipiens, 31
  and ultimate fact, 31
cognition, 81
  act of, 59
  and apprehension, 62
  and experient occasion, 81
  and general scheme, 81
  of itself, 64
  and Kant, 81
  and knowledge, 22
  and occasion, 22, 59, 64
  and one versus many, 13
  and relatedness, 32
  and Whitehead, 81
cognitor, 58
cognitum, 58
  analysis of, 78
  characteristics of, 60
  defined, 31
  described, 58–9

  and eternal objects, 60
  and knowing, 31, 78
  as known, 78
  as percipiens, 31
  and subjects, 60
Cohen, Felix S., 193–4n5
Cohen, Morris Raphael, 192, 193–4n5
coherence, of ideas, 177
coherence criterion, 355
coincidence
  and present occasions, 23
  measurement as, 273, 274
collision theory, 89
color patch, and table, 76
Columbia University, 435, 435n4
Commentary to Kant's 'Critique of Pure Reason' (Kemp Smith) (1918), 8, 8n2, 52
Committee of Four (Harvard), xxx
common sense
  and common place, 307n2
  in Descartes, 360
  and rationalism, 174
  and reasoning, 305
  and science, 49, 409
Common Sense of the Exact Sciences (Clifford) (1885), 327, 327n1
communion of electrons, 216
communion of saints, 216
community see also scheme, general
  as abstract, 93
  as actual, 32
  and actual occasion, 82
  and analysis of real world, 81
  and being and not-being, 32
  and beyondness, 59
  defined, 13
  differentiation in, 153
  dimensional, 155
  and diversity, 160, 160n2
  and durational relationships, 153–4, 154fig
  and entity, 93, 115
  and event, 14–15
  and experient occasion, 65
  and extension, 156, 160, 163
  extensive, 153, 163
  of extensiveness, 150
  and extensive relation, 160
  and historical route, 101n5
  and Hume, 58
  ideal, 114
  and immediate occasion, 13, 14, 168
  and individual, 93, 115–16, 153
  and induction, 58
  and *it*, 114
  and limitations, 21
  lower, 61

450

and metaphysics, 18
and multiplicity, 13, 14
necessity of, 58
as never finished, 32, 81
and occasion, 10, 13–14, 19, 32, 56, 61, 68–9
partial, 59
and perceiving, 93
and physical world, 160, 160 *n*1
and process, 146
and reality, 146
relations of occasions in, 20
relationships of entities to, 153, 279
and subject, 60
total, 21, 22
and truth, 58
units in, 32
and unit occasion, 32, 81
unit multiplicities in, 93
and unity, 18, 69
upper, 61
of value, 62
of world, 21, 160, 333
community of durations, and approximation, 157
community of entities, constitution of, 144
community of occasions *see* occasions, community of
comparison
and imagination, 230
no form of, 251
and theory of knowledge, 219
and theory of morals, 219
yes and no forms of, 226
yes or no form, 230
compass, invention of, 408
complete in itself, 211, 256, 359
completeness
in community of occasions, 253
of entity, 257
as eternal form, 351
nature as abstraction from, 335
objectivity as abstraction from, 335
of past, 352
and time, 349, 349*n*1
versus totality, 349
completion, and prehension, 344–5
complex, explained by simple, 100, 100*n*5, 100*n*6
complexity
in entity, 260
of logically simple things, 128
possibility in, 261
and time, 250
of universe, and time, 250
complications, and simplicity, 128
compresence
in Alexander, 262*n*4
and causal dependence, 263

of entity, 262
possibilities of, 263, 263*fig*
and presupposition, 262
conation
and inheritance, 106
and value, 12
concept
and actual world as a possibility, 167
and analysis of percept, 176, 251
as analytic and correlative, 400
defined, 354
and eternal object, 199, 289, 354–5, 400
as function, 352*n*1
and functioning, 198, 219, 354–5
and identity, 347
matter of, 198
and mental occasion, 199
as mental, 166
as mind analysing, 355
in occasion, 172–3, 199
and percept, 219, 224, 224*n*1, 251, 377
synthesised in immediate occasion, 165
synthesising itself, 251
universal, value of, 174
Concept of Nature (Whitehead) (1920), viii, 7, 150, 150*n*1, 201, 251, 313, 341
as assigned reading, 3, 46, 121, 293
eternal objects in, 351
perceptivity as physical in, 217
supersession in, 351
and Tarner lectures, xxviii, 189*n*3
Concept of Time (Heath) (1936), xxxvii
concepts
as analytical, 354
causal efficacy prior to, 337
classes of, 173
discovery of, 173
exemplification in, 172–3, 174
exceptionally applicable to occurrences, 173
and history of philosophy, 55
and history of science, 173*n*8
importance of, 174
infinity of, 172–3
and laws, 173, 174*n*2
as modes of functioning, 195
and perspectivity of body, 167, 167*fig*
science as system of, 50
taste for, 173
truth of, 50
concepts, dramatic, 173–4
concepts, fundamental, analysis and definition of, 189

concepts, general, 173
disciplined method for, 176
exemplification of, 186
and language, 174
specific determinations of, 175
concepts, generic, 175, 176
concepts, necessary, 173, 173*n*4
concepts, ordinary, 173, 173*n*4
concepts, philosophical, 176
concepts, relevant, 173
concepts, scientific, 176
concepts, universal, 173; *see also* concepts, generic
conception
and substance, 341*n*4
in Descartes, 341*n*4
versus perception, 193
conceptivity, analysing perceptivity, 162
conceptual
origin of, 299
and perceptual, 299
conceptual activity
of Kant, 317
and physical sensibility, 359
conceptual analysis, supersession of perception by, 249
conceptual functioning
and analysis, 355
and abstract forms, 193
and eternal objects, 193
and mental occasion, 197
and perceptual functioning, 197
and perceptual ingression, 230
and synthesis, 377
conceptual harmony, 221, 222
conceptual vagueness, 186, 186*n*4
concomitance, and correlation, 374
concrescence
activity of, 213
of actual entity, 196, 217
actual occasion as, 216, 216*n*10
and creativity, 207
and demonstration, 226
in Descartes, 206
doctrine of, 216
and entity, 364, 365
how of, and eternal object, 352
under limitation, 206
and objectification, 226
occasion as, 399
process of, 230, 230*n*1
of universe, 196
and value, 207, 207*n*1
concrete
and abstract, 43, 387
abstraction as factor in, 151*n*1
occupying abstract, 127, 127*n*4
thought as analogue of, 126

451

Index

concreteness
  and abstractness, 113n8
  idea of, 128–9
  concretion
    actual occasion as, 401
  and abstraction, 104, 105
  and actual thing, 207, 207n1
  components of, 53
  of concrete, 53
  and creature versus creativity, 104
  datum for, 104
  defined, 53, 104
  as emergent entity, 9
  as essence, 53
  and eternal objects, 104
  how to describe, 9
  mental occasion as, 165
  of mental, physical, and perceptual functioning, 198
  objectification, prehension of, 344
  occasion as, 58
  of occasions, 55
  as possibility, 9
  and possible world, 104
  as real, 9
  versus synthesis, 104
conditions
  general versus particular, 131
  partial versus impartial, 19
  partial, and occasions, 20
  relationships between, 131
conformation
  versus diversity, 100n4
  versus otherness, 44
  of present to past, 254
  and primitive experience, 337
confusion, versus harmony, 113
Conger, George Perrigo
  biographical sketch of, xlvii
  career of, xlvii
  diary entry of, 435–7
  evaluation of Whitehead by, 435
  example of notes of, xlix
  friendship of, with Whitehead, xlvii
  importance of lecture notes of, xlvii
  lecture notes of, xlvii–l
  notes of, for Philosophy A, lx–lxi
  seminary notes of, xlviii, lvi–lvii, l
  state of notes of, xlviii–l
  and Whitehead lectures, 435
  and Whitehead seminars, 435
  and Whitehead Sunday evenings, 435
congruence, 338, 338fig
  in Euclid, 117
  as general relationship, 117

  and parallel lines, 283–4, 283fig
  of space, 284
  and structure, 284
  of time, 284
conic sections, 118, 410
conjunction, of propositions, 368
conjunctive complex, 369
connection
  in continuity, 160
  external, and extensive entity, 309
  internal, 308n6, 309
conscience
  and authority of state, 406
  nature without, 398
consciousness, 381
  and brain, 96n3
  and conceptual functioning, 219
  in Descartes, 53
  and distinction between verified and non-verified, 379–9
  emergence of, with trial and error, 378
  and fact, 237
  as imaginal occasion, 79n4
  as incomplete, 254
  and mental and physical occasion, 344
  nature without, 398n2
  occasion of, as physical occasion, 96
  origination of, 298–9
  and perception, 79n5, 298
  versus perceptiveness, 79, 79n3, 79n4
consequences, existence of, 393
consequent
  as actual, 105
  versus antecedent, 11
  and causal mode, 109
  defined, 104
  and epochal occasion, 105
  and eternal object, 105
  and ground, 102, 102fig, 102n2, 105, 109, 247, 247n7
  and incompleteness, 256
  and simultaneity, 257
conservation, and duration, 359
consistency, 193
contact, ways of, 306
containing, 321n2
context
  and meaning, 202, 344
  and object, 386
contiguity, relation of, 80
contingency
  belief in, 68
  and immediate experience, 56
  and occasion, 20
  and possibility, 18

  and potentiality, 218
  and unity, 21
continuity
  approach to, 126–127n6
  versus atomicity, 147, 153, 182, 295–6, 350
  and becoming, 261, 261n6, 268, 346, 347, 366
  and becomingness, 85fig
  of Cantor, 209n2
  and chemistry, 182
  in Chinese philosophy, 182
  connection in, 160
  and creativity, 84–85, 85fig
  of Dedekind, 209n2
  versus density, 328
  and divisibility, 218, 347
  and electromagnetism, 182
  and enduring object, 72
  of entity, 268, 268fig
  of events, 147
  and extension, 147, 310
  and extensive relation, 160
  as extra dense property, 328
  and flux, 182
  as fundamental, 347
  in Indian philosophy, 182
  of *natura naturata*, 85
  in nature, 366
  in past, 153
  and physics, 112, 366
  and φύσις, 268
  and potentiality, 218
  in psychology, 268
  and quanta, in nature, 297
  and science, 11, 35, 35n5, 48, 182
  and time, 88
  and vicious infinite regress, 346
  and Zeno, 84–85, 85fig
continuous function, theorem of, 180, 180n3
continuous, versus atomic, 149
continuum
  epochs in, 94
  extensive, versus realisation, 11
  four-dimensional, versus realisation, 11
  and potentiality, 296, 297
  scheme of, and realisation, 57
  and structure of loci, 278
  and supersession, 346
contradiction
  as error in problem solving, 128
  and Hegel, 245
  impatience with, 126, 126–7n6
  and philosophy, 129
  in science, 50
contradictories, and duration, 44
contrariety, in occasion, 101, 101n7

Index

contrast
 and actuality, 101
 and identity, 102*fig*, 103
 between past and present, 241
 no form of, 355, 356
 vividness of, 243
 yes form of, 355
controversy, in rationalism versus pragmatism, 180
convergence
 of abstract sets, 149
 of durations, 156–7n8
 equality of, 321
 equivalent, 324
 modes of, and point, 323
 to nothing, 148
 to a point, 149
 prime and antiprime as, 156
 proposition for, 321
 sharpest, 323—5, 325*fig*
 sharpness of, 323
 types of, 149
coordinates
 defined, 133
 and line, 360
 as logically prior, 274
 system of, 273, 274, 274*fig*
 and systematic structure, 274
Copernicus, Nicolaus, 317, 317n2, 409, 409n2
cork in infinite ocean, 40, 92
corpuscular theory, 295, 295n4
correlation, 326
 of citizens and constituencies, 142–3
 of cardinal numbers and fractions, 143
 and concomitance, 374
 in infinite class, 141
 of instantaneous space, 276, 276*fig*
 of magnitude, 338, 338*fig*
 and matching, 140, 140*fig*
 of measurements, 275
 and multiplicity, 140, 140*fig*, 141
 number as, 123
 and order, 140
 of parts of classes, 141, 142
 of parts of classes, proof for, 142–3
 of quantity, 338, 338*fig*
 of segmental numbers and fractions, 143
 of subclasses, 330
 and eternal objects, 373
cosmological epoch, 218
cosmological order, 163
Cotes, Roger, 295, 295n1
Coulomb's law of electrostatics, 413n1
Council of Trent, 6, 6n1
counting
 and number, 140, 326

and order, 140
and relationships of number, 326
covering
 and abstractive class, 321, 321*fig*, 324
 defined, 320
creation
 in actual entity, 251
 and character, 34
 and completion, 84
 and creature, 107
 and creature, 210
 data for, 97–98, 98n4
 diversity in, 100
 and eternal objects, 18
 how of, 99, 198
 and ideal, 34
 and impress, 18
 and limitation, 18
 and matter, 87
 of nature, 84
 as not finished, 83
 origination in, 251
 in philosophy, 144
 as process of activity, 210
 starting point for, 35
 versus supersession, 247
 and synthesis, 18
 time depth in, 35, 41
creative achievement
 as actual with reversion, 102
 occasion as, 101
creative act
 and atom, 41
 and epoch, 94
 immortality of community, 94
creative activity
 and creature, 83
 and immortality of past, 83
 and past, 34, 83, 270
creative advance
 and alternative serial systems, 162
 and creature, 162
 order through analysis of, 162
 sides of, 163
 of time systems, 162
creative character
 added to world, 298
 of entity, 269, 298
 of thing in itself, 256
creative diversity, and epoch, 100, 101
Creative Evolution (Bergson) (1907), 11–12n2, 150n5
 as assigned reading, 4, 47
creative identity
 defined, 101n6
 and epoch, 100, 101
creative individual, 210
creative individuality, principle of, 215, 217–18, 220

creative objectifications, and creature, 256–7
creative passage, 249, 249n6
creative successiveness, and measurability, 103, 103n4
creative synthesis, and eternal objects, 103, 103*fig*
creative transmission, and relationship of entities, 258
creativity, 34; *see also* process
 and act, 94, 232
 and actuality, 110, 209
 in Aristotle, 100
 and character, 214, 268
 and concretion, 104, 207
 and continuum, 84–5, 85*fig*
 and creative process, 230
 and creator, 34
 and creature, 34, 35, 84, 93, 94, 99, 100n4, 103, 104n7, 106, 107, 162, 210, 215, 220, 232, 252, 252n5, 256, 290, 268, 344
 and data, 108
 defined, 84, 344
 and entity, 209–10, 213, 213n1, 222, 230
 and envisagement, 95
 and eternal objects, 95, 344, 357
 and fact, 34, 213
 and functioning, 199
 and future, 34, 83, 270
 and general character, 230
 of God, 212
 ground and consequent in, 102
 and historical route, 42, 95
 how of, 99
 and individualisation, 213, 344
 knowledge of, 169
 under limitation, 98, 98–9n10
 and metaphysical principles, 230
 and mind, 355
 and objectification, 247
 in occasion, 84
 and other, 101, 102
 and past, 84, 95
 and philosophy, 123–4
 and φύσις, 268
 and potency, 290
 and present and future, 95
 and substance, 212
 and supersession, 252n5, 344, 354
 and supreme creature, 220
 and synthesis, 104
 and thing for itself, 166 n1
 and time, 34, 94, 100, 100n4, 245
 and universe, 213, 348

453

Index

creator
and creativity, 34
defined, 84
what of, 99
creature
actuality of, 99, 216, 220
analysis of, 43
and act, 290
and activity, 100n4
assimilation of, to other creatures, 261
becoming of, 290
character of, 214, 221, 256
and concretion, 104
and creation, 107, 210
and creative advance, 162
and creative objectifications, 256–7
and creativity under limitation, 98, 98–9n10
and creativity, 34, 35, 83, 84, 93, 94, 99, 100n4, 103, 104n7, 106, 106n8, 107, 162, 210, 215, 215n4, 220, 232, 252, 252n5, 256, 268, 290, 344
creating universe, 232
creation of, 35, 94–5
defined, 210
as end in itself, 219
elements of, 43
emergence of, 104
entering of the process into, 197
entity as, 210
epochal occasion as, 101
experience as, 168
experient, 98
experient occasion as, 95, 108
extensiveness of, 101n7
and fact, 34
future as, 35
God as, 210, 214
harmonious relationship of, 221
and ideal creature, 210, 215
ideal reference to, 219
and individuality, 219
and knowledge, 94, 223
and laws of nature, 162
limitations of, 220
and matter, 87
and mental occasion, 198
and mode, 238
and nature, 94, 366
and negative, 101n7
and opportunity, 108
as passing beyond itself, 165
physical, 197
and potency, 290
and potentiality, 238, 239, 366
as predicate, 162
relation of, to all creatures, 220
self-analysis of, 219
as self-creating, 210, 220, 261

space as, 94
as subject, 162
supersession of, 252n5, 344
and synthesis, 42, 43, 104
time as, 107
time depth of, 35, 85
ultimate, 102
and universe, 355
and world, 100, 243
creature, supreme *see also* God
argument for existence of, 256
existence of, 218–20
and creativity, 220
as end in itself, 220
and ideal creatures, 220–1, 221n1
in ideal relationship, 220–1, 221n1
and metaphysical principles, 220
ontological antecedent of, 220
and other creatures, 220
as self-creating, 220
and supersession, 220
creatureness, active, 213
cricket, and mathematics, 126–7n6
criteria, purge of obviousness by, 359
Critical Account of the Philosophy of Kant (Caird) (1877), 172n1
Critical Philosophy of Immanuel Kant (Caird) (1889), 172n1
criticism, rational standards for, 179–81, 183–4, 183n6, 186
Critique of Practical Reason (Kant) (1788), 29
Critique of Pure Reason (Kant) (1781), 29, 35, 84, 84n4, 194n2
Curtis, Charles P., xxx
curve, filling area, 338

Dalton, John, 39, 88, 90
Dante Alighieri, 212, 212n1
Darwin, Charles, 213, 394
Darwin, Horace, 322, 322n3
data
classification of, 74, 75*table*
created, 108
for creation, 97–8, 98n4
and creativity, 108
and occasion, 98, 109
and possibility, 98, 98n5
and realism, 98n4
relatedness of, 98, 98n4
sense, and relation, 70
sensory, 342
specific, 108
synthesis of, 108
datum
versus abstraction, 96
as chaotic, 192n4, 193

for concretion, 104
as fact, 70, 252
final, and behaviour, 33
ground as, 104
and inspection of mind, 74
and knowledge, 96, 108
and object, 79
and occasion, 69, 70, 96, 109
in private psychological field, 70
sense prehension as, 70
De George, Richard, xliv
De humani corporis fabrica libri septem (Vesalius) (1543), 409, 409n1
de Laguna, Theodore, 304, 304n3
and connection, 307
and extensive abstraction, 321, 321n2
De Magnete, Magneticisque Corporibus, et de Magno Magnete Tellure (Gilbert) (1600), 408
De revolutionibus orbium coelestium (Copernicus) (1543), 409, 409n2
Dedekind, Richard, 328, 328n1
and continuity, 138, 143
and irrational numbers, 124, 209n2
and real numbers from rational numbers, 136–7, 136*fig*, 136n3, 137*fig*, 137n1
Dedekind cut, 137n1, 138n1, 209n2
deduction
elegance of, 186
from false proposition, 186
in test of belief, 181
deductive reasoning, and entity, 149
definiteness, criteria for, 104
definition
accuracy of, 205
essence of, 310
importance of, 306
order of, 324
Democritus, and atomic theory, 90
demonstration
as animal faith, 242, 242n1
and concrescence, 226
defined, 225, 226
and description, 228–9
of entities, 224, 224–5n3, 289
of eternal object, 224, 224–5n3
and identity, 225, 225n1
and knowledge, 225, 225n1, 229n1
under limitation, 224, 224–5n3
and objectification, 225, 226, 230, 231
and perception, 242

Index

and perceptivity, 226
and supersession, 249, 249*n*3
demonstrative phrase, 228
Demos, Raphael, xxxi, lv, xlvii, 32, 32*n*2, 260
dense series, of points, 328
density
  and continuity, 328
  at a point, 147
Department of Social Ethics (Harvard), lvii, lviii, 391, 391*n*2
dependence
  of entity, 353
  and substance, 352
depth, of actuality, 104
Descartes Réné, 133, 231; *see also under* Cartesian
  and *a priori*, 52
  and actual entity, 212, 213–14, 246, 261, 268
  alternative to, 398
  and analysis, 90
  and analytic clearness, 188
  and Aristotle, 114
  assigned reading from, xxviii, 4
  background of, 182
  body and mind in, 99
  and body, 353
  and Christianity, 63
  and class theory, 74
  cogitating subjects in, 53
  cogitating substance in, 53
  and concept of whole, 89
  cogito of, 12, 30, 57, 74, 359
  concrescence in, 206
  consciousness in, 53
  consistency in, 193
  and context, 171
  versus Dewey, 183*n*6
  difficulties in, 13
  doctrine of individual substances of, 112
  doctrine of perception of, 206
  dualism of, 18–19, 31, 77
  and *ego*, 62
  and endurance, 240, 247, 266, 307
  and epochal occasion, 361
  and epochal time, 36
  and ethics, 63
  and experience, 360
  and extended material, 89
  and extension, 74, 148, 160, 162, 183, 266, 300, 307
  extensive quantity in, 300, 300*n*6
  external in, 360
  and fallacy of misplaced concreteness, 38
  and force, 87, 88
  and geometry, 124, 205, 206*n*2, 207
  geometrical method of, 207
  and God, 206, 209, 210, 266, 359, 376, 398
  and grammar, 201
  heritage of, 114
  and Hume, 359–60
  and imaginal occasion, 69
  and immediately given, 6
  independence in, 207
  and individuality, 204
  influence of, 112, 170, 395, 397
  inspectio of, 73, 73*n*1
  and knowing, 30, 78
  and knowledge, 58, 360
  and Locke, 170*n*4, 188, 188*n*5, 353
  and logic, 63
  and many versus one, 13, 78, 78*n*3
  and mass, 183
  mathematics of, 133–4, 133*n*4, 183, 410*n*6
  and matter, 37, 41, 75, 87, 348*n*2
  and mentality, 360
  merits of, 395
  and metaphysics, 60, 63*n*2, 94, 108, 200, 207, 291, 291*n*5, 360, 375
  method of doubt of, 184*n*2
  and mind, 12, 77, 266, 347–8*n*7, 353
  modes of, 360
  morals in, 208*n*8, 209
  morphological view in, 76
  and mysterious side of universals, 43
  versus new rationalism, 205*n*2
  objective and formaliter in, 14
  objectivism in, 53
  and occasion, 50, 53, 61, 61*n*1
  ontology of, 398
  and perception, 74, 217*n*5
  and permanence, 347, 347–8*n*7
  and philosophy of nature, 53, 207
  and philosophy of science, 10
  physical fact in, 297
  and physics, 10, 160, 183, 291, 291*n*5, 294
  and Plato, 347–8*n*7
  point in, 307
  and potential, 343
  and private world, 196
  process in, 86
  rational insight in, 190
  real versus relational in, 207
  reduction to simplicity by, 184
  revolt against, 205*n*1
  and science, 86–7, 266, 267, 396
  and self, 298
  and sensa, 360
  and sense data, 76
  sixth meditation, 242
  and social ethics, 396
  and Socrates, 63*n*2
  and space, 127*n*7, 183, 278
  subjectivism in, 53
  and subject–predicate form, 202, 203, 205*n*1, 206, 266
  and substance, 10, 53, 57, 77, 86, 120, 146, 164, 172, 188, 201, 204, 205, 205*n*4, 205–6*n*5, 206*n*5, 208*n*1, 208*n*2, 212, 278*n*3, 299, 299*n*2, 341, 341*n*4, 352, 358, 359, 360, 361, 362, 396
  and substantiality, 209
  and Ten Commandments, 208*n*1
  and theory of ideas, 202
  and time, 12, 57, 85*n*4, 347
  and truth, 190
  and universal relevance, 209
  values in, 215, 215*n*5
  and wax, 28, 73*n*1, 74, 232, 360, 361
  and Whitehead, 172, 172*n*6, 341, 341*n*3
  world view of, 182–3
description
  and demonstration, 228–9
  of eternal object, 229
  and presupposition, 228–9
  and relationship, 228
detail, and originality of thought, 244
determinable
  defined, 117
  diversity in, 120
determinate, defined, 117
determinate relationship, 263
determinates, incompatibility of, 174
determination
  and future, 253
  and prehension, 253, 344–5, 345*n*1
  value as *how* of, 166 *n*1
determinism
  as arbitrary, 21
  and empiricism, 21
  and empiricists, 69
  evaluation of, 69
  and monism, 69
  and pluralism, 21
  and pluralists, 69
deus ex machina, in metaphysics, 60
Dewey, John, viii
  abstraction in, 342*n*3
  assigned reading from, xxviii
  versus Descartes, 183*n*6
  eternal in, 342, 342*n*3
  and eternal objects, 344

Index

like Locke, 341, 341*n*3
and logic, 171
and pragmatism, 180
as pragmatist, 171
and prehension, 343
versus rationalism, 183
and substance, 188
and Whitehead, 47n7, 170–1, 172*n*1, 172*n*6, 177, 341, 341*n*3, 341*n*6, 342*n*3
wisdom of, 341*n*3
diagram, versus language, 203
dialectic regeneration, 126
Dialogue Concerning the Two Chief World Systems (Galileo) (1632), 408
Dialogues of Alfred North Whitehead (Price) (1954)
Dickson, William J., xxxix
dictum de omne et nullo, 6
difference
   and resemblance, 347
   in entity, 100–1
   versus endurance, 28
differentiation
   in community, 153
   and entity, 153
   and occasion, 153
dimension, 41
   of concrete fact
   defined, 104–5
   and extension, 148
   generalised sense of, 104–5*n*8
   of historical route, 105
   and measurability, 104, 104*n*2
   of mentality, 104–5, 105*n*8
   and mutual inheritance, 351
   number of, 351
   and occasion, 105
   of space, 104*n*2
dipolarity
   of entity, 69*n*5, 299
   of facts, 100
   of knowledge of world, 223–4
   magnet as example of, 197
   of occasion, 97, 197, 342–3
disagreement
   as lack of correspondence with facts, 335
   as lack of internal coherence, 335
discernment, and thought, 9
discipline
   and imagination, 178
   necessity for, 176
   philosophical, 176
   scientific, 176
   stage of, in education, 402
   types of, 176
disjunctive complex, 369
dissection, 143, 144
   of duration, 156
   and events, 147, 147*fig*

and extensive connection, 311–12, 312*fig*
and overlapping, 147, 147*fig*
diversity, 174
   and abstraction, 237
   cogitation as consciousness of, 236–7
   and community, 160, 160*n*2
   versus conformation, 100*n*4
   of creations, 100
   and definiteness, 104
   in determinable, 120
   and eternal object, 237, 332
   in Euclid's axioms, 120
   as general waste basket, 115–16
   and historical route, 100*n*8
   and identity, 60, 199, 225, 225*n*1, 344
   and knowledge, 197, 199
   as mathematical concept, 137
   versus sameness, 100
   and similarity, 121, 121*fig*
   and space-time, 127
   by synthesis of differences, 102
   and totality, 145
   of universe, 115–16
   and whole and parts, 125
divisibility
   axioms of, 121
   and continuity, 218, 347
   potentiality, 347, 356
   proposition for, 310
   and spatio-temporal extension, 320
doctrine of causation, and irreversibility of time, 345
doctrine of types, 230, 436
drama
   influence of, on Aristotle, 292
   scientific experiment as, 174
dramatic, versus ordinary, 173–4
dream, versus knowledge, 132
dualism, 64–5
   of Descartes, 18–19, 31, 42, 164, 194, 239
   error of, 42
   of occasions, 21–2
duration
   and becoming, 260
   beliefs about, 154, 154*n*1
   complexity of, 153
   and conservation, 359
   and contradictories, 44
   defined, 155
   in Descartes, 341*n*4, 341*n*5
   dissection of, 156
   divisibility of, 155
   division of, 11
   and division of locus, 156
   and entities, 361
   and events, 154, 155
   and extension, 156
   of fact, 84, 84*fig*
   indivisibility of, 11, 11–12*n*2

and matter, 38
moment as, 157
parallel, 156
and past and future, 155
as physical fact, 153
present, and contemporary events, 156*n*1
present, defined, 152*n*3, 152*fig*
and present occasion, 70
and presentational relationships, 155
and reality, 153
and substance, 36–7, 36*n*5, 341*n*4
and time, 150
durations
   approaching convergence, 156–7*n*8
   class of, as fact, 154
   intersecting, 154, 154*fig*
   overlapping, 156
   parallel, 154, 154*fig*, 155, 155*fig*, 155*n*1
   in same time systems, 156
   and world lines, 154
durée (Bergson), 11*n*2, 85*n*4, 240, 240*n*3, 346, 361
dynamics, 411
   second law of, 38, 38*n*1
dynamo, as analogy, 239

e (Euler's number), 138
Earth, in universe, 81, 81*n*6
Eaton, Ralph Monroe, 186
eclipse, solar, 175, 175*n*3, 176*n*8
economic man, 394–5
economics, and political economy, 394–5
ecstatic vision, and memory, 346
Edinburgh Critical Edition of the Complete Works of Alfred North Whitehead, ix–x
Edinburgh, University of, viii, xi
education
   cycle of belief in, 401–2
   difference of, in epochs, 244
   and historical route, 402
   philosophy of, in work of Whitehead, viii
   and psychology, 403
   progress in, 403
   states in, 401–2
efficient causation
   apprehension of, 361
   defined, 210
   as principle of metaphysics, 210
   principle of, 215, 218, 220, 222
efficient cause
   actual entity as, 215
   and final cause, 13, 49, 56, 57
   and force, 10–11

and potentiality, 238
in science, 50, 56
and time, 11
ego
 cognitive, 95*fig*
 and experient occasion, 98, 98*n*7
 perceptive, 95, 95*fig*
Egypt
 geometry in, 177 177*n*2
 applied mathematics in, 123, 123*n*3
 physics in, 173*n*3
Egyptian language, and philosophy, 174
Einstein, Albert, vii, 133, 274, 327
 and acceleration, 154
 and common conditions for all formulae, 134
 and common space, 277
 and contemporary occasions, 24
 contribution of, 124
 and electron, 41
 and immediate presentation, 280
 and internal and external relations, 24
 predictions by, 49
 and presented occasions, 24
 and quantitative relation, 273
 and relativity, 23, 24, 134, 154, 155, 264, 267, 269, 273, 274, 287
 space-time principle of, 286
elastic solid, theory of, 295
electricity
 and atoms, 90, 295, 295*n*8
 and energy, 30
 and matter, 29–30
electromagnetic equations, 287–8
electromagnetic theory, 90
electromagnetism
 as continuous, 182
 description of, 295
 and molecule, 295
 study of, 408
 variance in equations in, 287
electron, 90
 and abstract and actual world, 128
 and body, 263
 characteristics of, 39, 40
 as convenient fiction, 314
 defined, 39
 divisibility of, 40
 and Einstein, 41
 as element in body, 248
 energy of, 90, 90*fig*, 40, 92, 92*eq*, 267
 as fundamental, 39
 mass of, 40
 and occasions, 79*n*7

relation of, with other electrons, 256
shape of, 256, 256*fig*
electrons
 arrangement of, 41, 41*n*2
 throngs of, 405
electrostatics, 413, 413*n*1
element
 aboriginal, 261
 activity of, 209
 geometrical, and abstractive class, 148
 of, 342, 342*n*1
 and proposition, 368
 self-created, 261
 ultimate definite, 313
elements
 atomic, 90
 in biology, 341–2, 342*n*1
 classes of, 343
 comparison of, in universe, 273
 in complex unity, 263
 concretion of, 343
 gradation of, 242
 as ideas, 43
 in logic, 341–2, 342*n*1
 not-actual, predicates as, 379
 plurality of, 57
 relation of, to other elements, 272
 relational, and knowing, 112
Elements of Euclid 135*n*7, 306, 306*n*2
emergence, and relatedness, 373
Emergent Evolution (Morgan) (1923), 3*n*6, 46–7*n*7, 293*n*2, 299*n*5
 as assigned reading, 293
Emerson, Ralph Waldo, 210, 210*n*1, 409*n*4
emotion
 and action and belief, 191
 metaphysical basis of, 106
 and observation, 192
 and rationalism, 191
 source of, 65*n*4
 and types of order, 135
emotional intensity
 and self-consciousness, 378*n*1
 and self-judgment, 377
 and synthesis, 377, 377*n*6
empiricism
 and *a priori*, 8, 52
 English, mind in, 194–5, 195*n*1
 future in, 32, 80
 future and past in, 82
 and Hume, 132*n*1
 and metaphysics, 44
 number in, 326
 occasions in, 50
 organic, 9
 and rationalism, 5
 sceptical, and *a priori*, 52

and scepticism, 9
and what is known, 132
empiricists
 and determinism, 69
 and past and future, 32
 and time, 58
end
 versus beginning, 11, 56
 experient occasion as, 17
 infinite, 346
 occasion as, 62
 and progress, 113
 relevance of, 216, 216*n*6
 self as, 216
end in itself
 actuality as, 14
 art as, 62, 63
 creature as, 220
 entity as, 210, 215, 223, 398, 404
 individuality as, 219
 occasion as, 62, 197, 197*n*1, 224
 supreme creature as, 220
 value as, 15
endurance
 and antecedent, 74
 and art, 16, 63
 character of, 72
 as characteristic, 361
 as creative passage, 249, 249*n*6
 defined, 25, 33, 33*fig*, 240*n*3
 and Descartes, 240, 247, 266, 307
 and difference, 28, 82, 82*n*1
 and effect, 151
 and entity, 104*n*5, 247, 365
 and environment, 27
 and ethics, 15, 63
 and existence, 36
 and extension, 300, 300*n*5, 348
 and future, 82
 grades of, 27, 27*fig*
 and historical route, 72, 247
 and identity, 17, 28
 and inheritance, 72
 as instants, 25
 as internal characteristic, 361
 and occasion 16, 25, 37, 245, 247, 361
 and potentiality, 240, 240*n*3, 241
 present, defined, 152, 152*fig*
 process of, 33
 and repetition of structure, 72
 route of, 25
 and space, 266
 and space-time, 361
 and spatial extension, 267
 and specious present, 240
 and structure, 25, 72, 74
 of substance, 36, 85, 94
 and time, 36, 240, 300, 300*n*7

457

Index

energy
  and activity, 89, 91
  of atom, 92, 92n7
  as atomic, 40
  atomic primates as, 91
  concept of, 89
  constancy of, 295
  distribution of, 92
  divisibility of, 40
  and electricity, 30
  of electron, 40, 90
  flow of, 29, 29n8
  as functional, 76
  as fundamental, 39
  individualisation of, 89
  and inertia, 90
  intrinsic, 91
  kinetic, 29, 91, 295
  location of, 90, 92
  and mass, 29, 40, 77, 89, 295
  and matter, 89, 91
  and Maxwell, 40
  and period of atom, 93, 93eq
  potential, 29, 89, 295
  properties of, 29, 92
  quantity of, 77
  structure of, 92
  and time, 41, 93
  types of, 29
English language, as abstract, 126
enjoyment, types of, 373n7
Enquiry (Berkeley) *see Siris*
Enquiry Concerning the Human Understanding (Hume) (1748), as assigned reading, 4, 47
Enquiry Concerning the Principles of Natural Knowledge (Whitehead) (1919), viii, 46
entities
  class of all, 370
  class of disparate, 367–8
  classes as, 367
  classification of, 65
  continuum of, and perspective, 303
  and eternal objects, 234
  eternal objects as, 65
  individual, as physical entities, 53
  occasions as, 65
  systematic relationship of, 255–6
entity, 174; *see also* entities; *see also under types of entity*
  as abstract, 93
  and abstraction, 149, 237
  as acting, 213
  actualisation of, 262
  and activity of production, 344
  and activity of world, 230
  and actual world, 344
  for another entity, 335
  and antecedent, 213, 299

antecedent and subsequent, 260
anticipation of, 262
and artists, 18
and attribute, 202
becoming of, 260
and binding relation, 367
in blind spot, 263
body and mind in, 249n4
and causal dependence, 301
and causal relation, 255–6, 263, 272, 272n1
and causation, 348
character of, 233
character of generality in, 223
and community, 93, 115
as complete, 257, 349
as complete fact, 342n5
complexity of, 249, 249n9, 249n10, 260
conceptual analysis as, 351n4
and concrescence, 364, 365
concurrence of, 280
concurrent events for, 272
conformation of, 257, 261
continuous, 268
creation of, 129, 129n5
as creative, 301
creative character of, 269, 298, 301
as creative determinants of other entities, 301
and creative process, 398
and creativity, 213, 213n1, 230, 348
as creature, 210
criterion for, 129
and deductive reasoning, 149
defined, 115, 237
demonstrated, and prehension of entity, 250
and demonstrated entity, 250
demonstrating, 249
as denotation of demonstrative phrase, 227–8
dependence of, 353
derivation of, 247
derivative, mutual relevance of, 212
description of, 228–9
determinate, 34, 270, 369
as determination of entities, 269
as determined by natural relations, 270
difference and sameness in, 100–1
and differentiation, 153
divisions of, 17–18
and duration, 361
and endurance, 104n5, 365
as end in itself, 404
entering into another entity, 272

and environment for other entities, 234
essence in, 115
and eternal objects, 233, 233n2
exemplification of, 234
in experient occasion, 17
and extension, 365, 366, 367
and extensive connection, 249, 309
and fact, 235, 365
field of, 305, 305n1, 305n2
as finished, 365
as future event, 272
and future entity, 213
in future of other entities, 271
generality of, and ontological principle, 223
and historical route, 100–1, 101fig
history of, 255
how to describe, 13
how to know about, 370
how to point to, 367
identity of, and knowledge, 228
and immediate predecessor, 265
included in occasion, 250, 250n5
inclusion of other entities in, 249, 249n10, 250
incompleteness of, 257
importance of environment to, 214–15
individual character of, 257
individual experience of, 270
individual realisation of, 260
individuality of, 228, 269
internal relationships of, to community, 153
as individual, 216
for itself, 335
and knowledge, 223, 360
less complex, 18
under limitation, 364
in logic, 128
and logical simplicity, 128
logical stability of, 227
and logical truth, 235
locus of immediate presentation of, 281
and mathematicians, 18
as member of a class, 120–1, 120fig, 121
mind as creative of, 317
minor versus major, 248
and modes of functioning, 227–8
moment as, 158
more complex, 17–18
motion of, 259, 259n7
multiplicity of, 233, 250
mutual relevance of, 212, 213
from natural ground, 334

nature as, 100n4
none as dead, 230
non-substantial, 396
not-actual, 212, 233
objectified, 225, 234, 234n1, 255, 255n3, 257, 258, 262, 270, 271, 272, 383
occasions as, 65
and organism and function, 153
and other entities, 250
as object of perception, 229
as organism, 258
origination of, 298
as part of itself, 305
parts of, 279
and past, 232, 232fig, 270, 301
and patience, 363, 386
and perception, 298, 365
as perspective of another entity, 168
and φύσις, 268
and point, 149
and play and interplay, 213
plurality of, 144
and possibility, 270
postulation of, 129, 129n5
potential, 333
potential division of, 248, 248fig
and potentiality, 296–7
and predicate, 270, 271, 366
prehension of, 262, 353
and presentational immediacy, 271, 274, 278, 301
presupposition of, 262
primary character of, 348
and proposition, 366, 369
pure perceptivity as, 351n4
and its qualities, 116
and quantum, 337
realising itself, 272
reference to, 363
relations within, 308
relationships to, and accuracy, 116
requiring nothing but itself, 188, 188n5, 231, 261, 342n5, 353, 360
at rest, 158, 158fig
relations of, 128, 131, 146, 305, 305n3, 334, 353, 360
relationships of, 116, 131, 257, 258, 260, 303, 304–5
and self-creation, 296
self-dissatisfaction in, 404
self-enjoyment of, 352
and self-generation, 267
self-identity of, in occasions, 225, 225n1
self-knowledge of, 230, 296
self-realisation of, 263
self-satisfaction in, 404
self-sufficiency of, 261
sequence of, 121–2

and simultaneity, 257
simultaneous, independence of, 258
as social, 120
social, and social ethics, 405
as something for itself, 213, 352
solidarity of, 233, 257, 259
and solidarity of universe, 233, 234, 235
and space, 284, 284n6
and spatio-temporal relations, 270, 271
square root of 2 as, 129, 129n5
and standpoint, 271, 271fig, 303, 303n3
and structural relation, 280
as subject, 115
substance as, 204
as succession of experiences, 298
successive, 232
and supersession, 246, 248, 269
as synthesis of *how* and *what*, 115
synthesised into occasion, 78
and systematic character, 257, 272–3, 274
and systematic relationships, 271, 274
systematic relevance of, 272, 272fig
and time, 284n6, 255
and totality, 237
truth about, 151n1
types of, 65–6, 228
and types of order, 134–5
types of status of, 209
unified by predicate, 378n5
universal relevance of, 209
and universals, 146
and universe, 237
what and *how* of, 116, 233, 233n2
what counts as single, 326
world of, 279
and world as social, 348
entity, abstract, 93, 326
and mathematics, 184
point as, 185
entity, actual, 228, 351n4
and act of analysis, 376n6
as act of percipience, 229
and activity, 213, 296
as actual occasion, 277
and actual world, 229
as atomic, 218
attempt to define, for paper, 252n6
buildup of, 297, 375
as Cartesian substance, 233
as character conditioning creativity, 222
and *cognita*, 30
as complete, 349, 401
complete, paradox of, 269

as completed class, 246, 246n4
as complex, 260, 269, 300
complex unity of, 376
concrescence of, 196, 217
conditions for existence of, 210
contributions of, to other entities, 269–70
control of, 297
coordinated subcommunities of, 280
and creative activity, 297
and creative process, 398
and creativity, 209–10
creature as, 210, 215
defined, 212
degree of actuality in, 246, 246n5
demonstration of, 224, 224–5n3, 253n4, 290
and Descartes, 212, 268
descriptive scheme of, 213
dipolarity of, 299
as efficient cause, 215
as end in itself, 210, 215, 398
endurance in, 247
and eternal objects, 228, 229, 230, 250
and entities, 298, 376
existence of, 212
and experience, 226, 226n4, 290, 298, 299, 376, 377
and experiential philosophy, 223
and extension, 300
features of, 398
foci of original creation in, 251
as fundamental, 234, 297
future as, 34
in greater organism, 412
imaginal occasion as, 64–5
and incompleteness, 251
individuality of, 231, 261
inferred, 222
and internal relationship, 268
and limitation, 215, 221
as limited occasion, 296
and logical relationships, 184
meanings of, 213
measurement of, 289
mental pole of, 219
and metaphysics, 233
and modes of functioning, 196
modes of ingression into, 225
and monad, 362
and motions, 260
mutual relevance of, 212
in nineteenth century, 213–14
as not simple, 185
objectification of, 225, 235, 354
and other acts of experience, 377
and other entities, 212, 213, 217, 398
and otherness, 100

459

Index

ourselves as, 297
and past, 296, 299
as patient of being objectified, 235
and perceptivity, 299, 353
perceptum as, 78, 78n4
as point, 259, 259n7
at a point, 247
potential fractions of, 241, 241n1
potentialities in, 333
predicate of, 362
presupposition by, of other entities, 261, 261fig
and proposition, 382
and process, 146, 210, 215, 217–18, 398
production of, 296
as quantum, 296, 297
and real world, 258
realisation of, and potentiality, 239
relations among, 85
relationships of, 184, 267, 268, 278–9
as result of activity, 209
requiring other entities to exist, 215
self-satisfaction of, 231
as self-sufficient, 188
as social, 353
socialised, 353
society in, 398
and solidarity, 258, 398
as something by itself, 335
as soon as you get hold of it, you lose it, 249
and space, 278
spatio-temporal perspective of, 261
status of, 209
as stretch, 259, 259n7
and substance, 36, 201, 203, 204, 209, 212, 353
and supersession
as synthesis, 337
synthesis of, with potentialities, 334
and time, 258, 258n7, 196, 401
and time depth, 30, 78
time relations between, 361
togetherness in, 261
and ultimate fact, 31
and world, 100, 231
world as solidarity of, 298
entity, approximating, postulated, 317
entity, complete, in philosophy, 269
entity, complex
actual entity as, 269
and experience, 378
unity of, 378, 378n5

entity, compresent, 262
and actual occasion, 52
and Aristotle, 13
change in, 246
final, as ultimate occasion, 21–2
as immediate occasion, 13
ineffective, 264, 264fig
and particularity, 229
and perception, 41
and presentational immediacy, 264, 264fig
presupposition of, 265
and relativity, 264
supersession of, 342
and time, 264, 264fig
entity, corporeal
nature as, 278
and space, 278
entity, enduring
achievement in, 404
and antecedents, 299, 299n7, 404
and Aristotle, 13, 63n2
community of occasions as, 11
defined, 299, 299n7
destruction of, 404–5
earning by, 404
and epochal occasion, 100n6
and evolution, 111
and experient occasion, 100n6
historical route of, 27, 404
inheritance from past, 404
life history of, 100n6
mechanism of, 27
versus physical entities, 53
and physical occasion, 14
relation of, to other entities, 249
robbed, 404
entity, epochal
occasion as, 361
potentiality in, of many entities, 241n1
entity, eternal, ingression of in occasion, 224, 224n2
entity, experient, line of, 103
entity, extended
defined, 307
versus real entity, 267
relationships of, 316
and sharpest convergence, 324, 324fig
entity, extensive
defined, 303
events in, 313, 313fig
and external connection, 309
whole and part of, 307–8
entity, extra-temporal, 261
entity, finite, and physics, 88
entity, fundamental, 233
entity, general, God as, 261
entity, high-grade, 213
in constitution of actual, 215
as eternal objects, 217

entity, physical
relations of, 160
and relationship, 353
entity, physical–mental, 351, 351n4
entity, real
as event with extension, 267
versus extended entity, 267
as individual, 396–7
mind as, 267
multiplicity of, 204
on its own, 396–7
entity, relational
eternal object as, 66
green as, 66
entity, self-contained, 348
entity, self-created, 261
entity, self-creative, 210
entity, substantial, 127, 127n4
entity, ultimate
and abstraction from whole, 78
and achieving, 78
as achievement, 30
and activity, 30, 78
and becomingness, 86
bipolarity of, 64–5
as dipolar, 69n5
as experient occasion, 79
how to describe, 78
and prehension, 78
and product, 78
and process, 86
real, 204
sensitive occasion as, 75
and synthesis, 78
and time, 78
time depth in, 30
entity, voluminous, and geometry, 307, 307fig
environment
and antecedent route, 299
and endurance, 27
evolution of, 294
favorable, 299, 405
harmony in, and depth of actuality, 231–2
importance of, to entity, 214–15
importance, of, to science, 214–15, 215n1, 215n2
inheritance from, 350
molecule in, 111
of occasion, 227
and organisms, 294
reference as interaction to, 374
systematic character of, 356
unfavorable, 299
envisagement
and actual world, 95
and creativity, 95
defined, 42
and eternal objects, 42, 95
and future, 42
and knowledge, 42

460

epic (literary)
    as adventure, 292n6
    defined, 292
    and universe, 292
epiphenomenon, knowledge as, 96
epistemology
    as foundation of philosophy, 190n6
    and metaphysics, 195
    problem of, 190–1
    problems in, 342
    rejection of, 12
epoch, 41
    as actual with reversion, 102n3
    and becoming, 84, 85n4
    common, and individual epochs, 85
    in continuum, 94
    and creative act, 94
    and creative diversity, 101
    and creative identity, 101
    and experient occasion, 44, 44fig
    and historical route, 101n5
    and identity, 101
    immediate occasion as, 57
    individual, and common epoch, 85
    new versus old, 44, 100
    and otherness, 101, 101fig
    present as, 153
    and specious present, 35n3, 241
    and substance, 36, 85
    time as, 35, 36, 57
    unit of, and actual occasion, 45
epochal difficulty, 38
equal, defined, 322
equality, 338
    and addition, problem of, 125
    defined, 337
    in Euclid, 117, 117n3, 337
    and reflexivity, 337
    symbol for, 321
    and symmetry, 337
    and transitivity, 337
Erasmus, as magnificent teacher, 244
Erasmus: A Study of His Life, Ideals and Place in History (Smith) (1923), 44, 44n5
error
    causes of, 152
    in induction, 152
    and perceptual immediacy, 336
    and symbolic reference, 336
    theory of, 199–200
    and truth, 337
error, statis, 83
error of misplaced concreteness *see* fallacy of misplaced concreteness

Essay Concerning Human Understanding (Locke) (1689), 341, 341n3
    as assigned reading, 170
    influence of Descartes on, 188n5
    importance of, 170
Essays in Radical Empiricism (James) (1906), as assigned reading, 4
Essays in Science and Philosophy (Whitehead) (1948), viii
Essays on Truth and Reality (Bradley) (1914), 167n3, 223, 223n1
esse est percipi, 30–1, 78, 78n2
essence, relational
    defined, 224
    limitation of, 224
essences, 373
    as predicates, 378
essential, versus actual, 62
eternal
    capture of, 16
    in Dewey, 342, 342n3
    identity as, 65–6
    relevance of, 16, 63
eternal good, 222, 222n3
eternal recurrence, 107, 107n3
ether (classical element), 29, 294, 413
    and atom, 92, 92n3
    as continuous, 295–6
    Earth moving through, 287
    of events, 296
    and force, 88
    and immediate experience, 296
    and matter, 38, 267
    and Maxwell's equations, 287
    origin of, 295
    and rest, 287
    scientific notion of, 267
    stationary, 38
    test for existence of, 287, 287n5, 287n7
ethics, 61
    and appeal to alternatives, 56
    and Aristotle, 63, 397
    versus art, 10, 15–16, 60
    and Descartes, 63
    and endurance, 15, 63
    evil in, 63
    and given, 60
    and God, 60
    and independence, 208
    and individualism, 396
    and metaphysics, 16, 60
    and occasions, 15, 63
    philosophical implications of, 15
    and philosophy, 397–8
    and possible worlds, 10
    and privacy, 208n3
    and progress, 15, 63

and realised values, 15
    and requiring nothing but itself, 208n3
    social *see* social ethics
    and Socrates, 60, 63
    and substance, 397
    and survival value, 63
    Whitehead's view of, lvii
Euclid in Greek (Heath) (1921), 313, 313n2
Euclid, 133
    axioms of, 117, 120
    congruence in, 117
    equality in, 117, 117n3, 337
    first sentence of, 306, 306n1
    geometry of, 157
    line in, 326
    mathematics of, 133, 135, 135n7
    and organic theory of nature, 307
    and point, 127, 306
    and self-evidence, 180, 180n2
Euler diagrams, 368
Europe
    philosophy of science in, 5
    science as intellectual pursuit in, 177, 177n2
events *see also under* occasions
    abstractions of, and time, 255
    and beyond, 147
    versus bodies, 160
    causal relations of, 352
    and *cognitum*, 60
    common future of, 161
    common past of, 161
    and community, 14–15
    completed series of, 253
    conditioning of, 152, 161
    connected by antecedents, 68
    constituting organism, 372
    continuity of, 147
    creative emergence of, 21
    description of, 14–15
    and dissection, 147, 147fig
    and duration, 154, 155
    and emerging value, 15
    ether of, 296
    exclusion from, 62
    and extensiveness, 145, 153
    history of, 255
    how to define, 61
    and ideas, 14
    and incompatibility, 15, 62
    independence of, 68
    indivisibility of, 147
    knowledge of, 225
    limitation by, 14
    locus of, 153, 155–6, 155fig, 156fig
    membership of, 14
    memory of antecedent event in, 254
    and metaphysics, 14

461

Index

objective immortality of, 255
order of, and perception, 70
and overlapping, 147
parallel, 156*n*5
parts of, 145, 145*table*
past and future in, 161
pasts of, as identical, 334*n*1
as physical occasions, 207, 207*n*3, 351
as physical pole, 343
and potentiality, 351
and presentational relationship, 152, 161
and process, 207*n*3
as real, 146
relationships of, 155
relativity of, 68
repetition of, as objectification, 254
with same status of immediacy, 152
society of, 234
and space and time, 272–3
succession of instantaneous, 289
and unboundedness, 147
and universe, 9
and value, 15
value as, 62
events, actual, concretion of, 9
events, causal, and parallel duration, 156
events, concurrent, 272
events, conditioned, 152
events, contemporaneous, 23, 24
events, contemporary *see also* occasions, contemporary occasion
and present duration, 156*n*1
as present events, 68
as presented events, 24
relations of, 68, 68*fig*
events, physical, 14
events, present
as contemporaneous events, 23
as contemporaneous events, 24
as contemporary events, t8
and measurement, 70–1
succession of, 70–1
events, presented
contemporary events as, 24
events, simultaneous
and causal independence, 255
conformation of, 257
independence of, 257, 345
and relativity, 23
every actual thing, 79, 79*n*5
evil
defined, 354d, 399
as destructive, 399–400
in ethics, 63
examples of, 63, 63n5
and God, 222
and good, 222
and war, 406

evolution
toward better, 208
course of, 27
emergent, 299
and enduring entities, 111
of environment, 294
interpretation of, 208
of laws of nature, 290
and opportunity, 108
of organisms, 294
social, 243–4
and structural coordination, 281
and Tennessee, 315
theory of, 394
example, versus abstraction, 134
exclusion
art as, 44
from event, 62
and prehension, 62
of undefined things, 323
and value, 62, 63
exemplification
as faith, 184
of general concept, 186
in geometry, 184
of ideas, 177, 179, 181, 192
as test of belief, 181
existence
and endurance, 36
and extension, 300
inertia of, 33
and logic, 382
material, 103
mutual advantage in, 280–1
and proposition, 381, 382
and relation, 145
right to, 399
and substance, 204
existences
classification of, 381
reality of, 389
relations of, 388
existing, as inappropriate word, 212
experience (word), senses of, 176
experience
and actual entity, 226, 226*n*4, 290, 298, 299, 376, 377
analysis of, 176, 333
and act of analysis, 376, 376*n*6
and complex entity, 378
and conceptual hypothesis, 377
and Descartes, 360
and extension, 300
fronting of, 6
and Hume, 75
and knowing, 52
and knowledge, 149, 176, 195, 195*n*6, 333
as leaky, 374
measurability of, 104
and metaphysics, 298–9, 376
and mind, 195, 195*n*2, 195*n*3

and morphological view, 77, 77*n*1
objectification of, 378
obviousness of, 334
and other acts of experience, 377
in philosophy, 289
and precision, 114, 114*n*1
and proposition, 379
and reason, 8
relation between, 378
and scheme of ideas, 191
and self, 298
and sense data, 223
and space, 289
succession of, entity as, 298
as synthesis, 45
and thought, 6
versus universal, 317
and universal ideas, 6
and *what*, 115
and words, 205*n*3
experience, act of, 298
and fact, 267
and proposition, 380, 380*n*5
and subject
experience, antecedent, 282*n*4
experience, blind, 176
experience, causal, 27
experience, concrete, 129
experience, direct, infallibility of, 336
experience, immediate
Bradley on, 167, 167*n*3
as creature, 168
description of, 65–6
and ether, 296
and fact, 200, 200*n*4, 200*n*5, 277
as non-relational, 167
and philosophy, 393
and practice, 191, 393
qualities of, 167–8
as subjective world, 162
and universe, 376
experience, immediate (phrase), meanings of, 200
experience, physical, 176
experience, previous, 349
experience, primitive, and conformation, 337
experience, vulgar, 297
Experience and Nature (Dewey), 170*n*7, 341, 341*n*3, 341*n*6
as assigned reading, 171, 171*n*9, 172*n*6
and Locke, 170–1
experiment
accuracy of, 294
defined, 175
information from, 305
and philosophy, 189, 189*n*6
and progress, 175

purpose of, 189
and science, 5
explanation
    and action, 177
    boundaries for, 178
    and meaning, 256, 256n3, 317
    as motive for progress, 177
    in science versus philosophy, 177
explanatory, in antecedent, 262
expression, clear, and test of belief, 180
expression, elliptical, 374
expression, essence of, 252, 252n3
expression, theory of, and philosophy, 186
expressive vagueness, 186
extension
    extension, 263, 269–72
    as abstract, 300
    and accuracy, 294
    and actual entity, 300
    and approximation, 319
    and atomism, 88
    as attribute, 162, 304
    and axioms, 293
    as basis of world as community, 163
    and character of creativity, 268
    as characteristic, 361
    and classification, 113, 113n5
    and community, 146, 156, 160
    and continuity, 147, 310
    defined, 11, 150, 300
    and Descartes, 74, 148, 160, 162, 266, 300, 307
    and dimension, 148
    dimensionless, 315
    and divisibility, 310, 310fig, 312–13
    and division, 369
    and duration, 156
    as element of structure, 125
    and endurance, 300, 300n5, 348
    and entity, 365, 366, 367
    and existence, 300
    and experience, 300
    as fundamental, 148
    and geometry, 148, 149–50, 293, 300
    and mass, 75
    as matter, 41, 88
    and measured time, 161
    non-reflexive, 385–6, 388
    and organic relationship, 263
    as overlapping, 102n1
    in philosophy, 291
    and physical world, 160, 160 n1
    and point, 148
    and predicate, 148, 367
    as property of matter, 28, 29
    and real, 11

as relation, 148, 150
as relational complex, 358
relation of, 144
and relations between points, 306
and relationship, 161, 300
and route of approximation, 147
in science, 293
and space, 266, 370
and space and time, 144, 150, 267, 301
and substance, 160–1, 300
and synthesis, 369
and time, 300, 300n7, 347
for Whitehead, 148
extension, genus, 294
extension, spatial-temporal, and real entity, 267
extensional perspective, and π (punct), 152
extensive abstraction
    methods of, 313–16
    propositions for, 319, 319n3
    theory of, 319
extensive character
    of epochal occasion, 102, 102n8
    and time and space, 267
extensive complexity, 369
extensive connection, 304–12
    of class, 308
    and continuity, 311, 311n5
    and dissection, 311–12, 312fig
    propositions for, 304, 305, 306, 307, 308, 309, 310
    relationship of, 304
    and tangency, 308
    types of, 306, 306fig, 307, 307fig, 309, 309fig
extensive continuity, in past, 153
extensive element, time as, 36
extensive occasion, and M, 151
extensive quantity, 84
    defined, 35, 35n1
    in Descartes, 300, 300n6
    and Kant, 35
    and shading, 319
    and time, 12, 259n2
extensive relation
    as absolute, 162
    covering in, 320–1
    and potentiality of subdivision, 241
    propositions for, 321
    shading in, 321
    and tangency, 321, 323, 323fig
extensive relationships, 73, 262, 262n2
extensiveness
    abstraction from, 151n1
    and accuracy and precisions, 113n6
    community of, 150

and containedness, 310, 310fig
of creature, 101n7
and event, 153
as relationship, 304–5
and space and time, 57, 151n1
of world, 38
extent, devolution of, and simplicity, 148
external, defined, 360
external connection, 308, 309, 309fig
extrusion, and art, 62

fact
    as abstraction, 166 n1
    and act of experience, 267
    analysis of, 164
    and analytic proposition, 382
    and Aristotle, 124
    awareness as, 236
    balanced with ideas, 409
    canalised by factors, 237
    clear versus shadowed, 179, 179n7
    and cogitation, 237
    conceptual analysis of, 198
    and consciousness, 237
    creativity as, 213
    and creativity and creature, 34
    as datum, 70, 252
    defined, 150
    as definite, 168
    dipolarity of, 100
    disagreement as lack of correspondence with, 335
    and entity, 235, 365
    enunciated by sentence, 266
    and eternal objects, 164
    and experient, 100
    and experient occasion, 96
    fitting our systems, 181, 181n6
    form fused with, 166
    four dimensions, 159
    generalising from particular, 333
    and growth of mind, 194
    happening as, 267
    in ideal world, 98
    and ideas, 193–4
    and immediate experience, 200, 277
    immortality of, in future, 253
    importance of exceptional, 173, 173n8
    infinitely complex, 388
    at an instant, 144
    and knowing, 100
    versus knowledge of fact, 96
    and logical nominalism, 225
    limited by factor, 237
    and mentality, 97, 326
    and objectification, 365
    and occasion, 162
    patience of, 99

Index

perceptivity as, 349
and perspective of universe, 164
and philosophy, 176
physical occasion as, 166 $n1$
as physical and mental, 165, 239, 239$n5$
physical world and, 195
and picture, 385, 387
and possibility, 99$n2$, 225
and potentiality, 225, 239
prehension as, 348
versus principles, 193–4$n5$
and proposition, 372, 385
proved wrong, 180, 180$n3$
relations of, 87
as relationship of factors, 236
versus relationships, 146
requiring nothing but itself, 150, 246$n3$, 342$n5$
and science, 124, 124$n3$, 176
sense data as, 387
and sign, 386
and solipsism, 225
structure of, 387
and subject–predicate view, 266
as substance, 209
succession of, and change, 246
and symbol, 384, 386
synthesis as ultimate, 108
and theory, 193–4$n5$
and thought, 388, 388$n1$
treatment of, 239–41
and truth, 222
as unknowable, 389
value as, 17
and world, 388
fact, actual
 completion of, 99
 possibility in, 260
 as social, 145
 unity of, 31
fact, atomic, 385, 388, 389
fact, blind, anticipation as, 344
fact, concrete
 actual simplicity as, 128
 dimensions of, 149
fact, definite, 246
 and accuracy, 125
fact, detached, not ultimate, 99
fact, experient, 100
fact, metaphysical, 177
fact, natural, and datum versus abstraction, 96
fact, physical
 in Descartes, 297
 genus of, 163, 297, 297$n3$
 and nature, 299
 perceptivity as, 346
 space as, 299–300
fact, private, 203
fact, real, description of, 164

fact, superreal, of relation of time points, 241
fact, ultimate
 and actual entity, 31
 and *cognita*, 31
 knowledge of, 108
factor
 examples of, 237
 facts canalised by, 237
 as limitation of fact, 237
faith, and science, 5, 184
fallacy of misplaced concreteness, 18, 38, 52, 66, 66n1, 127, 127$n2$
 and actual world, 128$n7$
 and points, 127$n2$
fallacy of the average, 149
falling body, equations for, 38, 38$n1$
falsehood, and logic, 370
falsity
 in actual world, 165
 in proposition, 171
Faraday, Michael, 177, 177$n3$, 267
feeling
 and experient occasion, 107
 metaphysical basis of, 106
 and mind, 176
 and physical world, 176
fiction, 314–15, 317
field, as synonym for domain, 305, 305$n2$
figure, and background, 257
final cause
 and actual occasion, 16
 and efficient cause, 13, 49, 56, 57
 in science, 50
 and time, 11
 as value, 13
final reality, as enduring subject, 172
finite distance, exclusion of, 338
finitude, and limitation, 237
first law of motion, 33, 411
flexibility, 74
flow, and Bergson, 57
flowing, 53
flux
 and continuity, 182
 as fundamental, 347
 and ideas, 10
 of occasions, 17, 65
 versus permanence, 182
 and philosophy, 182
 truth in harmony of, 56
fluxions, in Newton, 12
flying, progress in, 403
force
 as action at a distance, 87
 as change in momentum, 38
 and change of motion, 412
 defined, 37, 87, 88

and Descartes, 87, 88
and efficient cause, 10–11
equation for, 412
and ether, 88
and mass, 37, 413
and matter, 87, 88, 88fig, 89, 353
and momentum, 87, 88
and *natura naturans*, 87 $n1$
in Newton, 88, 267, 294
and occasion, 10
origin of, 88
origin of idea of, 56
at a point, 38
as presentational relationship, 110
as product of mass and acceleration, 87
in space, 267
and stress, 87, 412
as stuff, 79
in third law of motion, 412
ways of expressing, 37
force, gravitational, equation for, 37
Ford, James, 404
Ford, Lewis, xlii, li
Foreign Policy Association, 70$n1$
form
 as entity, 396
 eternal, and completeness, 351
 exemplified by actual occasion, 165
 fused with facts, 166
 as perceptivity, 167fig
 and proposition, 389
 universal potentiality of, 165, 165$n6$
 and universality, 166
formal cause, and actual occasion, 16
formaliter
 defined, 14, 168
 versus objective, 14
 as point of view, 168, 169
forms
 ingression of, and mental occasion, 165, 165$n4$
 limitation on, 165$n4$
 as unknowable, 389
forms, ideal, and God, 222
formula
 describing relations, 135$n3$
 and historical route, 247
 induction leading to, 49
 and intensity of transmission, 247, 247$n4$
 and measurement, 134, 134$n2$
 as pattern, 247
 precision in, 171$n8$
 proposition as, 171, 171$n5$
 as relative knowledge, 135
formulae, common condition for all, 134

464

Foundations of a General Theory of Manifolds (Cantor) (1883), 129*n*6
fractions
 in continuous series, 330
 correlation of, with cardinal numbers, 143
 defined, 143
 density of series of, 136–7
 insufficient for continuous series, 329
 and order of points, 130–1
 order type of, 130*n*1
 as relations between numbers, 331
 versus segmental numbers, 143
fractions, classes of, 136, 136*fig*, 328
 limit in, 148
 logical consistency of, 328
fractions, dense series of, infinite series in, 329
fractions, ordinal, 136
 and cardinal numbers, 138
fractions, series of, as route of approximation, 317
Frankfurter, Felix, xxix, xxix*n*8, 193–4*n*5, 221*n*4, 437, 437*n*1
freedom, 166
 as concept, 7
 and gap between possibility and occasion, 99*n*2
 and individual, 208
 and knowledge of future, 389
 and limitation, 69
 and mentality, 106
 and occasion as end in itself, 197, 197*n*1
Frege, Gottlob
 and irrational numbers, 124
 and names, 387
Fresnel, Augustin-Jean, 29, 29*n*7
fronting
 of experience, 6
 of world, 7
function
 and actuality, 36
 bijective, 330–1
 as category of scientific thought, 48
 of cell, 90
 concept as, 352*n*1
 defined, 76
 and depth of time, 56
 and energy, 76
 and entity, 153
 and external relations, 89
 injective, 330–1
 and James, 11
 and knowledge, 76*n*3
 and mass, 90
 of matter, 88
 and morphology, 76–7
 and Newtonian physics, 77
 object as, 347
 and philosophy of science, 11, 56
 and physical occasion, 55
 of presented structural scheme, 71
 reality as, 55
 and science, 11, 57
 in structure, 125
 in structure of universe, 132
 subject as, 347
 and time, 37
 and world, 76*n*3
function of knowing, 51
Function of Reason (Whitehead) (1929), viii
functional view
 difficulties in, 77–8
 versus morphological view, 76–7
 and reality, 77
 and science, 77–8
functioning
 and actual entity, 196
 concept as, 354
 concrescence of, and mental occasion, 355
 and creativity, 199
 and entity, 227–8
 and eternal object, 199, 379
 as essence of matter, 39
 and identity, 227, 347
 and logical stability, 227
 and proposition, 379
 and relationship, 347
 and universe, 379
functioning, conceptual *see also* mental pole
 and blind intuition, 219, 219*n*3
 and complete occasion, 199
 and consciousness, 219
 defined, 223
 function of, 199
 how of, 217
 and knowledge, 223
 and occasion, 219
 origination of, 219
 and perceptual functioning, 198–9, 206, 217, 217*n*3, 378
 and possibility, 302
 and proposition, 380
 as ripple, 219
 supersession of, 249*n*4
 as test of physical ground, 199
 yes form dominant in, 378
functioning, mental
 as analytic of mentality, 219
 and mental occasion, 198
 originality of, 355
 and perception, 290
functioning, modes of
 and common past, present, and future, 198
 concept as, 195, 198
 knowledge as concrescence of, 197
functioning, perceptual *see also* physical pole
 and conceptual functioning, 198–9, 206, 217, 217*n*3, 378
 defined, 223
 and occasion, 199, 219
 and possibility, 302
 types of, 378
functioning, physical, and mental occasion, 198
functioning, relational, prehension as, 253
functioning organism
 concretion of, 9
 and philosophy of science, 9
fundamental, explanation of, by less fundamental, 76
fusion, as value, 164
future, 32–4, 80–3; *see also* occasion, future
 ability to know, 32
 abnormality in, 152
 as abstract, 33
 actuality of, 34, 83, 84
 and actual occasion, 82
 attempt to define, 262
 becoming of, 34
 and causal relations, 352
 characteristics of, 33–4
 conditioning by, 198
 contingency on, 34
 creative passage into, 249, 249*n*6
 and creativeness, 83
 and creativity, 34, 95, 270
 as creature, 35
 as definite, 33, 82, 84
 and determination, 253
 as determinate, 34
 and determined character, 34
 and duration, 155
 and empiricism, 32, 80
 and endurance, 82
 in event, 161
 existence of, 80, 245, 251
 foreshadowed in present, 32–3
 and freedom, 389
 in immediate occasion, 107
 immortality of fact in, 253
 immortality of occasion throughout, 253
 and immortality of past, 83
 inability to measure, 274
 as incomplete, 252, 253, 352
 and inertia, 82
 influence of, on envisagement, 42

465

Index

information about, 71
knowledge of, 82, 107
meaning of, 290
and metaphysics, 160
and nature, 270
as not actual, 33, 160n3
as nothing, 271
and occasion, 344
occasions modified by, 70
and past, 32, 82, 83, 84, 160, 245, 255
and past and present, 36, 81, 108, 152, 153, 269, 289, 333
past as transition to, 83
as possibility, 81
potentiality of, 252
and present, 71, 77, 77n1, 83, 252
and process, 34
and proposition, 381
qualification of, 251
and reflective reference, 375
relationship of, to eternal objects, 81
relationship of, to past, 73, 268
relative, and causality, 156n5
and systematic character, 274
and timetables, 251
transition to, 34, 34*fig*
uncertainty of, 80
as undetermined, 349

Galileo Galilei
and astronomy, 394, 403, 411
and celestial mechanics, 317n2
and discovery of laws of science, 173n3
and final ends, 397
and gravitation, 412
and laws of motion, 411
and mass, 37, 87, 183n1
and matter, 28, 37, 87
and primary and secondary qualities, 74n3
sensitive body, 74, 75
as physicist, 410, 410n6
perceptivity in, 217n5
gases, kinetic theory of, 118, 118n7
Gauss, Carl Friedrich, 382, 382n1, 413, 413n1
Gauvin, Marshall J., 184n1
general
and particular, 117, 117n3, 211, 212
and specific, 81, 195–6
generality
Earth as level of, 265
and potential mentality, 226, 226n5
higher level, function of, 265
layers of, 116
levels of, 265

and occasion, 63
problems of, 132, 132n1
generic, and specific, 243
genus
of physical fact, 297, 297n3
realisation of, 238–9
variation of, 244
geometrical element
and abstractive class, 322
defined, 322
in moment, 158
geometry
axioms of, 185
beginning of, 306
as certain, 131–2, 317
derived from creative advance of time systems, 162
of Descartes, 124
and differences of time systems, 159
and Egyptians, 177 177n2
elements of, and routes of approximation, 315
exemplification in, 184
and extension, 148, 149–50, 293, 300
and extensive community, 153
and Greeks, 184, 185
how it exists, 157, 158
ideals in, 313
and language, 127
and measurement, 155, 158
necessity for, 155
and philosophy, 184
versus physical relationship, 149
projection in, and language, 384, 387
pure, and numbers, 133
of Pythagoreans, 124
qualitative relationships in, 133, 133*fig*
and rationalistic method, 184
and reasoning, 205, 205n2, 205n3
and relationship between moments, 158
type of order in, 133–4
and voluminous entity, 307, 307*fig*
geometry, Euclidean, 306–7
German merits, 74
Gestalt psychology, 257, 257n1
Gifford lectures
of Alexander, 46–7n7
invitation for, xxxii
and *Process and Reality*, xxxii
Whitehead, viii, xi, 261n6
Gilbert, William, 408, 408n3, 409
Gilson, Étienne, xxxi, 267, 267n1, 347–8n7, 358
given
as chaotic, 12, 65, 166
and different occasion, 7
and ethics, 60

and immediate occasion, 51
and impress, 60
and Kant, 65, 166
and knowing, 65
knowledge as analytic for, 166
limitation of, 64
in mathematics, 251
nature of, 60
organisation of, 7
and present, 7
real, 65
and space, 12
and specious present, 7
and Whitehead, 12, 65, 166
Glueck, Sheldon, 406, 406n2
God *see also* creature, supreme
as actuality, 216
and art, 60
as concept, 7, 233
creativity of, 212
as creature, 210, 214, 216
defined, 214, 360
and Descartes, 206, 209, 210, 266, 359, 398
and ethics, 60
and evil, 222
existence of, 218–20
as general entity, 261
goodness of, 220, 221
history of, in world, 221
as ideal, 114
and ideal forms, 222
incompleteness in, 251
independence of, 209
in Kant, 166
limitation of, 218
logical side of, 166
and metaphysics, 60, 216, 360
and mind, 266
and morals, 208–9, 208n8
nature of, 5, 216
nature as ideas in the mind of, 31
as non-actual, 216, 216n3
as obeying laws, 230
objectification of, 221
as occasion, 198
origins of, 216
and physical value, 222
as principle of order, 113
and proposition, 388
purpose of, 221
relation of, to other substances, 204, 204n4
and relationship, 146
religious value of, 216
as saviour, 357
scholastic approach to, 166
and Spinoza, 166, 268
Stoic view of, 220, 230
and substance, 172n2, 204, 205, 205n4, 205–6n5, 209, 341, 341n5, 352, 353, 360, 396

466

Index

as supreme creature, 218–222
as ultimate, 166
and universe, 376
will of, 397–8
good, and evil, 222
grace, inevitability of, 292
grades
  in occasions, 71
  grades, in relations, 71
graduality
  and achievement, 101n3
  and becoming, 101n3
grammar
  abstraction from, 114
  and Aristotle, 114
  and epochal occasions, 114, 114n4
  and eternal objects, 114
  it in, 114
  and philosophy, 114, 174, 174n3, 201
  and reality, 125
  subject in, 114
  and synthesis, 114
granite, history of particle of, 91
gravity, law of, 38, 38n1, 412–13, 413n1
  flux theorem for, 413
  proof for, 413
Greek drama, and science, 5
Greek language, and truth, 183
Greeks
  and accuracy, 117, 117n1
  and analysis of belief, 188, 188n2
  and becoming, 251
  and Chinese language, 114, 174, 174n3, 201
  and clarity, 127
  and difficulties in mathematics, 123
  and geometry, 184, 185
  influence of, on science, 48, 170
  and language, 174, 174n3
  and logic, 183, 214
  and logical coherence, 188, 188n2
  logical thinking of, 170
  and mathematics, 123, 123n4, 183
  naiveté of, 170, 170n3
  and rationalism, 183
  and relationships between conditions, 131
grinningness, and universe, 235
grins without cats, 235, 235n4
ground
  abstraction from, 114
  and attributes, 336
  and causality, 110
  and causal mode, 109
  conceptual functioning as test of, 199

and consequent, 102, 102fig, 102n2, 105, 109, 247, 247n7
  as continuous, 335
  defined, 104, 335, 366
  and epochal occasion, 105
  and eternal object, 105
  and historical route, 105
  and imaginal occasion, 105
  natural, entity from, 334
  from occasions, 105
  and opportunity, 108
  and past, 335, 335fig
  phases of, 335–6
  physical occasion as, 165, 198
  and potentiality, 335, 336
  reversion of, 105, 105n4
  satisfaction and criticism phase of, 335
  substantial and perceptual phase of, 335
  undefined, 366
Grundlagen einer allgemeinen Mannigfaltigkeitslehre (Cantor) (1883), 129n6

h (Planck's constant), 41, 91, 93–4, 93n1
Haldane, John Burdon Sanderson, 103n4
Haldane, Richard Burdon, 103n4
hallucination, error in, 374
Hamelin, Octave, 372
Hamlet, 235
Hamlet (Shakespeare), 235
happening, 267
harmony
  in actual occasions, 56
  versus confusion, 113
  hypothesis of, 358
  in medieval philosophy, 87
  in Plato, 56
Hartshorne, Charles, 327n2
  as note-taker
    biographical sketch of, xli
    career of, xli
    edits to notes of, xlii
    guest lectures by, xxxi, xlvi–xlvii, lv
    history of notes of, xli–xlii
    organisation of notes of, xlii
    quality of notes of, xli–xliii
    as Whitehead scholar, xli
Harvard lectures
  adjustments to, xxvii
  assigned reading for *see* assigned reading
  attendance at, xxxi
  comparison of notes for, xxxiii–xxxiv
  content of, xxix–xxx, xxxv
  dates for, xxxv

development of Whitehead's thought in, x, xi–xii, xxvii–xxviii, xxix–xxx
  enrolment in, xxvi, xxviii
  nature of, x, xi, xxvii–xxviii
  notetakers for, xxv, xxxvi–lv
  reading aloud in, xxxvi
  salary for, xxviin6, xxx
  schedules for, xxvii
  students in, xxvi
  topics of, x–xi, xxvii
  Whitehead's evaluation of, xxvi
Harvard lectures, notes for
  dating of, xxxv
  discovery of, ix, x–xii
  editorial conventions for notes from, xiii–xv
  expansion of abbreviations in, xxxvi
  integration of, xxxiii–xxxiv
  for 1926–7, xlvi–lv
  for, 1925–6, xxxix–xlvi
  nature of, xxxiii
  selection of, xxxii–xxxiii, xxxv
  sources for, xxv, xxvn1
  standardisation of, xiii–xv, xxxvi
  state of, xxv
  style of, xxxvi
  unused, xxxv
Harvard seminars, xxvii
  notes for, sources for, xxvn1
Harvard University
  independence of departments at, lviii
  Whitehead's appointment to, vii
Harvey, William, 409, 410n1
Hawthorne experiments, xxxix
Heath, Louise Robinson, 313, 313n2
  biographical sketch of, xxxvii
  conferences of, with Whitehead, xxxvii
  as graduate student, xxxvii–xxxviii
  quality of notes of, xxxviii–xxxix
Heath, Thomas Little, 7n3, 118, 118n5
Hegel
  and absolute, 208n2, 397n1
  and contradiction, 245
  and epochal unit of actual occasion, 45
  in history of philosophy, 172
  and mathematics, 126–7n6
  and negative, 101, 101n7
  and not-being, 6
  and principle of contradictories, 44
  rejection of, 205n1
  and relatedness, 235, 236n1
  and substance, 188
  and Whitehead, 172n1
Hegelians, 251

467

Index

heliocentric hypothesis, 394, 409
Henderson, Lawrence J., xxvii, xxx, 391
Henry IV, Part 1 (Shakespeare), 129, 129n5
Heraclitus
  consciousness in, 53
  flowing in, 53
  and particular occasion, 10
  and physical occasion, 9, 10
  and scepticism, 10, 55
  and time, 347
here and now
  and immediate occasion, 13
  and known, 12
  and occasion, 61
  and self, 13
  versus there and then, 13, 59
  and unity, 12
Hexter, Maurice Beck, 404
higher, explained in terms of lower, 97
historical revolt, and cause and effect, 48
historical route, 232, 264
  and action, 357
  and child development, 402
  and community, 101n5
  and concurrence, 357
  and congruity, 357
  and creativity, 95
  defined, 73–74
  dimension of, 105
  and diversity, 100n8
  and endurance, 72, 247
  and enduring object, 25, 28, 72, 111, 352, 401
  of enduring entity, 27, 404
  and entity, 100–1, 101fig
  and epoch, 101n5
  and epochal occasion, 101, 105
  and experient occasion, 73–4
  formed by occasions, 71, 71fig
  formulae for, 246–7
  and ground, 105
  and identity, 100, 100n8
  and individual, 246
  and inheritance, 107, 352
  inspectional relationship along, 79–80
  of mental route, 106
  as microcosm, 100n7
  of occasions, 72, 100n6, 246, 399
  perception of, 80
  perceptual object as, 73–4
  and point inheritance, 280
  points in, 247
  and rest, 277
  and sense data, 361, 362
  and spatio-temporal relations, 360
  and transmission, 247
  as tropism, 110, 110fig

History of European Morals (Lecky) (1869), 230n2
History of Greek Mathematics (Heath) (1921), 313, 313n2
history *see also under subfields of history*
  as conformation to event, 255
  of entity, 255
  integration of, 356
  of objectification, 255
  and privacy, 203
  and rise of scientific mind, 5
  and science, 5
  time as, 107
Hitchcock, Curtice, xxx, 3n3, 46n3, 93–4n4
Hobbes, Thomas, and subject and predicate, 381
Hocking–Cabot Fund for Systematic Philosophy, lx
Hocking, Richard, lx
Hocking, William Ernest, lix
Hoernlé, Augustus Frederic Rudolf, 187, 187n2
  as neo-idealist, 187n4
  and new rationalism, 187
  as realist, 187
  and substance, 187
Homer, epics of, 292
Hooton, Earnest, 403, 403n2
how
  and abstraction, 114–15
  and entity, 115
  versus *how not*, 73
  of possibility, 99
  of relation, 115
  and *what*, 115
humans, as intrusive organism, 294
Hume David, 337
  and *a priori*, 52
  and appeal to action, 191
  and appeal to practice, 209, 371, 393
  assigned reading from, xxviii, 4
  and Berkeley, 171n10
  and Cartesian metaphysics, 108
  and cause, 75, 107, 108, 393, 400
  and cogitation, 57
  and consciousness of causation, 254
  and Descartes, 359–60
  as empiricist, 132n1
  and experience, 75
  and impression, 12, 58
  and induction, 49
  and internal relations, 99
  and Kant, 6, 7, 172, 193n4
  and knowing, 50, 112
  and mathematics, 382
  and memory, 75, 76, 345
  metaphysics, 99
  method of, 360

  mind versus matter in, 75
  and morphological view, 30, 76, 77
  and observation versus induction, 6
  and occasion, 50, 63, 63n1, 80
  and perceptivity, 108
  present versus past in, 75
  and presentational relations, 110
  and private world, 196, 196n1
  and properties of matter, 28
  and rationalism, 5, 382
  and relatedness, 235–6, 236n1
  and scientists, 48
  and spatial relationships, 28
  and time, 58
Husserl, Edmund, and possible worlds, 10
hypotheses non fingo, 194, 194n3, 195, 412
hypothesis
  conceptual, and experience, 377
  importance of, 409
  and Newton, 194, 194n3, 195
  publication of, 377

icthyosauri, number of, 326
ideal
  and actual, 62, 212
  approximating to, 313
  as archetype, 166
  and creation, 34
  God as, 114
  logic as realm of, 214, 214n
  in nature, 114
  non-actual entities as, 212
  progress towards, in rationalism, 191
  as set of non-actual entities, 212
ideal comparison
  and mentality, 219
  as principle of metaphysics, 210
  defined, 210
  principle of, 215, 218, 219–20
idealism
  and knowing, 112
  versus realism, 19
idealism, absolute, 211
  and Bradley, 208, 208n2
  and Kant, 193
  idealism, German
    catastrophe of, 205
    move from, 205n1
    and science, 291, 291n3
idealist
  and realist, 19
  Whitehead as, 187
ideality, realm of, 14
ideals, imported into nature, 113, 113n10

ideas
  actual thing existing in, 206
  balanced with facts, 409
  bundle of, 6
  distinctness of, 179
  as elements, 43
  and event, 14
  exemplification of, 192
  and facts, 193–4
  and flux, 10
  how to design, 322–3
  and mind, 409
  new, as muddled, 182, 182n7
  and objectification, 206, 206n6
  particular, 6
  and Plato, 10, 14, 43, 56
  private world of, 333
  progress in breakdown of, 136, 136n2
  qualifying subject, 202
  recasting of, 76
  relevance of, 79
  revisions of, 207
  and rigid logicality, 192, 192n2
  search for, 173
  stages of, 96
  system of, 195
  tests for, 177, 179–81
  theory of, 202
  and thought, 6
  on universe, 291
  unobvious, 128, 128n2
  and Whitehead, 14
ideas, scheme of
  and experience, 191
  imaginative suggestion of, 191
  and obviousness, 192
ideas, universal
  and experience, 6
  in Kant, 6
  versus particular, 6
identity
  versus attribute, 362
  and change, 247, 247n3
  and concept and percept, 347
  and contrast, 102fig, 103
  defined, 17
  and demonstration, 225, 225n1
  and diversity, 160, 199, 225, 225n1, 344
  and endurance, 17, 28
  enduring, 65
  and epoch, 101
  and eternal objects, 332
  and functioning, 347
  and historical route, 100, 100n8
  and knowledge, 197, 199, 217
  and modes of functioning, 227
  nature of, 102fig, 103
  of objects, 18
  and objectification, 225
  and occasions, 17, 65

  patience of relationship of, 225
  in *Principia Mathematica*, 347n3
  and relation, 347
  and sense data, 65
  of type, 102–3
  use of, 17
ignorant man, 124
Illinois, University of, lectures at, xxx
illusion
  as genuine perception, 219, 219n4
  and memory, 346
image
  of memory, 345
  in present, 345
  and presentational immediacy, 356
imagination, 251
  and attentiveness, 199
  and comparison, 230
  conscious perception as, 224
  defined, 243
  discipline of, 175
  and disciplined mind, 178
  and flexibility, 74
  and Greek tragedy, 292
  and infinity, 74
  and knowledge, 192, 198, 199, 356
  and memory, 346
  and mental potentiality, 226
  and metaphysics, 194, 194n4
  no form dominates in, 378
  and nature, 244
  and observation, 377, 377n1
  and perception, 192
  and philosophy, 175, 178, 178n2, 393, 395
  and progress, 200
  as pure potentiality, 334
  and real world, 207
  with relevance, 244
  and science, 194, 194n4, 291–2
  and sense perception, 345
  and thought, 244
  and trained mind, 244
  useless, 244
  variation of genus in, 244
imaginative and stimulating, 409
imaginative origination, defined, 230
immediate prehension, and art, 15
immediate presentation
  of actual entity, 277
  and Einstein, 280
  locus of, 281
  in organism, 281
  as private, 275
  as receptacle, 277
  of sense data, 275

immediately given
  atomic nature of, 6
  and Berkeley, 6
  and Descartes, 6
immediately real, 161, 161fig
immortal, past as, 107
immortality
  and actual objects, 44
  and causation, 345
  of community, 94
  as concept, 7
  and eternal objects, 44
  of fact, 253
  and form of things, 100n4
  and metaphysics, 44, 44n3
  objective, 254, 355
  of occasion, 93, 100, 253, 345
  of past, 33, 349
  and sameness, 44
  theory of objective, 253
Imperial College London, vii
Imperial College of Science and Technology, vii
impress
  of art, 63
  creative, 18, 93
  and given, 60
  intuition as, 12
  limitation of, 93
  permanent, 63
  realisation as, 12
impression
  in Hume, 12
  on mind, 12
inaccuracy, knowledge of, 127
incompatibility, 174
  as essence of world, 174, 174n8
  and event, 15
incompleteness, 251–2
  and actual entity, 251
  of actual world, 125
  and antecedents and consequents, 256
  of atoms, 350
  in community of occasions, 253
  of consciousness, 254
  of entity, 257
  of future, 252, 253, 352
  and God, 251
  and objectification of entities, 255, 255n3
  of occasion, 349
  and physical memory, 253, 344
  of present, 252
  relative, 349
  and social relations, 349
  and time, 246, 251, 255, 343n2, 344
independence
  of contemporaneous occasions, 23
  in Descartes, 207
  and ethics, 208

Index

of God, 209
of individuality, 204
of mind, 353
and philosophy, 208, 208n2
of simultaneous entities, 258
of special characters, 255
indeterminateness
  of green, 18
  of occasion, 18
indetermination
  versus actuality, 18
  in eternal object, 66
  of occasion, 253, 253n5
India
  philosophy in, 182
  scientific state of mind in, 5
individual
  and community, 93, 115–16, 153
  entity as, 216
  and freedom, 208
  and good and evil, 216
  and historical route, 246
  individual, past of, 246
  publicity of, 335
  versus relation, 124
  and self-enjoyment, 243
  social environment, 208
  solidarity of, with universe, 216n4
  and space and time, 93
  and value, 207, 207n1
individualism
  defined, 396
  and ethics, 396
  and prohibition against stealing, 392
individuality
  and actual, 112
  of art, 63
  and Bosanquet, 15
  and Descartes, 204
  of entity, 228, 269
  heightening of, 219
  independence of, 201, 204
  and intensity, 248
  and limitation, 18, 112
  and mental pole, 231
  and occasion, 63, 63n4
  and percipience, 231
  principle of, 19
  and supersession, 216, 216n5
  and universe, 212
individualisation
  and actual, 220, 376
  and concretion, 351
  and creativity, 213, 344
  of energy, 89
  exclusive and inclusive character of, 220
  and transition, 34
induction, 333–4
  antecedent, 49
  and community, 58

error in, 152
example of, 132n3
giving new information, 235
and Hume, 49
information from, 235
in Kant, 6
leading to formula, 49
and memory, 49
method of, 49
and morphological view, 77
and number of instances, 49
versus object, 75n3
and occasion, 227
in philosophy of science, 4
possibility of, 234
and probability, 240
problem of, 6
and Russell, 49
in science, 112
theories of, 176n1
and universal judgement, 55
Industrial Worker: A Statistical Study of Human Relations in a Group of Manual Workers (T. N. Whitehead) (1938), xxxix
inertia
  and energy, 90
  of existence, 33
  and future, 82
  law of, 411
  and mass, 89–90
  as normality, 33
inevitability
  and religion, 292
  and tragedy, 292, 292n6
inexhaustibleness, 237
inexplicable
  drawing attention to, 175n5
  ignoring, 175, 175n4
inference, and proposition, 389
Inferno (Dante) (1472), 212n1
infinite, different sorts of, 389
infinite classes, and correlation, 338
infinitesimals, theory of, 88
infinities, distinctions among, 143
infinity
  approach to, 126–7n6
  axiom of, 332
  continuous, 329
  correlation of, 130n1
  defined, 218
  dense, 328, 329
  divisibility of, 388
  and imagination, 74
  as number, 327
  and order type, 143
  of possible changes, and flexibility, 74
  proof of types of, 329
  and reference, 374–5
  and time, 70
  time interval in, 375

types of, 328
versus unboundedness, 389
vicious regression to, 240
Inge, William, 216, 216n2
ingression, 381
  and actual occasions, 196
  and aesthetic individuality, 226
  defined, 251
  determination of, in occasion, 18
  diverse modes of, 225
  and eternal object, 79, 98n7, 196, 226, 227
  modes of, 197
  of objects in occasion, 66, 66n4
  and occasion, 18, 21, 224, 251
  into occasion, 18, 251
  and relationships of objects to occasions, 21
  and universals, 98n7
ingression, conceptual, and actual occasion, 165
ingression, concrete
  and actual occasion, 165
  as aesthetic element, 165
ingression, perceptive
  and knowledge, 197
  and physical occasion, 197
ingression, perceptual, 230
  and conceptual function, 230
inherent, derivation of, 359
inheritance
  and dimensions, 351
  and endurance, 72
  and enduring object, 25
  from environment, 350
  and historic route, 352
  and occasion, 25, 106, 106n5, 362
  principle of, 106, 106n8
  successive, 25
  from universe, 350
Inquiry (Berkeley) *see Siris*
insight
  in critical philosophy, 190
  in metaphysics, 231
  and philosophy, 192
  in rationalism, 190
  in religion, 231
inspectio, 73, 73n1, 209, 232, 242
inspection
  and class theory, 74
  of *cognita*, 32
  of internal character, 80
  of mind, 28, 74
  versus presentation, 78
inspectional relationship, 109
  causality as, 73n8
  and contemporary occasion, 73
  defined, 73
  of eternal objects, 73, 73fig
  along historical route, 79–80
  and immediate occasion, 110

470

Index

in knowledge, 79–80, 80n1
of occasion, 79–80
and presentational relationship, 80
instance
  beyondness of immediate, 49
  and induction, 49
  philosophy, 49
instantaneous space, 277
instants
  discrete, 260
  as everywhere dense, 350
  and fact, 144
  as happenings, 212
  defined, 86n1
  infinite number of, 260
  relation between, 144
  successive, in morphological view, 76
  and time, 153, 260
instrument, how to design, 322
integers
  order type of, 130n1
  relations of, 330
integration, of past, 232
intelligibility, and science, 5
intensity
  gradations of, 213, 243
  grades of, 263
  and individuality, 2478
  and universals, 263
  versus value
intensive quantity, 84
  and actuality, 98
interaction
  and perspective, 335
  of substances, 204
interconnection, in universe, 335
internal, realisation as, 21
Introduction to Mathematical Philosophy (Russell) (1919)
  as assigned reading, 126
  real numbers in, 209n2
Introduction to Mathematics (Whitehead) (1911), viii, 148
  as assigned reading, 293
intrusion, and prehension, 62
intuition, 245
  blind, 343
  and conscious perception, 355
  form of, 60
  as impress, 12
  and Kant, 12, 58, 353
  by occasion, 351
  and organised world, 353
  and physical world, 349
  and space, 12
  as time, 9, 12
  and time and space, 58
irrelevance, and relevance, 203
is, as pointing, 202

isolation
  and occasion, 59
  versus synthesis, 59, 60n2
  and togetherness, 94
it
  as abstraction, 114
  and community, 114
  as entity, 113, 114, 115
  nature of, 116
  occasion as, 61, 61n4
  versus other, 116

Jackson, Gardner, liv–lv
James, William, viii, 69, 251, 268
  assigned reading from, xxviii, 4
  biographical note on, 47n8
  and consciousness, 53, 97
  versus Descartes, 205n1
  and function, 11
  influence of, on Whitehead, 47n7
  and knowing, 96
  logical realism of, 18, 66n3
  and morphological view, 76
  and rationalisation, 251n5
  and subjectivism, 53
  and substance, 188
  and universe, 301
  value of, 175
  Whitehead's opinion of, 4n5
Jansen, Cornelius, 292n5
Jansenism, 292, 292n5
Jesuits
  and inevitability, 292
  view of universe of, 292
Johnson, William Ernest, 117–18n3, 119n4, 174n6
  propositions of, 372
Joule, James Prescott, 89, 89n4
judging, as a particular, 379
judgment
  and assumption of normalities, 258
  as conformation of thought to universal forms, 332
  and conscious perception, 355
  as perceptivity, 356
  and principle of analysis, 50
  and proposition, 371
  as psychological, 371
  synthesis of, 50
Jupiter, 373–4

Kant
  and *a priori*, 8
  and absolute idealism, 193
  action in, 12
  Anschauung in, 114n2
  versus Bacon, 193
  Caird's commentary on, 172
  and chaotic datum, 59, 192n4, 193
  and chaotic given, 65
  and cognition, 81

conceptual activity of, 317
consistency in, 193
and criteria of *a priori*, 52
criticism of, 7, 171, 171–2n12
defined instant of, 86n1
Ding an Sich of, 359
and discovery of world, 31
and extensive quantity, 35
and facts and ideas, 194
function of knowing in, 182
functioning of mind in, 193
given for, 166
and given occasion, 7
God in, 166
and Hume, 6, 7, 172, 193n4
induction in, 6
and intensive quantity, 98n3, 213
and internal relations, 99
and intuition, 12, 58, 343, 353
and knowing, 9, 42, 112, 193
and knowledge, 58
and knowledge of world, 195
Leibniz in, 171–2, 171–2n12
and logic of universe, 269
and mental occasion, 108
and monad, 29
and necessary belief, 180
and Newton, 171–2
and occasion, 50
and perception, 263
and perceptivity, 108, 192, 192n4
phenomenalism of, 31
and Platonic realism, 114n2
rejection of, 205n1
and relatedness, 235, 236n1
and space, 12, 150
and substance, 188
synthetic and analytic method of, 214
and synthetic propositions, 51
and time, 9, 12 58, 84, 252
transcendental aesthetic of, 176
value in, 12
and Whitehead, 172, 172n1
Whitehead's view of, 171–2n12, 172n1
work of, on Hume, 6
world in, 29
Kant's Theory of Knowledge (Prichard) (1909), 171, 171n11, 171–2n12
Keats, John, 16
Kelvin, Lord (William Thomson), 29, 295, 295n6
Kemp Smith, Norman, 8, 52, 358, 358n2
  biographical sketch of, 358n2
  as new realist, 187n4
  as realist, 187
Kennedy, Roy J., 287n7

471

Index

Kepler, Johannes, 118, 118*n*6, 409, 409*n*3
  and astronomy, 410, 412, 412*fig*
  and celestial mechanics, 317*n*2
  and laws of motion, 412, 412*fig*
Kerby-Miller, Sinclair, lvii, lx
Keynes, John Maynard, vii, 239–40, 239–40*n*7, 240*n*1
King, Lester Snow, lii–liii
Kingdom of Heaven, 208, 222
knowing, 52; *see also* cognisance
  of activity, 31
  and Berkeley, 30, 31, 78, 78*n*2
  and body, 76*n*3
  and *cognita*, 30
  and *cognitor*, 58
  and *cognitum*, 31, 78
  of total community, 22
  creating world by, 31
  and Descartes, 30, 78
  elements of, 42
  and experience, 30, 52
  of experient occasion, 22
  and fact, 100
  as function of order, 182
  about future and past, 32
  and given, 65
  and Hume, 50
  and imaginal occasions, 21–2
  and immediate occasion, 51
  in James, 96
  and Kant, 9, 193
  versus knowing *cognita*, 30
  and known, 12
  and matter, 87
  and morphological view, 76
  and occasions, 50
  organising faculty of, 51
  and perception, 31, 76
  and plurality, 52
  and process, 9
  process of, as general, 192–3, 193*n*1
  and reality, 31
  and relation of elements, 51
  and simple location, 52
  and spatiality, 12
  versus stuff, 96
  and temporal world, 112
  and temporality, 12
  value as, 17
  and world, 42
knowing, function of, 51, 182
  as attribute, 96
  and Bradley, 52
  and relational elements, 112
  and sense perception, 8
  and solipsism, 52
  and time, 9, 52
knowing, occasions of
  and cognition, 22
  and experient occasion, 69
  as imaginal occasions, 69

knowing-of-process, 52
knowledge
  knowledge, 42–3, 99–100
  absolute, and relative knowledge, 135*n*4
  and abstract versus concrete, 43
  and abstract versus experient, 43
  as abstraction, 45
  and actual, 219–20
  and actual occasion, 96, 217
  of actual world, 132, 195
  as analytic for given, 166
  antecedent, and analysis, 377
  and bodily senses, 96
  and character of creature, 223
  and cognition, 22
  as cognisance of perceptivity, 108
  and concept of identity, 17
  and conceptual functioning, 223
  as concrescence of modes of functioning, 197, 198
  and concretion of identity and diversity, 197, 199
  as creature, 94
  and datum, 96, 198
  defined, 42, 43, 94, 206, 223
  and demonstration, 225, 225*n*1, 229*n*1
  and Descartes, 360
  direct, of eternal object, 223, 223*n*2, 223*n*3
  versus dream, 132
  enjoyment of, 354
  and entity, 223, 360
  and envisagement, 42
  as epiphenomenon, 96
  erroneousness of, 97
  and eternal object, 197, 206, 351, 351*fig*
  of event, 225
  and experience, 149, 195, 195*n*6
  of experient occasion, 65, 110
  expression of, 252, 252*n*3
  and extensive abstraction, 304
  of fact, 29
  factors in, 42, 192
  fake, 192–3, 193*n*1
  forms of, 361
  and function of matter, 96
  as functional, 76*n*3
  of future, 107
  and given occasion, 96
  how it is possible, 94, 164, 191
  how to examine, 94
  of identity, 217
  and identity of entity, 228
  and imaginal occasion, 64, 69, 96, 105
  and imagination, 192, 198, 199, 356

  inadequacy of, 22, 71
  inspectional relationships in, 79–80, 80*n*1
  and instantaneous space, 277
  and Kant, 7
  of knowledge, 105
  and known, 82
  and language, 187
  limited by mind, 195*n*5
  and mathematics, 185
  meaning of, 164
  and memory, 270
  and mentality, 365
  and metaphysics, 94, 99
  and named points, 135
  and new rationalism, 195
  and objectification, 365
  and occasion, 58
  as outcome, 401
  and particular occasion, 8–9
  of past, 132, 361
  and perception, 108, 192, 232, 333
  and perceptive ingression, 197
  and perceptual relationships, 223
  and philosophy, 96
  and physical experience, 176
  possibility of, 12, 65
  and privacy, 203
  and process, 194, 401
  as question in modern philosophy, 42
  and reformed rationalism, 191
  and relatedness, 32, 81
  relational, 360
  and relations of entities, 360
  representation of, and presentational immediacy, 186
  requirements for, 33
  of self, 298
  by sense perception, 7
  from standpoint of physical occasion, 165
  subject–object theory in, 202
  and symbol, 360
  symbolism of, 186
  and system, 33
  and thing on its own, 120
  types of, 6–7
  of ultimate fact, 108
  and ultimate occasion, 69
  universal, from analysis, 50–1
  from universal standpoint, 166 *n*1
  of universe, 274
  of unobserved things, 132
  and value, 43, 95
  of values, 7
  of world, 333
  of world, origins of, 223
  world as datum of, 108

knowledge, natural, principles of, 304
knowledge, primary
 of antecedent life, 79–80, 80n1
 and secondary, 199–200
 as ultimate fact, 199
knowledge, relative
 and absolute knowledge, 135n4
 deduction from, 135, 135fig
 formula as, 135
knowledge, secondary, as believed fact, 199
knowledge, theory of, 94–6
 and deduction of absolute knowledge, 135n4
 and ideal comparison, 219
 and imaginal occasion, 96
 and relation of substances, 204
known
 for empiricist, 132
 and here and now, 12
 and knowing, 12
 and knowledge, 82
 and patience, 226
 universe as, 12
 versus unknown, 182
known things, tests for, 94
Köhler, Wolfgang, 257n1

Laertes, 235
Langmuir, Irving, 41, 41n2, 41n3, 92n5
language
 abstract, 126
 analysis of, 200
 as anti-metaphysical, 237, 237n2
 and concrete thing, 386–7
 versus diagram, 203
 equivocal meanings in, 198
 expression by, 384
 and general concepts, 174
 and geometry, 127
 and Greek philosophy, 200–1, 201n1
 inaccuracy of, 171n4
 inadequacy of, 238
 as inexpressible, 385
 information in, 211
 and knowledge, 187
 logic of, 384
 in mathematics, 297
 and meaning, 205
 and metaphysics, 210, 211, 237, 237n2
 and Mill, 382–3
 as misleading, 211
 multiplicity of meaning in, 201
 naïve trust in, 203
 nothing can be said in, 385
 ordinary, and reasoning, 304
 origins of philosophy in, 114
 and philosophy, 116, 186, 374, 385
 as pictures, 387, 390
 as pointing, 202, 364
 and projection in geometry, 384
 and projective geometry, 387
 and science, 126n4, 297
 and sense data, 361
 as symbolism, 186, 201
 technical, 96
 and thought, 174
 trust in, 212
 and truth, 211
 unfamiliar forms of, 203
 as unique case, 388
 as violent metaphor, 179
Laski, Harold, 221, 221n4, 222
Latin, and abstract language, 126
law
 conciliation of privacy and socialism by, 397
 as hypothetical, 174
 as principle of scientific thought, 48
law of attraction, and matter, 90
law of identity, and immediate occasion, 53
laws
 and concepts, 173, 174n2
 depth of, 302
 of science, 172
 search for, 173
laws of motion, 411
 and Galileo, 411
 invariance of, 286–7
 as revolutionary, 412
laws of nature
 and congruity of organisms, 405
 in different measurements, 286, 286n2
 as not eternal, 351
 as special to epoch, 177
laws of physics, and final ends, 397
Le Verrier, Urbain, 412, 412n3
League of Free Nations Association, 70n1
Lecky, William Edward Hartpole, 230, 230n2
Lectures on the Science of Language (Müller) (1863), 126n2
Leibniz, Gottfried Wilhelm
 and criteria of *a priori*, 52
 and geometrical reasoning, 205
 influence of, on Kant, 171–172, 171–2n12
 and monad, 9–10, 235–6, 236n1, 278
 perspectives in, 343
 and physics, 88
 point in, 307
 and possible worlds, 10, 55
 and problems in differential calculus, 137n1
 and substance, 171, 171–2n12, 352
 and theory of space, 307
 universe in, 358
 Whitehead's objection to, 172
Lewis, C. I., 98n9
Life and Adventures of Nicholas Nickleby (Dickens) (1839), 97n5
Life of Erasmus (Smith) (1923), 44
life
 accuracy as art of, 116
 as doing versus being, 77n1
 as functioning, 90
 slow secular change in, 244
 and universals, 253
light
 as bombardment, 294
 and sight, 296
 wave theory of, 295
likeness
 and proposition, 381, 382
 versus unlikeness, 381
limit
 and convergence of measurement, 148
 defined, 148, 313
 point as, 148, 148fig
 in scientific state of mind, 5
 space without thickness as, 276
 as type of order, 129, 129n4
limitation
 by abstraction, 33
 and achievement, 34, 103
 and actual entity, 215
 on actual occasion, 82
 and actual thing, 222
 of actual world in potentiality, 195
 and actuality, 116, 217–18
 antecedents as, 34
 and art, 18, 62–4, 63
 on beyond, 12
 in community, 21
 concrescence under, 206
 and creative synthesis, 103
 creativity under, 98, 98–9n10
 on datum in occasion, 109
 defined, 224
 demonstration under, 224, 224–5n3
 entity under, 364
 and eternal objects, 82, 103, 103fig
 by events, 14
 and finitude, 237
 and freedom, 69
 function of, 64, 64n2
 and future occasion, 81
 of given, 64
 happiness of, 217–18
 how it works, 93
 and immediate occasion, 110
 imposed by reality, 14

473

Index

of impress, 93
and individuality, 18, 112
and metaphysics, 61, 61*n*6
modes of, 59–60
modal, of being, 61
object under, 374
and objectification, 225, 343
and occasion, 14, 19, 19*fig*, 59–60, 59*n*6, 67, 101, 242
passage into occasion under, 165, 165*n*3
by past, 64
on *perceptum*, 78, 78*n*4
and physical event, 14
on plurality, 12
predicate in proposition as, 364
prehension under, 353–4
prime mover as, 34
of relational essence, 224
of relationships, 27
and religious art, 64
and spontaneous choice, 21
and synthesis, 31
and there and then, 59
uniformity as, 64, 64*n*2, 64
and unity, 21
and value, 15
for Whitehead, 15
limits
  measurements converging to, 149
  method of taking, 316*n*1
line
  as class of points, 325, 327
  closed, 325
  and coordinates, 360
  cut in, 314
  defined, 127, 326
  end of, 314
  generation of, 314
  how to define, 323
  importance of, 318
  as intersection of moments, 160
  neutral definition for, 322
  as ordered points, 129
  as route of approximation, 315, 316
  segment, defined, 325, 325*fig*
  as series of points, 324
  in space, 282
lines
  correlation of, 281
  intersection of, 314, 327, 327*fig*
lines, curved, and straight lines, 326
lines, parallel, and congruence, 283–4, 283*fig*
lines, straight
  extra density of, 328
  and motion, 283
  order type of, 138
  in time, 282, 282*fig*

linkage, poles in, 253
literary incompletion, 125
literary tradition, and science, 126
literature
  and philosophy, 129
  and reality, 50
  value of, 50
Lobachevsky, Nikolai, 180, 180*n*1, 180*n*2
localisation, sense data as, 337
locality
  and causal efficacy, 337
  and presentation, 337
location, simple, 90, 294
  and Descartes, 77
  and knowing, 52
  and matter, 77
  and mind, 77
Locke, John
  and Descartes, 170*n*4, 188, 188*n*5, 353
  like Dewey, 341, 341*n*3
  influence of, 170
  and knowledge, 58
  and metaphysics, 188, 353
  and mind, 267, 353, 359
  mind of, 195, 195*n*1
  nescio quid of, 359
  and Newton, 75, 188, 188*n*5
  perceptivity in, 217*n*5
  and perpetual perishing, 247, 249
  and properties of matter, 28
  and reflection, 359
  and substance, 203, 203*n*8, 358, 359
  and time, 247
  and Whitehead, 172, 341, 341*n*3
loci, structure of, and continuum, 278
locus
  division of, and duration, 156
  of occasions, and correlation, 276, 276*fig*
logic
  aesthetics of, 118*n*2, 119*n*1
  and accuracy, 171*n*4
  and Aristotle, 63*n*2, 149, 363
  deductive system in, 118, 119*n*1
  definite meaning in, 214, 214*n*2
  and Descartes, 63
  domain of, 184
  elements in, 341–2, 342*n*1
  and existence, 382
  and God, 166
  and Greeks, 183, 214
  inductive, and scientific method, 49
  influence of, on philosophy, 170–1
  and mathematics, 370

meaning in, 214
and medieval philosophy, 63
and metaphysics, 6, 60, 371
misapprehension in, 214
as not theology, 372
as objective, 183*n*7
occasion in, 51
and philosophy, 171
and proposition, 171, 171*n*5, 375
and psychology, 383
and rational standards for criticism, 183
and rationalism, 183
as realm of ideal, 214, 214*n*
relations in, 370
and Renaissance, 214
and right or wrong, 334
rigid, and ideas, 192
and sentence, 363
simplicity of, 185
and space, 370
and subject–predicate theory, 203, 211
symbols in, 214
and truth, 171, 334
and truth and falsehood, 370
value of, 238, 238*n*1
logic, Aristotelian
  and philosophy, 289
  revival of, 5
logic, mathematical, propositions in, 390
logic measurement, 269
Logic (Johnson) (1921–4), 117–18*n*3, 174*n*7
logical coherence
  and analysis of belief, 188, 188*n*2
  and analysis, 377
  and Greeks, 188, 188*n*2
  as test of belief, 181
logical constants
  and principles, 388
  and signs, 388
logical construct, physical space as, 275
logical contradictions, 102, 102*n*9
logical nominalism, and potentiality, 225
logical realism, 18
logical reasoning, certainties of, as hypothetical, 185
logical simplicity, in relationships, 128, 128*n*3
logical stability
  and entity, 227
  and modes of functioning, 227
logician, and plausibility, 155
Loomer, Bernard, xli
Lorenz, Hendrik Antoon, 101*n*4, 302, 302*n*2
Lowe, Victor, xxxviii

474

Index

Lowell, Abbott Lawrence, xxvi, xxx
Lowell lectures, xxvi
  of Whitehead, xxx, 113*n*1
lower segment
  defined, 138
  proof of, 139–40
Lowes, John Livingston, xxx
Luther, Martin, 73, 73*n*7

macrocosm, versus microcosm, 101
magnet, as example of dipolarity, 197
magnetic force, versus magnetic induction, 320
magnetic induction, 320
magnetism
  and matter, 29–30
  study of, 408
magnitude
  correlation of, 338, 338*fig*
  defined, 120
  extensive, in physics, 273
  versus quantity, 120
  and segmental number, 143
  symbol for, 122
Management and the Worker (Roethlisberger and Dickson) (1939), xxxix
manifold, point in, 313, 315
Mansel, Henry Longueville, 216, 216*n*1
many
  community of, 59
  and one, 9, 13, 31, 78, 78*n*2, 78*n*3, 113, 115, 376
  synthesis of, 115
  types of, 13
martyrdom, psychology of, 147
mass
  and activity, 90
  of atom, 90
  constancy of, 295
  defined, 29, 75
  and Descartes, 40, 183
  of electron, 40
  and energy, 29, 40, 77, 89, 295
  expression of behaviour of, 37
  extended, and external activity, 89
  and extension, 75
  and force, 37, 87, 413
  and function, 37, 90
  and Galileo, 37, 87, 183*n*1
  and inertia, 89–90
  laws of, 173, 173*n*3
  and matter, 29, 37, 87, 88
  and Newton, 37, 87, 89–90, 183
  as property of matter, 28, 29
  for Pythagoras, 37
  and space, 37
  and time, 37

mass × acceleration, 411
Massachusetts General Hospital social service department, lviii
matching, 119, 119*n*4
  and correlation, 140, 140*fig*
  and isoid relation, 119, 120
  mathematical, 140
  and multiplicity, 140
  and symmetry and transitivity, 337
material, extended, 89, 90
materialism
  in science, 291
  versus theory of values, 6
mathematical logic, propositions in, 390
mathematical physics *see* physics, mathematical
mathematical projection, 386
mathematician
  as artist, 186
  and entities, 18
  and eternal objects, 66n2
mathematics
  and abstract entities, 184
  abstraction versus example in, 134
  and actual world, 185
  aesthetics of, 186
  and accurate thought, 128
  application of, to universe, 132–4
  and Aristotle, 81
  axioms and premises in, 189*n*6
  beauty of, 124
  and certain knowledge, 185
  and classes, 370
  and creative power of human mind, 139, 139*n*3
  and cricket, 126–7*n*6
  defined, 10, 137
  of Descartes, 133–4, 133*n*4
  difficult problems in, 123
  domain of, 184
  elaboration of clear ideas in, 137, 137*n*2
  of Euclid, 133
  given in, 251
  goal of, 189
  and Greeks, 123, 123*n*4, 183
  and Hegel, 126–7*n*6
  as high grade of abstraction, 326
  and Hume, 382
  influence of, on philosophy, 170–1, 289
  influence of, on Plato, 292
  language in, 297
  and logic, 370
  matching in, 140
  measurement as applied, 123, 123*n*3
  and metaphysics, 235

and Mill, 382
  as objective, 183*n*7
  and order of points, 130
  and order types, 129, 135–6, 136*fig*, 136*n*1
  and philosophy, 129, 171, 183, 184, 184*n*2
  and Plato, 10, 81
  and possibilities of world, 185
  practical use of, 123, 123*n*3
  versus pragmatism, 182
  and presentational locus, 153
  and problem solving, 126–7*n*6
  problems of, 126–7*n*6
  progress in, 403
  proposition in, 214
  and rational standards for criticism, 183
  and rationalism, 183, 183*n*7
  and rationalists, 190
  and reasoning, 305
  and relationships in actual world, 134–7
  role of, 360
  as set of relations, 131
  solutions to problems in, 403
  and theory versus practice, 177, 177*n*2
  truth in, 179
mathematics, applied, 342, 410
  discovery of, 122
  and observation, 382
mathematics, pure
  abstraction in, 137
  versus applied, 382
  and experiment, 189
  and formal relationships, 149
mathematics, Pythagorean, 123, 123*n*4, 124, 129*n*4, 130–1, 135–6, 136*fig*, 136*n*1, 259, 259*n*6
matter, 348
  as atomic, 90
  atomic theory of, 88
  and atoms, 39, 90
  cell as unit of, 90
  changes in, 37
  as continuous, 295
  and creating, 87
  and creature, 87
  and Descartes, 75, 87
  defined, 61, 75
  divisibility of, 39
  and duration, 38, 348*n*2
  and electricity, 29–30, 295, 295*n*8
  electro-magnetic theory of, 90, 182
  and energy, 29, 89, 91
  and ether, 38, 267
  and experient occasion, 99
  and external world, 87
  and extension,, 28, 29 41, 88, 90, 348*n*2

Index

and force, 87, 88, 88*fig*, 89, 353
function of, 88
functioning as essence of, 39
as fundamental, 347, 347–8n7
and Galileo, 87
in Hume, 28, 75
as kink in space, 327
and knowing, 87
and law of attraction, 90
life history of, 91
and magnetism, 29–30
and mass, 28, 29, 75, 87, 88
and Mill, 382
and mind, 88
as morphological, 76
versus mind, 18–19, 28, 31, 75, 75*table*, 77, 88, 375
natural units of, 39
and Newton, 267, 353
and organism, 61, 61n4, 88
properties of, 28–30, 37
and simple location, 77
and space, 12, 127, 267, 294
spatio-temporal behaviour of, 87
stress as property of, 29
and time, 12, 127
matter, bits of
attraction between, 90, 412
in ether, 294
forces between, 38, 87
forces in, 10
and occasions, 10
relations among, 97
as free and equal, 411
versus mind, 75
relationship between 10, 88, 97
in space and time, 10, 56
in vortices, 294, 295
matter, extended, as electrical, 90
Matter, Life, Mind, and God (Hoernlé), 187, 187n3
Maxwell, James Clerk, 29, 327
biographical note on, 118n7
and electromagnetism, 295, 350
and energy, 40
force in space, 267
laws of, 177
and probability, 118
Maxwell's equations, 287, 351, 413n1
Mayo, Elton, xxxix
McDougall, William, 97n2
McGill University, lectures at, xxx
McGilvray, James, xlv
McTaggart, J. M. E., 388
biographical sketch of, 54n6
and substance, 54–5n6
time not taken seriously by, 259, 259n4

meaning
assigned to symbolism, 214n5
and community of symbols, 336
and context, 202, 344
and explanation, 317
and language, 201, 205
in logic, 214
and predication, 201
and proposition, 382
search for, 175
in sentences, 214
and symbol, 336
and words, 205, 382
measurability
and creative successiveness, 103, 103n4
of Dedekind continuity, 143
and dimension, 104, 104n2
and dimension of being, 103n4
of experience, 104
and time, 103, 103n4
measurement, 122, 139–41
and accuracy, 113n3, 294, 409
of actual entities, 289
application of, 130
as applied mathematics, 123, 123n3
of area, 134, 134*fig*
and classification, 124, 124n4
as coincidence, 273, 274
convergence of, 148, 149
correlation of, 275
defined, 113
of entities,
and extensive quantity, 130
and formula, 134, 134n2
of future, 274
general theory of, 123, 123n5
and geometry, 155, 158
how it is possible, 130
information about, 133
and isoid relationships, 130
and law of nature, 286, 286n2
made by presentational relationships, 71
methods of 134, 161
and objectification, 380
order type, 133, 133n3, 133*fig*
and presentational relation, 163*fig*
and presented occasions, 24
and presented space, 24
and quantity, 120, 120n3
and relation, 123
and relativity, 23
and science, 70, 286
and space and time, 161
and spatio-temporal relationships, 130
starting point for, 134, 134n2
and structure, 132, 134, 273
and succession of present events, 70–1

mechanics
celestial versus terrestrial, 317, 317n2, 411n3
as science of tropisms, 110n4
Meditations on First Philosophy (Descartes) (1641)
as assigned reading, 4, 47, 170, 187n1, 341, 341n4
importance of, 170
objective versus subjective in, 53
and solipsism, 53
Meeting of Extremes in Contemporary Philosophy (Bosanquet) (1921), 187, 187n4
Meland, Bernard, xli
memory
as analysis of causation, 254
of antecedent event, 254
in brain, 76, 349
and causation, 270, 349, 400
concurrence of, 180
and consciousness of causation, 254
and ecstatic vision, 346
and Hume, 75, 76, 345
and illusion, 346
as image in present, 254, 254n4
image of, 345
and imagination, 346
immediate, and sense perception, 345
and induction, 49
and knowledge, 270
and morphological view, 77
as objectification of past, 345
and past, 49, 270, 270*fig*
and physiology, 254
versus presentational immediacy, 356
remote, and image, 346
memory, conscious
defined, 254, 254n1
and conceptual analysis, 254n1
and physical memory, 349
memory, physical
as causation, 254, 345
and conscious memory, 349
and incompleteness, 344
and incompleteness and prehension, 253
men of genius, versus lesser men, 409
Menaechmus, 118, 118n5
Mencken, H. L., 409n5
mental
concept as, 166
and physical, 182, 239, 248, 248*fig*, 336
mental functioning *see* functioning, mental
mental pain, 400

mental pole *see also* functioning, conceptual
  and actual entity, 231
  and concretion, 355
  and eternal object, 355
  importance of, 343
  and individuality, 231
  and ingression, 230
  and knowledge, 193
  linkage of, with physical pole, 343, 355
  mentality as, 343
  and occasion, 342–3, 348
  of occasion
  versus physical pole, 224
  supersedes physical pole, 343, 348
  and supersession, 248
mental potentiality, and imagination, 226
mental relation, and time, 255
mental route, historical route of, 106
mentality, 104–5
  as analytic, 251
  as analytic of mental functioning, 219
  as analytic of physical synthesis, 219
  and Descartes, 360
  dimension of, 104–5, 105n8
  effective, 227, 227n2
  and experient occasions, 107
  and facts, 97, 326
  and freedom, 106
  functions of, 238
  and ideal comparison, 219
  idle, 280
  ineffective, 227, 227n2
  and knowledge of self, 365
  as mental pole, 343
  of occasion, 238
  original in, 251
  perceptivity in, 110
  and percipience, 365
  potential, and generality, 226, 226n5
  problem of, 164
metaphysical facts, 177
Metaphysical Foundations of Modern Physical Science (Burtt) (1925)
  as assigned reading, 293, 294n1, 408
metaphysical principles, 215–22
  and creativity, 230
  elucidation of, 217–18
  and inference of actual entity, 222
metaphysics *see also* philosophy
  and activity, 44
  and actual entities, 233
  and actual versus possible, 18–19

  adequacy of, 12
  adoption of, 395
  approach to, 125
  of Aristotle, 94
  and art
  and being actual, 207
  coherence of, 12
  and community, 18
  concept of God in, 233
  conditions for, 102
  crude, 375
  deep insight in, 231
  defined, 188
  definitions to be put at end in, 206
  and Descartes, 63n2, 94, 108, 207, 291, 291n5, 360
  and description of event, 14
  as descriptive, 44, 99
  and determinism, 21
  deus ex machina in, 60
  doctrine of experience world in, 112
  and empiricism, 44
  and epistemology, 12, 195
  and eternal objects, 44
  and ethics, 16, 60
  and experience, 298–9, 376
  failures in, 198
  fluffy, 238
  fundamental approach to, 94
  and future, 160
  and God, 60, 216, 360
  how it is possible, 197
  ideas in, 291
  and imagination, 194, 194n4
  and immortality, 44
  importance of, 375
  independence versus solidarity in, 204
  individual, 195
  and internal relations, 99
  and knowledge, 94, 96, 99
  and language, 210, 211, 237, 237n2
  and limitation, 19, 61, 61n6
  and Locke, 188, 353
  and logic, 6, 60, 371
  and mathematical symbols, 210
  and mathematics, 235
  metaphors in, 237
  nature of, 99
  and Newton, 188
  no final conclusion in, 204
  and old rationalism, 188
  and philosophy of nature, 207
  and physics, 291, 291n5
  of Plato, 94
  pluralistic, and determinism, 21
  and plurality, 18
  and pre-Socratics, 60
  and predication, 201
  and principle of otherness, 44

  principles of, 44
  reduced to definiteness, 238
  rejection of, 395
  in Renaissance, 297n4
  revolt against, 188, 189n1
  and science, 194, 194n4, 291, 297, 375, 395
  and scientists, 188
  and self-creative activity, 18
  sentences in, 205
  six main principles of, 210
  and social ethics, 208, 208n4, 208n5
  and subject–predicate form, 202, 203, 207, 212
  and substance and attribute, 211
  synthesis of, 204
  test of, 12
  and truth, 211
  as unexhausted topic, 198
  unfolding of, 200
  and universe, 232–3, 366
  as wheel, not stick, 207
  words in, 205
metaphysics, Cartesian
  alternative to, 210
  and Moore, 98n6
  and Russell, 98, 98n6
metaphysics, empirical, and determinism, 21
Methods of Ethics (Sidgwick) (1874), 375, 375n3
Methuselah, 304
Metz, Rudolf, 187n4
Michelson, Albert A., 287n5
Michelson–Morley experiment, 287
Michigan, University of, lectures at, xxx
microcosm, 100n7, 101
Mill, John Stuart, 6
  and beyond, 49
  as inductive, 382
  and language, 382–3
  logic of, 49
  and mathematics, 382
  matter and perception in, 382
  and probability of reign of laws, 49
  proposition in, 381–3
  sensa in, 358
Miller, Dayton Clarence, 287, 287n7
Miller, John C., xxx
Milton, John, 260, 260n1
mind, 381
  acting symbolically, 336
  and body, 164, 248, 352–7
  as complete occasion, 268, 268fig
  as creative of entity, 317
  and creativity, 355
  closed to nature, 97

Index

creative power of, 139, 139n3
and Descartes, 12, 99, 266, 347–8n7, 353
and eternal objects, 354
and experience, 195, 195n2, 195n3
and feeling, 176
functioning of, and Kant, 193
and God, 266
growth of, and facts, 194
and ideas, 409
and imaginal occasion, 99
impression on, 12
independence of, 353
inspection of, 28
irrational numbers as creation of, 129
knowledge limited by, 195n5
and Locke, 267, 353
and matter, 18–19, 28, 31, 75, 75table, 77, 88, 375
and mental activity, 198
and occasions, 12
pathology of, 354
qualities of, 75, 75table
as real entity, 267
and relatedness, 373
scientific state of, 4–5; *see also* scientific thought
as self, 298
and simple location, 77
as substance, 172n2, 204, 396
thought as property of, 28
types of actual, 125
and world, 76, 239
world as function of, 51
world ordered by, 171–2n12
mind, bits of, and beginning of philosophy, 56
versus bits of matter, 75
mind, creative, and philosophy, 123–4
mind, disciplined, and imagination, 178
mind, English, 194–5, 195n1
mind, medieval, and cause and effect, 48
mind, scientific, rise of, 5
mind, trained, and imagination, 244
Mind and Its Place in Nature (Broad) (1925), 189, 189n3
as assigned reading, xxix, 168
minding, types of, 373n7
mirror
as abnormality in environment, 152
and presentational immediacy, 257
and systematic relations, 271
misplaced concreteness, fallacy of
and actual world, 128n7
defined, 50
and Descartes, 38

and points, 127, 127n2
and problematic classification, 18, 52, 66, 66n1
mode, 17
and creature, 238
limitations of, and synthesis, 31
Modes of Thought (Whitehead) (1938), viii
molecule
in community, 160
and electromagnetism, 295
in environment, 111
kinetic energy of, 91
moment
abstractive class in, 157
defined, 157, 158
as duration, 157
as entity, 158
general set of, 159, 160
geometrical elements in, 158
intersection of, 159, 159*fig*, 160
parallel, and rest, 158
presentational, and rest, 158
relationship between, 158
and route of approximation, 156n5, 158, 159, 159*fig*
special set of, 159, 160
as three-dimensional space, 157n3
momentum, and force, 87, 88
monad
and actual entity, 362
defined, 29
enduring, 29
and Kant, 29
of Leibniz, 235–6, 236n1, 278
and physical occasion, 9–10
as point, 314
mongoose, 69, 69n3, 76, 349
monism, and determinism, 21, 69
monistic view, solidarity of entities in, 233
Montague, William P., 104–105n8
Moore, G. E., viii, 98n6, 187, 187n4
moral value, actual as basis for, 215
morality, and belief, cycle of, 401
morals
barbaric, 292
and Descartes, 208n8
and God, 208–9, 208n8, 397–8
and philosophy, 397–8
and privacy, 397
in religion, 292
and right to existence, 399
and self-building, 334
theory of, and ideal comparison, 219
and world, 208–9, 208n8

Morgan, C. Lloyd, xxxi–xxxii, 293, 293n2
and emergent evolution, 299
influence of, on Whitehead, xxxii, 46–7n7, 293, 293n2, 372
Morley, Edward W., 287n5
morphological view
and causality, 77
change from, 76
in Descartes, 76
difficulties of, 77
and experience, 77, 77n1
of function, 77
versus functional view, 76–7
and Hume, 76, 77
and induction, 77
and knowing, 76
and memory, 77
perception in, 76
in philosophy, 76
and scepticism, 76–77
in science, 76
sense data in, 76
successive instants in, 76
of world, 77
and Zeno, 77
morphology
and biology, 76
defined, 76
versus function, 76–7
and matter, 76
motion
and activity, 89
and attainment of ends, 411
change of, 411
and entity, 259, 259n7, 260
and force, 412
and instantaneous space, 6
natural, 7, 52
and Newton, 87
organic relationship of, 259
and parallel duration, 155
relative, 153, 154, 162, 277, 283, 285, 285*fig*
in space, 281, 283
third law of, 37
uniform, and rest, 276
violent, 52
Mount Wilson Observatory, 287, 287n7
Müller, Max, 126, 126n2
multiple, versus solitary, 204
multiplicity, 174, 176
as abstract quantity, 326
and community, 13
and correlation, 140, 140*fig*, 141
defined, 62
definite, and relation, 123
and definite number to, 331
of entities, 204, 250
of infinite numbers, 141
and matching, 140

478

and occasion, 13, 14
and order, 140
and order types, 329
and solidarity, 250
types of, 13
and unity, 60, 332
music
  doing things with, 383
  and number versus value, 136
  and symbol, 386
mysticism, and proposition, 384
myth, epic style of, 292

names
  and Frege, 387
  meanings of, 389
  method of giving, 122
  predicate as system of, 122
  and proposition, 382, 383
  and Wittgenstein, 387
Napoleon, and Waterloo, 81
natura naturata, 84, 87, 100
  and acceleration, 87n1
  and actual substance, 85–6
  as continuous, 85
  defined, 36
  and *natura naturans,* 37, 39, 91, 268
natura naturans, 84, 87, 100
  defined, 36
  as epochal, 85
  and force, 87 n1
  and *natura* naturata, 37, 39, 91, 268
natural selection, 394
Nature and Experience (Dewey) (1925), as assigned reading, 187n1
nature
  as abstraction from formal completeness, 335
  and accuracy, 113
  analysis of, as partial, 257
  and atomicity, 366
  and behaviour, 87
  as beyondness, 64
  bifurcation of, 73n5, 110, 217, 349, 366, 375
  as closed system, 351
  without conscience, 398
  without consciousness, 398n2
  continuity in, 366
  as corporeal entities, 278
  creation of, 84
  and creature, 94, 366
  Dewey's view of, 170–1
  as entity, 100n4
  evolution of laws of, 290
  and future, 270
  ideal in, 114
  ideals imported into, 113, 113n10
  as ideas in the mind of God, 31
  and imagination, 244

at an instant, 99
laws of, 6, 162
limits in, 17
materialistic view of, 299
mind closed to, 97
morphological view of, 99n5
order of, 10, 56
organic theory of, and Euclid, 307
organic view of, 372, 412
perceptivity as account of, 176, 175n5
philosophy of, 5
and physical fact, 299
and potency, 290
and potentiality, 333
and process
  quanta and continuity in, 297
  relatedness of, 235–6
  settled, from standpoint, 165, 165n2
  theory of, 49
  time in, 100n4
  and thought, 332, 333
  thought and science in, 244
  and unity from multiplicity, 332
  and value, 49, 64
necessity
  and *a priori,* 8, 52
  and proposition, 8, 52
  and universality, 8
negative
  and creature, 101n7
  and Hegel, 101, 101n7
Nelson, Everett John, l–lii, 1
neo-idealists, 187n4
neo-Platonists, and science, 81n5
Neptune, orbit of, 412
new rationalism, books about, 187n9
new realists, 187n4
new, related to old, 162
Newton, Isaac, 327
  and acceleration and rest, 154
  and astronomy, 403, 412
  and calculus, 88
  and celestial mechanics, 317n2
  as child playing by the ocean, 393, 393n2
  common space in, 277
  and concept of whole, 89
  and discovery of laws of science, 173n3, 318
  equation of, for gravitational force, 37
  fallacy in, 280
  first law of, 33
  fluxions in, 12
  force in, 88, 267
  and gravitation, 412–13, 413n1
  and hypotheses, 194, 194n3, 195

and Kant, 171–2
and law of gravity, 38, 38n1
and laws of mass, 173, 173n3
and laws of motion, 87, 411, 412
and Locke, 75, 188, 188n5
and mass, 37, 87, 89–90, 183
and mass plus extension, 75
and matter, 37, 353
and matter and space, 267
and metaphysics, 188
mind of, 195
and motion, 87
in Philosophy A, lx
physics of, 394, 401, 410n6, 412
and problems in differential calculus, 137n1
and properties of matter, 28
receptacle in, 294
and science, 266
second law of dynamics of, 38, 38n1
and space, 278, 294, 295
and space and time, 127
third law of motion of, 37
and time, 12, 401
and velocity, 158
nominalism, versus realism, 224, 224–5n3
nominative case, and science, 295–6
non-being *see* not-being
none, as a mathematical concept, 137
normality, 33, 258
not-being, 6; *see also* beyondness of actual occasion, 82
and Aristotle, 101n7
and being, 6, 32, 51, 81
as beyondness, 6, 51
and Hegel, 6
notions
  adequacy of, 175
  as inexhaustible, 173
noumena, concepts that qualify as, 7
Nova Persei, 271, 271n6
novelty
  time as becoming of, 112
  versus time, 245
now
  and before and after, 70, 375
  and present, 154
  and specious present, 154, 240, 241
  and theory of relativity, 154
nucleus, of atom, 90
number field, internal relationships in, 266
numbers, 174
  and abstraction, 124, 134–5
  as antecedent to classes, 326
  as class of predicates, 331

Index

classes of, 331, 331n2
and correlation, 123, 140, 327
and counting, 140, 326, 327
developing concept of, 326
and elucidating properties of things, 266
fraction as relation between, 331
infinite class of, 328
and isoid relation, 130
as instrument of thought, 326
order types in, 132, 133, 133fig
ordering of, 327, 327fig
origin of, 326
and Plato, 326
principle of, 388
and pure geometry, 133
and Pythagoras, 326
as relation between predicates, 331
and relations among quantities, 122, 122n8
and relationships, 124, 132, 133n3, 134–7, 139–40, 326
and science, 293
and space, 370
and structure of universe, 132, 133, 133fig
and value, 135, 135n3, 136
what it is, 326
numbers, cardinal, 140–1
  classes in, 141
  correlation of, with fractions, 143
  correlation of, with segmental numbers, 141, 141fig
  defined, 140
  infinite class of, 329
  and infinity, 331
  and order types, 143
  and ordinal, 327, 329
  as primary, 329
numbers, definite
  and philosophy, 177
  relation of, to multiplicity, 331
numbers, finite
  and Clifford, 329
  and science, 177
numbers, final, 327
numbers, ideal, 41
numbers, inductive, 331, 332
numbers, imaginary, 332n1
numbers, infinite, 388
  multiplicity of, 141
numbers, irrational, 123–4, 133, 133n3
  as creation of mind, 129
  as difficulty in mathematics, 123–4
  and Pythagoreans, 259, 259n6
  between rational numbers, 328
numbers, ordinal
  infinite, 367
  as prior to cardinal, 327

numbers, prime, proof of infinite, 331
numbers, rational, irrational numbers between, 328
numbers, real *see also* numbers, segmental
  constructed from rational numbers, 136–137, 136fig, 136n3, 137fig, 137n1, 209n2
  σ as, 332
numbers, segmental, 139–41, 139fig
  based on 10, 142
  based on 2, 142
  correlation of, with cardinal numbers, 141, 141fig
  correlation of sets of, 141–142, 142fig
  versus fractions, 143
  and magnitude, 143
  order type of, 139
  and quantity, 143
  as real, 140
numerosity, 174

object
  apprehension of, 68
  and context, 386
  demonstrated earlier, 372
  demonstrated to you, 372
  diverse modes of ingression of, 225
  as function, 347
  function of, 217
  identity of, 18
  versus induction, 75n3
  ingression external to, 21
  under limitation, 374
  objectifications of, 334
  in past occasion, 83
  relations of, to other objects, 334
  self-enjoyment of, 354
  as social, 354
  versus subject, 182, 196–7
  supersession of, 354
  and synthesis, 336
  and thought, 332
  under reference, and actual entity, 372
object, actual
  versus eternal object, 228
  and immortality, 44
  and otherness, 44
  and sameness, 44
object, concrete, 17, 387
object, enduring, 61, 159
  and continuity, 72
  defined, 25
  and endurance of structure, 27
  and eternal object, 25, 72
  enduring, examples of, 60n6

and historical route, 25, 28, 72, 111, 352, 401
inheritance of, 107
and self-inheritance, 25
structure of, 72
type of person interested in, 66
object, eternal, 163, 373
  and abstraction, 44
  activity of, 344
  and actual, 82
  and actual entity, 228, 229, 230, 354
  versus actual object, 228
  and actual occasion, 104
  and actual world, 95
  as always operative, 354
  and analysis, 355
  and another life, 225
  as antecedents, 34
  and artist, 66
  beyond all possibility, 302, 302n5
  and bifurcation of nature, 349
  and *cognitum*, 60
  complex, 105
  as component of concretion 53
  and concept, 199, 354–5, 400
  as concepts, 198
  and conception, 289
  and concrete occasion, 43
  and concretion, 104
  and consequent, 105
  and correlations, 373
  and creation, 18
  and creative synthesis, 103, 103fig
  as creativity, 95, 344, 357
  and data of activity, 100
  and datum, 79
  defined, 206, 353, 379
  as defining elements, 343
  demonstration of, 224, 224–5n3
  description of, 229
  as detachable from actual entities, 233, 233n2
  and Dewey, 344
  and diversity, 237
  versus enduring object, 25, 72
  entering occasion, 227
  and entity, 65, 228, 233, 233n2, 234
  and envisagement, 42
  and epochal occasion, 115n4
  and eternal relationships, 21
  examples of, 60, 396
  and experient occasion, 45, 69, 72–3, 98n7, 104
  expression of, 45
  and facts, 164
  and finite relations, 99n1
  and finite truth, 99
  as form of thought, 206
  and functioning, 354–5, 379

480

Index

and grammar, 114, 114n3
and ground, 105
higher, more tenuous, 224
as *how*, 217
and *how* of analysis, 352
and *how* of concrescence, 352
how to describe, 228
ideal entities as, 217
and identity and diversity, 332
and imaginal occasion, 45
imaginal occasion as, 104
and immortality, 44
incompatibility in, 357
indetermination in, 66
ingression of, 79, 98n7, 226, 227
ingression of, into actual occasion, 196, 219, 251, 251n4
inspectional relationships of, 73, 73fig
isolation of, 21, 94
and knowledge, 197, 198, 206, 351, 351fig
and limitation, 82, 103, 103fig
and mathematician, 66n2
as media of actuality, 250
and metaphysics, 44
and mind, 354
and mode of functioning, 199
and mode of ingression, 196
and multiplicity of actual entities, 250
mutual relevance of, 212
and objectification, 253, 253fig, 343, 344, 352
and occasion, 18, 66, 67, 355, 399
and organisation of occasion, 250
and particular occasion, 66
and past, present, and future, 81
pattern of, 233, 233n3, 234
and perception, 206, 289
as percepts, 198
and perceptual versus conceptual functioning, 193
and philosopher, 66
and physical and mental pole, 355
and physical occasion, 197n3, 355
and physical world, 343
and possibility, 66, 94
and potentiality, 195, 225, 333, 357
as predicate, 378
and prehension of occasion, 354
presentational relationships of, 73, 73fig
and realism, 98n9
realisation of, 104

realm of, 18
relational character of, 43
as relational elements, 289
as relational entities, 66
relational essence of, 228, 234
and relations, 18, 66, 68, 68fig, 99, 99n1, 347
relationship of, to occasion, 21, 66
relationships among, 19, 27
relative status of, 73, 73fig
as representing substances, 206, 206n3
and sameness, 100
sensa as, 86
as sense data, 345
and space and time, 94
status of, 209
synonyms for, 217
and synthesis, 164, 164fig, 334
and systematic character of world, 234, 234n2
and thought, 333
and togetherness, 43
as true object of perception, 80n4
and truth, 43
type of person interested in, 66
as universal, 18, 65
universals as, 343
value of relationships between, 19
and world, 69, 234
object, extended, and enduring identity, 65
object, immediate, 372
object, individual
  as occasion, 399
  past in, 399, 400
object, perceptual, 28–30, 72, 82
  as historical route, 73–4
  problem of, 79
  and subject, 72
  and substance, 72
object, physical, examples of, 356
objectification, 209, 263
  and actual entity, 235, 372
  anticipatory, 253, 253fig
  and concrescence, 226
  connected by relationship, 225
  and creativity, 247, 256–7
  defined, 221
  and demonstration, 225, 226, 230, 231
  effected by universals, 262
  of entity, 225, 234, 234n1, 258, 262, 270
  and eternal objects, 343, 344, 352
  of event, repetition of, as, 254
  of experience, 378
  and fact, 365
  finished, 379
  of God, 221

history of, 255
hypothetical form of, 379, 380
and idea, 206, 206n6
and identity, 225
and knowledge, 365
and limitation, 225, 343
mutual relevance of, 212
of object, 334
of occasion, 226, 242, 242n5, 253, 253 n5, 362, 399, 400
particularity of, 235
and percipience, 231
for percipient, 364
and perspective, 379–80
relevance of, 379
and scientific measurement, 380
species of, 269–70
of subject, 365, 380
and subject–predicate form, 364, 365
of successive entities, 232
and systematic background, 257
unification of, 258
and universal, 242, 242n5, 263
and vividness, 243
what of, 352
of world, 400
objectified acts, synthesis of, into objectified unity, 378, 378n4
objective
  defined, 14
  versus formaliter, 14
  as point of view, 169
  and subjective, 61n5, 93, 162
objective immortality, 344
  and time, 246
objectivity, as abstraction from formal completeness, 335
observation
  and applied mathematics, 382
  and Bacon, 176, 176n1
  defined, 176
  and emotions, 192
  and imagination, 377, 377n1
  and inductive reasoning, 290
  as integration of facts, 180
  versus reasoning, 5
  and science, 5
  and self-analysis, 377
observer, influence of, on observed, 373
obvious
  certainty of, 191
  and rationalism, 191
obviousness
  versus belief, 191
  of experience, 334
  purged by criteria, 359
  of rational system, 186
  and rationalism, 191
  and scheme of ideas, 192
  self-evident, as ultimate fact, 191

481

Index

occasion *see also under types of occasion*
absolute status of, 67
abstract, and dipolarity, 342–3
and abstraction, 10, 66n3
and achievement, 34, 101
activity and value in, 62
as always incomplete, 344
analysis of, 19, 102*fig*, 103, 107
and another life, 225
antecedent route of, 362
and Aristotle, 55, 61
and being, 299
biological, 22, 26
bipolarity of, 165
causal efficacy of, 362
character of, 253
characteristics of, 357
characters in, 112
and cognition, 59, 64
and *cognitum*, 60
community of occasions defined by, 19
concepts in, 172–173
as concrete, 18
as concretion, 55, 58, 343
and contingency, 20
contrariety in, 101, 101n7
as creative achievement, 101
creativity in, 84
data in, 109
datum for, 70
defined, 36, 58, 343
as defined from present, 344
definite occasion as, 67
and Descartes, 50, 53, 61, 61n1
and dimension, 105
dipolarity of, 342–3
distortion of contemporaneous, 71
and efficiency, 55
and electron, 79n7
and empiricism, 50
empty, 22
in empty space, 219
as end in itself, 62, 197
and endurance, 25, 37
as enduring, 245
in enduring structure, 79
entities included in, 250, 250n5
entities synthesised in, 78
as entity, 65
environment of, 227
essence of, 61, 61n4
and eternal object, 18, 66, 67, 227, 355, 399
and ethics, 15, 63
experienced, and universe, 53
and experient occasion, 71, 71*fig*
and flowing, 53

flux of, 17, 65
and force, 10
freedom in, 357
fundamental, 72
and future, 344
general scheme of, 81
and generality, 63
God as, 198
and ground, 108
and ground for contrast, 105, 105n1
and here and now, 61
historical route of, 71, 71*fig*, 72, 100n6, 246, 399
and *how*, 95
and Hume, 50, 63, 63n1
and identity, 17, 65
as immortal, 100, 253, 345
incompleteness of, 172, 172n5, 349
and incompleteness of future, 253
indeterminateness of, 18
indetermination of, 253, 253n5
individual, value of, 216n6
and individuality, 63, 63n4
and induction, 227
as infectious in universe, 398
and ingression, 18, 21, 224, 251
and inheritance, 25, 106, 106n5, 362
as inheriting universe, 350, 350*fig*
inspectional relationship of, 79–80
at an instant, 36, 77
intuition by, 351
and isolation, 59
as *it*, 61, 61n4
and Kant, 50
and knowledge, 58
and knowing, 50
of life history, route of, 275$6$, 275*fig*
and limitation, 14, 19, 19*fig*, 59, 59n6, 67, 101
under limitation, 242
limitation on datum in, 109
limitations on, 14
locus of, and correlation, 276, 276*fig*
and logic, 51
and measurable time, 104
medium for relating, 76
memory of antecedent occasion in, 253
mental side of, 243
mentality of, 238
and metaphysics, 19
as microcosm, 100n7, 101
and mind, 12
modification in, 27

modification of, 70, 71
multiple occurrences of, 107
as multiplicity, 13
multiplicity of, 50–1
objectification of, 196, 226, 242, 242n5, 253, 253*fig*, 253n5, 362, 399, 400
as organism, 61n6, 348
organisation of, 51, 250
and organisation of other occasions, 343, 343n3
and other occasions, 399
and otherness, 100n8, 101
and partial conditions, 20
passage into under perspective limitation, 165, 165n3
and past, 25–6
between past and future, 34
of perception, 108
perception of 80, 105, 105n7
and perceptiveness, 79
percepts and concepts in, 199
and perceptual and conceptual functioning, 219
and percipience, 231
physical and mental in, 243
and physical occasions, 10
and physics, 56
and Plato, 62
prehended by subject, 343
as prehension, 58
prehension by, 348, 351
prehension into, 251
prehension of, 253, 344, 345, 354
prehension of occasions by, 348
and present, 32
and presentational immediacy, 272, 272*fig*, 272n2, 275, 345
and presentational relation, 79
and production, 344
and real world, 8
and reality, 25
and realisation, 19, 239
and realised values, 15
reason to start with, 72
relation to, 81
relation of experient occasion to, 77, 80
relations of, in community, 20
relationship of, to eternal objects, 66
relationship of, with universe, 227
repetition of, 107, 107n3
and retention, 101
and sameness, 100n8
and self-enjoyment, 243n4
self-identity of entities in, 225, 225n1
and sense awareness, 351
and social relations, 349
and space, 10, 19, 60, 67

482

and spatio-temporal scheme,
  81
specific, 19
and spontaneity, 20–1, 68,
  68n3
and structure, 25, 74
and subject, 60
and subjective psychological
  fact, 162
subsequent, and antecedent
  occasions, 20
and substance, 10
and substantial activity, 34
and supersession, 172, 172n4,
  342, 343, 348
and synthesis, 61, 61n4, 96
and time, 10, 19, 60, 67, 105,
  105n8, 107
time as relation between, 245
time depth of, 85
types of, 64
and universal, 50, 243
and universality, 8
and universe, 242
and value, 34, 62, 63, 63n4,
  168, 216, 398
value in, and universe, 216
versus world, 62
world synthesised in, 166
occasion, actual
  and abstraction, 10, 112
  as actual entity, 277
  and actual substance, 85
  actuality of, 85
  and actuality versus
    indeterminations, 18
  analytical pole of, 197
  and apprehension, 242
  and art, 16
  and being and not being, 82
  and cause, 16
  and cognisance, 52
  and community, 82
  as component of concretion 53
  as concrescence, 216, 216n10,
    399
  and concrete entity, 52
  as concretion, 53, 401
  consciousness of, 79
  correlated with imaginal
    occasion, 104
  as creative activity, 210
  defined, 85n5
  elements of, 250
  emergence of final, 378
  and endurance, 16
  and entity, 228
  epochal unit of, 45
  and eternal objects, 104
  as finished, 81
  form exemplified by, 165
  functional theory of, 112
  and future, 82
  immediate, and real world, 8

immortality of, 93
ingression of eternal objects
  into, 196, 219
ingression of forms into, 165,
  165n4
and inheritance from past, 265
intrinsic reality of, 45
and knowledge, 96, 217
and life history of organism,
  279, 279fig
limitation on, 82
mental pole of, 351–2
morphological theory of, 112
and other acts of experience,
  377
and other occasions, 250
and perceptiveness, 45
physical pole of, 197, 351–2
and possibility, 99n2
and prehension, 242
process of, 82
and real world, 8
and realisation, 239
realm of determination of, 104
and realm of possibility, 68–9
of repetition, 107
represented in actual occasions,
  196
as retention, 44
and space, 299–300
stuffing of, 79
and successor, 104–5
and supersession, 347
and time, 196, 401
and universal judgement, 55
and universals, 250
as unity, 81
and world, 14
world patient of, 275
yes and no in, 45
occasion, antecedent, 79, 79fig,
  79n10, 79n11
  conditions by, 67
  and connection of events, 68
  and experient occasions, 106
  and mental occasions, 108
  and mentality of experient
    occasions, 106
  and subsequent occasions, 20
occasion, biological, as type of
  ultimate occasion, 22
occasion, complete
  mind as, 268, 268fig
  perceptual and conceptual
    functioning in, 199
occasion, concrete, 17
  dipolarity of, 197
  and eternal objects, 43
  and immediate experience,
    200
  physical and mental, 200
  poles of, 348
  time depth of, 84
  and togetherness, 43

occasion, definite
  and community of occasions,
    67
  as occasion, 67
  status of, 67
occasion, empty, as type of
  ultimate occasion, 22
occasion, epochal, 172n3
  as actual entity, 361
  analysis of, 103
  completeness of, 168
  and consequent, 105
  creativity of, 102
  as creature, 101
  dated from immediate
    occasion, 168
  and Descartes, 361
  and differentiation, 153
  and endurance, 361
  and enduring entity, 100n6
  and eternal objects, 115n4
  and experient occasion, 106
  extensive character of, 102
  and grammar, 114, 114n4
  and ground, 105
  and historical route, 101, 105
  as incomplete, 167
  life history as succession of,
    101
  and principle of identity, 102
  relationships of, 155
  and rest, 282, 282fig
  as synthesis, 102, 102n7
  as totality, 241
  as ultimate creature, 102
occasion, eternal, and particular
  occasion, 16
occasion, experient, 95fig, 100–1
  ability to describe, 17
  and abstract situation, 43
  and actual occasion, 79
  analysis of, 95–6, 97–8
  and antecedent occasions, 106
  biological, 22
  and biological occasion, 26
  causal independence of, 69
  classification of entities in, 17
  and cognition, 81
  and cognisance, 53
  as concrete, 17
  and community, 65
  creation of, 97–8
  as creature, 95, 108
  and data, 97–8
  as datum, 69
  defined, 17, 21–2, 73, 95
  duplicity in, 13
  and ego, 98, 98n7
  as emergence of superjicient
    value, 22
  and emotion, 65n4
  empty, 22
  as end, 17
  and enduring entity, 100n6

483

Index

and epoch, 44, 44*fig*
and epochal occasion, 106
and eternal object, 45, 69, 98*n*7, 104
and external relationships, 73
and fact, 96
and feeling, 107
and finite truth, 106, 106*n*5
and historical route, 73–4
how to describe, 17
and imaginal occasion, 17, 21–2, 24, 25–6, 25*fig*, 64–5, 69, 79, 94, 97
and internal relationships, 73
and inheritance, 106, 106*n*5, 107
knowing of, 22, 65, 79
knowledge of, 110
limitation on, 73
limitation on *perceptum* in, 78, 78*n*4
and material occasion, 26
and matter, 99
and mental occasions, 108, 108*fig*
and mentality of antecedent occasions, 106
as multiplicity, 13
and occasion of knowing, 69
and other occasions, 71, 71*fig*, 73, 73*fig*
perception as, 79*n*4
and physics, 96
possibility of, 26, 65
preceding imaginal occasion, 65
as primary, 78
rational, 22
and rational occasion, 26
relation between, 106
relation of, to other occasions, 77, 80
relationships of, 73, 73*fig*, 73*n*4
route of, 106, 106*n*3
and sensitive body, 75
spiritual, 22
and spiritual occasion, 26
and synthesis of world, 13
ultimate entity as, 79
and ultimate occasion, 71
and unit, 44
as unit, 13
and universal, 50
and value, 17, 58, 64, 65
and void occasion, 26
occasion, future *see also* future
characteristics of, 33–4
definiteness of, 82
and limitation, 81
nature of, 81
and past occasion, 33
and past and present, 20–1
versus present occasion, 82

occasion, given
datum as, 96
isolation of, 7
and Kant, 7
and knowledge, 96
occasion, imaginal, 95, 95*fig*
ability to describe, 17
analysis by, of experient occasion, 98*n*1
and biological occasion, 26
causal independence of, 69
and cognisance, 53
as concrete, 17
consciousness as, 79*n*4
correlated with actual occasion, 104
as datum, 69
defined, 17, 24, 65, 69, 71
and Descartes, 69
as emergence of superjicient value, 22
and emotion, 65n4
empty, 22
as entity, 64–5
and eternal object, 45
as eternal object, 104
and experient occasion, 17, 21–2, 24, 25–6, 25*fig*, 64–5, 69, 79, 94, 97
and ground, 105
as individual value, 65
and knowing, 21–2
knowledge as, 96
and knowledge, 64, 69, 105
and material occasion, 26
and mind, 99
as occasion of knowing, 69
and perceived occasion, 105
rational, 22
and rational occasion, 26
relative importance of, 81
and spiritual occasion, 26
status of, 102
and theory of causation, 69
and theory of knowledge, 96
and thought, 99*n*2
and time, 104
and ultimate occasion, 71
and value, 17, 22, 65
and void occasion, 26
occasion, immediate
as actual when fused with universal potentiality, 165
analysis of, 51
and art, 62
becoming of, 107
of bodily life, 22
and community, 13, 14, 166, 168
concept synthesised in, 165
as concrete entity, 13
defined, 6, 57
and efficient and final causes, 59–60

epochal occasions dated from, 168
and future, 68*n*1, 107
and general scheme, 81
and given, 51
and here and now, 13
and knowing, 51
and law of identity, 53
and limitation, 59–60, 110
and other occasions, 8
and past, 110
of perceptivity, 108
perspective in, 168
and philosophy of nature, 58
as prehension, 64
real as, 13
and real world, 8
and reality, 13
and relatedness, 32
relations of, 80–1
as reorganisation, 165
self as, 13
and substance, 53
as synthesis, 59, 59n7
unity of, 59
and world, 242
occasion, immediate actual, 8
and real world, 8
occasion, individual
and community of occasions, 11
and universal, 50
occasion, knowing, 95
occasion, limited, actual entity as, 296
occasion, limiting, and art, 16
occasion, living, as grade of reality, 25
occasion, material, 22
and experient and imaginal occasion, 26
as grade of reality, 25
as type of ultimate occasion, 22
occasion, mental, 342–3
and analysis, 354
and antecedent occasions, 108
community in, 165*n*6
and concept, 199, 354
and conceptual functioning, 197
and concrescence of functioning, 355
as concretion, 165
and consciousness, 344
and creature, 198
defined, 197
describing physical occasion, 165
and experient occasions, 108, 108*fig*
forms as concepts in, 165, 165*n*4
freedom in, 357
as grade of reality, 25

484

Index

and immediate experience, 200
and ingression of forms, 165, 165n4
inheritance of, by experient occasions, 106
of Kant, 108
and mental functioning, 198
and mental pole, 198
and mode of ingression, 197
and perceptual functioning, 198
versus physical, 238–9
and physical functioning, 198
and physical occasion, 163, 163fig, 165, 197, 198, 344, 354, 355
and process, 198
and real world, 206
relationships of, 108
route of, 106, 106n3
and self-knowledge, 198
and unity of body, 167
occasion, organised, 51
occasion, particular
of cognisance, 6
and eternal object, 66
and eternal occasion, 16
and Heraclitus, 10
and knowledge, 8–9
patience of, for physical relationship, 226
standpoint of, 166n1
occasion, past
as embodiment of creative activity, 34
and future occasion, 33
immortality of, 103
objects in, 83
and present and future, 20–1
occasion, perceived, and imaginal occasion, 105
occasion, physical, 9, 342–3
as abstraction, 351
analysis of, 192
as blind perceptivity, 165
and consciousness, 344
and concept, 354
defined, 58, 150–1, 150fig, 197
described by mental occasion, 165
and enduring entity, 14
epochal, 351
and epochal view of time, 37
and eternal object, 197n3, 355
events as, 207, 207n3, 351
as fact, 166 n1
freedom in, 357
and function, 55
general character of, 199
as ground, 198
and Heraclitus, 9, 10
and immediate experience, 200
knowledge from standpoint of, 165

and mental occasion, 163, 163fig, 165, 197, 198, 344, 354, 355, 356
and monad, 9–10
multiplicity of, 14
and occasion of consciousness, 96
and occasions, 10
and organism, 10
as organisation, 165
peculiar character of each, 14
and perceptivity, 163fig
and philosophy of science, 9
and physical world, 343
potentialities of, 199
and relationship, 353
and self-knowledge, 198
as settled ground, 165
occasion, physical–mental, 165
occasion, present, 24, 70–1, 70fig
and coincidence, 23
contemporary, 70
and contemporary occasions, 24, 70–1
and duration, 70
versus future occasion, 82
and past and future, 20–1
as process, 83
and relations of immediate occasion, 80–1
synthesis of
occasion, presented, 24
occasion, rational, 22
and experient and imaginal occasion, 26
as type of ultimate occasion, 22
occasion, sensitive, as ultimate entity, 75
occasion, spiritual, 22
and experient and imaginal occasion, 26
as grade of reality, 25
as type of ultimate occasion, 22
occasion, ultimate
dipolarity of, 71
and experient occasion, 71
as final concrete entity, 21–2
gradation of, 22
and imaginal occasion, 71
and knowledge, 69
types of, 22
as unity of experient and imaginal occasions, 69
occasion, unit
versus community, 32
as finished, 32
and general community, 81
occasion, void, and experient and imaginal occasion, 26
occasion of consciousness, 96
occasion of knowing, as imaginal occasion, 69

occasions
and community, 10, 13–14, 19, 32, 61, 63
conceptual relationship between, 226
conditions for, 19
congruity of, 405
connections between, 70
consequent, and knowledge of character, 67–8
definition by, of other occasions, 247–8
depth of actuality in, 73
dualism of, 21–2
harmony in, 56
plurality of, 53, 57
point as track of, 158, 158fig
presentational relationships of, 73
relations in, relative importance of, 81
relationship of, to other occasions, 70, 70fig, 72, 56, 79
relative status of, 19, 67, 80–1
self as summation of, 401
succession of, 10, 56
successive, and unity, 244
synthesis of, 17, 105
transaction between, 253
ultimate, mutual causal relations between, 22
unity of, 8, 65
world as community of, 241–2
world as system of, 172
world line of, 153
occasions, actual
community of, 21, 56, 68–9
plurality of, 52
relations between, 196
relationships of, to eternal objects, 21
occasions, community of, 8, 16, 56, 57, 62, 65, 81
as actual, 32
and actual community, 11
in Aristotle, 61
character defined by, 19, 67
completeness in, 253
defined by occasion, 19
and definite occasion, 67
in Descartes, 57, 61n1
epoch in, 57
in functional view, 57
and immediate occasion, 80–1
incompleteness in, 253
and individual occasion, 11
and induction, 227
lower, 61
and necessity, 8
as never actual, 32
as never finished, 32
occasions in, 32, 57, 61
and possibility, 68

485

Index

and present, 32
unit occasions in, 32
and *relata*, 32
standpoint of, 166n1
and subjectivism, 13–14
and substance, 57
and unity, 11
and universality, 8
upper, 61
and world, 57, 61, 81, 241
occasions, concurrent, 272
occasions, contiguous, as historical route, 73
occasions, contemporaneous, 22–3
defined, 23
distortion of, 71
independence of, 23
as internal, 71
occasions, contemporary, 70; *see also* occasions, independent
defined, 24, 70
and Einstein, 24
and inspectional relationship, 73
mutual independence of, 20
and present occasions, 24, 70–1
and presentational relation, 24
relations of, 21
occasions, non-contemporaneous, characteristics of, 23
occasions, non-contemporary, 71
occasions, non-continuous, internal relation of, 72, 72*fig*
occasions, relative, and realisation, 25
occurrence
concepts applicable to, 173
and general concept, 175
old rationalism, revolt against, 188
old, related to new, 162
omission, 50
On the Structure of the Human Body (Vesalius), 409
one
and *cognita*, 31–2
versus many, 9, 13, 31, 78, 78n2, 113, 115, 376
and *what*, 115
ontological principle, 215, 218, 221, 223
and character of generality, 223
defined, 210, 223
and entity, 223
as principle of metaphysics, 210
and supreme creature, 220
ontology
of Descartes, 398
and physics, 275
versus theology, 398

opportunity
and evolution, 108
and creature, 108
and data, 108–9
total, 108
order
analysis as introduction of, 166
and correlation, 140
and counting, 140
God as principle of, 113
idea of, 129–30
limit as type of, 129, 129n4
and multiplicity, 140
of points, 130
relationship in, 129
segmental, defined, 139n2
serial, dense and continuous, 328
theory of, conceived, 129
order type, 129, 130–2, 327, 328
and abstraction, 134–5
in aesthetic value, 135
and cardinal numbers, 143
comparison of, 137–8
of Dedekind continuity, 137–9
descriptions of, 131
in emotional value, 135
and entities, 134–5
in geometry, 133–4
information from, 132–3, 133n3
and infinity, 143
and multiplicity, 329
in numbers, 132, 133, 133*fig*
and Pythagorean mathematics, 135–6, 136*fig*, 136n1
and Pythagoreans, 129n4, 130–1
and relations of entities, 131
relationships between, 131, 135–6
and relationships in actual world, 134–5
rule of correlation between, 129–30, 130n1
of segmental numbers, 139
in spectrum, 135
of straight line, 138
and structure of universe, 132, 133, 133*fig*
symbols in, 131
theory of, 129
ordinal series, time as, 255
ordinal types, class of, 367
ordinary, versus dramatic, 173–4
organic determination
causality as becomingness of, 163
in creative advance, 163
organic empiricism, 9, 9n1, 52, 52n5, 61, 61n3
organic realism, 163, 258
organisation, physical occasion as, 165

organised occasion, 51
organism
as complex of elements, 258, 258n6
complexity of, as predicate, 362
constituted by events, 372
as coordination of organisms, 102, 102n4
different modes of, 373
electromagnetic, 302
and entity, 153, 258, 258n6
and environment, 294
evolution of, 294
examples of, 372
extensive relationship as condition of, 262, 262n2
and immediacies of presentation, 281
life history of, and actual occasions, 279, 279*fig*
and matter, 61, 61n4, 88
occasion as, 61n6, 348
and physical occasion, 10
and potentiality, 296
and regress, 102n4
and relatedness, 373
and science, 11
and sense presentation, 336
study of function of, 313
and superorganism, 247, 248n2, 263
organism, atomic, and quantum of time, 346
organism enduring, 101, 163
life of, 265, 265*fig*
life history of, 101
and presentational immediacy, 265, 265*fig*
organism, percipient, as component, 372
organisms
congruity of, and laws of nature, 405
relatedness of, 372
unity of, 301
violent activity of, 297, 297n4
world as system of, 343
Organization of Thought (Whitehead) (1917), viii
original sin, 208, 350, 405
and destructiveness, 399, 400
as foundation 396–7
and social ethics, 392
and social solidarity, 398
summary of, 399
original virtue
doctrine of, 400
as foundation, 396–7
and social ethics, 392
and social solidarity, 398
summary of, 399
originality
and science, 409
and self-creative character, 345

Index

origination, and conceptual functioning, 219
Oscanyan, Fred, xlv
other
   and creativity, 101
   versus *it*, 116
otherness
   and actual entities, 100
   and actual objects, 44
   versus conformation, 44
   defined, 100, 100n2
   and epoch, 101, 101*fig*
   and occasion, 100n8, 101
   and potentiality, 226
   principle of, and metaphysics, 44, 44n3
otherwise, what might have been, 67
Our Knowledge of the External World as a Field for Scientific Method in Philosophy (Russell) (1914), as assigned reading, 3, 46, 47n1
overlapping, 143–4
   and dissection, 147, 147*fig*
   of durations, 156
   and events, 147
overstatement, in science, 395

pain, destruction as, 400
painter, and presentational immediacy, 271, 271n4
Pappus, 118, 118n5
Paradise Lost (Milton) (1667), 260n1
paradox, method of eliminating, 367–8
parts
   and beyond, 125
   and quantity, 120
   sequence of, 121–2
   and spatio-temporal process, 125
   and whole, 30, 71, 71*fig*, 79, 89, 90, 125–6, 143, 147, 263, 303, 304, 304n4, 306, 307–8, 338
partial verification, and analysis, 377
particular
   fitting to abstract, 132
   and general, 117, 117n3, 211, 212
   and universal, 173n1, 333
particularity
   and concrete entity, 229
   as feature of perceptivity, 166
   of objectification, 235
Pascal, Blaise, and inevitability, 292
past
   ability to know, 32
   and actual, 34
   and actual entities, 296, 299

actuality of, 33–4, 83
antecedent to presentational immediacy, 276
and beyondness, 64
as capable of recreation, 221, 221n4
and causal relations, 352
change in, 253
completeness of, 352
conditioning by, 198
conformation to, 337
consequence of, for other entities, 257*fig*, 258
continuity of, 261–2
and creative activity, 83, 270
and creativity, 84
defined by causality, 67
as definite, 160n3
as determining present, 107
and duration, 155
and empiricism, 32
and entities, 301
in event, 161
existence of, 80
extensive continuity in, 153
as formative element, 400
and future, 32, 83, 82, 84, 160, 245, 255
and immediate occasion, 110
as immortal, 33, 35, 82, 83, 84, 95, 107, 221, 221n4, 349
of individual and world, 246
in individual object, 399, 400
information about, 71
inheritance from, 264
integration of, 232
as irrevocable, 107
knowledge of, 132, 361
limitation by, 64
and memory, 49, 270, 270*fig*
as never dead, 221, 221n4
objectification of, 345
and occasion, 25–6
and persistence, 373
philosophy's relationship to, 15
physical component of, 400
and physical relationship, 373
potentiality determined by, 297
and present, 71 75, 77, 77n1, 83, 107, 241, 254, 334, 337, 349, 400
and present and future, 36, 81, 108, 152, 153, 269, 289, 333
presentation correlated to, 151
and presentational relationship, 161
and proposition, 381
and reflective reference, 375
relevance of, 16, 63n7
as relative to present, 333
relationship of, to eternal objects, 81

relationship of, to future, 73, 268
repetition of, 107, 107n4
and sense data, 336
as transition to future, 83
uncertainty of, 80
past, harmonious, 399
past, settled
   conformation of present to, 334, 334*fig*
   and immediate activity, 333
pasts, of events, as identical, 334n1
patience
   and actual world, 99
   and entity, 363, 386
   and known, 226
   of ideal world, 99
   importance of, 124
pattern
   as formula, 247
   versus sense data, 386
paving stone, 125, 144, 173n7
Peabody, Francis Greenwood, lviii
Peano, Giuseppe, 338, 338n2
Peirce, Charles Sanders, 327n2
perceived
   objectified for percipient, 378
   and percipient, 378
   and philosophy of nature, 58
   and predicate, 378
   versus percipient, 78, 78n2
perceiving
   and community, 93
   process of, 6–7
percept
   and concept, 176, 219, 224, 224n1, 251, 377
   and eternal object, 289
   and identity, 347
   as internal relationship, 336
   in occasion, 199
   particular shape of, 335n1
perception, 382
   versus actual world, 76
   as appropriating a disembodied universal, 334
   as being, 41, 41n1
   and brain, 76
   character of, 298
   versus conception, 193
   and concrete entity, 41
   and consciousness, 79n5, 298
   defined, 298, 336
   and demonstration, 242
   and Descartes, 74, 341n4
   doctrine of, 206
   and entity, 298, 229
   as experient occasion, 79n4
   form of, of entities, 229, 229*fig*
   of historical route, 80
   illusion as, 219, 219n4
   and imagination, 192
   at an instant, 76–7

487

Index

and Kant, 263
and knowing, 31, 76
and knowledge, 108, 192, 232, 333
and mental functioning, 290
and Mill, 382
in morphological view, 76
of occasion, 80, 105, 105n7
and order of events, 70
pathology of, 23
and perceiver, 242, 242n3
as physical relation, 290
in physics, 79, 79fig
reciprocity of, 78n2
and reflection, 359
and sense awareness, 351
and state of body, 296, 296n1
and substance, 341n4
supersession of, 249
and symbolism, 336
time as form of, 252
and time and space, 263
and transmission theory, 151n3
true object of, 80, 80n4
perception, conscious
as blind intuition and conceptual functioning, 219, 219n3
defined, 224
and intuition, 355
and judgment, 355
perception, physical
and actual entity, 353
versus conscious, 192, 192n1
versus mental, 193
perception, pure
defined, 343
and mentality, 251, 251n1
and physical occasion, 251, 251n1
perceptiveness
and actual occasion, 45
versus consciousness, 79, 79n3, 79n4
defined, 79
and occasions, 79
perceptivity
as account of nature, 176, 176n5
and actual entity, 299, 353
analysed by conceptivity, 162
as basis of physical world, 163
conceptual analysis of, 298–9
concrescence of, and physical pole, 352
consciousness of, 299
and demonstration, 226
as fact, 349
form as, 167fig
how of, 217
and Hume, 108
immediate occasion of, 108
and judgment, 356
and Kant, 108, 192, 192n4

knowledge as cognisance of, 108
as knowledge of ultimate fact, 108
as mental, 166
in mental sphere, 400
in mentality, 110
particularity as feature of, 166
as physical, 166, 217, 217n5, 346, 400
and physical relations, 299, 299n1
in physical sphere, 400
and physics, 400
and predicates, 378, 378n2
as presentation, 163
as synthesis of data, 108
perceptivity, blind
versus cognitional, 110
as physical activity, 344
physical occasion as, 165
prehension as, 250, 250n5
perceptual, and conceptual, 299
perceptual functioning
and abstract forms, 193
and conceptual functioning, 197
and eternal objects, 193
and mental occasion, 198
universals in, 243
perceptual immediacy
and error, 336
and symbolic reference, 336
perceptum
as actual entity, 78, 78n4
limitation on, 78, 78n4
percipience
and actual entities, 229
and entities, 365
of entities, 365
and individuality, 231
and mentality, 365
and objectification, 231
and occasion, 231
percipience, pure, and self-percipience, 230
percipience, reflective, as self-percipience, 230
percipiens
and actuality, 30–1
versus *cognita*, 31
as *cognitum*, 31
percipient
objectification for, 364
versus perceived, 78, 78n2
perceived objectified for, 378
and predicate, 378
and proposition, 381
and symbolic reference, 336
and time, 381
percipient field, as unity, 78
period, and quantity of energy, 93, 93eq
periodicity, in vibration, 102

permanence
versus flux, 182
as fundamental in Descartes, 347, 347–8n7
and philosophy, 182
perpetual perishing, 247, 249
Perry, Ralph Barton, lx
persistence, and past, 373
personal peculiarity, independence of, 257–8
personalism, 5
perspective
and continuum of entities, 303
and interaction, 335
and objectification, 196–7, 379–80
and proposition, 380–1
and subject, 380
perspective relationships, 73
perspectivity, of body, and concepts, 167, 167fig
phenomena, sequence of, 256, 256n3
phenomenalism, of Kant, 31
Philo of Alexandria, 10, 10n4
philosophers
defined, 278
disagreement with, 200
and eternal objects, 66
misled by mathematics and logic, 171
narrowness of, 126
psychology of, 193
and space-time, 281
types of, 144
philosophic method, types of, 126
philosophical scheme, and appeal to practice, 191n1
Philosophical Works (Descartes) (1911), 26n4, 31n4
philosophy *see also* metaphysics; *see also under* types of philosophy
a priori, 195
and abstraction, 126, 175
accurate analysis in, 320
adequacy of notions in, 175
adequacy of thought in, 393
adequate scheme of, 191
adventurous, 292
aesthetics in, 192
American, viii
analytic, viii
antirationalist, 178
application of, 403
approach in, 245
assumptions in, 178, 178n5
authority of, 392
and belief, 179, 179n1
and belief versus practice, 191–2
Cartesian, divergence from, 291
in China, 182

488

Index

and common language, 374
and common sense, 371
complete entities in, 269
and concrete experience, 129
and contradiction, 129
creation in, 144
and creative mind, 123–4
and creative power of human mind, 139
as critic of science, 393
defined, 35, 179n1
defined ideas in, 392
and description of knowledge, 190–1
descriptive system in, 238
as discovery of ultimate meanings, 392
different schools in, 178, 178n5
differing emphases in, 181–2
difficulties in, 51–2
discipline in, 176
dual nature of time in, 85, 85n4
emphasis on matter in, 347
empiricist, time in, 12
epic view of, 292
epistemology as foundation of, 190n6
exemplification of ideas in, 192
experience in, 290
experiential, and actual entity, 223
and experiment, 189, 189n6
and explanation, 177
extension in, 291
and facts, 176
finished versus unfinished, 81
and flux, 182
formulations of belief in, 392
function of, 50
generalisation in, 250, 250n3
Glasgow school of, 172n1
goal of, 173, 177
and grammar, 114, 174, 174n3
and Greek geometry, 184
how questions arise in, 241
and imagination, 175
and immediate experience, 393
inadequacy of ideas in, 393
and independence, 208, 208n2
in India, 182
influence of logic on, 170–1
influence of mathematics on, 170–1, 289
influence of science on, 170–1
and insight, 189, 189n7, 192
and instance, 49
interaction of, with science, 178
and interesting things, 82
and interpretation of experience, 392
job of, 395

key problems of, 5
and knowledge, 96
and language, 116, 174, 174n3, 186, 385
and literature, 129
literary approach in, 320, 324
literary tradition in, 303
logical deductions in, 392–3
logical scheme of generic concepts in, 392–3
logical system in, 238, 238n1
materialism in, 291
mathematical method in, 192, 192n2
and mathematics, 129, 183, 184, 184n2
and method, 177, 178n5, 291
mind versus matter in, 75, 75$table$
misled by Plato, 10, 56
modification of ideas in, 393
and morals and ethics, 397–8
morphological interpretation of, 76
multiple routes in, 129, 129n2
nature of, 96
necessity for, in science, 50
new schools of, 175
Newtonian, divergence from, 291
and number, 177
objectivism in, 53
origins of, in language, 114
and permanence, 182
and physics, 102, 183, 397
pitfalls of, 175
pluralistic realism in, 352
and poetic imagination, 178, 178n2
and poetry, 178
and practice, 393
and problem solving, 403
process, xli, 144
progress in, 175, 178
as province of general concepts, 177
as pruning premises, 192
reasoning in, 304–6
and religion, 129, 178
revolt from, 206
role of, 175
and science, 56, 126, 129, 177, 215, 245, 250, 291, 391, 393, 394, 394, 395
and scientific attitude, 49
and scientific systems, 50
scope of, 392
search for general notions in, 173
Semitic, 182
and scepticism, 102
and social ethics, 391, 398
and social science, 393, 395
and sociology, 403

and spatial relationship, 144
and stimulus to imagination, 393, 395
as stimulus to poetry of thought, 393
stuff in, 291
and subject–predicate form, 289
subjectivism in, 53
substance in, 291
supplementing, 393
as survey of human interests, 392
system of internal relations in, 144
technical language in, 96
and theory versus practice, 177
and truth, 384
universal applicability in, 393
universality of ideas in, 177
philosophy, critical
and *a priori*, 52
analysis of truth and falsehood in, 190, 190n3
certainty in, 190n2
dangers in, 190n3
insight in, 190
role of, 189, 189n7
versus speculative philosophy, 189–90
Whitehead's view of, 189
philosophy Greek
and language, 200–1, 201n1
and mathematics, 289
philosophy, history of
and concepts, 55
explanation in, 177
function of, 55
importance of, 129
and space, 55
and time, 55
philosophy, literary, and contradiction, 126, 126–7n6
philosophy, mathematical
and Aristotle, 183
and Descartes, 183
versus literary, 244–5
and Plato, 183
philosophy, mediaeval
and beginning versus end, 11
harmony in, 87
and logic, 63
and subject–predicate theory, 203
and substance, 146
and universals, 43
philosophy, modern
and beginning versus end, 11
and physics, 56
philosophy, process, origins of, viii
philosophy, Renaissance
and beginning versus end, 11
and science, 266
entity in, 299
oversimplification in, 78n1

489

Index

philosophy, speculative
  absolute premises in, 190
  versus critical philosophy, 189–90
  happy guesses in, 189–90, 190n1, 190n2
philosophy, system of
  general and specific in, 195–6
  universals in, 181
Philosophy A: History of Philosophy, lx–lxi
  course content of, lx
  instructors for, lx
  notes for, lx
  quality of notes for, lx
philosophy of experience, viii
philosophy of history, in work of Whitehead, viii
philosophy of nature
  philosophy of nature, 5, 53, 58; see also philosophy of science
  approaches to, 53–4
  and Descartes, 207
  and immediate occasion, 58
  and metaphysics, 207
  and perceived, 58
philosophy of perception, 151n3
philosophy of science
  philosophy of science, 9, 53, 58; see also philosophy of nature, 53
  and Archimedes, 4
  and Aristotle, 4
  and Aristotelians, 9
  and Church, 5
  defined, 4, 170
  degeneration of, 48
  and Descartes, 10
  development of, 5
  development of Whitehead's, xi
  in Europe, 5
  and function, 11, 56
  and Greek drama, 5
  history of, 4
  induction in, 4
  origins of, 4
  and Roman Empire, 5
  and Roman law, 5
  and space, 11
  space and time in, 4
  and Stoics, 5
  and time, 11
  in work of Whitehead, viii
philosophy of scientific realism, 187
philosophy of value, 5
Philosophy 3b, xxxvi–xxxvii
  varying content of, xxxviii
φύσις, 268
physical
  versus mental, 182, 239, 248, 336
  pain, 400

physical pole see also functioning, perceptual
  as abstract, 356
  and blind perceptivity, 352
  and completion, 356
  and concrescence of perceptivities, 352
  and eternal object, 355
  event as, 343
  importance of, 343
  and knowledge, 193
  linkage of, with mental pole, 343, 355
  versus mental pole, 224
  mental pole superseded by, 343
  and occasion, 342–3, 348
  superseded by mental pole, 348
physical science, atomic conceptions in, 112
physics
  as abstraction, 58
  and abstractive class, 148
  of Aristotle, 7
  and astronomy, 411
  atomicity and continuity in, 366
  and continuity, 112
  defined, 102
  and Descartes, 10, 291, 291n5
  and differential calculus, 88
  and engineering, 411
  and existence of supreme creature, 256
  and experient occasion, 96
  explanation of function by, 77
  extensive magnitude in, 273
  and final ends, 397
  and finite entities, 88
  and functional view, 77–8
  laws of, 302
  and Leibniz, 88
  measurement in, 161
  and metaphysics, 291, 291n5
  of Newton, 394
  and occasions, 56
  and ontological concepts, 275
  and perception, 79, 79fig
  and perceptivity, 400
  and philosophy, 56, 102, 183, 397
  pluralistic realism in, 352
  and presentational locus, 153
  and presentational relation, 163fig
  and presentational relationships, 156n1
  and quantitative relation, 273
  Renaissance, 56
  scale in, 409
  as science, 75
  and simple location, 10
  and space, 10
  and study of universe, 132
  and succession of occasions, 10

and time, 10, 401
  transmission in, 247
  world line of occasions in, 153
physics, mathematical
  invariance of laws in, 287
  and modern rationalism, 185
  as possible, 286
  and reasoning, 305
Physics (Aristotle), 98–9n10
physiology, and memory, 254
π (punct), 138
  and extensional perspective, 152
picture
  and fact, 385, 387
  and language, 387, 390
  as model of reality, 384, 384n4
  and representation, 386
  in *Tractatus*, 390
Pilgrim's Progress (Bunyan) (1678), 292
Planck's constant *(h)*, 41, 91, 93–4, 93n1
planes
  defined, 157
  intersection of, 157
  as intersection of moments, 160
planes, parallel, 157
  order in space through, 162
  time system divided into, 162, 162fig
Plato
  and abstraction, 10
  actual and value in, 215
  and analysis of belief, 188, 188n2
  and Aristotle, 114
  beauty in, 56
  and Chinese language, 201
  Descartes reacting to, 347–8n7
  and general versus specific, 81
  harmony in, 56
  and ideal world, 98
  Ideas of, 10, 14, 43, 56, 378
  influence of mathematics on, 292
  inspectional point of view of, 32
  and language, 200–1, 201n1
  as mathematician, 183
  and mathematics, 10, 81
  and matter as extension, 41
  metaphysics of, 94
  and number, 326
  and occasion, 62
  philosophy misled by, 10, 56
  and point, 313, 314, 317
  and politics, 183
  profound truth in, 218
  reaction to, 183
  and relation, 98
  and relationships of numbers, 124

490

and science, 81
and spatial relationship, 144
and substance, 146
and time, 12, 57, 162, 218
and universals, 43
and view of universe, 292
Platonic myth, 19, 19*fig*, 19, 275, 351
Platonic realism, and Kant, 114*n*2
Platonic realm, 212
pluralism, doctrine of, 228
pluralistic view, multiplicity of entities in, 233
pluralists, and determinism, 69
plurality
  of entities, 144
  and knowing, 52
  limitation on, 12
  and metaphysics, 18
  of occasions, 57
poetry, and philosophy, 178
point *see also* points
  as abstract entity, 185
  abstractive classes of, 326
  actual entity at, 247
  Archimedean, 184
  versus area, 313
  convergence to, 149
  coordinates of, 274
  defined, 127, 159, 306, 313, 314, 323
  defined by class, 149
  density at, 147
  in Descartes, 307
  and entity, 149
  and extension, 148
  in Euclid, 127, 314, 322
  and fallacy of misplaced concreteness, 127*n*2
  as geometrical fiction, 314
  geometrical relations of, to other points, 160
  Greek views of, 313–14
  as historical route, 159
  how to define, 304, 304*n*3
  idea of, 127
  in impartial space, 283, 283*fig*
  importance of, 318
  indivisibility of, 160, 313–14
  information from, 133, 133*n*3
  inheritance of, 280
  as intersection of moments, 160
  knowledge from named, 135
  in Leibniz, 307
  as limit, 148, 148*fig*
  magnetic density at, 320
  magnitude of, 313–14
  in manifold, 313
  and modes of convergence, 323
  naming of, 133, 133*n*5, 135*n*3
  neutral definition for, 322
  as order type, 327
  origination of idea of, 320

physical information from, 149
  as postulate, 148
  as pure time dimension, 158, 158*fig*
  and route of approximation, 149, 315
  and simplicity, 148
  and space, 130
  in space, at rest, 283
  on surface, 326
  timeless, 158, 158*fig*
  as the track of occasions, 158, 158*fig*
  track of, 283, 283*fig*, 283*n*4
point-events, space-time as, 125
point instant, as intersection of planes, 157
point occasions, succession of, 276, 276*fig*
pointing, language as, 202
points *see also* point
  correlation of, with numbers, 140
  covered by line, 325
  density of, 328
  division of infinite, 327–8
  infinite points between two, 327
  line as class of, 327
  line as ordered collection of, 127–8, 128*n*2
  order of, 129, 130–1
  ordered in a line, 129
  ordering of, 130
  relation between, 127–8, 128*n*2, 306
  relationships of, 130
  spatial relations between, 131–2, 131–2*n*2
  universe as abstraction of set of, 135
pole, mental *see* mental pole; *see also* functioning, conceptual
pole, physical *see* physical pole; *see also* functioning, perceptual
politics
  and Aristotle, 183
  and Plato, 183
Pope Paul III, 6
possibility, 382
  and actual, 18–19
  and actual occasion, 99*n*2
  and actuality, 9, 66, 260
  and complexity, 261
  and conceptual functioning, 302, 302*n*8
  and contingency, 18
  and data, 98, 98*n*5
  defined, 18, 66
  and entity, 270
  and eternal object, 66, 302, 302*n*5
  and fact, 99*n*2, 225
  how of, 99

and immediate successor, 265
and perceptual functioning, 302, 302*n*8
and φύσις, 268
and thought, 99
possibility, impartial, 19
possibility, partial, 19
possibility, partial versus impartial, 67
possible
  and actual, 19, 32
  and metaphysics, 18–19
possible worlds, 10
postulate, point as, 148
postulates, discovery of, by Pythagoreans, 131
postulation, and existence, 317
potency
  and creativity, 290
  and creature, 290
  defined, 290
  and nature, 290
potential
  versus actual, and thought, 332
  exemplified by actual, 333
potentialities
  as eternal objects, 333
  multiplicity of, 333
  synthesis of, with actual entities, 334
potentiality, 238–41
  actual arising from, 337
  in actual entity, 333
  and actuality, 218, 218*n*4
  of alternative characters, 238
  ambiguous, 238
  and contingency, 218
  and continuity, 218
  and continuum, 296, 297
  and creature, 238, 239, 366
  definite, 238
  determined by past, 297
  and divisibility, 347, 356
  of division of entity, 248, 248*fig*
  as element, 251–2
  and endurance, 240, 240*n*3, 241, 252
  and entity, 296–7
  in epochal entity, 241*n*1
  and eternal object, 225, 357
  and event, 351
  and fact, 225, 239
  as genus, 238
  imagination as pure, 334
  as indeterminate, 349
  limitation of, 238
  limitation of actual world in, 195
  and logical nominalism, 225
  natural, 334
  and nature, 333
  and organism, 296
  and otherness, 226

Index

of physical occasion, 199
of potentiality, 333n1
and probability, 239
realisation of, 296
and realisation of actual entity, 239
realised, 239
and thought, 333
of universe, 268
unrealised, 238, 239
Poynting vector, 29n8
Poynting, John Henry, 29, 29n8
practice
  appeal to, 191, 191n1, 198, 393
  versus belief, 191–2
  and immediate experience, 191, 393
  ocean of, 393
  versus science, 191, 191n2, 393
  as supplement, 191
  what is assumed in, 371
pragmatic standpoint, and self-enjoyment, 243
pragmatics, as subjective, 183n7
pragmatism, 249
  and controversy, 180
  and Dewey, 180
  extreme form of, 180
  versus mathematics, 182
  versus rationalism, 183n6, 231, 231n2, 232
  versus science, 50
pragmatists, and substance, 188
pre-Socratics, 30, 60
precision
  and experience, 114, 114n1
  and extensiveness, 113n6
  in education, 402
  of topic, 334
predecessor, immediate, and entity, 265
predicate
  as affirmation, 383
  and class, 367, 370
  creature as, 162
  defined, 379, 383
  in Descartes, 202
  and entity, 270, 271, 362, 366, 396n1
  as essences, 378
  as eternal object, 378
  examples of, 212
  and extension, 148, 367
  in metaphysics, 202
  as non-actual elements, 379
  objectification of experience by, 379
  and perceived and percipient, 378
  and perceptivity, 378, 378n2
  as Platonic idea, 378
  and proposition, 201

in proposition, as limitation, 364
and solipsism, 363
and subject, 381
subject disjoined from, 235–6, 236n1
and subject, as trap, 235–6, 236n1
and substance, 146
as system of proper names, 122
unifying entities, 378, 378n5
and universe with time extension, 362
predication
  as fundamental, 201
  and meaning, 201, 202
  and metaphysics, 201
  and rational thought, 201
  versus relevance, 203
prehension, 108, 249–50, 381
  versus apprehension, 62n5
  apprehension as consciousness of, 243
  as blind perceptivity, 250, 250n5
  as blind physical perceptivity, 343
  and completion, 344–5
  as concrete fact, 348
  of concretion objectification, 344
  as converse of supersession, 249
  defined, 251, 343
  and determination, 253, 344–5, 345n1
  of entities, 250, 262, 353
  and exclusion, 62
  immediate occasion as, 64
  immediate self as, 13
  as inclusion of entities in occasion, 250, 250n5
  and intrusion, 62
  under limitation, 353–4
  and occasion, 58, 242, 251, 344, 345, 351
  occasion as, 58
  and organisation of world, 343
  and physical memory, 253
  as poles in linkage, 345
  as relational functioning, 253
  sense, as datum, 70
  versus synthesis, 62
  and time, 245, 343, 343n2
  and ultimate entity, 78
premises (logic)
  discovery of, 119
  fundamental, deduction from, 185, 185n1
  in mathematics, 189n6
  pruning of, 192
present
  and actuality, 83, 84
  actualisation in, 35
  versus antecedent, 285

and community of occasions, 32
and conditioned events, 152
conditioning by, 198
conformation of, to past, 334, 334fig, 337, 400
consequence of, for other entities, 257fig, 258
and creativity, 95
as epoch, 153
function of, 77, 77n1
and future, 77, 77n1, 83, 252
and future and past, 83, 333
future foreshadowed in, 32–3
and given, 7
in Hume, 75
image in, 345
incompleteness of, 252
information from, 71
meanings of, 285
and now, 154
and past, 77, 77n1, 83, 107, 241, 334, 337, 349
past as determining, 107
and past and future, 36, 71, 81, 108, 152, 153, 269, 289
past as limitation of, 64
versus presentational immediacy, 352, 352fig
and presentational locus, 152
versus private psychological field, 68
as relative to past, 333
relatedness in, 32
relationship of, to eternal objects, 81
and sense data, 336
types of, 7
ways of looking at, 269
present, specious
  and endurance, 240
  and epoch, 35n3, 241
  and given, 7
  and now, 154, 240, 241
  and presentational immediacy, 352
  and process, 58n2, 154
presentation
  correlated to past, 151
  versus inspection, 78
  and locality, 337
  as outcome, 163
  as perceptivity, 163
  and sense data, 337
  and spatialisation,, 252 252n3
presentational immediacy, 375
  and bodies, 349
  after causal efficacy, 337
  and compresent entities, 264, 264fig
  and concurrent events, 272
  as cone, 352
  crosscut of, 277–8
  defined, 337

and enduring organism, 265, 265*fig*
and entities, 271, 278, 301
and experience of world, 279
and image, 356
locus of, 275–6, 275*fig*
versus memory, 356
and mirror, 257
and occasions, 272, 272*fig*, 272*n*2, 275, 345
and painter, 271, 271*n*4
past antecedent to, 276
versus present and simultaneous, 352, 352*fig*
and private world, 350
and representation of knowledge, 186
schemes of, 279
and science, 279
and scientific observation, 275
and seeing double, 257
and sense data, 263
simultaneity as, 346
and space, 277
of space-time, 271
and specious present, 352
and systematic character, 275
and systematic relationship of entities, 274
and universals, 262–3
presentational locus
and mathematics, 153
and physics, 153
and present, 152
qualities of, 153
presentational relation, 109, 109*fig*
and Hume, 110
and relative status, 73
presentational relationships, 109
of eternal objects, 73, 73*fig*
example of, 73
fused to inspectional relationships, 80
locus of events with, 152
of occasions, 73
presupposition
and compresence, 262, 265
defined, 262
and description, 228–9
of entity, 262
Price, Lucien, 436
Prichard, Harold Arthur, 171, 171*n*11
prime mover, as limitation, 34
prime, as convergence, 156
Principia Philosophiæ (Descartes) (1644) *see Principles of Philosophy*
Principia (Philosophiæ Naturalis Principia Mathematica) (Newton) (1687), 295*n*1, 393*n*2
as foundation of modern science, 408, 412

and hypothesis, 194, 194*n*3, 412
Principia Mathematica (Whitehead and Russell) (1910–13), vii, 193*n*5, 390*n*3
and class, 367
and expression, 186
identity in, 347*n*3
introduction to, 383
and predicate, 367
theory of types in, 384, 436
Whitehead's evaluation of, 436
Principle of Relativity (Whitehead) (1922), vii, 207, 235, 235*n*6
as assigned reading, 3, 46
fact and limitation in, 98*n*2
principles
exemplification of, 388, 393
and logical constants, 388
versus facts, 193–4*n*5
and propositions, 388
supplementation of, 393
Principles of Logic (Bradley), 202*n*2
Principles of Natural Knowledge, An Inquiry Concerning the (Whitehead) (1919), xxviii
as assigned reading, 46
Principles of Philosophy (Descartes) (1644), 26*n*4, 31*n*4
as assigned reading, 4, 47*n*3, 172*n*6, 341, 341*n*4
substance in, 205, 205*n*4, 205–6*n*5, 396
privacy
and ethics, 208*n*3
and history, 203
and knowledge, 203
and morals, 397
rejection of, 203
requiring nothing but itself, 208*n*3
without robbery, 397
in social ethics, 397
versus socialism, 397
versus solidarity, 371
and subject–predicate form, 203–4
in world of thought, 203
private
versus common, 275
immediate presentation as, 275
private minds, 279
private psychological field, datum in, 70
private space, versus physical space, 23
private worlds, 279
probability, 118, 239
and induction, 240
of Keynes, 239–40, 240*n*1
and potentiality, 239
and self-repetition, 33

problems, for well-educated man, 85
Process and Reality (Whitehead) (1929), viii, xi
becoming of continuity in, 261*n*6
development of, xxxii
evaluation of, xxix
and Gifford lectures, xxxii
process philosophy *see* philosophy, process
process, 34; *see also* creativity
as activity, 146
and actual entity, 146, 210, 215, 217–18
of actual occasion, 82
and antecedent versus sequent, 156
and Aristotle, 6, 86
being and non-being in, 6
versus Cartesian philosophy, 146
and character, 401
and community, 146
and creative synthesis, 146
and creativity, 84
defined, 125, 146
in Descartes, 86
and entity, 210
and events, 207*n*3
every actual thing as, 79, 79*n*5
and future, 34
and knowing, 9, 52
and knowledge, 401
importance of, 146
and mental occasion, 198
and nature, 37
of perceiving, 6–7
in philosophy, 144
of physical world, 162
present occasion as, 83
and reality, 146
and specious present, 58*n*2, 154
versus substance, 86
and time, 401
and ultimate entities, 86
and world, 160, 160 *n*1
product, and ultimate entity, 78
production, and occasion, 344
progress
and end, 113
and ethics, 15, 63
and experiment, 175
and imagination, 200
in philosophy, 178
projection
method of, and proposition, 387
of principle of construction, 386
and proposition, 384, 387
and thing, 387
projection, logical, 386

Index

projection, mathematical, 386
proof, negative, versus failure, 141
property, and social ethics, 392
property, private, 397
property as robbery, 392, 397, 399
proposition
  about all propositions, 385
  and abstraction, 363–4
  and act of experience, 379, 380, 380n5
  and actual entities, 382
  ambiguity in, 368
  analysis of, 379
  atomic, 202, 376
  basic, 376
  belief in, 379
  and Bradley, 202
  and causation, 381, 382
  class as, 368
  and classes, 367
  and coexistence, 381, 382
  as complex entity, 375, 376
  complexity of, 368
  and conceptual functioning, 380
  conjunction of, 368
  connection in, 381
  defined, 168, 371, 383
  as description of fact, 372
  and element, 368
  as elliptical, 201
  and entity, 366, 369
  establishment of, 184, 185
  to establish truth, 289
  and existence, 381, 382
  existence of, before logic, 372
  expression by, 384
  and fact, 385
  falsity in, 171
  as formula, 171, 171n5
  and function, 171, 379
  and future, 381
  general form of all, 389
  and God, 388
  how to define, 371
  how to explain existence of, 375
  importance of, 212
  importance of context to, 171
  and inference, 389
  infinite form of, 385
  and infinity of negating processes, 390
  as intermediate universal, 379
  internal, 386
  about itself, 388
  and judgment, 371
  and likeness, 381, 382
  and logic, 375
  in mathematics, 214
  in mathematical logic, 390
  and meaning, 382
  and method of projection, 387
  in Mill, 381–3
  multiplicity of, 369
  and mysticism, 384
  and name, 382, 383
  and necessity, 8, 52
  and non-reflexive extension, 385–6
  as nonsense, 385
  and objectification of entity, 383
  and past, 381
  and patient universe, 363
  and percipient, 381
  and perspective, 380–1
  as picture of fact, 385
  and principle, 388
  and projection, 384, 387
  about propositions, 390
  and reality, 202, 384
  reference in, 202
  reference to world in, 211
  and relevance, 364, 379
  and Russell, 385
  saying nothing, 389
  and sense data, 387
  and sequence, 381, 382
  and structure, 202, 388
  subjects in, 380
  and subject and predicate, 201
  with synthetic unity, 369
  and tautology, 389
  temporal relevance of, 380
  and truth, 171, 171n6, 389, 390
  truth functions of, 389–90
  and truth value, 385
  types of, 368, 375–6
  and unity, 368, 369
  as universal, 365, 370
  and universality, 8, 52
  and universe, 364
  vagueness of, 202
  validity of, 384
  verification of, 119
  and words, 383
proposition, analytic
  and fact, 382
  and Mill, 382
proposition, complex, 369
  and truth function, 385
proposition, definite, and deductive reasoning, 214
proposition, elementary, 385
  and form, 389
proposition, extended, 375
  defined, 376
proposition, fake, 382
proposition, false, deductions from, 186
proposition, fictional, 380–1
proposition, logical, and subject, 380
proposition, molecular, 385
proposition, non-extended, defined, 376, 376n2
proposition, not extended, 375
proposition, not particular, 366
proposition, primitive, 304–12
  defined, 310
proposition, projective, 384
proposition, secondary, 385
  and form, 389
proposition, subordinate, 376n2
proposition, subsidiary, 385
proposition, synthetic, and Kant, 51
proposition, truth, symbol of, 390
propositional function, 384
Protestant civilisation, 396
proton, 90
  characteristics of, 39, 40
  defined, 39
  divisibility of, 40
  as energy, 267
  as fundamental, 39
  radius of, 91
  shape of, 92
Psalms, as universal, 188, 188n2
psychology
  as aesthetic sense, 118
  continuity in, 268
  and education, 403
  and functional view, 30, 77–8
  and logic, 383
  of martyrdom, 147
  and metaphysics, 96
  of philosopher, 193
  and progress, 403
psychology, Gestalt, 257, 257n1
publicity, how it is possible, 94
push, 88, 88fig
Pythagoras, 133
  mass and matter for, 37
  and number, 326
  and point, 314
Pythagoreans
  discovery of axioms by, 131
  geometry of, 124
  and irrational numbers, 259, 259n6
  and mathematics, 123, 123n4
  and order of points, 130–1
  and types of order, 129n4, 130–1
  as simple minded, 130

quality
  as category of scientific thought, 48
  as entity, 396
  versus substance, 75, 75table
quantitative measurements, series of, 317–18
quantitative permanence, 29
quantity
  and Aristotle, 140
  as category, 140
  complexity of, 140
  correlation of, 338, 338fig

Index

defined, 120, 120n3
extensive, 125, 130
as not a fundamental category, 273
infinite, 389
intensive, 213
versus magnitude, 120
measured, 266
nature of, 140
and number and relations, 122, 122n8
and parts and wholes, 120
and segmental number, 143
and structural relationships, 266
and structure, 266–7, 273
symbol for, 122
quantum
actual entity as, 297
and continuity, in nature, 297
life cycle as, 334
size of, 346
and specific entity, 337
time as, 350
in vibration, 102
quantum theory, 91–2
atomicity and continuity in, 182
and time, 346
Quine, W. V. O., xxx

Radcliffe lectures, xxxv, xxxviii
Radical Empiricism (James) *see Essays in Radical Empiricism*
railway timetables, 245n5, 251n7, 263, 270
Ramsey, Frank Plumpton, 385, 385n1
rational standards for criticism, fulfillment of, 186
rational tests, and ridiculousness, 212
rationalisation
procedure of, 191
and rationalism, 191
rationalism
and *a priori*, 8, 52
versus anti-rationalism, 289
and axioms, 185
belief in, 183–4
Cartesian versus modern, 185
and common sense, 174
confused with scepticism, 184
and controversy, 180
deterioration of, 178
versus Dewey, 183
dogmatic, 149
and empiricism, 5
as faith, 178, 184
and Greeks, 183
and Hume, 5
as an ideal, 183–4, 183n8
and knowledge, 179, 179n5
limitation of, 184

and logic, 183
and mathematics, 183, 183n7
and obviousness, 191
versus pragmatism, 183n6, 231, 231n2, 232
procedure of, 191n3
and progress towards ideal, 191
and premises, 185–6
and science, 5
spatialisation by, 251, 251n5
and truth, 183
rationalism, modern
and imaginative construction, 185
and mathematical physics, 185
rationalism, new
versus Descartes, 205n2
and knowledge, 195
and Whitehead, 188
rationalism, old, and metaphysics, 188
rationalism, reformed, and knowledge, 191
rationalist, Whitehead as, 171
rationalists, and mathematics, 190
rationalistic method, and geometry, 184
Ratzel, Friedrich, 64n2
reading, assigned *see* assigned reading
real
defined, 125
event as, 146
and immediate occasion, 13
multiplicity of, 51
versus relational, 207
real, as inappropriate word, 212
real world, defined, 60
realisation, 57–8
act of, versus continuum, 11
versus becomingness, 11
defined, 11
of eternal objects, 104
and four-dimensional continuum, 57
of genus, 238–9
as impress, 12
as internal, 21
and occasion, 19, 239
of potentiality, 296
and relative status of occasions, 25
and scheme of continuum, 57
stages of, 239
as succession, 57
and temporal series, 11
and togetherness, 21
and value, 21, 22
realised
divisibility of, 11
and time depth, 57
realised values
and ethics, 15
and occasions, 15

realism
and data, 98n4
and eternal object, 98n9
forms of, 225
versus idealism, 19
logical, 66, 66n3
naive, 206
versus nominalism, 224, 224–5n3
pluralistic, in philosophy, 352
pluralistic, in physics, 352
versus solipsism, 224, 224–5n3
as true, 201n4
realist, and idealist, 19
reality
and adventure, 125
and community, 146
and duration, 153
fronting of, 50
as function, 55
and functional view, 77
grades of, 25
and grammar, 125
and immediate occasion, 13
and individual substance, 125
and knowing, 31
limitation imposed by, 14
and literature, 50
and occasion, 25
and process, 146
of physical event, 14
picture as model of, 384, 384n4
and proposition, 202, 384
reasoning
cogency of, 149
and common sense, 305
and mathematical physics, 305
and mathematics, 305
versus observation, 5
and ordinary language, 304
in philosophy, 304–6
presupposition in, 306
by Russell, 304
and science, 5
reasoning, abstract, limitations on, 5–6
reasoning, circular, 206
reasoning, deductive
and definite proposition, 214
error in, 237
method for, 131
as not desired, 214
reasoning, geometrical, 205, 205n2, 205n3, 206n2
reasoning, inductive, 382
justification for, 290
and observation, 290
reasoning, symbolic, 304–11
Reconstruction of Philosophy (Dewey) (1926), as assigned reading, 46, 46n6
reference
and apprehension, 374
to entity, 363

495

Index

and influence, 374–5
  as interaction to environment, 374
  and physical relatedness, 374
reflection, and perception, 359
reflective space, 95*fig*
reflexivity, and equality, 337
regress, and organism, 102*n*4
relata, and universe, 237
relatedness
  abstracted and called mind, 373
  and British empiricists, 235–6, 236*n*1
  and Caird, 235, 236*n*1
  and emergence, 373
  fundamental types of, 372
  and Hegel, 235, 236*n*1
  and Hume, 235–6, 236*n*1
  and inspectional point of view, 32
  and Kant, 235, 236*n*1
  and knowledge, 32, 81
  logical, 32
  and organism, 373
  physical, 372
  and presentational point of view, 32
relatedness, referential, 373
  abstraction from, 373, 373*n*2
relatedness, scheme of
  and cognition, 32
  and immediate occasion, 32
  and meaning of world, 32
  and present, 32
relatedness, spatial, 372
relatedness, spatio-temporal, 32
relatedness, temporal, 372
relation
  and abstraction, 98
  and Aristotle, 98, 98*n*8
  and definite multiplicity, 123
  of entities, 146
  and eternal objects, 347
  and extension, 144, 148, 150, 358
  function of, 144
  how of, 115
  and identity, 347
  versus individual, 124
  and measurement, 123
  notion of, 66
  to occasion, 81
  and Plato, 98
  and sense data, 70, 98
  and simple notion, 358
  and space, 127
  what of, 115
relation, causal, of entities, 263
relation, extensive
  and community, 160
  and continuity, 160
  defined, 160
  and happening, 267

relation, external
  demonstration of, 24
  versus internal relation, 24
  and presented occasion, 24
  and sense data, 24
relation, fundamental organic, 163
relation, identity, and sameness, 347
relation, inspectional, and occasion, 79
relation, internal
  versus external relation, 24
  of non-continuous occasions, 72, 72*fig*
  and presented occasion, 24
  and relativity, 24
  and sense data, 24
relation, isoid, 117
  and correlation to numbers, 130
  finding instances of, 119, 119*n*1
  and matching, 119, 120
  reflexive, 119
  and reversion, 119
  transitive, propositions for, 120
relation, physical, and perception, 290
relation, presentational, 163*fig*
  and contemporary occasion, 24
  and measurement, 163*fig*
  and occasion, 79
  and physics, 163*fig*
relation, quantitative
  of Einstein, 273
  and physics, 273
  between point events, 273, 273*fig*
  and relativity, 273
relation, systematic, space and time as, 127
relational, versus real, 207
relations
  among bits of matter, 97
  described by formulae, 135*n*3
  of entities, 128, 353
  and eternal objects, 99, 99*n*1
  of facts, 87
  and function, 89
  grades in, 71
  in logic, 370
  in mathematics, 131
  among numbers and quantities, 122, 122*n*8
  of occasions, relative importance of, 81
  between points, 127
  between ultimate occasions, 22
relations
  external, 21
  in presentational relationships, 71

relations, finite, and eternal objects, 99*n*1
relations, internal, 21, 71
  doctrine of, 164
  versus external, 23
  and Hume, 99
  and Kant, 99
  and metaphysics, 99
  in presentational relationships, 71
  and Russell, 99
  and spontaneity, 23
  system of, 23, 23*fig*
  system of, in philosophy, 144
relations, physical, and perceptivity, 299, 299*n*1
relations, presentational
  and inspectional relationships, 28
  of occasions modifying *E*, 27
relations, spatial, between points, 131–2, 131–2*n*2
relations, spatio-temporal, relative importance of, 81
relations, sympathetic, of humans, 232
relations, systematic, and mirror, 271
relationship
  activity described by, 196, 196*n*2
  actual entity as, 278–9
  community of extension as, 146
  and description, 228
  of entities, 131
  of events, 145, 155
  and experient occasion, 73
  and extension, 161, 300
  and functioning, 347
  and God, 146
  in ideal world, 98
  of identity, 225
  logical simplicity in, 128, 128*n*3
  and number, 124
  of objects to occasions, 21
  of occasions, 28
  of ordered things, 129
  and physical entity
  and physical occasion, 353
  of points, 130
  preference for, 19
  and pure mathematics, 149
  and relatum, 164
  and space-time, 225
relationship, causal, 156*n*1
  and universals, 262–3
relationship, conceptual, between occasions, 226
relationship, concrete, abstract characteristics of, 303
relationship, conditioned, 151*n*1, 151*fig*

Index

relationship, conditioning, 151*n*1, 151*fig*
relationship, contemporaneous, 156*n*1
relationship, durational, and community, 153–4, 154*fig*
relationship, environmental, 227
relationship, eternal
　defined, 66
　and eternal objects, 21
relationship, extensive, 303
　as abstraction, 305
　characteristics of, 303–4
　and duration, 156
　and spatio-temporal relationships, 303
relationship, external, 73, 73*n*5
relationship, general, congruence as, 117
relationship, harmonious, of creatures, 221
relationship, inspectional, 71–2, 72*fig*
　defined, 27
　of occasions, 28
　and presentational relations, 28
relationship, internal, 73, 73*n*5
　and actual entity, 268
　causal relation as, 256
　in number field, 266
　of perceived thing, 336
　in structure, 266
relationship, isoid, 118
　as abstraction, 305
　limitation of, 27
　and measurement, 130
relationship, linear, and order of points, 130
relationship, logical, and actual entities, 184
relationship, organic, and extension, 263
relationships, perceptual, and knowledge, 223
relationship, physical
　versus geometry, 149
　and limits of series, 318
　patience of particular occasion for, 226
　and time, 255
relationship, presentational, 71–2, 72*fig*, 151*n*1, 151*fig*
　and conditioning of 'physical me', 151–2
　apprehension of, 153
　defined, 27, 71, 110
　and duration, 155
　and event, 161
　external relations in, 71
　internal relations in, 71
　and locus of events, 155–6, 155*fig*, 156*fig*
　measurements by, 71
　and past, 161

and physics, 156, 156*n*1
　reason for, 151–2
　and space-time, 110
relationship, qualitative, in geometry, 133, 133*fig*
relationship, reflexive, 118
relationship, spatial
　and Hume, 28
　and philosophy, 144
relationship, spatio-temporal
　defined, 130
　and entity, 271
　and extensive relationships, 303
relationship, structural, and quantity, 266
relationship, systematic
　and entity, 271
　versus fact, 146
　types of, 151*n*1
　uniformity of, 127
relationship of status
　defined, 26
　versus presentational, 26–7
relationships
　as complex of abstractions, 303
　between eternal objects, 19
relationships of community, and entity, 279
relative status
　and presentational relation, 73
　in relations of eternal objects, 73, 73*fig*
relativity, vii
　versus absolute, 134
　and compresent entity, 264
　of events, 68
　explanations of, 274
　and internal relations, 24
　invariance of laws in, 287
　and measurement, 23
　modern, and Cartesian science, 267
　and present events, 24
　of presented occasion, 24
　and quantitative relation, 273
　and simultaneous events, 23
　and ways of looking at present, 269
relativity theory
　and duration, 155
　of Einstein, 134
　and now, 154
　and rest, 284
　space-time in, 289
　special, and space and time, 284
　Whitehead's, 98*n*2, 207, 235–7, 235*n*6, 237*n*1, 320
relevance
　degrees of, 212
　grades of, 263
　of ideas, 79
　importance of, 203

intensity of, 203
　and irrelevance, 203
　of objectification, 379
　of physical subject, 354
　versus predication, 203
　and proposition, 364
　scales and stages of, 203
　styles of, 203*n*6
　and subject, 380
　and thought, 266, 332
religion
　and appeal to alternatives, 56
　expression of insight in, 231
　and inevitability, 292
　morals in, 292
　and philosophy, 129, 178
Religion in the Making (Whitehead) (1926), viii, xxx, 113*n*1
　as application of new rationalism, 187–8
　as assigned reading, 171, 171*n*3, 172*n*6
　God in, 221, 222
　publication of, xxxi
Renaissance
　and meaning in logic, 214
　and principles of progressive civilisation, 408
　sense perception in, 257
repetition
　actual occasion of, 107
　versus anticipation, 107
　of immortal past, 107, 107*n*4
　and inertia of existence, 33
　and structure, 125
　and structure of occasion, 25
representation
　and picture, 386
　sense as form of, 387
requiring nothing but itself in order to exist, 150, 188, 188*n*5, 204, 205*n*4, 208*n*3, 231, 246*n*3, 261, 342*n*5, 352, 353, 360, 396, 397
resemblance, and difference, 347
res vera, as actual, 209*n*4
rest
　absolute, 283
　and acceleration, 154, 154*n*3
　apparent versus actual, 277
　apprehension of, 277
　and common space, 282
　and correlation of space, 277
　defined, 158, 277, 289
　and epochal occasion, 282, 282*fig*
　and ether, 287
　and historic route, 277
　modes of, 277, 278
　and parallel duration, 155
　and parallel moments, 158
　point in space at, 283

497

Index

and presentational moments, 158
and relative motion, 277
relative, 154, 158, 162, 278, 285, 285*fig*, 285*n*1, 289
and relativity theory, 284
and space versus time, 285–6, 285*fig*
species of, 283, 284, 285, 285*fig*
types of, 278
and uniform motion, 276
and velocity, 158, 284
restatements, 107
retention, and occasion, 101
reversion
  in creative achievement, 102
  and epoch, 102*n*3
  and isoid relation, 119
  principle of, 101*n*7
  and vibration, 243
reversion, double, 243
Revue de Métaphysique, 321, 321*n*1
rhetorician, and plausibility, 155
ridiculousness, and rational tests, 212
Riemann, Friedrich Bernhard, 134*n*3
Riemann integral, 134*n*3
Robinson, Edward Schouten
  biographical sketch of, xlii–xlv
  career of, xliii
  editing of lecture notes of, xlvi
  fate of lecture notes of, xliv–xlv
  quality of lecture notes of, xlvi
  transcription of lecture notes of, xlv
  value of lecture notes of, xliv–xlv
Roethlisberger, Fritz
  biographical sketch of, xxxix
  notes of, xxxix–xli
Roman Empire, and science, 5
Roman law, and science, 5
romance
  as stage in education, 402
  versus thought, 174
Romans, influence of, on scientific thought, 48
root metaphor, 29*n*8
Ross, W. D., 47*n*2
  assigned reading of, 4
  biographical note, 4*n*1
route of approximation, 147
  defined, 319, 319*fig*
  equivalent, 320
  and leap to exact, 318
  limit of, 315
  meaning for, 320
  moment as, 158
  to nothing, 318
  and point, 149
  use of, 316

route, antecedent, and environment, 299
route, historical *see* historical route
route, of occasions of life history, 275–6, 275*fig*
routes of approximation, 316*n*1
  equal, 322
  interconnections of, 320, 320*fig*
  and moments, 159, 159*fig*
  to nothing, 316, 316*fig*
  propositions for, 322, 322*n*2
  simplification by, 316, 316*n*4
routes of convergence
  points as, 323
  use of, 320
Royal Society of Edinburgh, 126–127*n*6
Royce, Josiah, 211
Ruddigore; or, The Witch's Curse (Gilbert and Sullivan) (1887), 77*n*5
rule of safety, 368
Russell, Bertrand, vii, 304, 437
  and appeal to action, 191
  and appeal to practice, 371
  assigned reading of, xxviii, 3
  and Cartesian metaphysics, 98, 98*n*6
  class theory of, 74
  and induction, 49
  and internal relations, 99
  and irrational numbers, 124
  and nature of metaphysics, 99
  as new realist, 187*n*4
  and proposition, 385
  as realist, 187
  and relativity versus absolute, 134
  and sense-data, 98
  and substance, 86, 358
  and symbolic reasoning, 304
  Tarner lectures of, 189*n*3
  and *Tractatus*, 385, 385*n*3, 390
  and Whitehead, 436
  Whitehead's collaboration with, vii
  Whitehead's opinion of, 436

Sacco, Nicola, liv, liv*n*1
sameness
  and actual objects, 44
  and definiteness, 104
  versus diversity, 100
  in entity, 100–1
  of eternal objects, 100
  and identity relation, 347
  and immortality, 44
  and occasion, 100*n*8
Santayana, George, 209, 242, 373, 389, 437
  aesthetics of, 235
  and conceptual functioning, 219

  essences in, 378
  and experience, 297
  and real is any *res*, 209
sceptic, gullibility of, 371
scepticism, 384
  confused with rationalism, 184
  and empiricism, 9
  and Heraclitus, 55
  and morphological view, 76–7
  and organic empiricism, 9
Scepticism and Animal Faith (Santayana) (1923), 209, 235, 242
Scheherazade, 33, 33*n*3
scheme, general, 81; *see also* community
  and cognition, 81
  danger of overemphasising, 81
  of occasions, 81
scheme, spatio-temporal, and occasion, 81
Scholasticism, 5
Schroeder, Ernst, 330*n*4
science, 50; *see also* system of concepts
  and action, 177
  adequacy of notions in, 175
  aesthetic pleasure of, 118
  aesthetics of, 124, 124*n*3
  approach in, 245
  and Aristotle, 81
  and arithmetic of finite numbers, 177
  atomicity in, 11, 182
  atomism in, 90
  and atomism versus continuity, 153
  and Bacon, 193–4, 193*n*3, 193–4*n*5
  and Berkeley, 291
  and Bradley, 291
  and causal relations, 274
  causality in, 112
  certainty in, and abstract demonstration, 184
  in China, 177, 177*n*2
  clarity in, 178
  and common sense, 49, 409
  continuity in, 11, 182
  and continuity and atomicity, 35, 35*n*5
  creature and creativity in, 256
  defined, 50
  and Descartes, 266, 396
  description in, 112
  determination of synthesis by, 113
  discipline in, 176
  discovery of concepts in, 173
  discovery of laws of, 173, 173*n*3
  efficient cause in, 50
  elaboration of principles in, 394–5

Index

and epochal theory of time, 86–87
and experiment, 5
and explanation, 77, 100n5, 177, 256, 256n3
extension in, 293
and extensive magnitude, 293
and facts, 124, 124n3, 176
and faith, 5
final cause in, 50
and function, 11, 57, 77–8
general aim of, 413
and German idealism, 291, 291n3
and history, 5
history of see science, history of
ideas in, 291
ignoring the inexplicable, 175, 175n4
and imagination, 194, 194n4, 291–2
importance of environment to, 214–15, 215n1, 215n2
induction in, 112
inevitability of contradictions in, 50
influence of Descartes on, 112
influence of Greeks on, 170
influence of, on philosophy, 170–1
interaction of, with philosophy, 178
and language, 126n4, 297
laws of, 172, 173, 173n2
literary approach to, 409
and literary tradition, 126
mathematics in, 289
and measurement, 70
and metaphysics, 194, 194n4, 291, 297, 375, 395
mind versus matter in, 75, 75*table*
morphological interpretation of, 76
in nature, 244
and natural whole, 89
necessity for philosophy in, 50
necessity of knowing facts in, 409
and neo-Platonists, 81n5
new period of, 408
and Newton, 266
nominative case in, 295–6
and observation, 5
and organism, 11
and originality, 409
origins of, 173n8
and philosophy, 56, 126, 129, 177, 215, 245, 250, 291, 391, 393, 394, 395
physics as, 75
and Plato, 81
versus practice, 191, 191n2, 393, 394

versus pragmatism, 50
and presentational immediacy, 279
progress in, 408–9
as province of specific concepts, 177
purpose of, 172n7
and rationalism, 5
and reasoning, 5
reformulation of principles in, 394, 395
and Renaissance philosophy, 266
scope of, 112
search for general laws by, 172, 172n7
search for relevant concepts in, 173
simplicity in, 124, 124n3
space and time in, 71, 245, 266
and subject–predicate view, 203, 267
and theory versus practice, 177 177n2
time in, 85
time versus becomingness in, 162
transmission in, 247
and value, 58, 62
variety of conceptions in, 30
science, history of, 394–5
concepts in, 173n8
scientists in, 410–11
in work of Whitehead, viii
science, modern, 170
and Descartes, 266
energy in, 29
and epochal view of time, 37
mass in, 29
Newtonian physics as, 408
versus Renaissance science, 294
time depth in, 77
science, philosophy of. See philosophy of science
science, Renaissance, 170, 409
difficulties in, 266
and final ends, 397
versus modern, 294
and time, 37
Science and Civilizations (Marvin) (1923), 408
Science and the Modern World (Whitehead) (1925), viii, ix, 693, 93–4n4, 227, 227n3, 293, 293n2, 320, 408
analysis of, xxxi–xxxii
as assigned reading, xxviii, 3, 46, 171, 172n6, 178n4
Braithwaite's review of, 233n1
and Greek tragedy, 292
and Lowell lectures, xxvi, xxvii
number and thought in, 326n1
publication of, 3n3, 46n3

scientific attitude, and philosophy, 49
scientific experiment, as prearranged drama, 174
scientific ideas, epochs in, 170
scientific imagination, as principle of scientific thought, 48
scientific method
as imaginative muddled suspense, 334
particular to general in, 49
procedure for, 49
scientific mind, rise of, 5
scientific observation
and presentational immediacy, 275
and private world, 280
scientific state of mind
and Church, 5
and civilisation, 5
defined, 4–5
development of, 5
in Europe, 5
and Greek drama, 5
limit in, 5
and Roman Empire, 5
and Roman law, 5
and Stoics, 5
scientific systems, and philosophy, 50
scientific theories, 86–7
elucidation of, 29
test of, 29
scientific thought, 4–5, 48; *see also* scientific attitude; scientific state of mind
accuracy and precision as principles of, 48
categories of, 48
examination of, 48
facts in, 48
importance of details in, 48
influences on, 48
origin of, 48
principles of, 48
Renaissance, 48
Scientific Thought (Broad) (1927), 189, 189n2, 189n4, 189n6
as assigned reading, xxix, 3, 46, 189n2, 293, 293In3
mathematical method in, 192n2
sensa in, 86n3
scientists
authority of, 413
importance of Hume to, 48
job of, 394–5
and metaphysics, 188
narrowness of, 126
overstating scope and validity by, 395
perceptivity for, 108, 108n1
role of, 89
Scopes, John, 315n4

Index

second law of motion, 411
seeing double, and presentational immediacy, 257
segment, greater, 138
segment, lower
   defined, 138
   proof of, 139–40
segment, measurable, 139–140
segment, upper, defined, 138
selection
   and architecture, 63, 63n6
   art as, 63
   and Chinese literature, 63
   and emergence of creature, 104
self
   in beyondness, 13
   and body, 298
   for Descartes, 298
   as end, 216
   and experience, 298
   as experient, 13
   and here and now, 13
   as immediate occasion, 13
   knowledge of, 298, 365
   mind as, 298
   permanent knowing, 64
   as summation of antecedent occasions, 401
   unity of, and historical route, 167
self, immediate, as prehension, 13
self-analysis
   of creature, 219
   and observation, 377
self-creation, of entities, 296
self-creative character, and originality, 345
self-creativeness, process of, 335
self-enjoyment
   and individual, 243
   and occasion, 243n4
   and pragmatic standpoint, 243
self-evidence
   belief in, 180
   danger of overstatement in, 180
   of ideas, 179, 180
   and test of belief, 180
self-judgment, and emotional intensity, 377
self-knowledge
   of entity, 230, 296
   and occasions, 198
   of physical creature, 197
self-percipience
   and pure percipience, 230
   as reflective percipience, 230
self-realisation
   of entity, 263
   social, 243–4
   of value, 298
seminaries, 1926–7, lvi–lx
   format of, lvi
   notes for, lvi
   social aspect of, 436

Semites, poetry of, as philosophy, 188, 188n2
sensa
   and Descartes, 360
   as eternal objects, 86
   and sentence, 383
   and state of body, 263
   and Whitehead, 86
sensa values, 303
sensation, external cause of, 74, 74n4
sense, as form of representation, 387
senses, species of, 337
sense awareness
   and occasion, 351
   and perception, 351
   as physical, 351
sense data
   and Bradley, 223
   and brain, 76
   and causal efficacy, 337
   characteristics of, 66, 66n1
   and Descartes, 76
   eternal objects as, 345
   and experience, 223
   and external relation, 24
   as fact, 387
   and function of knowing, 51
   and historic route, 361, 362
   and identity, 65
   immediate presentation of, 275
   and internal relation, 24
   and language, 361
   as localisation, 337
   in morphological view, 76
   mystical form of, 386
   organisation of, 29
   and past and present, 336
   versus pattern, 386
   and presentation, 337
   and presentational immediacy, 263
   and presented occasion, 24
   private psychological space of, 275
   and proposition, 387
   as relational, 23
   and relation, 98
   relations of, to world, 232
   and Russell, 98
   and spatio-temporal relatedness, 361
   and table, 76, 195, 195n6
   and time, 76
   as useful, 361
sense data, chaotic, 29
sense experience, meaning in, 114
sense perception
   and function of knowing, 8
   knowledge by, 7
   and physical imagination, 345
   and presentational immediacy, 337

   in Renaissance, 257
   and simultaneity, 257
sense presentation, 272
   and organism, 336
sensibility, physical, and conceptual activity, 359
sensitive body (Galileo), 74, 75
sentence
   abstraction from, 114
   construction of, 386
   deficiencies in, 266
   enunciating fact, 266
   and logic, 363
   in metaphysics, 205
   and sensa, 383
   structure of, 387
   temporal order in, 114
   temporal synthesis in, 114
   vague meaning in, 214
sequence
   of entities, 121–2
   and proposition, 381, 382
   of parts, 121–2
   time as, 57
sequent, versus antecedent, 156
serial advance, and physical world, 162
serial systems, alternative, and creative advance, 162
series
   converging to nothing, 318
   how to discriminate, 318
   how to find, 318
series, continuous
   of fractions, 329
   rational and irrational numbers in, 328
series, dense, 260
   types of, 328
series, dense and continuous, 346
series, infinite, in dense series of fractions, 329
series of fractions
   cut in, 331, 331*fig*
   discontinuous gaps in, 329
   fractions between, 329
   infinite irrationals between, 329
set theory, 316n1
seventeenth century
   philosophy in, 170, 297n4
   science in, 294, 297n4, 397
   scientific state of mind in, 4
   scientific thought in, 48
shading, 306, 308, 308n1, 308n6, 308n8, 309, 309n2, 312
   and extensive quantity, 319
   and extensive relation, 321
   interior, 309, 309n1*fig*, 309n2
   of itself, 308
   of whole and part, 308
Shahryār, 33, 33n3
Shakespeare, William, 129n5
sheep, versus mutton, 91, 182, 182n5, 312, 313

Sheffer, Henry Maurice, 383–4*n*3
Sheldon, Wilmon Henry, 44*n*3, 252, 252*n*7
Shelley, Percy Bysshe, 271, 271*n*5
shielding, 306
ship, and ship builder, 83, 210
Sidgwick, Henry, 375, 375*n*3
σ (condition of abstractive set), 149–50, 332, 332*fig*
σ-antiprime, 150
  defined, 157
σ-prime, 150, 332, 332*fig*
sign *see also* symbol
  and fact, 386
  and logical constants, 388
similarity, and diversity in class, 121, 121*fig*
simple location, 52
  difficulties of, 77
  and physics, 10, 56
  and subjectivism, 53
simple, explained by complex, 100, 100*n*5, 100*n*6
simplicity
  and accuracy, 147
  and complication, 128
  and convergence to nothing, 148
  and devolution of extent, 148
  distrust of, 7
  kinds of, 128
  of logic versus simplicity of application, 185
  and point, 148
  pursuit of, 128
  in science, 124, 124*n*3
  and truth, 128
  and universe, 128
  and whole, 147
simplicity, actual
  as concrete fact, 128
  defined, 128
simplicity, logical
  and actual world, 185
  defined, 128
  examples of, 128
simplicity, psychological, 128
  defined, 128*n*6
simultaneity, 257–8, 345–6
  and antecedent and consequent, 257
  versus before and after, 22
  and causal relationships, 255
  meanings of, 346
  non-causal, 346
  and past and future, 255
  and physical causation, 257
  and presentational immediacy, 346, 352, 352*fig*
  as relationship of entities, 257
  and time, 246
  and time and space, 272
sin, original, 166*n*1, 208, 216*n*8, 350, 392

Singer, Charles, 408
Siris: A Chain of Philosophical Reflexions and Inquiries (Berkeley) (1744)
  as assigned reading, 4, 47
situation
  dramatic, 173–4
  immanent, 174
  transcendent, 174
sixteenth century
  philosophy in, 54
  science in, 294, 397
  scientific state of mind in, 4
Sixth International Congress of Philosophy, xxix–xxx, xxxi
Skinner, B. F., xxx
Smith, John Alexander, 354*n*1
Smith, Norman Kemp. *See* Kemp Smith, Norman
Smith, Preserved, 44, 44*n*5
Smith, Robertson, 126–7*n*6
Social Ethics 20a: Fundamentals Underlying the Social Sciences, lviii
social
  actual fact as, 145
  entity as, 120
  world as, 120
social ethics
  conciliation of privacy and socialism by, 397
  and Descartes, 396
  doctrine of, 405
  doctrines founded on, 392
  and ethics, 395
  independence and solidarity in, 208, 208*n*4, 208*n*5
  and metaphysics, 208, 208*n*4, 208*n*5
  and original sin, 392
  and original virtue, 392
  and philosophy, 391, 398
  privacy in, 397
  and property, 392
  socialism in, 397
  and society of social entities, 405
social ethics seminary
  format of, lviii–lix
  notes for, lvii–lx
  questions for, 402*n*1
  role of students in, lix
  stenographer for, lix
social relations, and incompleteness, 349
social sciences
  approaches to, 391
  limits of achievement of, 403
  and philosophy, 393, 395
  progress in, 403
social solidarity
  doctrine of, 398
  and original sin and virtue, 398

social work, teaching of, lviii
socialism
  versus privacy, 397
  in social ethics, 397
society
  and favorable environment, 405
  in actual entity, 398
  maintenance of, 406
Society of Fellows (Harvard), xxx
sociology
  and philosophy, 403
  in Whitehead's work, viii
sock repaired until it's new, 247, 247*n*3, 362, 362*n*1
Socrates
  and Descartes, 63*n*2
  and ethics, 63
  and ethics versus metaphysics, 60
  mortality of, 202
solidarity
  defined, 210, 298
  of entities, 258, 259
  and multiplicity of entities, 250
  principle of, 215, 217, 218, 220
  as principle of metaphysics, 210
  versus privacy, 371
  social, doctrine of, 216, 216*n*8
  of universe, 213, 235, 269
solipsism, 211, 384
  and fact and potentiality, 225
  and function of knowing, 52
  and predicate, 363
  and private world, 196, 196*n*1
  versus realism, 224, 224–5*n*3
  and subject–predicate theory, 203
solipsist moment, 223
solitary, versus multiple, 204
some, as a mathematical concept, 137
sound, and presentational immediacy, 271
space, 93, 163; *see also* space-time; spatiality
  as abstract conception, 127
  as abstraction, 127
  and accuracy, 127
  and actual entities, 278
  and actual occasion, 299–300
  and Alexander, 159
  and Bergson, 150
  and beyond, 272–3
  as category of scientific thought, 48
  congruence of, 284
  and corporeal entity, 278
  corpuscular theory of, 295*n*4
  and creative impress, 93
  as creature, 94
  curvature of, 24

501

Index

and Descartes, 183, 278, 341*n*4, 341*n*5
dimensions of, 104*n*2
distribution of energy in, 92
diversity of physical, 289
as empty, 294–5
and endurance, 266
and entity, 284, 284*n*6
and eternal objects, 94
and events, 272–3
and experience, 289
and extension, 144, 150, 266, 301, 370
as extensive, 57, 267, 368
force in, 267
and given, 12
and history of philosophy, 55
and individual, 93
infinity of three-dimensional, 281, 281*fig*
and intuition, 58
and Kant, 12, 150
knowledge of, 130
lines in, 282
and mass, 37
and matter, 12, 127, 267
matter and force in, 294
and measurement, 161
motion in, 281
and Newton, 127, 267, 278
and occasion, 10, 60, 71
order in, 162
origin of, 150
and perception, 263
and philosophy of science, 4, 11
as physical fact, 299–300
and physical world, 160, 160 *n*1
and physics, 10
as plenum, 294*n*3
and points, 130, 283, 283*fig*
and presentational immediacy, 277
as receptacle, 294, 375
and relation, 29, 127
relational theory of, 307
and rest, 282, 285–6, 285*fig*
in science, 71, 266
and simultaneity, 272
and status of occasions, 19, 67
study of, 126–7*n*6
and substance, 127*n*7, 144, 341*n*4, 341*n*5
as systematic relation, 127
table occupying, 127, 127*n*4
theory of, and Leibniz, 307
without thickness, 276
and time, 11, 23, 245, 301
and universe, 127
space, common
and Einstein, 277
as logical construct, 278
and modes of rest, 277
in Newton, 277

space, empty, as grade of reality, 25, 25*n*3
space, instantaneous, 152, 158
correlation of, 276, 276*fig*
geometry of, 160
at a limit, 282
and motion, 276, 276*fig*
in universe, 278
space, physical
as complex, 278
differences in, 284
as logical construct, 275
modes of rest in, 278
versus private space
space, presented, 24
space, timeless, 158, 159
geometry of, 160
space relations, 23
space system, alternative, 162
Space, Time, and Deity (Alexander) (1920), 46–7*n*7, 124, 293*n*2
as assigned reading, 3, 46
influence of, on Whitehead, 46–7*n*7
spaces, instantaneous, correlation of, 276, 276*fig*
space-time, 93
character of, 45
classical versus modern, 289
contingency of, 81
and diversity, 127
empty, 213–14
and endurance, 361
geometry of, vii
as how things are, 101–2, 102*fig*
nature of, 126
and philosophers, 281
and philosophy fundamentals, 348
as point events, 125
presentational immediacy of, 271
and presentational relationships, 110
principle, 286
qualities of, 32
relationship of, 225
in relativity theory, 289
and state of body, 263
structural character of, 289
units, 113*n*6
as universe, 220
spatial extension, and endurance, 267
spatial facts, evolution of, 281
spatial relation, outside universe, 249
spatialisation, and presentation, 252, 252*n*3
spatiality. *See also* space
as abstraction from extensiveness, 151*n*1

and knowing, 12
versus temporality, 11
spatio-temporal, universe as, 202
spatio-temporal activity, 124
spatio-temporal behaviour of matter, 87
spatio-temporal continuum, time in, 265
spatio-temporal extension, and divisibility, 320
spatio-temporal perspective, of actual entities, 261
spatio-temporal process
and parts, 125
character of, 125
spatio-temporal relatedness, and sense data, 361
spatio-temporal relations
and entity, 270
and historical route, 360
in molecules, 110*n*6
spatio-temporal structure, 125
spatio-temporal uniformity, 159
specific, versus general, 81, 243
Spencer, Herbert, and unknowable, 49, 208*n*2, 359, 359*n*3, 397*n*1
Spinoza, Baruch, 87
and activity, 18
and Alexander, 124
and geometrical reasoning, 205
and God, 166, 268
as misunderstood, 210
modes in, 53
monads of, 362
in Philosophy A, lx
φύσις in, 268
and substance, 53, 205–6*n*5, 278*n*3, 352
spontaneity
and internal relations, 23
and occasions, 20–21, 68, 68n3
spontaneous choice, 21, 69
square root of 2, 148, 317
as constructed number, 136, 136*n*3, 137, 138, 139
and dense series, 328, 328*fig*, 329
as mind-created entity, 123–4, 124*n*1, 129, 139
and postulation versus existence, 317
as real entity, 129, 129*n*5
and route of approximation, 315
standpoint
universal, knowledge from, 166*n*1
universe from, 169
Stanley, Philip Edwin, 80*n*6, 383*n*1
State of Tennessee v. *John Thomas Scopes* (1925), 315*n*4

502

Index

state
  authority of, 405–6
  fixing responsibility on human beings, 406–7
statements, exact, logical simplicity of, 128, 128n7
Stetigkeit und irrationale Zahlen (Dedekind) (1872), 328n1
Stevin, Simon (Stevinus), 410, 410n3
stigma (prick), as point, 314
Stoics
  doctrine of God of, 220, 230
  and philosophy of science, 5
  and scientific state of mind, 5
strain, 38
  and energy, 89
  and force, 87
Strait of Dover, 299
stress, 38
  defined, 88
  and force, 87, 412
  in physics, 412
  as property of matter, 29
Strife of Systems and Productive Duality: An Essay in Philosophy (Sheldon) (1918), 44n3
structural coordination, and evolution, 281
structural relation, 280
structure
  and causal experience, 27
  and congruence, 284
  and endurance, 27, 72, 74, 79, 80n4
  extension as element of, 125
  of fact, 387
  formal, and concrete object, 387
  function in, 125
  internal relationships in, 266
  and measurement, 134, 273
  and occasion, 74
  and principle of construction, 388
  and propositions, 388
  and quantity, 266–7, 273
  and relationship, 132
  and repetition, 25, 125
  of sentence, 387
  and substance, 125
  and synthesis, 27
  and system of coordinates, 274, 275, 289
stuff
  and consciousness, 97
  forces as, 79
  versus knowing, 96
  in philosophy, 291
stuffing, of occasions, 79
subclasses
  correlation of, 330
  number of, always greater than class, 330

subdivision, infinite, 338
subject
  and community, 60
  creature as, 162
  in Descartes, 202
  disjunction of, from predicates, 235–6, 236n1
  enduring, examples of, 60n6
  as entity, 115
  examples of, 60
  as function, 347
  in grammar, 114
  in metaphysics, 202
  versus object, 182, 196–7
  and occasions, 60
  and predicate, 201, 381
  and predicate, in logic, 211
  and predicate, as trap, 235–6, 236n1
  as prehending occasion, 343
  private predicates of, 203
  and proposition, 201
  in proposition, objectification of, 364
  qualified by ideas, 202–3
  and unity, 60
subject (grammatical), absolute, 114, 114n3
subject, logical
  objectification of, 380
  and perceptual subject, 380
  percipient subjects, 380, 380n3
  and proposition, 380
subject, perceptual, and logical subject, 380
subject, percipient
  and acts of experience, 380
  and logical subject, 380, 380n3
  objectification of, 380
  and proposition, 380
subject, physical, relevance of, 354
subjective, and objective, 61n5, 93, 162
subjectivism
  in Aristotle, 53
  and community of occasions, 13–14
  defined, 14
  in Descartes, 53
  in James, 53
  in philosophy, 53
  and simple location, 53
subject–object theory, 202–3
subject–predicate complex, and metaphysics, 207
subject–predicate fallacy, 237
subject–predicate form
  and Aristotle, 203
  atomic view of, 202, 203
  and Descartes, 203, 206
  metaphysics, 203, 212
  misuse of, 203
  and objectification, 365
  objection to, 203

  and philosophy, 289
  and privacy, 203–4
  and relation, 358
  and science, 203
subject–predicate propositions
  and objectification, 364
  and solipsism, 362–3
  complex, 364
subject–predicate theory
  and Descartes, 203, 205n1
  and logic, 203
  and medieval philosophy, 203
  problems in, 207
  and solipsism, 203
subject–predicate view
  and actual world, 251
  and atomism, 266
  and Descartes, 266
  and fact, 266
  and science, 267
  and time, 246
substance
  and absolute idealists, 188
  and actual entity, 36, 201, 203, 204, 209, 212, 233
  actual fact as, 209
  actuality of, 246n5
  and activity, 297
  and adventure, 348n2
  in Aristotle, 86, 146
  and attribute, 211
  body as, 172n2, 204
  bodily, 341, 341n4, 341n5
  in Broad, 86
  as category of scientific thought, 48
  and Christianity, 146
  and cogitation, 94, 164
  as complete in itself, 256
  corporeal, 53, 164, 299
  and creativity, 212
  defined, 10, 120, 146, 206n5, 396
  and dependence, 352, 353
  and Descartes, 10, 53, 57, 77, 86, 120, 146, 164, 172, 188, 201, 204, 205, 205n4, 205–6n5, 206n5, 208n1, 208n2, 212, 278n3, 299, 299n2, 341, 341n4, 352, 358, 359, 360, 361, 362, 396
  and Dewey, 188
  duality of, 42
  versus duration, 36–7, 36n5
  and endurance, 36, 85, 94
  and epoch, 36, 85
  and eternal objects, 206, 206n3
  and ethics, 397
  examples of, 396
  and existence, 204
  extended, 29
  and extension, 160–1, 300

503

Index

and God, 172n2, 204, 205, 205n4, 205–6n5, 209, 341, 341n5, 352, 353, 360
and Hegel, 188
and Hoernlé, 188
and immediate occasion, 53
independence of, 208n1, 208n2, 396–7
as individual, 396–7
and James, 188
and Kant, 188
knowledge of existence of, 341n4
and Leibniz, 171, 171–2n12, 352
and Locke, 188n5, 203, 203n8, 358, 359
in McTaggart, 54–55n6
and mediaeval philosophy, 146
mental, 94, 341, 341n4
as metaphor, 237
mind as, 172n2, 204
as mystery, 203
and occasion, 10
in philosophy, 291
and Plato, 146
plurality of, 9
and pragmatists, 188
and predicate, 146
primary, 146
versus process, 86
versus quality, 75, 75 table
as real entity, 204
and reality, 125
requiring nothing but itself, 204, 205n4, 352, 396
in Russell, 86
as sense data, 358
as social, 353
and space, 127n7, 144
and Spinoza, 53, 205–6n5, 278n3, 352
and structure of universe, 125
as term, 298
and time, 86, 86fig, 359n5
and understanding of world, 396–7
unity of, 278n3
substance, actual
and actual occasion, 85
and *natura naturata*, 85–6
substance, cogitating, 53
substance, enduring,
and becomingness, 36
and Descartes, 77, 85
substance, individual, as ultimate real, 53
substances
interaction of, 204
relationships between, 146
substances, system of, actual occasion as, 85n5
substantiality, 209
substantive activity, and actual, 82

substantivism, defined, 396
subtraction, defined, 139
succession
art as, 15
and coexistence, 381
realisation as, 57
and time, 255, 264, 337
successor, immediate
immediate, conditions for, 265, 265fig
and possibility, 265fig
superject
defined, 334
origination of, 298
superjicient value, 22, 22n4
superorganism, 247, 248n1
and organism, 247, 248n2, 263
supersession, 342
and actual entity, 222
and actual occasion, 347
and becoming, 346
and causation, 218
and continuum, 346
as converse of prehension, 249
of conceptual functioning, 249 n4
of concrete entity, 342
versus creation, 247
of creature, 344
of creature by creativity, 252n5
and creativity, 344, 354
defined, 249n1
demonstration as instance of, 249, 249n3
direction of, 247–8
and entity, 246, 248, 249n1, 269
and individuality, 216, 216n5
and infinite end, 346
internal, 248, 248fig
modes of, 248
mutual, 248
of object, 354
of perception, 249
and occasion, 342, 343, 348
and supreme creature, 220
and time, 245, 246, 249, 343n2, 354
transcending time, 343
of universe, 269
and vicious infinite regress, 346
superstition, defined, 389
supreme creature *see* creature, supreme
surface, 326
importance of, 318
neutral definition for, 322
origination of idea of, 320
point on, 326
as route of approximation, 315, 316
survival value, and ethics, 63

symbol *see also* sign
determined by experience, 336
and fact, 384
for idea, 310
and knowledge, 360
and meaning, 336
and music, 386
and relation of fact, 386
symbolic reference
and actual thing, 337
defined, 336
and error, 336
and perceptual immediacy, 336
and percipient, 336
symbolism
and knowledge, 186, 187
language as, 186, 201
meanings assigned to, 214n5
and perception, 336
as temporal synthesis, 114n5
Symbolism: Its Meaning and Effect (Whitehead) (1927), viii, xxxii, 335n1, 336n2
Symbolism and Truth (Eaton), 186
symmetry, 337
synthesis
as achievement, 31
and actuality, 335
and aesthetic intensity, 377, 377n6
and analysis, 336
and beyondness, 59
of conceptive and perceptive, 162
and conceptual functioning, 377
versus concretion, 104
and creation, 18
creative, 103, 146
and creature, 42, 43, 104
determination of, 113
as efficient cause, 59–60
and emotional intensity, 377, 377n6
entity as, 115
of entity into occasion, 78
and eternal objects, 164, 164fig
exclusion in, 64
experience as, 45
of experient and imaginal occasions, 65
and grammar, 114
of *how* and *what*, 115
immediate occasion as, 59, 59n7
versus isolation, 59, 60s2
of judgement, 50
and limitations of mode, 31
of many, 115
mental, 164–5, 164fig
modal, 65
necessity for limitation in, 73, 73n7
and object, 336

504

and occasion, 17, 61, 61*n*4, 96, 105
of opposites, in occasion, 102, 102*n*7
versus prehension, 62
in sentences, 114
and structure, 27
and symbolism, 114*n*5
and temporal order, 114
and truth and error, 337
and ultimate entity, 78
as ultimate fact, 108
of world, 13
synthesis, physical
and mental synthesis, 164–5, 164*fig*
mentality as analytic of, 219
synthesised things, 17
synthetic, and analytic, 381–2
synthetic propositions, and Kant, 51
synthetic truth, 6
system
and knowledge, 33
universe as, 202
system of concepts, 50; *see also* science
system of coordinates, and structure, 275, 289
system of presentations, physical world as, 162
system, standard, existence of, 154
system, temporal-spatial-physical-referential (TSPR), 373–5, 373*n*2
examples of, 373
systematic character
and actuality, 274
and entities, 274
of environment, 356
and future, 274
and presentational immediacy, 275

tangency, 306, 319
deceitfulness of, 323
difficulties of, 323
and extensive connection, 308
and extensive relation, 321, 323
Tarner lectures, xxviii–xxix, 189*n*3
tautology, and proposition, 389
Taylor, A. E.
as neo-idealist, 187*n*4
and necessary thought, 180
as realist, 187
Taylor, Henry Osborn, xxvi, xxx
Taylor, Julia Isham, xxx
teachers, magnificent versus pedantic, 244
teleology, external, 168
teleology, internal, 168
temporal order
and synthesis, 114
in sentences, 114

temporal relation, as relative, 162
temporal series, and realisation, 11
temporality *see also* time
as abstraction from extensiveness, 151*n*1
and knowing, 12
versus spatiality, 11
Ten Commandments, 208, 208*n*1, 396
Tennyson, Alfred, 390
theology, versus ontology, 398
theology, medieval, 5
theology, process, xli
theology, transcendental, 166
theory
and fact, 193–4*n*5
verification of, 186*n*4
where to begin, 173, 173*n*8
there and then
as actual, 59
versus here and now, 59
as limitation, 59
thing
and creativity, 166 *n*1
and projection, 387
thing, actual, and concretion, 207, 207*n*1
thing in itself, creative character of, 256
thinking, and corporeal substance, 299
third law of motion, 37, 412
Thomson, J. J., 437
Thomson, William (Baron Kelvin), 29, 295, 295*n*6
thou shalt not steal, 392, 397, 399, 404
thought
as abstract, 6, 50, 335
and act of nature, 333
and actual creatures, 99
and actual versus potential, 332
as analogue of concrete, 126
description of, 43
as dimension, 45, 103
and discernment, 9
and eternal objects, 333
and experience, 6
and fact, 388, 388*n*1
generic versus detailed, 244
history of, 173
and ideas, 6
and imaginal occasion, 99*n*2
and imagination, 244
initiative of, 244
kind of content of, 332–3
and language, 174
laws of, 10
narrow versus imaginative, 175
number as instrument of, 326
and nature, 244, 332
and object, 332
originality of, and detail, 244

out of time, 103, 103*n*3
poetry of, 393
popular, habit of, 335
and possibility, 99
as property of mind, 28
relations in topics of, 391
and relevance, 266, 332
and relevant potentialities, 333
versus romance, 174
separation by, of entity from exemplification, 250–1
and unity from multiplicity, 332
what and *how* of, 332
and Wittgenstein, 388
thought, accurate, and mathematics, 128
thought, mediaeval, and spatial relationship, 144
thought, rational, and predication, 201
Three Dialogues between Hylas and Philonous (Berkeley), as assigned reading, 47
time, 36–37, 84, 84*fig*, 163; *see also* space-time; temporality; time, measured
as abstraction, 127
and abstractions of event, 255
and accuracy, 127
activity through, 93
and actual entity, 196, 258, 258*n*7, 361, 401
and actual occasion, 196, 401
as adjective, 259
and Alexander, 159
alternative routes of, 265
alternative systems of, 155
analysis of, 245, 248
in Aristotle, 100
aspects of, 57
and antecedent and succession, 255
as atomic, 85
as atomic entity, 11
awareness of, 58
and becoming, 88, 94, 350
as becoming of graduality, 36, 37
as becoming of novelty, 112
and becomingness, 84, 162
and Bergson, 57
and beyond, 272–3
and calculus, 12
as category of scientific thought, 48
causal element in, 245
and causation, 255
and chaotic given, 12
classical view of, 281
and completeness, 342*n*5, 349, 349*n*1
and complexity, 250

505

Index

and complexity of universe, 250
and conformation to past, 337
congruence of, 284
and continuity, 88, 94, 350
as continuous, 85, 94, 245
as continuous flow, 258, 258n7
and correlation of substance to 86, 86fig
and creative impress, 93
as creative passage of nature, 218, 218n1
and creativity, 34, 84, 94, 100, 100n4, 245
as creature, 107
defined, 107
as dense series, 240–1
depth of see time depth
and Descartes, 12, 57, 85n4, 341n4, 341n5, 347
difference in, in different universe, 286
difficulties in, 132
discreteness of, 260, 260n2
distinctions in, 22
as divisible, 57, 94
double notion of, 57
and duration, 36, 150
as *durée*, 85n4
and efficient and final causes, 11
in empiricist philosophy, 12
and endurance, 36, 240, 300, 300n7
and energy, 41, 93
and English empiricists, 58
and entity, 284n6
as epoch, 35
as epochal, 57, 94, 246, 346–7, 350–1
and eternal objects, 94
and events, 272–3
and extension, 11, 144, 150, 300, 300n7, 301
and extensive character, 267, 347
as extensive element, 36, 85
and extensive quantity, 12, 259n2
and extensiveness, 57
as fact of epoch, 270
as form of perception, 252
and function, 37
and function of knowing, 9, 52
as fundamental, 347
as graduality of becomingness, 36, 37
and Heraclitus, 347
as history, 107
and history of philosophy, 55
and Hume, 58
as illusion, 84, 246
and imaginal occasion, 104
as immediate activity, 36

and incompleteness, 246, 251, 255, 343n2, 344
and individual, 93
and influence of past on present, 107
and inheritance, 44, 44fig
versus instant, 153
as instants, 260
internal versus external, 245
and intuition, 9, 58
as irreversible, 254, 345
and Kant, 9, 12, 58, 84
and Locke, 247
and mass, 37
and matter, 12, 127
as measurable, 12, 36, 85, 85n4, 104, 269
versus measured time, 245
and measurability, 12, 58, 103, 103n4
and measurement, 161
and mental relation, 255
moment of, 281
natura naturans as, 85
in nature, 58, 100n4
and Newton, 12, 127
not becoming of the actual, 259
versus novelty, 245
and objective immortality, 246
and occasion, 10, 60, 71, 105, 105n8, 107
order of, 252
as ordinal series, 255
origination of, 12
paradox of, 36
and perception, 263
and percipient, 381
as perpetual perishing, 247, 249
and philosophy of science, 4, 11
in philosophy versus science, 250
and physical influence, 70
and physical relationships, 255
and physical world, 160, 160 n1
physical universe with, 251
and physics, 10, 401
and Plato, 12, 57, 218
as pluralistic system, 259
as point instants, 125
and predicate, 362
and prehension, 245, 343, 343n2
and present, 255
and process, 401
as quanta, 346, 350
and relative completeness of entities, 255
as relation, 85, 246
as relational, 107, 107n2
relations in, 29

and Renaissance science, 37
and rest, 285–6, 285fig
in science, 71, 85, 266
and sense data, 76
as sequence, 57
as serial, 245, 252n2, 270
as serial succession, 250
and Sheldon, 252
and simultaneity, 246, 255, 272
and something happening, 259, 259ff, 259n2
and space, 245, 301
versus space, 11, 23
in spatial-temporal continuum, 265
and status of occasions, 19, 67
straight lines in, 282, 282fig
study of, 126–127n6
and subject–predicate view, 246
and substance, 341n4, 341n5, 359n5
and succession, 245, 246, 249, 264, 337, 343n2, 354
as systematic relation, 127
taken seriously, 246, 252, 259, 342, 342n5
theory of, 285
thought out of, 103, 103n3
transcended by supersession, 343
and transmission, 247
and ultimate entity, 78
and universe, 240
and universe as totality, 246, 246n2, 246n3
and vicious regression, 259, 259n2, 260
as what actual is enjoying, 259
Zeno difficulty in, 112
time, epochal theory of, 36, 84–5, 112
and science, 86–7
time, epochal view of, 34
defined, 36
and Descartes, 36
and modern science, 37
and physical occasions, 37
time, measured, 218
versus *durée*, 240, 240n3
and extension, 161
and measured space, 300
and point, 304
versus time, 100, 245
time depth, 11
in activity, 77
and actual entity, 30, 78
in becomingness, 85
in biology, 77
characteristics of, 30
in concrete occasion, 84
in creative act, 35, 41
in creature, 35, 85

506

Index

and function, 56
necessity for, 153
in occasion, 85
of Planck's constant, 93
in ultimate entity, 30
and what is realised, 57
time points
  and previous point, 240, 240*fig*
  relation between, 241
time quantum, 346, 350
  origination of, 346
time relations, 23
time systems
  alternative linear, 162
  defined, 156
  division into planes, by moment, 162, 162*fig*
  differences of, and geometry, 159
  durations in, 156
  geometry derived from, 162
  intersection of, 157
  and parallel duration, 156
time thickness
  of an act, 240
  of a happening, 212
  and space, 276, 281, 281*fig*
  versus succession of instants, 275–6, 281
times, differences in, 284
timetables, 245*n*5, 251*n*7, 263, 270
togetherness
  and concrete occasion, 43
  and eternal objects, 43
  and isolation, 94
totality
  versus actual universe, 237
  versus completeness, 349
  and diversity, 145
  and entity, 237
  epochal occasion as, 241
totemism, 177, 177*n*4
Tractatus Logico-Philosophicus (Wittgenstein) (1921), 186, 383–7, 389
  picture in, 390
  and Russell, 385, 385*n*3, 390
tragedy (literary)
  defined, 292
  and imagination, 292
  and inevitability, 292, 292*n*6
  and universe, 292
transitive, as point of view, 169, 169*fig*
transitivity
  and equality, 337
  and matching, 337
transmission
  and historical route, 247
  intensity of, and formula, 247, 247*n*4
  in physics, 247
  and time, 247

transmission theory, and perception, 151*n*3
trap
  philosophical methods leading to, 203, 205*n*3
  subject–predicate view as, 203–4, 235–6, 236*n*1
Treatise Concerning Human Understanding (Locke) *see Enquiry Concerning Human Understanding*
Treatise of Human Nature (Hume) (1739), as assigned reading, 4
Treatise on Conic Sections (Apollonius), 7
Treatise on Probability (Keynes) (1921), 239–40, 240*n*1
Treatise on Universal Algebra (Whitehead) (1898), viii
trenchant man, 124
Trinity College, Cambridge, vii
tropism, historical route as, 110, 110*fig*
truth, 170
  as absolute, 168
  accuracy as, 120
  accurate, 128
  in actual world, 165
  adventurous, 292
  analytic versus synthetic, 6
  and community, 58
  as correspondence, 356
  correspondence theory of, 230
  distribution of, 50
  about entity, 151*n*1
  and error, 337
  and eternal objects, 43
  and facts, 222
  grades and scales of, 171*n*8
  and Greek language, 183
  in harmony of flux, 56
  history as validation of, 171*n*6
  how to establish, 289
  in language, 211
  and logic, 334, 370
  in mathematics, 179
  and metaphysics, 211
  and philosophy, 384
  and primary proposition, 389
  and proposition, 171, 171*n*6, 390
  and rationalism, 183
  as relative, 168
  and simplicity, 128
  uncertainty in, 147
truth, abstract, and facts of history, 222, 222*n*3
truth, definite, 128
truth, final, 292
truth, finite, 93
  and Bosanquet, 99*n*1
  and Bradley, 99*n*1
  and eternal objects, 99

and experient occasions, 106, 106*n*5
  possibility of, 127, 145
truth, logical, and entities, 235
truth, synthetic, 6
truth, theory of, 217*n*3
truth function, 384
  and complex proposition, 385
  defined, 385
  nature of, 389–90
truth operation, application of, 389
truth proposition, symbol of, 390
Truth Seeker, 184*n*1
truth value, and proposition, 385
TSPR *see* system, temporal-spatial-physical-referential
two faces, 212
Tycho Brahe, 317*n*2, 409, 409*n*3, 410
Tyndall, John, 96, 96*n*3
types
  combinations of, 132, 132*n*4
  definiteness and contrast in, 104*n*6
  doctrine of, 230, 436
  theory of, 368

unbounded, 64; *see also* bounded
unboundedness
  and events, 147
  versus infinity, 389
uncertainty, and truth, 147
Underhill, Robert L. M., notes by, lx
understanding
  attainment of, 175
  in Descartes, 341*n*4
  and substance, 341*n*4
uniform state, 154
uniformity, as limitation, 64, 64*n*2, 64
uniqueness, principle of, 67
units
  becoming of, 44
  complex, 376
  and experient occasion, 44
  how to describe, 39
  versus community, 32
unity
  abstract types of, 376
  of actual fact, 31
  and actuality, 101, 366
  as choice, 69
  and class, 368
  and community, 11, 18, 21, 69
  conceived, 78
  defined, 78, 78*n*4
  and here and now, 12
  imposition of, 59
  and limitations, 21
  and multiplicity, 60, 332
  and occasion, 11, 59, 246–7
  percipient, 78

Index

percipient field as, 78
and proposition, 368
self-created, 261
and subject, 60
and successive occasions, 244
and total community, 11, 21
versus whole, 69
universal
   as abstract, 18
   and activity, 333
   and actual occasion, 250
   and analysis, 58
   and Aristotle, 43
   and causal relationship, 262–3
   effecting objectification, 262
   eternal object as, 18, 65, 343
   versus experience, 317
   function of, 242, 242n5
   and ingression, 98n7
   and intensity, 263
   as irrelevant, 165
   and life incidents, 253
   limits of, on past life, 253
   and medieval philosophy, 43
   and objectification, 242, 242n5, 263
   and occasion, 50, 243
   versus particular, 173n1
   in perceptual functioning, 243
   and Plato, 43
   predicates as, 271n2
   and presentational immediacy, 262–3
   proposition as, 365, 370
   reality of, 389
   relational character of, 43
   and relations of entities, 146
   versus relative, 73
   as true object of perception, 80, 80n2
   and wax, 361
Universal Algebra (Whitehead), 186
universal judgement
   and actual occasion, 55
   and induction, 55
universality
   and *a priori*, 8
   as criterion for *a priori*, 8, 52
   and form, 166
   gradations in, 174
   and necessity, 8
   and occasion, 8
   and proposition, 8, 52
universals, system of, omission in, 50
universe *see also under* world
   as abstraction of set of points, 135
   as background, 363
   and Bacon, 291
   canalised, 237
   character of entity shared with, 257

comparison of elements in, 273
complexity of, and time, 250
as complicated, 115
concrescence of, 196
as concretion of events, 9
contingency of, 261
and creativity, 213, 348
and creature, 355
creature creating, 232
defined, 12
democratic view of, 411
difficulty of understanding, 128
diversity of, 115–16
Earth in, 81, 81n6
and entity, 237
epic view of, 292
and events, 9
essential incompleteness of, 169, 169*fig*
and experienced occasion, 53
extension in, 150
feudal view of, 411
and functioning, 379
fundamental doctrine of, 228–9
general ideas on, 291
and God, 376
Greek view of, 292
and grinningness, 235
how to study, 132–133, 133*fig*
identical loci in, 279, 279n3
and immediate experience, 376
and individuality, 212
individualising of, 212
as inexhaustible, 173
infected by occasion, 398
information about, from type of order, 133
inherited by occasion, 350, 350*fig*
instantaneous space in, 278
interconnection by abstraction in, 335
knowledge of, 53, 274
in Leibniz, 358
as logical, 269
mathematics applied to, 132–4
mechanistic account of, 413
and metaphysics, 232–3, 366
mind outside, 238
morphology versus function of, 301
and occasion, 242
patience of, 363–4
perpetual creation of, 376
perspective of, and fact, 164
as pluralistic, 200, 200n2
point of view in, 279
potentiality of, 268
and predicate, 363
propositions in, 375
and proposition, 364
before proposition, 372

as rational, 128
and reference in proposition, 202
relationship of occasion with, 227
relationship underlying, 303
and relationships becoming actual, 164
and relationships of numbers, 132
self-limitation of, 269, 269n4
self-presentation of, 196
and simplicity, 128
and space, 127
as space-time, 220
spatialisation of, 161–2
as spatio-temporal, 202
from a standpoint, 169
static, 301
structural system of, 281
study of general laws in, 291n6
study of specifics in, 291n6
supersession of, 269
and system of relata, 237
systematic character of, 202, 272–3
systematic investigation of, 137
and time, 240
as totality, and time, 246, 246n2, 246n3
versus totality, 237
tragic versus epic view of, 292
transience of, 269
as unfinished, 301
and value in occasion, 216
view of, as system, 266
universe, physical
   extended, 249
   relation of, to existence, 325
   special relation outside, 249
   with time, 251
universe, solidarity of, 213, 269
   with entity, 234, 235, 257
   with individual, 216n4
universe, structure of
   functions in, 132
   and numbers, 132, 133, 133*fig*
   and substance, 125
   and types of order, 132, 133, 133*fig*
universe, study of, and physics, 132
University College London, vii
University of London, vii
university, as creature, 232
unknowable, 397n1
   and Spencer, 49, 208n2
unknown, versus known, 182
unlikeness, versus likeness, 381
upper segment, defined, 138

vagueness
   conceptual, 186, 186n4
   expressive, 186

value
  abstraction of, 135, 135*n*2
  actual as basis for, 215
  and alternative, 21
  and art, 16, 62, 63, 63*n*8
  community of, 62
  and conation, 12
  and concrescence, 207, 207*n*1
  defined, 298
  as end, 62
  and event, 15, 62
  and exclusion, 62, 63
  and experient occasion, 17, 64, 65
  as fact, 17
  as final cause, 13, 59–60
  fusion as, 164
  germ of, 59–60, 59n8
  gradations of, 65
  graded experience as, 115, 115*n*4
  as *how* of determination, 166 *n*1
  in ideal world, 98
  and imaginal occasion, 17, 22, 65
  and individual, 207, 207*n*1
  of individual occasion, 216*n*6
  versus intensity, 435
  in Kant, 12
  as knowing, 17
  and knowledge, 43, 95
  and limitations, 15
  and nature, 64
  and number, 135, 135*n*2, 136
  and occasion, 34, 62, 63, 63*n*4, 168, 216
  philosophy of, 5
  and realisation, 21, 22
  of relationships between eternal objects, 19
  in science, 62
  self-realisation of, 298
  superjicient, 22, 22*n*4
value, achieved, defined, 15
value, emerging, and event, 15
value, physical, and God, 222
values
  in Descartes, 215, 215*n*5
  grades of vividness of, 73
  versus nature, 49
  practical knowledge of, 7
  theory of, versus materialism, 6
values, individual
  and property as robbery, 399
  and thou shalt not steal, 399
Vanzetti, Bartolomeo, liv, liv*n*1
velocity, 174
  versus acceleration, 286
  and rest, 158, 284
velocity, constant, equation for, 278
verification, as pragmatic, 356
Vesalius, Andreas, 409, 409*n*1

vibration
  periodicity and quanta in, 102
  and reversion, 243
vicious infinite regress, and supersession and continuity, 346, 346*fig*
vicious regress, 35
  and time, 259, 259*n*2, 260
  and Zeno, 153
Virginia, University of, lectures at, xxxii
vivid intensity, 298
vividness
  and art, 243
  and generic and specific, 243
  grades of, 73
  and objectification, 243
volume
  and architecture, 16, 63n6
  and art, 16
vortex
  in Descartes, 294
  in Kelvin, 295
vortex rings, 29, 29*n*5
vortex theory
  failure of, 92, 92*n*3
  and force and momentum, 38

war
  and evil, 406
  justification for, 406
Ward, James, 268, 268*n*2
was, and existence of past, 80
watch, as analogy, 114
watchmaker metaphor, 83, 84, 107, 210
water, self-creation of, 296
Watkins, Frederick M., xxx
wave motion, uncertainty about, 186, 186*n*4
wave theory, of light, 295
wave-form, of energy, 29
wax, of Descartes, 28, 73*n*1, 74, 232, 360, 361
Weierstrass, Karl, 88, 88*n*6, 316, 316*n*1
  approximation theorem of, 180
  and number, 326–7
Weiss, Paul, xli
  biographical sketch of, li
  career of, li
  and Harvard lecture notes, xliv
  and Whitehead, li–lii
  and Yale Philosophy Club, li
  seminary notes of, lvii
welfare of all, contribution to, 208
Western Electric worker productivity study, xxxix
what
  and abstraction, 114–15
  and entity, 116
  and experience, 115, 115*n*4

  and *how*, 115
  and one, 115
  of relation, 115
Wheeler, William Morton, 248*n*1
Whewell, William, 193–4, 194*n*1
White, Alfred T., lviii
Whitehead, Alfred North
  activities of, xxv–xxxii
  Alexander's on, 46–7*n*7
  and analysis, 90
  Bergson's influence on, 47*n*7
  Broad as foil for, 46n5
  Cabot's introduction of, 391
  career of, vii
  and *cogito*, 12, 57
  and cognition, 81
  in Committee of Four, xxx
  communistic point of view of, 145
  conferences of, with Heath, xxxvii
  and Conger, 435–7
  Conger's evaluation of, 435
  courses of, differences in, 3
  critical edition of works of, viii–ix
  and Descartes, 172*n*6
  and Dewey, 170–1, 172*n*6, 177, 342*n*3
  Dewey's influence on, 47*n*7
  doctoral papers of, 174*n*6
  evaluation by, of *Principia Mathematica*
  and extension, 148
  Gifford lectures of, viii, xi, 261*n*6
  and given, 12, 65, 166
  and Hegel, 172*n*1
  as idealist, 187
  and Ideas, 14
  influences on, xxix, 124*n*8, 172*n*1
  James's influence on, 47*n*7
  and Kant, 172*n*1
  knowing and world for, 42
  law of gravitation of, 413*n*1
  lecture style of, 435
  life of, xvi–xix
  and limitation, 15
  Lowell Lectures of, xxvi, 113*n*1
  and McDougall, 97*n*2
  as mathematician, 113
  Morgan's influence on, 46–7*n*7, 293, 293*n*2
  and mutual form of things, 100*n*4
  Nachlass of, viii–ix
  and new rationalism, 188
  as new realist, 187*n*4
  objection of, to philosophy, 235
  panpsychism of, 435
  and presented occasions, 24
  as rationalist, 171

509

Index

and Russell, collaboration with, vii
and sensa, 86
Sunday at homes of, 435
Tarner lectures of, 189n3
and value in actual world, 98
Whitehead, Alfred North, philosophy of
  characterisation of, 436
  influences on, viii
  themes of, viii
Whitehead, Alfred North, thought of
  development of, in lectures, x, xi–xii, xxvii–xxviii, xxix–xxx, xxxii
  early versus late, xi–xii
  evolution of, x–xii, xxviii–xxviii
Whitehead, Jessie, xxvii, 437n2
Whitehead, Margot, xxxi, 437
Whitehead, T. North, xvi, xxxi, xxxix, 315n4, 335
Whitehead Research Project, ix
whole
  versus all, 125
  and analysis, 90
  and part, 30, 71, 71fig, 78, 89, 90, 125–6, 143, 147, 263, 303, 304, 304n4, 306, 307–8, 338
  and part, equation for, 122
  and quantity, 120
  and simplicity, 147
  in science, 89
  versus unit, 69
Wieman, Henry Nelson, xli
will be, and existence of future, 80
Williams, Daniel Day, xli
Wilson, E. Bright, Jr., xxx
Wisconsin, University of, xxx–xxxi
Wittgenstein, Ludwig, viii, 383–4n3
  concrete versus abstract in, 387
  methodology of, xi
  and names, 387
  and propositions, 384
  says what can't be said, 385
  as sceptic, 372
  and thought, 388
  truth function in, 384
  and validity of propositions, 384
  world in, 384
Woods, James Haughton, xxvii, 347–8n7, 435, 435n2
  influence of, on Whitehead, xxix
  Whitehead's attendance at lectures of, xxix
words, 360
  defining, 205
  doing things with, 383
  and experience, 205n3
  and meaning, 382
  in metaphysics, 205
  and proposition, 383
  technical, 368
world see also under universe
  abstraction from, 18
  versus abstractions, 99
  and actual entity, 100, 231
  actual experience of, 279
  analysis of, and community, 81
  bonds of sympathy in, 243, 243n4
  character of, 212, 302
  community of, 21, 333
  components of, 160n1
  comprehensibility of, 173
  conceptual, as abstraction from real world, 77
  considered under scheme, 116
  created by knowing, 31
  creative character added to, 298
  and community, 160, 160 n1
  and community of occasions, 61
  as continuous and atomic, 160, 218, 218n4
  as creature, 100
  and creatures, 243
  as datum of knowledge, 108
  defined, 61, 384
  determined, 84
  diagram of, 95fig
  discovery of, and Kant, 31
  divisibility of, and potentiality, 356
  and entity, 348
  and envisagement, 95
  and eternal objects, 69
  evolution of, 243
  experienced, metaphysical doctrine of, 112
  as extended bodies with endurance, 160
  extensiveness of, 38
  and facts, 388
  as four-dimensional, 34
  as five-dimensional, 45, 104, 104n1
  fronting of, 7
  as function of mind, 51
  as functional, 30, 76n3
  general laws in, 8
  harmony of, and principle, 357
  ideal, 98, 99
  and immediate occasion, 242
  incompatibility as essence of, 174, 174n8
  infected by substance, 397
  interaction in, 113n3
  and knowing, 42
  knowledge of, 75, 187, 223–4
  and limitations of language, 116
  and matter, 87
  meaning of, and relatedness, 32
  and mental world, 102
  and mental and physical, 238, 375
  mind in, 76, 239
  and morals, 208–9, 208n8
  morphological view of, 30
  as multiplicity of actual occasions, 14
  and natural potentiality, 334
  objectification of, 400
  and occasion, 8, 62
  occasion of perception in, 108
  order of, 399–400
  order and destruction in, 400
  ordered by mind, 171–172n12
  organisation of, and prehension, 343
  organised, and intuition, 353
  original sin in, 397
  original virtue in, 397
  outside, demonstrated by spatial relations, 249
  past of, 246
  patient of actual occasions, 275
  versus perception, 76
  perceptively organised, 166
  as phenomenon of appearance, 259
  Platonic view of, 113
  possibilities of, and mathematics, 185
  as presented instantaneously, 152
  and process, 160, 160 n1
  reference to, in proposition, 211
  relational side of, 94
  relations of sense data to, 232
  as social, 120
  as solidarity of actual entity, 298
  structure of, 94
  subjective, immediate experience as, 162
  synthesis of, 13
  synthesised in occasion, 166
  as system, 250
  as system of occasions, 172
  as system of organisms, 343
  systematic character of, and eternal objects, 234, 234n2
  as totality of facts, 387
  understanding of, and substance, 396–7
world, actual
  and actual entities, 229
  as always spacey, 132
  as community of occasions, 241
  and concept as possibility, 167
  completeness of, 251
  construction of, 379

510

defined, 241
and entity, 344
and exact statement, 128, 128n7
and ideal world, 99
incompleteness of, 125
knowledge of, 132, 195
limitation of, in potentiality, 195
and logical simplicity, 185
and mathematics, 185
and patience, 99
and relation of abstract, 128
relationships in, 134–7
relative importance of, 81
as repetition of cycles, 107
revising notions of, 185
solidarity of, 232, 233
truth and falsity in, 165
and types of order, 134–5
value in, 98
world, common, 11–12
versus phenomenal, 29
versus private, 275
world, physical
as community, 160
error in, 354
and eternal objects, 343
evil in, 354
and extension, 300
and fact, 195
and feeling, 176
as intuition, 349

perceptivity as basis of, 163
and physical occasions, 343
process of, 162
and serial advance, 162
as system of presentations, 162
and unity of organisms, 301
world, possible, and concretion, 104
world, private
and Descartes, 196
and Hume, 196, 196n1
and scientific observation, 280
as solipsism, 196, 196n1
world, real
abstraction from, 164
and imagination, 207
measure in, 98
and mental occasion, 206
as multiplicity of actual entities, 258
world, temporal, and knowing, 112
world, timeful, and incompleteness, 251
world as we find it, 205n1
world line
accelerative, 154, 154n3
adjustment to, 151
collision of, 151
durations connected with, 154
of occasions, 153
uniform, 154, 154n3
world view, new, 409

worlds, like bubbles on river, 271, 271n5

Yale Philosophy Club, and Harvard lecture notes, xliv, xlv, xlviii, li
Young, Allyn Abbot, 403, 403n1
Young, Thomas, 29, 29n7
youth
versus age, 182
revolt of, 241

Zeno of Elea
Achilles paradox of, 84–5, 346
Achilles paradox of, solution to, 86, 86n2
arrow paradox of, 346
and becoming, 153
and continuity, 84–5, 85fig
and morphological view, 30, 77
and time as continuous, 258, 258n7, 259, 259n3
and vicious regress, 153
Zeno argument (continuity), 366
Zeno difficulty, 35, 35fig, 36, 84–5, 350
source of, 89–90
in time, 112
zeppelin raids, 182
Zermelo, Ernst, 330, 330n4

EU Authorised Representative:
Easy Access System Europe Mustamäe tee 50, 10621 Tallinn, Estonia
gpsr.requests@easproject.com

Printed and bound by CPI Group (UK) Ltd, Croydon, CR0 4YY
02/03/2026
02063697-0013